Global Politics

Dean A. Minix
University of Houston, Downtown

Sandra M. Hawley
San Jacinto College

West / Wadsworth

 I T P® **an International Thomson Publishing Company**

Belmont, CA • Albany, NY • Bonn • Boston • Cincinnati • Detroit • Johannesburg
London • Los Angeles • Madrid • Melbourne • Mexico City • Minneapolis / St. Paul • New York • Paris
San Francisco • Singapore • Tokyo • Toronto • Washington

History editor: Clark Baxter
Text design: Merry Obrecht Sawdey, Shade Tree Designs
Copyediting: Beth Bulger
Composition: Parkwood Composition Service, Inc.
Cartography: CartoGraphics; Maryland Cartographics
Illustrations: CartoGraphics
Indexing: Northwind Editorial Services
Cover design: Tom Heffron
Cover photograph: Sean Ellis/Tony Stone Images

Printed in the United States of America
1 2 3 4 5 6 7 8 9 10

For more information, contact Wadsworth Publishing Company, 10 Davis Drive,
Belmont, CA 94002, or electronically at http://www.thomson.com/wadsworth.html

International Thomson Publishing Europe
Berkshire House 168-173
High Holborn
London, WC1V 7AA, England

International Thomson Editores
Campos Eliseos 385, Piso 7
Col. Polanco
11560 México D. F. México

Thomas Nelson Australia
102 Dodds Street
South Melbourne 3205
Victoria, Australia

International Thomson Publishing Asia
221 Henderson Road
#05-10 Henderson Building
Singapore 0315

Nelson Canada
1120 Birchmount Road
Scarborough, Ontario
Canada M1K 5G4

International Thomson Publishing Japan
Hirakawacho Kyowa Building, 3F
2-2-1 Hirakawacho
Chiyoda-ku, Tokyo 102, Japan

International Thomson Publishing GmbH
Königswinterer Strasse 418
53227 Bonn, Germany

International Thomson Publishing
Southern Africa
Building 18, Constantia Park
240 Old Pretoria Road
Halfway House, 1685 South Africa

Library of Congress Cataloging-in-Publication Data

Minix, Dean A.
    Global politics / Dean Minix, Sandra Hawley.
       p. cm.
    Includes bibliographical references and index.
    ISBN 0-314-06767-1 (soft : alk. paper)
    1. International relations. 2. World politics. I. Hawley,
Sandra. II. Title.
JX1308.M56 1997
909.82—dc20

96-38395
CIP

 This book is printed on acid-free recycled paper.

It is with the utmost appreciation that we thank our families. My wife, Barb, was understanding when I was away from her and my newborn son, Matt. There is absolutely no way that this book could have come to fruition without her love and support. Add to her my dad, Willard Minix, who never forgot to ask, "How's it coming?" His support, added to Barb's, was just enough to keep me going. To these important people in my life, Barb and my dad, plus the memory of my mother, Frances, I dedicate my portion of this book.
Dean A. Minix

My daughter, Lee Anne Hawley, both regretted and understood the time this book took away from her; her support was invaluable. James D. Heil, as ever, gave freely both moral and technical support. Like Dean, I dedicate my portion of this book to my family: my daughter, Lee Anne, my mother Margaret McNair, and the memory of my world-class dad, Ralph S. McNair.
Sandra M. Hawley

Photo Credits

6 Superstock; **12** UPI/Bettmann; **12** Reuters/Bettmann; **16** UPI/Bettmann Newsphotos; **18** UPI/Bettmann; **19** AP/Wide World Photos; **39** AP/Wide World Photos; **41** AP/Wide World Photos; **49** AP/Wide World Photos; **49** UPI/Bettmann Newsphotos; **50** AP/Wide World Photos; **50** AP/Wide World Photos; **90** Reuters/Bettmann; **101** Reuters/Bettmann; **102** Reuters/Bettmann; **148** Reuters/Bettmann Newsphotos; **160** Courtesy Dean A. Minix; **168** Reuters/Corbis-Bettmann; **181** The Bettmann Archive; **183** The Bettmann Archive; **194** The Bettmann Archive; **196** The Bettmann Archive; **197** AP/Wide World Photos; **199** AP/Wide World Photos; **201** Reuters/Bettmann; **201** AP/Wide World Photos; **211** UPI/Bettmann; **233** UPI/Bettmann Newsphotos; **248** Reuters/Bettmann; **262** AP/Wide World Photos; **284** AP/Wide World Photos; **288** UPI/Bettmann; **296** UPI/Corbis-Bettmann; **297** AP/Wide World Photos; **333** AP/Wide World Photos; **354** SuperStock; **366** The Bettmann Archive; **371** UPI/Bettmann; **411** AP/Wide World Photos; **414** Reuters/Bettmann; **414** AP/Wide World Photos; **421** Sygma; **425** AP/Wide World Photos; **473** SuperStock; **475** UPI/Bettmann; **483** The Gamma Liaison Network © John Chiasson; **503** The Bettmann Archive; **508** AP/Wide World Photos; **519** AP/Wide World Photos; **536** AFP/Corbis-Bettmann; **548** UPI/Bettmann.

Contents

x　◆　*Contents*

PART IV

Rules of the Game • *319*

CHAPTER 10
*The Game of Nations: Intelligence
and the Making of Policy*   **320**

PART V

New Problems, New Players   •   455

CHAPTER 13
The Web of Global Communications   456

Introduction   457

Preface

This is a fascinating time to study global politics. The end of the Cold War has produced numerous repercussions in the world's political and economic systems, leaving many observers bewildered and confused. *Global Politics,* a comprehensive textbook on international relations for the twenty-first century, is one of the first such books not shrouded in the rhetoric of the ideological tensions between communism and capitalism.

As teachers of international relations, we believe that students must understand the historical underpinnings of the international political and economic system in order to grasp contemporary conditions. Both past and present systems are vividly depicted in this book. Students also need to visualize the physical relationships between nations; accordingly, a full-color map section has been included. In addition, each chapter provides abundant examples and non-European perspectives. *Global Politics* also offers the reader clear, engaging, jargon-free writing.

Global Politics provides an introduction to some of the vital new components of world politics. One of these is communications. In chapter 13, we discuss the impact instantaneous communication has upon international decision-makers and the policies that result from the rapid heartbeat of news reporting, electronic mail, and the information superhighway.

Also included is a chapter on intelligence and policy-making. Many international relations texts do not discuss intelligence as a vital part of the formation of public policy. Chapter 10 details the cycle of intelligence and compares the U.S., British, Russian, and Chinese intelligence agencies.

Another unique feature of *Global Politics* is its study of the social psychology of international relations, found in chapter 5. This chapter looks at decision-making, and particularly crisis decision-making. By examining the interplay within small groups and tendency of small groups to reach either riskier or more cautious decisions than the group members would reach individually, the chapter raises this question: Which decisional unit, the individual or the small group, is best suited for crisis decision-making?

Chapter 6 on ideologies, is another distinctive feature of the text. This chapter focuses on the impact of various political ideologies on global politics, and on the recent "triumph" of democracy and capitalism. It also addresses the question, Is this the end of history?

Global Politics also contains two chapters that examine international economics and the transformation of the geoeconomic system in depth. A chapter devoted exclusively to the current issues of global population, the environment, and disease is also included.

Global Integration and Disintegration: A Unifying Theme

The summary to chapter 1 says that "international relations provide an essential backdrop to our daily existence—but because they do not occupy the foreground of our attention, assuming that life as we know it will go on as usual, we can safely ignore global affairs." But we may in fact be far from safe in our ignorance. The world contains many more uncertainties today than it held during the halcyon days of the Cold War.

Politically and economically, the world is undergoing both integration and disintegration. Economic integration can be seen in the European Union, the North American Free Trade Agreement (NAFTA), the ASEAN group, and other regional economic unions and associations. There is unprecedented economic cooperation between rich states (or those who are at least in the take-off stage). This fact has led many to predict that the concerns and tensions of the global elite in the twenty-first century will be more economic and less political than they have been. In contrast, the newly created or unleashed states, such as those that once composed the Soviet Union and Yugoslavia, see the world through the lens of disintegration and dissolution. These states tend to be poor and riddled with revolutionary nationalism. Economic cooperation via integration is not part of their present agenda.

Students should be aware of these two crosscurrents and their importance in defining geopolitics today.

Organization of the Book

Global Politics is divided into five parts. Part One, "Principles," contains the book's introduction, "The Environment of International Relations" (chap. 1); "Power" (chap. 2); and "Who We Are: States, Nations, and Nationalism" (chap. 3). In Part Two, "Players," we present "The Galaxy of Global Actors on the International Horizon: IGOs, NGOs, and MNCs" (chap. 4); "How to Get Your Way in the World: The Social Psychology of International Relations" (chap. 5); and "Ideas that Make the World Go Round" (chap. 6). Part Three is entitled "How the Game Is Played." It includes these chapters: International "Political Economy" (chap. 7); "The Geo-Economics of Today: Integration and Disintegration" (chap. 8); and "Diplomacy and International Law" (chap. 9). Part Four, "Rules of the Game," contains "The Game of Nations: Intelligence and the Making of Policy" (chap. 10); "War: Its Types, Culture, and Causes" (chap. 11); and "Weapons: The Technology of Death" (chap. 12). In Part Five are found these chapters: "The Web of Global Communications" (chap. 13); "Global Issues" (chap. 14); and "The Dynamics of the Post–Cold War World" (chap. 15).

Currency

Global Politics offers a unique blend of the historical with the most current scholarship. Its academic sources span the ages, from the writings of Thucydides to citations downloaded from the World Wide Web. Needless to say, this subject matter is so dynamic that professors and students will have to do their own updates until the second edition is published!

Accessibility

The first goal of this text was to produce a readable, understandable book about a very complicated discipline. Without minimizing the complexities of today's global society, the text tackles the issues using a clear, conversational tone. To help students, margin definitions have been provided, along with a complete glossary, for all significant terms. Plentiful maps, tables, and graphics clarify complex issues.

Ideological Balance

Global Politics is a "straight-down-the-middle" introductory textbook on international relations. Any biases are unintentional. The goal is to educate, not indoctrinate; educated persons can make their own reasoned judgments in the public policy arena.

Special Features

This text incorporates a number of special features:

A clear writing style. Clear writing should not be confused with a dearth of scholarship. As mentioned earlier, marginal definitions and a glossary are provided for key terms and concepts.

Historical examples balanced with the most contemporary scholarship. The past and the present have been uniquely juxtaposed in this text. Many students will have no recollection of or formal training in the history that set the stage for the post–Cold War world. This text gives them the background they need to understand how the world works now.

KEY TERMS. At the end of each chapter is a list of key terms. These terms are defined in the glossary.

THOUGHT QUESTIONS.

"GLOBAL PERSPECTIVES" These features, found in each chapter, examine interesting and relevant issues on today's international scene. They provide an excellent basis for critical analysis or classroom discussion.

A GLOBAL PERSPECTIVE. The authors strive to avoid a purely Western focus in the text, and instead to introduce the perspectives of many world actors.

Ancillaries

INSTRUCTOR'S MANUAL. An excellent instructor's manual for *Global Politics* has been prepared by John Soares. It includes key terms with definitions, fully annotated chapter outlines, lecture notes, critical thinking exercises, classroom presentation ideas, and suggestions for using transparencies and other media supplements.

TEST BANK. This document, also prepared by John Soares, includes more than 1500 objective, short-answer and essay questions.

WESTEST 3.1.

Acknowledgments

Writing a textbook on international relations during a great shift in the plate tectonics of world politics is quite a project. Many would wait until the dust of the Cold War had settled a bit more, and there was some stable pattern to the "New World Order." But we authors believe that we undertook this venture at a most propitious time. The world was simultaneously spinning quickly out of control and coming together like never before. Explaining these phenomena to both ourselves and our students was difficult. As one of us commented, "When you're in the midst of a hurricane, it's hard to get the charts out." But such a task was also imperative. In part, our attempt to make sense of the whirlwind of events unfolding before our very eyes, and then to put it together for class in a semicoherent fashion, was the impetus to begin this project.

Our acquisitions editor at West, Joan Gill, and developmental editor Becky Stovall agreed with the timing and the approach of this book. Along the way towards publication we picked up two other editors, production editor Amy Hanson and copy editor Beth Bulger. All these people helped us stay on track and out of trouble. We are eternally indebted to them for their professionalism and assistance. This text is certainly more solid and more polished because of their invaluable work.

Of course, *Global Politics* has profited in rigor and accuracy from the wisdom of our colleagues around the nation who viewed all or part of the manuscript. We are deeply indebted to them for their insights and comments. While we could not incorporate all of their suggestions, we have included many. These reviewers are as follows:

Renee Scherlen
Appalachian State University

Michael Preda
Midwestern State University

Gregory Hall
University of Central Florida

Howard Carey
Kennesaw State University

Peter Howse
American River College

Phil Meeks
Creighton University

Lynn Rigsbee
Marshall University

Wei-Chin Lee
Wake Forest University

Michael Kelley
University of Central Arkansas

Roslyn Simowitz
University of Texas-Arlington

William Greene
Florida International University

Frances Wayman
University of Michigan-Dearborn

Ramsey Kleff
Virginia Union University

John Freeman
University of Minnesota

Richard Clinton
Oregon State University

Eric Mlyn
University of North Carolina-Chapel Hill

Richard Harknett
University of Cincinnati

H. J. Maitre
Boston University

Carol Leff
University of Illinois-Urbana

Greg Russell
University of Oklahoma

Stephen Burgess
Hofstra University

Harvey Feigenbaum
George Washington University

Kim Spiezio
Virginia Tech

Martin Hillenbrand
University of Georgia

David Forsythe
University of Nebraska-Lincoln

Robert Rood
University of South Carolina

William Carroll
University of North Texas

Cecilia Lynch
Northeastern University

We received much behind-the-scenes help from local colleagues, as well as friends from other institutions. We have attempted to include all these individuals; any omission is unintentional.

Dean Michael R. Dressman, University of Houston–Downtown

Dr. Dragan Stefanovic', Appalachian State University

Dean Dan R. Jones, University of Houston–Downtown

Dr. Vinny Prince, Wilmington College

Dr. Cindy J. Kistenberg, University of Houston–Downtown

Dr. Mike Kelley, University of Central Arkansas

Dr. Leena Thacker-Kumar, University of Houston–Downtown

Dr. Michael Preda, Midwestern State University

Dr. William E. Brigman, University of Houston–Downtown

Dr. Lynn Rigsbee, Marshall University

Dr. Abdulah Al-Kurd

Professor James Hall, San Jacinto College

Dr. Jeffrey Roet, San Jacinto College

Ms. Carolyn Waddles, University of Houston–Downtown

Dr. Dennis Toombs, San Jacinto College

Ms. Vanessa Peveto

Ms. Linda Whitfield, San Jacinto College

Ms. Cassandra Abbajay

Ms. Ellen Everett, San Jacinto College

Mr. Michael Bradley

Dr. James Semones, San Jacinto College

And finally, thanks to all of our past and present students who contributed to this book through their questions and comments.

DEAN A. MINIX
University of Houston–Downtown

SANDRA M. HAWLEY
San Jacinto College

Part One

Principles

Chapter 1

The Environment of International Relations

Introduction:

What Is International Politics and Why Study It?

You pick up the paper, or turn on the radio or television, and what you see or hear is bits of war, mayhem, and misery occurring in distant parts of the world in a repetitive dance that has no rhythm. Just one *foreign* event after another—all unrelated to one another, or to you. Right?

The study of world politics is so fascinating because this field is unlike any course in American national government, comparative politics, or state and local government that the average American student has taken. It is much more inclusive, much more comprehensive, and, we believe, much more complicated, than any study of politics you may have engaged in previously. Aristotle described politics as the master science; the bedrock of this crucial discipline is the study of international relations, because it is global in nature, not country- region- or issue-specific. The study of international or world politics encompasses all human political behavior in the world.

It is this comprehensiveness that leads many to say, "Well, it's too complicated to me. I don't see the relationship between the sale of U.S. missiles to Saudi Arabia and the price of Coca-Cola in Israel." Such relationships are indeed complicated, yet lifting the lid of a proverbial black box reveals that these connections between many different, frequently competing actors—all with their own agendas—are sometimes understandable. But only sometimes. Einstein, the father of modern physics, once was asked, "Why is it that when the mind of man has stretched so far as to discover the structure of the atom we have been unable to devise the political means to keep the atom from destroying us?" He replied, "That is simple, my friend, it is because politics is more difficult than physics" (Herz 1962, 214n.).

So **international politics** is difficult to understand. Then why do we study it? Because it is important. It affects each and every one of us in terms of *how* we live, *where* we live, *why* we live, and even *whether* we live. Think of world politics as a huge spider's web of political relationships. If you were to pluck one strand of that web, you would send vibrations throughout the entire web system, bouncing actors and issues all over the place. Some strands would be more affected than others, depending upon how hard you plucked the web and where you plucked it. Nonetheless, the entire web would feel the jolt. Such is the political world. We need to know who is connected to whom, why, and what it means for us. We need to know how, when, and why some political action in another part of the world will affect us, so that we may be prepared for any shock waves to follow. Events as minor as a price increase in the cost of Toyotas in America or as major as the war between Serbia and Bosnia all affect us in various ways. The price increase in Toyotas is felt in terms of more money spent on a car; the war between Serbia and Bosnia could have meant your jumping from a C-130 air transport plane with other American troops in the Balkans. One example would cost you just a few dollars; the other could cost you your life. This is why the study of global politics is not only relevant, but the most fundamental study of human behavior in the world. At the very least, international relations are important to us because what we don't know *can* hurt us!

international politics A term often interchanged with international relations, world politics, or global politics that denotes the sum of all political interchange within the world at a given time. In its strictest sense, international politics is the accumulation of all politics that emerge between nations of the world.

The issues and the actors in international politics have changed tremendously over the past fifty years. In fact, some of the more dramatic changes have occurred just since 1989.

Today's issues are less geostrategic than ecostrategic. Since the fall of the communist wall in Eastern Europe, the confrontation between East and West is not a military, but an economic one. Particularly in Eastern Europe, the focus is on economic and **political integration** and reconstruction. In Western Europe and on the North American continent, the discussion centers on how nations can integrate economically, and to a certain degree, politically.

In other quarters of the world **political** and economic **disintegration** seem to be prevailing over integrative forces. Ancient ethnic, tribal, and racial animosities are resurfacing, producing a virulent form of nationalism that is quickly engulfing the Balkans, parts of sub-Saharan Africa, the Middle East, Latin America, and Asia in a tsunami of civil war and unrest.

When we contrast the economic and political integration going on in Europe, North America, and to some extent the nations of the Pacific Rim to the disintegration of virtually the remainder of the world, we see chaotic change worldwide. But this is not the only development since 1989.

As mentioned above, the actors themselves have also changed. No longer is the sole actor of the political world the **nation-state.** Actors today include stateless nations such as the Kurds and the Basques, nongovernmental actors, such as the International Red Cross, **transgovernmental actors** like the European Union, multinational corporations like McDonald's, and **supragovernmental organizations,** such as the United Nations. All of these parties, plus countless other groups and individual players we haven't yet mentioned, constitute a galaxy of new global actors.

Global issues today are complex, in the sense that many of them cannot be treated solely from the perspective of just a single nation or other player. Additional actors, because they have a stake in the political outcomes, must be included.

In a world that is simultaneously integrating and disintegrating along economic and political dimensions, one tremendously important factor is **technology,** which we could define as the making and use of tools to enable us to live a better and more productive life. Technology is the fuel that propels the world today. It fans the fires of war, and, at the same time, quells them. Through advances in instantaneous global communication, wars appear live and in color in the living rooms of those not directly involved. Technology produces both drought-resistant vegetation and life-threatening diseases.

Clearly, the milieu of world politics today is a dynamic one. Fueled by the technological revolution that characterizes the modern world, simultaneous economic and political integration and disintegration are occurring. Meanwhile, the issues and the actors have been changing rapidly since the days of the Cold War between the East and the West (see Fig. 1.1).

We have examined *what* world politics is and *why* we study it. Now we must look at *how* to study world politics. Let us turn to a very helpful framework.

Levels of Analysis

One of the more enduring and important organizing frameworks in the modern study of international relations is called **levels of analysis** (see Fig. 1.2). The world can be seen through three (some say four or more) lenses. Much like the microscope with its varying fields of vision, the levels-of-analysis approach offers

political integration The composition of forces within a society or system to bind it together.

political disintegration The explosion of political order and symmetry.

nation-state A nation with a political construct, i.e., territorially defined boundaries, legal government, foreign recognition, etc.

transgovernmental Term denoting usually agreements, exchanges between governments or sub-units of a government working with their counter-parts with other governments.

supragovernmental Political dealings at a level that transcends the nation-state(s), e.g., at the level of the United Nations. In other words, politics at a plateau above the nation.

technology The practical application of knowledge and the application of tools which are used to make work easier.

levels of analysis Perspectives (individual, state, or systemic) from which to view and analyze international politics.

A Quick Global Tour

To illustrate how the U.S. CIA describes the world in statistics, we have captured some eclectic "facts" about the world we live in:

World Geography:

- *Total Area:* 510.072 million km²
- *Land Area:* 148.94 million km²
- *Water Area:* 361.132 million km² (comparative area: 16 times the size of U.S.) *Note:* 70.8% of the world is water; 29.2% is land
- *Land Boundaries:* 250,883.64 km (not counting shared boundaries twice)
- 42 nations are landlocked
- *Terrain:* highest elevation is Mt. Everest at 8,848 meters; lowest is Dead Sea at 392 m below sea level. Greatest ocean depth is Marianas Trench at 10,924 m
- *Natural Resources:* the rapid using up of nonrenewable mineral resources, the depletion of the forest areas and wetlands, the extinction of animal and plant species, and the deterioration in air and water quality (especially in Eastern Europe and the former USSR) pose serious long-term problems that governments and peoples are only beginning to address
- *Arable Land:* 10%
- *Permanent Crops:* 1%
- *Meadows and pastures:* 24%
- *Forest and woodland:* 31%
- *Environment:* large areas subject to severe weather (tropical cyclones); natural disasters (earthquakes, landslides, tsunamis, volcanic eruptions); overpopulation; industrial disasters; pollution (air, water, acid rain, toxic substances); loss of vegetation (overgrazing, deforestation, desertification); loss of wildlife resources; soil degradation; soil depletion; erosion

World People:

- *Population:* 5,733,687,096 (May 1996 est.)
- *Population Growth Rate:* 1.6% (July 1993 est.)
- *Birth Rate:* 24 births/1,000 population (1996 est.)
- *Death Rate:* 9 deaths/1000 population (1996 est.)
- *Infant Mortality Rate:* 64/1,000 population (1996 est.)
- *Life Expectancy at Birth:* total population: 62 yrs.; male: 60 yrs; female: 64 yrs. (1993 est.)

GLOBAL PERSPECTIVES

- *Total Fertility Rate:* 3.2 children born/woman (1993 est.)
- *Administrative Divisions:* 265 sovereign nations, dependent areas, and miscellaneous entries
- *Legal System:* varies by individual country; 186 are parties to the United Nations International Court of Justice

World Economy:

- *Gross World Economy:* $30.7 trillion (1994 est.)
- *National Production per capita:* $5,400 (1994 est.)
- *Inflation Rate:* developed countries 5%; developing countries 50% (1992 est.)
- *Unemployment Rate:* developing countries 5–12%; developing countries *extensive* unemployment
- *Exports:* $4.0 trillion (1994 est.)
- *Imports:* $4.1 trillion (1994 est.)
- *External debt:* $1 trillion for less developed countries (1993 est.)
- *Industries:* industry worldwide is dominated by the onrush of technology, especially in computers, robotics, telecommunications, and medicines and medical equipment; most of these advances take place in OECD nations; only a small portion of non-OECD nations have succeeded in rapidly adjusting to these technological forces, and the technological gap between the industrial nations and the less developed countries continues to widen; the rapid development of new industrial (and agricultural) technology is complicating already existing environmental problems;
- *Agriculture:* the production of major food crops has increased substantially in the last 20 years; the annual production of cereals, for instance, has risen by 50%; production increases have resulted mainly from increased yields rather than increases in planted areas; while global production is sufficient for aggregate demand, about one-fifth of the world's population remains malnourished, primarily because local production cannot adequately provide for large and rapidly growing populations, which are too poor to pay for food imports; conditions are especially bad in Africa, where drought in recent years has intensified the consequences of overpopulation;
- *Defense Expenditures:* decline of 5–10% to 3/4 of trillion dollars (1994 est.).

Source: *CIA World Fact Book.*

Unlikely revolutionaries: workers on a microchip assembly line are part of the technology revolution that continues to change international relations.

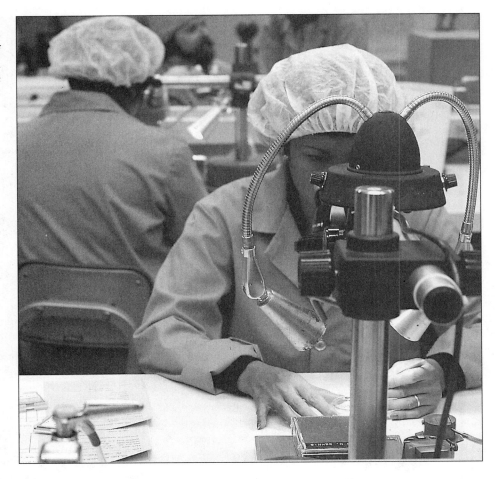

much insight into the behavior of the various actors or players in the world through its use of varying perspectives. The wider the field of vision, the less specificity is obtained; the narrower the field, the greater the specificity. So it is with levels of analysis.

Systems Level

systems level The level of analysis that focuses on global actors and conditions, e.g., geopolitics and geoeconomics, world technology, etc.

The most inclusive level is the **global, or systems, level,** which focuses upon the international system's actors, primarily nation-states, and their interactions. However, also included at this level are other actors such as international organizations like the United Nations, nongovernmental organizations such as the International Red Cross, and multinational corporations such as McDonald's. Analysis at this level focuses on the relative power and geographical position of such actors in the world. It encompasses all global political interactions from the perspective of a single large "system." The international system, so the analogy goes, is just like any other system, in that the whole is greater than the sum of its parts. For example, the automotive system of your car is much more than just engine, tires, steering gears, computers, and so on. The automotive system functions as a whole because of the interaction and cooperation of all of its functioning parts. When one of your car's system stops functioning, the entire system is weakened or

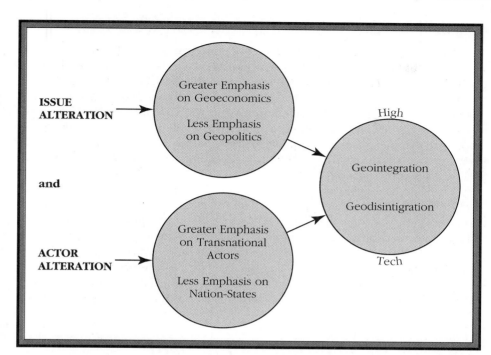

Figure 1.1
The Post–Cold War World

breaks down. The same is true, it is alleged, for the international political system. The components of the system, primarily nation-states and sundry international governmental and nongovernmental actors and organizations, work together to achieve certain political goals, such as conflict resolution or trade relations. In doing so, these actors tend to follow some rather vague assumptions about how they are supposed to behave with one another.

Nation-State Level

The next most specific level is the **nation-state level.** Here politics is viewed from the perspective of the aggregation of individuals within a defined territory, the nation-state. Various societies are arranged and managed differently in terms of both their domestic affairs and their international relations. State organizations, which are leading variables in determining how states behave, run the gamut from liberal, participatory democracies to one-person dictatorships. Liberal, Western democracies act differently toward one another in terms of trade or foreign policy than do dictatorships or monarchies, which can act faster, but sometimes more belligerently, than deliberative democracies.

  The nation-state is probably the most familiar analytical level to the reader. States have been the principal organizing concept in the world since the Peace of Westphalia was signed in 1648 to end the Thirty Years' War. We are accustomed to looking at the state as the major player and provider in the world arena. After all, it is the state to which we pay allegiance. It is the state that traditionally binds peoples together (although fervent, revolutionary nationalism, as we shall learn, has split many states in the history of the world). It is states, in the minds of many, that produce world politics, not some ethereal large "system" incorporating nebulous "other actors" that are offsprings of states to begin with.

nation-state level The level of analysis that focuses upon the sovereign state as the primary player of international relations.

Social-Psychological Level

social-psychological level
Level of analysis that
focuses on the intersection
of variables between the
individual and society.

The third, and most specific, level is the **social-psychological level** of analysis, which looks at the interaction between individuals and groups as they behave politically. *People* behave politically; states and other such political constructs do not act by themselves. For instance, some say that there would have been no Russian Revolution without Lenin, and no World War II without Hitler. Nations or systems are merely abstract political constructs. Political social psychologists emphasize that the *person* as the political actor, especially in the context of group interaction, makes the world tick politically—not artificial political constructs such as global systems or nation-states.

Which is the best level at which to understand international relations: the level of the international system as a whole functioning unit, that of the competition between individual nation-states, or that of human political actions, performed both individually and in groups? Which level explains more varieties of political behavior? The answer sometimes depends upon which question is being asked, and how much specificity one desires. But the most exhaustive analysis would encompass investigations at all three levels. (See J. David Singer 1961; Ken Waltz 1954; Knorr and Rosenau 1969 for further discussion of the levels of analysis in world politics.)

Towards International "Political Meteorology"

International relations scholars must attempt to become political meteorologists. We must *describe* oncoming changes in the political climate. We need to *explain*

Figure 1.2
Levels of Analysis

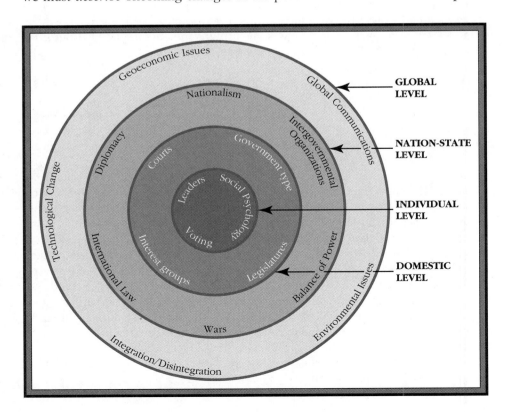

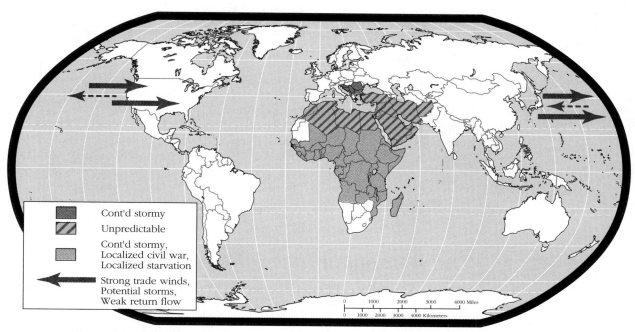

Figure 1.3 **Global Meteorology**

these changes in our political environment so that we can evaluate and categorize them for future use. And finally, based upon our analysis of the events, and the changes they signify, we can hope to *predict* over time any future occurrences of a similar nature and how these *political patterns* will affect our lives.

In the midst of all of the political windstorms in the world, it seems futile to pull out the charts to see where we are going. But what appears to be mayhem and chaos, crisis upon crisis, is to the trained analyst something other than mere randomness, disorder, and disarray.

Picture yourself watching the local television weather report on a given evening. The world map in Figure 1.3 appears on the screen. But instead of using meteorological terms, we employ international relations terms to describe, explain, and possibly predict *political* "weather patterns" for today and the next few days.

The forecast might sound like this:

Tonight we see increasing political haziness over the *Balkans* due to increased Russian troop deployments on the former Yugoslav front, with an influx of arms shipments from the European Union and the United States. There is an unstable rising tide of nationalism complicating the Balkan's map. Forecast is for more violent, revolutionary storms for the foreseeable future.

In Asia, we see trade winds continuing to blow from the Pacific towards the U.S. creating economic low pressure systems within the American economy. There is a rising tide of protectionism on the part of the U.S. Forecast: continued strong trade winds, with some counterclockwise motion back across the Pacific.

In the Middle East, blowing sands of Islamic fundamentalism continue to wreak havoc on burgeoning democracies and societies in transition. Forecast: continued cloudiness and unpredictability.

> *In Africa,* an occluded developmental front with extensive poverty, human misery, and environmental destruction. Forecast is for continued storminess, locally heavy civil war, and starvation.

theory In the political context, the scientific attempt to describe, explain, and predict political phenomena.

The source and the object of this political meteorologist's skill is solid political **theory.** Theory is the goal of political science, and of international relations study in particular. Political theory attempts three things: it *describes* a certain political event; it *explains* the event; and, if the theory is well developed, it *predicts* future political events of the same or similar nature. It is the authors' view that the world of political behavior can and should be studied systematically. And, as with any scientific endeavor, from medicine to nuclear physics, the purpose is to build theory. For in the study of international relations, events are *always* describable, *frequently* explainable—and even *sometimes* predictable. And even when they are not predictable, then, at the very least, the study of world events is fascinating.

The Dynamic International Environment

International relations do not take place in a vacuum; like everything in human affairs, they take place within a set of ideas and circumstances that often dictate their course. In other words, international relations have a framework of concepts and settings that limits what individual actors can do and often determines what they *will* do.

The End of the Cold War

Cold War The period between 1945 and 1989 in which the world was basically bipolar and marked by loyalty to either the United States and its allies or the USSR and its allies.

In this first chapter we will explore the international political environment and define as clearly as we can the dynamics of contemporary international relations. As recently as six or seven years ago, describing this environment would have been simple: international relations were still understood within the framework of the **Cold War**. During this forty-five-year period of hostility which verged upon but never deteriorated into a "hot" war, much of what happened globally was defined by the duel between the two superpowers, the Soviet Union and the United States. In fact, many actors on the international stage, nations and individuals alike, found themselves caught up in the larger drama of the Cold War, and their major concerns—ideological, nationalistic, religious, or otherwise—overshadowed by the tensions and competing ideologies of the superpowers. Thus, civil wars in Angola or Vietnam or Afghanistan became theaters for Cold War confrontations, with one or another superpower assuming that its rival was at the heart of the conflict and that it must respond. Both the United States and the Soviet Union intervened in such conflicts, often with horrendous results for both the superpowers and the lesser actors, which in effect had lost control of their own internal problems.

However, the Cold War has all but ended, and it is unlikely that it will ever reappear in the same all-consuming form it took from 1945 until 1989. The former Soviet Union has disappeared, in all probability forever, although there may well be attempts to recreate a Russian empire that includes the territories claimed by both the old Tsarist and the more recent Soviet empires. However, it is unlikely that the ideological fires that fed the Cold War will rekindle in the same virulent forms they took before. This is not to say, however, that ideological wars or ideologically motivated nations cannot resurface with a vengeance in the future.

With the Cold War structure shattered probably far beyond the ability of all to resurrect it, we must now try to discover what organizing principle has replaced the Cold War and to understand how this new environment may affect international relations as the world moves toward the twenty-first century. The political picture in this new global environment is incomplete. But what is apparent is that the world is simultaneously integrating and disintegrating on different fronts. Why such a profound reaction?

The End of World War I

A historical precedent to give us some understanding of our contemporary framework can be found early in this century, in the period of chaos and instability that followed World War I. Modern wars are incredibly destructive, smashing not only millions upon millions of lives but also nations and empires, leaving behind wreckage that the victors, or at least the survivors, must attempt to fashion into new configurations. World War II is the exception to this in our century, since world affairs moved almost immediately into the superpower confrontation constituting Cold War. Tensions between the United States and the Soviet Union had been rising steadily throughout the war itself; despite a superficial atmosphere of cooperation and even conviviality, the economic and political systems of the two nations were vastly different and generally antagonistic. Even in the heat of World War II, some American and British leaders had toyed with the idea of allowing Nazi Germany to destroy the Soviet Union, and these two Allies had specifically excluded the Soviet Union from key decisions and key projects like the development of the atomic bomb. The wary, often superficial, cooperation of the World War II allies all too readily yielded to superpower confrontation, first in central and eastern Europe, and then on the global stage.

A far more accurate model of the typical postwar period is provided by the time following World War I. During that period, great attempts were made to establish a global system within which nations could work for their mutual benefit, and could suppress those forces they found inconvenient. Both these attempts and their varying degrees of success can help us understand the forces unleashed by the ending of the Cold War.

The great empires that slid into World War I had erected what they considered a secure framework for international relations in the nineteenth century: a balance of power system in which each empire enjoyed virtually unquestioned control of affairs in its own domain, and in effect agreed not to interfere with the affairs of any other empire. Within each one, imperial issues dominated and often submerged the concerns of individual groups, whether these were defined in terms of religion, ideology, or ethnicity. However, when World War I finally ended, four of the six great empires that had begun fighting in 1914—the Austro-Hungarian empire of the Hapsburgs, the Russian empire of the Romanovs, the German Empire of the Hohenzollerns, and the Ottoman empire of the Turks—lay shattered and destroyed, their political structures gutted, their economies ruined, and their territory up for grabs. The other two great empires, those of France and Britain, had survived the Great War more or less physically intact, but the war had exacted a terrible toll whose real magnitude would become apparent only in the 1930s and 1940s, as those empires too began to crumble. Turmoil and instability thus were the dominant features of the postwar world, as new leaders, new ideas, and new systems battled one another for control.

sovereignty The fundamental right of the state to perpetuate and govern itself, subject to no higher political authority.

In many ways our present situation is very similar to that which followed World War I. The empire knit together by the Soviet Union after World War II—containing the client states of central and eastern Europe as well as the great physical realm of the USSR itself—has collapsed. The central and eastern European countries have reclaimed their **sovereignty,** and the constituent republics of the Soviet Union have split up as well. A decentralized and highly unstable structure, the Commonwealth of Independent States (or, in Russian terms, the "Near Abroad"), attempts to provide a framework for continued economic cooperation to replace the centralized economic dictatorship that characterized the old Soviet Union.

NATO North Atlantic Treaty Organization: Body established at the end of World War II by the United States and its Western European allies to guard against the encroachment of Soviet communism.

The United States' alliance system, never as brutally imposed or ruthlessly controlled as the Soviet empire, is also showing signs of strain and instability. The western European nations whose economies were closely linked to that of the United States are now attempting to develop their own economic community, the European Union, which specifically excludes the United States. The North Atlantic Treaty Organization, **NATO,** the great military alliance developed as a counterpoise to the armed strength of the Soviet empire, has in effect won the Cold War, and is now searching for other missions to carry out. One indication of how greatly the world has changed in the past few years is the talk, however loose and improbable, about the possibility of the central and eastern European states, and perhaps even Russia itself, cooperating with or even joining NATO. Virtually paralyzed by its internal problems—primarily the huge burden of debt incurred at least in part in order to win the Cold War—the United States seems destined for a fairly prolonged period of navel-gazing withdrawal from the passionate leadership it has

The seismic shifts resulting from the end of the Cold War are clearly visible in these two photographs of the Berlin Wall. The photo on the left, taken in 1962, shows the early stages of the Wall; ultimately the rows of barbed wire would flank a huge concrete barrier snaking its way through Berlin. In the photo on the right, a schoolgirl balances atop the rubble that is all that remained of the wall by early 1990.

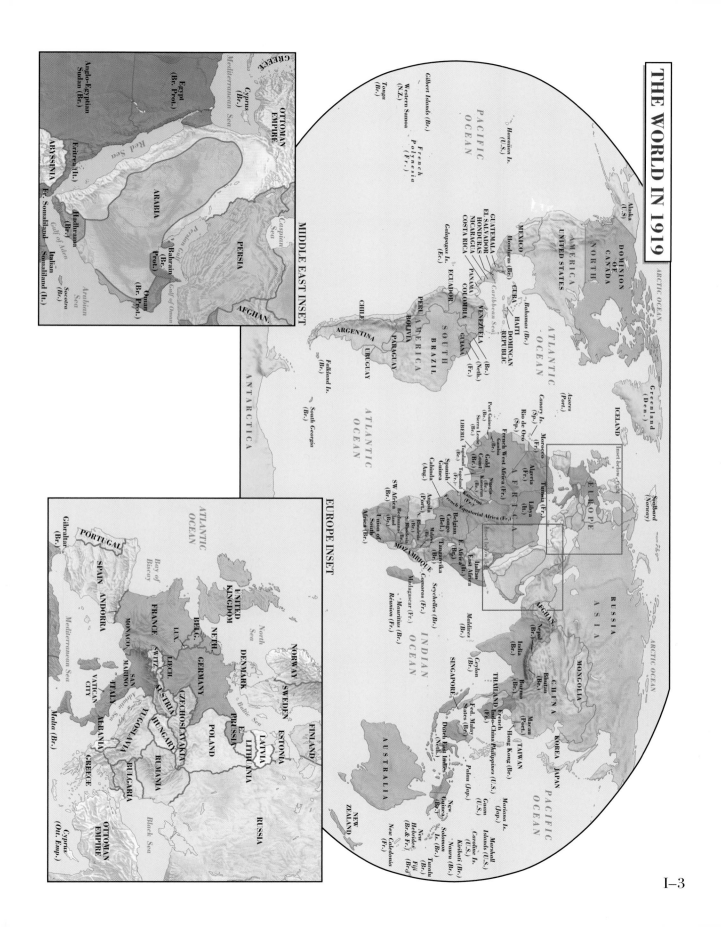

THE WORLD IN 1919

I–3

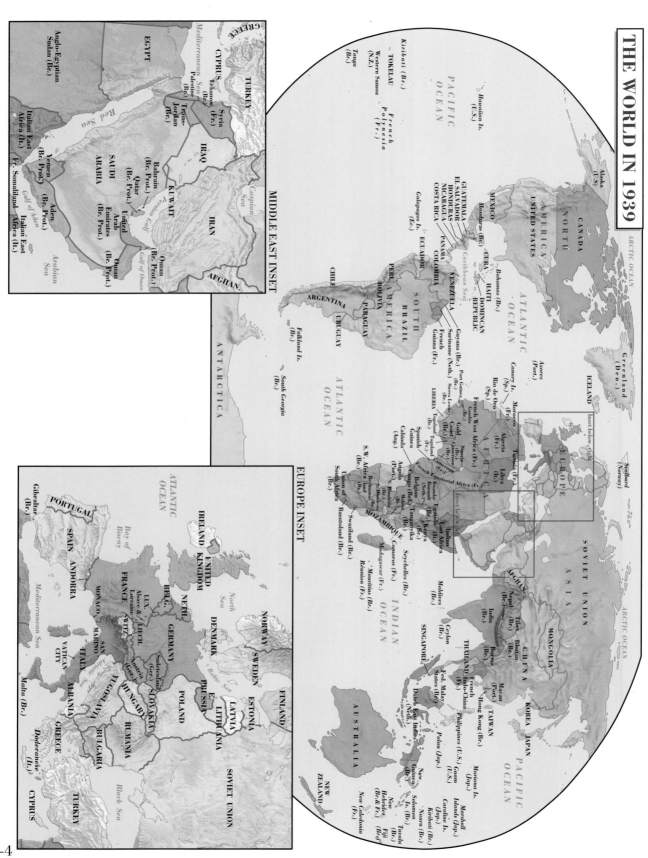

THE WORLD IN 1939

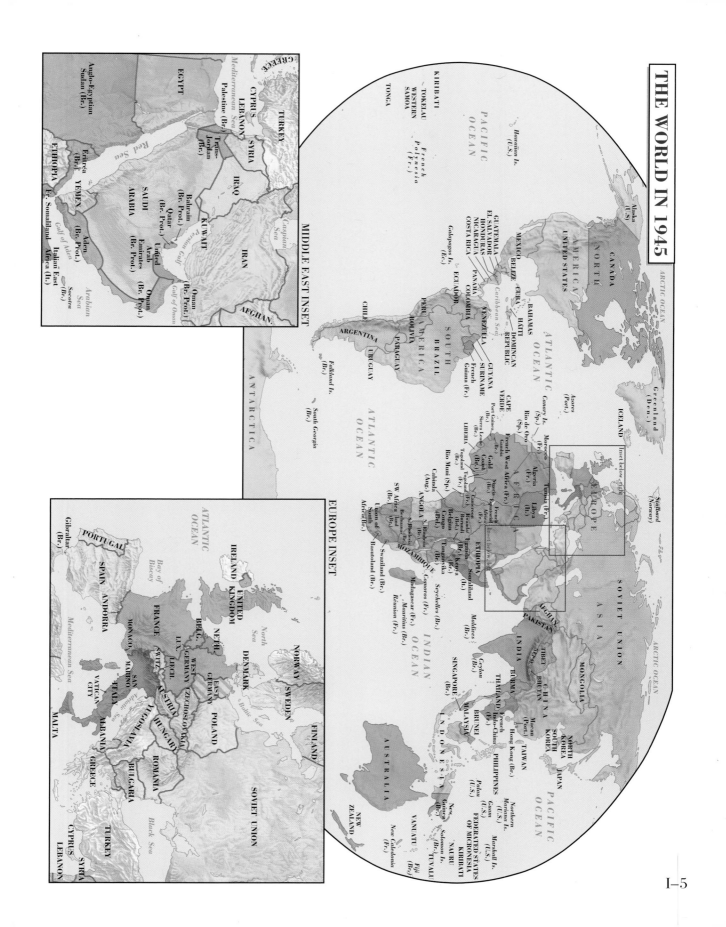

THE WORLD IN 1945

THE WORLD IN 1996

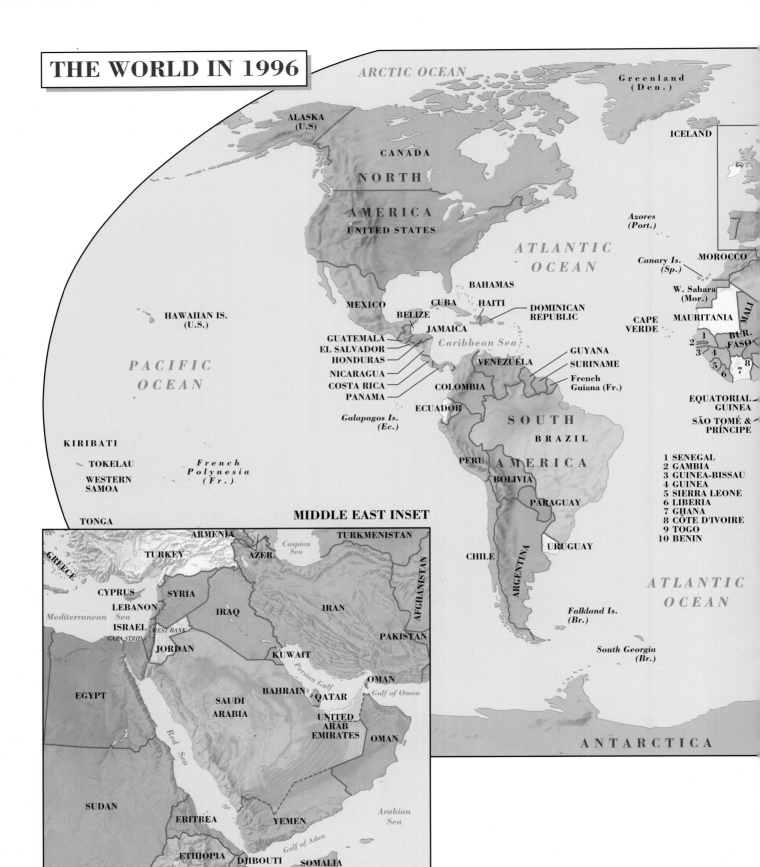

ARCTIC OCEAN

Greenland (Den.)

ALASKA (U.S)

CANADA

NORTH

AMERICA

UNITED STATES

ICELAND

Azores (Port.)

ATLANTIC OCEAN

MOROCCO

Canary Is. (Sp.)

W. Sahara (Mor.)

BAHAMAS

MEXICO   CUBA   HAITI

BELIZE   JAMAICA   DOMINICAN REPUBLIC

GUATEMALA

EL SALVADOR

HONDURAS

NICARAGUA

COSTA RICA

PANAMA

Caribbean Sea

CAPE VERDE

MAURITANIA

MALI

BUR. FASO

2 1

3 4

5 6 7 8

EQUATORIAL GUINEA

SÃO TOMÉ & PRÍNCIPE

HAWAIIAN IS. (U.S.)

PACIFIC OCEAN

VENEZUELA

GUYANA

SURINAME

French Guiana (Fr.)

COLOMBIA

ECUADOR

Galapagos Is. (Ec.)

SOUTH

AMERICA

BRAZIL

KIRIBATI

TOKELAU

WESTERN SAMOA

TONGA

French Polynesia (Fr.)

PERU

BOLIVIA

PARAGUAY

URUGUAY

1 SENEGAL
2 GAMBIA
3 GUINEA-BISSAU
4 GUINEA
5 SIERRA LEONE
6 LIBERIA
7 GHANA
8 CÔTE D'IVOIRE
9 TOGO
10 BENIN

ATLANTIC OCEAN

CHILE

ARGENTINA

Falkland Is. (Br.)

South Georgia (Br.)

ANTARCTICA

MIDDLE EAST INSET

GREECE

ARMENIA

TURKEY   AZER.

Caspian Sea

TURKMENISTAN

CYPRUS

LEBANON

ISRAEL

SYRIA

IRAQ

IRAN

AFGHANISTAN

Mediterranean Sea

GAZA STRIP

WEST BANK

JORDAN

KUWAIT

Persian Gulf

PAKISTAN

EGYPT

SAUDI ARABIA

BAHRAIN

QATAR

OMAN

Gulf of Oman

UNITED ARAB EMIRATES

OMAN

Red Sea

SUDAN

ERITREA

YEMEN

Arabian Sea

ETHIOPIA   DJIBOUTI   SOMALIA

Gulf of Aden

ARCTIC OCEAN

Svalbard (Norway)

RUSSIA

EUROPE

ASIA

Inset below right

AZERBAIJAN

GEORGIA

ARMENIA

KAZAKSTAN

MONGOLIA

UZBEKISTAN

KYRGYZSTAN

TAJIKISTAN

NORTH KOREA

SOUTH KOREA

JAPAN

PACIFIC OCEAN

TUNISIA

ALGERIA

LIBYA

AFRICA

NIGER

CHAD

NIGERIA

CAMEROON

GABON

CONGO

CABINDA (Ang.)

ANGOLA

NAMIBIA

BOTSWANA

SOUTH AFRICA

LESOTHO

SWAZILAND

ZAMBIA

ZIMBABWE

MOZAMBIQUE

MALAWI

BURUNDI

TANZANIA

RWANDA

KENYA

ZAIRE

UGANDA

CENTRAL AFRICAN REP.

ETHIOPIA

SOMALIA

Inset below left

AFGHAN.

PAKISTAN

CHINA

NEPAL

BHUTAN

INDIA

BANGLADESH

BURMA (MYANMAR)

LAOS

THAILAND

VIETNAM

CAMBODIA

Macau (Port.)

Hong Kong (Br.)

TAIWAN

SRI LANKA

MALDIVES

BRUNEI

MALAYSIA

SINGAPORE

PHILIPPINES

Northern Mariana Is. (U.S.)

Guam (U.S.)

PALAU

MARSHALL ISLANDS

FEDERATED STATES OF MICRONESIA

KIRIBATI

NAURU

SEYCHELLES

COMOROS

MADAGASCAR

MAURITIUS

Réunion (Fr.)

INDIAN OCEAN

INDONESIA

PAPUA NEW GUINEA

SOLOMON IS.

TUVALU

VANUATU

FIJI

New Caledonia (Fr.)

AUSTRALIA

NEW ZEALAND

EUROPE INSET

FINLAND

NORWAY

SWEDEN

ESTONIA

LATVIA

RUSSIA

North Sea

DENMARK

LITHUANIA

RUSSIA

BELARUS

IRELAND

UNITED KINGDOM

NETH.

POLAND

UKRAINE

ATLANTIC OCEAN

BELGIUM

LUX.

GERMANY

CZECH REP.

SLOVAKIA

MOLDOVA

LIECH.

AUSTRIA

HUNGARY

Bay of Biscay

FRANCE

SWITZ.

SLOVENIA

CROATIA

ROMANIA

Black Sea

MONACO

SAN MARINO

BOS. & HERZ.

YUGO.

BULGARIA

PORTUGAL

SPAIN

ANDORRA

ITALY

VATICAN CITY

ALBANIA

MACEDONIA

GREECE

TURKEY

CYPRUS

SYRIA

LEBANON

Gibraltar (Br.)

Mediterranean Sea

MALTA

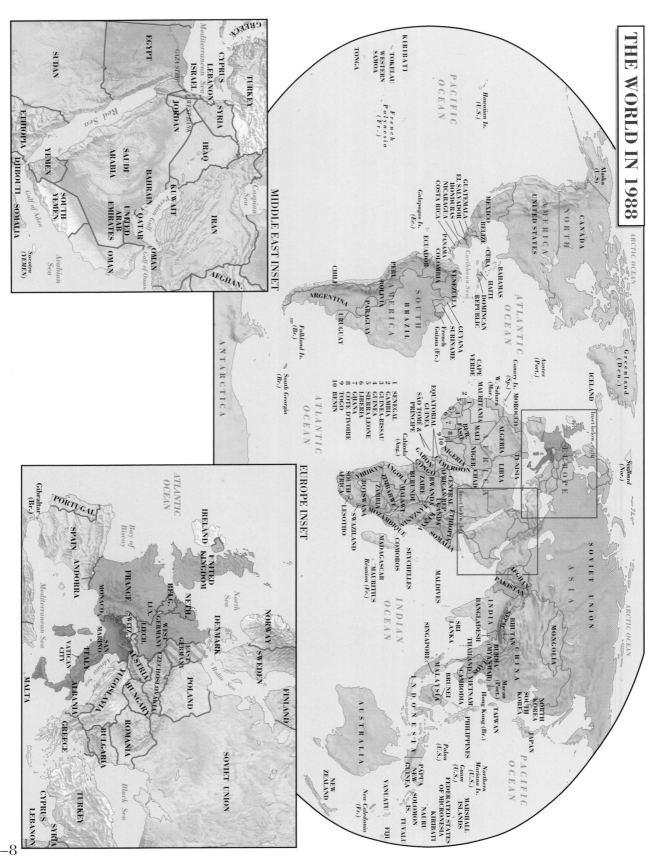

exercised for the past fifty years, during both World War II and the Cold War. American allies are being told to take on increasing responsibility for their own defense in this "new world order," and the hard-and-fast guidelines that once determined who these allies were—any nation or individual against the Soviet Union or communism was more or less automatically assumed to be a friend of the United States—have vanished, leaving a playing field on which no one has scorecards that tell who the players are. Leaders of the United States intelligence committee proclaim that although the Soviet dragon has been slain, the United States now confronts dozens of smaller snakes presenting varying degrees of danger.

In other words, the certainties of the Cold War that shaped international affairs for most of the last half-century are gone. The world is entering a new stage of uncertainty and instability, and the milieu within which international relations will take place in the future is less a finished structure than a collection of partially completed and loosely joined pieces. The war may well be over, but the peace is anything but assured. The world of the 1990s thus looks surprisingly—and dismayingly—like the world of the second and third decades of the twentieth century. During those years after World War I, global actors grappled with the problems created by the collapse of empires and the emergence of long-submerged forces and new players. All these problems challenged, and ultimately overcame, the ability of the world's leaders to create a framework that would preserve peace.

Versailles: Making a New World

To understand what is happening in today's world, we can look first to the past, to the chaos that followed World War I and the attempts to tame that chaos, particularly the great peace conference at **Versailles** in 1919. The problems that loomed so large in the world of the Versailles conference, and that were in large part submerged by the superpower confrontation of the Cold War, have once again burst loose and are threatening to plunge the world into a period of protracted instability and danger. Even as the Cold War ended, some students of international politics were saying, not entirely tongue in cheek, that we would soon miss the Cold War and the certainties it brought. An excursion back to the end of World War I and the attempts to build a new framework for international relations will reveal all too well how accurate this gloomy assessment may be.

World War I, which its participants called the Great War (never suspecting that the next generation would cynically start labeling its Great Wars), changed both the map of the world and the conduct of world politics irrevocably.

A map of the world in 1914, on the eve of the Great War's eruption, is completely foreign to the contemporary viewer; it represents accurately the world of the nineteenth century but bears little resemblance to the world in the rest of the twentieth century. This prewar map shows most of Europe divided up among great continental empires: the Austro-Hungarian empire of the Hapsburgs, the Russian empire of the Romanov tsars, the German empire of the Prussian Kaisers, and the teetering Ottoman empire of the Turks, which extended from the edge of Europe into the heart of the Middle East. These great polyglot empires, crazy-quilt structures of languages, peoples, and religions, encompassed virtually all of the land east of France and north of the Mediterranean. Much of the rest of the world is colored in shades of pink and green and blue, to signify that great chunks of Africa and Asia exist only as parts of one global empire or the other—of the British, French, and German empires especially, but of lesser entities like the Belgian and Dutch and Italian empires as well. (See full-color map inserts.)

Versailles conference The Paris Peace Conference of 1919, which concluded World War I and set the stage for nationalistic expectations around the world.

Yet a map of the world drawn in 1919, only five short years later, looks more or less familiar to the modern viewer: the great continental empires are either gone—neither the Austro-Hungarian nor the Ottoman Empire appears at all—or greatly diminished: both Russia and Germany are considerably shrunken. In place of the massive empires, the map of Europe is now a patchwork of nation-states, both large and small, drawn along lines that seem to have little to do with geography. The Middle East is now divided up among the remaining Great Powers, England and France, while Africa and Asia retain their pastel tints (although the green shade of Germany is now gone, replaced by the pink of the British and the blue of the French empires). Even now, on the edge of the twenty-first century, this world that appeared on the maps of 1919 is still recognizable.

There's nothing surprising about this. The map of 1919 reflects forces either unleashed or accelerated in the turmoil of the Great War, forces that have shaped and dominated international relations for the past seventy years and seem likely to go on doing so. Just as the map of 1919 is far more complex, filled with far more states and borders than that of 1914, so too international relations in the twentieth century has been far more complex than the state and imperial relations of the nineteenth.

To understand the world in which we live today, and the world we will inhabit tomorrow, we must examine the complex factors that played such a large role in shaping the world of 1919 and will play an equally important role in shaping the world of 2019. These factors—the emergence of new players with new **ideologies, nationalism** of all varieties, **ethnicity,** shifting balances and concepts of power, religion, revolution, the struggle for control of resources, geography, economics, the simultaneous integration and disintegration of international actors, the interplay of personality and policy—became more and more important during the Great War and dominated the conference at Versailles. Today, this proliferation of players and issues is equally important, and ever since the Great War has been exacerbated by another potent, driving force: technology. The impact of technology was felt on the battlefield of Verdun, as it is felt in today's instantaneous trading of stocks on the New York Stock Exchange. Through using as referents the Versailles conference and the related events that swirled across the world of 1919, we can begin not only to identify many of the major dynamics of late-twentieth-century international relations, but also to grasp the tangled complexity of the web-like relationships among these dynamic modern forces.

ideology A finely honed belief system of how the world works or should work.

nationalism A state of mind in which the individual's loyalty is directed totally toward the nation-state on behalf of a nation.

ethnicity The sense of shared historical, linguistic, and socio-religious heritage among a particular group of people.

New Players in World Affairs

The Versailles conference witnessed the first emergence of the United States as a dominant world power, with Woodrow Wilson's Fourteen Points outlining the soaring ideals around which he had tried to mold American participation in the Great War and hoped to mold the kind of future world that could justify the struggle and sacrifice just passed. America's debut at the center of world politics would end ingloriously with an attempted retreat across the safe fastness of the Atlantic; still, Versailles foreshadowed the role, in terms of both ideals and practical power, that the United States would play in the future and continues to play now.

Also among the participants at Versailles were other players not seen before at the gatherings of the Great Powers. China and Japan, in particular, began to take their places in world affairs. Although their roles would waver uncertainly over the next half century, the great Asian states would never again remain aloof from or ignored by the dance of nations. For the first time in hundreds of years, the Middle East began to take a shape independent of one or another of the great Muslim empires that had wielded power for more than a millennium; although they were temporarily under the domination of the European states, these Islamic states would soon play a powerful and critically important role in global politics.

Nationalism

The gathering at Versailles differed from earlier international relations not only in personnel but also in style.

Throughout the nineteenth century, international relations had been conducted by individual states, many of them dynastic empires and monarchies. This system of state relations dates back to the end of the Thirty Years' War and the Westphalia conferences of 1648 that ended that war and fractionalized Germany. In some cases international relations resembled a troubled family quarrel, as monarchs and emperors were tied to one another through an intricate series of blood relationships. Cousins ruled three of the six Great Powers that entered World War I, all of them grandsons of Victoria of England: King George V of England, Kaiser Wilhelm II of Germany, and Tsar Nicholas II of Russia. France was again a republic, the Ottoman Empire was a rickety combination of ancient empire and revolutionary "Young Turks," and the Austro-Hungarian Empire was a tottering imperial relict of the late Middle Ages.

By the time the Versailles conference began, both Nicholas II and Wilhelm II had lost their thrones, the last vestiges of Ottoman **imperialism** had been banished from the Middle East, and the Austro-Hungarian empire had collapsed into a confused turmoil of peoples demanding their own nationhood. The imperial and monarchical states that had begun the war had yielded or were about to yield to the major structure that would dominate twentieth-century international relations, the modern nation-state. Although both the French and the British empires remained intact at war's end, the war effort itself had drained them psychologically as well as financially, and their collapse was less than a generation away.

Certainly one of the most vital consequences of Versailles was the validation of the nation-state as the principal form of state organization, reflected especially in the redrawn European map at the end of the conference. Nationalism, generally defined as the desire of a people sharing language, history, and culture to form a state unique to themselves, has played a dynamic role throughout the twentieth century, and has shaped much of international relations. The emergence of nationalism in the nineteenth century had in fact helped set the stage, at least in part, for the Great War: various nationalities and peoples caught within the great continental empires—Russia, Austria-Hungary, Turkey—had longed and agitated for self-determination in nation-states of their own. It was in part their struggle to overthrow the polyglot multinational empires that had undermined European stability since late in the nineteenth century; specifically, the nationalistic dreams of peoples in the Balkans led to the assassination of the Austro-Hungarian heir, Archduke Franz Ferdinand, precipitating the Great War itself.

Nationalism and the fulfillment of nationalist dreams would likewise dominate many of the proceedings at Versailles. The new map of Europe would reflect Woodrow Wilson's ringing statements that every people had a right to **national self-determination,** with over a dozen small nation-states emerging from the ruins of the Austro-Hungarian and Russian empires (along with large parcels of land carved from the German empire). Generally small and weak, these new states presented problems for twentieth-century international relations. Lying as

imperialism Economic theory founded by Hobson, and later refined by Lenin to connote the highest stage of capitalism. Belief that surplus capital seeks external markets, raw materials, and cheap labor to the detriment of host nations.

national self-determination One of the principles called for in Wilson's Fourteen Points which advocated the right of people to assert their nationalistic claims to a particular territory and to subsequently establish self-rule or sovereignty over their territory.

Amidst Belgian ruins, President Woodrow Wilson speaks to war-weary Europeans, who must surely share his hope that the "Great War" will have been "the war to end all wars."

they did between the large and aggressive states of Germany and Russia, they were open invitations to mischief-making and ultimately invasion, first from the west and then from the east.

While President Wilson proclaimed the right of all people to national self-determination, he clearly meant to confine this right to European nations. In the Fourteen Points Address, in which he enunciated this doctrine of national self-determination, Wilson did not call upon his fellow leaders to dismantle the colonial system they had imposed on much of the non-European world, but merely implored them to mind their manners, to engage in "equitable redistribution of colonial claims." This "redistribution" clearly would entail not colonial peoples' assumption of the mantle of self-determination, but rather the continuation of the existing imperial systems, suitably modified to replace German rule with other, more trustworthy European rule.

Revolutionary Nationalism

While Wilson and his great power colleagues may have understood perfectly well the qualifications put on the term "national self-determination," those very words galvanized many individuals Wilson did not intend to address, who were already under colonial or imperial rule. Wilson spoke eloquently throughout the war of the great ideals of democracy, proclaiming that the ultimate purpose of the war was both to end all wars and to make the world safe for democracy. While some of this was undoubtedly the kind of superpatriotic hyperbole necessary to mobilize a modern democratic society and energize a mass conscript army, people throughout the world thrilled to Wilson's rhetoric and shared his lofty ideals. The great empires were in many cases already seething with unrest, but Wilson's ringing phrases would give shape to that unrest and provide even greater impetus to the cause of independence in the colonial peoples.

Revolutionary nationalism would emerge full blown at the Versailles conference and become one of the main engines of both change and chaos in the twentieth century. Symptomatic of the emergence of revolutionary nationalism and prophetic of the problems it would create was the attempt by a Vietnamese nationalist to speak to Woodrow Wilson at Versailles in order to plead his people's case for independence. Wilson's American entourage refused the young Vietnamese access to the American president, who had far more important matters to attend to at Versailles than to listen to the importunings of an unknown Asian. Disillusioned and embittered, the young Vietnamese nationalist ultimately turned to Marxism as the best hope for his people; leaving Versailles, he ended up in the Soviet Union and later returned to Vietnam as leader first of the anti-Japanese, then of the anti-French, and finally of the anti-American resistance. The kind of revolutionary nationalism personified by that young Vietnamese patriot, best known by the revolutionary name he adopted, Ho Chi Minh, might have been largely ignored at Versailles, but it would become one of the main engines driving international relations throughout the twentieth century.

revolutionary nationalism Desire for independence, self-determination, and social, political, and economic reform that generally culminates in a revolt against the existing regime.

Power and Its Uses

The Versailles conference also provided a nearly perfect illustration of a conflict that is still raging over the definition of **power** and its use: the conflict between **realism** and **idealism.**

Realism, the belief that nations should deal with one another primarily on the basis of national interest and use any necessary force to gain their ends, had dominated European thinking since the Vienna Conference had effectively terminated the Napoleonic period. European diplomats had considered the ideas embodied in the French Revolution to be at the heart of the turmoil unleashed on the continent in its aftermath; at Vienna they had attempted to restore Europe on the basis not of ideology and ideals, but of what they saw as the hard facts of life. The **Balance of Power theory** set in place at Vienna reflected their "realistic" view that if every nation had just enough but not too much power, stability and peace would endure.

Simultaneously fearing and disdaining ideals, realists had worked to maintain the balance of power throughout the nineteenth century with what they thought was substantial success. Toward the end of the century, the great German chancellor, Otto von Bismarck, had callously used this "realistic" approach to diplomacy, *realpolitik,* to justify waging a series of wars whose ultimate purpose was German unification. By the end of the century, many understood "realism" as the naked use of force with no regard to morality, and the prospect of this philosophy coupled with the awesome weapons provided by modern technology was genuinely appalling.

Idealists, in contrast, argued that realism was essentially suicidal; if wars had to be fought, they must be "just" wars fought for a reasonable purpose. Human beings were above the beasts, the idealists argued, and aggression pure and unrestrained was not worthy of them; men might have to be sent to fight and die, but the purpose had to be worthwhile. Idealists were also beginning to understand what Napoleon had known: a huge modern army could not be ordered to go into the field and fight purely for reasons of power. Ideals could motivate human beings to heroic sacrifice far more readily than such prosaic considerations of national interest as extending boundaries.

power The core concept of international relations; the totality of a nation's international capabilities, stemming from natural, synthetic, and social-psychological components.

realism School of international relations political theory that concentrates on power relationships; power is seen as the essential element of maintaining stability within the international system.

idealism The theory of international relations in the twentieth century that states that human beings are essentially good in nature and peace depends upon the appropriate concentration of international power.

Balance of Power Theory Theory of international relations stipulating that peace will ensue when there is a configuration of military power so that no one power dominates the system.

Woodrow Wilson would be perceived as the chief architect and spokesperson of idealism not only at the Versailles conference, but also throughout the twentieth century. Seeking reasons for America's entry into the war, and spurning self-interest as inadequate, the American president (reflecting both traditional American idealism and his own religious background) boldly and brilliantly articulated the idealist position. Civilization itself was at stake in the Great War, Wilson argued; the ultimate purpose of that war must not be to restore the old order, which had led to war in the first place (the ultimate idealist critique of realism). Instead, this "war to end all wars" would, in Wilson's words, "make the world safe for democracy."* Trying to galvanize the American people into support of a war they regarded with suspicion, the American leader provided an essentially apocalyptic view of the stakes of the conflict; it was not about boundaries and grudges and the balance of power, but about ultimate human causes and purposes. Like many idealists, Wilson was also a moralist, strict in his judgment of himself and even sterner in his judgment of others. He had called America to the great crusade of Progressivism and now he sought to enlist the rest of the world in a similar crusade; a crusade that would lead to "peace without victory" and would remove all causes for war. To rally the people of Europe to his ideals (he was rather more skeptical about rallying their leaders), Wilson proposed his Fourteen Points, a blueprint for Americanizing and saving the world that would endure as a basis for American foreign policy throughout the century.

Georges Clemenceau best expressed the cynicism that he and other European leaders felt about this newcomer with the great ideals and puny experience: "Moses gave us ten commandments and we have broken them all," he said; "Wilson has given us fourteen, and we shall see." To Clemenceau, the only legitimate point of this great war was to make sure it would never happen again; that meant

---

*Although Woodrow Wilson is generally credited with the phrase "the war to end all wars," he never actually said it. The first to use the phrase was H. G. Wells, in a 1934 magazine article. Since it caught the spirit of Wilsonian idealism so well, "the war to end all wars" has been associated with Wilson, not with Wells.

Here, at a working session of the Versailles conference, the American president faces an audience of "realist" European leaders much more skeptical about his idealistic vision of the future than the Belgians he had addressed earlier.

(Left to right) Italy's Vittorio Orlando, England's Lloyd-George, France's Georges Clemeneceau, and America's Woodrow Wilson pose for photographers before settling down to negotiations at the Versailles conference.

not only crushing the aggressive Germany of Bismarck and Kaiser Wilhelm II, but also removing forever Germany's ability to threaten France. Old scores, particularly the humiliation that France had suffered during the disastrous Franco-Prussian War, would be settled, and lands legitimately French reclaimed—but it was far more important to destroy Germany's ability ever again to make war. International institutions like Wilson's proposed League of Nations could not do that; only the complete destruction of German industrial and military power could accomplish it.

David Lloyd George, the British prime minister who had orchestrated England's war effort, was equally skeptical of Wilsonian idealism. England's role as a great power rested on its empire; the preservation and, if possible, the strengthening of the empire had to take precedence over everything else. Germany's aggressive expansionism on the continent of Europe had not immediately threatened England, but its equally aggressive expansionism in Africa had posed a direct threat to the British Empire. This could not be permitted in the future. Describing his goal for dealing with Germany at Versailles, Lloyd George said that his government would squeeze the German orange "until the pips squeak." Like other European leaders, Lloyd George was resentful of the criticism of traditional European diplomacy implied in the Fourteen Points, particularly in Wilson's goal of "open covenants openly arrived at." Secret diplomacy had worked for hundreds of years, and the powers had entered World War I dragging a variety of secret treaties with them. Diplomacy was far too delicate for public scrutiny, Europeans insisted.

To Wilson, the keystone to the better world that would justify the suffering of the Great War was the League of Nations, a congress of the world's nations where reason would prevail and rational dialogue would solve problems. The idea of substituting words for bullets, rhetoric for strategy, was enormously attractive to a world reeling from the carnage of the Great War. But to Clemenceau and Lloyd George, this vision was pure utopianism in a real world where military power rather than moral suasion was the key to attaining national goals. However, they acceded to the establishment of a League of Nations, at least in part so that they could achieve their own goals at Versailles; as they hoped would happen, Wilson accepted provisions in the Versailles treaties that he personally regarded as disastrous, because he believed that they could be improved and their impact softened through future actions of the League. The terrible irony, of course, was that the United States never joined the League of Nations and thus never provided the leadership and moral vision that Wilson considered essential.

Interpretations of the ultimate failure of the Versailles conferences to produce a just and lasting peace reflect the continuing struggle between realists and idealists. In the idealist view, Versailles failed and the Second World War engulfed Europe because of the harsh terms realists like Clemenceau and Lloyd George imposed on Germany, terms so harsh they virtually guaranteed anger, resentment, and revenge. In contrast, realists believe that Wilsonian idealism corrupted the diplomatic process and led to both unachievable goals and unworkable means; Germany had been treated not too harshly but not harshly enough, and had not learned its lesson. Throughout the rest of this century, realists and idealists have wrangled about how power ought to be used and what its ends ought to be without arriving at any absolute answers. This argument is above all an echo of the debates that raged throughout the Versailles conference, the great confrontation between those who believed that power must be used for moral purposes and those who argued that power must be harnessed to ensure the survival and prosperity of the nation, itself an ultimate moral good.

Ideologies

One of the most important events of 1919 happened not at Versailles but a thousand miles from the elegance of Louis XIV's Hall of Mirrors, in the vast reaches of what had been the Russian Empire. That empire, in disarray long before the Great War erupted, had collapsed under the strains of the war. In February 1917, Tsar Nicholas II, recognizing that he and his government were no longer capable of running the Russian Empire, had abdicated, turning government over to a cousin with the stipulation that a democracy would be created. That democracy, with very shallow roots, had appeared by the summer of 1917; however, the newborn Russian government rashly overextended itself by attempting to achieve three major goals: the creation of a totally reformed democratic government within Russia; massive social reforms long overdue to bring Russia more in consonance with the twentieth century, both socially and industrially; and the continued involvement of Russia as a major ally in the war. Any one of these three tasks would have been difficult; achieving all three was probably impossible.

In October 1917 the overextended democratic experiment fell apart as a result of a coup d'état led by Vladimir Ilyich Lenin, who, with a small group of dedicated revolutionaries known to history as the Bolsheviks, set in its stead a revolutionary Marxist government.

The appearance of a Marxist government in Russia represented a dual nightmare: both Russian withdrawal from the war, which would permit Germany to transfer up to a million troops to the western front, and, even more frightening in the long run, a communist state on the fringes of Europe, positioned to carry out the Marxist revolution. In an attempt to deal with this, the Allies dispatched armies to both European and Asiatic Russia in a desperate attempt at a counterrevolution. That this counterrevolution was doomed to failure was becoming more and more evident even as the Versailles conference met; by the time the conference ended in the early summer of 1919, the Allies already had begun to withdraw their armies from the newly formed Union of Soviet Socialist Republics, admitting their defeat and reluctantly accepting the continued existence of a Marxist state in Europe.

The new USSR was in many ways far more experimental than the nation-states being carved out of the old European empires at this time. In contrast to the spirit of nationalism that stimulated the redrawing of much of Europe, it was ideology that undergirded the formation of the Soviet Union. This represented a great experiment, an attempt to create a utopian society based on the revolutionary ideology of **Marxism.** The establishment of a Soviet state would almost immediately provide a counterforce to the emergence of the United States as the largest and most powerful of the industrial democracies; much of the history of the last half of the twentieth century would unfold in the context of the rivalry between these two great nations. Equally important, the Soviet Union would often represent a touchstone for emerging nations outside of Europe, with its ideology that promised a better world for all and its example of going at it alone, outside the framework created by the industrial democracies of Europe and the West.

Through the Third International, the Soviet Union would also spread revolutionary doctrine and support revolutionary nationalism worldwide for much of the twentieth century. Its motives were not always pure and unmixed; clearly, much of this effort was designed less to aid the struggling peoples of the imperial colonies than to cause problems for the imperialist nations.

Although absent from the Versailles conference, Russia nevertheless cast a long shadow over the proceedings. The Russian Revolution continued to boil across the vast landscape of the old empire and the great powers—England, the U.S., and France—admitted their failure to contain it. They had to acknowledge the existence of a powerful new force in European and world affairs, the militantly Marxist Union of Soviet Socialist Republics. The Soviet Union represented a nightmare come true for the rest of the Great Powers: not only had the physically largest and potentially most powerful of the nation-states fallen victim to an ideology implacably hostile to the capitalism and democracy that most of them espoused, but also it could now serve as a launching pad for secret agents and agitators to fan out through the world and spread this pernicious gospel of a Marxist utopia. The threat of the Soviet Union would shape and often disrupt international relations from the Versailles conference to the present.

Marxism The ideology named after Karl Marx, the nineteenth-century German philosopher. With Georg Hegel, Marx emphasized the dialectical progression of history—thesis, antithesis, synthesis—which, according to the theory, yielded a higher stage of human being, who is seen as merely an economic animal.

Resources and Regions

More than earlier wars, the Great War had underlined the importance of natural resources, particularly of a resource that few would have stopped to consider even twenty years earlier: oil. One of the most important changes that took place on the eve of World War I was the decision by Britain's Royal Navy to transform all of its coal-burning ships into an oil-burning fleet. From the moment First Lord of the Admiralty Winston Churchill made that decision in the summer of 1914, the industrial world would no longer be dependent for its energy solely on supplies of coal and iron ore; a brand new factor—oil—had entered the resource picture. There was a problem with this: much of the world's known oil supply lay not within the boundaries of Europe, but in the Soviet Union, along the Iranian plateau, and within the United States. Consequently, the shift to greater and greater dependence on oil would accelerate the rise of the United States, create new problems for a Europe that now found itself cut off from the rich sources of oil in the Soviet Union, and bring into new prominence the Middle East, long a crossroads of controversy but destined to become throughout the twentieth century the holder of resources upon which most of the rest of the world depended.

Until the eve of World War I, much of the Middle East and virtually all of its oil-bearing territory had been within the realm of the Ottoman Empire, the so-called Sick Old Man of Europe. Unwisely, that empire had chosen to enter the war on the side of the Central Powers (whose other members were Germany, Austria-Hungary, and Bulgaria). The newly established Turkish government that succeeded the Ottoman Empire was as unable to consolidate power, carry out reform, and wage a great war as the newly formed Russian government would be. The result was that much of the Middle East was up for grabs; the Versailles conference parceled out large parts of that vital area among the various great powers. Largely artificial lines were slashed across the map. Under the auspices of the League of Nations, France was given control of Lebanon and Syria, and England received control of the vital belt that stretched from the Mediterranean coast of what was then Palestine to the edges of the British Empire in Afghanistan. Under the mandate system established at Versailles, England controlled Palestine and Mesopotamia. Since Iran was largely an English protectorate at that time, this put much of the world's known supply of oil under the control of England, not exactly an accident. Britain's interest in much of the Middle East was related not solely to oil, but also to its strategic position as guard of the Suez Canal, acknowledged as the lifeline of the British Empire. In fact, although the Arabian Peninsula became loosely a British protectorate after the war, and in the early 1920s England would help Ibn Saud organize a government there, nothing was yet known of the vast oil reserves that lay under the peninsula; the first great Saudi field would not be discovered and explored until the 1930s.

England's coming to power in the Middle East would have far-reaching consequences for many people besides its own, and would play a major role in creating the long-term problems that still bedevil the Middle East.

In 1917, England made a poorly-thought-out attempt to win support in the old Ottoman Empire by announcing the Balfour Declaration. Under the terms of this declaration, the British government came out in favor of the principle of Zionism, that is, the establishment of a Jewish homeland in the biblical land of Israel. The British government was careful to hedge this statement with the disclaimer that it would support this idea only so long as it did not displace the current Arab population. Hailed by European Jews, the Balfour Declaration would become the basis for the movement of a substantial Jewish population to the state of Palestine. This migration brought Jews into conflict with Arabs, whose claims to the land of Palestine were nearly as ancient as, and whose absolute residence was far longer than, those of the Jews. The stage was set for both the emergence of the modern state of Israel and the conflict between Israel and its Muslim Arab neighbors that has dominated so much of Middle Eastern politics in the last half of the twentieth century.

Clearly, the seeds of the Arab-Israeli conflict were sown in the period of Versailles, by both the Balfour Declaration and the parceling out of the Middle East to France and England under the mandate system.

Personalities

The dominant personality at Versailles was Woodrow Wilson, the American president. Austere, rigid, idealistic, the scholarly Wilson sought to reinvent international relations on his own terms, according to his own soaring idealism and his

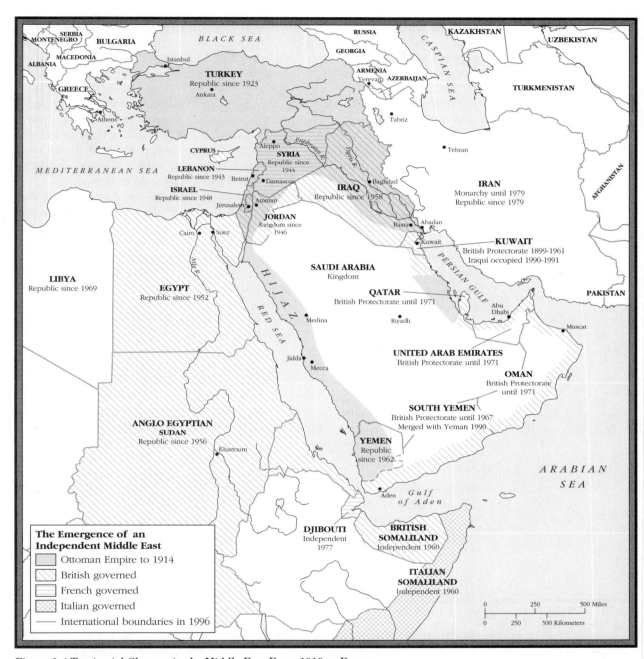

Figure 1.4 **Territorial Changes in the Middle East From 1918 to Present**

vision of a world order based not on power but on morality and justice. In part by sheer force of personality and determination, and in part because he was backed by the military and industrial strength of the United States, Wilson was able to dictate the boundaries of the Versailles discussions and to force his reluctant British and French allies to accept at least parts of his vision of a new world. But at the same time, that very rigidity and austerity also undermined Wilson at what should have been his greatest moment of triumph, the presentation of his treaties to the American people. The same sense of righteousness that had enabled him to shape the Versailles treaties was a major factor in his failure to win approval of those treaties from the United States Senate.

Although historians and political scientists will continue to debate the reasons for both Wilson's failures and his successes well into the future, they also agree that the Versailles conference would have been a very different process indeed had another American president been involved. For example, it is almost impossible to envision the ebullient Teddy Roosevelt playing the role Wilson took at Versailles, and fully impossible to imagine the highly skilled but very pragmatic Richard Nixon molding the conference according to Wilson's vision.

Far from Versailles, another powerful individual was simultaneously demonstrating the force of one will: Vladimir Ilyich Lenin, architect of the Bolshevik Revolution. Charismatic, brilliant, and utterly ruthless, Lenin seized control of a small and virtually powerless faction of a minor Russian political party and used it to seize power in the chaos of the revolution. Lenin had not started the Russian Revolution, but he alone had the clarity of vision, determination of purpose, and amoral ruthlessness to take it over and remake it. Like Wilson, Lenin was animated by ideals, although antithetical ones. And like Wilson, Lenin was able to force complex events along paths he dictated. And finally, like Wilson, Lenin was ultimately unable to mold the unruly forces of either international or domestic politics as surely as he believed he could.

The Russian Revolution, of course, was an enormously complex event, but no one can deny that its result, and the course of the next sixty years of international relations, would have been far different had there not been a Lenin, or had the German government not sent Lenin and his followers back to Russia in a Pandora's box railroad train. Likewise, it is hard to imagine the course of twentieth-century history without Adolf Hitler, Joseph Stalin, Mao Tse-tung, or Mikhail Gorbachev.

As we stated at the beginning of this chapter, there are strong arguments for using each of the three levels of analysis to examine world affairs, and equally strong arguments that true understanding of international relations can come only by studying and combining the three levels. Certainly, the Versailles conference justifies examination of the social-psychological level, as it illustrates vividly how strong-minded individuals can bend history to their own wills.

Summary

International relations provide an essential backdrop to our daily existence—but because they do not occupy the foreground of our attention, we frequently take them for granted, assuming that life as we know it will go on as usual, and that we can safely ignore global affairs. This is not necessarily the case. We have attempted to point out that what you do not know can, and frequently will, hurt you. Events in a part of the world that you have never even heard of could affect your life—could even end it!

Coming to grips with such a complex discipline as global politics requires careful and sometimes tedious analysis. Political scientists have devised the "levels of analysis" framework to help them examine the political behavior of the world's actors. The three levels on which to analyze such behavior, listed from the most comprehensive level to the least, are the global/systems, the nation-state, and the social-psychological levels. By carefully examining global behavior, political scientists hope to develop theory, and then in turn to use such theory to describe, explain, and predict political behavior.

In this chapter, we have likened this interplay of events and theory to meteorology. A political meteorologist must be familiar with the "lay of the land." The political world at the beginning of the century looked somewhat similar to today's world. However, several shifts in the Earth's underlying political plates and climatic conditions have occurred since that time, to leave us with the distinctive global political landscape of the late twentieth century.

The century began with the preeminence of vast European and Middle Eastern empires—empires whose remnants lay in ashes by 1919, to be replaced by nation-states forged out of the new ideal of nationalism: the demand of peoples to form their own particular nations and create their own destinies. The Great War, World War I, had unleashed the forces of nationalism, which were to be quelled only temporarily by the ideological contest that followed World War II.

World War II gave birth to the Cold War. During this era, ideology overshadowed nationalism, pitting two systems of thought—communism and liberal democracy—against each other. The United States and the USSR were the principal antagonists, with the world's other nations looking on—or sometimes up, to see who was trampling them! The Cold War brought a peace of sorts. The United States and the Soviet Union did not engage each other directly in military conflict; instead, in this era of high tension, each superpower used its smaller allies as their pawns. With two superpowers armed to the teeth with nuclear weapons, there was grave cause for concern about any direct confrontation between the East and the West.

We have noted that the world we see today is somewhat similar to the Europe of the 1920s. It is a world experiencing the birthpangs of nationalism. Yet even as some nations are forming, others are disintegrating. It is also a world experiencing (especially in the developed nations of the West) economic integration through huge trading blocs. Today's world is different.

In this maelstrom of change, it is easy to overlook the fact that people are at the core of political behavior. To a great extent, political personalities have shaped the world we live in today. People have a history; they also have ideas. Thus we analyze international relations at various levels rather than focusing on nation-states or international systems.

Key Terms

International politics
Political integration
Political disintegration

Nation-state
Transgovernmental actors
Supragovernmental organizations

Technology
Levels of analysis
Global/systems level of analysis
Nation-state level of analysis
Social-psychological level of analysis
Theory
Cold War
Sovereignty
NATO
Versailles conference
Ethnicity

Ideology
Nationalism
Imperialism
National self-determination
Revolutionary nationalism
Power
Realism
Idealism
Balance of Power theory
Marxism

Thought Questions

1. Describe how the Paris Peace Conference of 1919 helped to set the stage for global politics in the latter part of the century.
2. Discuss the relevance of nationalism to world politics in the twentieth century.
3. Comment on the role of natural resources in international relations.
4. What is the impact of technology on world politics today?

References

CIA World Fact Book (Washington, D.C.: Central Intelligence Agency, 1996), Internet.http://www.odci.gov/cia/publications/95fact. Downloaded May 10, 1996.

Herz, John H. *International Politics in the Atomic Age*. New York: Columbia University Press, 1962.

Knorr, Klaus, and J. N. Rosenau. *Contending Approaches to International Politics*. Princeton: Princeton University Press, 1969.

Singer, J. David. "The Levels-of-Analysis Problem in International Relations." In Klaus Knorr and Sidney Verba (eds.). *The International System*. Princeton: Princeton University Press, 1969.

Waltz, Kenneth. *Man, the State, and War*. New York: Columbia University Press, 1954.

Chapter 2

How to Get Your Way in the World: Power

Introduction

What Is Power?

Power is simultaneously the single most important and the single most elusive concept in international relations. While political scientists would agree that power is central to political relationships, they often disagree on what constitutes power. One of the most practical definitions comes from President Harry Truman: "Power is the ability to get someone to do something that they wouldn't otherwise normally do." And Hans Morgenthau, a leading scholar of international politics, holds that "when we speak of power, we mean man's control over the minds and actions of other men . . . . Political power is a psychological relation between those who exercise it and those over whom it is exercised" (Morgenthau 1979, 32).

Even a working definition of power in general fails to list its components; defining and calculating the relative power of nations is even more complex. For example, we might confidently assume that military power is an obvious component of a nation's power. And it is comparatively easy, at least in democratic societies, to count ships and soldiers and tanks. Governments love to publish long lists of such measures of power (generally the ones that make them look best). But there are other elements that aren't published. How well trained are these soldiers? How well maintained are these ships? How do these tanks measure up against another country's tank-killing weapons? Unless we know the answers to questions like this, we don't know how much power the statistics really represent, and we certainly can't compare the power of two nations with precision. Yet diplomats and military planners must work with these unnervingly inexact figures every day.

During the 1970s and 1980s the United States and the former Soviet Union each spent enormous amounts of time and energy trying to prove itself more powerful than the other. One component of military power officials counted and recounted was missiles. The Soviet Union had more missiles than the United States, and they were huge, with enormous destructive power. However, the United States' missiles were far more sophisticated and accurate than those of the Soviet Union, and the United States had a far more varied ballistic arsenal, including land-based, air-based, and sea-based missiles. But the land-based missiles of the former Soviet Union were mobile. Which country was more powerful? Luckily, the all-out nuclear war that would have answered that question did not occur.

In this chapter we will approach power in several different ways. First, we will present some of the key sources of national power, and venture to judge relative power relationships in today's world. Then we will examine two different ways diplomats and political leaders have looked at power: the idealist and the realist perspectives. Finally, we will discuss how power is distributed globally, tracing various, historical expressions of the idea of the balance of power, and examining recent shifts in the relative power of nations.

Sources of National Power

Political scientists generally distinguish three different sources of national power: natural sources (geography, natural resources, and population), social-psychological sources (national stability, leadership, and political will), and synthetic sources (industrial capacity and military capacity). In this section we will examine all three components of national power and attempt to rank the world's largest and most populous nations in terms of their relative power.

Natural Sources of Power

Geography

Geography, which we will define as land and location, has always played a major role in determining power, although the extent of its importance has varied and can be affected by other considerations.

Size.   One major element of geography is *size,* or land mass. Throughout history, and particularly in the modern era, the size of a nation has been a major factor in determining its power. For example, both the United States and Russia possess huge physical size; the old Soviet Union extended across eleven time zones, almost halfway around the world. Russia's great size has been a key factor in protecting it from invaders: both Napoleon and Hitler came to grief on the vast expanse of Russian soil. However, size alone does not guarantee power. Despite its great size, Canada has not emerged as a major international power, largely because of its relatively small population and because so much of its land mass lies in far northern regions whose forbidding climates make agriculture impossible.

Table 2.1 lists some of the world's more important nations according to physical size. The positions of Russia, the United States, and China at the very top of the list conforms to the concept that power is related to land mass. However, India's fifth-place ranking, like Canada's third-place position, denotes potential rather than actual power. And some of the more powerful nations of the twentieth century—Japan, the United Kingdom, Germany, and France—appear far down on this list. Clearly, while sheer size is important, it is not the only major ingredient of national power.

Table 2.1
Land Mass

Country	Size in square miles
Russia	6,592,846
China	3,962,244
Canada	3,849,672
USA	3,787,425
India	1,269,345
Saudi Arabia	900,000
Mexico	756,065
Iran	636,296
Turkey	300,948
France	210,026
Iraq	167,925
Japan	145,870
Germany	137,817
UK	94,247
Israel	8,000

Source: Central Intelligence Agency, *World Factbook 1995.*

A large land mass usually also implies rich natural resources, another important component of power, and one we will discuss later in this section. But size is not the only way to judge the value of land mass. China, for example, is about 10 percent larger physically than the United States and possesses plentiful natural resources, although their nature and extent are still being explored. But much of China's land mass consists of mountainous or desert terrain; estimates are that as little as 15 percent of China's land is arable, that is, level enough, fertile enough, and receiving enough rainfall to be cultivated for food production. Vast expanses of Russia's land also are not suited for agriculture, primarily because they lie too far north to permit food crops to grow successfully. In contrast, as much as 85 percent of the land mass of the United States is arable, and thus capable of supporting a huge agricultural enterprise.

Location is also critical to national power and not just for the climatological reasons mentioned above. *Borders* are important as well. A nation that borders on hostile states is insecure, if not powerless. For example, the massive nations of China and Russia have faced one another along five thousand miles of hostile border since the middle of this century. The enormous amounts of money they have spent in fortifying and protecting this border have sapped the strength of both. On the other hand, the United States has been fortunate in enjoying essentially peaceful relations with both its northern and its southern neighbors for most of the last two centuries; neither Canada nor Mexico constitutes a military threat against which Americans have had to arm themselves. Because its other borders are the great waterways of the Atlantic and Pacific Oceans and the Gulf of Mexico, the United States has enjoyed an essentially sheltered location that has given it both time and room to develop into a major power. In addition, its long coastlines also permitted early and easy American entry into international trade. In contrast is Russia, which despite its vast bulk, historically has had no direct outlet to the major oceans. Much of Russia's history can be seen as an attempt to seize control of warm-water ports. Nineteenth-century imperialism enabled Russia to gain a Pacific port when it seized a narrow strip of land from China and built the great port of Vladivostok—but even Vladivostok is thousands of cold and treacherous miles from European Russia and its major industrial and population sites.

A general rule of thumb among students of international relations is that there is a strong correlation between the number of national borders a state has and the frequency of conflicts it is involved in. This correlation has been particularly evident on the continent of Europe, but the experiences of both Lebanon and Israel in the Middle East also seem to support it. In contrast, England and the United States, with relatively few borders, can more or less choose the wars in which they will participate.

strategic location The politically important geographical characteristics and position of a nation.

Lebanon and Israel are also examples of the way **strategic location** can affect a nation. Both nations lie at the historic crossroads of the Middle East, on that strip of land along the eastern Mediterranean that has been a pathway for trade, expansion, and war almost since civilization itself arose just to the east, on the banks of the Tigris and Euphrates Rivers. A nation's location in a strategically significant area can increase its power, as has tended to happen for Israel, or turn it into a battleground for everyone, as has tended to happen for Lebanon.

chokepoint A narrow body of water or land whose possessor can exercise great power through controlling communications.

A vital concept when discussing the importance of strategic location to national power is the idea of the **chokepoint.** A chokepoint is a narrow body of water or land whose possessor can exercise great power by controlling communications. Major chokepoints are identified in figure 2.1.

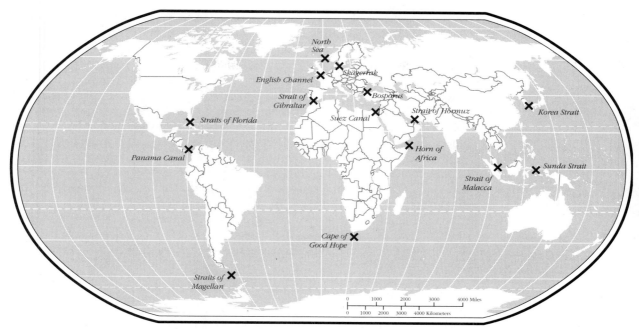

Figure 2.1 **Global Chokepoints**

The Strait of Gibraltar, the gateway between the Mediterranean Sea and the Atlantic Ocean, has through history been one of the world's most important chokepoints; a great deal of Britain's nineteenth- and twentieth-century political and military strategy was geared to maintaining control of this chokepoint and thus access to critical waterways. More recently, the Strait of Hormuz between the Persian Gulf and the Red Sea has been a critical chokepoint because of its importance to oil tanker routes. In the late 1980s, the United States sought to demonstrate its power and protect its interests by dispatching substantial navy units to patrol the Persian Gulf and keep the Strait of Hormuz open. This action, sometimes interpreted as a mere sideshow or prelude to the 1991 Gulf War, was both a recognition and a demonstration of the strategic significance of this chokepoint.

Other narrow bodies of water also have been critical chokepoints: the English Channel; Tsushima Strait between Korea and Japan; the Bosporus, separating Turkey from continental Europe; the Strait of Malacca, threading its way from the Indian Ocean to the South China Sea; the Panama Canal, linking the Atlantic and Pacific Oceans; and the Suez Canal, stretching from the Mediterranean to the Red Sea.

The strategic significance of South Africa and its potential power are derived partly from its position astride the turbulent waters connecting the Indian and Atlantic Oceans, one of the most important routes for heavily laden tankers carrying Middle Eastern oil to Europe and the Americas.

Chokepoints change. The Suez Canal, once the lifeline of the British Empire, has shrunk in importance partly because it cannot accommodate modern supertankers carrying oil, and partly because of the decline of the British Empire. The Panama Canal is arguably less important in this era of supertankers than it has been in the past; today, many of the most important ships in the American navy can barely squeeze into its narrow and thus antiquated locks.

One of the ironies of these chokepoints is that the nations whose lands they border have often found themselves to be victims rather than players in power games, as larger and more powerful states have found it advantageous to control these vital chokepoints. For example, the Panama Canal passes through what used to be the territory owned by Colombia. That country lost rather than gained power because of the canal's strategic location, as its far more powerful northern neighbor, the United States, sought to protect and increase its own power by establishing control over the Isthmus of Panama. Likewise, neither Malaysia nor Indonesia has profited from bordering on the crucial Strait of Malacca, connecting the Indian Ocean to the South China Sea and eventually to the Pacific Ocean. Instead, for the last four hundred years, control of the Strait of Malacca has rested with one of the powerful, expansionist European nations, first Holland and then Britain. In addition, the city-state of Singapore at the edge of the strait is acknowledged as one of the "dragons" of Asia, at least in part because of its control of the strait. The strait's importance is highlighted by the recent U.S. decision to base part of its Pacific fleet in the Singapore navy yards abandoned by England as its power declined.

Geopolitics

geopolitics World affairs viewed primarily from a national security perspective.

Late in the nineteenth century a group of strategists and players in the game of nations attempted to create a new "science," **geopolitics,** that would relate the importance of land and location to local and global power.

In 1890, just as steam power and steel armor were revolutionizing the world's navies, an American navy captain and strategist, Alfred Thayer *Mahan* wrote one of the first major works of geopolitics, *The Influence of Seapower upon History*. According to Mahan, the great empires of history have been built on control of the seas. The paths that ships cleave across these waters comprising five-sixths of the earth's surface ultimately determine the power of a nation. True power requires fleets of merchant ships to carry the nation's goods along these trade routes, vast navies to protect and keep open vital shipping lanes, and far-flung naval bases. Only a navy, Mahan argued, can truly project a nation's power great distances from its borders. Not surprisingly, Mahan's theory of the importance of the seas both described the greatest of nineteenth-century powers, Great Britain, whose mighty empire depended on control of the seas, and prescribed the path to global power for the United States, 60 percent of whose borders are lapped by ocean waters. Mahan's works on seapower quickly became required reading in naval academies around the world, and there is no question that his ideas contributed to the development of American naval power. His theories were also influential in Japan, an island nation seeking sources of wealth and power, and in Germany, clawing its way upward in a struggle for European and global power. The combination of new naval technology and the cogency of Mahan's ideas played a major role in touching off the great naval arms race of the late nineteenth and early twentieth centuries, and in turn this arms race was a major trigger for World War I. (For a more detailed discussion of this process, see Massey 1992).

Scarcely a decade later, the second great geopolitical thinker of the modern world, Sir Halford *Mackinder,* posited a very different geopolitical key to power: control of essential areas of the Eurasian continent. He maintained that improvements in land transportation, and particularly in railroads, had made the seas comparatively less important. The key to power, Mackinder believed, lay in control of the "pivot area," illustrated in figure 2.2, that stretched from eastern Europe across the steppes and forests to the Siberian plains (in other words, much of the Russian empire). The "Heartland," as Mackinder called this vast Eurasian interior, contained both great resources and vital communications. The Heartland was surrounded by an "inner crescent" that included Germany, Turkey, India, and China, and an "outer crescent" that included outliers such as Britain, South Africa, and Japan. Dividing the world as he did in this way (note that the United States is so far away that it isn't even accorded the status of "outer crescent"), Mackinder formulated three classic rules for the wielding of power on a global scale:

Who rules East Europe commands the Heartland.
Who rules the Heartland commands the World Island [Eurasia].
Who rules the World Island commands the World. (Morgenthau 1979, 62)

Although many give Mackinder credit for predicting the rise of the Soviet Union as a superpower, since it in fact controlled the Heartland, others point out that there are major flaws in the Heartland theory. Among other omissions, the Heartland theory fails to account for air power, which makes the Heartland more penetrable than Mackinder believed, and also for the terrible difficulties of developing the tundra, taiga, and desert that constitute much of the Heartland. One such difficulty is dealing with the permafrost that underlies substantial parts of this area (Jordan and Rowntree 1990, 142–43).

Mackinder's Heartland theory stimulated another major attempt to link geography and global politics, Nicholas Spykman's "rimland theory." *Spykman* agreed with Mackinder that Eurasia was the key to world conquest, but Spykman emphasized the importance of the "rimland," the vast coastal area that encircled the heartland (see fig. 2.3). Two-thirds of the world population inhabited that rimland, Spykman emphasized, and the rimland itself was far more hospitable than the environmentally harsh Heartland. Furthermore, the rimland had multiple pathways into the Heartland. To counter Mackinder, Spykman wrote

Who rules the rimland rules Eurasia.
Who rules Eurasia rules the world.

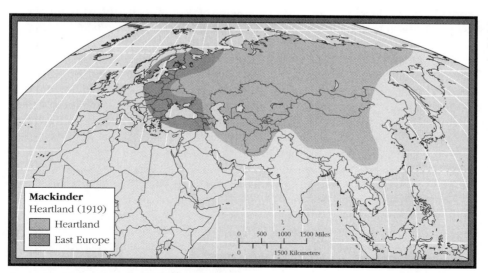

Figure 2.2
Mackinder's Heartland Theory

Source: Mackinder, Sir Halford. (1919). *Democratic Ideals and Reality.* New York: Henry A. Holt.

Figure 2.3
Spykman's Rimland Theory

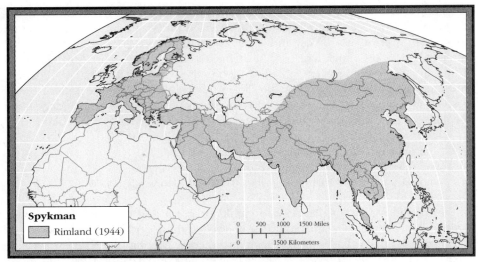

Spykman

Rimland (1944)

0   500   1000   1500 Miles

0   1500 Kilometers

Source: Mackinder (1919). *Democratic Ideals and Reality.* New York: Henry A. Holt.

In addition to being a neatly phrased rebuttal to Mackinder, Spykman's parody presented a view of global balance that was to underlie much of U.S. foreign policy after World War II (DeBlij and Muller 1988, 181–82; Jordan and Rowntree 1990, 142–44).

Some students of modern international relations believe that Mackinder's theories influenced, among other things, the realist policies of Cold War American foreign policy. Some argue, that as the "rimland" or "outer crescent" of Eurasia became more and more important because of changes in technology, the idea of containment that was the basis of America's Cold War policy toward the Soviet Union basically restated Mackinder by claiming that power could run two ways, both from the Heartland out and from the rimland in. By controlling the rimland, and through building a series of alliances in western Europe, across southern Asia, and in Southeast Asia, America could dominate the rimland and thus prevent full Soviet exploitation of its position in control of the Heartland. Other students of modern geopolitics point out that the foreign policy of Richard Nixon and Henry Kissinger, both geopoliticians and "realists," emphasized in large part "playing the China card." That is, by exploiting the rivalry and even hostility between the two largest communist nations, the Soviet Union and the People's Republic of China, the Americans sought to prevent their reconciliation and thus their united control of the Heartland.

By the end of the nineteenth century the most devastating critique of these theories had already appeared, long in advance of either Mackinder or Spykman. In 1899 a British scientist, Sir William Crookes, emphasized that aggression and seizure of land was not necessary for a nation to increase its living standard. The key, he emphasized, was technology (Bergman 1995, 347). In recent years, technology, in the form of everything from airplanes to intercontinental ballistic missiles, has indeed rendered much of the strategic thinking behind both the Heartland and the rimland theories obsolete.

The New Geopolitics. Far more sophisticated versions of geopolitics have emerged since Mahan and MacKinder enunciated their theories. *The new geopolitics* is a complex mixture of concepts including realms and regions, shatterbelts and gateways (see fig. 2.4).

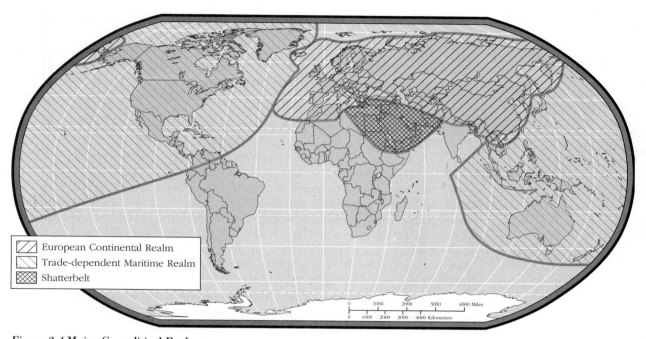

Figure 2.4 **Major Geopolitical Realms**
This map shows how Saul B. Cohen sees the world geopolitically in terms of two major realms, the European Continental and the Maritime realms. Note that most of South America, Africa, and South Asia lie outside these realms, in what Cohen calls the "quartersphere of marginality." Note too the "shatterbelt" caught between the realms.

According to Saul B. Cohen, a former president of the Association of American Geographers, today's world is divided into a geopolitical hierarchy whose elements are, in descending order, realms, regions, nation-states, and subnational units (Cohen 1991). There are two geostrategic realms, or arenas of strategic place and movement: the Maritime realm and the Eurasian continental realm. The two realms differ in many ways; for example, while the Maritime realm is open to specialized exchange, the Eurasian continental realm is inward-oriented. Each realm in turn contains several regions, the result of contiguity and political, cultural, military, and economic interaction. The Maritime realm contains a number of regions: Anglo-America and the Caribbean, Maritime Europe and the Maghreb, offshore Asia, South America, and sub-Saharan Africa. In contrast, the Eurasian continental realm contains only two regions, the Russian heartland and East Asia. Nation-states and subnational regions, the most specific constructs in the geopolitical world, are already familiar.

Cohen introduces several other geopolitical concepts as well. One of the most important is the idea of **shatterbelts,** "politically fragmented areas of competition between the maritime and continental realms." (Cohen 1991) Southeast Asia, once a shatterbelt, has now been politically and economically integrated into the offshore Asia region of the maritime realm. The last remaining shatterbelt is the Middle East, which seems to be moving toward the maritime realm as well, especially as a result of the collapse of the Soviet Union. The high degree of political fragmentation in the Middle Eastern shatterbelt—it contains six major regional powers, Egypt, Iran, Iraq, Israel, Syria, and Turkey—may keep it in shatterbelt status for quite a while.

shatterbelts Flashpoints of geostrategic contention.

gateway Geographical term for key passages of (usually, but not exclusively) water for shipping of goods.

Another concept Cohen stresses is the **gateway** region. Gateways have several distinct characteristics: they are generally distinct historic culture hearths, they are often economically more developed than surrounding areas, they are small in both population and area, and they lie athwart key access routes. According to Cohen, today's gateways have often been unstable conflict zones, but the relative peace created by the end of the Cold War has allowed them to change their function and their status. Because they straddle geopolitical borders, gateways readily serve integrative functions between the realms and among the regions, with specialized manufacturing, trade, tourism, and financial services available to the realms. At present, the most important gateway consists of the band of Central and Eastern European countries that stretches from the Baltic to the Adriatic, caught but not crushed between the maritime and continental realms. Figure 2.5 illustrates Cohen's predicted future gateways. Cohen believes that the Middle East possesses the ability to become a gateway, as does the Caribbean, which could become a gateway between Anglo-America to the north and Latin America to the south. The more gateways the better, in Cohen's view, because they will become major contributors to a peaceful and stable global system by linking together otherwise separate regions and realms.

Lying outside the major realms and regions is what Cohen calls "the quartersphere of marginality." Two major areas fall into this category: sub-Saharan Africa, with the exception of the Union of South Africa, and South America, with the exceptions of Brazil, Argentina, and Chile. The marginal areas, which are depicted in figure 2.4, share common problems: grinding poverty, overpopulation, low life expectancy, poor diet, dependence on the export of raw materials no longer

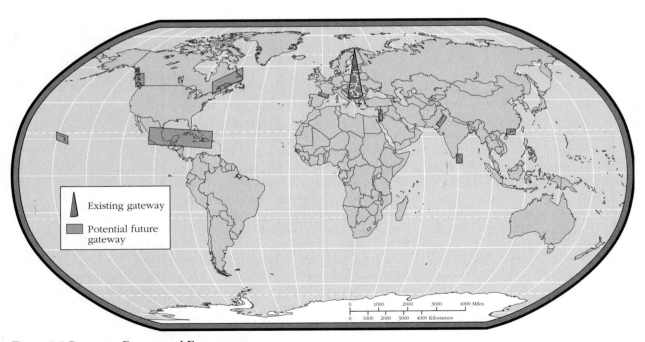

Existing gateway

Potential future gateway

Figure 2.5 **Gateways, Present and Future**
This map shows the major existing Gateway in East Europe, according to Cohen, as well as areas that he feels will emerge as twenty-first century gateways: the Caribbean, British Columbia, Hawaii, Quebec, the Basque region, Kashmir-Punjab region, Sri Lanka, the Gaza-West Bank area, and the Hong Kong-Shenzen area.

regarded as strategic by the developed world, and massive debt. Cohen has little hope that these areas will be able to join either the maritime or the continental realm without massive infusions of capital, technology, and aid. However, he fears, the quarter-sphere will "not receive substantially new help unless there is a sea-change in the attitudes of the wealthy of the world . . . [through which] strategic and economic disinterest give way to humanitarian considerations"—or unless some quarter-sphere nation acquires weapons of mass destruction and uses them to demand consideration by the two realms. Without such aid, the quarter-sphere will remain conflict-prone and destabilizing (Cohen 1991).

Natural Resources

Quite logically, natural resources are a major determinant of a nation's power. The state with vast internal resources can be virtually autonomous, that is, dependent on no outside suppliers of materials, and need not fear having vital materials denied in the midst of crisis. However, as with virtually every other facet of national power, the role played by natural resources in determining national power has varied widely.

The United States possesses bountiful natural resources; it is the world's leading producer of molybdenum and phosphates, its second leading producer of silver and copper, and its third leading producer of gold. It also has abundant energy resources: the U.S. is the world's largest producer of both electricity and petroleum, second largest producer of natural gas and uranium, and third largest producer of coal (Chaliand and Rageau 1992, 93). Russia, by virtue of its enormous size, also possesses enormous natural resources, although exact statistics are impossible to obtain at this point. In contrast, Japan, although a major industrial and financial power, is terribly deficient in natural resources: it must import 100 percent of its copper and uranium, 99 percent of its oil, 92 percent of its iron, 89 percent of its coal, and 92 percent of its other required minerals (Chaliand and Rageau 1992, 171).

Food. One of the most important natural resources is *food*. When calculating national power, students of international relations ask whether a given nation can feed itself, and if so, how good that diet will be. Obviously, great continental powers like Russia, Germany, and the United States, potentially self-sufficient in food production, enjoy great advantages over smaller powers like England and Japan, which must import substantial amounts of their food and are thus vulnerable to boycotts or to interdiction of imports. However, Russia's potential for self-sufficiency has been seriously compromised by major problems of production and distribution, as disturbingly long food lines have testified over the last few years—and therein lies danger. A population either hungry or worried about hunger is a dangerous population: lack of bread, a staple in the diet of most commoners, played a major role in precipitating both the French Revolution of 1789 and the Russian Revolution of 1917. Even today the potential power of major nations such as China and India is severely compromised because their food production lags behind or barely keeps step with population growth. On the other hand, food production is not all-important: Canada and Argentina, although major exporters of foodstuffs, have not become major powers because of different limiting factors.

Figure 2.6 shows the average daily number of calories available in the world's major nations. Again, there are few surprises. The leading industrial nations—France, Italy, Germany, the United States, and Japan—all enjoy diets providing far

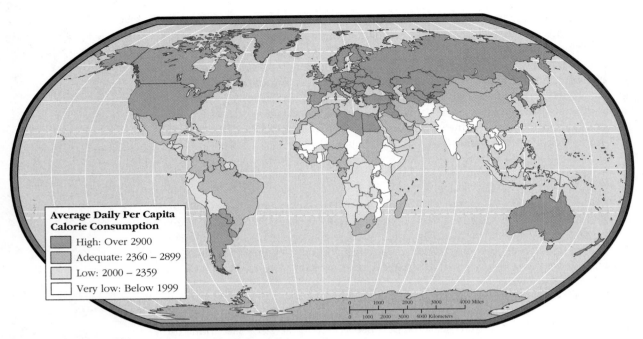

Figure 2.6 World Average Daily per Capita Calorie Consumption
Source: Data from United Nations, Food and Agriculture Organization Statistics. Figure modified from H. J. deBlij and P. O. Muller, *Human Geography: Culture, Society, and Space,* 3rd ed. (New York: John Wiley & Sons, 1986), pp. 60–61.

more than minimal requirements. China, despite its vast size and population, is able to sustain an adequate caloric level (2360 calories per day is considered optimum for a working adult), while India falls far below that level.

The United States enjoys a dominant position as the world's largest producer and exporter of food, accounting for over half the world's supply cereal grains (wheat, oats, corn, barley, sorghum). It ranks first in world production of soybeans, corn, and millet-sorghum, second in cotton lint and sunflowers, and third in wheat, barley, and hogs (Chaliand and Rageau 1992, 92). On the other hand, two nations with real claims to international power, Russia and Japan, have been importing vast amounts of grain in order to feed their populations. Clearly, they lack the autonomy in food supply that the U.S. enjoys, and are comparatively vulnerable to interruptions in their food supply. The recent disruptions caused by the continuing political crisis in Russia has certainly worsened that nation's already precarious position.

Energy, Raw Materials.   *Energy* and the *raw materials* used to produce it are perhaps the most important natural resources after food. In the eighteenth and nineteenth centuries, the latter took the form of iron ore and coal. These resources were the key to industrial revolution, and the nations with bountiful amounts of them—England, France, and Germany—were both the leading industrial nations and the leading "great powers." The United States' emergence as a major world power was linked at least in part to its vast troves of iron ore and coal; in contrast, Japan's emergence as a great power was always endangered because it had to rely on other nations for virtually all of its iron and coal.

The opening of the great Spindletop oil field in Texas in 1900 and subsequent discoveries helped make the United States a major global power in the twentieth century.

The Oil Age. The late nineteenth and early twentieth centuries saw the beginning of the *oil age*. Both widespread use of the internal combustion engine and its diesel cousin and the development of the petrochemical industry—producing textiles, plastics, and pharmaceuticals—made oil the most desired resource of the twentieth century. Those nations that enjoyed abundant pools of oil (as well as iron ore and coal) within their borders became the world leaders: the United States and the Soviet Union, with their abundant sources of oil, surged ahead of traditional powers like England and France that were dependent upon imported oil.

The emergence of oil as a dominant resource also created a whole new series of power equations, as much of the world's known reserves of oil are in the Middle East (see table 2.2). While most Middle Eastern countries—Saudi Arabia and Kuwait, for example—lack the other resources necessary to become major powers, they have become extraordinarily important players in world politics because of their control over world oil markets. Oil-producing nations banded together in the early 1960s to try to protect their interests by controlling both production and pricing of this vital resource. The cartel they formed, the Organization of Petroleum Exporting Countries (OPEC), was relatively powerless for the first decade of its existence, largely because its members lacked the political will to exert power.

However, oil politics changed radically in 1973, when the Arab OPEC countries united because of the Yom Kippur war between Israel and its Arab neighbors. Flexing their petro-muscles, the Arab OPEC states proclaimed an embargo on the sale of oil to any country deemed "too friendly" to Israel. The effects were immediate. In the United States, gasoline prices skyrocketed almost instantly to three times their pre-embargo levels; as gasoline became a scarce commodity, the United States instituted an informal rationing system, and motorists spent hours in line waiting to purchase fuel. Still, as hard as the United States was hit by the embargo, it was protected to some extent because over half of American oil needs were still being supplied by domestic production. Many developing countries

---

Table 2.2
World Crude Oil Reserves

Country	Oil Reserves (billions of barrels)
Saudi Arabia	262.5
Iraq	100.0
Kuwait	98.4
Iran	62.5
Russia	57.9
United Arab Emirates	55.7
Mexico	52.0
USA	26.5
Libya	22.8
China	21.5
Nigeria	16.7
Indonesia	12.3
Norway	11.0

Source: *Grolier Academic Encyclopedia*. Prodigy Online Service. Armonk, New York. Downloaded May 15, 1993.

were virtually devastated by the embargo: not only did transportation costs of all imported goods soar, but also petro-based products like fertilizer, essential to their efforts to feed themselves, suddenly were priced beyond their ability to pay (see Yergin 1992 for more information).

Japan has always had a shaky relationship to oil. Its drive to modernization in the late nineteenth and early twentieth centuries made it dependent on oil, but the nation lacked both domestic oil sources and access to oil through an overseas empire. Japan's desperate need for oil and the American decision to embargo sales of oil to the Japanese empire in the summer of 1941 were key elements in the Japanese decision to go to war in December 1941. The 1973 OPEC oil embargo was even more threatening to a Japan that, like most industrial powers, was more dependent than ever on oil, and the country quickly began shifting its foreign policy from friendship towards Israel to a far more pro-Arab position.

A second round of oil embargoes in 1979 sent prices soaring once again, causing still greater misery for developing nations and once again reminding the industrialized nations how fragile their oil-dependent economies were. The price of oil climbed to stratospheric heights: this "black gold," which had sold for roughly three dollars a barrel in 1962, was selling on the "spot market" for as much as thirty-nine dollars a barrel by 1984. The economies of the industrialized nations reeled under this sort of inflationary pressure. Happily, the price of oil soon plunged downward as a combination of conservation and sheer lack of money showed that even wealthy industrial nations could afford to spend only so much for oil.

Recently the oil markets have been relatively stable, as the major leaders of OPEC, particularly the Saudis, have recognized that it would harm them almost as much as it would harm the industrial nations if oil prices continued to skyrocket. After all, the oil-soaked monarchies of the Middle East have invested large portions of their petrodollar incomes in industrial nations such as England and the United States, and oil policies that harm the assets of those two nations ultimately harm Middle Eastern investments as well.

Retreating Iraqi forces torched hundreds of Kuwaiti oil wells in 1991 both as a gesture of defiance and as an attempt by Saddam Hussein to destroy what he could not have.

Nonetheless, the oil embargoes of the 1970s announced clearly that control of oil resources constitutes a major source of power in an industrial world heavily dependent on petroleum products. Further evidence of the power of oil is seen in the American patrols of the Persian Gulf; the struggle between environmentalists and oil companies over the production and transportation of oil in many of the world's last great wildernesses (such as the Arctic and various coastal waters); and the continuing global concern about instability in the Middle East.

Foreign policy analysts remain deeply concerned that vast oil resources lie under the control of Saddam Hussein in Iraq and Iran's governing mullahs, still vitriolically anti-American. Saddam's invasion of oil-rich Kuwait in the summer of 1990 and the American-coordinated Gulf War in the late winter of 1991 demonstrated two things clearly: the vulnerability of a large amount of the world's oil reserves, and the fiendishly intertwined power relationships created and nurtured by oil.

Tables 2.3 and 2.4 reveal fascinating facts about the distribution and consumption of oil throughout the world. As table 2.3 shows, the United States is far and away the world's leading consumer of oil, using nearly three times as much of this valuable resource as China, its nearest competitor. (No reliable figures are available for Russia, however.) But, the U.S. is also the world's second leading *producer* of oil, as table 2.4 shows. Japan's insecure position is clear: although it is the second highest importer of energy, after the United States, it possesses no measurable energy resources of its own. Coal remains an important energy source

Table 2.3
Oil Consumption

Country	Consumption (gallons of oil)
USA	1,707,152,400,000
China	610,879,200,000
Japan	577,713,600,000
Germany	316,758,000,000
UK	206,635,000,000
India	169,459,200,000
France	148,167,500,000
Mexico	104,187,600,000
Saudi Arabia	75,467,726,000
Iran	53,670,300,000
Turkey	41,380,800,000
Iraq	9,481,244,000
Israel	9,287,088,000

Source: Kidron and Segal, 1991. pp. 26–27.

worldwide, and the U.S., China, and Russia enjoy in terms of both coal production and coal reserves.

Other Resources. *Other resources* besides oil and coal are critical in the late twentieth and early twenty-first centuries. Diamonds, particularly industrial diamonds, are valued not because of their importance in jewelry, but because they are essential to complex and sophisticated manufacturing processes, as are gold, silver, and platinum. Other, still rarer, metals, such as chromium and uranium, are also necessary to an industrial economy. The avid interest with which industrial nations have watched the political unraveling of the various South African nations derives far more from fascination with their rich deposits of these vital minerals than from political voyeurism alone.

Again, we must note that the mere possession of natural resources does not translate immediately, or even necessarily, into power. For example, Indonesia is a major oil-producing nation but has played a relatively minor role in world politics; the same can be said of Venezuela, Nigeria, and Mexico. And while the great

Table 2.4
World Oil Production, 1989

Country	Oil Produced (in millions of tons)
Former Soviet Union	605
USA	425
Saudi Arabia	270
Mexico	145
Iran	145
Iraq	140

Source: Chaliand and Rageau, 1992 p. 192.

wealth of the Middle Eastern oil producers like Saudi Arabia and Kuwait has not made them into major powers, ironically, it has made them even more vulnerable.

Population

A nation's population is a major component of national power, but the relationship of population to power is an extremely complex one. For one thing, large *numbers* of people permit nations to form large armies and thus exert power over others. France was long the most powerful nation in Europe, in large part because it was also the most populous nation. The consolidation of Germany in the late nineteenth century meant that almost instantly Germany replaced France as the chief mover in European politics, at least in part because Germany's population was 25 percent greater than that of France. The large populations of both the United States and the Soviet Union were important factors in their emergence as superpowers after World War II. So important has sheer size of population been to various nations that at times they have instituted policies of rewarding families for high birth rates: France, Germany, and Russia have all provided both cash awards and lavish praise to large families.

However, other countries in which large families have been valued now face enormous problems brought on by the very sizes of their populations. The cultural systems of both India and China, for example, have long stressed the value of large families; those two nations are now the most populous in the world. And yet their huge populations have translated into not power, but problems. Simply producing enough food to keep up with the rate of population growth has strained the resources of both nations. We will discuss the implications of population for the future in chapter 14; for now, let us note that there is no consistent link between population and power. Two of the world's most heavily populated areas, the United States and Russia, rank as the world's most powerful nations; yet nations of even greater population, India and China, are still powers in the making rather than major global powers, at least in part because of the problems created by their huge populations. Table 2.5 shows national rankings by population. Figure 2.7 illustrates projected population growth rates; note that the highest

Table 2.5
Characteristics of Global Population

Country	Population	Percentage Urban	Percentage Rural	Percentage Growth	Percentage Under 15 Years	Percentage Over 65 Years
China	1,203,097,268	26	74	1.04	26	6
India	936,545,814	26	74	1.77	35	4
USA	263,814,032	74	26	1.02	22	13
Russia	149,909,089	74	26	0.20	22	12
Japan	125,506,492	77	23	0.32	16	15
Mexico	93,985,848	71	29	1.90	37	4
Germany	81,337,541	83	17	0.26	16	16
Iran	64,625,455	54	46	2.29	45	4
UK	58,295,119	90	10	0.27	19	16
France	58,109,160	74	26	0.46	19	16
Iraq	20,643,769	73	27	3.72	48	3
S. Arabia	18,729,576	77	23	3.68	43	2
Israel	5,433,134	91	9	1.40	29	10

Source: CIA, *World Factbook 1995*, and Hepner and McKee pp. A2–A9, 1992.

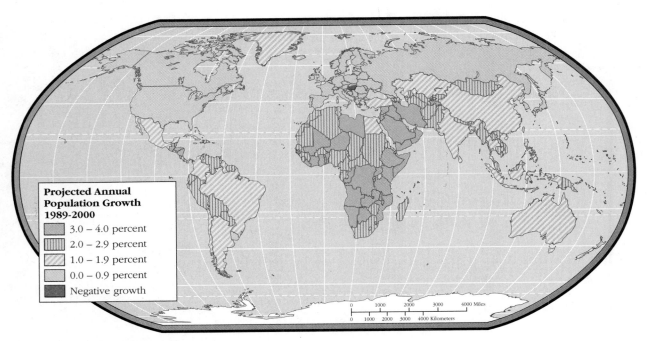

**Projected Annual
Population Growth
1989-2000**

  3.0 – 4.0 percent
  2.0 – 2.9 percent
  1.0 – 1.9 percent
  0.0 – 0.9 percent
  Negative growth

Figure 2.7 **Population Growth Rate**

growth rates are occurring in many of the world's poorest nation, what Cohen terms the "quartersphere of marginality."

Demographics are more important than sheer numbers in the way population characteristics influence national power. Two obvious demographic factors are age and education.

Clearly, a population with too young a median age—many nonindustrialized nations in Africa and South America count half or more of their populations under the age of twenty—poses serious problems. Too young to fully contribute to their nations' industrial or military prowess, these huge groups of children and youths are a drain on scarce national resources as they must be nurtured, fed, and educated until they can become fully productive citizens. Table 2.5 shows the large youthful populations of many countries. Nearly two out of every five Indians, for example, are under fifteen years old; and this figure represents some 343 million people not yet ready for full-time adult employment, and requiring huge expenditures for education and training to become productive workers. Even though only 27 percent of China's population is under fifteen, that nation nevertheless must cope with the problems of educating and training 314 million people under the age of 15.

Other nonindustrialized or just-industrializing nations like Pakistan, Bangladesh, Iran, Iraq, and Ethiopia also must deal with the drain on resources represented by 45 percent or more of their populations. And virtually all of these nations have high rates of population growth, which means that these problems will endure and perhaps even worsen.

In contrast, the most highly developed industrialized states stand on the opposite side of the demographic gap: increasing percentages of their populations are older than the nominal retirement age of 65. In Germany, the United Kingdom, and Switzerland, 15 percent of the population is aged sixty-five or older; in

Italy, France, Japan, and the United States, 10 percent or more of the population is in this age group. Low population growth rates—less than 1.0 percent per year—in these nations could foreshadow enormous future problems, as fewer and fewer young workers struggle to support an ever-larger elderly population. (For a more extensive discussion of population issues, see chap. 14, "Global Issues.")

Education. *Education* levels are also vital in determining how much a nation's population contributes to that nation's power. As we begin moving into what many call the Third Industrial Revolution, one based on information and technology rather than iron or steel, there are obvious demands for a more and more educated population. There is little doubt that Japan, for example, has partially offset its lack of natural resources by producing a highly educated and highly motivated population. Traditional Japanese culture was derived from Chinese Confucianism, which emphasized the importance of education at least for the elite. Then, the leaders who brought Japan from feudalism to industrialism in the late nineteenth century saw that education for all would be essential. All schools were brought under the control of the central government, and attendance became compulsory. By 1900 Japan boasted (although the claim was impossible to confirm) a literacy rate of 99 percent, higher than the rates of any of its western competitors. Even today, Japan continues to enjoy the highest literacy rate and to possess one of the toughest education systems in the world.

Claimed literacy rates are often dubious. For example, a recent American study states that although the United States claims an adult literacy rate of 98 percent, 47 percent of the adult population "ha[ve] difficulty performing at the lowest literacy levels" (Roth and Rugeley 1993). Clearly, the literacy levels shown in figure 2.8 must be used cautiously. However, even allowing for inaccuracies, we

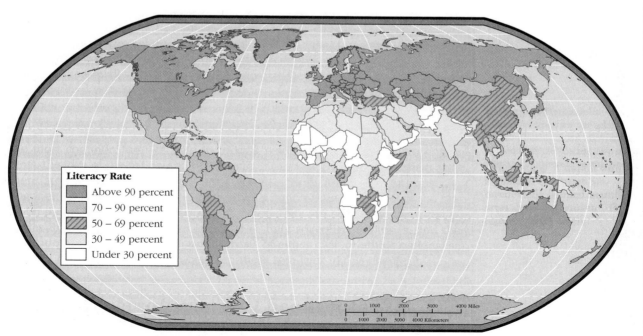

Figure 2.8 **Literacy of World Population**
Source: Modified from *Goode's World Atlas* (Chicago: Rand McNally, 1990).

find the highest literacy levels in the most powerful industrial nations and the lowest levels among the poorest industrializing nations. Educating a nation's population is an expensive proposition, and there is some concern that poorer nations will never have enough money to cover this education gap.

The United States recognized the link between power and education as early as the Civil War, when Congress passed laws promoting "agricultural and mechanical colleges." However, American education policy has been decentralized and American education levels consequently have been uneven. Recently there has been a great deal of national soul-searching about how effective the American educational system really is, as standardized tests show American students scoring substantially lower than Japanese, Korean, and other Asian students in math and science. The debate over how to improve the American educational system will probably rage far into the next century.

Even among educated populations, there are major differences in the educational emphases that influence nations' economic success and hence their power. For example, the United States and Japan enjoy a strong advantage over their major economic competitors in terms of absolute numbers of scientists and engineers and in terms of the relative numbers of these essential figures in the general workforce. While Japan has a higher percentage of scientists and engineers overall, the United States' much larger population gives it a decided edge in total numbers, reflected in a higher ratio of scientists and engineers to each thousand workers overall. These high numbers virtually guarantee that as the world moves deeper and deeper into the information age, the already-industrialized nations will maintain and perhaps increase their margins of economic and military superiority over those nations and areas that lack sufficient numbers of scientists and engi-

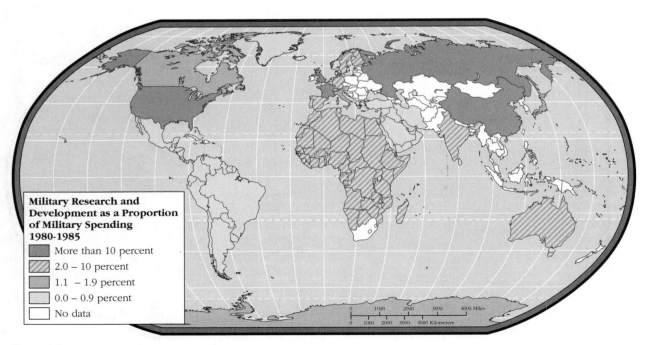

Military Research and Development as a Proportion of Military Spending 1980-1985

More than 10 percent
2.0 – 10 percent
1.1 – 1.9 percent
0.0 – 0.9 percent
No data

Figure 2.9

neers. Figure 2.9, "Science Power," shows graphically the worldwide distribution of scientific power used in military research and development (R&D).

It should be clear from this discussion of natural sources of national power that there is no single factor that can be isolated and pointed to as *the reason* country A is powerful while country B is weak. Many of the factors that account for power can work both ways: while geographic location remains fixed, the importance of geographic location shifts with new technologies; possession of rich natural resources can either add to a country's power or make it a tempting target for predators; and large populations can be sources of either strength or weakness. A small, physically isolated island nation like England or Japan can take its place among the great powers; vast continental states like the United States and the Soviet Union can be, for a while, superpowers; and large, densely populated nations like India and China can remain comparatively weak.

Of course, natural resources are not the only factors to consider in calculating a nation's power; power also is built on social-psychological forces like national unity and leadership, and on "synthetic sources" such as a nation's industrial capacity.

Social-Psychological Sources of Power

National Stability

A nation's ability to assert its power, and thus a nation's power, is heavily dependent on its internal stability, that is, the extent to which people trust their government and are willing to follow the requests or demands of that government.

Stability itself is clearly the product of many of the same factors that determine power (such as the ability of the nation to feed itself), but it includes other components as well. For example, a major element in any government's stability is whether or not it can guarantee the personal security of its people at a price the people are willing to pay. The trade-off between individual liberty and order has always been one of the most difficult issues any government confronts, but the stability of a nation can rest on how a government addresses this dilemma. Obviously, a nation whose citizens are shooting one another in the streets and in which anarchy has replaced orderly processes of government is not one that those same citizens are likely to put their faith in. Even if the government of Lebanon possessed nuclear missiles, for example, it is unlikely that Lebanon could arise from chaos to exert any substantial power. Terrorism is in large part an attempt to create so much chaos that a people's faith in their government will evaporate and that the government in turn will be unable to use its other power assets.

On the other hand, a government that creates order in its streets by the use of oppression, secret police, informers, and the other tactics of totalitarianism we have witnessed in the twentieth century is ultimately an unstable government as well. For example, while the Soviet Union deployed an army of over four million men at the height of the Cold War, there were always concerns about how far that army could be trusted to do the bidding of its commanders; we saw during the collapse of the Soviet system that the soldiers would not obey their commanders if they ordered the wholesale slaughter of civilians. China is likewise an inherently unstable state, as the events in Tiananmen Square in 1989 testify.

In table 2.6 we have attempted to categorize the world's major nations according to their inherent political and economic stability. Rather than ranking

Table 2.6
National Stability

Stable Nations	Moderately Stable Nations
United States	India
Japan	Saudi Arabia
Germany	Iran
United Kingdom	Mexico
France	
Israel	

Unstable Nations
China
Iraq
Russia

these nations, we have divided them into three major categories: stable nations, moderately stable nations, and unstable nations. The classifications are based on our understanding of the internal dynamics of each state. Not surprisingly, industrial democracies such as the United States, the United Kingdom, and Japan are in the category of stable states, while dictatorial and generally poor regimes constitute most of the unstable states. We have classified China and Russia as unstable because of the current problems each is enduring in terms of leadership and of transition or attempted transition to a market economy.

We have to be careful not to overstate our case: fear and intimidation can be extremely effective, at least in the short run, and a government that depends not only on them but also on a sophisticated propaganda apparatus can exert great power. Both the Iraqi and the Iranian governments, however distasteful their structures are to Western advocates of democracy, were able to mobilize their people and demand enormous self-sacrifice during the ten-year war between them. This illustrates that even what we perceive as oppressive and fundamentally unstable governments can consolidate their power against foreign foes. Hitler's Germany is another prime example of the way a repressive, totalitarian regime could, at least in the short run, mobilize the nation's resources to exert enormous power. So too is Stalin's Russia.

Leadership

Leadership, the ability to galvanize a state's people and mobilize them for hardship, struggle, and sacrifice, is another key component of national power. Chapter 5, "The Social Psychology of International Relations," will examine in detail the role that personality plays in international relations. We can make a few observations here.

A society facing hard economic times, social chaos, or war will respond to strong leadership with an almost desperate eagerness; conversely, a relatively stable society drifting without adequate leadership will become increasingly unwilling or unable to exert power of any significant sort.

Outstanding leadership is not necessarily based on conventional, Western standards of morality. There have been great leaders who met these standards—and perhaps as many great leaders whom we would have to regard as morally loathsome. A leader's charisma, charm, speaking ability, ideology, and ruthlessness all contribute to his or her ability to mobilize and use national power. Adolf Hitler was personally charming and charismatic, was capable of virtually hypnotizing masses of people, and had a coherent if irrational ideology that offered Germans both scapegoats for their present problems and visions of glory in the future. Germans who were floundering in the mire of the Depression gratefully listened to Hitler's promises, watchfully observed the fate of those who opposed Hitler, and ultimately followed Hitler and National Socialism for over a decade. This leader's rhetoric and pageantry constituted a lifeline for desperate people, and they eagerly seized it.

On the other side of the Atlantic, Franklin Delano Roosevelt was galvanizing the American people to pull themselves out of the Depression by offering not scapegoats, but hope. In his personal ebullience, FDR was a reminder to Americans that at least by the American credo, there was no such thing as an unsolvable problem. Winston Churchill rallied the English people with his unquenchable confidence and brilliant rhetoric in 1940 and convinced them that their nation, reeling on the brink of military collapse, could accomplish the impossible by single-handedly continuing to stave off Hitler. A France that had been militarily stronger but poorly led had already collapsed.

Strong and confident leadership both creates and reinforces national morale, the sense that the nation can accomplish anything. Gamal Abdel Nasser was able to rouse a poverty-stricken but proud Egyptian population to oppose what he proclaimed to be the twin evils of imperialism and Zionism, and to temporarily unite much of the Arab world in this struggle. And Mahatma Gandhi mobilized

There is little doubt that World War II would have been entirely different had not Adolf Hitler (left) been leading the German People and Franklin Delano Roosevelt (right) the American leader.

the masses of his vast subcontinent to resist English colonialism by the quiet example of nonviolent resistance.

It is virtually impossible to predict when and how this kind of mesmerizing and mobilizing leadership will appear. Who would have predicted that an American aristocrat would lead his country out of the Depression, or that an Austrian corporal would lead the German nation into the world's most destructive war? Or that an austere college professor would emerge as the leader of a coalition to make the world safe for democracy? Or that a peasant from Hunan, the Chinese equivalent of Appalachia, could unite China's hundreds of millions of people, give them hope, and lead them into the modern era? Or that a peasant's son from Siberia, a man with a reputation for recklessness and too great a fondness for vodka, could mobilize the Russian people by climbing atop a tank and daring anyone to stop Russia's headlong drive toward democracy? But FDR, Hitler, Woodrow Wilson, Mao Tse-tung, and Boris Yeltsin did emerge as vital leaders. Each of these men seized a defining moment in his nation's history, revitalized national morale, and convinced millions upon millions of people to follow him. Personal power embodied in these leaders became the means for mobilizing national power.

Political Will

Political will, or the will to use power, is another intangible but essential factor. After its defeat in Vietnam, the United States often seemed unwilling to use its vast power, in military or other ways. Many Americans and others welcomed the Gulf War in 1991 as a sign that this national paralysis had finally lifted and that the United States would once again behave like a superpower. However, the will to use power rests on many intangibles, such as the national perception of danger,

Two charismatic leaders: Mao Tse-tung (left) shaped the communist revolution and state in China, while Boris Yeltsin (right) played a crucial role in the dismembering of the Soviet Union and the abandonment of communism in Russia.

the ability of the leader to mobilize the population, and the support given to the leadership in its attempt to influence public opinion.

National stability, leadership, political will—all are key factors in any nation's power, and yet all are as difficult to define as power itself. Although we may not be able to quantify them in neat, easily manipulated formulas, we can readily appreciate how vital these components are to this elusive entity of national power.

Synthetic Sources of Power

In addition to natural and social-psychological sources of power, students of international relations also recognize a third type: what they call "synthetic" sources of power. In this context, "synthetic" means not "artificial," but "having been transformed or synthesized." A nation's natural and social-psychological power sources can be transformed or galvanized into more complex sources of power. The two most widely recognized synthetic sources of power are industrial capacity and military capacity.

Industrial capacity

The Industrial Revolution that began in mid-eighteenth-century England transformed virtually every element of life, from the way people worked and lived to what constituted national power. Since at least the beginning of the twentieth century, a nation's industrial capacity has been a major measurement of its power, in both its own estimation and the estimation of others.

For one thing, the factories that produce sewing machines and automobiles can easily become the factories that produce bombs and bombers and tanks. Techniques used to manufacture one thousand rifles a month can be expanded to produce ten thousand a month. The American Civil War showed the extent to which industrial capacity translated into military capacity, and most subsequent wars have confirmed that the most industrially powerful nation is also, in the long run, the most militarily powerful nation as well.

Industrial capacity also increases national strength by providing jobs and security for people, thus contributing to the stability so essential for the creation and exercise of power. While national morale is not totally a function of material well-being, a nation that is well fed and well housed, enjoying a high standard of living with such commodities as televisions and automobiles and microwave ovens, is a demonstrably happier nation. Admittedly, there is an ongoing debate about whether possession of such an abundance of consumer goods makes a people more willing to struggle to protect them or more likely to become complacent, but all will agree that some material security does contribute to national stability.

Finally, industrial capacity can translate into a strong position in the international marketplace by allowing a nation to export surplus goods and thus import whatever it wants. We will discuss this process in chapter 7, "International Political Economy"; for now it is enough to observe that powerful nations will become even more powerful if they can maintain favorable **balance of trade,** that is, if they can export more than they import. A nation that shows a continuing imbalance by buying from others far more than it sells to others hemorrhages hard currency. Ultimately, the economic and industrial strength that are key factors in its overall power deteriorate, as does national self-confidence.

balance of trade The ratio between what a nation exports compared to what a nation imports.

The importance of industrialism can also be seen in the equation of relative power between the industrial nations and the nonindustrial nations. Lacking the ability to produce manufactured goods, the nonindustrial nations must export almost exclusively raw materials: bauxite, tin, coffee, sugar, magnesium, and oil, for example. Generally speaking, this puts the nations exporting these raw materials at the mercy of the industrial nations that purchase them, for the market system tends to operate in favor of the purchaser. If there is a strong market for a particular raw material, nations producing this raw material may appear both prosperous and powerful; but if that market crashes, the exporters are usually devastated. Producers of raw materials attempt to offset this by forming cartels such as OPEC, but not even this is always effective. For example, in the 1950s and 1960s, the worldwide price of tin was controlled by the London Tin Cartel; the prosperity of average workers in Thailand or Malaysia, and thus the stability and power of their governments, rested directly on the ability of the London Cartel to limit the world supply of tin and thus keep the world price as high as possible. In the mid-1970s the tin cartel crashed, resulting in economic devastation in the tin-producing areas of southeast Asia. National economies reeled and governments collapsed until some kind of economic stability was restored, largely by inviting the establishment of foreign manufacturing establishments.

This dependence on exporting raw materials leaves a nation dependent on importing the consumer goods its population wants or demands. A nation that can't sell its raw materials in a glutted international market can't afford to import even the more common luxuries, like motorcycles and television sets, that the population has begun to take for granted. There is not only an economic downturn but also a decline in perceived standard of living, and thus in national morale, confidence in the government, stability, and total national power. We discuss these ideas more fully in chapter 8, "Geo-Economics."

Table 2.7 shows several important elements of national economic strength. Clearly the United States has a major advantage in one key component, gross national product; the nearly $6 trillion American economy is more than twice as large as that of its nearest competitor, Japan, and three and a half times greater than that of third-ranking Germany. Figure 2.10 graphically illustrates the worldwide distribution of sheer economic strength.

In terms of a second key element, per capita income, the United States also holds a margin of 10 percent or more over the other large industrial countries. Although Switzerland's per capita income is close to that of the U.S., Switzerland's small size and population effectively disqualify it as a major power.

However, when we examine a third key component of national economic strength, the balance of trade, a different picture emerges. The United States is the world's largest exporter of goods and commodities—but it is also the world's largest importer nation, with an overall negative trade balance (the difference between the value of exports and of imports) of nearly $90 billion. Japan, in contrast, has a positive trade balance of $270 billion, by far the largest favorable balance of trade of any nation. We will discuss the causes and consequences of such trade balances in chapter 7. However, it is obvious that continuous large trade deficits will ultimately weaken national power. A quick glance at table 2.7 shows that only a handful of nations other than Japan—including China, Saudi Arabia, Iran, and Iraq (according to pre–Gulf War figures) enjoyed positive balances of trade, a fact with potentially ominous long-range consequences.

Table 2.8 compares another important element of national economic strength: the distribution of labor. While the world's poorer countries tend to con-

Table 2.7
National Economies, 1994

Country	GDP (in billions of U.S. dollars)	National Product Per Capita (in U.S. dollars)	Exports	Imports	Trade Balance
			(in billions of U.S. dollars)		
USA	6,738.4	25,850	513.0	664.0	−151
China	2,978.4 (b)	2,500 (b)	121.0	115.7	+5.3
Japan	2,527.4	20,200	395.5	274.3	+121.2
Germany	1,344.6	16,580	437.0	362.0	+75.0
India	1,253.9	1,360	24.4	25.5	−1.1
France	1,080.1	18,670	249.2	238.1	+11.1
UK	1,045.2	17,980	200.0	215.0	−15.0
Mexico	728.7	7,900	60.8	79.4	−18.6
Russia	721.2	4,820	48.0	35.7	+12.3
Iran	310.0	4,720	16.0	18.0	−2.0
S. Arabia	173.1	9,510	39.4	28.9	+10.5
Israel	70.1	13,880	16.2	22.5	−6.3
Iraq	NA	NA	10.4 (c)	6.6 (c)	+3.8 (c)

(a) Figure used by CIA; roughly equivalent to per capita income.
(b) Extrapolated from World Bank estimates; may be as much as 25% too high.
(c) 1990 figures; no post-Gulf War statistics available.
Source: CIA, *World Factbook 1995*.

tinue to employ most of their workforces in the most basic economic sector, agriculture, many of the advanced industrial states have already seen their labor forces shift out of the manufacturing and into the service sectors of their economies. In Ethiopia, the poorest country we have included in this table, 90 percent of the workforce is involved in agriculture, while China and India, the two largest nations in the world, still have more than half their workforces deployed in the agricultural sector. In contrast, the industrial states like the United States, the United Kingdom, France, and Germany still employ only a small fraction of their workforces in agriculture. This fact is particularly startling regarding the United States when we remember that the U.S. is nonetheless the world's leading food exporter. The relatively large size of Japan's agricultural population—9 percent of its workforce—is largely the result of cultural and historical pressures rather than economic necessity. The mature economic states of Israel, France, Italy, the United States, and Japan all employ more than half their workers in the service sector: banking and finance, trade, communications, and the provision of services ranging from medical care to teaching to restaurant work.

Military Capacity

As we have said before, one of the elements that makes industrial capacity so important is that it can easily be translated into military capacity. Since the earliest days of civilization, a nation's military capacity has been a major element of a nation's power.

Much of this equation is so self-evident that there is little need to belabor the point; clearly, a nation that can produce more bullets, more bombs, more tanks and trucks and rifles and field rations has a tremendous military and thus power advantage over a nation producing less of these, *as long as both are fighting the*

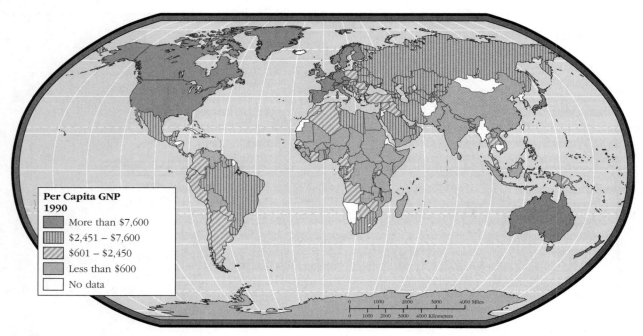

Figure 2.10 **Total GNP and GNP Per Capita**

same kind of war. (We'll return later to the importance of this statement.) In the American Civil War, generally regarded as the first industrialized war, the South generally had better generals and, man for man, superior soldiers. Northern superiority lay in two factors: the superior leadership of Abraham Lincoln and the massive industrial edge enjoyed by the Union. Ninety-five percent of all iron in the prewar United States had been produced in northern factories, and the Civil War

Table 2.8
Workforce Distribution
(in percentages of working populations)

Country	Agriculture	Manufacturing & Construction	Service, Professional
China	60	25	15
India	65	14	11
USA	2.9	25.5	71.6
Russia	14	43	16
Japan	7	33	54
Germany	6.7	47.5	45.8
Iran	33	21	N.A.
UK	1.2	25	62.8
France	7.2	31.3	61.5
Ethiopia	90	3	7
Iraq	30	22	48
S. Arabia	16	28	22
Israel	3.5	28.6	53.4
Mexico	28	21	31.7

Source: CIA, *World Factbook 1995; Grolier Academic Encyclopedia* (Prodigy Online Service), 1993.

was fought with iron cannons and rifles, transported by iron trains along iron rails. The manufactured goods the South expended could not be replaced: a bullet shot was a bullet gone. In contrast, the North cold produce four, six, even ten bullets for every one expended. Thus, when the Civil War became not a war of mobility but a war of attrition, Northern victory was inevitable.

Attempting to quantify this principle, one political scientist examined 39 wars fought from 1815 to 1945, and determined that 75 percent of them, 31 out of 39, were won by the side with the greater industrial capacity (Wright 1964, 237).

However, the ability to train an army, equip it, and put it into the field does not guarantee the ability to motivate that army to fight or to lead it well against an enemy force. Sheer numbers don't necessarily predict anything. Again, we return to the examples of Vietnam and Afghanistan; although in each case one side, the United States or the Soviet Union, enjoyed overwhelming industrial superiority, the other side won, or at least created a stalemate that equalled victory. Simply put, the two sides were fighting different wars. Both the United States and the Soviet Union tried to fight conventional wars in which they could bring their military and industrial capacity to bear in the most efficient manner. But their opponents fought guerrilla wars, wars of national liberation, in which what counted most was not industrial capacity but cunning, tenacity, will—social/psychological rather than traditionally military factors.

These two wars clearly show that no matter how powerful a nation may feel, seem, or actually be, war is always a matter of risk, for it always leaves room for the unquantifiable or unpredictable. William II of Germany knew exactly what he was saying when he proclaimed at the start of World War I, "Let the Iron Dice roll!"

Although power and the determination of relative power are elusive, and although what constitutes power in one set of circumstances may be irrelevant or even self-defeating in another set of circumstances, nations have never stopped attempting to build up their own power and measure it against that of other nations. Nor have students of international relations stopped trying to clarify both the meanings and the sources of power. One factor both groups study often is military spending.

Figure 2.11 shows world military spending as of 1989. Not surprisingly, the United States and the Soviet Union, at that point the two world superpowers, ranked first and second respectively. We must use such figures with caution, as they are notoriously inaccurate. Although the United States publishes its military budget as part of the national budget, there are often items that are not published but become part of what is known as the "black budget," which deals with classified items not to be made public. Figures for the Soviet Union are more unreliable still; recently the Central Intelligence Agency admitted that it has often grossly exaggerated Soviet military spending. The collapse of the Soviet Union, disputes about who owns or is responsible for components of the former USSR arsenal, and continued economic turmoil in Russia and the Congress of Independent States today make it virtually impossible to determine exact figures. However, the proportions of military expenditures should remain fairly much the same, since Russia will probably end up with most of the former Soviet military machinery.

It has not always been clear exactly what nations have obtained in return for these high levels of military spending—one recent study claims that high levels of military spending have largely been responsible for the collapse of most modern empires (Kennedy 1989). It is important to note, in any case, that relative levels of military spending are not necessarily reflected in relative sizes of armed forces. China, for example, has a large armed force, despite lower spending levels, that

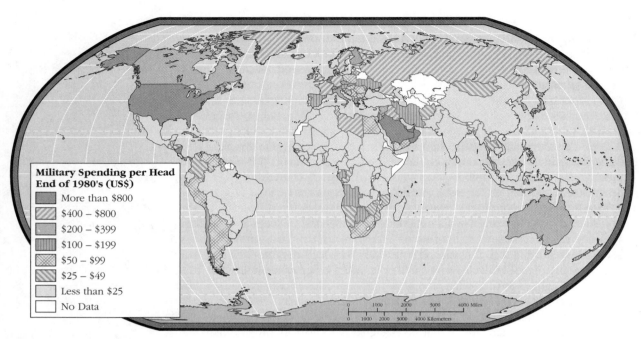

Figure 2.11
As late as the end of the 1980s, military spending accounted for one out of every twelve dollars spent worldwide, an average of $160 per individual—approximately one thousand times the United Nations budget.

reflects both recent Chinese-Russian tensions and China's enormous size. Still, relative to its population, China has a much smaller armed force than either the Soviet Union or the United States.

Most of the numbers in figure 2.11 reflect conventional military forces, that is, armies, navies, and air forces. However, since 1945 nonconventional weapons, that is, nuclear and thermonuclear weapons, have played a major role in determining relative military strength. In 1989, on the eve of the disappearance of the Soviet Union and the end of the Cold War, enormous numbers of warheads were held by the Soviet Union and the United States. This explains in part why those two nations were considered to be superpowers. These nuclear arsenals have been downsized since the end of the Cold War and as a result of the Strategic Arms Reduction Treaties signed by the Soviet Union and the United States. Much greater reduction will take place in the near future, although it will be accompanied most probably by the acquisition by other, smaller powers of nuclear weapons. Not all of these smaller nations publicly admit possessing nuclear arsenals. Many such nations—Pakistan, India, and Israel, for example—have, probably have, or are in the process of developing nuclear weapons. Iraq, for example, has been attempting to acquire them for years. While the global trend has been for nations to seek nuclear power, recently there have been some shifts in the opposite direction. For example, the government of South Africa did develop nuclear weapons, but destroyed them and has since signed the Nuclear Non-Proliferation Treaty. Brazil and Argentina have moved bilaterally to reject nuclear arms possession. However, the nuclear genie has not yet been pushed back into the bottle, and may never be.

Table 2.9
Relative Gauges of National Strength

Country	A	B	C	D	E	F	G	H	I	J	K	L	M	N	O	P
China	2	12	7	20	6	1	12	2	7	6	22	9	5	2	113	3
India	5	12	20	20	6	2	19	5	6	8	10	10	15	4	132	5
USA	3	1	6	2	9	3	4	1	1	13	1	1	2	3	53	1
Russia	1	7	4	1	1	6	2	9	9	3	22	2	15	15	71	2
Japan	19	6	20	20	10	7	1	3	3	1	1	6	15	15	140	7
Germany	20	12	20	20	8	12	1	4	2	2	1	3	15	10	135	6
Iran	9	3	20	5	4	15	16	10	12	9	10	11	15	8	152	10
UK	16	12	20	20	6	18	1	7	5	11	1	5	3	14	147	9
France	16	2	20	20	6	19	2	6	4	4	1	4	4	9	121	4
Iraq	18	2	20	6	3	24	15	13	13	7	22	8	6	15	183	13
S. Arabia	6	12	3	2	6	25	14	11	10	5	10	7	15	15	141	8
Israel	26	12	20	20	6	27	5	12	11	10	1	13	15	15	191	12

The numbers in each column indicate the relative ranking of the various nations in terms of these gauges of material power. A number one ranking is best. The last column P, shows overall national power rankings.

Key

A Land Mass	G Literacy Rates	M Nuclear Weapons
B Food Production	H Gross National Product	N Armed Forces
C Crude Oil Reserves	I Exports	O Total
D Oil Production	J Trade Balance	P Power Ranking
E Energy Export/Import	K Stability	
F Population	L Military Spending	

Global Power Distribution

Table 2.9 "Relative Gauges of National Strength," provides a cross-national comparison of power in its various manifestations.

The Ideologies of Power

Opinions about how power ought to be used range across a wide spectrum, from what is called the "idealist" or "utopian" view to the "realist" view. In fact, few actual uses of power can absolutely follow one or the other of these schools, but it is useful to examine each one in order to understand the tensions that exist in trying not only to define but also to use power.

Idealism

The idealists rely on thinkers of the Enlightenment for their basic understanding of the nature of human beings and thus the way they should use power. To these thinkers, human beings were above all rational beings, creatures that used their minds and reason rather than force or violence to achieve their ends. Reason enabled people to understand problems and thus to solve them.

John Locke (1632–1704), the greatest of all Enlightenment philosophers, described the human person essentially a thinking machine, a being with no preconceived or innate ideas but with the gift of reason, the ability to organize perceptions into ideas and then use ideas to create a better self and a better world. Humans were educable beings, Locke argued, and thus capable of improvement, of becoming better and better. Late in the Enlightenment, Voltaire would satirize the intense optimism of the period by having characters in his novel *Candide* mindlessly parrot, "Every day in every way I am getting better and better." While there was a certain degree of this mindlessness involved in the Enlightenment faith in reason, its advocates did sincerely hold out the possibility of using reason to make things better, in both the individual and the national life.

Reasonable persons fashioned livable societies, Locke proclaimed, by recognizing one another's rights and then creating and abiding by governments designed to protect those rights. Government was a humanly created institution designed solely for the protection of reasonable persons and their rights. After all, there was nothing that reason could not accomplish, no problem so great that reason could not ultimately solve it. Education would be the vehicle for the improvement of both the individual self and the collective society, for the education of reasonable humans would lead to wisdom.

The reasonable person tended as well, Enlightenment philosophers believed, toward the good; echoing the ideas of the Chinese scholar Confucius some two thousand years earlier, members of the Enlightenment argued that this tendency toward the good could be reinforced by education. If individuals could be taught what was right and good, their own natures would incline them to adopt the good and strive for the perfect.

Twentieth-century idealists have tended to share this Enlightenment faith both in the basic good nature of human beings and in the ability of reason to solve problems. To the idealist fully grounded in the rationalist tradition, there are no insoluble problems, no insurmountable dilemmas, neither irresistible forces nor immovable objects. All are amenable to the force of reason.

War is thus an affront to human nature itself, not simply because of its destructive violence but also because it is so completely avoidable, at least in the idealist view. Wars are unnecessary: they occur only because human beings either forsake reason altogether or because they have not yet acquired the wisdom to build institutions that can solve problems and eliminate violence between states, just as domestic government eliminates violence between its reasonable citizens. (For further discussion of the relationship between war and democracies, see chapter 11, "War.")

Idealists tend to place a great deal of faith in institutions, expecting treaties or other international structures to bring reason to bear on problems among nations. To the idealist, the practice of international relations is basically a question of problem-solving, using reason to build solutions acceptable to reasonable persons on all sides of an issue. Thus Woodrow Wilson put his faith in the League of Nations as a forum in which quarreling states could settle their problems; in the 1920s his successors signed treaties limiting the number of weapons nations could possess, and finally even declaring war itself to be illegal. The Kellogg-Briand Treaty of 1928, perhaps the high point of idealist action in the twentieth century, proclaimed that all decent nations would join together in outlawing war, and promised that reasonable individuals in reasonable nations would work to solve their problems rationally.

In political science parlance, idealists tend to be normative; that is, they attempt to prescribe what ought to be and then work to shoehorn reality into that prescription. Thus, even as World War I raged, Woodrow Wilson could solemnly speak of a "just peace" and offer to serve as an "honest broker" among the nations of Europe. Believing that he was in the service not only of reason but also of superior morality, Wilson sternly lectured the leaders of Europe on their short-comings and proposed to solve all their problems through American leadership, the League of Nations, and the Fourteen Points. Not surprisingly, the Europeans were less than thrilled to be lectured by the Americans about the rightness of their actions; after all, it was the European allies who had done most of the fighting and most of the dying, and they expected that blood would count for something. It didn't—not to Wilson and the other idealists. What counted for them, what had to count if the terrible carnage of the war were to have any meaning, was using reason to restrain vengeance and construct a peaceful world.

Wilson could talk all he wanted of peace without victory and warn his allies over and over of the pitfalls of a "victors' peace," but the French and the British in particular were far more eager to revenge for the horrors of the war than to piece together international structures of peace. Consequently, the Versailles set-tlements were far more punitive of Germany than Wilson thought wise; Germany was forced to admit its "guilt" for starting the war, and to accept the loss of pop-ulation, territory, property, military capacity, and perhaps worst of all, pride. Twenty years later, it appeared that Wilson and the idealists had been correct, for angry and resentful Germans had embraced the vitriolic nationalism of Adolf Hitler and were once again a major threat to world peace.

Idealism tends to shade into moralism, the belief that there are fundamental, universal, natural moral principles that must be followed not only in national life but also in international life. The idealist would argue, for example, that in the same way that the true measure of a nation's worth was how well it treated its poorest and least citizens (as Franklin Delano Roosevelt once proclaimed), the true measure of a nation's foreign policy was how well it conformed to an ulti-mate test of morality. In the late 1970s, American president Jimmy Carter attempted to introduce universal moral concepts into American foreign policy by focusing not totally on issues of power, but also on what he termed "human rights" issues. Carter demanded that other countries, particularly those of the then Soviet bloc, grant to their citizens the basic human rights enshrined in the Amer-ican Bill of Rights: freedom of speech, freedom to worship, freedom of emigra-tion, and so forth. He announced that the United States would link other elements of its foreign policy, such as trade, to how well other countries' human rights records held up under American scrutiny. For this insistence on human rights and morality, Carter was scoffed at by many in the United States and regarded with genuine puzzlement by many outside it. However, in his memoirs, former CIA chief Robert Gates adds a new perspective to the Carter human rights policy. According to Gates, Soviet leaders found frightening Carter's vocal support for human rights in general and for Soviet dissidents such as Andrei Sakharov in par-ticular. "This really just drove them crazy," writes Gates. "They really thought it was going to destroy the system, and maybe they were right." (Gates 1996, 283)

Idealism as a foundation for international relations finds expression not only in the rationalistic and moralistic tendencies we have already discussed, but also more extreme philosophies. Pacifism, the belief that all war is wrong, is probably the most extreme form of moralistic idealism. While most idealists would ulti-mately accept that sometimes a nation may be forced into war, pacifists argue that there is never a reason to go to war. To support this position, many pacifists rely on the early Christian emphasis on the doctrine of turning the other cheek. While pacifism is often an appealing doctrine for the individual, and while it has flour-ished in societies at times, for example, in the United States during the 1960s and in England during the 1920s and 1930s, it has never become the basis for any state's foreign policy.

Idealists present the student of international relations with a genuine dilemma. Idealism is enormously appealing because it is based on the assumption that human beings will operate out of their very best characteristics, characteristics formed by the use of reason. And yet rationality comes to a screeching halt when it confronts massive irrationality. The paralysis of many leaders of the European and American communities in the face of the monstrous outrages and lies of the Hitler regime testifies all too well to the terrible problems rationalists and idealists have in dealing with the irrational or the downright evil.

Realism

Far from the idealists on the political spectrum are the theorists and political leaders known as *realists*. Realism began to come into its own as a theoretical system in the late nineteenth century. To some extent its rise was linked to the rise of Social Darwinism. Taking Charles Darwin's ideas of natural selection and competition from his *Origin of Species,* Social Darwinists tried to explain political and economic processes in the same terms. All life is competition, they proclaimed, a "tooth and claw" process in which ruthlessness is essential and moral or ethical considerations are counterproductive. Just as a Darwinian struggle would lead to the "survival of the fittest" among biological species, the Social Darwinists proclaimed, so too it would lead to the emergence of superior types of human beings. There was a price to pay for this, however: subscribers to Social Darwinism admitted that the losers of the struggle must be discarded and allowed to suffer and die. "It may be difficult for the individual," one nineteenth-century industrialist proclaimed, "but it is best for the [human] species, because it ensures the survival of the fittest in every department." Human misery and suffering were inevitable, according to the Social Darwinists, and therefore to be accepted. "Tough-minded" individuals would not shrink from the consequences of their ideas and would not permit "soft-headed sentimentalism" to get in their way.

These ideas of "tough-mindedness" and "survival of the fittest" meshed well both with existing international practices and with the views of Thomas Hobbes (1588–1679), a seventeenth-century English philosopher who took a deeply pessimistic view of the nature of the human being and of life. The majority of people were innately corrupt, Hobbes argued: they would cheerfully perform the most dreadful acts if they thought they could prosper as a result. Life was short and brutish, a merciless struggle in which anything was fair, and often necessary. Hobbes's ideas of human nature and human society were strongly opposed to the sunnier views of the Enlightenment, and far better suited to a Darwinian perspective on the world. (Hobbes's dark view of human nature and the drive of human beings for power echoed the ideas of Renaissance philosopher Niccolo Machiavelli, who wrote that the leader of a state, the "Prince," must do whatever is necessary to protect his power and the interests of the state. Even today, we use the word "Machiavellian" to describe a political theory or act that is cunning, amoral, or duplicitous.)

In the late nineteenth century, the German chancellor Otto von Bismarck wove together the Hobbesian concept of human nature, the Darwinian idea of absolute struggle, and what he saw as the needs of his own state; he called the resulting synthesis *realpolitik,* the politics of realism. Morality was an outmoded concept, Bismarck believed, and certainly one that had no place in international relations. Success went to the strong and the ruthless; *macht macht richt* ("might makes right") became both Bismarck's motto and his operating creed. Matters of state are settled not by reason, he proclaimed in a famous speech, but by blood and iron.

Following his own rules, Bismarck cynically and calculatingly manipulated European politics not for any long-range goal such as international peace, but solely for whatever benefited Germany. In 1866 he provoked a war with Austria, and in 1870, a war with France. These wars were not the result of deep-rooted and genuine grievances that could be solved by no other means; they were tools by which Bismarck planned to achieve the unification of Germany and to make Germany the strongest power on the continent of Europe. Bismarck's cynical manipulation of politics and his willingness to use military force to achieve his ends was derived in part from one of the greatest theoretical studies of war, Clausewitz's *On War*. In addition to being a study of the changes in war that industrial technology had brought about, Clausewitz's book was also a meditation on war. He concluded that war was simply a continuation of politics by other means; in effect, war was a rational tool in the armory of the modern state, a tool that would enable a state to achieve militarily what it had not been able to achieve diplomatically or politically. (For more information on Bismarck, see Crankshaw 1981.)

Neither Bismarck nor Clausewitz nor most of their realist successors saw war as an inherently wrong and irrational event, as did the idealists; instead, war was simply an extension of normal politics, and therefore itself normal.

As we said in chapter 1, idealists believed that the cynicism and calculation of *realpolitik* were responsible for the carnage of the Great War, and thus attempted to create a postwar world that reflected the best of human characteristics rather than the worst, that reflected reason and moral standards rather than the selfish and irrational scramble for power. Power for its own sake is wrong, the idealists thought; power is legitimate only when it is harnessed to worthwhile goals, like the creation of a better world.

When the rise of Hitler, Mussolini, and the ultranationalists in Japan plunged the world into a second "great war" (in reality simply a continuation of the first "Great War"), many political theorists and diplomats rejected what they saw as the failed doctrines of idealism and instead turned to a modified version of Bismarckian *realpolitik*, which they now termed "realism."

Three men played particularly important roles in the development and application of realist political theory in the United States: George F. Kennan, Hans J. Morgenthau, and Henry Kissinger. Kennan became both a formulator and a practitioner of realism as a leading State Department analyst of Soviet policy, the creator of America's containment policy, and finally a historian and critic of American foreign policy. His *American Foreign Policy, 1900–1950* (1951) is one of the most important realist critiques of idealism in the United States' global relations. Morgenthau was primarily an academician; his *Politics Among Nations* (1979) is one of the most important studies of international relations and a detailed explication of realist theory. Kissinger first made his mark as an academic realist with his study of the balance of power in nineteenth-century Europe, entitled *A World Restored;* he then became one of the most powerful national security advisors and secretaries of state in recent American history. The discussion of realism that follows is based primarily on the work of these three men.

Generally speaking, realists reject the sunlit view of human nature put forth by the idealists in favor of the darker view of *realpolitik*. People are not always rational, nor do they always seek the good, realists argue. Instead, they are capable of great irrationality and great evil (this idea is now a given, in a world still reeling from the atrocities of Hitler's Germany). Politics is a jungle, realists believe, and in a jungle anything goes.

The state, which is the principal actor in international relations, is if anything even less good than its people. The state is essentially amoral. "A sleepless, opportunistic, and necessarily ruthless entity, a state has neither a soul, a conscience, an enemy, nor a friend," writes one commentator. "Cruel by nature and dishonorable by definition, the state recognizes no law other than its own need. Were the state to be cast in an animal form it would be seen as a hideous and mutant thing—reptilian, stupid, rapacious, and half-blind" (Lapham 1989, 268, 231). While most realists would probably argue that this bleak view is overly dramatic, they would agree that it is a logical extension of their view of the modern state.

While idealists are constantly seeking the "philosopher's stone" that will remake the world, realists proclaim that they deal with the real world. "What the seekers after the magic formula want is simple, rational, mechanical; what they have to deal with [the real world] is complicated, irrational, incalculable," warns Morgenthau (1979, 47). Realists, Kennan adds (1951, 95–96), are concerned with "taking the awkward conflicts of national interest and dealing with them on their own merits with a view to finding the solutions least unsettling to the stability of international life". Realists pride themselves on dealing with "human nature as it actually is, and with the historic processes as they actually take place" (Morgenthau, 1979, 3–4).

Not surprisingly, realists, with their emphasis on facing the real world rather than trying to achieve an ideal one, also emphasize "tough-mindedness." For example, one of the most important realist books about nuclear policy during the Cold War was titled *Thinking the Unthinkable*. Statesmen must learn to think not about moral ideals but about political realities, the realists maintain; there is "a sharp distinction between the desirable and the possible—between what is desirable everywhere and at all times and what is possible under the concrete circumstance of time and place" (Morgenthau 1979, 4).

According to Kennan, realists must order their policy by this tough-mindedness, this concentration on power and reality, and consign international law and morality to their proper place, assigning them "the unobtrusive, *almost feminine* [italics added] function of the gentle civilizer of national self-interest" (1951, 54). This equation of tough-mindedness and masculinity, and its concurrent dismissal of all else as "almost feminine," has reached both mythic and hysterically funny extremes, particularly in American thinking.

In addition to being tough-minded, realists also proclaim themselves to be guided by history, since neither human nature nor the nature and needs of the state have changed. "Human nature, in which the laws of politics have their roots, has not changed since the classical philosophies of China, India, and Greece endeavored to find these laws." "Novelty is not necessarily a virtue in political theory, nor is old age a defect," according to Morgenthau. Again and again in setting forth his theories of realism, Morgenthau illustrates his ideas by citing historical examples, generally taken from European history. "A theory of politics must be subjected to the dual test of reason and experience," he explains, and students of international relations must deal "with the historic processes as they actually take place" (1979, 3–4). In the sense that it looks to the past for both theoretical formulation and affirmation, the realist theory of international relations is profoundly conservative.

The goal of international relations is not the making of a better world, realists proclaim: international relations is not about morality but about power. "Statesmen think and act in terms of interest defined as power," Morgenthau writes. "International politics, like all politics, is a struggle for power. Whatever the ultimate aims of international politics, power is always the immediate aim" (1979, 7, 31). Morgenthau goes on to say that "all political policy seeks either to keep power, to increase power, or to demonstrate power" (1979, 52). Kennan also points to power and what he terms "power realities" as key to the understanding and practice of international relations.

Although there sometimes seems to be a tendency among realists to advocate the exercise of power for its own sake, most realists say that in international relations power is applied in pursuit of what they call the "national interest." In other words, a nation should not and does not use its power to pursue altruistic or idealistic goals; the only legitimate use of power is to advance the interest of the nation. Interest, especially national interest, writes Morgenthau, "is the perennial standard by which political action must be judged and directed" (1979, 12). In effect, the realist argues that this concern with national interest and its central role in determining policy places desirable limits on any state's policy. "We will have," Kennan writes, "the modesty to admit that our own national interest is all that we are really capable of knowing and understanding," and thus of pursuing. There's nothing wrong with this pursuit of national interest, Kennan believes: "If our own purposes and undertakings here at home are decent ones, unsullied by arrogance or hostility toward other people or delusions of superiority, then the pursuit of our national interest can never fail to be conducive to a better world" (1951, 103).

The realist is in fact arguing that in order for the international system to work properly, each state has a *duty* to pursue its own national interest, rather than wasting its resources on what must be a futile attempt to pursue unrealistic goals like those prescribed by the idealists. Pursuit of the national interest will not result in the creation of a perfect world, but that is not possible; states and individuals, according to Morgenthau, must accept "the realization of the lesser evil rather than of the absolute good" (1979, 4).

Morgenthau believes that determining the national interest is a simple process: national interest "encompasses the integrity of the nation's territory, of its political institutions, and of its culture" (Dougherty and Pfaltzgraff 1993, 961). Although pursuit of the national interest can bring about greater stability for the nation, it will not necessarily bring about peace or even stability on the international level: "The concept of the national interest presupposes neither a naturally harmonious, peaceful world nor the inevitability of war." National interests will of necessity often conflict with one another, as the needs of one nation seldom completely parallel those of another. Smoothing out these conflicts between national interests is the job of the diplomat, the person the realist believes should be trusted with the conduct of foreign policy.

War thus becomes an ever-present possibility in a world dominated by these conflicting or even clashing national interests. Rather than condemning war as irrational, realists accept it as inevitable. "All history shows that nations active in international politics are continuously preparing for, actively involved in, or recovering from organized violence in the form of war," according to Morgenthau (1979, 52). Kennan comments that while it might be natural for Americans, used to both governmental and social systems based on compromise and reasonableness, to think in terms of international stability and reason, this view just does not match up to the real world. "The idea of the subordination of a large number of states to an international [law], limiting their possibilities for aggression and injury to other states, implies that these are all states like our own." This assumption results in serious errors of policy, he adds, for Americans "tend to underestimate the violence of national maladjustments and discontents elsewhere in the world" (1951, 98).

The best way to avoid instability and resulting war is the prudent application of realist principles by diplomats skilled at recognizing and seeking the national interest. Recognizing these limits and responding to them cannot be handled by idealists or well-meaning amateurs, even those who control nations. Only those who are skilled in defining the national interest and who can see when the national interests of other states must be taken into account ought to run foreign policy. Kennan writes that besides protecting the national interest, the true purpose of conducting international relations is "to temper the asperities to which [this protection] often leads, to isolate and moderate the conflicts to which it gives rise, and to see that these conflicts do not assume forms too unsettling for international life in general" (1951, 98).

To achieve this kind of delicate balancing, the diplomat must be cautious and prudent; the crusader-idealist will be too set on the goal of a better world to deal well with the existing one. "Prudence—the weighing of the consequences of alternative political actions—[is] the supreme virtue in politics," Morgenthau writes; "political ethics judges action by its political consequences" (1979, 12). Maintenance of this prudent balancing act in world politics, Kennan agrees, "is a task for diplomacy, in the most old-fashioned sense of the term. For this, law is too abstract, too inflexible, too hard to adjust to the demands of the unpredictable and unexpected" (1951, 98).

The idealist or the amateur cannot be trusted with carrying out policy, Morgenthau argues, for such an individual utterly lacks a realistic understanding of the world, and therefore of the prudence with which the world must be approached. "The utopian internationalist," Morgenthau writes rather sneeringly, "has no direct contact with the international scene. His thought, if it is sufficiently general, can roam over the globe without ever risking collision with the stark facts of politics." Proclaiming utopian or idealistic goals, Morgenthau says, "is sufficiently general to avoid contact with historic realities and political facts,"—but it is certainly not the way to formulate or to conduct diplomacy. Any attempt to infuse international relations with the universal moral principles so beloved by Wilson and other idealists is doomed to fail, and fail dramatically. "The carrying-over into the affairs of states of the concepts of right and wrong, the assumption that the state is a fit subject for moral judgment" will inevitably lead to disaster (1979, 48). Convinced that his or her policy represents absolute right, and that those who oppose it of necessity represent absolute wrong, the idealist will feel both morally superior to the transgressor and justified in resorting to unlimited violence, total war, against the transgressor. Kennan calls for his fellows to accept a realistic view of the rest of the world and accept the limitations of what can be accomplished: Americans must adopt, he writes, "an attitude more like that of the doctor toward those physical phenomena in the human body that are neither pleasing nor fortunate—an attitude of detachment and soberness and readiness to reserve judgment" (1951, 98). Otherwise, he warns, both statesmen and states will fall into the trap of absolutes, of moral judgments that can lead to war: "the legalistic [and moralistic] approach to world affairs, rooted as it unquestionably is in a desire to do away with war and violence, makes violence more enduring, more terrible, and more destructive to political stability" than the realistic approach ever could (1951, 100–101).

Global Distribution of Power

One of the major issues that occupies students of international relations is how power has been or should be distributed among states. What kind of distribution of power is best suited to creating stability and preventing major wars? What kind of distribution of power is most likely to lead to war? How do these systems of distribution occur, and what happens when they get out of balance?

The attempt to answer these questions has led political scientists to examine major systems of power distribution that have characterized the last three centuries. We will discuss these power systems both historically and in contemporary terms.

Balance of Power and Its Many Variations

According to both political scientists and historians, the first balance of power system was put together in Europe in the early eighteenth century. France's attempts to expand its power and territory, especially during the reign of Louis XIV, had led to a deadly and expensive series of wars involving most of the major states on the continent of Europe. After one of those wars, the War of the Spanish Succession, representatives of the major powers met at Utrecht to hammer out a treaty that would both end French adventurism and restore stability to a battered Europe. The result was the Treaty of Utrecht and the creation of a balance of power system on the continent of Europe.

To maintain a balance of power, each major state in Europe essentially accepted the status quo. In order to prevent future war as much as possible, the European monarchies agreed to curb their own impulses to expand and to accept their existing borders; if each state could be satisfied with matters as they stood, war could be prevented more easily. In many ways the balance of power system supported John Locke's ideas on the nature of government: each state gave up some of its fundamental rights in order to gain more protection and more stability than it could create individually.

Looking back, political scientists agree that this balance of power system worked because a unique set of conditions existed on the continent of Europe. There were no major ideological disputes among the "Great Powers:" each was a monarchy committed to the preservation of its current dynasty. Consequently, the alignment of these states was fluid; not tied to one another by major ideologies (such as capitalism or communism), the powers could form ever-shifting coalitions to deal with changing circumstances. If power A showed signs of becoming difficult, powers B, C, and D could easily form a new alliance designed to keep power A under control.

Obviously, this constantly shifting series of alliances and coalitions would work only if two other conditions were met: there must be enough Great Powers in existence to carry on this balancing act, and they must continue to see the balance of power as essential to their survival and prosperity. Some students of balance of power politics have drawn up elaborate sets of "rules" that must obtain, while others have created equations and statistical tables to show when and how correct conditions for a balance of power system arise (see, for instance, Kaplan 1969).

Generally speaking, balance of power politics worked, for a variety of complex reasons, for most of the eighteenth century. The system collapsed only when one of the major players, France, plunged into the chaos of revolution and emerged from it as an expansionist, ideologically driven state determined to challenge the balance of power and create a new world. Under Napoleon, French armies carrying the banner of revolutionary ideology, "Liberté, egalité, fraternité," marched across Europe for fifteen years, devastating existing states and raising fears that his antimonarchical disease of the French might become an epidemic.

When a broad European coalition finally defeated Napoleon on the battlefield, the great powers once again met, as they had at Utrecht, to put together a new and more durable balance of power system. Gathered at Vienna, the powers invited France, their recent enemy, to rejoin their ranks as a "great power" if it would accept in essence status as an equal. Concerned with restoring stability

Becoming a Great Power May Be the Easy Part . . .

GLOBAL PERSPECTIVES

History testifies that acquiring great power status may well be easier than holding on to it! In a controversial best-seller, *The Rise and Fall of the Great Powers* (1989), historian Paul Kennedy examines the dynamics of power in the modern world, tracing the rises and falls of the European great powers from the end of the Renaissance to today.

Kennedy maintains that the same dynamics are involved in every rise of a great power, regardless of the time period. Of particular importance is rapid economic growth coupled with increasing military strength. From the beginning of a nation's rise to great power status, this vital economic-strategic link is dominant. However, Kennedy continues, virtually every great power of the modern era has been unable to maintain great power status. Every rise has preceded a fall.

Two factors are most important in explaining the fall of great powers: the tendency of these great powers to overextend themselves militarily and economically, and the constantly shifting relative positions of nations' economic bases. In many ways, overextension seems inherent in the nature of Great Powers: they will continually try to enlarge and consolidate their spheres of influence. Ultimately the military and economic costs of this expansion become more than a power can sustain, usually because the power's economic base has been shrinking relative both to the demands upon it and to the economies of its rivals. The result: one great power begins to decline even as another begins to rise in its stead. And the dance goes on.

Kennedy's thesis implies a kind of historical inevitability that he explicitly denies. There are many variations upon this theme of rise, overextension, and fall, he contends, and one consistent principle: power, whether economic or military, is always relative. He quotes a seventeenth-century German writer:

Whether a nation be today mighty and rich depends not upon the abundance and security of its power and riches, but principally on whether its neighbors possess more or less of it. (Von Horncyk, quoted in Kennedy 1989, xxii)

Kennedy also cautions that his tale has validity for today's great and would-be great powers, warning that the key is not a fatalistic acceptance of the inevitable loss of power, but the exercise of skill and insight by national leaders in order to maintain power.

Source: (Kennedy 1989)

and order after three decades of revolution and warfare, the French government agreed. Thus a new balance of power system was created, very much along the lines of its eighteenth-century predecessor. The same "rules" prevailed: all the powers accepted limits on their ambition (at least on the continent of Europe itself), there were enough players to ensure that the game could proceed smoothly, and the powers allied themselves in fluid coalitions driven not by ideology but by the desire to maintain the status quo.

Like the balance of power created at Utrecht, the new system created at Vienna worked well as long as these essential conditions were met. To be sure, there were some minor wars—as when several of the powers allied to foil Russian ambitions during the Crimean War—but for nearly a century Europe enjoyed relative peace and stability.

However, this system of balance began to collapse in the late nineteenth century, as the German states coalesced into a nation determined to assert itself without regard to the maintenance of the balance of power. The deciding moment came when the young German emperor, William II, fired the Iron Chancellor, Bismarck, who had been a genius at the balance of power game. (In a remarkable illustration of how fluid the balance of power system was, and what a minor role ideology, even nationalism, played in this system, Italy then offered Bismarck the opportunity of directing *its* foreign policy! This would be the equivalent of the Soviet Union's openly offering a retired American Secretary of State a job!)

The collapse of the 19th-century balance of power system took a while to accomplish; Bismarck was fired in 1891, but the system itself had either strength or inertia enough, that it took nearly twenty-five more years for war to erupt. Many of the leaders who assembled at Versailles in 1919 saw the failure of the balance of power system to prevent World War I as indication that the system itself was inherently flawed and should be replaced with something more reliable. The League of Nations represented a first attempt to create an international structure that would simultaneously replace the sometimes cynical balance of power system and move toward an international politics designed to create a better world.

For a complex series of reasons that historians are still sorting out, including the emergence of Adolf Hitler as a "wild card" never foreseen in the calculations of diplomats and politicians, and also the failure of the United States to lend its great power and prestige to the League, this attempt at replacing the balance of power failed miserably, and the world plunged once more into bloody war.

Unipolarity

It is at least theoretically possible to have a unipolar world, that is, one in which a single nation is so powerful that it dictates global activity. However, given the spread of modern technology, it seems unlikely that any nation will find itself in that dominant role. The United States, for example, may now be the only superpower, but in no way can it claim to control or dictate global politics.

Bipolarity

When World War II ended, most of Europe lay in shambles, devastated by the ferocity of the war; in Europe itself as many as 35 million people had died, while the worldwide toll soared to as many as 60 million. The total collapse of most of the former great powers was enough in itself to doom any attempt to revive the balance of power. However, another factor also changed the dynamics of power relations worldwide: the ideologically driven struggle between the United States and the Soviet Union. (For a full discussion of the role played by ideology in international relations, see chapter 6, "Ideas That Make the World Go 'Round.") Further complicating the matter was the development of awesomely destructive nuclear weapons, held almost exclusively by the two ideological enemies.

At least for a while, the result was the division of the players in international relations into two and only two spheres of influence: the United States with its allies, and the Soviet Union with its allies. The two mighty nations became known not as great powers but as superpowers, a far more accurate description of the disparity between their power and that of other, lesser nations.

Political scientists call this division of the world between two superpowers **bipolarity.** Like "balance of power," this term is both ambiguous and not always accurate. However, it is a good description of the way most Europeans, at least, thought of global politics from World War II until 1989: as a division between two contending and enormously powerful states. One historian vividly described the American-Soviet struggle as resembling "two scorpions in a bottle" while philosopher/theologian Reinhold Niebuhr referred to it as a contest between "the children of light and the children of darkness." Much of the realist view of international relations was forged during this Cold War period.

Crucial to the concept of a bipolar world is the concept of a "zero-sum" game; in the struggle between superpowers split by ideology, each certain that it represents the truth, each determined to prevail and conquer in the name of that truth, there can be only one winner. Consequently, there must be a loser as well. Cooperation of the sort that made the balance of power system work is impossible in a world split between warring camps—or so it seemed for nearly five decades. In fact, in the vocabulary of American politicians and diplomats, "coexistence" was a dirty word. It represented the unthinkable idea that the two superpowers could simultaneously occupy the same world in relative stability. The prevailing belief was that the Cold War and the bipolar world system must end in victory for one side, defeat for the other. This essentially apocalyptic view, combined with the thirty thousand or so nuclear warheads in the hands of the superpowers, made the stakes of the struggle high and the price of loss intolerable. It also made for a great deal of nervousness, both in the nonaligned nations and within many citizens of both superpowers.

Stability

For years political scientists have argued about the relative stability of a bipolar world. Several streams of ideas have emerged. To some, bipolarity, at least nuclear bipolarity, is even more stable than the earlier, European balance of power was, since the two sides do not dare play their trump card by using their nuclear weapons. In such a world there may be (and during the Cold War were) many "small wars" fought either by clients of the superpowers or by nonaligned nations (the Israeli-Arab wars, the Pakistani-Indian wars), but there will be no cataclysmic major war. In this view, the existence of two superpowers possessing nuclear arms is the best guarantee against instability and the cataclysm of global nuclear war. Deterrence, as much a psychological concept as a strategic doctrine, works.

In discussing stability, Morton A. Kaplan distinguishes between "loose" and "tight" bipolar systems. In a "loose" bipolar system, Kaplan argues, supranational actors such as the United Nations can play a major role in the balancing process as mediators or integrators. Kaplan also says that loose bipolar systems will tend

bipolarity A world configuration in which there are two centers of power.

to be ideologically defined. In his opinion, a loose bipolar system is somewhat stable (Kaplan, 1969, 297–98). In contrast, a tight bipolar system, that is, one with no outside or supranational actors to play mediating roles, will be very unstable, with a "high degree of dysfunctional tension" (Kaplan, 1969, 298).

Kenneth Waltz (1969) argues that in many ways the bipolar system is the balance of power system revisited, what he elegantly terms "the formation and perpetuation of a balance *a deux*." Such a system, he maintains, is far more stable than a multipolar system.

Other students of international relations have argued that the bipolar world is an inherently more dangerous one than the world of the balance of power. Small wars will proliferate, they agree, but there is too much risk that small wars will escalate into larger and larger wars as client states in trouble appeal to their superpower mentors for help. The balance of power was replaced by the "balance of terror," they argued; such a balance is inherently unstable and doomed to catastrophic failure.

Multipolarity

In an important behaviorally oriented study of systems stability, Karl W. Deutsch and J. David Singer argue that as the world now moves from bipolarity to **multipolarity,** the global political system will become more stable, and both the frequency and the intensity of wars will decrease. They define stability as the "probability of [a nation's] continued political independence and territorial integrity without any significant probability of becoming engaged in a 'war for survival'." This stability will increase with the number of independent actors within the system, and thus with the opportunities for interaction among them. When the system includes more than five actors, "the stability-enhancing increment begins to grow very sharply." Each actor must allocate less of its attention to any other given actor; thus the possibility or at least the intensity of conflict decreases, and the system becomes more stable. In such an ideal multipolar system "arms increases by a rival power, which in a bipolar world might pose a fatal threat, might call in a multipolar world for little more than a quick adjustment of alliances." However, Deutsch and Singer argue, history has shown that multipolar balancing systems have normally not lasted more than a few centuries; thus, over a long time, a multipolar system will tend to break down into a bipolar system and become more and more unstable (Deutsch and Singer 1969, 315–24).

multipolarity Two or more centers of global power.

Of course, some would argue that the term "bipolar," referring to a world divided between two diametrically opposed ideologies, never did accurately describe much of the world beyond Europe. Nations emerging from colonialism or revolution—India and Indonesia, for example—tried to steer clear of involvement with either side by pursuing policies of neutrality. Other centers of power began to emerge in the shadow of the superpowers; both Japan and China became increasingly powerful, although neither had the necessary combination of population, resources, industrial power, and nuclear weapons to directly challenge the superpowers.

Other political scientists have agreed that the idea of bipolarity is too simplistic to describe reality. Noting the emergence of these nonaligned nations and of powerful states within the camps of the superpowers (Japan in the American realm, China in the Soviet sphere), these political scientists have tried to elaborate on the idea of bipolarity to describe a world in which the balance of power no longer exists. They have developed a bewildering array of terms to describe this world: strong bipolarity, weak bipolarity, multipolarity, bi-multipolarity, and so forth. An equally bewildering array of charts and diagrams have been drawn up to support and to illustrate these descriptions of power distribution (see also chapter 11, "War").

Billiard Balls and Cobwebs

cobweb model The model of international relations that asserts that the world is intricately connected. What happens in one part of the world has repercussions in every other quarter of the world no matter how insignificant the event.

A quite different approach to global power distribution is the **cobweb model** of J. W. Burton, who argues that trying to understand the world solely in terms of individual nation-states and their alignment is too simplistic. In this overly simple view, nations clash and carom off one another as if they were billiard balls, Burton says—but the world just doesn't work that way. In reality, the world is composed of a series of systems interacting with one another, systems that are indeed composed of nation-states, but also of actors, at both the supranational and the subnational levels. Burton advocates analyzing separately the various systems—communications, trade, science, tourism—that constitute global politics, and then superimposing these systems upon one another to get an accurate picture of the complexity of global interactions. How would this picture look? "The map of world society would be one cobweb of transactions imposed on another, and the image of world society would be one of concentrations of interactions at some points, and linkages across national boundaries, sometimes clustered, sometimes infrequent" (Burton 1974, 5–6). The starting point for such a cobweb system, Burton states, is relationships. "No progress can be made in the study of any level of behavior unless there is description and an explanation of relationships, how they evolve, how they are learned, what patterns emerge, and why there is observance and deviance from them." In other words, the billiard balls that represent nations do not have absolute freedom of movement; they are caught up in and often moved around by the cobwebs of relationships that span the earth (Burton, 7–8). (For a discussion of actors other than states, see chapter 4, "The Galaxy of Actors on the Global Horizon: IGOs, NGOs, and MNCs.")

An Emerging Multipolar System?

The sudden collapse of the Soviet Union and its carefully crafted alliance system in Eastern Europe, dubbed the "quiet cataclysm" by John Mueller, has apparently ended both the system of bipolarity and the debate over its meaning. Today's world has only one superpower, the United States, and it is mired in domestic economic problems, created at least in part by the massive spending necessary to maintain superpower status. The Soviet Union no longer exists; republics of varying degrees of strength have broken out of the former Soviet structure to proclaim their independence and take their places on the world stage. Neither does the Warsaw Pact, the military and political alliance forged by the old Soviet Union, exist any longer: virtually all of the states once linked together by the Warsaw Pact have broken free of Soviet dominance and are now trying desperately to build democratic political systems and free-market economies to replace the vanished communist structures.

To some, there is a large amount of comfort to be derived from these rapid changes. The possibility of global nuclear war and thus global destruction seems to be rapidly receding, levels of military tension are diminishing, and no longer do hostile superpowers stand toe to toe, "eyeball-to-eyeball," on the brink of destruction.

Others see these rapid changes as unnerving, for they raise the inevitable question, "What next?" Can there be some kind of global balance of power created to bring about worldwide stability? Will we see the emergence of a multipolar system of nuclear powers in which hostile states confront not one but multiple "enemies"? Will the United States somehow maintain its position as the world's one and only superpower, and use that status not just to restore stability but also to spread prosperity? Will we see global conflict shift to a confrontation between industrialized and prosperous states on one side and poverty-stricken, nonindustrial states who control vital natural resources on the other?

In the following chapters, we will return to these questions and draw some conclusions about not only the sources, use, and distribution of power, but also the actors, dimensions, and dynamics of contemporary international relations. In our quest to examine how the world works politically in the modern age of high technology, we will investigate the simultaneous currents of global power integration and world power disintegration.

Summary

What Is Power?   At the heart of international relations lie issues of power: how one nation achieves what it wants and how it forces others to yield to its demands. Expressed crudely, power means getting your way.

Sources of National Power: The power of a nation-state rests on three different sources: natural, social-psychological, and synthetic. Natural sources include geography, natural resources, and population. Social-psychological sources are intangibles such as stability and leadership that determine how successfully a country can utilize its resources. Synthetic sources of power include the industrial and military capacities developed from a nation's resources. A given nation may rank very high in terms of one or two of these sources of power but still be relatively powerless because of shortcomings in other areas.

The Ideologies of Power: The question of how power should be used has perplexed statesmen and philosophers for many centuries. The two basic positions are idealism and realism. Idealism demands that power be used for a purpose that lies beyond the narrow interests of an individual actor or state. Thus idealists look toward the humane use of power to build a better, more peaceful world and to improve the lot of the average human being. Realists, on the other hand, believe that the only practical, and the only defensible, use of power is to meet the national interest of the individual nation-state. Realists tend to scorn the argument that morality and humane interests should play a role in the formulation of national policy. The debate continues.

Global Distribution of Power: Political scientists discern a number of ways in which power may be distributed globally. The principal models of power distribution include a balance of power system, unipolarity, bipolarity, and multipolarity.

Key Terms

Strategic location
Chokepoint
Geopolitics
Shatterbelts
Gateway

Balance of trade
Bipolarity
Multipolarity
Cobweb model

Thought Questions

1. What are the three major sources of power? Give examples of each.
2. Outline the debate between idealists and realists about the use of power. Choose a topic from today's news and explain how an idealist and a realist would deal with such a problem.
3. Which of the following do you think most accurately describes the global distribution of power: unipolarity, bipolarity, multipolarity, or a cobweb? Why?
4. Describe the idea of the national interest. Analyze the national interest of the United States, Great Britain, Russia, and Turkey in the former Yugoslavia conflict. On the basis of that national interest, what should each nation do?

References

Bergman, Edward. *Human Geography: Cultures, Connections, and Landscapes*. Englewood Cliffs, N.J.: Prentice Hall, 1995.

Burton, John. "International Relations or World Society?" In *The Study of World Society: A London Perspective*. Pittsburgh, Pa.: University of Pittsburgh International Studies Association, 1974.

Central Intelligence Agency. *World Factbook 1995*. Internet. http://www.odci.gov/cia/publications/95fact. Downloaded May 10, 1996.

Chaliand, Gerard, and Jean-Pierre Rageau. *Strategic Atlas: A Comparative Geopolitics of the World's Powers*. New York: Harper Collins, 1992.

Cohen, Saul. "Global Geopolitical Change in the Post-Cold War Era." *Annals of the Association of American Geographers,* (81) 4, 1991.

Crankshaw, Edward. *Bismarck*. New York: Penguin Books, 1983.

deBlij, Harm J., and Peter O. Muller. *Geography: Regions and Concepts*. New York: John Wiley and Sons, 1988.

Demko, George J. *Why in the World: Adventures in Geography*. New York: Doubleday Anchor, 1992.

Deutsch, Karl W., and J. David Singer. "Multipolar Power Systems and International Stability." In James N. Rosenau (ed.). *International Politics and Foreign Policy*. New York: The Free Press, 1969.

Dougherty, James E., and Robert L. Pfaltzgraff, Jr. *Contending Theories of International Relations* (3rd ed.). New York: HarperCollins, 1993.

Fisher, James S., ed. *Geography and Development: A World Regional Approach.* 4th ed. New York: Macmillan, 1992.

Gates, Robert. *From The Shadows: The Ultimate Insider's Story of Five Presidents and How They Won the Cold War.* New York: Simon and Schuster, 1996.

Getis, Arthur, Judith Getis, and Jerome Fellmann. *Introduction to Geography.* 2d ed. Dubuque, Iowa: Wm. C. Brown, 1988.

Hepner, George F., and Jesse O. McKee. *World Regional Geography: A Global Approach.* St. Paul, Minn.: West, 1992.

Isaacson, Walter. *Kissinger: A Biography.* New York: Simon and Schuster, 1992.

Kaplan, Morton A. "Variants on Six Models of the International System." In Rosenau.

Kennan, George F. *American Diplomacy, 1900-1950.* Chicago: University of Chicago Press, 1951.

Kennedy, Paul. *The Rise and Fall of the Great Powers.* New York: Random House, 1989.

————. *Preparing for the Twenty-First Century.* New York: Random House, 1993.

Kidron, Michael, and Ronald Segal. *The New State of the World Atlas.* 4th ed. New York: Simon and Schuster Touchstone, 1991.

Kidron, Michael, and Dan Smith. *The New State of War and Peace: An International Atlas.* New York: Simon and Schuster Touchstone, 1991.

Kissinger, Henry. *A World Restored: Metternich, Castlereagh, and the Problems of Peace, 1812–1822.* Boston: Houghton Mifflin, 1992.

Luard, Evan, ed. *Basic Texts in International Relations: The Evolution of Ideas about International Society.* New York: St. Martin's Press, 1992.

Massey, Robert. *Dreadnaught: Britain, Germany, and the Coming of the Great War.* New York: Ballantine Books, 1992.

Morgenthau, Hans. *Politics Among Nations.* 6th ed. New York: Alfred A. Knopf, 1979.

Rosenau, James N., (ed.). *International Politics and Foreign Policy.* New York: The Free Press, 1969.

Roth, Bennet, and Cindy Rugeley. "Land of the Illiterate." *Houston Chronicle,* September 9, 1993.

Waltz, Kenneth N. "International Structure, National Force, and the Balance of World Power." in Rosenau.

Wright, Quincy. *A Study of War.* Chicago: University of Chicago, 1964.

Yergin, Daniel. *The Prize: The Epic Quest for Oil, Money, and Power.* New York: Simon and Schuster, 1991.

Chapter 3

Who We Are:
States, Nations,
and Nationalism

Introduction

From space, Earth is a planet of breathtaking beauty, a blue globe swathed in white clouds, alternately bathed in brilliant sunlight and cloaked in darkness. Astronauts of all nationalities have pointedly remarked that when they look back at this fragile globe, they see no national borders drawn on the earth. In fact, in physical terms, most national borders are more fiction than fact: the earth itself is unmarked by the neat dividing lines drawn clearly and geometrically on maps.

Should extraterrestrials ever land on earth, they would see a planet teeming with carbon-based, oxygen-breathing, erect bipeds. They would be unlikely to notice the distinctions between Japanese, Angolan, and Danish populations, much less the far finer distinctions between Germans, French, Croats, Slovenians, and Ukrainians. Even people of one ethnic or racial group often have trouble drawing distinctions between members of other groups.

For most of us, nationality is a vital element of our sense of identity. We boast of being Americans or Nigerians or Chinese; we carry passports identifying us as citizens of particular nations, not residents of Earth; we salute as our national flags are carried past; and we talk in terms of national interest, national economies, and national policies. And all too often, we have gone to war on behalf of our own nations, killing others for the sin of belonging to different nations.

What is going on? Why are so many people so passionately concerned about differences that, from many perspectives, do not even exist?

Nationalism

The answer is **nationalism,** one of the most powerful, most creative, and most destructive forces in modern international politics. As an idea, nationalism is relatively new, dating to the late eighteenth and early nineteenth centuries; as a reality, nationalism and its fellow traveller, the nation-state, were confined almost exclusively to Europe and such European offspring as the Americas until after World War II. In fact, even after World War II, in the nearly half-century when the Cold War divided the world into pro-American and pro-Soviet camps, many scholars were ready to write nationalism's obituary and consign the nation-state to the graveyard of obsolete political systems. Today, however, nationalism has reemerged as a dynamic force, simultaneously uniting people behind a particular flag and pitting them against others who do not share that flag or the ideals, values, and history that it represents. New nations have proliferated in the last half-century: United Nations membership has increased from the original 54 members to the present 184, and the process of creating new nations continues. Czechoslovakia fissions into the Czech Republic and Slovakia, Yugoslavia dissolves into six warring states, Basques demand separation from Spain and Ibos from Nigeria, and Bolivia reiterates a century-old claim to parts of contemporary Colombia.

Driving this often dizzying pace of change is nationalism, "the greatest emotional-political force of the age" (Moynihan 1993, 111). Above all, nationalism is an *idea,* the idea that people who share the same language, same history, same religion, and same culture constitute a distinct group united by these common ties—that they are a "nation." Furthermore, nationalism goes on to claim that these people, the members of this **nation,** deserve their own nation-state, their own country, to express this sense of special nationalism. Hans Kohn, one of the keenest students of nationalism, defines it as "a state of mind in which the

nationalism A state of mind in which the individual's loyalty is directed totally toward the nation-state on behalf of a nation.

nation A body of people who believe that they have racial, ethnic, religious, linguistic, or cultural reasons for a common political identity or purpose.

supreme loyalty of the individual is felt to be to the nation-state." Nationalities, he writes, possess "certain objective factors distinguishing them from other nationalities, like common descent, language, territory, political entity, customs and tradition, or religion." Finally, Kohn asserts, "the most essential element [of nationalism] is a living and active corporate will . . . [that] asserts that nationalism is the ideal and the only legitimate form of political organization" (Kohn 1965, 1–2). This vital element of will can often unite people that might seem otherwise divided: Belgians who speak two distinct languages, Kurds who likewise speak two distinct languages and are partitioned among several states, Chinese who speak mutually unintelligible dialects but still consider themselves Chinese. Will and emotion can unite immigrants from many countries and continents into a single nation, as in the United States, or it can create a single nation from more than 120 nationalities, as in contemporary Russia.

Usually nationalism is based on shared characteristics of a people that separate them from others and link them together. Language is one of the most common bonds of nationalism; others are religion, history, ethnic sameness, culture, territory, and propinquity. Nationalism can be an integrating force, providing cohesion and a sense of belonging, or it can be a destructive force, separating peoples and classifying them into "our kind" and "aliens." Nationalism is more than merely ideological; it is also profoundly political, demanding that people unite to create their own state, a state that will express their unique values and sense of self. Nationalism is thus, according to a recent examination of the subject, "both an ideology and a political movement which holds the nation and the sovereign nation-state to be crucial in dwelling values, and which manages to mobilize the political will of a people or of a large section of a population." Nationalism exists, then, "wherever individuals feel they belong primarily to the nation, and whenever affective attachment and loyalty to that nation override all other attachments and loyalties" (Alter 1989, 8–9).

In all its capacities—as a uniting principle, as a destructive force, as an ideology, and as a political movement—nationalism has been one of the most vital forces in shaping modern international politics. Even today, despite the rise of multinational organizations like the United Nations or the Red Cross and transnational corporations like ITT or General Motors, nationalism remains the dominant organizing force in the states that constitute the chief actors on the global stage. Even the term we apply to global politics, "international relations," attests to the centrality of the nation-state. Although there are signs that the forces of nationalism are beginning to fade in some places—with the rise of the European Union, for example—in many others nationalism is as powerful, and sometimes as virulent, as ever.

In this chapter, we will examine first of all the rise of nation-states and their role as the exemplification of nationalism; then, we will look at the varieties of nationalism in today's world. Finally, we will see how difficult it is to shoehorn the world into nationalist molds by examining two problems: nations without states, such as the Kurds, and states that consist of multiple nationalities, including, most tragically, Yugoslavia, as well as the former Soviet Union and the United States.

The State

state A legal geopolitical entity that has a permanent population, defined territory, and a legitimate government.

Before we go on, it will be useful to set out some important definitions and distinctions. Although we tend to use the terms interchangeably in ordinary conversation, "nation" and "state" have quite different meanings, and their combination as "nation-state" has yet another. A **state** is an organized political entity that exerts its will upon those within its boundaries. A state may take a wide variety of forms, from a monarchy to an empire to a democracy. Three elements determine the existence of the state: institutions, boundaries, and rule-making ability. First, the state is composed of institutions; in turn, these institutions possess means of violence and coercion, such as police forces or armies. The state's own personnel staff such institutions, and the institutions endure beyond changes in government. The inauguration of a new president does not require the creation, or the re-creation, of the United States Army, for example. Second, the state controls a specific geographic area within which it exercises power. Finally, the state monopolizes rulemaking or lawmaking within its boundaries (Hall 1993, 878–83). In addition, states participate in international affairs as the representatives and guarantors of their people. Consequently, although we in the United States use the term "states" to refer to subnational political entities such as Montana and Connecticut, only the federal government constitutes a *state* in the formal sense used in international relations. Iowa does not develop its own foreign policy; nor does Texas issue its own currency—and laws made by both are superseded by federal laws.

The Nation

Nation refers much more specifically to a group of people who feel themselves bound together by strong cultural, historical, religious, or linguistic ties. Members of a nation consciously distinguish themselves from other peoples or other nations. One of the strongest human needs is the need to belong, to be identified with a larger force or group that can both justify and enable the individual, as well as reinforce a basic sense of identity. At the most basic level, the family provides a sense of belonging; in a much broader way, the nation does so. Thus it is legitimate to speak of a "nation" as a distinct ethnic group (the Czech nation), or as any other self-defined and self-conscious group (the "Woodstock nation"). The concept of "nation" is double-edged; while the nation is inclusive for those individuals who meet the necessary criteria to belong, it also excludes far more people, and too often defines those excluded not only as different but also as inferior and dangerous to the nation. As a political and emotional movement, nationalism rises from both wellsprings: the strong sense of identity and belonging on the one side, and the equally strong sense of "us versus them," with all those not of the nation defined as "alien," on the other.

The Nation-State

The most common form of state in today's world combines these two components, the idea of the nation and of the state, into a single entity, the **nation-state.** There are still states that are not nation-states—Saudi Arabia, for example, is a kingdom, and Iran is a theocratic rather than a nation-state—but most of the players on the world stage are in fact nation-states. They are politically organized territories that recognize no higher law, that is, fully sovereign territories, and their population identifies with them on the basis of either civic or ethnic nationalism. (We will discuss the distinction between these two later in this chapter.)

nation-state A nation with a political construct, i.e. territorially defined boundaries, legal government, foreign recognition, etc.

From Universalism and Localism to Sovereign States

Historically, nationalism is very much a latecomer among ways that people and governments have organized themselves. Far more common have been much smaller and more rigid systems, such as the tribe or clan, or much larger and more inclusive systems, such as the empire. The tug-of-war between the universalism of an empire and the particularism of local entities has shaped European politics for more than twenty-five hundred years. Nation-states are relative newcomers, with the modern sovereign state basically a seventeenth-century creation and the nation-state the product of the nineteenth century. Because so much of our twentieth-century political awareness has been shaped by nationalism and the interaction of nation-states, it is often a shock to realize how recent both nationalism and the nation-state are. Since nationalism was originally a European phenomenon, we will first trace its development within Europe and then examine how nationalism spread beyond Europe into Africa and Asia, often with enormous consequences.

Imperial Universalism: Rome

During the classical period Europe experimented with both the particularism of local organization and the universalism of empire. During the earliest stage of this period, the Greeks organized themselves by *polis,* or city-state. These political units were generally small and exclusive, with citizenship dependent upon birth. The polis was physically united and confined to a small area. Even though the Greeks shared a common language, culture, and religion, they chose to divide and define themselves locally. Rome, the successor to Greece as the dominant force in the classical world, was built on a diametrically opposed organizing principle: the idea of universal empire. Sprawling across much of Europe, the Middle East, and North Africa, the Roman empire incorporated all or part of thirty-nine modern nations within its frontiers. Citizenship in the empire was defined by allegiance, not birth.

As Rome demonstrated, empire offers powerful advantages to the state. Empires by definition can incorporate and accommodate multiple ethnic groups speaking a wide variety of languages. Each group brought great strengths to the Roman Empire, as warriors, traders, or farmers. Furthermore, an empire is in theory infinitely expandable: its borders depend on the strength of its armies and the ambition or ability of its rulers, not on the much more constricting nationality of the people inhabiting its territory.

Ecclesiastical Universalism: The Christian Church

The rise of the Christian Church reinforced within the Roman Empire the sense of universalism, that is, the sense that the religious and political structures were both large enough and strong enough to accommodate virtually any group or any people. In fact, the word *catholic* in the title given later to the Roman Catholic Church means "universal." Whether as members of the Roman Empire or of the Christian church, by the end of the classical age most Europeans saw themselves as part of systems that encompassed all of civilization and that stretched far beyond the narrow compass of their own area and language.

The collapse of the Roman Empire did not destroy this European concept of universalism. Europeans continued to see themselves as the heirs of the Roman Empire, and there were multiple attempts to re-create that empire, particularly in the Holy Roman Empire. Overarching all political institutions in its continued realization of universality was the Christian church, which found expression as "Christendom" in the Middle Ages. All Europeans, no matter who their king or emperor, were members of Christendom, united in their loyalty to the Christian church and capable of being galvanized into such enormous enterprises as the Crusades on its behalf. The Church remained a universal institution, part of no kingdom or state, but above all. Feudalism divided Europe into thousands of local entities claiming the loyalty of Europeans, but the Holy Roman Catholic Church pressed and often realized its claim to universalism.

Even as individual kingdoms and smaller empires rose to replace the Roman empire, they remained expansive. Gradually the idea grew that the kingdom was in fact the personal property of the king, and its residents were "subjects" of the king. However, the identification of kingdoms as the personal property of the rulers still allowed kings to blur boundary lines. Thus, both English- and French-speaking monarchs could claim control of much of France—with the deadly result of the Hundred Years' War—and a Russian monarch like Peter the Great could expand his empire's borders to lands previously ruled by Swedish or Polish monarchs. Catherine the Great could rule Russia at the end of the eighteenth century even though she was born in a German-speaking territory, and an Italian named Mazarin could serve as principal advisor to the young French king Louis XIV.

Universalism began to collapse with the rise of strong centralized European governments in the late Middle Ages. And it vanished almost completely from Europe with the split of Christendom itself in the furies of the Protestant Reformation. The last great convulsion of the Reformation raged across central Europe from 1618 to 1648, as Protestant and Catholic battled for superiority within the Holy Roman Empire, the last remnant of the idea of Christendom. It says a great deal about the collapse of universalist religious principles that during this war the Catholic French supported many Protestant European states, more concerned about French interests than about the fate of Catholicism.

The Modern Sovereign State

From the ruins of the Holy Roman Empire and its tattered claims to universalism rose the first important steps toward the modern state system: the signing of the **Treaty of Westphalia** in 1648 signaled not only an end to bloody religious warfare in central Europe, but also the recognition of a completely new political entity, the sovereign state. Crucial to the Westphalian settlement was the concept of the sovereignty of the individual state. No longer were states defined as the personal property of kings and emperors, with other kings and emperors possessing the right to intervene and meddle in their affairs. Instead, after Westphalia each major state was accepted as sovereign—that is, its borders were impermeable, and whatever happened within those borders was not the concern of other states. This concept of **sovereignty** lies at the heart of our modern state system even today, and is one of the most important defining aspects of nationalism. The exact location of sovereignty has been defined differently, from the monarchical view that the monarch is himself or herself sovereign, God's agent on earth, to the view of Thomas Hobbes that the state constitutes the sovereign agent, to the Enlightenment view that sovereignty arises from the consent of the people—but its meaning has generally been agreed upon. Each sovereign state stands alone and is answerable to none for its domestic conduct; what happens within the sovereign state's borders is literally no one else's business. There is no institution beyond the sovereign state capable of forcing the state into doing what it does not want to do. As sovereigns, states control and act upon their own populations without any outside interference: they issue their own currencies, create their own

Treaty of Westphalia The 1648 peace treaty that concluded the Thirty Years' War and ultimately led to the establishment of the current nation-state system.

sovereignty The fundamental right of the state to perpetuate and govern itself, subject to no higher political authority.

flags and anthems, demand and receive the loyalty of their own citizens, and control their own borders, deciding who or what may enter. Each sovereign state also deals as it wishes—or as it can—with all other sovereign states.

Today, however, some of these aspects of sovereignty are hotly debated or under attack. For example, does sovereignty give a state the right to brutalize its citizens? Are repressive regimes to be tolerated simply because they are sovereign, or are there general human rights that must override all claims to sovereignty? Increasingly, the international community has proclaimed that human rights must take precedence over sovereign rights, and thus the United States intervenes in Haiti and the United Nations attempts to intervene in the Balkans. Furthermore, modern communications and economics have often overtaken the concept of sovereignty; borders long impermeable to armies are porous to radio waves, and few modern states can effectively control the ideas to which their people are exposed. Modern states cannot isolate their economies from the global economy and enjoy any degree of prosperity; nor can they control the value of their own currencies. (See chapters 4, 7, and 13 for more thorough discussions of these issues.)

Although the concept of sovereignty is in many ways simply not applicable to an increasingly global international system, this concept that emerged from the Treaty of Westphalia remains the principal organizing idea of the modern state. We shall examine how in the nineteenth century this concept of the sovereign state would merge with a new and often explosive idea, the idea of the nation, to forge the modern nation-state.

The Birth of Nationalism and Nation-States

Seventeenth-century England, racked by civil war between Puritans and Cavaliers, produced one of the basic foundations of modern nationalism in the work of John Locke. Many of Locke's ideas are so fundamental to our thinking that we take them for granted, but they were both product and stimulator of revolution. For example, Locke maintained that the rights of the individual to such basic elements as life, liberty, and property were neither the gift of a benevolent king nor the creation of any government, but were innate, **natural rights.** The desire to protect those rights drove people to bind themselves to one another in states, Locke wrote, and to create governments that would guarantee this protection. States and governments were neither ordained by God nor granted to kings, but were created by the people in order to protect their natural rights. Should government threaten rather than protect the people's natural rights, the people possessed the right to rebel, to overthrow that government (which they had, after all, created), and to replace it with a new government that would fulfill its responsibilities more faithfully.

During the intellectual revolution of the eighteenth century known as the Enlightenment, many political philosophers, particularly in France, elaborated on Locke's basic ideas. One of the most important was Jean-Jacques Rousseau, who developed the concept of the **social contract** binding together people of a single nation, and the idea of the "general will" of the people.

The first conscious attempts to fuse the concepts of nation and state came during the French Revolution, and the dual creative and destructive nature of nationalism became immediately apparent. Successive revolutionary governments, desperate to mobilize a hitherto passive population both to carry out the Revolution and to battle external enemies, enlisted *all* the people of France in its

natural rights Inalienable rights innate to human beings; these are not given by government, and hence cannot be taken away by government.

social contract Rousseauian construct of the "general will" linking the governed and the government, upon which government rested.

defense, calling upon the young men to form armies and all others, from the very young to the very old, to do whatever they could on behalf of France. Napoleon would wage war against most of Europe in the name of the French nation, using the concept to marshal and hold together huge citizen armies. The monarchs he threatened appealed in turn to the nascent nationalism of their subjects in order to meet the Napoleonic threat. Then, recognizing the Pandora's box they had opened, conservative European leaders spent the rest of the nineteenth century trying to suppress nationalism. They ultimately failed.

Romantic Nationalism

In the nineteenth century, nationalism became intertwined with Romanticism, which emphasized emotion and intuition. Nationalist writers began to romanticize "lost causes" of the eighteenth century and nationalist rebellions of the nineteenth. Under the romantic rubric, poets like Byron and Shelly wrote about resurgent Greek nationalism and the heroic struggle of the Greeks to free themselves from their Turkish masters; Byron even went off to die in Greece with the patriots. One of the most influential of the romantic nationalist writers was Sir Walter Scott, who glorified the Scotland of the highland clans and their long, and futile, struggle to overthrow English rule. Nothing better epitomizes the fusion of nationalism and romanticism than Scott's highly charged introduction to *The Lay of the Last Minstrel:* (1805):

> Breathes there the man, with soul so dead,
> Who never to himself hath said,
> This is my own, my native land!
> Whose heart hath ne'er within him burn'd
> As home his footsteps he hath turn'd,
> From wandering on a foreign strand?
> If such there breathe, go, mark him well;
> For him no minstrel raptures swell;
> High though his title, proud his name,
> Boundless his wealth as wish can claim—
> Despite those titles, power, and pelf,
> The wretch, concentred all in self,
> Living shall forfeit far renown,
> And, doubly-dying, shall go down
> To the vile dust, from whence he sprung,
> Unwept, unhonour'd and unsung.
> (Scott, 1805)

During the nineteenth century, nationalism in Europe showed both its most creative and its most destructive faces. Its creative influence was seen in the emergence of new, unified nation-states like Italy and even Germany. However, as Kohn points out, the nature of nationalism itself began to shift. "Nationalism changed in the middle of the nineteenth century from liberal humanitarianism to aggressive exclusionism, from the emphasis on the dignity of the individual to that on the power of the nation, from limitation and distrust of government to its exaltation" (Kohn, 1961, 50). In Germany, in particular, the romantic "rediscovery" of Germanic mythology and the idea of the *volk* created an increasingly intense nationalistic fervor. *Volk*, according to a student of German nationalism, "expressed what was felt to be a much more comprehensive and emotionally charged German experience, imperfectly understood . . . by those content to describe themselves as 'peoples' or 'nations.'" The term "signified the union of a group of people, bound together in a common racial identity that was the source of their individuality and creativity" (Bullock 1992, 69). (Later, in Hitler's hands, the idea of the German *volk* would have terrible consequences for all of Europe.)

The destructive face of nationalism was seen in the threat it posed to the polyglot, multinational empires of central and eastern Europe: the Austro-Hungarian, Russian, and Ottoman (Turkish) Empires, all essentially relics of the late Middle Ages. In all three empires, already weakened by incompetence, corruption, and inertia, nationalism became a highly dangerous force, since it demanded that the empires be dismembered into new states that reflected individual nationalities. The instability created by nationalists within these empires played a major role in bringing on World War I. Then, the various Treaties of Versailles that constituted the postwar peace settlement institutionalized nationalism. This virtually guaranteed continuing instability, because of both the very nature of nationalism and the difficulties of creating states that actually embodied specific and unique nations. In the aftermath of Versailles it became clear that nationalism could no longer be confined to Europe, and in the next forty years nationalist longing for independence and self-determination tore apart the great empires that had ruled much of the world when World War I began. Now, after having been suppressed somewhat by the powerful forces of the Cold War that attempted to compress all international relations into an East-West matrix, nationalism has once again emerged as a powerful force.

Nationalism as a Cultural and Moral Force

While the most obvious component of nationalism is political—the belief in the right of national self-determination, the right of a nation to govern itself—Michael Ignatieff points out that nationalism incorporates moral and cultural elements as well. In moral terms, nationalism represents "an ethic of heroic sacrifice," and justifies the use of force in defending the nation against both internal and external enemies. Culturally, nationalism proclaims that an individual's primary form of belonging, or fundamental identity, comes from the nation; among the multiple identities we all possess, the national identity is the most important. These three elements of nationalism are intertwined and mutually reinforcing. The moral justification of the use of violence to defend the nation springs from the cultural claim that only the nation can fulfill an individual's need for identity, belonging, and security. And both the political demand for self-determination and the moral claim that struggle for nationhood justifies violence rise from the cultural claim that each people is unique and this uniqueness must be fulfilled, and can only be fulfilled, by nationhood, the creation of a state that fully expresses the nationalism of its people (Ignatieff 1994, 5).

Civic versus Ethnic Nationalism

civic nationalism Nationalism predicated upon a shared sense of political ideals; national identity is based upon beliefs, not blood.

Students of nationalism distinguish between civic and ethnic nationalism, generally viewing civic nationalism as positive and ethnic nationalism as negative and often dangerous.

Civic nationalism maintains that the sense of nation must rest on a shared political creed. National identity is a matter of belief, not of blood. Civic nationalism thus "envisages the nation as a community of equal, rights-bearing citizens, united in patriotic attachment to a shared set of political values and practices." Such civic nationalism is by definition democratic, since it vests sovereignty in the people (Ignatieff 1994, 6). The United States, with its wide mixture of peoples, embodies civic nationalism.

Ethnic nationalism is very different. Emerging from nineteenth-century romanticism, ethnic nationalism is the nationalism of blood. According to this view, the state rose "not [from] the cold contrivance of shared rights but [from] the people's pre-existing ethnic characteristics: their language, religion, customs, and traditions." An individual's passionate attachment to the nation is born of blood, inherited rather than chosen. The national community defines the individual (Ignatieff 1994, 7–8).

ethnic nationalism Fervent loyalty to one's cultural, ethnic, or linguistic community within the nation or nation-state.

There is a problem here. Although shared ethnicity may link individuals at one level, it does not prevent them from fighting at other levels over jobs, spouses, or food. Since ethnic nationalism does not stem from a shared sense of the values and principles that undergird law, the regime created by ethnic nationalism must attempt to forge unity by imposing laws from above, and must maintain that unity by force rather than consent; consequently, ethnic nationalist regimes tend to be far more authoritarian than civic nationalist regimes.

Furthermore, the ethnic nationalist state often finds excuses to rid itself of all who do not share the same blood. Ideas may be learned, but blood and inheritance are immutable. Any who do not share the same blood thus pose a threat to the community. They can never belong. For the community to be preserved, ethnic nationalists have argued, it must be purified, purged of all alien elements. Thus the horror of the Holocaust or the current spectre of "ethnic cleansing" in the Balkans seems eminently logical in the eyes of the ethnic nationalist. In contrast, civic nationalism recognizes that mere ethnicity does not of itself erase difficulties or resolve tensions. Common roots do not hold a society together. Law does. The rationalism of the Enlightenment, not the emotionalism of the romantic era, informs civic nationalists. "By subscribing to a set of democratic procedures and values, individuals can reconcile their right to shape their own lives with their need to belong to a community" (Ignatieff 1994, 7). Somewhat like the classic empire, the state built on civic nationalism is in theory infinitely expandable.

Problems in Creating Nation-States

Language

The greatest problem of modern nationalism is more or less self-evident: how do people organize a nation-state? If the chief determining factor is language, there are incredible problems. Some languages have far too many speakers, spread too far over the globe, to be shoehorned into a single nation. For example, English-speaking peoples have formed dominant, separate nations not only in Europe but also in North America, where two predominantly English-speaking nations exist, and in the Pacific, where two more English-speaking nations can be found. Virtually the same pattern of language diffusion is true of Spanish. Speakers of such global languages may well form communities of mutual history and culture, but they constitute neither nations nor nation-states.

On the other side of the coin, many physical regions have a surfeit of languages. According to the Summer Institute of Linguistics, there are 6,170 languages worldwide (Moynihan 1993, 72). The island of New Guinea, which is divided into only two nations at present, has more than eight hundred distinct languages. Africa alone is home to anywhere between one thousand and three thousand distinct languages (Oliver 1991, 38). In many cases, these languages have only a few thousand or a few hundred thousand speakers, but they nonetheless qualify as distinct and separate languages.

One study of the congruence between linguistic boundaries and national boundaries found that the national borders of fewer than 10 percent of current nations fit more or less exactly over linguistic boundaries (Connor 1970, 36). Most people in the world are, according to one authority, "disenfranchised or disadvantaged linguistically." Only 86 of the world's languages are official national tongues, and 5 languages—English, French, Spanish, Portuguese, and Arabic—serve as official languages in 124 states. Some 27 nations have minority languages spoken by 10 percent or more of their populations, and in only 69 of the present 183 nations do more than three-fourths of the people speak the dominant or official language as their mother tongue. In at least 50 nations (many of which are in Africa), less than 25 percent of the population speaks the dominant or official language as its mother tongue (Kidron and Segal 1991, 70–71). In India, there are two all-Indian languages, English and Hindi, and 14 officially recognized regional languages. English is also an official or semiofficial language in 90 states besides India. One estimate places the number of reasonably fluent English speakers worldwide at more than one billion people, roughly one-fifth of the world's teenage and adult population. Over two-thirds of the world's scientists write in English, and 80 percent of all information stored in electronic retrieval systems is in English (Kidron and Segal 1991, 142–43).

Religion

Religion is also a difficult standard for determining national boundaries. For one thing, many modern peoples are intensely secular—that is, they live in societies in which religion is less important than it traditionally has been. Furthermore, there are serious difficulties in defining "religion" itself as a basis for nationalism. For example, is Christianity a religion? Or are Catholicism and Protestantism so different that they constitute two separate religions? In the Muslim world, is Islam a single religion, and thus the basis for an enormous Islamic state, or are sects such as Sunni, Shia, and Wahabi so different that states should be built around them rather than around Islam in general? The Israeli attempt to construct a state on the basis of the Jewish religion has encountered not only the practical problems associated with a substantial domestic Islamic Arab population, but also difficulties arising from differences among multiple sects within Judaism. The power given in Israel to Orthodox Jewish religious courts, for example, often angers less strict religious adherents. All of these are only a sample of the many obstacles faced in the attempt to define a nation by religion.

Culture and History

"Culture" is a concept that is key to nationalism, but again, is difficult to pin down. Clearly, culture encompasses language and religion—but it goes beyond these into the realms of mythology, folktales and other literature, music, art, and many other expressions of life that are influential but hard to measure. "History" is equally difficult to pin down. As a collective biography of a particular group or people, history can tell either a story of a shared past or a tale of conflict, struggle, and blood. In other words, a shared history may be the history of a cohesive nation acting together, or it may be the shared history of hatreds and wars. We may talk of a Polish past, which has been an essential ingredient in Polish nationalism, but we may also talk of European history, which records far more conflict than accord.

Race and Ethnicity

Race or ethnicity are other ways of defining nationalism, but again, these concepts are either so broad—clearly not all Asians could be wedged into a single Asian nation—or so narrow—a New Guinea tribe of two hundred may in fact be a distinct group—that they become almost meaningless as ways of defining a nation. European imperialism further complicated the issue of nationalism by drawing colonial boundaries, often later translated into national boundaries, that reflected the needs of the European masters rather than the realities of the colonial peoples. The boundaries of modern African nations reflect far more the geopolitical games of European imperialists than tribal or ethnic distinctions among the African people. (Compare fig. 3.1, showing major African tribes, to figs. 3.2 and 3.3, which

Figure 3.1
Major African Tribes
Source: George Demko, *Why in the World: Adventures in Geography* (New York: Doubleday, 1992), 39.

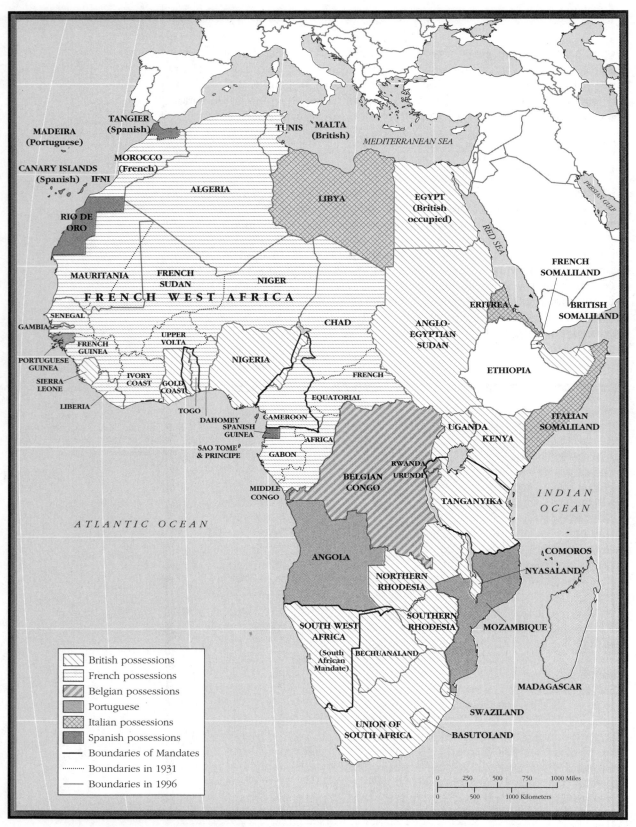

Figure 3.2 Colonial Africa Between the Two World Wars

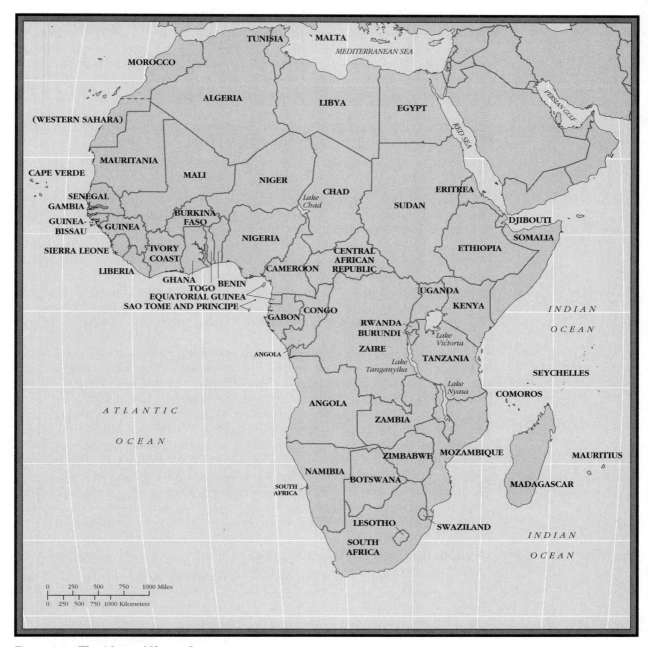

***Figure 3.3*   The Africa of Nation-States**
Source: Roland Oliver, *The African Experience: Major Themes in African History from Earliest Times to the Present* (New York: Harper Collins, 1991), 284.

depict colonial and modern national political divisions in Africa.) The Middle East, where Arab-speaking Islamic peoples were divided up into a series of nations, has been a victim of the same process.

Despite the immense difficulties of clearly defining these elusive concepts, nationalist sentiment rises when enough of these factors are present that a number of people, preferably a large number, begin thinking of themselves as united in a single nation. Nationalism is thus more than a collection of facts or of narrow criteria that can be measured scientifically. It is a collective act of will, a decision made in concert with a large number of other people to regard those others as essentially identical to oneself, and, just as important, to exclude a much larger number of people by proclaiming them fundamentally different from oneself. The role of consciousness and will in the creation of nationalist sentiment greatly overshadows any other individual component of nationalism.

The Two Faces of Nationalism

Nationalism as a Positive Force

Obviously, a phenomenon that has spread so rapidly must provide many benefits—and nationalism does. In the modern world, nationalism has been an organizing mechanism for strong states, empowering governments to use its appeal to galvanize both their populations and their economies. Both great modern wars, World Wars I and II, were wars of nationalism in which total mobilization, and total war, were possible largely because governments could call upon the nationalist sentiments of their populations. Even leaders of a state organized more on the basis of ideology than nationalism, the Soviet Union, recognized the value of the appeal to nationalism, and World War II became the "Great Patriotic War" for the Soviet people.

Nationalism also fulfills a need on the part of human beings, providing them with both an intense sense of identity and an equally intense sense of belonging. The individual with a strong national identification is part of something far larger than himself or herself—and sometimes believes that this cause is far more important than the individual as well. Nationalism is also inherently egalitarian: all Italians are equal in being Italian, all Guatemalans equal in being Guatemalan. Throughout the nineteenth century, nationalism was generally regarded as a liberating idea, linked to the concept of citizenship and equality. Although the rise of a conservative and militaristic Germany late in the nineteenth century, and the perversions of nationalism in the twentieth century, have generally undermined that concept, many peoples still look to nationalism as a means of liberation. Certainly nationalism did provide a vehicle for the overthrow of colonialism.

Nationalism as a Destructive Force

Unfortunately, the twentieth century has provided an almost endless list of the kinds of problems that can be created by nationalism. Among them are the tendency of modern nationalism to be more exclusive than inclusive, the way nationalism can be manipulated by the unscrupulous, and the difficulties presented both to and by people who consider themselves a nation but who lack a nation-state, or must share one.

Minorities within the Nation-State

The difficulties of constructing national boundaries along strictly nationalist lines can lead to two virtually opposite problems, each one of which has caused acute misery in our own time. First, nation-states often include linguistic or ethnic minorities. In addition, the process of state creation through war and conquest has incorporated into existing nation-states conquered groups who still dream of their own, lost nation—often through a romantic haze that makes the idea of nationalism even more powerful than it ordinarily is. One of the most striking examples of this problem in the contemporary world, and one that illustrates how nationalist grievances can have profound international consequences, is the dilemma of the Palestinian Arabs within the borders of the Jewish state of Israel. For more than four decades the Palestinians have dreamed of achieving their own nationhood, largely by destroying the Israelis and reclaiming Palestine for themselves. Arab nations have often manipulated this Palestinian nationalism for their own ends, attempting far more to destabilize Israel than to aid the Palestinians. Today, as Israel is granting limited autonomy to some Palestinian areas, the Palestinians are discovering that nationalism provides very little in the way of preparation for the actual creation of a state, with the institutions, laws, and habits that permit a people to live together and rule themselves. Whether in fact the Palestinians will be able to make the transition from ethnic nationalism with its negative and destructive tendencies to civic nationalism with its nation-building elements is a vitally important question, for much of the future of the Middle East may well depend on their success.

Irredentism

A second problematic way the drawing of national boundaries interacts with nationalism is that sometimes these boundaries separate people who consider themselves members of the same nation. This can lead to what is called **irredentism,** the desire to reclaim lost territories and lost peoples. Adolf Hitler used the irredentist claims of the Sudetenland Germans, who had been included in the new state of Czechoslavakia, as justification for his forcible entry into Czechoslovakia in 1938, one of the major steps on the road to World War II.

irredentism The desire by one nation to annex territory belonging to another, but that the first nation believes is historically or ethnically linked to itself.

Separatism

Nation-states that include substantial minority groups recently have found themselves facing *separatist* movements: organized factions that want to claim independence, by either becoming autonomous within the existing nation-states, or breaking away completely to establish separate nation-states. Often separatism has become extremely violent.

You Remember the Bolivian Navy, Don't You?

Nations often cling to their irredentist claims to land long lost, looking back a century or more to define their once and future territory.

For example, in March of each year Bolivia, a landlocked South American state, celebrates Maritime Day. The Maritime Museum in La Paz is one of Bolivia's most popular tourist attractions. Both commemorate the

GLOBAL PERSPECTIVES

Pacific coastline that Bolivia lost to Chile in 1878. The dream to regain that coastline is called a Bolivian "obsession," and Bolivia even maintains a navy in anticipation of the day that its lost coastline is finally restored. "Our main mission," says a Bolivian navy captain, "is to promote in the consciousness of the Bolivian people that we had a coast and that one day we will return" (Marx 1992).

A largely nonviolent separatist movement exists in Canada, where a large French-speaking minority inhabits a physically compact area, the province of Quebec. Quebec originally was colonized by France and later ceded to Britain as a result of war. Although the province has a sizable minority of English-speaking Canadians, which constitute a majority in Canada's other provinces, the *Québecois* (French-speaking residents of Quebec) long have seethed with resentment against the province's English speakers, and with the desire to preserve French culture, especially the French language.

In the 1960s a powerful separatist movement emerged in Quebec, fueled in part by a visit from the president of France, Charles de Gaulle, who supported the idea of an independent Quebec. The Quebec parliament eventually passed a law making the use of any language but French illegal in public life. Shops, schools, and businesses had to operate solely in French; street and highway signs had to be in French alone.

The separatists even went so far as to hold two referenda on whether or not Quebec should secede formally from Canada. Secession lost in 1992, and even the French language movement began to be challenged widely. However, in October 1995 the voters of Quebec rejected secession by only a paper-thin margin—less than one percentage point—and the new premier of Quebec, upon taking office in January 1996, vowed to continue the struggle for independence from Canada.

The overwhelming rejection of a proposed constitution that would have made substantial concessions to the separatists in October 1992 did not lead to civil war, and some experts even claimed that the rejection of the constitution relieved all Canadians (Serrill 1992, 48). After the much narrower defeat of separatism in 1995, there is still a peaceful, if uneasy, coexistence of the two factions in Quebec.

Nationalism has spawned more violent separatism elsewhere. Basques seeking independence from Spain have resorted to terrorism, as have Tamils in Sri Lanka and the Irish Republican Army in Northern Ireland. Russia did not hesitate

The ethnic unraveling that has accompanied the end of the Cold War: Russian soldiers patrolling a burned-out street in Grozny, capital of rebellious Chechnya.

to use force to attempt to suppress Chechen nationalism in what it painted as an internal Russian problem. Smoldering nationalist tensions erupted into violence in the Balkans at the end of the Cold War, and similar problems are likely elsewhere.

Variations on a Theme: Revolutionary Nationalism and Ultranationalism

Revolutionary Nationalism

Revolutionary nationalism has been one of the most important and dynamic forces in twentieth-century world politics, fusing as it does two of the century's most important themes, revolution and nationalism. When this century began, much of the non-European world was controlled, either directly or indirectly, by the great European imperial powers. One historian estimates that 84 percent of the world's land surface was controlled by Europeans at the onset of World War I (Kennedy 1989, 76). Today, as the century nears its end, those great empires have vanished. In their place stand independent states created in the fires of revolutionary nationalism, the incendiary combination of the desire for independence, the desire for self-determination, and the desire for social, political, and economic reform. This revolutionary nationalism not only created nearly two-thirds of the world's existing nations, but also determined their internal dynamics and their relations with the rest of the world. One of the most important, and most successful, examples of revolutionary nationalism is modern China, now the world's largest nation-state.

The Chinese Example

China has the longest continuous history of any nation in the world, as well as the world's largest population. For most of that history, however, the Chinese defined their state in terms of culture, not nationalism. The boundary between civilization and barbarism, between China and everything else, was not political, military, or governmental, but cultural. The Chinese written language and the Confucian culture defined and unified China. Even when political power was fragmented and China's physical territory was divided among several would-be empires, the idea of China as a single cultural entity endured. So strong was this cultural identification that throughout history China absorbed and sinicized its alien conquerors, from the Mongols to the Manchus.

At the center of a vast civilization and perceiving themselves as the definition of culture itself, the Chinese failed to recognize the challenge posed by the European nations and their technology when the Europeans began to intrude more and more into China in the eighteenth century. In the nineteenth century China suffered a series of humiliating military defeats, at the hands first of the Western powers and then of the Japanese, who had adopted Western technology, culture, and ultimately imperialism in the middle of the century. The result was the partition of China among the imperialist powers, including Japan, in what was vividly if inelegantly called "carving up the Chinese melon." As a result of military defeats and partition, the Chinese lost control of their own nation: foreign troops patrolled Chinese cities, foreign navies ruled not only China's coastal waters but also its great rivers, and foreign traders and manufacturers exploited the Chinese people.

After the Manchu dynasty was overthrown in 1911, China's first elected president, Sun Yat-sen, lamented that the Chinese were not a nation but "a heap of sand," a people not united by national sentiment. Sun created what he called the Kuomintang, or "Nationalist Party," to attempt to unify China, but these attempts ultimately failed.

By the mid-1930s the communist leader Mao Tse-tung had begun to formulate and implement in China a new revolutionary strategy based on the peasantry instead of the urban proletariat. Although this was a radical departure from traditional Marxism, it was brilliantly suited to a country composed largely of peasants. When the Japanese attacked China in 1937, Mao quickly recognized that he could direct both anti-Japanese feelings and peasant discontent simultaneously into what became known as **revolutionary nationalism.** As part of this strategy, Mao devised highly successful guerrilla tactics that could be used against any foe that held China's cities, the Kuomintang or the Japanese. The guerrilla strategy depended on cooperation between the peasants and the communist forces, which in turn dictated a communist policy based on rural reform: land redistribution, peasant education, and mobilization of the peasants against the Japanese. In eight years of this combined guerrilla warfare and moderate reform, the communists gained the loyalty of the peasants.

> **revolutionary nationalism** Desire for independence, self-determination, and social, political, and economic reform, which generally culminates in a revolt against the existing regime.

Essentially, Mao and his communist forces were able to merge together two extraordinarily powerful forces. One was the force of revolution, both social and economic; the other was the rising force of nationalism, the desire of the Chinese people, especially the peasants, to rid themselves of foreign domination and assert their own rights. In revolutionary nationalism, these two forces combined in an entirely new ideology, one that would carry the communists to victory in 1949 and permit them to begin forging a new nation. The communist victory in China in 1949 and the establishment of the People's Republic of China owed much less to traditional Marxism than to revolutionary nationalism (Johnson 1967, *passim*).

It is interesting to note that in spite of intense Chinese nationalism, within the borders of modern China, fifty-six "National Minority Peoples" continue to exist along with the five major nationality groups (Han, Tibetan, Hui, Mongol, and Manchu) first recognized by Sun Yat-sen. (see fig. 3.4.) These nationalities are found on the fringes of the ancient Chinese empire, particularly in the Tibetan borderlands and the far western provinces of Chinese central Asia. They number some ninety million and occupy more than 60 percent of China's territory (Moynihan 1993, 156).

Ultranationalism

> **ultranationalism** Hypernationalism that goes beyond xenophobia to an active attempt both the eliminate those who are not of the same nationality and to extend national power.

Ultranationalism is an extreme and often dangerous form of nationalism that exalts the nation above the individual and degrades anyone not of the nation. Sometimes referred to as hypernationalism, ultranationalism goes beyond xenophobia, the fear or hatred of foreigners, to an active attempt both to eliminate those who are not of the same nationality and to extend national power. It was a powerful destructive force in the mid-twentieth century, particularly in its Japanese, Italian, and German manifestations, and played a major role in precipitating World War II in both Asia and Europe.

Japanese Ultranationalism

Japan's unique culture had long been a source of both pride and strength to Japan's elite, especially the military elite. For centuries Japan had been essentially

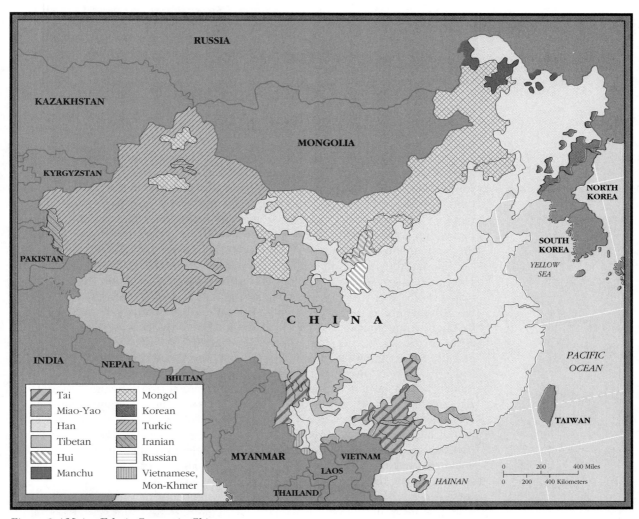

Figure 3.4 **Major Ethnic Groups in China**

a feudal society in which the *samurai* ethic, *bushido,* had dictated the actions of Japan's nobility. Emphasizing military virtues, loyalty to one's superiors, emperor-worship, and honor, *bushido* had at least in theory governed the actions of Japan's ruling class for nearly six hundred years before the arrival of Westerners in the mid-nineteenth century. Shinto, Japan's official religion, was essentially nationalistic, emphasizing the special nature of Japan and particularly exalting the emperor, considered to be the direct descendant of the Sun Goddess and thus a deity himself.

After the American navy forced Japan to open itself to foreigners, key members of this elite decided that the nation must abandon its traditional feudal ways and modernize. The result was the Meiji Restoration, one of the great transformations of any modern society. The Meiji Restoration had substantially achieved its goals of military, economic, and political modernization by the end of the nineteenth century, propelling Japan into modern world politics at the height of global imperialism (perhaps the Japanese decision later to become imperialist itself should be no surprise).

Some Japanese scholars detect the beginnings of ultranationalism during the Meiji period, in the period's emphasis on total submissiveness to imperial authority. From 1890 onward Japanese schoolchildren opened each school year with a reading of the *Imperial Rescript on Education,* which was designed "to turn out citizens who spontaneously and enthusiastically supported national policies. A willingness to die for the country in time of war was stressed as 'loyalty to the emperor and love of country.'" In addition, children were taught to venerate the emperor's photograph. (Ienaga 1978, 21–22).

The Meiji period also saw the emergence of a number of patriotic societies that would play a major role in fostering Japanese ultranationalism. The best known of these were the Kokuryukai or Black Dragon Society (named after the Amur River, which its members felt should be Japan's mainland boundary) and the Genyosha, which carried on espionage and even assassinations in Korea as part of a program to encourage Japanese expansion. Members of these societies played key roles in early Japanese expansion efforts like the penetration of Korea, the Sino-Japanese War (1894–95), and the Russo-Japanese War (1904-1905).

During the 1920s, after what many Japanese viewed as their failure to gain what they deserved as a result of their victory over Russia in 1905 and their participation in World War I, many military officers became involved in an ultranationalist attempt to revive what was called *kokutai,* or "national polity," the belief that the nation constitutes a family with the emperor at its head. The ultranationalists of the 1920s, even more than the earlier Black Dragon and Genyosha groups, were often violently anti-Western, despising both democracy and capitalism. One historian points out that this ultranationalism was essentially "atavistic in that it looked back to a simpler, more harmonious, more agrarian, and more authoritarian past" (Reischauer 1974, 186). Thus it united peasants, military officers, disenchanted intellectuals, and others fearful that Japan had lost far more than it had gained in its rapid modernization. They swore exaggerated loyalty to the emperor, still seen as divine, and began to view his chief advisors as traitors who had sold out Japan in adopting Western values and attitudes. Increasingly frustrated by what they saw as the weakness and pacifism of the civilians who surrounded the emperor and ran the government, ultranationalists gained particular strength in the armed forces, particularly among the younger, lower-ranking officers.

The depression that began with the collapse of the U.S. stock market in 1929 and spread worldwide had a devastating impact on Japan, wiping out much of its export trade and sending unemployment skyrocketing. Ultranationalists within the military saw this depression as confirmation of their worst fears about the dangers to Japan of dependence on foreign trade and international goodwill. In 1930 a group of younger officers established the Sakurakai (Cherry Society), composed primarily of army officers from the War Ministry, the General Staff, the military training schools, and Tokyo units. "Two phrases occurred frequently in their statements, 'the imperial way' *(Kodo),* and 'the Showa restoration.'" Both phrases were magnificently vague, but "there could be no question about who were the targets of attack: the political parties . . . and big business." The ultranationalists' combination of intimidation, pamphlets, newspaper articles, protests, and demonstrations, "all harping on the theme of patriotic duty," made it increasingly difficult for Japanese officials to oppose this ultranationalism, as did the willingness of the ultranationalists to resort to assassination (Beasley 1974, 240–41). Another ultranationalist group, the Blood Pledge Corps, carried out a series of assassinations and attempted assassinations, ushering in what would be called a period of "government by assassination" (Harris and Harris 1991, 178).

The mid-1930s saw an explosion of ultranationalism throughout Japan, and its expression through a series of political assassinations and assassination attempts against civilian leaders viewed as not nationalist or Japanese enough, the men who were "giving the Emperor bad advice." Three of Japan's eleven prime ministers from 1918 to 1932 were victims of assassination, and February 26, 1936, saw a virtual epidemic of successful and attempted assassinations as young officers, profoundly influenced by ultranationalism and its glorification of the military, carried out a series of attacks that struck even the emperor's inner council. Put on trial, these young officers used the courtroom as a stage to popularize their ideas and to denounce and denigrate democracy. Although many of those involved or implicated were executed, the ultranationalists essentially succeeded in their goal of removing civilian constraints from military operations, a major factor in the outbreak of World War II in the Pacific.

In line with the increasingly hysterical ultranationalism that swept Japan, foreign books were proscribed, textbooks rewritten in nationalist terms, and many Western customs attacked; as an example of the latter, golf was condemned as an unnecessary game of luxury (although baseball emerged unscathed). In 1937 the Ministry of Education issued *Kokutai no Hongi (Principles of the National Polity)*, which became the centerpiece of a major campaign directed at schoolchildren. Two million copies were sold, and special commentaries on the *Kokutai no Hongi* issued to schoolteachers. Its "doctrines became the basis of an intensive propaganda directed at the young, . . . anti-liberal in the extreme. Individualism was anathema, service to the State was service in its highest form. Moreover, patriotism taught that what was bad was foreign" (Beasley 1974, 255). *Kokutai* became the subject of such a vast literature in the late 1930s and early 1940s that libraries devoted an entire classification to it.

The concentration of ultranationalism in the military was a major factor in alienating the Japanese military from the civilian government and in driving the Japanese to expand their "Greatest East Asia Co-Prosperity Sphere" throughout the Pacific, an expansion that led to World War II in the Pacific. During the war this ultranationalism continued to prevail, primarily expressed as absolute and unquestioning loyalty to the emperor and seen in such phenomena as the *kamikaze* pilots.

Ultranationalism also played a major role in World War II Italy and Germany, where it became the basis for fascism and Nazism; we will discuss this in detail in chapter 6.

Is Ultranationalism Back?

The last decade has witnessed the resurgence of ultranationalism in Japan, Germany, and, to a lesser extent, Italy. The depth or breadth of this resurgence is hotly debated—is it a genuine national phenomenon or merely an attempt by an alienated segment of the population to gain a sense of control over their own destiny?—but the reappearance of ultranationalism in any degree is disturbing.

Japan's failure in the war discredited ultranationalism, and the occupying Americans did everything they could to crush it, including having the emperor formally denounce any claims to his divinity. Still, many Japanese continued to be fascinated by their past. Recent years have seen the partial resurfacing of ultranationalism in Japan at several different levels. One of the most interesting was the career of novelist and flamboyant personality Yukio Mishima, whose books, such as *Runaway Horses,* glorified the ultranationalists of the 1920s and 1930s, and whose films explored traditional Japanese values. Mishima even formed a society to train an ultranationalist force in the ways of traditional Japan and attempted to form a private army. However, his fascination with one aspect of traditional culture, *seppuku* (ritual suicide), was distasteful to many Japanese, and his self-dramatizing *seppuku* in 1970 after a failed uprising left his nascent movement leaderless.

A second, in many ways far more disturbing, symptom of possibly reemergent ultranationalism is the book *The Japan That Can Say No,* written by Shintaro Ishihara, a well-known right-wing politician, and Akio Morita, former chairman of Sony. Although Morita's authorship seems more honorary than actual, it is disturbing to many that he endorses the ultranationalism of the book. *The Japan That Can Say No* is a strident denunciation of the widespread adoption of Western culture in Japan and a call for return to traditional Japanese ways. Its vehemence has shocked many Westerners, as has the widespread acclaim the book has enjoyed in many circles of Japanese society. The book was not sold to American publishers; the most widespread version is a pirated copy translated by the Pentagon and published in the *Congressional Record.*

Frighteningly enough, the past few years have also seen a resurgence of ultranationalism in Germany, with a rise in neo-Nazi groups in other areas of

Soccer Nationalism

One of the most interesting phenomena of contemporary ultranationalism is its fascination for young people, not only of Germany but of other European nations as well. In a frightening book, *Among the Thugs,* American journalist Bill Buford, explores the culture of England's "soccer hoodlums," the young men responsible for terrible violence at soccer matches, both in England and particularly on the continent of Europe. Many of these young men, he finds, paint their faces with the British Union Jack, wear Union Jack T-shirts and even Union Jack boxer shorts (sometimes on their heads), and see soccer matches as a kind of war. On their way to foreign matches, the "soccer hooligans" sing chorus after chorus of "Rule Britannia" and another song, "England," that consists simply of endless repetition of the word "England."

Buford also explores links between the "soccer hooligans" and protofascist organizations like the National Front or the decidedly unorganized skin-

GLOBAL PERSPECTIVES

heads. He finds few direct ties, but recognizes that both soccer fans and protofascists share what he calls a "violent nationalism," expressed by these fans as fury against anyone non-English, whether in England or on the continent. This violent nationalism, Buford concludes, is often responsible for the riots that break out when English soccer teams travel overseas. "These fools, despised at home, ridiculed in the press, incapable of being contained by any act of impulsive legislation that the government had devised, want . . . an England to defend. They [don't] want Europe; they [don't] understand Europe and [don't] want to. They want . . . a war. They want . . . a nation to belong to and fight for" (Buford 1992, 305).

One can argue that modern sports encourage nationalism, what with the playing of national anthems for Olympic victors and the promotion of "World Championships" left and right, but certainly the cases discussed above represent a far darker version of nationalism than the simple use of sports to express patriotism.

Europe as well. In 1992 in Germany alone right-wing youths, many of them self-proclaimed neo-Nazis, carried out eighteen hundred attacks on foreigners and on Jewish synagogues and monuments (Lane and Breslau 1992, 30).

Throughout Europe, foreigners have become targets of anger, hatred, and often violence. In Austria, for example, the New Freedom party has prospered by playing on Austrian fears of being swamped by waves of immigrants from southern and southeastern Europe. Chillingly, the New Freedom party's polished young leader, Jorg Haider, sometimes called the "Yuppie Fascist," also talks about the necessity of a "final solution" to Austria's political problems, and about "total war" (Breslau 1992, 32).

Analysts of this phenomenon observe that skinhead and neo-Nazi bands throughout Europe now beat out a message of hatred of foreigners and openly use Nazi symbols. German skinhead rock bands proclaim that Hitler was a hero and that the German race, still pure, faces defilement from foreigners. Note the words of a song by *Endsieg* (Final Victory), a skinhead band:

> When you see a Turk in a tram
> > And he is looking at you annoyingly
> Just stand up and give him a good punch
> > and stab him seventeen times.
> (Masland and Breslau 1992, 53)

Recent attacks against Turks in Germany have cost several lives and caused Germany to revoke its constitutional guarantee of asylum to anyone fleeing political oppression. In May 1993 German legislators, concerned about both the rising level of violence and the wave of asylum seekers—over 440,000 entered Germany

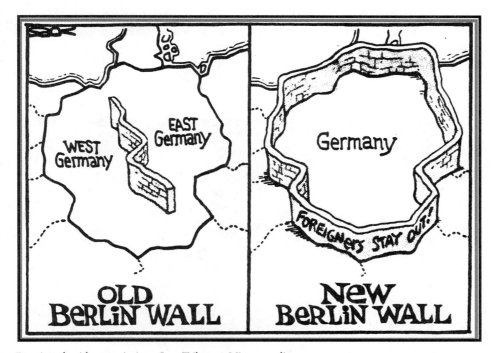

Reprinted with permission, Star Tribune, Minneapolis.

in 1992—voted to allow border guards to turn away anyone seeking to enter Germany for political asylum from a neighboring country. Article 16 of the German constitution had expressed the world's most liberal asylum policy, adopted to atone for Nazi crimes and show gratitude to the countries that accepted 800,000 Germans seeking political asylum during the Nazi years (Fisher 1993). It is important to keep two almost conflicting thoughts in mind: these ultranationalists represent only a tiny fraction of the German population, but any reappearance of German ultranationalism, given its power in the past, must make us concerned for the future.

Nations without States: The Kurds

The people known as the Kurds provide a tragic illustration of the problems facing those who consider themselves a nation but are physically dispersed among other nation-states. Although the numbers are open to dispute, the contemporary Kurdish population is approximately twenty-five million, making the Kurds the largest nation on earth with no state of their own. Instead, the Kurdish domain, called Kurdistan, which occupies about the same area as France, is parceled out among five separate nation-states: Turkey, Syria, Iraq, Iran, and the southern Caucasus republic of Azerbaijan (see fig. 3.5). Iraq's 3.5 million Kurds constitute 25 percent of its population, while Syria's 1 million make up 10 percent of that country's people. Most of the Kurds live in the Taurus and Zagros mountains, although perhaps as many as 40 percent of the Kurdish people have been driven from their mountain homelands in recent years (Krieger 1993, 518). The history and present plight of the Kurds illustrates some of the paradoxes of nationalism, as well as the vulnerability of nations lacking states to manipulation by other powers.

Are the Kurds a nation? As we have seen, they do not constitute a physical nation-state, but are spread out among other nation-states. Linguistically, there is only the most tenuous Kurdish unity: although all Kurds speak variations of an Indo-Iranian language called Kurdish, the two main dialects of Kurdish, Kurmanji and Sorani, are mutually unintelligible, and Kurds in Turkey and parts of Iran speak other very distinct dialects. (The argument is made, however, that the var-

Figure 3.5
Kurdistan
This map clearly shows how "Kurdistan" overlaps the boundaries of five other nations. Halabja, just inside the Iran-Iraq border, was the site of a lethal poison gas attack in 1988.
Source: Adapted from John Bulloch and Harvey Morris. *No Friends but the Mountains: the Tragic History of the Kurds.* New York: Oxford, 1992.

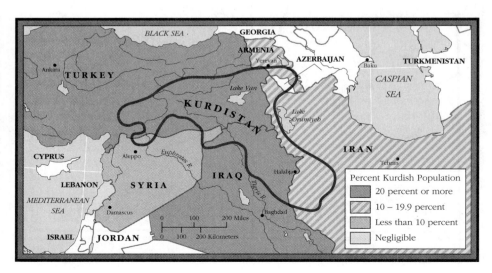

ious Kurdish dialects are no more distant from one another than the Beijing and Cantonese dialects of Chinese or the distinct dialects of Italy before it unified in the nineteenth century—Bulloch and Morris 1992, 56.) Religion does serve as a unifying factor among the Kurds, since they are virtually all followers of Islam, although there are several heretical sects of Kurds in Turkey, and some mystical sects as well. Most Kurds are Sunni Muslims.

However, although the Kurds are scattered across several other nation-states, although their language is not unified, and although there are substantial variations in Kurdish religion, two factors key to nationalism anywhere serve to unite these people: first, their history, and second, their own fierce belief that they constitute a single nation and ought to constitute a single nation-state as well.

Early History

Kurds trace their origins several thousand years back to the ancient Medes, rivals of the early Persians. As early as the third century A.D., the name Kurds was applied to the people of modern Kurdistan (Bulloch and Morris 1992, 57). In the seventh century, a long struggle between Arab and Kurd resulted in the conversion of most Kurds to the new religion of Islam. The next few centuries saw the formation of several distinctly Kurdish states and dynasties that controlled substantial portions of Kurdistan as well as other territory, but ultimately the Kurds were absorbed by the sprawling Ottoman Empire.

The Rise of Nationalism

In 1880 the leader of a major revolt against the Ottomans wrote the first generally acknowledged statement of Kurdish nationalism: "The Kurdish nation is a nation apart. Its religion is different from that of others, also its laws and customs . . . . We want to take matters into our own hands. We can no longer put up with the oppression which the governments [of Persia and the Ottoman empire] impose upon us" (Bulloch and Morris 1992, 73).

During World War I, the Kurds were divided in their allegiance: some supported the remnants of the Ottoman empire, rapidly evolving into a Turkish nation-state, while others, in hopes of Kurdish independence, supported the British-French-American allies. President Woodrow Wilson's Fourteen Points address referred to the establishment of independent nation-states from the ruins of the Ottoman empire, and many Kurds optimistically assumed that this included them. However, although in the Treaty of Sèvres (1920) the Turkish government agreed to a separate Kurdistan that would be basically under British protection, the treaty was never ratified, and in the Treaty of Lausanne (1923), all reference to Kurdish autonomy was dropped. Instead of receiving an independent state, the Kurds found themselves partitioned in effect among Turkey, the British mandate of Mesopotamia (later Iraq), and the British protectorate of Persia (later Iran) (Fromkin 1989, 560). Nonetheless, the Kurds continued to nurture the dream of an independent Kurdistan, a dream that left them vulnerable to manipulation in "great power" politics.

The Manipulation of Kurdish Nationalism

Most tragically for the Kurds, they have been caught up in the politics of oil and of the Persian Gulf. The fate of the Kurds demonstrates that when nationalism confronts major forces in international relations, nationalism often loses. For example, in the early 1970s the United States encouraged Kurdish rebellion in Iraq, hoping to weaken the Iraqi government and thus strengthen the Iranian government of the Shah, then very much an American client. Huge quantities of arms were transferred surreptitiously from the United States to Iran and then to the Iraqi Kurds. But the American goal, despite what CIA agents may have told the Kurds, had never been to achieve Kurdish autonomy. That, after all, might pose a threat to Iran, which also contained a substantial Kurdish minority. Instead, the American purpose was to keep the Kurds of Iraq strong enough to fight and to preoccupy the Iraqi army, but not strong enough to win. In 1975, the Iraqi and Iranian governments reached an accord, part of which called for immediate suspension of any aid to the Kurds. After the agreement was secretly signed—the Kurds were not told of it—there was to be a two-week "grace period" in which Kurds were to be allowed to cross the border into Iran. However, the Kurdish leaders were not told of this until almost the instant that the Iraqi army, now free from fear of any attack from Iran, shifted their maximum forces against the Kurds. Thousands of Kurds were killed, thousands "relocated" to the deserts of southern Iraq, and thousands more forced across the borders into Iran and Turkey. In the aftermath of the Watergate scandals, much of the American role in first encouraging the Kurdish rebellion, then arming it (with approximately $16 million worth of modern weapons), and finally betraying it became public. The investigating committee quoted Henry Kissinger, a chief architect of the American Kurdish policy, as saying that "covert action should not be confused with missionary work." The senatorial investigating committee summarized: "Even in the context of covert operations, ours was a cynical enterprise" (Bulloch and Morris 1992, 134–39).

Anti-Iraqi Rebellion and Genocide

The Kurdish rebellion against the Iraqi government flared up again in the 1980s as the Iraqis became more and more oppressive, and this renewed rebellion led to one of the most ghastly chapters in the long and tragic history of Kurdish nationalism: the use of chemical weapons against unarmed civilians at Halabja. Once again, the slaughter of Kurds came at least in part as the result of international events—in this case, the long and devastating war between Iraq and Iran that had begun in the summer of 1980, in the aftermath of the fall of the Shah and the creation of the Iranian Islamic state under the Ayatollah Khomeini. Again the Kurds were caught between the two warring states, with much of the war carried out in Kurdistan. During the war, the Kurds were divided: some supported Iran as a means of gaining independence, some supported Iraq, and an even larger third group attempted to use the war as a means for finally gaining Kurdish independence.

On March 16, 1988, in apparent retaliation for Kurdish opposition to Saddam Hussein's government, Iraqi planes carrying bomb-loads of mustard gas, nerve gas, and cyanide dropped their deadly cargoes on the Kurdish village of Halabja. As many as five thousand civilians died almost immediately from these chemical weapons, whose use had been outlawed since the Geneva Convention of 1925 as inhumane. Gruesome pictures showed the streets of the village littered with the bodies of civilians. In one of the most poignant, the body of a Kurdish man was stretched out, one arm wrapped around a dead baby in a futile protective gesture.

Appallingly, Halabja was neither the first nor the last time that the Iraqi government used these outlawed weapons against its Kurdish population. And while

A Kurdish Iraqi guerrilla fighter and his colleagues rest in mountain fastnesses of the Kurdistan that they dream of creating.

people of other nations were shocked by pictures of Halabja, virtually nothing was done to sanction Iraq for use of the chemical weapons against the Kurds. The long war between Iran and Iraq was finally winding down, and there was apparently widespread fear that condemnation of the Iraqis and sanctions against them might rebound to the benefit of Iran. In a typical incident, a Kurdish delegation appealed to Kuwaiti leaders to protest the use of poison gas against innocent civilians. A Kuwaiti official responded, "What did you expect to be sprayed with, rosewater?" (Bulloch and Morris 1992, 143). Not until September 8, 1988, safely after the war between Iraq and Iran had ended, did the United States government announce that Iraq had used chemical weapons against the Kurds and label that use "abhorrent and unjustifiable" (Clark 1992, 19–20).

The Persian Gulf War

The outbreak of the Persian Gulf War provides another illustration of great powers manipulating Kurdish nationalism for their own purposes. When Operation Desert Shield became Operation Desert Storm, the United States government openly encouraged the Kurds to rebel against Saddam Hussein's government, as it also encouraged the Shi'ite Muslims of southern Iraq to rebel. However, after the Kurds had done so, the United States and its Persian Gulf allies did virtually nothing to stop the Iraqi army from savagely turning against them and carrying out a combination of genocide and expulsion. Over one million Kurds were forced out of northern Iraq completely, many of them fleeing to the almost equally inhospitable Turkey, and millions more were made homeless by the Iraqi attack. The bitter winter of 1991–92 caught hundreds of thousands of Kurdish refugees in the open, and pictures of freezing and starving Kurds briefly dominated Western television and magazines. Ultimately the United States and its allies ordered the Iraqi government to cease its war against the Kurds, and American army units entered Iraqi Kurdistan to build tent cities as shelters and provide food to prevent even greater starvation. A no-fly zone for the Iraqi air force was proclaimed in Kurdistan, and American combat aircraft began to enforce it from Turkish bases. Nearly 3.5 million Kurds live in Iraqi Kurdistan, still partially guarded by Allied planes enforcing the no-fly zone. However, the thousands of U.N. guards and Allied troops deployed over the bitter winter of 1991–92 have dwindled to a handful.

It now appears that the Kurds have been taking advantage of available Allied support to begin the process of actually building a Kurdish nation-state. In May 1992 they created Kurdistan and elected a parliamentary government. Observers report that the Kurds have gradually toned down their differences and begun to work together, although the various militia forces still maintain separate commands and guard separate areas (Chabra 1993). A recent visitor to Kurdistan reports that Suleimaniya, abandoned when the Kurds fled before Saddam Hussein's forces in 1991, has been repopulated; schools are open in the town and a university is now functioning. "The Kurds are setting up something that looks, every day, more like an independent, democratic state," writes another observer (Brooks 1993).

However, the fate of Kurdistan remains uncertain, not only because of the constant threat posed by Saddam Hussein, but also because of the skepticism of Kurdistan's neighbors, especially Turkey. An estimated 12 million Kurds live in

A twelve-year-old Kurdish boy in a Turkish refugee camp displays facial wounds he attributes to an Iraqi army bombing of his home-town in Iraqi Kurdistan.

Turkey, making up roughly 20 percent of its population. Kurdish rebellion against Turkey has flared intermittently since 1984, and the Turkish army even today is conducting operation against the Kurdish Workers' Party (PKK), which has used northern Iraq as a launching point for attacks against Turkey (Chabra 1992). In turn, Iraqi Kurds have voted to expel the PKK and have begun cooperating with Turkish forces against the PKK. "They're causing us a hell of a problem," an Iraqi Kurd says. "We're dependent on the good will of Turkey to keep international protection. That's a part of life" (Nordland 1992).

Terrorism and Frustrated Nationalism

Particularly in Turkey, frustrated Kurdish nationalists have turned to terrorism, exploding bombs and attacking Turkish troops in Turkish territory. Inevitably this has provoked Turkish responses, including the bombing of Kurdish camps, even within Iraq. The enormous complications of this problem have heightened tensions between Turkey, deeply concerned about Kurdish separatism as well as Kurdish terrorism, and its NATO ally, the United States, still guarantor of Kurdish safety in northern Iraq. At this point, there is no solution in sight (Lippman, 1995; Erdem, 1995; "Kurds Ambush Turkish Soldiers," 1995).

The Multinational State in Collapse: Yugoslavia

Certainly the most devastating example of ethnic nationalism in contemporary world politics is the former Yugoslavia. The death of strongman Josef Broz Tito in 1980 began Yugoslavia's unraveling process, and the collapse of ideology that accompanied the dissolution of the Soviet Union and the Soviet bloc accelerated this process. The clash between the desire of individual republics to form nation-states and that of the largest republic, Serbia, to maintain its dominant position, even to create a "Greater Serbia," led inexorably to what has been called the Third Balkan War. (The first two in the early twentieth century played a major role in precipitating World War I.) Tragedy mounted upon tragedy and horror upon horror as brutality, rape, the killing of civilians, concentration camps, and "ethnic cleansing," all eerily reminiscent of Nazi Germany, spread across the Balkans and threatened once again to engulf all of Europe in a major war.

The Balkans

The Balkans, the ruggedly mountainous area that contains the former Yugoslavia as well as Albania, Bulgaria, and much of Greece, constitute a geopolitical shatterbelt, an unstable collision zone between empires and peoples. Historically the Balkans have been the dividing line between the Slavic and Mediterranean peoples, the Roman and Byzantine empires, Christian Europe and the Islamic Ottoman empire. Armies have marched and countermarched over its rugged mountains while religions, cultures, and empires have all claimed its peoples and fought over them. The language, literature, and religions of the Roman and Byzantine empires shaped the Balkan peoples, who were then reshaped, first by waves of Slavic migration and then by the Islamic Turks in centuries of conquest and rule. Even the name "Balkans" testifies to the influence of non-European culture in this southeasternmost European area: the word is not Greek, Roman, or even Slavic, but instead is derived from the Turkish word for mountains.

Despite the early hegemony of the Greeks and Romans, the modern Balkans began in the sixth and seventh centuries with the onslaught of Slavic peoples from the steppe lands to the east, submerging the earlier Graeco-Roman culture. Today, at least north of Greece, virtually all the Balkan peoples speak one or another Slavic language and share a Slavic heritage. (Albania and the Albanian language constitute the major exception to this; Albanian is related only very loosely to any other modern European language, occupying its own solitary branch on the Indo-European language tree.)

Slavic empires waxed and waned on the Balkan peninsula for centuries, with both the Serbs and the Croats at various times claiming control of vast amounts of territory. One reporter observes that a best-selling map in Zagreb, the capital of Croatia, is a reprint of tenth-century maps showing a Croatian kingdom stretching from the banks of the Danube to the Adriatic Sea. However, similar maps sold in Belgrade, Serbian Yugoslavia, show maps of the fourteenth-century Serbian kingdom, on the eve of the Ottoman invasion, also stretching from the Danube to the Adriatic (Gay 1992).

The eruption of the Ottoman empire into Europe in the fourteenth century submerged the Slavic empires and left the Balkans more divided than ever. Many Balkan peoples were conquered and absorbed into the Turkish empire; some remained militantly Christian, while others adopted the new Islamic religion. Still, other Balkan peoples remained within the boundaries of the Austro-Hungarian empire, keeping their Roman Catholic faith and their strong ties to Europe intact.

Yugoslavia

Modern Yugoslavia took shape in the ashes of the Austro-Hungarian and Ottoman Empires immediately after World War I. Even the term "Yugoslavia" is slippery, for there have been at least three Yugoslavias in the twentieth century. The first Yugoslavia was shaped in part by pan-Slavism, in part by the desire of Slavic leaders to reunite the long-separated Orthodox and Roman Catholic churches, and in part by Croatia's hopes to avoid being gobbled up by Italy, which had advanced claims to large parts of the old Dalmatian coast (Gay, 1992). From the beginning the new state, which claimed to serve southern Slavic self-determination, was in turmoil. Croatian nationalists almost immediately began to seek autonomy within the newly created Kingdom of Serbs, Croats, and Slovenes, ruled by Alexander I of the Serbian royal house. After the leader of the Croatian nationalist movement and two of his followers were shot and killed on the floor of Parliament in 1927, King Alexander stepped in, proclaimed a royal dictatorship, changed the name of the state to Yugoslavia, and reorganized the land into new provinces, named after rivers in hopes of defusing the intense nationalism that threatened the nation. In 1934 Alexander was assassinated by Macedonian terrorists on a visit to Marseilles. (IMRO, the principal Macedonian terrorist organization, is considered the first modern international terrorist group.) Attempted reforms in 1939 were aborted by the outbreak of World War II.

Had there been any chance of saving "Yugoslavia" in any recognizable pre-World War II form, that opportunity was lost in April 1941, when German armies crashed into Serbia. The Croats immediately proclaimed their own independent Croatia under the leadership of Ante Pavelic, a pro-fascist leader and founder of the Ustashe, the Croatian terrorist organization formed in the late 1920s. The

Ustashe in effect proclaimed war on all non-Croats in the new Croatia (which contained a large slice of Bosnia-Herzegovina). A systematic campaign exterminated tens of thousands of Serbs, Jews, and gypsies; Pavelic boasted that he would convert one-third of the Serbs to Catholicism, expel one-third, and kill the remaining one-third. The exact number slaughtered by the Ustashe is still debated; conservative scholars place the number at 350 to 450 thousand. Croats use figures as "low" as seventy thousand, while contemporary Serbian leaders have inflated the figures to as high as one million.

While the slaughter continued in Croatia, Germany and Italy divided the rest of Yugoslavia among themselves and their Bulgarian allies. Two resistance groups were formed to fight the fascists: the Serbian-dominated Chetniks and the multiethnic Partisans. The Chetniks proclaimed themselves supporters of democracy, but ceased major anti-fascist actions when faced with a dramatic reprisal policy against civilians. The Partisans continued fighting; in fact, they carried out two simultaneous wars, one of national liberation and one to crush anticommunists, many of whom conveniently fit into the pro-fascist category. Ultimately the Allies, led by the British, threw their support behind the Partisans and their communist leader, Josef Broz Tito.

When World War II ended with the liberation of Yugoslavia, Tito and his supporters established control of the nation and staged a series of show trials that terminated with guilty verdicts and executions for thousands of Ustashe and Chetniks alike. With all possible opposition thus eliminated, Tito reorganized Yugoslavia and ruled for the next thirty-plus years largely by pursuing a policy of "divide and conquer," setting nationalities against each other to maintain his own control. In 1974 a new Yugoslav constitution created a series of six federal republics, each one with a dominant nationality. However, the boundaries put about one-third of all Serbs outside the borders of the Serbian republic, making them instant minorities, with what they saw as diminished rights. Tito's death in 1980 left a precarious Yugoslavia rocked by mounting nationalistic quarrels, and the dissolution of the Soviet bloc in the late 1980s opened the way for the dissolution of Yugoslavia as well.

The Yugoslavian Republics and Their Collapse

Tables 3.1 and 3.2 illustrate the divisions that separated the Yugoslav republics and have formed the basis for the current turmoil. Table 3.1 "Diversity in 'Yugoslavia,'" shows clearly how fragile the foundations of Yugoslavian nationality were. The six republics shared only their common Slavic ethnicity. Serbo-Croatian was the dominant language in four of the six republics, but the two largest and most contentious states, Serbia and Croatia, used different alphabets reflecting their religious difference. Orthodox Serbia used and still uses the Cyrillic alphabet for written Serbo-Croatian, while Roman Catholic Croatia uses the Latin alphabet. Theoretically, Serbs and Croatians might be able to speak to one another but unable to read each other's street signs! Three of the six republics—Serbia, Macedonia, and Montenegro—are largely Orthodox; two of them—Croatia and Slovenia—are predominantly Roman Catholic; and one, Bosnia-Herzegovina, is primarily Islamic. No two of the six share an identical history. Only one, Montenegro, has a long history of independence, although four others have histories of independence in the early middle ages. Three were part of the Ottoman Empire; three part of the Austro-Hungarian empire (Bosnia managed to be part of both); and one, Slovenia, part of the Holy Roman Empire. Consequently, when

Table 3.1
Diversity In "Yugoslavia"

	Ethnicity		Language		Religion			History					
	Slavic	Serbian Majority or Dominant Minority	Serbo-Croatian	Other	Eastern Orthodox	Roman Catholic	Muslim	Independent	Independent Before 1400	Independent After 1800	Ottoman Empire	Austro-Hungarian Empire	Holy Roman Empire
BOSNIA	✓	✓	✓				✓		✓		✓	✓	
CROATIA	✓	✓	✓2			✓			✓			✓	
MACEDONIA	✓			✓	✓				✓4		✓		
MONTENEGRO	✓		✓		✓			✓3					
SLOVENIA	✓			✓		✓						✓	✓
SERBIA	✓	✓	✓1		✓					✓	✓	✓	

1-Uses Cyrillic alphabet
2-Uses Roman alphabet
3-Part of Serbia 1100-1400 Independent afterwards
4-Part of Bulgaria until 1300
Source: (Dragnich, 1992)

we look at the primary factors we defined earlier in determining nationalism—ethnicity, language, history, and religion—we can find virtually no unity in "Yugoslavia," and little in common among the largest and most powerful Yugoslav states.

Table 3.2 "Population by Ethnic Group, 1991," offers a further clue to the savagery of the fighting in the Balkans and the chilling prospect of its extension. It clearly shows how scattered the various ethnic groups of the Balkans are in the former Yugoslavia. In the 1991 census Yugoslavs could choose from among twenty-five national or ethnic identities to describe themselves, or could opt for "Yugoslav." In the city of Sarajevo not even this smorgasbord of nationalities was enough; Sarajevans identified themselves by over forty different ethnic or national denominations (Thompson 1992, 105).

This table also reveals potential flashpoints in the Balkans. Of greatest concern at the moment is the Serbian province of Kosovo, cultural heartland of the Serbs and scene of an epic 1389 battle against the Turks. Today the population of Kosovo is overwhelmingly Albanian and Muslim, although the region is considered an autonomous province within Serbian Yugoslavia, the rump state formed in 1991 by Serbia and Montenegro. Serious fears exist that should the Serbs attempt to purse the same kind of "ethnic cleansing" policies that they have undertaken in Croatia and Bosnia, Albanians from across the border will intervene to protect their kinsmen, and the Balkan fighting will spread beyond the boundaries of the old Yugoslavia (Kamm, 1993). Reinforcing this sense that war could easily spread are the claims of Serbian leader Slobodan Milosevic, who proclaims historic rights to a "Greater Serbia." Milosevic told United Nations peace negotiators, "You may have forgotten your roots, but we are still living our history" (Gay, 1992).

In fact, it is very clear that much of the current bloodshed and suffering in the Balkans rises from the determination not only to live, but to correct Serbian

Table 3.2
Population by Ethnic Group, 1991
(in percentages of total populations)

	Serbs	Croats	Macedonian	Yugoslavs	Albanian	Bulgarian	Turks	Gypsies	Muslims	Slovenians	Romanians	Hungarians
BOSNIA (4,365,000)	35	17	6						44			
CROATIA (4,704,000)	15	75		9								
MACEDONIA (2,034,000)	5		64		21	3	5	2.5				
MONTENEGRO (616,000)	89			6	4							
SLOVENIA (1,975,000)	3	3		3						91		
SERBIA (5,754,000)	96	1					1	1	2			
KOSOVO (1,955,000)	13				84			2				
VOJVODINA (2,013,000)	70	5									3	23

Source: (Dragnich, 1992)

history. Milosevic's recent career has been built on Serbian nationalism, beginning with an incendiary speech to Serbian nationalists at the Kosovo battlefield in 1987, in which he played upon old Serbian dreams of glory and reignited new Serbian fears of being left out or ignored (Graff 1992). Most analysts agree that Milosevic is neither a fervent Serbian patriot nor a fervent reformed communist; instead, they see him as a man seeking to maintain power by virtually any means, with extreme Serbian nationalism and the scheme of a "Greater Serbia" as his primary vehicle on the road to power.

Whether Milosevic is an opportunist or a genuine nationalist, he clearly has touched a nerve. Belgrade television broadcasts hours and hours of horrific film from World War II on a daily basis. An eighty-page book published by the Serbian government, *Never Again,* features photographs of Ustashe atrocities during the war. On the book's cover, Croatian fascists pose for the camera, holding down a struggling Serb prisoner as they prepare to saw off his head. Other photographs show concentration camp inmates bound in barbed wire, grotesque arrangements of decapitated bodies, and Croatian officers standing over corpse-filled trenches. "We have to make people aware of why the Serbs in Croatia have such fear, to make it understood that Serbs endured so much during the last war . . . that they can never be faced again with such a threat," states an official of the Serbian Information Ministry. (Ironically, in Croatia, a large-format paperback called *War Crimes Against Croatia* contains 161 pages of photographs. The grisly photographs are taken not from World War II but from the current conflict between Serbia and Croatia—Williams 1991.)

The past is still very much part of the present in Bosnia as well. There, Christian Serbs now proclaim that they are fighting not on behalf of a "Greater Serbia," but on behalf of the Christian world itself. "This goes back to the Field of the Blackbirds [Kosovo]," claims to a Serbian policeman. "These Muslims aren't Slavs," he continues. "They're not like us or like cultured Westerners. They are barbarians. Hey, after all, who gave Europe the knife and fork? The Serbs." An elderly grandmother echoes the policeman's sentiments: "I would rather eat [nettles] for the rest of my life than live again with Turks," she says, referring to the Bosnian Moslems. Another woman adds, "This province will never, never be Muslim again . . . . We won't live again with the Turks" (Pomfret 1993).

Other Multiethnic States

Of course, Yugoslavia is not the only modern example of a multiethnic state, but the recent fate of most other European ones is anything but reassuring. Until very recently, the largest and most important of the European multiethnic states was the Soviet Union. The USSR's sixteen republics, divided somewhat along ethnic lines, contained not a mere sixteen separate nationalities, quite enough to provide plenty of mischief (the current Balkan problems stem from essentially seven distinct nationalities), but a staggering 120 separate national and ethnic groups. Figure 3.6 gives some idea of this diversity. The seventy-year history of repression of nationalist stirrings and exaltation of ideology concealed the sharpness of the distinctions among the Soviet nationalities from many onlookers, but there is little question that the collapse of Soviet ideology opened the way for the rapid rise of nationalist sentiments and the equally rapid unraveling of the Soviet Union (Smith 1990; d'Encausse 1993).

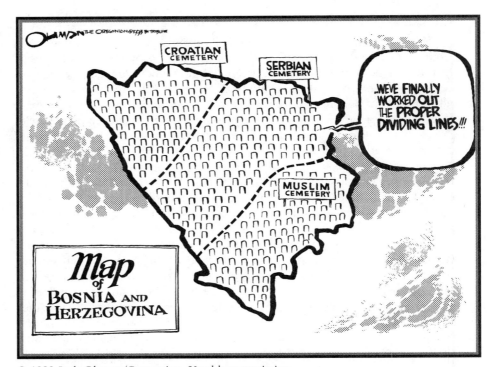

© 1993 Jack Ohman/Oregonian. Used by permission.

ED STEIN Reprinted by permission of Newspaper Enterprise Association, Inc.

Not surprisingly, a general rule of thumb seems to be that the fewer are the nationalities cobbled together to form a multiethnic state, the fewer are the possibilities of utter chaos. For example, Czechoslovakia, created after World War I by combining the very different Czech and Slovak peoples (and a large population of Germans in the Sudetenland), split apart fairly amicably on New Year's Day, 1993, into the Czech Republic and Slovakia.

At this moment, the United States remains one of the few apparently successful multiethnic states. A great deal of the credit for this goes to three factors: the dominance of a fundamental English heritage despite overlays of multiple other nationalities, the fact that the multiple nationalities that comprise the United States are widely scattered rather than occupying a single historic homeland, and the general prevalence and acceptance of American ideology as the most important uniting factor.

Today the United States reluctantly faces the problem of how, and even whether, to integrate huge numbers of new immigrants into the American synthesis. For some, multiculturalism is an exciting ideal of recognizing the value and contributions of all the different ethnic groups living in the United States rather than demanding that all forsake their own cultures and blindly accept the current amalgam. For others, multiculturalism is a dirty word that implies there is no such thing as a genuinely American culture and threatens to split America among warring tribes divided by language and heritage (Schlesinger 1992). However, after examining the problems of multinationalist states in Europe, one tends to see American problems as relatively minor. Further, the strength and resilience, as well as the universal appeal, of American civic nationalism cannot be overlooked.

The Future of Nationalism

We seem to find ourselves today back near the beginning of the twentieth century; once again we are seeing the terrible dynamic of nationalism rip apart countries and

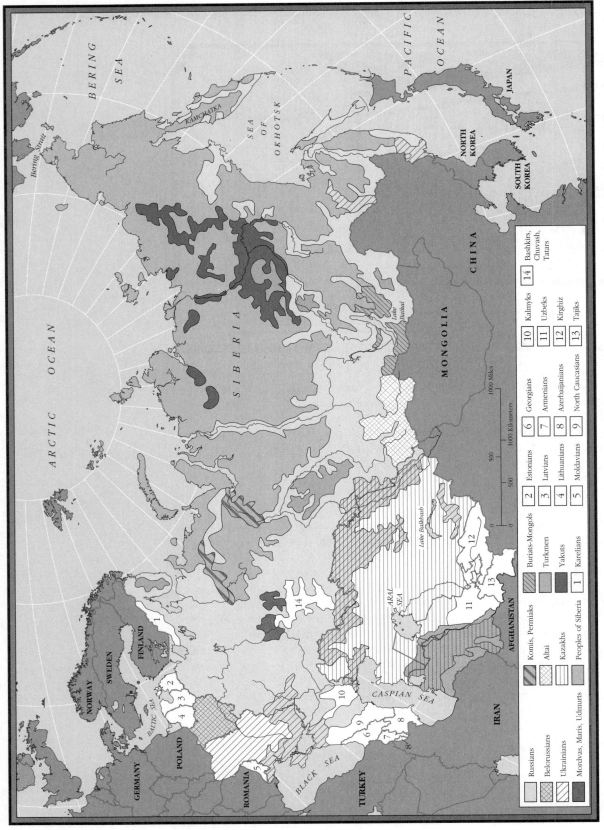

Figure 3.6 Peoples of the Soviet Union
Many of the ethnic groups within the former Soviet Union have now become independent republics, but there remains tremendous overlap between peoples and borders.

Legend:

Russians	Komis, Permiaks
Belorussians	Altai
Ukrainians	Kazakhs
Mordvas, Maris, Udmurts	Peoples of Siberia

Buriats-Mongols	2 Estonians	6 Georgians	10 Kalmyks	14 Bashkirs, Chuvash, Tatars
Turkmen	3 Latvians	7 Armenians	11 Uzbeks	
Yakuts	4 Lithuanians	8 Azerbaijanians	12 Kirghiz	
1 Karelians	5 Moldavians	9 North Caucasians	13 Tajiks	

destroy lives at a terrible pace. And we must ask what the future of nationalism will be this time.

In many ways, nationalism is clearly outmoded. Many fundamental modern problems transcend national and even continental boundaries: pollution, global warming, environmental issues, and population growth, to name just a few. And many current global trends—the borderless, twenty-four-hour economy and the growth of international communications, for example—weigh heavily against nationalism. The optimist will look at these problems and trends and say that humanity has little alternative but to move beyond nationalism and begin grappling with these issues on a global scale.

The pessimist will look at the carnage done in the name of nationalism and ask what mechanism, if any, can erase all the years, even centuries, of hatred. And what can replace nationalism as an organizing principle? Empires clearly seem passé, and a single, united global state remains a distant vision for some, a distant nightmare for others. Yet it is clear that in some cases multiple nationalities can live together successfully and have been doing so for long periods of time. Economically, regionalism seems to be emerging as a major organizing principle; perhaps regional blocs like the European Community represent not only a viable economic future but a viable political one as well.

Summary

Nationalism has been one of the most powerful forces in twentieth-century international relations, for both good and bad. To understand its power, we must first understand the concepts of nation and state, and how they combine to create the nation-state. In addition, it is important to distinguish between civic nationalism, usually a constructive force, and ethnic nationalism, often a destructive force.

From Universalism and Localism to Sovereign States:
Power has historically been distributed in a variety of ways, ranging from the universalism of the Roman Empire and the Christian church to the localism of the feudal structure. From the ruins of feudalism emerged the concept of the sovereign state as the principal actor at the state level. Nationalism slowly grew to be the organizing principle of the modern state, reaching its present form in conjunction with the rise of romanticism in the late eighteenth and nineteenth centuries.

Problems in Creating Nation-States: Although we generally see a handful of shared characteristics—language, religion, and culture primary among them—as the basis for modern nationalism, drawing national boundaries that actually reflect these characteristics is extraordinarily difficult and often impossible. For that reason the fulfillment of one group's nationalist aspirations has frequently been at the expense of another group.

The Two Faces of Nationalism: As a positive, integrating force, nationalism has been responsible for the emergence of many of the most successful states in the modern world. At the same time, however, nationalism can be destructive of the rights of minorities within the nation-state; it can lead to demands for the return of "lost" territory and for separation of minority groups from the nation-state to create nation-states of their own.

Various Cases of Nationalism: Revolutionary nationalism, combining the impulse of nationalism with anticolonialism or anti-imperialism, has been a powerful force in Asia, Africa, and Latin America throughout this century. Ultranationalism has also been a major international force, particularly in the dynamics of World War II; there are also signs of resurgent ultranationalism in many states today. The long and tangled history of the Kurds illustrates the dilemma of a nation that has yet to achieve its own nation-state, while the still unfolding tragedy in the Balkans illustrates what happens when a multinational state such as Yugoslavia begins to spin apart.

The Future of Nationalism: There are many political scientists and others who believe that nationalism is a spent force throughout most of the world and that integrative forces, such as communications and trade, will gradually erode nationalism, just as the concept of sovereignty is gradually being eroded. Others, however, point out that while the forces of nationalism may seem to be declining in Europe, even that continent is far from full integration, with nationalist opposition to the European Union becoming more prominent. Further, the forces of nationalism are still powerful in areas where they have not yet been fulfilled—in separatist struggles, for example—and ultranationalism seems on the rise in many areas of Europe as well.

Key Terms

Nationalism	Social contract
Nation	Civic nationalism
State	Ethnic nationalism
Nation-State	Irredentism
Treaty of Westphalia	Revolutionary nationalism
Sovereignty	Ultranationalism
Natural rights	

Thought Questions

1. Although it sounds contradictory, nationalism can be simultaneously a constructive and a destructive force. Explain and illustrate this paradox.
2. In what ways are revolutionary nationalism and ultranationalism similar? In what ways are they different?

3. Compare and contrast the situations of the Palestinians and the Kurds.

4. What do you think will happen to nationalism in the twenty-first century?

References

Abramowitz, Morton. "A Kurdish Country: How Long Can It Last?" *Newsweek,* September 21, 1992.

Alter, Peter. *Nationalism.* London: Edward Arnold, 1989.

Beasley, W. G. *The Modern History of Japan.* New York: Praeger, 1974.

Benjamin, Daniel. "Foreigners, Go Home." *Time,* November 23, 1992.

Breslau, Karen. "Europe's New Right." *Newsweek,* April 27, 1992.

Brooks, Geraldine. "Out of Harm's Way: For Kurds, at Least, 'Safe Area' Designation Provides Protection." *Wall Street Journal,* May 19, 1993.

Buford, Bill. *Life Among the Thugs.* London: Mandarin, 1992.

Bulloch, John, and Harvey Morris. *No Friends But the Mountains: The Tragic History of the Kurds.* New York: Oxford, 1992.

Bullock, Alan. *Hitler and Stalin: Parallel Lives.* New York: Alfred A. Knopf, 1992.

Chabra, Hans. "Will Kurds Ever Have Country of Their Own? There's a Chance." *Houston Post,* October 30, 1993.

Clark, Ramsey. *The Fire This Time: U.S. War Crimes in the Gulf.* New York: Thunder's Mouth Press, 1992.

Connor, Walter. "Nation-building or Nation-destroying?" In Fred Sonderman, David. S. McLellan, and William C. Olson, eds. *The Theory and Practice of International Relations.* Englewood Cliffs, NJ: Prentice-Hall, 1979. Cited in John T. Rourke, *International Politics on the World Stage,* 4th ed. Guilford, Conn: The Dushkin Publishing Group, 1993, 182.

Darnton, John. "Serbs Feel Invincible." *New York Times,* June 5, 1993.

Demko, George. *Why in the World: Adventures in Geography.* New York: Doubleday, 1992.

d'Encausse, Helene Carrere. *The End of the Soviet Empire: The Triumph of the Nations.* New York: Basic Books, 1993.

Dobbs, Michael. "Soviets, Eastern Europeans Embrace Nationalism." *Houston Chronicle,* December 1, 1991.

Dragnich, Alex N. *Serbs and Croats: The Struggle in Yugoslavia.* New York: Harcourt Brace Jovanovich, 1992.

Engelberg, Stephen. "Carving Out a Greater Serbia." *New York Times Magazine,* September 1, 1991.

Erdem, Susan. "Turkish Raid on Kurds in Iraq Raises Concern about Refugees." *Houston Chronicle,* March 22, 1995.

Fisher, Marc. "Germany Ends Right of Asylum." *Houston Chronicle,* May 27, 1993.

Fromkin, David. *A Peace to End All Peace: The Fall of the Ottoman Empire and the Creation of the Modern Middle East.* New York: Avon, 1989.

Gay, Lance, "Croat-Serb War Rooted in Centuries of Bloodshed." *Houston Chronicle,* August 16, 1992.

Glenny, Misha. *The Fall of Yugoslavia: the Third Balkan War.* New York: Penguin, 1992.

Graff, James L. "The Butcher of the Balkans." *Time,* June 8, 1992.

Greenfeld, Leah. *Nationalism: Five Roads to Modernity.* Cambridge: Harvard University Press, 1992.

Hall, John A. "State." In Joel Krieger, ed. *The Oxford Companion to Politics of the World*. New York: Oxford, 1993.

Harris, Meirion, and Susie Harris. *Soldiers of the Sun: The Rise and Fall of the Imperial Japanese Army*. New York: Random House, 1991.

Ienaga, Saburo. *The Pacific War: 1931–1945*. New York: Pantheon, 1978.

Ignatieff, Michael. *Blood and Belonging: Journeys into the New Nationalism*. New York: Farrar, Strauss, and Giroux, 1994.

Ishihara, Shintaro, and Akio Morita. *The Japan That Can Say No*. In Genie [electronic bulletin board]. Japan roundtable. [cited May 15, 1992].

Jansen, Marius. *Japan and China: From War to Peace, 1894–1972*. Chicago: Rand McNally, 1975.

Johnson, Chalmers A. *Peasant Nationalism and Communist Power: The Emergence of Revolutionary China 1937–1945*. Stanford, Calif.: Stanford University Press, 1967.

Kamm, Henry. "Albania Fears 'Ethnic Cleansing' May Spread to Kosovo Next." *New York Times,* June 13, 1993.

Kaplan, Robert D. *Balkan Ghosts: A Journey through History*. New York: St. Martin's Press, 1993.

Kaufman, Jonathan. "What's in a Name?" *Houston Chronicle,* January 7, 1993.

Kennedy, Paul. *The Rise and Fall of the Great Powers*. New York: Vintage, 1989.

Kidron, Michael, and Ronald Segal. *The New State of the World Atlas*. New York: Simon and Schuster, 1991.

Kohn, Hans. *The Idea of Nationalism*. New York: MacMillan, 1961.

————. *Nationalism: Its Meaning and History*. New York: Van Nostrand Reinhold, 1965.

Krieger, Joel. *The Oxford Companion to Politics of the World*. New York: Oxford University Press, 1993.

"Kurds Ambush Turkish Soldiers." Associated Press, April 15, 1995.

Lane, Charles, and Karen Breslau. "Germany's Furies." *Newsweek,* December 7, 1992.

Lane, Charles, and Theodore Stanger. "The Ghosts of Serbia." *Newsweek,* April 19, 1993.

Lippman, Thomas W. "The Kurd Quagmire." *Houston Chronicle,* April 9, 1995.

Masland, Tom, and Karen Breslau. "Muffling the Music of Hate." *Newsweek,* December 14, 1992.

Marx, Gary. "A Sea, A Blue Sea for Bolivia." *Houston Chronicle*. December 15, 1992.

McAllister, J. F. D. "Ever Greater SERBIA," *Time,* September 28, 1992.

Moore, Molly, and John Ward Anderson. "Little Noticed in the Rest of World, Kashmir War Escalates." *Houston Chronicle,* June 9, 1993.

Morgenthau, Hans. "Another 'Great Debate': the National Interest of the United States." *American Political Science Review*. December 1952. 961. Quoted in James A. Dougherty and Robert L. Pfaltzgraff, Jr. *Contending Theories of International Relations*. 3rd ed. New York: Harper Collins 1990. 96.

Morrow, Lance. "A Moral Mystery: Serbian Self-Pity." *Time,* April 11, 1993.

Moynihan, Daniel Patrick. *Pandaemonium: Ethnicity in International Politics*. New York: Oxford University Press, 1993.

Murphy, Kim. "'It All Started a Long Time Ago . . . .'" *Houston Chronicle,* June 13, 1993.

Nordland, Bob. "Brother vs. Brother: The Kurds Are Bloodied Again—By Other Kurds." *Newsweek,* November 9, 1992.

Oliver, Roland, *The African Experience: Major Themes in African History from Earliest Times to the Present*. New York: Harper Collins, 1991.

Pomfret, John. "History, Tradition Steel Bosnian Serbs to Fight 'the Turks.'" *Houston Chronicle,* May 7, 1993.

Reischauer, Edwin O. *Japan: the Story of a Nation.* New York: Alfred A. Knopf, 1974.

Rosza, Lori. "Computerized Hate Enters Superhighway." *Houston Chronicle,* March 18, 1995.

Schama, Simon. *Citizens: A Chronicle of the French Revolution.* New York: Vintage, 1989.

Schlesinger, Arthur M., Jr. *The Disuniting of America.* New York: W. W. Norton and Sons, 1992.

Schneider, Keith. "90s Neo-Nazis Have Developed 'New Model for Purveying Hate.'" *Houston Chronicle,* March 19, 1995.

Scott, Sir Walter. *Lay of the Last Minstrel.* 1805. In *Bartlett's Familiar Quotations.* Boston: Little, Brown, 1995.

Serrill, Michael S. "Back on Track." *Time,* December 21, 1992.

Shafer, Boyd. *Faces of Nationalism: New Realities and Old Myths.* New York: Harcourt Brace Jovanovich, 1972.

Smith, Graham. *The Nationalities Question in the Soviet Union.* London: Longman, 1990.

Thompson, Mark. *A Paper House: The Ending of Yugoslavia.* New York: Pantheon, 1992.

Tutt, Bob. "Serbs Use Tribalism to Mask Grab for Power, Scholars Say." *Houston Chronicle,* May 9, 1993.

Walsh, James. "Yugoslavia: The Flash of War." *Time,* September 30, 1991.

Will, George F. "Bedeviled by Ethnicity: The Itch to Fix the World, and the Perils of 'Self-determination.'" *Newsweek,* August 24, 1992.

Williams, Carol J. "Horrific Images Appear from Past: Photos Feed Yugoslav Fight." *Houston Chronicle,* October 27, 1991.

Part Two

Players

Chapter 4

The Galaxy of Global Actors on the International Horizon: IGOs, NGOs, and MNCs

Introduction

Much of our discussion of world politics has centered on the nation or nation-state. However, while the state remains a primary actor today, other players are now emerging to take their place at center stage. In this chapter we will examine three types of new actors: intergovernmental organizations (IGOs), such as the United Nations, the European Community, and NATO; nongovernmental organizations (NGOs), such as the International Red Cross and Amnesty International; and multinational corporations (MNCs), such as Ford, EXXON, and Nestlés. All three types of nonstate actors now have prominent places in the international landscape and are steadily increasing in power. While nation-states have been the dominant form of political organization since the seventeenth century, there are no guarantees that states as we know them today will continue to exist tomorrow, or that they will play the same dominant role they have played for the last two and a half centuries.

In examining this new alphabet soup of political and economic structures, we will focus on two major areas. First, we will examine the nature of the new structures. We are presented with a virtually endless array of actors that, luckily for our analytical purposes, share common characteristics. Second, we will look at the impact of these truly global actors on worldwide politics. After all, these new international entities often share, or even compete for, the same interests held by nation-states. The contemporary game of world politics is infinitely complicated by the addition of all these new players, who tend to make up the rules as they go along. With more layers, there are inevitably more points of contact, ranging from peaceful cooperation to conflict. This new world scheme is conceptualized as a *"complex conglomerate system"* by Mansbach, Ferguson, and Lampert (1976, 42).

Why Are IGOs and NGOs So Important?

Functionalism

One important way to analyze and describe the actions and impacts of these actors on the global stage is to use the theory of functionalism. **Functionalism** is an attempt to describe organizations in terms of their functions, particularly looking at how individuals or groups begin to act together at various levels. Functionalism posits that "individuals and groups become functionally linked as they discover that they share common interests and common needs that transcend existing organizational frontiers. They may then develop common views and even cooperative approaches to the problems that they confront" (Mansbach, Ferguson, and Lampert 1976, 32). As these groups or individuals form systems linked to one another, they spread out to form an intricate lacework that encircles the globe. "Linked systems tend to consolidate into administrative units . . . [and], once consolidated, . . . linked systems and their administrative controls acquire an identity and a legitimized status within their environment" (Burton 1968, 9).

In this sense, the traditional nation-state is a functional unit whose primary function since 1648 has been the administrative control of its particular area or domain. Within the nation-state, subunits perform specific, limited functions such as tax collection, road construction, and education; all subunits ultimately answer

functionalism An attempt to foster political integration in a bottom-up approach through transnational organizations and shared sovereignty.

to the larger organ, the state. We might be tempted to describe the modern globe as a set of subunits: nation-states, made up of their own subunits, deal with one another across political, geographic, or cultural boundaries, in the complex spiderweb of traditional world politics. However, the NGOs, IGOs, and MNCs we will deal with in this chapter represent new functional units that link people together in new structures that either subsume or ignore traditional national boundaries.

Functionalists optimistically believe that cooperation can become a habit. By working together in functional units that transcend national boundaries or causes (such as the IGOs and NGOs we discuss in this chapter), individuals or states can become accustomed to working together on specific problems with little regard for these boundaries or causes. Then, functionalists argue, cooperation can "spill over" from one set of issues or problems to others, producing greater international harmony and even greater integration across national boundaries. Adherents of **neofunctionalism,** who have revised functionalism, argue that such processes are not so automatic as functionalists seem to assume, but require conscious political will, and thus action by political as well as technical experts. However, neofunctionalists generally share the fundamental optimism of the functionalists about the possibilities of international cooperation.

Not everyone accepts the functionalist view, however. John J. Mearsheimer argues that this "article of faith" that international institutions promote global stability is simply wrong. Instead, Mearsheimer concludes that "institutions have minimal influence on state behavior, and thus hold little promise for promoting stability in the post–Cold War world" (Mearsheimer 1994/95).

neofunctionalism Political factors directly assessed in a re-constituted functionalist approach to politics.

The Decentralization of Loyalty

Among the most important issues raised by the explosive growth of non-state actors in the global drama is the question of loyalty. In a less complex world, individual loyalty was fairly easily focused on family, church, and state. Before the technological revolution that increased both global communications and global travel, nation-states could effectively limit the number and kinds of transactions between their own subunits and foreign subunits, even exerting such control at the level of the individual citizen. Today, largely because of the communications web that now encircles the world, that sort of control is out of the question. Furthermore, in this complex matrix of interlocking and interacting functional units, subunits within a state may well not be in agreement with other subunits or even with the policies of their own states. The modern world consists of various centers of power at all levels competing for the loyalty of the population.

In today's world, individuals often form their chief psychological attachment not to the nation-state but to other global or subglobal systems that take precedence over it. For example, a French farmer may have a greater interest in the agricultural commodities market that governs his vineyard and the price of his grapes than in the government of France. Not only economic but also cultural, religious, or ideological ties may compete with his loyalty to the French state. In short, political geography has much less to do with the individual's psychopolitical ties than it did just a few years ago. The list of opportunities to expand beyond one's own state is seemingly endless. An individual may study for a semester abroad in Germany, do a tour of military duty in Somalia, log on to a computer network that spans the globe, work for a multinational corporation that sends the entire family to Bahrain or Thailand, or simply fly to London or Rio for a vacation.

National loyalties tend to be vertical; that is, they extend in an up-and-down direction from the state to the individual and back again. However, in today's web of complexity, more and more individuals find themselves in horizontal relationships that spread across or ignore national boundaries. The Jews of the world, for example, whether they live in Europe, the United States, or South America, are at least interested in, if not tied to, the Jewish state of Israel. Likewise, Palestinians, Kurds, and Irish tend to retain a deep interest in the affairs and fates of their native lands and fellow nationals; the Irish Republican Army, for example, sends fund-raisers to cities like Boston that are host to large populations of Irish ancestry. Religious organizations, from the Roman Catholic Church to the Unification International Church, reach across national borders to engage the loyalty of their members. And other organizations, like the international environmental group Greenpeace, call upon their members to transcend national boundaries as well. Even though people may live in and be citizens of a given state, their allegiance may in fact also be to other organizations that function internationally. What kind of impact does this have on the stability of the international system?

The question of stability and multiple loyalties has become particularly important since the end of the Cold War and the disappearance of the Soviet Union. Regionalized and localized conflicts have increased since the lid placed on them by the superpowers has been lifted. We are now in an era in which conflict at the periphery of the geopolitical landscape, rather than conflict between the superpowers at its core, will probably predominate. The continued increase of new global actors will only enhance such peripheral conflict. This possibility calls into question the very *raison d'être* of the state. Should the state not be able to provide security for its citizens, then the principal rationale for its sovereignty would be lost. And with citizens having less and less psychological attachment to the state, what would replace it?

The Explosive Growth of Non-State Actors

There has been almost geometric growth in the number of NGOs and IGOs since the end of World War II. The number of IGOs has increased eightfold, while the number of NGOs has soared to almost seven hundred times its 1945 count. Admittedly, there has been a 400 percent increase in the number of countries during the same period, largely as the result of decolonization, but that in itself does not explain the mushrooming of NGOs and IGOs (Rourke 1993, 313). In addition, never have there been so many organized political actors on the global stage. We must ask why so many new organizations have come into being, and what ramifications the interactions of all these actors have for global or regional peace and stability.

The increasing interdependence of the world is the primary reason for this proliferation of international actors. Faster travel and enhanced communication have shrunk the globe: if you can't be somewhere physically within a matter of hours, you can be there almost instantaneously via television, fax, computer network, or amateur radio. Just as significantly, not just the physical but also the economic world has both shrunk and become much more intertwined. Trading among nations and international actors of other sorts has become more voluminous as well as more profitable, and money rockets around the globe literally at the speed of light, via electronic networks.

Another major reason for the proliferation of multinational and international organizations is the increasing inability of the nation-state system to provide security. The advent of the intercontinental ballistic missile, which easily penetrates national borders, has rendered the nation-state superfluous in the minds of some analysts. In addition, many of the problems faced by today's world—population increase and migration, pollution, the greenhouse effect, epidemic diseases such as AIDS—demand transnational cooperation and research.

This process of change and growth seems to feed upon itself. As the number of international actors has increased, this increase has spawned even more international actors. For instance, the creation of new Arab states in the Middle East, and the arrival of so many Jews in their midst, led in turn to the rise of the Arab League.

A profound sense of vulnerability to global forces also has given birth to many global organizations. With the concentration of political, military, and economic power in the hands of the few, primarily the rich industrialized nations of the North, many smaller states and interest groups within those states have formed alliances to promote their particular political, economic, social, and military interests. For example, the Organization of Petroleum Exporting Countries (OPEC) enabled oil-producing nations to wield tremendous clout because of the producers' tight grip on production quotas. OPEC in turn showed other nations possessing other resources how to pursue their own plans for creating commodity cartels. In this way, OPEC became a political-economic role model for international, transgovernmental cooperation. Such cooperation trickled down to other nongovernmental actors in the global arena. For example, Latin American nations have formed Mercosur (Spanish for Common Market of the South) and the Andean Pact, in order to both facilitate trade and cope with the operations of MNCs.

While these hypotheses about why the number of international actors has increased so dramatically are intuitively appealing, they will still leave us with other questions. Where are all these actors going? What kind of impact have they had and will they have on the international system, as well as upon individual nation-states? Will the still-dominant nation-states continue to tolerate such a proliferation of competitors? If not, what can they do about it? These and related questions are significant, but the answers to them remain elusive. Three trends seem possible.

Views of the Future

One vision of the future sees the world as truly a single complex system, with interrelated problems that can only be solved by ever greater cooperation across increasingly unimportant national borders. In this kind of future, the sovereignty of the nation-state would continue to erode, while transnational or even supra-national organizations, such as a United States of the World, would ultimately replace these outmoded structures.

A second vision of the future postulates enlarged influence for the current world powers (e.g., the United States, Russia, China, the European Community) so that they can maintain peace and stability for the immediate future. The maintenance of strong nation-states guiding world politics would neither simplify international politics nor eliminate all crises, but with the preservation of time-tested nation-states, important elements such as national distinctions and national oneness would be preserved.

A third route to the future could well integrate these two views. Nation-states will endure and will continue to be the most important international organizations or constructs, but they will be supplemented by a vast array of transnational and nongovernmental organizations to deal with the political, economic, and military baggage that accompanies world politics. This scenario, or some reasonable variation on it, is the most likely world picture for at least the first half of the coming century.

Intergovernmental Organizations (IGOs)

In this section we will examine the gradual development of international cooperation, from the rise of the nation-state system to the present. Much of our focus will be on the largest and arguably most important IGO, the United Nations, but we will also discuss both NATO and the European Union, to illustrate the rapidly changing problems that IGOs must confront today.

History

Until 1648, Europeans maintained the fiction that the emerging states of Europe were still part of a single, unified Christendom. European rulers still saluted the natural law tenet advocated by St. Thomas Aquinas, the belief that all persons were governed by a higher law than that made by man. However, the Thirty Years' War that ravaged the German-speaking Holy Roman Empire from 1618 to 1648, into which many of the other European monarchs piled with enthusiasm and ferocity, clearly manifested the total breakdown of "Christendom." That generation-plus of warfare was followed by the emergence of a state system undergirded by the belief in national **sovereignty.** This state system included territorial integrity (fixed borders with relatively stable populations), separate and autonomous governments (no intervention from outside), and sovereign equality (the ability of each state to conduct its own relations with other nations according to its will).

> **sovereignty** The fundamental right of the state to perpetuate and govern itself, subject to no higher political authority.

Since the establishment of this new order in the Treaty of Westphalia (1648), the sovereign state has been the primary, and virtually unchallenged, actor in world politics. If this state system has been stable and effective enough to endure since 1648, what has happened in the twentieth century to breed our present multiplicity of international actors? To a large extent, the blossoming of international organizations had to await a period of relative peace and tranquillity. That took some doing. Quincy Wright, for example, traces sixty-seven European wars involving the major powers from 1050 to 1800. But for constructive international contact to occur, the international environment had to be calm: political subdivisions within the individual states had to have a measure of time and peace to contact their counterparts, and, most important, states had to recognize that cooperation was in their own best interest, and would be more valuable to them than continued conflict. Until the beginning of the nineteenth century, international organization took place only in the most rudimentary form, when sovereign nations acted diplomatically to end war.

The Concert of Europe

In this turbulent atmosphere, it took the havoc and chaos of the Napoleonic years to prod the major states of Europe into acting together. Out of the devastation of more than two decades of Continental war, these major states met at the Congress of Vienna in 1814 and again in 1815 to fashion a system of diplomatic collaboration. In addition to ultimately bringing an end to the Napoleonic Wars, the great powers—England, Austria, Prussia, and Russia—agreed to "concert" together: to meet regularly to discuss matters of international concern, in order to renew the stability of the European monarchical state system, so nearly shattered by Napoleonic nationalism and protestations of democracy.

For nearly a century Europe would avoid further major wars. Both the idea of "concert" and the rigorous assertion of a balance of power system limited wars and gave the Continent a virtually unprecedented period free of general war. However, prolonged peace, and the emergence of a dynamic new German state determined to force its way to the forefront of European power, gradually eroded the Concert of Europe and replaced it with a series of tightly interlocked alliances that would finally drag the Great Powers into the carnage of World War I.

The League of Nations

As we noted in chapter 1, the Versailles conference of 1919 was seen by many as a chance to start anew, to fashion permanent international structures that would guarantee future peace. Clive Archer points out, "the participants at the Paris Peace Conference [also known as the Versailles conference] had the dual task of making a settlement of victor over vanquished and of establishing a functional international system after the disturbances created by a world war" (1983, 15). To some degree, the "Big Three," American president Woodrow Wilson, British prime minister David Lloyd George, and French prime minister Georges Clemenceau, shared a collective vision for the postwar world of an organization to promote international peace, cooperation, and security. To bolster this, they desired relations among states to be open, lawful, just, and peaceful (Archer, 16).

League of Nations A global intergovernmental organization that was the predecessor of the United Nations.

The embodiment of this vision was the **League of Nations.** Articles incorporated into the League covenant included provisions to limit arms and to limit the private (as opposed to governmental) manufacture of arms (Article 8). Article 10 of the Covenant stated that members of the League would "respect and preserve as against external aggression the territorial integrity and existing political independence of all Members of the League." To achieve this goal, Article 11 provided the basis for collective security: "Any threat of war . . . is hereby declared a matter of concern to the whole League and the League shall take any action that may be deemed wise and effectual to safeguard the peace of nations."

disarmament A process that would remove the possibility of nuclear war by abolishing nuclear weapons altogether. Today the term is used primarily in conjunction with nuclear weapons.

The League's Covenant also addressed the problem of conflict resolution. Article 14 established a Permanent Court of International Justice, while Articles 12, 13, and 15 addressed arbitration, conciliation, and mediation (Archer 1983, 16). The idealism of the time found expression in Article 18, in which Wilson's desire for "open covenants openly arrived at" was incorporated. Treaties were to be registered with and published by the League's secretariat. Territories held as colonies were placed under the mandate system established in Article 22, under which member nations would "undertake to secure just treatment of the native inhabitants of territories under their control" (Article 23).

collective security The original peacekeeping doctrine of the United Nations, which held that an attack against one was an attack against all and should be defeated by the collective action of all.

The League's Covenant, in short, was an attempt at international social and political engineering. The goal was peace, the intended price collective collaboration. However, the international system fashioned in 1919 could not prevent the outbreak of a second Great War, World War II, in 1939. Despite the desires and dreams of the founders of the League, this international organization faltered on the empty promises made about **disarmament, collective security,** and conflict resolution. Furthermore, without the active participation of such major international players as the United States and the Soviet Union, the League was doomed.

By the time the USSR did enter the League in 1934, it was far too late to make any real difference. The two major European shapers of the League, France and Britain, had divergent purposes. The French were interested almost exclusively in securing their borders against a potentially resurgent Germany, and the British proved unwilling to meddle in matters Continental.

The most lethal blow to the League was the disenchantment of the future aggressors of World War II: Germany, Japan, and Italy. All three considered themselves *victims* of the existing international system, and would finally, one by one, stalk out of the League. These nations' disenchantment with the League arose fundamentally from their disdain for liberal, democratic European values such as treaties, diplomacy, international law, and international economics. They saw the system created at Versailles stacked against them, refused to cooperate with it, and finally rebelled against it. It was easy enough to predict future turmoil. Noncooperation and rebellion against the system soon culminated in war. In this unstable system, the rise of Adolf Hitler and Nazism represented a joker in the deck, transforming an already volatile European order into one careening out of control.

Equally unsettling was the League's inability to deal with, and lack of interest in, matters non-European. Japan's aggression against Manchuria and China in 1931 and again in 1937 and Italy's aggression against Ethiopia in 1935 are two cases in point. To be truly a global organization, the League (or its successor) would require major changes at its most fundamental level. All the major powers would have to participate in such an organization from the very beginning, and a revivified League, to be successful, would have to implement its goals and strategies on a global, not just a Eurocentric, level.

The United Nations and Its Role in the International System

The United Nations in Historical Perspective

The international system that emerged after 1945 still rested on the concept of national sovereignty, but this time its members shared a belief in the efficacy of the European-crafted system of international institutions, diplomacy, and law. After all, the United Nations (UN), keystone to the new international order, was forged by the Allies, which had defeated the antisystem Axis powers (Germany, Italy, and Japan). As the successor to the League of Nations, the UN embodied the same beliefs on which it had rested.

The Development of the United Nations

The United Nations in some ways rose phoenixlike from the ashes of the League of Nations. Although the League had failed to maintain the peace, the idea of collective security remained attractive, and seemed more and more imperative as the carnage mounted in World War II. Collective security is "an arrangement among states by which all are committed to aid any country threatened with armed attack by any other country." The goal of collective security is to prevent war by confronting any potential aggressor with overwhelming power, and, if war occurs anyhow, to defeat the aggressor as quickly as possible. An alliance consists of states joined together looking outward at potential aggressors; a collective security arrangement, in contrast, consists of states joined together against threats from within the system. In theory, all members of a collective security arrangement are friends until one of them becomes an aggressor; the aggressor then becomes the enemy of all within the system (Riggs and Plano 1994, 100). As early as the fall of 1941, American president Franklin Delano Roosevelt and British prime minister Winston Churchill implied the necessity of a renewed international congress when they issued the Atlantic Charter. On January 1, 1942, soon after the United States entered the war, twenty-six nations issued the "Declaration by the United Nations"; this reaffirmed the goals of the Atlantic Charter and established the United Nations military alliance. Eventually twenty-one other nations would join this alliance. In October 1943 the foreign ministers of the "Big Four" (the U.S., the USSR, Britain, and China) signed the Moscow Declaration on General Security, pledging continuance of wartime cooperation "for the organization and maintenance of peace and security," and proclaiming "the necessity of establishing at the earliest practicable date a general international organization." Further wartime conferences at Dumbarton Oaks in Washington, D.C., from August to October 1944, and at Yalta in the Soviet Crimea, in February 1945, produced general agreement among the major powers about the general shape of such a postwar organization. President Roosevelt expressed a prevailing American and European opinion when he said, "This time we shall not make the mistake of waiting until the end of the war to set up the machinery of peace" (Riggs and Plano 1994, 11–14).

The various strands of League success, wartime necessity, and hope for future peace were finally woven together at the UN Conference on International Organization, which opened in San Francisco on April 25, 1945. Fifty nations participated in writing the Charter of the United Nations, and a fifty-first joined in signing the completed Charter on June 26, 1945. The speed with which the process was completed—writing the UN Charter took only half the time it took to write the Constitution of the United States—testifies to careful preparation by and wide agreement among the nations of the world. The United Nations officially drew its first breath on October 24, 1945, and the first General Assembly convened in New York on January 10, 1946 (Riggs and Plano 1994, 14–15).

From its inception, the United Nations has faced dual missions in order to achieve its central purpose, the preservation of peace: the establishment and maintenance of collective security, and the promotion of human rights and social welfare. The United Nations conceives of international security in the broad sense of the general well-being of the world's people, rather than in the strictly narrow sense of preventing wars. One can make the argument that in many ways the UN has been far more successful in its efforts to promote at least some aspects of general social welfare than in its collective security efforts. For example, UN agencies have played key roles in the virtual eradication of such global killers as smallpox (see chap. 14), but the UN has had relatively little success in preventing the two or three hundred wars and police actions that have erupted since the end of World War II. Much of that failure, of course, lies less in the structure and goals of the UN than in the hard fact of the Cold War, which virtually guaranteed that for most of its existence the UN would not enjoy the political cooperation of the major powers necessary for its success in preventing war.

In its broadest scope and mission, the newly formed United Nations paralleled the League of Nations: to preserve the established international system. While the issues and structures of the new organization differed from those of its predecessor, the fundamental goal did not. The state system was to remain intact. Hence, like the League, the United Nations was to be an inherently conservative institution designed to preserve the dominance of its membership and the continuity of their legacy: national sovereignty.

World government was not the goal of the founding nations of the Charter. Instead, they went to great lengths to preserve the integrity of the existing state system. The United Nations had as its primary mission the reduction of international war and the establishment of mechanisms that would avert a third cataclysmic global war. Radically reconfiguring the state-based system of global relations was out of the question.

The Structure of the United Nations

The UN Charter created six major organs to carry out the international organization's primary functions: the Security Council, the General Assembly, the Secretariat, the Economic and Social Council, the Trusteeship Council, and the International Court of Justice. Figure 4.1 shows the relationship of these six organs to the multiple other groups that also constitute the United Nations.

The Security Council

Charged with the maintenance of international peace and security, the **Security Council** consists of five permanent members—the United States, the Soviet Union (later Russia), Great Britain, France, and China, the great powers, without whose

Security Council The fifteen-member main peacekeeping body (with five permanent members) of the United Nations.

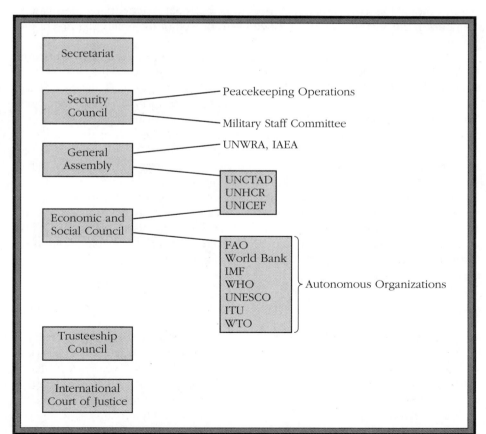

Figure 4.1
The United Nations
This diagram illustrates the six major UN bodies and some of the agencies and programs that they oversee. There are many more such agencies as well as numerous standing and ad hoc committees. Note, too, that the General Assembly and the Economic and Social Council jointly oversee several agencies.
Source: Adapted from "The United Nations System," United Nations, May 1995. Internet. http://www.pan.cedar.univie.ac.at. downloaded March 2, 1996.

Table 4.1
Vetoes in the Security Council, 1946–1992

TIME PERIOD	China	France	United Kingdom	United States	Soviet Union
1945–55	1	2	0	0	77
1956–65	0	2	3	0	26
1966–75	4	2	9	12	11
1976–85	17	9	11	37	7
1986–90	0	3	8	23	0
1991–92	0	0	0	0	0
Total	22	18	31	72	121

Source: Reprinted by permission of the publisher, from Robert E. Riggs and Jack C. Plano, *The United Nations: International Organization and World Politics,* 2nd ed. (Belmont, Calif: Wadsworth, 1994), 58.

cooperation virtually nothing would be possible—and originally six and then ten other nations, elected by the General Assembly. Intended as the primary enforcer of peace, the Security Council was charged in the Charter with settling disputes peacefully, and, when necessary, meeting threats to peace with coordinated action—that is, carrying out the ideas of collective security. Underlining the state-oriented nature of the UN and the recognition of its founders that cooperative action among the permanent members was essential, each of the permanent members in the Security Council received veto power, or the ability to prevent the passage of any resolution by opposing it.

During the Cold War, the Security Council was often in deadlock; at first the Soviet Union and later the United States made extensive use of the veto power. From 1945 until 1975 the Soviet Union exercised its veto power 114 times, while the United States used its own only 12 times; however, from 1976 to 1990, the Soviet Union exercised the veto power only 7 times, while the United States did so 60 times (Riggs and Plano 1994, 58). Not surprisingly, with the end of the Cold War, use of the veto power has decreased dramatically; in 1991–92, not one of the Big Five exercised the veto power in the Security Council (Riggs and Plano, 58). Table 4.1 traces the changes in the use of the veto power by the U.S. and the USSR.

Generally, the Security Council has been more successful at protecting great power interests than in fulfilling the overall mission originally envisioned for it. In addition, the changing global balance of power has raised questions about whether the Security Council should be reordered, with the possible addition of Germany and Japan as permanent members, to reflect the realities of the post–Cold War world.

The General Assembly

General Assembly The "legislative" body of the United Nations, composed of all constituent members.

The **General Assembly,** which functions as a quasi-legislative, quasi-policymaking body, includes all members of the United Nations as equals. Each nation has one vote and, in contrast to the Security Council, no state holds a veto power. Each nation is also a member of each of the seven main committees that organize the work of the General Assembly. While the Security Council meets several times a month, the General Assembly meets once a year, generally remaining in session from September to December. In many ways the General Assembly's most important function as a body is providing a forum for debate and discussion of issues; although it passes resolutions on a variety of topics, none of these resolutions are considered binding on the GA's constituent members. The General Assembly can also make recommendations for economic or military sanctions if the Security Council is unable to act. Another of the most important functions of the General Assembly is its supervisory role. The Security Council reports to but is not supervised by the General Assembly, but both the Economic and Social Council and the Trusteeship Council operate under the authority of the General Assembly.

In the immediate postwar years, the General Assembly was dominated by the United States and its principal allies, frequently at odds with the Soviet Union and its main allies, but long before the Cold War ended the texture of the General Assembly changed radically. With **decolonization,** new nations entered the UN, more than tripling its membership (from 51 in 1945 to 184 in 1994). Many of these new nations were desperately poor and struggling simultaneously with the problems of nation building and economic development, and they eventually recognized that they had far more in common with one another than with the industrialized nations that courted their votes. The East-West Cold War split began to yield to the North-South split, that is, the split between the industrialized and prosperous North and the nonindustrialized and poor South. In this case, the UN political configuration foreshadowed the state of the world after the Cold War.

The most dramatic manifestation of the growing North-South confrontation at the United Nations has been the emergence of two dominant, largely interlocking blocs within the General Assembly: the **Group of 77 (G-77)** and the Non-Aligned Movement. The G-77 (since then grown to 130 members) originated at the UN Conference on Trade and Development in 1964, as the developing nations, known then as the "Third World" (the Western, capitalist societies were the "First World" and the Soviet Union and other communist states the "Second"), attempted to unite in order to pressure the industrialized nations into what amounted to a redistribution of wealth in order to raise the general standard of living of the G-77 nations. This desire was embodied in the call for a "New International Economic Order," studiously ignored or scoffed at by the North. The G-77 also often played the role of general irritant to the United States, which in the 1970s seemed to regret its agreement to give equal weight to all UN members in the General Assembly. Despite attempts to maintain cohesiveness, the G-77 has understandably faced an identity crisis since the end of the Cold War and the virtual disappearance of economic alternatives to the market system (Rothstein 1993, 370; Riggs and Plano 1994, 60–63).

The Non-Aligned Movement (NAM) duplicates much but not all of the G-77 membership, listing 105 states and the Palestine Liberation Organization (which has observer status at the UN) as its members. The NAM, which began with a meeting called by Marshall Josef Tito in Belgrade, Yugoslavia, in 1961, arose from the desire of many nations to steer clear of the East-West confrontation. On economic issues, the NAM position has generally paralleled that of the G-77, but it has extended its interests far deeper into the general political realm. The NAM has been particularly interested in the Middle East and southern Africa, and has tended to take an anticolonial, anti-Western line, often quite shrilly. Like the G-77, the NAM is now struggling with the aftermath of the collapse of the Cold War; it is extremely difficult to remain nonaligned when there is no longer an East-West split to use as a reference point for nonalignment (Riggs and Plano 1994, 63–64). Figure 4.2 shows some of the consequences of the rise of the G-77 and the NAM, with the United States increasingly opposing measures in the General Assembly

decolonization The withdrawal of former colonial powers after World War II, primarily from Africa, Asia, and Latin America.

Group of 77 Group of 77 Third World nations that called for a reordering of global economic relations in North-South trade, aid, and investment, in a New International Economic Order.

after 1956 and the Soviet Union increasingly supporting such measures. (For more on the developing nations and their political and economic ideas, see chapter 8, "Geoeconomics.")

The Secretariat

The Secretariat constitutes the professional bureaucracy that runs the UN. Its sixteen thousand employees, primarily at the UN headquarters in New York, take care of the administrative, budgetary, secretarial, linguistic, and general housekeeping duties without which the UN could not function. The secretary-general oversees the operations of the Secretariat and has also assumed larger functions as general UN spokesman. The choice of secretary-general, an arduous process beginning with nomination by the Security Council and a two-thirds vote of confirmation by the General Assembly, leads to a five-year term. President Roosevelt envisioned the secretary-general playing a large role, as a kind of "world moderator." Early secretary-generals—Trygve Lie and Dag Hammarskjöld, for example—tended to be individuals of considerable ability who could assert power through a number of informal means, but in recent years secretary-generals often have been chosen more for acceptability to all factions than for general ability. In effect, the secretary-general is now "an increasingly powerless figurehead whose good offices are regularly by-passed" (Segal 1991, 15; Riggs and Plano 1994, 36). Table 4.2 shows the six men who have served as secretary-general, and their backgrounds.

Figure 4.2
Soviet, U.S. Voting with General Assembly, 1946–1990
Note how rapidly U.S. agreement with the majority declined after the emergence of the G-77, and how quickly the Soviet percentage of agreement rose.
Source: Reprinted by permission of the publisher, from Robert E. Riggs and Jack C. Plano *The United Nations: International Organization and World Politics,* 2d ed. (Belmont, Calif.: Wadsworth, 1994), 68.

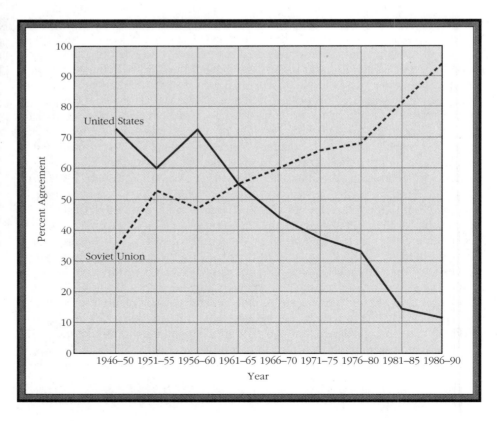

Table 4.2
UN Secretaries-General, 1946–1992

SECRETARY-GENERAL	Nationality	Term of Office	Previous International Experience
Trygve Lie	Norway	1946–53	Norway Foreign Minister at time of appointment; head, Norway delegation to San Francisco Conference (1945), former Minister of Justice, Commerce; politician and trade union negotiator
Dag Hammarskjöld	Sweden	1953–61	Minister of State (Finance) of Sweden at time of appointment; former chairman, Bank of Sweden; high-level civil servant, academic (political economy)
U Thant	Burma (Now Myanmar)	1961–71	Permanent Representative of Burma to United Nations at time of appointment; former government press director, free-lance journalist, high school teacher
Kurt Waldheim	Austria	1972–81	Permanent Representative of Austria to United Nations at time of appointment; former foreign minister, ambassador to Canada, foreign service officer; unsuccessful candidate for President of Austria (1971)
Javier Pérez de Cuéllar	Peru	1982–91	Representative of UN Secretary-General in Afghanistan at time of appointment; former UN Undersecretary-General; Representative of UN Secretary-General in Cyprus; Permanent Representative of Peru to United Nations; ambassador to Switzerland, Poland, Venezuela; foreign service officer, professor of international law and relations
Boutros Boutros-Ghali	Egypt	1992–	Deputy Prime Minister of Egypt at time of appointment; Egypt's minister of state for foreign affairs; diplomat, law professor, author, journalist

Source: Reprinted by permission of the publisher, from Robert E. Riggs and Jack C. Plano, *The United Nations: International Organization and World Politics,* 2d ed. (Belmont, Calif.: Wadsworth, 1994), 89.

Other Major Organs

In terms of policymaking and direct exertion of power, the three other major organs of the UN are substantially less important than the Security Council, the General Assembly, and the Secretariat, but two of them still perform vital functions. Least important of the structures is the Trusteeship Council, originally organized to ease the transition from colony to statehood for the collapsing European empires. However, most of that transition took place outside the Trusteeship Council almost completely; only eleven trusteeships were actually created, and today only one, the U.S. strategic trust over Palau in the south Pacific, endures (Riggs and Plano 1994, 34–35).

The Economic and Social Council (ECOSOC), which reports directly to the General Assembly, enjoys a broad mandate to deal with the multiple global issues of health, welfare, and development. ECOSOC has established functional commissions to deal with human rights, drugs, population, and regional economic and social development, among other issues. In addition, ECOSOC oversees the functions of such UN agencies as the World Health Organization (WHO), the

Food and Agricultural Organization (FAO), the International Labor Organization (ILO), and numerous international coordinating agencies, such as the International Civil Aviation Organization (ICAO), the International Telegraph Union (ITU), and the Universal Postal Union (UPU). Such major players in the international economic system as the World Bank and the International Monetary Fund also fall under ECOSOC's purview (Riggs and Plano 1994, 32–33, 200–231).

Finally, the last of the six principal organs of the United Nations is the International Court of Justice, also known as the World Court. Although it is linked to the UN, the World Court functions as a semi-independent agency, with its headquarters at The Hague, Netherlands. It is the direct lineal descendant of the Permanent Court of International Justice, which from 1922 to 1946 served as the world's chief judicial organ. The fifteen judges who sit on the World Court are chosen by the Security Council and the General Assembly for nine-year terms. Because only nations willing to have their controversies adjudicated by the World Court are parties to cases before the court, its jurisdiction is limited, and its ability to enforce its decisions even more limited. Nonetheless, the World Court represents at the very least an attempt to tame the anarchic international system and substitute a world of law. Given the persistence of the nation-state system and the tendency of nation-states to go their own way, every decision handed down by the World Court and every advisory opinion it issues represents a genuine victory for the rule of law (Riggs and Plano 1994, 35–36). (See chapter 9, "Diplomacy and International Law," for more on the World Court.)

Collective Security and the United Nations

Although the UN was designed to operate as a collective security system, it has in fact functioned in that way only twice in its history: in 1950, when war erupted on the Korean peninsula, and in 1990–91, when it broke out in the Persian Gulf. With the exception of these two cases, the rivalries and tensions of the Cold War precluded any effective attempt at exercising collective security. In 1950 the UN was able to act in concert to deal with the outbreak of war in Korea largely because the Soviet Union was temporarily boycotting the Security Council, and thus the Security Council could implement collective security unhindered by the Soviet veto. It didn't hurt that the United States had a large military force in Japan, at Korea's doorstep, and took the lead in reacting to the invasion of South Korea by communist North Korea. In many ways, despite its UN cloak, the Korean War was primarily an American show, with the United States and South Korea contributing more than 90 percent of the military force involved.

The end of the Cold War in 1989–91 cleared the way for further collective security actions by the United Nations, and the invasion of Kuwait by Saddam Hussein's Iraqi army provided the occasion. Again, the military force deployed was overwhelmingly American, although many other nations contributed troops and economic support. However, economic sanctions ordered by the Security Council also constituted a major part of the collective security response.

In the jubilant aftermath of the Persian Gulf War, Secretary-General Boutros Boutros-Ghali proposed the establishment of a more-or-less standing military force for use in collective security arrangements. Article 43 of the UN Charter provides for "armed forces, assistance, and facilities" to be made "available to the Security Council, on its call." The secretary-general also suggested placing such forces under the UN Military Staff Committee, as Article 47 stipulates. The future of this proposal is uncertain. In practice, the Military Staff Committee has been quite moribund, largely because of the Cold War. However, even with the Cold War over, many nations, especially the United States and the European powers, have given the idea of a standing UN force a cool reception. Furthermore, future aggression is unlikely to be so clear cut and so obviously in violation of the UN Charter; nor are American and Western interests necessarily going to be clearly threatened as they were in the Persian Gulf. As careful students of the United Nations observe, "In the post-cold-war system there may be more agreement than before on the kind of world that is to be made secure, but many practical obstacles to a functioning collective security system remain" (Riggs and Plano 1994, 108–9).

Peacekeeping

Even though the United Nations has enjoyed only limited success at one of its principal original functions, collective security, it has been considerably more successful in a role never mentioned in the charter: peacekeeping. **Peacekeeping** seeks not to deter aggression, but instead to place neutral, United Nations forces between two warring foes in order to police a cease-fire, enforce borders, serve as a buffer between hostile forces, supervise troop withdrawal, and maintain order during transitional periods.

peacekeeping An attempt by the United Nations to place itself between international belligerents to maintain an agreed peace.

Although the term "peacekeeping" had not yet come into use, the United Nations deployed what were essentially peacekeeping forces as early as 1947, when UN "observers" were dispatched to the Balkans to monitor the Greek border, and to Indonesia to help wind down the Indonesian war for independence and oversee the repatriation of Dutch forces. Both the Balkans and the Indonesian missions wound down quickly. However, two other early UN missions continue in operation today: the UN Truce Supervision Organization, created in 1948 to police conditions between Israel and its Arab neighbors; and the UN Military Observer Group in India and Pakistan, which has monitored the cease-fire over Kashmir and tried to keep the lid on conflict along the Indo-Pakistani border. Figure 4.3 illustrates current UN peacekeeping operations.

Peacekeeping per se began in 1956, when UN forces were sent into Egypt in the wake of England, France, and Israel's abortive Suez invasion. Nearly six thousand UN troops monitored the withdrawal of the invading forces and served as a buffer between Egypt and the invaders. Interestingly, in this case two permanent members of the Security Council were on the receiving end of the peacekeeping mission, and thus the peacekeeping mission was authorized not by the Security Council but by the General Assembly. The General Assembly continued to authorize peacekeeping missions until 1962, when the Security Council took over the establishment of peacekeeping forces.

Since peacekeepers almost by definition are not combat soldiers, the success of peacekeeping missions depends on a number of conditions. Students of peacekeeping outline three preconditions that must be met for it to succeed. First, successful peacekeeping requires the agreement of both, or all, warring parties. This consent derives entirely from the belligerents' perceptions of the impartiality and moral authority of the United Nations. Second, the great powers, especially the United States, must support the peacekeeping endeavor. Third, "peacekeeping requires a prior alteration of the local parties' basic objectives, from winning everything to salvaging something; a frequent corollary of attitude change is combat exhaustion or battlefield stalemate" (Durch 1993, 12).

Because of the necessity of maintaining impartiality, peacekeeping forces usually have been drawn from small, neutral nations not involved in Cold War

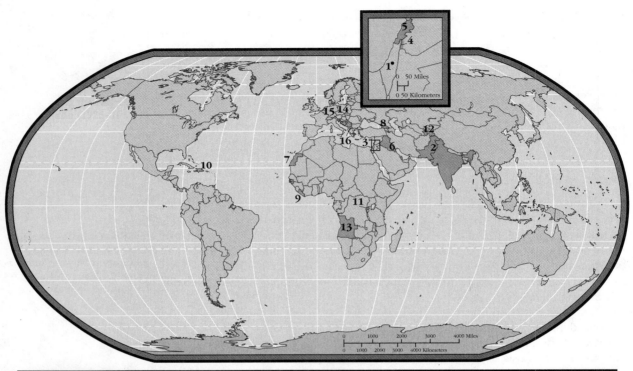

United Nations Peacekeeping Missions as of July, 1995									
	Location	Begun	Approximate Annual Cost	Fatalities	Current Strength		Location	Begun	Approximate Annual Cost	Fatalities	Current Strength
1.	Jerusalem	6/48	$28.6 million	18	218	14.	Bosnia***	3/95	$1.6 billion	11	39,789
2.	Pakistan/India	1/49	$7.2 million	6	39	15.	Croatia***	3/95			
3.	Cyprus	3/64	$42.3 million	163	1,183	16.	Macedonia***	3/95			
4.	Golan Heights, Syria	6/74	$32.2 million	37	1,030						
5.	Lebanon	3/78	$142 million	200	5,146						
6.	Iraq/Kuwait	4/91	$63.1 million	3	1,142						
7.	Western Sahara	9/91	$40.5 million	4	334						
8.	Georgia	8/93	$10.9 million	0	134						
9.	Liberia	9/93	$1.1 million	0	84						
10.	Haiti	9/93	$1.1 million	0	74						
11.	Rwanda*	10/93	$195.5 million	16	5,522						
12.	Tajikistan	12/94	$1.1 million	0	17						
13.	Angola**	2/95	$25.5 million	4	135						

* The UN mission to Rwanda was scheduled to be closed in March 1995.

** This is the third UN mission to Angola; the first was authorized in January 1989 and the second in September 1991.

*** The original UN mission to the Balkans began in March 1992; originally located in Croatia, it was expanded to include linked missions in Bosnia in June 1992 and Macedonia in December 1992. It was divided into three separate missions in March 1995. The figures given here represent the combined totals of all three missions.

Figure 4.3 UN Peacekeeping, March 1996
Source: "United Nations Peace-Keeping Operations" (1995) and "United Nations Current Peace-Keeping Operations" (1995).

strife. Although the end of the Cold War has removed the necessity of neutrality, it seems likely that future peacekeepers will continue to be from smaller nations. Thus, among the most frequent members of peacekeeping forces have been Canada, Finland, Sweden, Norway, New Zealand, and Ireland (Norton and Weiss 1990, 54–55). U.S. participation in UNOSOM, the mission dispatched to Somalia, represents an unusual American role made possible largely by the end of the Cold War.

Problems of Peacekeeping

Peacekeeping is often a fairly perilous venture. Sir Brian Urquhart, UN undersecretary for special political affairs and a major participant in peacekeeping ventures, wrote recently that "there have been times when the peacekeeping function was more like that of an attendant in a lunatic asylum, and the soldiers had to accept abuse and harassment without getting to physical conflict or emotional involvement with the inmates" (in Norton and Weiss 1990, 4). UN peacekeepers in particularly volatile locations, such as Lebanon, have been beaten, kidnapped, and even murdered. UN troops are under orders to turn the other cheek, although occasionally, as in Lebanon in the early 1980s, their function has become more that of a militia than that of a peacekeeping force. Not surprisingly, the Lebanon mission was a total failure, culminating in suicide bombing attacks on U.S. and French forces that led to 350 deaths and the withdrawal of the UN force.

How Peacekeeping Comes About

UN peacekeepers can end up in action in three different ways: as the result of Security Council initiatives, as the result of requests by belligerents or local participants, or as the result of brokered arrangements (Durch 1993, 16–17).

Proposals to Change Peacekeeping

One approach to improving UN peacekeeping functions would be the revitalization of the Military Staff Committee, an organ composed of the chiefs of staff of the five permanent members of the Security Council. For obvious reasons, this committee lay dormant during the long years of the Cold War, but recently a number of prominent figures, including Mikhail Gorbachev, former president of the Soviet Union, and Sir Brian Urquhart, UN undersecretary for special political affairs, have dusted off the concept of a combined military committee as a way of enhancing the role of the UN in global peacekeeping (Papp 1994, 81).

A second proposal would see the establishment of a standing "on-call" UN force composed of troops from several member nations. Rather than continuing to rely on the current ad hoc approach to peacekeeping missions, this concept would permit the rapid deployment of UN peacekeepers to trouble spots. However, attempting to forge operational multinational military forces is always difficult. In addition to the problems of language, command structures, incompatible munitions and vehicles, and sovereignty, there is the ever-present issue of money to support such a force. And there are such problems as ensuring that former enemies or belligerents do not end up in the same units, or that if they do, they are willing to cooperate.

There also has been a call recently to establish a $1 billion contingency fund for the rapid deployment of UN peacekeepers. Given the current state of the global economy, and the arrears in UN payments in which many members find themselves, this too seems unlikely.

Finally, some have proposed that the United Nations increase its use of force in peacekeeping missions, moving from peacekeeping (that is, interposition at the request of the belligerents) to **peacemaking** (imposing or forcing cessation of hostilities). This suggestion is problematic: a third party's increased use of force usually elicits a like increase in force from those the peacemaker is attempting to separate. Peacemaking may bring a transitory imposed peace, but unless the

peacemaking Imposing or forcing the cessation of hostilities between two or more conflicting parties.

United Nations can regain its intended role as conciliator and mediator, the period of peace will probably be short.

The prospects for an enhanced UN peacekeeping or peacemaking role are gloomy at best. However, increased opportunities to separate warring nations and warring factions may provide the practice and successes the United Nations needs in order to overcome the obstacles posed by its nature and its members. Perhaps one day the members of the UN will see that having UN forces occupy the lines between combatants is in the best interest of all. Until then, while the prospects of UN-imposed cease-fires and increased peacekeeping activities may not be bright, the prospects of UN-imposed and policed peace settlements are far dimmer.

NATO

Another major intergovernmental actor that is undergoing massive changes as the result of the end of the Cold War is the North Atlantic Treaty Organization (NATO). Founded in 1949 as part of the Western bloc Cold War effort against the Soviet Union and the Eastern bloc, NATO originally consisted of ten European nations, Canada, and the United States, its dominant member. The original European members—Belgium, Britain, Denmark, France, Iceland, Italy, Luxembourg, the Netherlands, Norway, and Portugal—were later joined by Greece, Turkey, West Germany, and Spain. NATO's major purpose was to repel an armed attack on Western Europe by the Soviet Union and its military-political alliance system, the Warsaw Pact. In addition, NATO was formed to develop a high degree of political cooperation among its members in order to forestall any potential conflict within Western Europe. In the eyes of the West, the greatest danger was the spread of international communism, and any crack in the wall of resistance would permit the Kremlin to disintegrate the alliance politically and conquer Europe without firing a shot.

NATO's forces consisted of the members' military forces, but the Allied Commander Europe was always an American. Politically, NATO is under the command of the North Atlantic Council, composed of ministers from each of the member states and a permanent ambassador in residence in Brussels, Belgium, the location of NATO headquarters.

Now That the War Is Over . . .

The poet Carl Sandburg once asked, "What if they gave a war and nobody came?" In some ways, this phrase summarizes NATO's current plight. What is NATO's enemy now that the Cold War is over? From whom is NATO now to protect Europe?

In the attempt to answer this question, NATO officials have considered a number of solutions, including forming closer ties with a number of non-European nations, widening NATO membership, and even shifting focus to a new enemy, militant Islam.

Partnership for Peace

The most fully developed of these alternative concepts for NATO is the creation of the Partners for Peace program, which aims for the inclusion of most of NATO's former enemies within NATO itself. In January 1994, NATO announced the opening of the **Partnership for Peace** (PFP), "a major initiative directed at increasing confidence and cooperative efforts to reinforce stability." The major goals of PFP include the maintenance of good relations with Russia (preferably a democratic Russia), assistance in guaranteeing the independence of Eastern Europe, and eventual integration of central Europe and perhaps the Baltic (Latvia, Lithuania, and Estonia) into the West. Any state that joins the PFP must commit itself to the preservation of democratic societies and the maintenance of the principles of international law, and must also reaffirm its allegiance to the United Nations, the Universal Declaration on Human Rights, and the disarmament and arms control processes ("Partnership for Peace" 1994; Williams 1995).

As of this writing, twenty-five nations had signed the PFP accords. Four of those nations, Poland, Hungary, the Czech Republic, and Slovakia, seem to be on a "fast track" for admission as full NATO members, and the Baltic states are arguing their case for full membership in quick order (see fig. 4.4). However, critics are now beginning to question the wisdom of granting any of the PFP signatories membership in the UN. Thomas Friedman, an astute political commentator, maintains that a recent House of Representatives vote to add the Visegard nations treated the UN "as if it were the Young Men's Christian Association." Friedman argues that undertaking this kind of potential life-and-death commitment—all NATO members are under the American nuclear umbrella—deserves far more thought than this "impulse-shopping." "My daddy always said to me," Friedman writes tongue in cheek, "'Son, never go into a global thermonuclear war to protect a country you can't find on the map'" (Friedman 1995).

A more extensive criticism of these actions comes from a German political scientist, Karl-Heinz Kamp. He asks some critical questions: "Is NATO politically willing and able to implement security guarantees to new members in the East? Is it possible to maintain alliance cohesion in an expanded NATO? How will an enlarged NATO handle the issue of nuclear weapons?" The most important problem of all, writes Kamp, is Russia. "What would be the Russian response to hasty expansion of NATO, which would move it closer to Russia's borders?" Bringing NATO to Russia's western borders would surely create new problems by risking Russia's feeling isolated and even endangered. "Explaining to a humiliated Russian military establishment that an extension of NATO for the sake of stabilizing Russia's western periphery would be a net gain for them, not another defeat, would probably exceed the ingenuity of even the most eloquent NATO expansionists" (Kamp 1995, 116–26).

Kamp recommends postponing rapid expansion, pointing out that "it is far from clear that quick NATO membership is the most urgent precondition for stabilizing the new democracies in Eastern Europe domestically. A very strong case can be made that economic cooperation through full access to West European markets is a much more promising approach." Seven major issues must be resolved, he writes, before NATO should be expanded. First, an evolving NATO must complete redefining itself as presently constituted. Second, the relationship of the United States to both NATO and Europe must be clarified. Third, there must be more progress in European unification. Fourth, Europeans must clarify the future role of nuclear weapons in European security. Fifth, there should be political and military improvements in Eastern Europe. Sixth, "the process of defining the new international role of Germany" should be completed. And finally, the domestic politics of Russia and Ukraine must become more stable, and their relationships to the West more stable and better defined. Once these changes have taken place, Kamp concludes, then it will be time to consider expanding NATO in Europe (Kamp 1995).

Partnership for Peace Association with NATO that may or may not serve to qualify for NATO membership—primarily nations of the former Warsaw Pact and Soviet Union.

Figure 4.4 **Contemporary Europe: NATO, Candidates, and PFP**
This map of Europe shows current NATO members as well as candidates for early membership and Partnership for Peace (PFP) members, who may well never actually join NATO. Several Central Asian states are also members of PFP.
Source: "Partnership for Peace." NATO. Internet. http://www.un.org/depts/dpko/pko.html. Downloaded March 2, 1996.

Somewhat the same tone of caution has recently been expressed by NATO leaders as well. In a March 1995 article, General George A. Joulwan, Supreme Allied Commander Europe, admits that "clearly, the Partnership for Peace initiative has come a long way in just one year. But equally as clear," he adds, "is the fact that it still has a long way to go." Joulwan points out that not all PFP members actually want to join NATO; "several desire simply to exercise with NATO in order to develop the capability to operate with the Alliance on future peacekeeping, humanitarian relief, or search and rescue missions." Joulwan takes a functionalist approach when he says that by working through PFP, NATO "can build mutual trust and confidence, develop common standards and procedures, and even work on common doctrine. In doing so, we will impart the ideals and values associated with military service in a democratic political system." He asserts that it takes a long time for the institutions of a working democracy—the political, economic, judicial, social, and military components of democratic nations—to evolve and develop. "Partnership for Peace focuses on the development of one of those institutions—the military—and, in doing so, nurtures the prospects for stability with progress towards democracy" (Joulwan 1995).

NATO and Russia

Future relations between NATO and its former nemesis, Russia, present complications and potential dangers. NATO's former counterpart, the Warsaw Pact, has vanished; many of the one-time Warsaw Pact members, and even former states within the USSR, are knocking on NATO's door, asking for admission. These states constitute what Russia considers the "Near Abroad," the territories along Russia's western edge through which Napoleonic and Nazi armies marched to wreak havoc on Russia. At the end of 1994 the Russians angrily suspended their membership in PFP because of concerns about NATO expansion to Russia's doorstep. Six months later, at the end of May 1995, the Russians announced that, while they continue to oppose quick membership for the "Near Abroad," they are now willing to forge closer ties with NATO and to resume their membership in PFP. Russia's foreign minister, Andrei V. Kozyrev, said that many Russians still view NATO as essentially an anti-Russian alliance; he asked that NATO become less a military alliance and more a political one, in order to ease Russian qualms. Kozyrev also stressed that NATO must make it clear that it no longer considers Russia its enemy, and added that Russia continues to oppose NATO expansion (Greenhouse 1995; "Russia Signals It's Ready for NATO Ties" 1995).

We suspect that this will be a continuing drama. Clearly, Russia is ready neither to abandon its historic edginess about its western borders nor to become a military ally of the Western nations. At the same time, Russia is anxious for the West to acknowledge the changes brought about by the end of the Cold War, especially the end of the enmity between itself and the United States. And with its former, if forced, allies clamoring to join the West, Russia must act to ensure that it is not isolated in Europe. And it is clearly in the best interests of the United States to ensure that a Russia still possessing huge nuclear stockpiles is a friendly Russia.

NATO and the Rest of the World

NATO also has expressed concerns about stability and security beyond its European venue. In October 1994, NATO leaders met with Japanese leaders for the third time since 1990 to discuss security topics. Three major concerns drive these meetings: the accelerating pace of deregulated global trade and commerce, the implications of the breakup of the Soviet Union, and the threat of nuclear proliferation in the wake of the collapse of the Soviet Union. ("NATO and Japan: Common Concerns for World Order" 1994).

At the same time, NATO also began reaching out to states on its southern flank, the nations of North Africa. Concerned about growing instability in that area, NATO began to pursue closer ties to Egypt, Tunisia, Morocco, Mauritania, and Israel. But just before meetings between NATO officials and representatives of these states took place in February 1995, newly appointed NATO Secretary-General Willie Claes touched off a firestorm by proclaiming that Islamic fundamentalism was "at least as dangerous" as communism had been. Claes also tied the rise of Islamic fundamentalism to threats of terrorism and the dangers of nuclear proliferation. "We cannot underestimate the risks coming from this fundamentalism," he concluded. Howls of outrage from Islamic nations led to an almost immediate retraction of the statement, along with claims that it had been misunderstood. "Religious fundamentalism, whether Islamic or of other varieties, is not a concern for NATO," Claes wrote. Typical of the reactions within NATO was a statement by a Spanish representative, "The purpose [of NATO] is to spread security, not find new enemies." Nonetheless, it is clear that instability on the southern shore of the Mediterranean is dangerous to the northern shore, which is NATO turf, and that NATO's new outreach to North Africa and Israel represents an attempt at some kind of "preventive alliance" (Clayton 1995; "NATO Wants Closer African Ties" 1995). (For further discussion of Islamic fundamentalism, see chapter 6, "Ideas That Make the World Go Round.")

The European Union

One of the potentially most important intergovernmental organizations is just coming into its own: the European Union (EU). Like NATO, the EU traces its roots to the chilliest days of the Cold War, and like NATO it is now transcending its Cold War identity and moving rapidly toward entirely new functions.

At the close of World War II, Europe, especially Western Europe, found itself facing a disastrous postwar depression and a de facto separation of the Continent that left it adrift. Eastern Europe was locked behind an iron curtain of tight political and economic control by the Soviet Union, while Western Europe found itself under the domination of the United States for its military and economic security. NATO quickly provided the military and even nuclear umbrella necessary to shelter Western Europe from Soviet threats, and throughout the Cold War provided both a collective defense system and a laboratory in collaborative security (Unwin and Paterson 1990, 2).

With its military security guaranteed by the American presence in NATO, Western Europe began to consider the second dimension of its security concerns: economics. By definition, superpowers like the United States and the former Soviet Union can sustain themselves without much reliance on other nations for raw materials, food, and so forth. Most nations are not in this comfortable position; instead, they must trade and interact with one another for survival. Western Europe falls into this category. Gradually, the Europeans began to recognize how interdependent they were, for not only military but also economic reasons. The United States also moved to foster **interdependence** and cooperation; in the original Marshall Plan schema (see chap. 7, "International Political Economy"), receipt of aid from the U.S. was contingent on the European nations' taking steps toward greater economic cooperation.

United in their common security interests and growing prosperity, and still searching for ways to prevent a resurgent German threat to European peace, Western Europeans began to forge functional economic-political ties within five

interdependence A situation of mutual dependence.

years of the end of World War II. The first small step toward functional integration was the formation of the European Coal and Steel Community in 1951. Its focus was the expansion of production and the reduction of costs, relying on cooperative common management instead of traditional competition among the member states. The Treaty of Paris in 1951 instituted a degree of supranationalism by establishing, alongside the ECSC's governmental Council of Ministers, a High Authority empowered to fix prices; this was financed by levies on production. A third component of the ECSC was the community's Assembly, a quasi-parliamentary body of extremely limited authority (Calvocoressi 1991, 213).

Thus Europeans took their first halting steps toward functional integration, at least in the realm of coal and steel. Over time, the strict limits of the coal and steel community gave way, as another form of functionalism, evidenced in the Treaty of Rome (1957), produced the European Common Market and eventually the European Community and European Union. The Treaty of Rome began a three-stage process toward European integration: a commercial and customs union, an economic union, and gradual political integration. The European Common Market, which essentially extended the ECSC's principles of a free trade market and a customs union, was the first step toward greater economic integration, with the establishment of a barrier-free market for goods, services, capital, and labor. Then came the establishment of a common agricultural policy. Expansion followed, as the Common Market extended its tentacles of association to parts of the Middle East and former colonial outposts in Africa and Asia. Simultaneously, western Europeans sought economic stability through curbing currency exchange rate fluctuations.

The path to greater integration and ultimate union has not always been a smooth one. For example, Great Britain was shut out of the Common Market for many years, in large part at the insistence of France's Charles de Gaulle, who felt that Britain's ties to the British Commonwealth and to the United States might interfere with its Common Market responsibilities. However, it was obvious that there could be no integrated Europe without Britain, one of its largest industrial powers, and after DeGaulle's death Britain joined the Common Market. Nationalism and national rivalries continue to tug against the emerging supranationalism of the European community, but for the most part they have been overcome.

Nowhere was the insistent problem created by nationalism more evident than in the struggle for ratification of the **Treaty of Maastricht** (1991), the instrument for the creation of a much more integrated supranational European Union. The treaty provided for, among other things, a single European currency, a European central bank, and community-wide citizenship. All seemed smooth sailing until the summer of 1992, when voters in Denmark rejected the treaty by a narrow margin. Despite later French and British approval of the treaty, Denmark's balk, although later reversed, decidedly slowed European integration. Figure 4.5 indicates 1994 members and membership candidates in the European Union.

Supporting the European Union are two independent but coordinating bodies: the European Political Cooperation (EPC) and the European Council. The EPC functions primarily as a means for the various member states to coordinate their international relations policies. Since its decisions are not binding on any member that does not join the majority consensus, the EPC's actions are limited, but there has been some success in coordinating policies toward Eastern Europe and the former Soviet Union. The European Council, consisting of the heads of state or government of the member states, meets twice a year to discuss general issues relating to the EC and to the European Political Cooperation.

Treaty of Maastricht Treaty signed by members of the European Union in December 1991 that stipulated greater economic and political unity.

***Figure 4.5* The European Union and Candidates for Membership**
Compare this map to Figure 4.4.
Source: Based on European Union Homepage. Europa. Internet. http://discover-net.net/master/Europa

We will discuss the potential economic impact of an integrated European community in chapter 7; in this chapter we want to discuss some of the political issues attached to the EU. In terms of potential political integration, certainly the most important unit of the EU is the European Parliament, with 518 members directly elected by universal suffrage throughout the community. Although membership is allocated roughly by national population, members of the EP are expected to vote along not national, but transnational political lines; several transnational European political parties are already represented within the EP. The EP is the EU's public forum, debating issues, approving or rejecting the European Commission's annual budget, and moving, however slowly, in the direction of transnational law making. However, to some extent the strong state-based nature of the European Commission has offset the transnational nature of the EP. According to Wise and Gibb, "This body grouping the governmental leaders of Member States has taken over much of the strategic thinking and goal-setting role originally reserved for the Commission, which often finds itself working out detailed proposals to achieve an objective fixed by the European Council" (1993, 24).

Despite the current problems, which are probably inevitable given the magnitude of the task—molding more than a dozen states with long histories of often passionate differences into a cooperative community—the EU has certainly made massive strides toward greater integration. Although national governments lie at the heart of the EU, it is definitely not just another international organization. Its founders deliberately chose the term "supranational" to denote a different form of international organization. The EU represents the most important attempt to date to achieve **integration** at a plane higher than bilateral or even multilateral levels. The attempt in the union to speak and act with a single voice represents a leap of faith into the future. The only other intergovernmental relationship even remotely similar, the North American Free Trade Agreement (NAFTA), is solely about trade and seems to have not only no political agenda but also no desire to move closer to any sort of political union. And by its very charter the United Nations remains unwaveringly an organization of decidedly unintegrated governments; there seems to be virtually no possibility in the foreseeable future that the UN will assume any kind of transnational, supranational, or integrative role.

integration In terms of political science, integration is the melding together of various units, sometimes sovereign nation-states to form a large supra-national unit, e.g., the European Union or NAFTA.

Nongovernmental Organizations (NGOs)

International nongovernmental organizations (NGOs) are both plentiful and potent forces in the global arena, composing about 90 percent of all international organizations. Most, not surprisingly, are to be found in the developed world, with its high degree of pluralism.

NGOs can be thought of as intersocietal organizations that help states to achieve agreement on matters of international policy. NGOs also work collaboratively with many IGOs. This is particularly the case with the United Nations, which has a plethora of NGOs working in conjunction with it. For example, the distinction between the United Nations Children's Fund (UNICEF), as well as the United Nations Fund for Population Activities (UNFPA), and the United Nations itself is often blurred. Veteran journalist and correspondent Robert Kaplan believes that NGOs are actually at a pivot point in the evolution of a little-noticed but vitally important change in global foreign policy. "As human disasters multiply on account of ethnic wars, famines, the collapse of states, and refugee migrations, NGOs have filled the gap left vacant by Western governments and their militaries." Kaplan notes that NGO workers often serve as primary sources of information for both diplomats and journalists about events outside national capitals. Furthermore, he sardonically observes that while nations like the United States are less and less willing to put their soldiers at risk, they do not object to their citizens' putting themselves at risk in international relief efforts (Kaplan 1996, 408).

Classifying NGOs is a difficult task, due to their number and the diversity of their aims. The Union of International Associations lists 4,600 NGOs. Of these, 9 percent are classified as universal membership organizations. The remaining 91 percent are classified as intercontinental or regionally oriented membership organizations (Union of International Associations, 1993–1994, vol. 2, 1667).

A prominent NGO is Amnesty International (AI). Founded in 1961 by British lawyer Peter Benenson, Amnesty International is an international nongovernmental human rights organization that works for the release of prisoners of conscience, fair and prompt trials for political prisoners, and the abolition of the death penalty, extrajudicial killings, and all forms of torture. According to the *Oxford Companion to Politics of the World* (1993, 26), "Amnesty International has set the standards for research and organizational expertise. It is also by far the largest NGO. In 1990 it claimed 700,000 active or dues-paying members in more than 150 countries, as well as a headquarters staff of more than 250 . . . . Amnesty International maintains an active and successful lobbying presence on issues within its mandate at the UN, the United Nations Educational, Scientific, and Cultural Organization, and the Council of Europe, as well as with the Inter-American Commission on Human Rights and the Organization of African Unity."

Clearly, Amnesty International is a global organization lobbying governments in the general area of human rights, as AI defines these. Amnesty International accomplishes its mission, in part, by sending delegations to nations to investigate alleged violations of human rights, and issuing an annual nation-by-nation survey of alleged human rights violations. It conducts publicity campaigns on topics associated with human rights violations, and has mobilized world public opinion on behalf of specific prisoners of conscience.

Another illustration of NGOs at work was provided in the aftermath of the Rwandan civil war. At least eleven different relief and humanitarian organizations were involved in the transnational relief effort spearheaded by the United States government to aid almost 1.5 million Rwandan refugees. According to *Newsweek* (August 1, 1994), NGOs assisting humanitarian efforts in the Rwandan refugee crisis included the Adventist Development and Relief Agency (providing a medical team and water trucks); the American Red Cross (the primary organization distributing food to 100,000 daily); AmeriCares (which airlifted 210,000 pounds of antibiotics and supplies); CARE (supplying eight truckloads of plastic sheeting and blankets); Catholic Relief Services (donating food and supplies for 150,000); Church World Services (airlifting 14 tons of food); Concern Worldwide (which supplied one relief flight and a truck convey carrying 1,000 tons of food); Doctors without Borders U.S.A., Inc. (which sent 190 volunteers to the region, and enough medicine to help 300,000); Oxfam America (donating two planeloads of water purification equipment and food); Save the Children (leading efforts to document and reunite displaced families); and the U.S. Committee for UNICEF (spearheading a vaccination drive for children, and trucking 100,000 liters of water daily). The global distribution of NGOs often reflects the desperate needs of developing nations. For example, Catholic Relief Services, which ministers to the most helpless and most destitute, has eighteen bureaus in Africa, eleven in Latin America, two in Haiti, and one in India. Such NGOs provide vital aid. According to an American Peace Corps doctor, "If the NGOs pulled out [of Africa], disease would explode out of all proportion" (Kaplan 1996, 54). Cambodia, shattered by war and revolution, has more than 90 NGOs operating within its borders, staffed by more than one thousand volunteers (Kaplan 1996, 408).

We often assume that NGOs are primarily found in the developed nations, but that is not necessarily so. In his study of the World Bank's environmental record, Bruce Rich stresses the importance of the "green" NGOs in calling the world's attention to environmental problems. In Indonesia, for example, Rich found that by 1983, more than 320 NGOs were participating in the Indonesian Environmental Forum, and more than a dozen other NGOs were establishing the Movement Against Forest Destruction. As early as the 1991 World Bank conference in Bangkok, Thailand, NGOs from both Thailand and other nations established a "People's Forum" to present environmental issues and protest their neglect. Rich notes that during the 1980s, more than two hundred NGOs developed in Thailand, most of them small and focused on a single issue, such as health, village development, or human rights. Most of these NGOs had staffs of ten or fewer, but they had developed links not only to one another but also to other NGOs around the world. India, Brazil, and the Philippines are also home to flourishing networks of NGOs that are linked both nationally and globally (Rich 1994, passim).

The NGO Forum

One of the most fascinating recent developments in the area of NGOs is the NGO Forum. Beginning with the Earth Summit in Rio de Janeiro in 1992, every UN gathering has been complemented by an NGO Forum, attended by NGOs from around the world interested in what the UN is doing and often possessing considerable expertise. A recent example took place in Copenhagen, Denmark, where the UN was holding the World Summit for Social Development. Dozens of NGOs established their own forum, holding hearings, issuing statements, and even running a "Global Village." While UN delegates labored, and sometimes bickered, over issues, the NGO Forum issued its own Alternative Declaration of Principles for fighting poverty and rectifying social wrongs. The thousands who thronged through the Global Village could see women's associations from Africa selling handicrafts, neocommunists distributing literature, descriptions of a Pakistani self-help program, Zapatista rebels from Mexico discussing their grievances, and an exhibit on slave labor in India. Blond schoolchildren sang earnest songs. People raised money to help refugees, talked to European advocates of greater AIDS awareness, or picked and chose from a multitude of causes and groups, all of them NGOs, that had come to Copenhagen to make their views known. Some who held earlier NGO Forums have become specialists for governments and consultants to various IGOs. Boutros Boutros-Ghali, secretary-general of the United Nations, has acknowledged that the importance of the NGO Forums is growing. Boutros-Ghali added that he would like to see such NGOs take an active part in building democracy at the grass-roots level (Crossette 1995).

As we can see, the significance of NGOs in the global arena is unmistakable. Such organizations have been in existence for more than a century, and more than a thousand are politically active today. More than three hundred have entered into arrangements as consultants to ECOSOC. These important players, which run the gamut from consumer and producer groups to humanitarian organizations such as those described in this chapter, promise to grow only stronger and more numerous in the future.

Multinational Corporations (MNCs)

Another of the most important forms of international organization is the multinational corporation (MNC), or transnational corporation (TNC). MNCs/TNCs are businesses with headquarters in one nation but with activities (manufacturing plants, mining ventures, stores, product distribution, etc.) in other nations. MNCs generally have a much broader international impact than they would if they were simply selling or producing products in the home state. They have truly global viewpoints, coupling hierarchically arranged corporate structures with central profit-maximizing strategies that cross national boundaries (Huntington 1973, 335). MNCs tend to occur in oligopolistic sectors of the economy, that is, areas of manufacturing and production dominated by a handful of extremely large corporations (Gilpin 1987, 232). For example, the world's largest corporation, General Motors, with some $123 billion in wealth, ranks twenty-third in a listing of the world's wealthiest entities; while it lags behind such nations as the United States ($5,465 billion), the former Soviet Union ($2,660 billion), and Japan ($2,115 billion), it ranks immediately behind tiny Switzerland and ahead of the former nations of Yugoslavia and Czechoslovakia, the most prosperous of the Eastern European states (see table 4.3).

The History of MNCs

However, MNCs are nothing new in global economics. The first MNCs appeared during the sixteenth and seventeenth centuries, during the first great era of European expansion, when Dutch, Spanish, and English adventurers carried their flags

Table 4.3
The World's Largest Economic Units, 1991
($U.S. Billions)

1.	U.S.A.	3,465	27.	**Royal Dutch/Shell Group**	**104**
2.	Soviet Union	2,660	28.	**Exxon**	**103**
3.	Japan	2,113	29.	South Africa	102
4.	Germany	1,137	30.	Indonesia	94
5.	France	873	31.	**Ford Motor**	**89**
6.	U.K.	938	32.	Argentina	82
7.	Italy	844	33.	Iran	80
8.	Canada	316	34.	Saudi Arabia	79
9.	Spain	435		Thailand	79
10.	China	413	36.	Denmark	78
11.	Brazil	388		**Toyota**	**78**
12.	Australia	234	38.	Finland	77
	India	234	39.	Greece	76
14.	South Korea	238	40.	Norway	74
15.	Mexico	236	41.	Romania	70
16.	Netherlands	218	42.	**IBM**	**63**
17.	Turkey	178	43.	**IRI**	**64**
18.	Poland	158		Hong Kong	64
19.	Taiwan	130	45.	Hungary	61
20.	Belgium	144	46.	**General Electric**	**60**
21.	Sweden	137	47.	**British Petroleum**	**58**
22.	Switzerland	126		Portugal	58
23.	**General Motors**	**123**	49.	**Daimler Benz**	**57**
24.	Czechoslovakia	120		**Mobil**	**57**
	Yugoslavia	120	51.	**Hitachi**	**56**
26.	Austria	111			

Note: Figures for states are gross domestic or gross national products as provided by the U.S. Central Intelligence Agency. *The World Factbook 1991* (Washington, DC: U.S. Government Printing Office, 1992). Figures for corporations are for total sales as provided by *Fortune,* July 27, 1992.

to the New World and parts of Asia. Establishing mines and plantations, these Europeans "in most cases plundered and exploited the native peoples for their mineral and other riches." England's East India Company, a prototypical MNC, also played an important political role in undermining local rule on the Indian subcontinent and opening the way for English domination. The second great wave of European expansion, the imperialist frenzy in the late nineteenth century, carried colonialism to Africa and Southeast Asia as Britain, France, Germany, and other nations established great empires. In this second wave of expansion, Europeans continued to exploit native wealth and work (Gilpin 1987, 246–47).

In this long-range view, the surge of MNCs that began in the 1960s and continues today represents the third wave of global expansionism, one that has depended more on economic than on military or political force. Driven in part by the communications revolution, this third wave of expansion continues virtually unabated today; in the last thirty years, the number of MNCs has soared from some seven thousand in the mid-1960s to more than thirty-seven thousand today (Barnet 1994, 473). Even within this recent pattern, there have been substantial shifts in the way MNCs operate. Most important, today's MNCs rely far more heavily on joint ventures, licensing arrangements, and a variety of other relationships known collectively as "strategic partnerships" than on wholly owned subsidiaries of the sort that dominated the global economic landscape just a decade ago. The need to generate enormous amounts of capital, the potential dangers of nationalization, the great cost of research and development, and the desire to avoid nontariff barriers to import trade—all of these have changed the basic strategies of the great MNCs.

Recent Trends

An astute scholar of MNCs, political economist Robert Gilpin, sees three major trends emerging. First, he notes that instead of locating all manufacturing and production facilities in a single nation, MNCs are now focusing on vertical foreign direct investment: the manufacture of components in several different nations and their final assembly in yet another nation. In this way MNCs, with relatively small investments in any single place, can move rapidly to relocate, should political conditions change or should they be able to tap into an even cheaper source of labor someplace else. Even now, components produced elsewhere by American manufacturers may account for as much as 60 percent of American imports. Second, Gilpin foresees a steadily increasing number of intercorporate alliances in the kinds of licensing agreements and "strategic partnerships" outlined above. Finally, he also anticipates much greater reliance by MNCs on "off-shore" production and "outsourcing" of components, intermediate goods, and even services. The day is past, Gilpin states, when MNCs could operate freely in less developed countries and often dominate their economies; instead, MNCs now see the less developed countries not as exporters of raw materials but as expanding local markets, industrial partners, and even potential rivals (Gilpin 1987, 254–56).

Like any powerful entity on the global stage, MNCs are a mixed blessing to the global economy and world stability. For many years, the debate about MNCs centered around the question of whether they influenced international politics. Today it is clear that the answer to that question is yes; the question to ask about MNCs today is not whether but *how* they influence international relations. Just how have these non-state actors affected states, which are the traditional global actors? How have they affected the relations between states? How have they affected global trade patterns and processes? In short, what is the impact of MNCs upon world politics?

Characteristics of MNCs

A conservative estimate puts the number of MNCs at the beginning of the 1990s at 37,000 entities, controlling almost 170,000 affiliates. Over 90 percent of these MNCs originate in developed nations—the United States, western Europe, and Japan. About 1.0 percent of parent corporations are based in central and eastern Europe, with the remainder headquartered in developed countries. In total, MNCs account for more than 80 percent of the world's trade in economies that are not centrally planned. This pattern reflects decades of capital accumulation, economic growth, and technological change that have strengthened the competitive advantages of firms in developed nations. The five major home countries—France, Germany, Japan, the United Kingdom, and the United States—are host to over half of the developed nations' total of MNCs. Among developing countries, parent MNCs are based mainly in newly industrializing and larger economies like South Korea, Taiwan, and Singapore. Judging from the data for the United States and Japan, it seems that nearly 60 percent of MNCs are in manufacturing, 37 percent are in services, and only 3 percent are in the primary sector (e.g., extractive industries such as mining).

Since MNC activity is so highly concentrated in relatively few companies, it is instructive to look at these corporations more closely. The largest one hundred MNCs (excluding those in banking and finance), ranked by the size of their foreign assets, owned about $3.2 trillion in global assets as of 1990; of this, $1.2 trillion was outside their own home countries, and accounted for one-third of the worldwide stock of Foreign Direct Investment (FDI).

Patterns of Foreign Direct Investment

foreign direct investment
Direct investment of capital by foreign nations in a host country.

In the first three decades after World War II, the chief participants in **foreign direct investment** were the United States and a handful of western European nations—Britain, France, and West Germany—in what was in many ways a bipo-

How do you say "a Big Mac and fries" in Russian? This Moscow McDonald's, which can feed up to fifteen thousand customers daily, shows the global spread of business from fast food to computers.

lar arrangement. The consolidation of Europe into the European Union and the emergence of Japan as a major player led to a major shift, from bipolarity to triangulation. By the start of the 1990s, the triangle composed of the U.S., the EU, and Japan accounted for 80 percent of the world's FDI, but only 59 percent of the world's trade (Center on Transnational Corporations 1991, 32). This new triangular relationship, or competition, stems from three main sources. First, the integration of the western European nations into the European Community and then the European Union has created the largest trading bloc in the history of the world. Second, Japan has emerged as a major player in international economics because of its technological expertise and its accumulation of wealth. Finally, the United States has undergone a relative decline as the world's dominant economic engine. No longer is it the world's primary source of global investments; instead, it has become a primary host nation for FDIs. "By the end of the decade [the 1980s], Europe was on par with the United States in terms of the stock of foreign direct investments, while Japan had surpassed the United States as a major source of foreign investment in terms of flows, with much of its outward investment direct to the United States itself" (Center on Transnational Corporations 1991, 221).

Today we are experiencing not only a consolidation of such MNC market shares within the triangle, but also regionalization or clustering within given industries. Within the automobile industry, for example, intraregional multinational dealings with the host country abound. Various components of the Toyota line are produced within the ASEAN (Association of Southeast Asian Nations) groups: stamped parts in Thailand, transmissions in the Philippines, and steering gears in Malaysia (Center on Transnational Corporations 1991, 62). Similarly, Ford Motor Company, almost the ultimate *American* firm, recently announced new operations to create international teams to develop cars and trucks. Each of five Ford Vehicle Production Centers (VPCs) will have worldwide responsibility for design, engineering, and development of a new line of vehicles. Under this proposal, VPCs based in Dunton, England, and Merkenich, Germany, will assume responsibility for small front-wheel-drive cars, while another VPC based in Dearborn, Michigan will be responsible for large front-wheel-drive cars, rear-wheel-drive cars, and personal-use trucks. Ford's Asia-Pacific and Latin American operations will remain separate for now. Ford's component group will be folded into the new Ford Automotive Operations unit, which will run all the company's automotive business in North America and Europe (*Houston Post,* April 14, 1994).

Defining the "nationality" of a particular vehicle has become a nightmare of hair-splitting definitions that make the medieval debates about how many angels could dance on the head of a pin look downright simple. In the 1980s, Monsanto urged its workers to "buy American," and offered a $1,000 bonus to any worker who bought an American car. Did that include a Geo Prizm, a Toyota Corolla made in California by General Motors? Or a Geo Metro, actually made by Suzuki and Isuzu? Or a Jaguar, manufactured in England by a wholly owned American company? Or a Mazda Navaho, which is actually the Ford Explorer manufactured in Kentucky? (Barnet and Cavanagh 1994, 279).

And if it is true that politics makes strange bedfellows, the politics of multinational corporations is no exception. For example, the Japanese government observes the Arab boycott of Israel. And the governments of Taiwan and South Korea ban the importation of Japanese cars. But, by a miracle of globalization, Honda Accords manufactured in Ohio become "American" automobiles and are thus shipped, with no problems, to Israel, Taiwan, and South Korea. *Business*

Week marvels at these MNCs' "chameleon-like abilities to resemble insiders no matter where they operate . . ." (Barnet and Cavanagh 1994, 280–81).

Tangled Relationships: MNCs, Home Countries, and Host Countries

The explosive expansion of MNCs owes its dynamism to many factors: the constant search for tax and labor advantages, the need to get "inside" nations in order to avoid tariff or other barriers, the general growth of the global economy in the past twenty years, and the encouragement of overseas expansion by national governments. In this section we will examine the tangled relationships between MNCs, their home countries, and their host countries.

Generally, MNC home nations have encouraged their expansion, believing that foreign expansion serves national interests. American officials, for example, have seen MNCs as a positive force in the balance of payments. During the Cold War, MNCs were viewed as mechanisms both for global economic development and for spreading the ideology of the free enterprise system; U.S. government officials saw both these roles as vital for combating international communism. The U.S. government has also attempted to use MNCs "in order to induce or coerce other governments to do its bidding," Gilpin notes, "in most cases to the displeasure of their business leaders." Other nations have tended to follow the American lead in encouraging multinationals to expand, for political as well as economic reasons (Gilpin 1987, 241–44).

However, while home countries have almost always regarded MNCs as an unalloyed good, host countries, the nations to which MNCs extend their activities, have been more skeptical. Since MNCs have tended until recently to expand largely into less developed countries, many of the misgivings and criticisms about their operations focus on issues of development and political stability. For example, critics charge that MNCs tend to distort developing economies and interfere with development in a number of ways: by soaking up local capital that could be used for development; by exploiting local labor forces; by transferring only out-of-date technology to the developing countries; by encouraging maldistribution of income; and by preventing the rise of local entrepreneurs by transferring profits abroad. In political terms, critics charge, MNCs tend to support authoritarian regimes that promise stability at any cost, and thus to create alliances between international capitalism and domestic reactionary elites rather than encourage democratic development. In addition, MNCs are accused of "cultural imperialism" by undermining traditional values in advertising and introducing new values "inappropriate" to the host nations (Gilpin 1987, 247–48).

Assessing this clash of views about the benefits versus the threats of MNCs to their host countries, Robert Gilpin concludes that "on the whole, the record of the multis in the developing countries is a favorable one." In fact, Gilpin observes that as MNCs have been increasingly wary of making substantial investments or long-term commitments in less developed countries and have shifted their investments to rapidly developing areas like South Korea, Brazil, Taiwan, Singapore, and Hong Kong, a new battle cry has been heard from the less developed countries: the refusal of corporations to invest in the less developed countries is now being termed "a new form of capitalist imperialism" (Gilpin 1987, 253).

Other students of MNCs are considerably less sanguine in their assessment of MNC impact, on home as well as on host countries. Richard J. Barnet and John Cavanagh, coauthors of a major study of MNCs (*Global Dreams,* 1994), view MNCs as potentially very dangerous. They point out that MNCs often export high-

The Virtual Corporation

The impact of the communications revolution on multinational corporations has been enormous, allowing the creation of a "virtual corporation" linked globally by computers and telecommunications. The virtual corporation offers enormous advantages to the MNC. Teleconferencing eliminates travel and the time, expense, and physical wear and tear associated with it. Telecommuting permits workers to stay at home and use their computers to do their work and share their ideas, as well as to join in virtual conversations and conferences. The implications of these new technologies for the international business world are tremendous: more rapid exchange of ideas, a much greater and more open flow of information, greater efficiency, and the flattening of hierarchies, as information once available only to high-level executives is distributed throughout the corporation. In fact, the communications revolution has even spawned a new kind of executive, the global information officer (GIO). Three MNCs illustrate the potential of the communications revolution: M. W. Kellogg, Schlumberger, and Citibank.

GLOBAL PERSPECTIVES

M. W. Kellogg

When this oil industry contractor agreed to join two others, Bechtel and Foster Wheeler, in a major project involving the expansion of a remote petroleum-producing site in Venezuela, it immediately recognized the danger of communications snafus, especially given the uncertain Venezuelan telephone system, and began designing its own comprehensive telecommunications system, dubbed Vennet. Six million dollars later, Vennet combines computers, e-mail, video-conferencing, and a direct satellite link into a telesystem that serves all three contractors and permits instantaneous transmission of information. Efficiency is up, decision-making time is down, travel costs are much lower, and the virtual conference is a daily occurrence. Kellogg's vice president in charge of the Venezuelan project sees teleconferencing as the future of the MNC: "That's why I've sold my shares in American Airlines and bought stock in Microsoft" (Silverman 1994).

Schlumberger

A multinational corporation since the 1920s, Schlumberger employs more than forty-eight thousand people in more than one hundred countries. Tying them all together is a telecommunications system based on the Internet and backed up by a proprietary net. Using the Internet connection, Schlumberger can send e-mail both in-house and to clients globally. At an annual cost of roughly thirty-five cents per employee, the oil-field services company not only provides many virtually instantaneous global communications but also allows some of its workers to telecommute. As one student of telecommunications explains, "the workplace is no longer a fixed place—it's often anywhere you want to work." Schlumberger also encourages its employees to use the Internet as a research tool. The company maintains a second system, the Schlumberger Information Network (SINet) to handle sensitive voice, video, and data transmissions for which security is vital. The MNC also maintains its own Internet Homepage (www.slb.com), which provides information about its own activities, as well as hypertext links to information about the petroleum industry in general (Silverman 1995).

Citibank Asia Pacific

To take full advantage of its place in the booming Pacific Rim marketplace, Citibank Asia Pacific has embarked on an ambitious project to centralize its "number-crunching" in one location. Designed to phase in over a four-year period, at an estimated $200 million cost, this centralization will locate all back-office processing in Singapore. It is hoped that sending their heavy processing to Singapore will free the Citibank Asia Pacific operations in fifteen separate countries to become "centers of excellence" focusing on the development of new and profitable products and services. For example, Citibank India is developing on-site computer terminals for processing car loan applications, and the Hong Kong and Australia locations will develop home banking by telephone. According to the technology officer overseeing the centralization project, "the priority is on delivering our products to market in half the time. The fact that we're going to save a fortune is secondary" (Wilder 1995).

paying manufacturing jobs from home countries; industrial workers in Australia or Ireland can be hired for 60 percent of U.S. wages, for example, and industrial workers in Mexico, Brazil, or South Korea for as little as 10 percent of the U.S. wage. Barnet and Cavanagh cite MNC exportation of jobs as partially responsible for the shrinking of manufacturing jobs in the U.S., from employing nearly 35 percent of the workforce in 1950 to occupying approximately 16 percent today (Barnet and Cavanagh, 1994, 275–76). MNCs also can present serious economic problems for their home countries, Barnet and Cavanagh note, especially in the area of taxes. "In the age of globalization a basic problem for government is how to collect enough revenue when the most powerful institutions that shape the economy have the mobility, expertise, and political clout to minimize their tax obligations." Barnet and Cavanagh observe that from 1984 to 1986, foreign-owned firms in the United States saw their profits increase 50 percent, but their U.S. taxes increase only 2 percent. In the boom year of 1987, he adds, 59 percent of foreign-owned firms in the U.S. reported no American profits and paid no American taxes (Barnet and Cavanagh 1994, 345).

transfer pricing The trading of commodities between a parent company's subsidiaries in different countries in order to record profits in jurisdictions where taxes are low.

Transfer pricing, that is, the importation and exportation of components within the MNCs themselves, poses special problems. A large percentage of international transactions take place within the MNCs as sales between one branch and another, so that the MNCs, not market forces, set these transfer prices. Consequently, "transfer prices are set with tax returns in mind; profits (or losses) show up where they will do the most good for the corporation's bottom line." According to Barnet and Cavanagh, the U.S. Internal Revenue Service found overwhelming evidence that Toyota had consistently overcharged its American subsidiaries for parts; Toyota denied any impropriety, but paid a reported $1 billion settlement (Barnet and Cavanagh 1994, 345).

Another problem that multinationals can present to home countries is in the area of national security. Many critics worry that "MNCs collaborating with foreign firms may transfer strategic technology abroad—technology that has often been heavily subsidized by the state" (Jenkins 1993, 607).

Perhaps the most damaging criticism leveled at the MNCs is that they are inherently destabilizing at a global level. According to Barnet and Cavanagh, "the most disturbing aspect of this [MNC] system is that the formidable power and mobility of global corporations are undermining the effectiveness of national governments to carry out essential policies on behalf of their people." Barnet and Cavanagh maintain that "national leaders no longer have the ability to comprehend, much less control, these giants because they are mobile, and . . . constantly changing appearances to suit different circumstances" (Barnet and Cavanagh 1994, 19). With the rise of "stateless" corporations, national governments no longer can use traditional methods to control or stimulate national economies. "National governments lack both the strategic vision and the management tools to play an integrative role in the societies they are elected to govern because to a considerable extent they have lost control of the levers of economic change" to MNCs (Barnet and Cavanagh 1994, 340). Barnet and Cavanagh go on to state that "in an integrated world economy the line between public authority and private power has grown murkier." They say that "the decline in effective public authority is introducing instability into the international economy," with potentially disastrous political and economic consequences. "Governments that are unable to address basic human needs and appear callous in the face of widespread economic injustice cannot govern democratic societies," Barnet and Cavanagh flatly state (1994, 348–57).

The result of this, Barnet and Cavanagh conclude, is that political disintegration seems to be triggered by economic integration, and "the world faces an authority crisis without precedent in modern times" (1994, 421–22). Unless new political and economic theories can be developed to balance the needs of peoples and nations with those of MNCs, Barnet and Cavanagh foresee disaster. Starvation will continue to rise and the ecology will continue to collapse. "Neither politicians nor corporate managers have been willing or able to make resource conservation balance central political values," they write. "The result has been a bizarre sacrifice of what is needed to sustain life, beauty, and the natural order. Every day real wealth—breathable air, drinkable water, human imagination and energy, and the health and development of children—are sacrificed for mere symbols of wealth, mostly pieces of paper and bits of electronic data that tell us how rich we are" (Barnet and Cavanagh 1994, 428). Another critic of MNC behavior characterizes it as a form of "neo-medievalism" in which the MNC is connected or loyal to nothing but itself (Roet 1995).

Even those who do not agree with this essentially apocalyptic view of the impact of MNCs on the globe must take its criticisms and concerns into account.

Controlling the MNCs

Control of MNCs has posed difficult dilemmas for both the mother countries and the host countries. Professors Kegley and Wittkopf point out that "it is clear that multinationals have become important actors in world politics in that decisions critical to nation states are now made by entities over which those nations may not have control. Thus, the question of control of MNCs constitutes a significant issue in the debate about the costs and benefits of multinational corporations" (In Olson 1994, 291).

Control over the dealings of MNCs is a central issue today: both host nations (many of whom are in the Third World) and home countries may find MNCs' actions running counter to their own domestic and foreign policy interests. Tracking the Byzantine web of transactions of just one MNC can become a life's work. For example, General Electric, which is headquartered in the United States, has production licenses with Nuovo Pignone of Italy, Mitsubishi Heavy Industries and Hitachi of Japan, Mannesmann and AEG Telfunken of Germany, John Brown Engineering of Great Britain, and Thomassen Holland of the Netherlands (Office of Technology Assessment 1981). As Barnet and Cavanagh quip, "You can't finger targets anymore, and if you aim at a target, you often find it's yourself" (1994). In an early, and often critical, study of MNCs, Barnet and Muller stated,

> The global corporation is the most powerful human organization yet devised for colonizing the future. By scanning the entire planet for opportunities, by shifting its resources from industry to industry and country to country, and by keeping its overriding goal simple—worldwide profit maximization—it has become an institution of unique power. The world managers are the first to have developed a plausible model for the future that is global . . . . In making business decisions today they are creating a politics for the next generation (1974, 363).

Third World nations have tried to control the behavior of MNCs within their borders principally through the UN Commission of Transnational Corporations. Through creating a code of behavior, Third World nations have sought to monitor the behavior of these global giants in terms of transfer pricing, taxation, ownership and control, and environmental protection. Other attempts to control MNCs include the Convention on the Settlement of Investment Disputes and the Declaration on International Investment and Multinational Enterprises.

However, in recent years, most developing nations have not sought to control MNCs as rigorously as they did in the past. During the 1960s, a favorite method of control was nationalization. But since the rise of OPEC in the early and mid-1970s (see chapter 7), there has been a 180-degree shift in Third World thinking about nationalization. The heavily indebted Third World nations have begun to think more like the industrialized northern tier of states. They have placed greater emphasis upon privatization and have begun to welcome the benefits associated with global corporations. FDI, once denounced as merely a sophisticated form of imperialism, is now often viewed as a means by which an impoverished nation can acquire capital, technology, and management skills from the rest of the world.

As this chapter makes clear, the growth and development of the complex web of international relationships—IGOs, NGOs, MNCs, and all their related forms—has made the world of the 1990s far more complex, far more challenging, and potentially far more integrated than the globe has been in its entire history. There is a pressing need to examine and understand the consequences, both positive and negative, of these forms of global integration, and the potentially lethal problems should we fail to understand and control these forces and use them to shape global politics for the better.

Summary

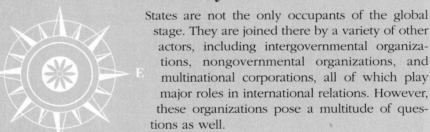

States are not the only occupants of the global stage. They are joined there by a variety of other actors, including intergovernmental organizations, nongovernmental organizations, and multinational corporations, all of which play major roles in international relations. However, these organizations pose a multitude of questions as well.

Intergovernmental Organizations: Created by states, these organizations reflect the needs of states to cooperate in vital areas such as security. The United Nations, successor to the League of Nations and other attempts to create international stability and security, is now in transition as a result of the end of the Cold War and the greater importance of functions such as peacekeeping. Other major IGOs, such as the North Atlantic Treaty Organization and the European Union, also illustrate both the drives behind intergovernmental organizations and the problems such organizations are encountering in the post–Cold War world.

Nongovernmental Organizations: Formed by individuals rather than states, the NGOs usually represent specific interests—disaster relief, human rights, or the environment, for example—and can play major roles both in lobbying governments and IGOs and in carrying out specific plans.

Multinational Corporations: Having emerged as a dominant force in international economics, the multinational corporations are major players in the modern world in terms of both their productive capacity and their political influence. MNCs pose serious questions about the limits of sovereignty, potential exploitation of less developed nations, and the ability of nations to deal with such structures.

Key Terms

Functionalism
Neofunctionalism
Sovereignty
League of Nations
Disarmament
Collective security
Security Council
General Assembly
Decolonization

Group of 77 (G-77)
Peacekeeping
Peacemaking
Partnership for Peace
Interdependence
Treaty of Maastricht
Integration
Foreign direct investment
Transfer pricing

Thought Questions

1. What is the difference between horizontal and vertical loyalties? In your own life, which of your loyalties are horizontal? Vertical? Do you feel any conflict between them?
2. To what extent has the United Nations been able to fulfill its original purposes? Why? What do you see as the future of the UN?
3. If you were running NATO, how would you deal with the Partnership for Peace? Russia? European security overall?
4. As the president of a small, developing nation, what steps would you take to attract MNCs to your nation? How would you deal with the issues of control and sovereignty raised in this chapter?

References

"A Race with Death," *Newsweek.* August 1, 1994, 26–31.

Archer, Clive. *International Organization.* Boston: Allen & Unwin, 1983).

"Baltic States Want NATO Tie." In Associated Press [database online]. downloaded February 8, 1995. Available from Prodigy. White Plains, New York.

Barnet, Richard J., and John Cavanagh. *Global Dreams: Imperial Corporations and the New World Order.* New York: Simon and Schuster, 1994.

Barnet, Richard J., and Ronald Muller. *Global Reach: The Power of the Multinational Corporations.* New York: Simon and Schuster, 1974.

Burton, John. *Systems, States, Diplomacy, and Rules.* New York: Cambridge University Press, 1968.

Calvocoressi, Peter. *Resilient Europe: 1870–2000*. New York: John Wiley, 1991.

Claes, Willy. "NATO and the Evolving Euro-Atlantic Security Architecture." *NATO Review* (December 1994/January 1995).

Claude, Inis. *Swords into Plowshares*. New York: Random House, 1971.

Clayton, Jonathan. "NATO Opens Talks with Mideast, African Nations." *Houston Chronicle,* February 25, 1995.

Coate, Roger A., and Donald J. Puchala. "Global Policies and the United Nations System." In Friedrich Kratochwil and Edward D. Mansfield, *International Organization*. New York: Harper Collins, 1994.

Crossette, Barbara. "Private Groups Show Strength at UN Events." *New York Times,* March 12, 1995.

Daugherty, James E., and Robert L. Pfaltzgraff, Jr. *Contending Theories of International Relations*. New York: Harper Collins, 1990.

Diehl, Paul F. "Institutional Alternatives to Traditional U.N. Peacekeeping: An Assessment of Regional and Multinational Options." *Armed Forces and Society* (Winter 1993).

Durch, William A., ed. *The Evolution of UN Peacekeeping: Case Studies and Comparative Analysis*. New York: Henry L. Stimson Center/St. Martin's Press, 1993.

"Ford Goes Global," *Houston Post*. April 14, 1994.

Friedman, Thomas L. "Congress Should Realize That Joining NATO Is Not Like Joining the YMCA." *Houston Chronicle,* March 11, 1995.

Gilpin, Robert. *The Political Economy of International Relations*. Princeton, New Jersey: Princeton University Press, 1987.

Greenhouse, Steven. "NATO, Russia Officials Try to Forge a Closer Link." *Houston Chronicle,* June 1, 1995.

Huntington, Samuel. "Transnational Organizations in World Politics," *World Politics,* April 1973.

Jenkins, Barbara. "Multinational Corporations." In *Oxford Companion to Global Politics*. New York: Oxford, 1993.

Joulwan, General George A. "NATO's Military Contribution to Partnership for Peace: The Progress and the Challenge." *NATO Review* (March 1995).

Kamp, Karl-Heinz. "The Folly of Rapid NATO Expansion." *Foreign Policy* (Summer 1995).

Kaplan, Robert D. *The Ends of the Earth: A Journey at the Dawn of the 21st Century*. New York: Random house, 1996.

Kratochwil, Friedrich. "The Challenges of Integration." In Friedrich Kratochwil and Edward D. Mansfield, *International Organizations*. New York: Harper Collins, 1994.

Krieger, Joel, ed, *The Oxford Companion to Politics of the World,* New York: Oxford University Press, 1993.

Mansbach, Richard, Yale H. Ferguson, and Donald E. Lampert. *The Web of World Politics: Non-State Actors in the Global System*. Englewood Cliffs, N.J.: Prentice Hall, 1976.

Mearsheimer, John J. "The False Promise of International Institutions." *International Security* (Winter 1994/1995).

"NATO and Japan: Common Concerns for World Order." Brussels, Belgium: NATO Office of Information and Press, December 1994.

"NATO Wants Closer African Ties." In Associated Press [database online]. Downloaded February 8, 1995. Available from Prodigy. White Plains, New York.

Norton, Augustus Richard, and Thomas George Weiss. *UN Peacekeepers: Soldiers with a Difference*. New York: Foreign Policy Association, 1990.

Olson, Mancur. *The Rise and Decline of Nations*. New Haven, CT: Yale University Press, 1982.

Papp, Daniel S. *Contemporary International Relations: Frameworks for Understanding.* New York: Macmillan, 1994.

"Partners for What?" *The Economist.* September 24, 1994.

"Partnership for Peace." Fact Sheet No. 9. Brussels, Belgium: NATO Office of Information and Press, June 1994.

Office of Technology Assessment, *Report on Transnational Corporations.* 88th United States Congress. Government Printing office Washington, DC: 1981.

Rich, Bruce. *Mortgaging the Earth: The World Bank, Environmental Impoverishment, and the Crisis of Development.* Boston: Beacon, 1994.

Riggs, Robert E., and Jack C. Plano. *The United Nations: International Organization and World Politics.* 2d ed. Belmont, Calif.: Wadsworth, 1994.

Roberts, Adam. "United Nations." In *Oxford Companion to Politics of the World.* New York: Oxford, 1993.

Roet, Jeff. "The Geopolitics of the Global Economy." Unpublished speech at San Jacinto College, Jan. 10, 1994.

Rothstein, Robert. "G-77." In *Oxford Companion to Politics of the World.* New York: Oxford, 1993.

Rourke, John T. *International Politics on the World Stage.* Sluice Dock, Conn.: Dushkin, 1993.

"Russia Signals It's Ready for NATO Ties." *Houston Chronicle,* May 30, 1995.

Segal, Gerald. *The World Affairs Companion.* New York: Simon and Schuster, 1991.

Silverman, Dwight. "Remote Meetings for Firms Turning into Virtual Reality." *Houston Chronicle,* January 9, 1994.

___. "Digital Nation: Computer Networks Redefine Workplace." *Houston Chronicle,* February 7, 1995.

"Transnational Corporations, 1990," United Nations: Center on Transnational Corporations, 1991.

Union of International Associations, ed. *Yearbook of International Organizations, 1993–94.* London: K. G. Saur.

"United Nations Current Peace-Keeping Operations," United Nations, May 1, 1995. Internet. Gopher://gopher.uudp.org:70/00/unearth/pko/carol. Downloaded March 17, 1996.

"United Nations Peace-Keeping Operations." United Nations, July 1995. Internet. http://ralph.gmu.edu/cfpa/peace/toc.html. Downloaded March 17, 1996.

Unwin, D. W., and W. E. Paterson. *Politics in Western Europe Today.* New York: Longman, 1990.

Wilder, Clinton. "Making Borders Disappear: Citibank Asia-Pacific Pushes Centralization from Turkey to Guam." *Informationweek,* February 27, 1995, 41–49.

Williams, Geoffrey Lee. "NATO's Expansion: the Big Debate." *NATO Review* (May 1995).

Wise, Mark, and Richard Gibb. *Single Market to Social Europe: The European Community in the 1990s.* New York: John Wiley, 1993.

"The World Economy in Charts," *Fortune.* July 27, 1992, 61–81.

Chapter 5

The Social Psychology of International Relations

Introduction

To what extent does an individual decision-maker's personality affect a nation's behavior? Can the motivations of just a single leader move a nation into war or peace? Were the personalities of Jimmy Carter, Anwar Sadat, and Menachem Begin instrumental in achieving a rapprochement between Israel and Egypt, for example? Did the motivations of a single leader, Adolf Hitler, lead Europe and the rest of the world into World War II? Was it Stalin's alleged paranoia that contributed to the onset of the Cold War? More recently, was the Gulf War caused by Saddam Hussein's single-minded quest to control Kuwait?

On the more positive side, was it something in Gorbachev's psyche that compelled him to restructure the Communist Party of the Soviet Union, resulting ultimately in the fall of the Berlin Wall and the end of the Cold War? Was it the *persona* of George Bush to send food relief to the starving in Somalia? And what of Boris Yeltsin? Did something in his psychological makeup cause him to restructure radically Russia's political and economic systems?

What do we really know about leaders' cognitions and perceptions and their impact upon world politics? The scientific answer is mixed, but intuition says that the two are not unrelated.

Political observers have long questioned and studied the relationship between psychology and politics. The Greek historian Thucydides, writing twenty-four centuries ago, was perhaps the first to question the impact of personality upon politics. In his *History of the Peloponnesian War,* Thucydides examined the decisions of city-state leaders in matters of war and peace. He focused not only on the systemic, or environmental, factors that affected the leaders' choices, but also on the role of their psychological fears and ideas of honor in motivating them.

Part of the problem in assessing the impact of personality upon political decision-making is access to the principal decision-makers themselves. How many leaders would allow a political psychologist to inspect, probe, and question them during even routine, let alone critical, decision periods? Necessarily, most of the scientific data that we possess is from surrogate sources or subjects. Just how accurate, reliable, and representative of the real world these subjects are is not known. However, the possible relationship between psychology and politics is far too critical to go unstudied in a scientific fashion.

The purpose of this chapter is to examine the political individual. Since nations, multinational corporations, and sundry IGOs are merely constructs of human beings, the study of politics must include the study of these human beings as political actors. Richard Snyder, H. W. Bruck, and Burton Sapin have taken this position: "It is one of our basic methodological choices to define the state as its official decision-makers—those whose authoritative acts are, to all intents and purposes, the acts of the state. State action is the action taken by those acting in the name of the state" (1963, 65).

We do not mean to imply that **idiosyncratic** personality or social-psychological variables are the *sine qua non* of unraveling the riddles of international politics. But we do believe that examining the individual human being, acting both alone and within a group, is the logical starting point for addressing such riddles. It is illuminating to hybridize several disciplines—political science, psychology, sociology, and **social psychology**—to personality and group effects

idiosyncratic Personality-level variables.

social psychology The intersection of two academic disciplines, sociology and psychology, that focus upon the role of the individual within a group setting.

Is Saddam Hussein Crazy?

Is Saddam Hussein mad? Definitely not, says Jerrold Post of George Washington University. He is not irrational and unpredictable. He is not psychotic, or completely out of touch with reality.

If Saddam is not crazy, then what is he? Says Post, he is self-absorbed and grandiose. He has no empathetic ability. Moreover, he has no conscience. His loyalty is only to himself—not even to Iraq. He uses aggression to serve his personal needs. Weapons of mass destruction fit only too nicely into the cowboy mentality of the Iraqi collective psyche, and of Saddam's own.

Saddam is, though, a bit paranoid. For example, in his mind Kuwait was to blame for the economic woes of Iraq after the Iran-Iraq war, even though Kuwait had been a loyal supporter and underwriter of the Iraqi war effort.

But this question can be asked: If Saddam is rational, why has he miscalculated so frequently? There are several possible reasons. First, his world view and political agenda are not the same as those in western capitals. This does not mean he is miscalculating, only that his agenda is different. Also, Saddam has traveled outside of the Arab world only twice. His only foreign influencers were the Russians. Finally, Saddam has surrounded himself with sycophants who will not cross or disagree with him.

Therefore, to call Saddam Hussein insane or mad is simply not true. His own personal and political survival is of utmost importance to him. Political causes are useful only insofar as they help Saddam.

A word of caution is in order. Psychobiography, as it is called, is a relatively new approach to

GLOBAL PERSPECTIVES

studying politics, and can be helpful. However, it is an imperfect tool, as political leaders (especially ones already dead!) are not inclined to lie on an analyst's couch for intensive psychotherapy. Researching individuals' life stories for clues as to how and why they behave as they do is fraught with scientific danger. While many such armchair psychoanalytical studies are highly interesting and intriguing, the student is encouraged to take them with the proverbial grain of salt.

Is this the portrait of a madman? Despite a sneaking suspicion on the part of most Americans, Saddam Hussein is not "Saddam Insane"—especially when we look at him from *his* rather than *our* perspective. Jumping to this kind of conclusion can lead to serious miscalculation in global politics.

upon power relationships. In so doing, we look at a more fundamental level of world politics: the individual as political actor within the sociological/political milieu. Of course, we must keep in mind that it is impossible to explain world politics, or anything else for that matter, in terms of just a single variable. Hitler alone did not begin World War II, and Yeltsin did not by himself restructure Russia. But their political personalities were important, perhaps highly so, in those two epochal political events of the twentieth century.

Viewing international politics from a social-psychological perspective provides the analyst with several methods of contributing to the scientific study of world society. Such a perspective can aid in "counteracting and correcting the tendency of analysts (principally systems-level theorists) who reify the state and treat it as a human agent" (Kelman 1965, 586). In addition, when foreign policy behavior is viewed social-psychologically, it is possible to scrutinize in detail the processes that contribute to such behavior. In both cases, the analysis of the social dynamics between individuals and groups provides a fresh perspective for the analysis of international politics and foreign policy (Minix 1982, 10).

Personality

The concept of political personality is like mercury: most difficult to corner. Hence, definitions of political personality abound. For our purposes here, we define one's **political personality** as the sum of all attitudes, opinions, and beliefs that one holds about politics. **Attitudes** can be defined as a relatively enduring way of reacting to a *class* of objects. **Opinions** is similarly defined, but is a reaction only to a specific object, i.e., a *sharpened* attitude. **Beliefs** are the assertion that something exists or does not exist. You may have an attitude concerning the people of the United States, but only an opinion about its president. And if you have never seen the leader in person or on television, you still may believe that he exists, on the basis of other news accounts.

(A word of caution: it is possible to talk of a *political personality* only in the confines of an academic discussion. In other words, it is impossible in real life to distinguish or separate one's political personality from one's complete personality. This would be akin to describing the weather in Cleveland, Ohio, and somehow ignoring the fact that the same weather system was accounting for various weather patterns in the entire Midwest.)

The question is not whether personality is important to the study of world politics. Clearly, personality does matter. We want to examine the extent of its significance in political decision-making. A host of questions spring forth. Do individuals behave differently during routine versus nonroutine, or crisis, periods? How does stress affect a leader's decisions? What effect do perceptions play in shaping a leader's **belief system,** or image of self, nation, and others in the political world? Relatedly, are political decisions usually rational and objective, or are humans rationalizing animals who seek the best spin on their actions? Do people behave differently when acting as individuals than they do when acting within the context of groups? Which unit—person alone or person-in-group—affords the optimal **decision quality**? Which decisional unit tends to make the most extreme decisions? These and other issues in the social psychology of world politics will be explored in this chapter.

political personality The sum of an individual's political beliefs, attitudes, and opinions.

attitudes Predispositions to react favorably or unfavorably toward a class of objects or people.

opinions Relatively stable predispositions to react favorably or unfavorably to particular objects or persons.

beliefs Feeling or convictions that given entities either exist or do not exist.

belief system Sum of beliefs, attitudes, and opinions an individual holds.

decisional quality The *processes* used in coming to a final group decision and the successful implementation of the decision.

Do Clothes Make the Man or Does Man Make the Clothes?

Did you ever wonder if the role or position that a person occupies—the office of president, prime minister, or secretary of state—has greater influence than the individual's personality on political decision-making? Upon assuming office, does a person leave the personality baggage outside the door, only to reclaim it when he or she is no longer in office? Will the office make the person something he or she normally is not?

**psychological predisposi-
tions** Individual perceptions of the world.

cognitions Beliefs about
the world.

This question of the relative importance of psychology (the personality) versus sociology (the social role) is really a conceptual question rather than an empirical one. We know from experience and we illustrate using the phenomenological
paradigm S—O—R (stimulus-organism-response) that environmental factors
(stimuli) are mediated through a person's predispositions. But we also assume
that these predispositions are dependent on one's environment. Therefore, social
and psychological characteristics are not mutually exclusive, but compatible.
Social characteristics can cause psychological characteristics, but cannot substitute for
them. To what extent is the converse true? To what extent do the **psychological
predispositions** (perceptions) and **cognitions** (beliefs) that a leader brings to the
office of power determine how that leader will act on the environment?

Some analysts would answer, "Not at all." Their position is challenged by one
of the preeminent researchers in the field of cognitions and political decision making, Ole Holsti. In the article "Cognitive Process Approaches to Decision-Making:
Foreign Policy Actors Viewed Psychologically" (Holsti, 1976, 11–32), Professor
Holsti questions the assumption that explanations centering on cognitions and
perceptions (i.e., the psychology) of elites are *not* likely to expand our knowledge significantly. In this article, Holsti establishes three *straw* arguments *against*
studying political psychology, only to rebut each one successfully.

Straw Argument One, says Holsti, asserts that foreign policy decisions are
made within complex bureaucratic structures that severely constrain the individual's capacity for uniqueness. Organizational memory, prior policy commitments,
standard operating procedures (SOPs), normal bureaucratic inertia, and conflict
resolution by bargaining all, limit the decision-maker's impact on policy.

To this argument Holsti offers the rebuttal that the focus on bureaucratic politics need not exclude a concern for belief systems. In other words, conflict and
bargaining may result from divergent diagnoses and prescriptions, which in turn,
are derived from different beliefs about the nature of politics, the character of
opponents, and so on. These differences may not be correlated perfectly with
bureaucratic position. Furthermore, bureaucratic politics may be useful in explaining *slippage,* or the difference between what is intended and what actually occurs.
But bureaucratic politics does not necessarily explain the decision itself.

Straw Argument Two goes like this. Foreign policy is a manifestation of domestic institutions, ideologies, and other attributes of the polity. While names and faces
may change, interest and policies do not. This argument assumes a single, strong,
and unified national interest that suppresses individual political beliefs because of
intense socialization pressures for conformity to whatever national norms exist.

Holsti argues that while all of this is true to a degree, personality characteristics and belief systems still emerge as important variables in explaining *how*
decisions are derived. Moreover, this argument assumes a strong correlation of
beliefs within and among the various foreign policy actors. But, as we have discussed previously, there is *no* single national interest within any nation.

Straw Argument Three states that structural and other attributes of the international system shape and constrain policy choices to such an extent that this
broadest level is the logical starting point for most analyses. Those who believe
this would favor extending analysis to national and domestic levels of analysis,
but not to examination of the cognitive processes of even the highest leaders.
According to this reasoning, after one has examined systemic, governmental, soci-
etal, and bureaucratic constraints, most of the variance in decision-making has
been explained. The leaders' cognitions are merely a residual or "leftover" category of unexplainable variance.

This might well be true if it were not for one important element: people. It is *human* political behavior that we are analyzing. International systems, governments, societies, and bureaucracies do not act by themselves; they act because people are behaving politically. Therefore, leaders' cognitions and belief systems are highly valuable in unlocking the secrets of unexplained variation in political acts.

Shapiro and Bonham (1973, 161) acknowledge that studying leaders' predispositions is difficult: we are "short of comparative studies that might reveal the circumstances under which alternative premises, e.g., beliefs of foreign policy decision-makers, are central to the study of decisions, and these probably account for more of the variance than any other single factor."

But regardless of its difficulty, there may be good reason to look at the social-psychological level of analysis when one or more of the following conditions are present:

1. *Non-routine situations* that require more than standard operating procedures (SOPs) and mechanized decisional rules, e.g., the outbreak of war or any crisis situation;
2. *Decisions made at the pinnacle of government* by leaders who are free from organizational and other restraints;
3. *Long-range policy planning;*
4. *Situations that are highly ambiguous* and open to a variety of interpretations (crises again);
5. Circumstances of *information overload,* in which decision-makers are required to use a variety of strategies (arranging and weighing decision options, filtering information, omitting and reducing decisional categories, etc.—crises again);
6. *Unanticipated events* in which initial reactions are likely to reflect *cognitive sets,* i.e., decision-makers' belief systems/personalities (frequently crises, but not necessarily);
7. Circumstances in which complex cognitive tasks associated with decision-making may be interpreted or otherwise significantly affected by various types of *stress* that impinge on top-ranking executives.

Group Dynamics and Decisional Quality

This section is concerned primarily with the *quality* of decisions produced during international crises. In particular, it discusses some of the salient variables that impel small groups to reach more extreme choices than those reached by isolated, individual decision-makers. Since it is impossible to verify objectively quality from decision output, the term is generally reserved for the *processes* contributing to the final decisional outcomes. It is generally assumed that certain procedures lead to increased decisional success, that is, to the meeting of the decision-maker's objectives and to having them adhered to in the future. High-quality decisions, according to Irving Janis and Leon Mann, are characterized by "vigilant information processing," which stems from following a seven-point checklist of "ideal procedures." For example, these procedures include the following:

1. thoroughly canvassing a wide range of alternatives;
2. surveying all objectives to be fulfilled and the values implicated by choice;
3. weighing the costs and benefits of each alternative;
4. intensively searching for new, relevant information;

5. correctly assimilating this new information—even if it opposes initially pre-ferred choices;

6. reexamining the positive and negative consequences of all known alternatives; and

7. making detailed provisions for implementation of the chosen course of action, with contingency plans available should known risks materialize. (Janis and Mann 1977, 11)

These procedures—*if followed*—tend to decrease the "postdecisional regret" that frequently accompanies important or stressful decisions. If these criteria are sidestepped, defective information processing can arise, in such forms as

Cloak, Dagger, and Couch

One of the most esoteric, and at the same time most fascinating, areas of intelligence is the attempt to understand individual leaders and what motivates them—and thus to predict, however gingerly, what they might do in given situations.

In the late 1960s the CIA established the Center for the Analysis of Personality and Political Behavior, later renamed the Political Psychology Center, but generally known as the Psychology Shop (or PsyShop). Its director, Jerrold Post, assembled psychiatrists, psychologists, political scientists, historians, and anthropologists to compile interdisciplinary studies of world leaders. The portraits produced by the PsyShop were often entertaining, laced with interesting, gossipy tidbits, but were sometimes woefully inaccurate. Even Post admits that long-distance psychological analysis is extremely dicey, particularly when the analyst has virtually no information about the subject's formative childhood and adolescence. In the late 1980s the PsyShop fell victim to budget cuts and bureaucratic infighting. Ceasing to function as an independent center, it now operates with a greatly reduced staff under the aegis of another CIA unit. Jerrold Post has left the CIA to become a professor at George Washington University.

Because of such problems, in recent years analysts have turned to the quantitative study of a leader's language, or psycholinguistics. In addition to reflecting a current widespread preference in the social and behavior sciences for numbers rather than intuition, psycholinguists are far more con-

GLOBAL PERSPECTIVES

cerned about a subject's current motives than about the psychodynamics of his or her personality. Psycholinguists pore over recent speeches and interviews, using a coding manual to "score" the subject's rhetoric in terms of power, achievement, and affiliation. They maintain that careful quantification provides insight into such crucial issues as a leader's predisposition to violence in a certain situation; in this fashion, psycholinguists claim, they can provide at least conditional (if/then) predictions.

The value of psychological profiling is still hotly debated. While leaders such as presidents and cabinet secretaries seem to rely upon such profiles, many intelligence professionals distrust psychological profiles as "squishy" in comparison to satellite imagery or other "hard" information. These skeptics cite limited information, cultural misperceptions, and a tendency for Americans to personalize policy rather than analyze power and other motivations (Omestad 1994, 105–22).

The truth is a mixture of the two positions. Certainly national leaders are important; Iraq without Saddam Hussein might be a very different nation. Nonetheless, as we have stressed throughout this text, a wide range of factors drive national policy: power, perception and misperception, and ideology, to name just a few. While understanding a nation's history and national goals may be vital, it is equally critical to understand the psyche of a leader. Policy-making that attempts to take into account the other side's motives and possible reactions will of necessity be "squishy," but policy-making that fails to do this will generally be wrong.

defensive avoidance (avoidance of making the decision), **bolstering** (magnifying the attractiveness of the chosen alternative), or **hypervigilance** (panic)—Janis and Mann 1977, 6, 82). Though it is possible to produce successful outcomes from low-quality decision-making procedures, maladaptive coping mechanisms like those cited are likely to surface.

Decisional extremization, on the other hand, is the phenomenon whereby small groups adopt choices that are more risky or more cautious than the individual preferences contained within the group. In focusing on decisional quality, the analyst is forced to look closely at both intrapsychic and interpsychic, or social, factors that may impinge on the policy-making process. Since a **crisis** is a stressful condition, it is likely that reactive social processes and coping reactions will be related to either the process or the form of the final outcome. The amounts and types of effects crisis situations have on individual decision-making processes and group deliberations is the focus of this section.

The social interaction and intellectual interchange between the individuals aggregated in a nation's foreign policy apparatus is highly significant, because these individuals—arranged in **small groups**—frequently thrash out, argue, and "politick" matters of the highest concern during a foreign policy crisis. And it is quite likely that the final group decision—regardless of its degree of risk—will be quite different from what "a simple aggregation of individual preferences and abilities might otherwise suggest" (George et al. 1975, 40). It is such a possibility that compels this investigation of small-group versus individual foreign policy decision-making behavior.

The purpose of this section is to shed light upon the decisional polarization or extremization phenomenon as it relates to small-group crisis decision-making in the foreign policy-making process of a nation. This is no small task, and not all pertinent ground can be covered. Nonetheless, we believe that the factors and variables discussed here contribute significantly to the added amount of risk or caution (decisional extremization) a small group, as opposed to an isolated decision-maker, is willing to adopt during a crisis.

It is important to note that the findings in this chapter seem to transcend various political cultures. Therefore, it is anticipated that this synthesis of findings from psychology, sociology, social psychology, and political science will illuminate potential sources of small-group decisional polarization in the crisis decision-making of any nation.

It is not size of the group alone that we will investigate. In addition to the reduced size of the decisional unit, the membership composition and role structure of the group are likely to influence the extremity, and, in general, the "quality," of a decision made in a period of crisis-induced stress. As we begin this discussion, remember that we are focusing upon *international crisis* decision-making. We will examine whether the fact that such decisions are made in the context of unnatural risk to the nation involved will cause the nation's leadership to "shrink" in number, so that only those closest to and most trusted by the top echelon participate. We will demonstrate that it is within such a small-group context that the potential social-psychological pathologies associated with group polarization are to be found. To these potential pathologies we now turn.

Size of Decision-Making Group

Even during normal or routine periods of foreign policy decision-making, the size of the decisional unit is generally restricted to a small coterie of individuals in the

defensive avoidance Avoidance or veering away from making a decision.

bolstering Shoring up the attractiveness of a decision once it is made.

hypervigilence Panic behavior.

decisional extremism The tendency of small decisional groups to reach more extreme decisions (either riskier or more cautious) than would be predicted from the sum of individual preferences.

crisis An international situation characterized by high threat to system stability, short decision time, and surprise to the foreign policy makers of a nation.

small groups Units ranging usually in size from three to twenty members who make decisions on behalf of the nation, bureaucracy, etc.

foreign policy apparatus. For example, the "routine" decision by the Carter administration to cancel funding for the full-scale production of the B-1 bomber included no more than a handful of top government officials at any given time: the president, the vice-president, the secretary of state, the secretary of defense, National Security Advisor Brzezinski, and the President's top-echelon subordinates. During crises, however, the number of involved personnel frequently becomes even more restrictive. Research indicates that the size of the decision unit is generally between two and seven members (Snyder and Paige 1958, 362).

In *International Crises: Insights from Behavioral Research,* edited by Charles Hermann (1972), the nature of a nation's foreign policy machinery is examined. One contributor to this volume, James Robinson, contends that "a crisis tends to bring a problem or an issue to the top of an organization's hierarchy, it permits bypassing much of the bureaucratic lethargy that often characterizes foreign offices. A crisis decision will be taken by officials near the top and, given the demands of time, they can afford to bypass many customary procedures in making decisions" (Robinson 1972, 34).

Glenn Paige reinforces Robinson's remarks by investigating two substantive examples: the Korean War and the Cuban Missile Crisis (Paige 1972, 45–56). In the former case, the officials involved in the decision numbered fourteen; in the latter, they numbered about sixteen. Moreover, Paige, among others, notes that these crisis groups are generally ad hoc in nature—committees assembled because of talent and trust on the part of the leader. For example, the National Security Council, the conventional United States national security machinery devised to handle crisis situations, was bypassed in the Cuban Missile Crisis in favor of a coterie of individuals both within and outside of the government who were respected for their expertise on a particular subject, or for their general abilities in dealing with foreign policy matters. These participants also were held in close regard by the chief executive. Former Secretary of State Dean Acheson quickly comes to mind in the case of the Cuban Missile crisis. No doubt, Acheson was chosen because of his former positions in government and his link to Democratic presidents, as well as his knowledge of foreign affairs.

In his perceptive analysis of crisis-handling by State Department officials, Howard Lenter, buttresses this "consolidation of decision-making" thesis (Lenter 1972, 130–31). His figures show that State Department officials, when asked to respond to the two statements in table 5.1, were found to believe overwhelmingly that (a) crisis precipitates concern at a higher level, and (b) crisis decision-making takes place at a higher level than is customary.

Lenter's data reveal that State Department officials who believe that crises "always" precipitate concern at a higher level (68.4%) are more assured of this belief than those who replied that this was "often" the case (27.8%). If these two categories are combined and compared with the "sometimes" and "never" classifications (3.8% and 0% respectively), then it can be concluded that an overwhelming majority (96%) of those State Department officials queried feel that crises do indeed create concern at higher levels than is normal for "routine" or customary decision-making in the Department of State.

The same data are supportive of the "reduced crisis decision-making set" thesis. Responding to the second statement—"a crisis precipitates decision-making at a higher level than normal"—51 percent recalled that crises "always" generate decision-making at higher levels, while 47 percent stated that this was "often" the case. Only one individual (1.3%) felt that this phenomenon occurs "sometimes."

Table 5.1

Frequency of Involvement of High-Level Officers in Crises

	No Response*	Always	Often	Sometimes	Never
a) A CRISIS PRECIPITATES CONCERN AT A HIGHER LEVEL THAN NORMAL	0 —	54 (68.4%)	22 (27.8%)	3 (3.8%)	0 —
b) A CRISIS PRECIPITATES DECISION-MAKING AT A HIGHER LEVEL THAN NORMAL	1 —	40 (51.3%)	37 (47.4%)	1 (1.3%)	0 —

*Excluded in calculating percentages.
Source: Howard Lenter, "The Concept of Crisis as Viewed by the United States Department of State," 112–135, in *International Crises: Insights from Behavioral Research,* edited by Charles Hermann (New York: Free Press, 1972).

No individuals felt that crises "never" rise in the bureaucratic decision-making hierarchy.

In his own simulation research, Charles Hermann substantiates the claim that crisis decision-making is handled by a rather small group of participants. For example, he found that (1) as time decreases, the number of participants in a decision tends to decrease, and that (2) the larger the nation is, the fewer decision-makers are engaged in all situations (Hermann 1972, 192).

Therefore, it is taken as a given that during crises, the decision-making unit will be considerably smaller in size than it is during the making of "normal" or "routine" foreign policy decisions. And this very smallness may introduce other factors that, if present, affect the internal group dynamics of the deliberation process, as well as the quality of the decision being rendered. Membership composition and role structure are two of the salient variables most scholars agree will affect internal structure and interaction patterns in committees (George 1972, 783).

Group Composition and Role Structure

Robert Bales, a prominent scholar of small-group interaction processes, states that committees tend to form "informal power prestige offerings" from the outset (1950). That is, individual members engage in a perceptual evaluation of the membership's early contributions and then form preliminary personal judgments of everyone's relative "worth" to the committee. From this analysis, members form expectations regarding one another's potential committee contribution; moreover, opportunities to participate in the discussions are differentially allocated by the members to each other (George et al. 1975, 41). This evaluation of committee members by one another leads to a status ranking with respect to various members' contributions to discussion. And this perceptual ranking establishes the informal power and influence structure in a group, which of course affects the **group dynamics.** For example, high contributors are more powerful and influential than low contributors. Moreover, "high participators interrupt others, but are

group dynamics The interpersonal working relationships that transpire within a small decisional unit.

Former United States President Jimmy Carter arrives in Haiti to begin his diplomatic mission; behind him are General Colin Powell, former U.S. chairman of the Joint Chiefs of Staff, and Senator Sam Nunn, D-Ga., chairman of the Senate Armed Services Committee. Their success illustrates how individuals and individual personalities can influence international politics.

not interrupted; they tend to get agreed with more than others; and they have more control over the interaction process than low participators" (George et al. 1975, 41).

Bales's model offers help in understanding a small group or committee's role structure and interaction. But small-group decision-making has other attributes, as well. For example, smaller groups tend to have simpler role structures, which reflect less differentiation of tasks, less division of labor and specialization, and less formalized modes of procedure than are found in larger, more complex organizations (George et al. 1975, 42). One of the consequences of this simplified role structure is conformity to group norms, practices, and procedures, resulting in increased group cohesion.

Conformity: Group Pressures on the Individual

cohesion The bonding of individuals in a small group setting generally with the feeling that the group is superior to other groups.

Cohesion among group members refers to "the members' positive valuation of the group and their motivation to continue to belong to it" (George et al. 1975, 41). According to psychologist Irving Janis, cohesion "looms very large and exerts considerable influence on [an individual's] choice when [that person] is participating in a group decision—namely, the social approval or disapproval [the individual] anticipates receiving from the leader or from fellow members" (Janis 1972, 133).

There are two sides to this issue of group cohesion, as Janis intimates. As an asset, cohesion reflects group solidarity, mutual good will, and a high feeling of task participation. Moreover, highly cohesive groups, according to Kurt Lewin and his followers, provide members "with a source of security, with solace and support against anxiety or distress, and help them to maintain self-esteem" (George et al. 1975, 44).

But as a liability, "highly cohesive groups are not necessarily high performance groups" (George et al. 1975, 44). This seems particularly true with respect to the phenomena under investigation: foreign policy crises. During a crisis, the

Jimmy Carter's Haiti Mission

GLOBAL PERSPECTIVES

Reviews of the press show on an almost daily basis that the foreign policy decision-making process in even the most broadly defined crisis situations involves just a small group of advisors to a nation's leader. Such was the case with the U.S. invasion of the island nation of Haiti. For three years, American policy had been directed at restoring power to the democratically elected president of Haiti, Jean-Bertrand Aristide, who had been ousted in a coup led by Lieutenant General Raoul Cedras.

In an address to the American people, President Clinton boldly told the Haitian ruling junta, "Your time is up!" However, immediately after the televised address, Mr. Clinton summoned his *closest* advisors to the Oval Office for one last-ditch effort to avoid bloodshed. Present were National Security Advisor Anthony Lake, Vice President Al Gore, and Leon E. Panetta, White House Chief of Staff. President Clinton then decided, upon the recommenda-tion of this small group of advisors, to send one last diplomatic mission, which would be headed by former U.S. president Jimmy Carter. Carter would be accompanied by retired U.S. General Colin Powell, and U.S. Senator Sam Nunn (*New York Times,* September 19, 1994). Thus, commissioned by a small decision-making unit within the White House, a still smaller group traveled to Haiti to negotiate the reinstatement of President Aristide.

One can only speculate as to the group dynamics involved in either of the two high-level small groups assembled to deal with this international crisis. But it is abundantly clear from the elite U.S. press reports that the factors of short decisional time (as perceived by the decision-makers), high stress, and reduced size of the unit played important parts in this decision to (1) attempt yet another diplomatic maneuver in spite of previous failed attempts, and (2) reinstate the ousted president of Haiti.

group may realize the fundamental threat to national values, goals, and lives, and subsequently reduce in-group conflicts in favor of converging upon a particular course of action. In other words, in a crisis situation, it is believed better to have a quick consensus on a national policy than to have protracted debate, minority reports, and so on, which waste valuable time and energies. According to George and his colleagues,

> the policy consensus arrived at under these conditions may be more than sim-ply the convergence of individual opinions on a particular issue; rather it may also express fundamental individual needs and group values that transcend nor-mal canons of objectivity, and it may reflect a tacit agreement within the group to agree unquestioningly upon whatever course of action causes least interper-sonal strife (George et al. 1975, 44).

For example, Chester Cooper, in *The Lost Crusade,* describes part of the Viet-nam policy-making process in the Johnson administration:

> The NSC meetings I attended had a fairly standard format: The President, in due course, would announce his decision and then poll everyone in the room—Council members, their assistants, and members of the White House and NSC Staffs. "Mr. Secretary, do you agree with the decision?" "Yes, Mr. President." "Mr. X, do you agree?" "I agree, Mr. President." During the process I would frequently fall into a Walter Mitty-like fantasy: When my turn came I would rise to my feet slowly, look around the room and then directly at the President, and say very

quietly and emphatically, "Mr. President, gentlemen, I most definitely do not agree." But I was removed from my trance when I heard the President's voice saying, "Mr. Cooper, do you agree?" And out came a "Yes, Mr. President, I agree" (Cooper 1972, 273–74).

conformity The propensity of a small decisional group to gel around certain norms of operation. Conformity is used by the group to repel outsiders who disagree with the group's norms and values.

By Cooper's own account, the pressure leading to **conformity** to the administration's Vietnam policy was immense. In order to reduce cognitive dissonance, dissenters quietly conformed. When dissent did surface, other group members attempted to force the dissident to conform by making him the center of attention, invoking collegial "peer pressure." If these efforts failed, the dissident, as George and his colleagues state, "may be isolated by the group, being placed in the distressing position of having either to maintain his unpopular stand without support, or to withdraw into silence and inactivity. In extreme cases the deviant member may be rejected altogether by the group" (George 1975, 45).

This was apparently the case when George Ball began to question administration policy on Vietnam. President Johnson at first tolerated Ball's deviance by jocularly greeting him thus: "Here comes Mr. Stop-the-bombing." At that point, Ball was useful to Johnson, because he could be counted on to plot an alternate, though highly unfavorable, course in Vietnam strategy, thereby allowing the administration to deflect the criticism that all sides of the war issue were not being given just attention. But as the war dragged on, Ball's usefulness had run its course. In-house dissent began to grow, and with it, the need to close ranks with like-minded advisors. This persuaded the President that Ball (and others, like Robert McNamara, who shared his views) should leave. As Halberstam relates, McNamara's departure to join the World Bank was indicative of the group-induced pressures for conformity to the administration's bombing policy in Vietnam (Halberstam 1972, 604–5).

norms The standards or values by which a small decisional group operates.

The tendency to conform to group **norms** has been confirmed repeatedly, both in scientifically controlled laboratory experiments and in everyday interpersonal relations (Sherif 1936). Norms are rules of behavior, defined corridors for a group member's acceptable conduct. Such norms are generally derived from the group itself and the goal(s) that the group has selected. Hare states that

> when the norms refer to the expectations for a single individual they constitute the individual's role. The norms are then, in effect, the expectations for the role of an undifferentiated group member. Each person has within him a set of norms and goals which are a composite of his own idiosyncratic ideals, the expectations of other groups of which he is also a member. (Hare 1976, 19)

When either the individual or the group feels that a member has transgressed the normal codes of behavioral conduct, there are but four options for the person: (1) change the group norms, (2) remain a deviant, (3) leave the group, or (4) conform. Conformity is the likely behavior in small, elite foreign policy-making bodies because of the cohesiveness of the group to begin with, as well as the intrapsychic pressure to remain in such a powerful, prestigious group.

Accompanying the pressures of group cohesion is the danger that the chief executive will become isolated by myopic advice. Such pressures led Robert Kennedy to recall in his memoirs on the Cuban missile crisis that he "had frequently observed efforts being made to exclude certain individuals from participating in a meeting with the President because they held a different point of view"

(Kennedy 1969, 117). And according to Townsend Hoopes, Vice President Humphrey's attempt to stop the bombing of North Vietnam in February 1965 was received by the White House "with particular coldness, and he was banished from the inner councils for some months thereafter, until he decided to 'get back on the team'" (1969, 31). Hoopes remarks,

> It was my impression that the President's sense of incongruity reflected the extent to which he had become the victim of (1) Rostow's "selective briefing"— the time honored techniques of underlining, within a mass of material, those particular elements that one wishes to draw to the special attention of a busy chief—and (2) the climate of cozy implicit agreement on fundamentals which had no longer characterized discussions within the inner circle on Vietnam, wherever was never heard a disparaging word. (Hoopes 1969, 218)

Groupthink: Stress-Induced Cohesion

Social psychologist Irving Janis begins his seminal book *The Victims of Groupthink* by questioning Arthur Schlesinger, Jr.'s account of the Bay of Pigs incident. "How," Janis wonders, "could bright, shrewd men like John F. Kennedy and his advisors be taken in by the CIA's stupid, patchwork plan?" (1972, iii) Janis's research led him to note that this foreign policy "fiasco" (and others) were characterized by group decision-making processes that inhibited the Kennedy team from debating the issues. Specifically, Janis noted a high degree of concurrence-seeking behavior, which resulted in a feeling of invincibility among group members. **Groupthink** is the concept employed by Janis to refer to a deterioration in the quality of group decision-making processes.

groupthink The inclination of decisional groups to promote consensus, conformity, and insularity, resulting in a lack of vigilant information-processing, moral judgment, and reality testing.

Groupthink, according to Janis, is a quick and easy way to refer to a mode of thinking that people engage in when they are deeply involved in a cohesive in-group, "when the members' strivings for unanimity override their motivation to realistically appraise alternative courses of action . . . Groupthink refers to a deterioration of mental efficiency, reality testing, and moral judgment that results from in-group pressures."

The so-called pathology of the groupthink phenomenon stems from neither the individual nor the organizational setting. Rather, the pathology arises from the cohesiveness often found in small foreign policy decision-making groups. As Janis states, "the cohesion of small in-groups engenders a concurrence-seeking tendency, which fosters excessive optimism, lack of vigilance, and sloganistic thinking about the weaknesses and immorality of out-groups." These symptoms are conducive to different forms of behavior, such as risk taking, being aggressive, stereotyping adversaries, and poor information processing (Janis 1972, 40).

Janis finds evidence of the groupthink effect in many recent U.S. foreign policy decisions. His examples are drawn from the response to the attack on Pearl Harbor, the entry of the U.S. into the Korean War, the Bay of Pigs fiasco, and the escalation of U.S. bombing attacks on North Vietnam. Other decisions can also be culled for potential pathologies regarding small-group decision-making.

The Bay of Pigs episode, which Janis labels "a perfect failure," is characteristic of the deficiency in reality testing that accompanies high-level policy-making within such closed groups. The illusion of invulnerability was marked in the "New Frontiersmen." As Robert Kennedy later related to a colleague in the Justice Department, on the day that the CIA launched its plan against Cuba,

It seemed that, with John Kennedy leading us and with all the talent he had assembled, nothing could stop us. We believed that if we faced up to the nation's problems and applied bold, new ideas and hard work, we would overcome whatever challenged us (Guthman 1971, 88).

According to Arthur Schlesinger, Jr., "the dominant mood in the White House was buoyant optimism. It was centered on the 'promise of hope' held out by the President. *Euphoria reigned; we though for a moment that the world was plastic and the future unlimited*" (italics added—Schlesinger 1965, 258–59). However, the spirit of Camelot led the planners of the Kennedy administration to misperceive the strength and support of Castro as an adversary. They thought him weak and stupid, a hysterical leader of a Third World nation who would do nothing to neutralize the Cuban underground (Schlesinger 1965, 293).

A shared illusion of unanimity is also symptomatic of the stress-induced cohesion of group think. Sorenson relates that no strong voice of opposition was raised in any of the key meetings, and no realistic alternatives were presented. And Schlesinger adds that

> the massed and capricious authority of his senior officials in the realm of foreign policy and defense was unanimous for going ahead. Had one advisor opposed the venture, I believe that Kennedy would have canceled it. No one spoke against it. (Schlesinger 1965, 258–59).

In addition to the illusions of invulnerability and unanimity, groupthink also can prohibit dissenters of policy from making their feelings known. Whether this censorship is self-imposed or performed by others, it may prevent a just hearing of an important perspective on a matter of policy.

According to Janis, Schlesinger was not hesitant about showing his discontent over policy, but he did so only via memoranda. In top-level White House meetings, Schlesinger was mute. As Schlesinger himself recalls,

> In the months after the Bay of Pigs I bitterly reproached myself for having kept so silent during those crucial decisions in the Cabinet Room though my feelings of guilt were tempered by the knowledge that a course of objection would have accomplished little save to gain me a name as a nuisance. I can only explain my failure to do more than raise a few timid questions by reporting that one's impulse to blow the whistle on this nonsense was simply undone by the circumstances of the discussion. (1965, 255).

This concurrence-seeking behavior among group members—in this case, foreign policy decision-making groups—is fostered by group-induced cohesion. Political decision-making is often stressful, but it is particularly so in foreign policy areas, where the demand for a quick and often forceful national option brings undue pressures upon the executive and the lieutenants. Such extremely stressful conditions as international crises pull the leadership together in order to permit a quick resolution to the crisis and to return operations to a less stressful, "normal," or "routine" state. But to Janis, this cohesion induced by **stress** can be pathological—one more element driving members into groupthink.

As George and his colleagues point out, the groupthink literature developed by Irving Janis is reminiscent of Leon Festinger's theory of informal social communication, which Stanley Schachter later used in his studies of conformity pres-

stress The anxiety an individual experiences in a situation he or she perceives as posing a severe threat, either to the individual or to one or more values.

sures. Schachter stresses that when there is no empirical referent for an issue, the sought-after referent then becomes the opinions of those around you. Thus, when individuals are confused or perplexed, they look to other group members in order to establish the validity of their own opinions. (Festinger et al. 1956)

As Janis admits, just the fact that a foreign policy decision turns out to be a fiasco does not automatically mean that it was the result of groupthink or defective decision-making. Conversely, not every defective decision arising from groupthink will produce a fiasco. It is indeed possible to make successful decisions under poor decision-making conditions. But in general, the way foreign policy decisions are rendered can, and will, affect the tone and the implementation of the nation's policy. Decisions produced without conscious attention to excessive group cohesiveness, the channeling of information toward or away from a chief executive, and the membership composition and role structure of the group usually do not permit the proper conditions for a rational consideration of the crisis at hand. While complete rationality in political decision-making is unobtainable, improving the decision-making process can enhance the probabilities for successful implementation and decrease postdecisional regret.

Are Groups More Extreme?

Conventional wisdom dictates that small groups ameliorate the extreme positions of their members and hence produce less "risky" decisions than do individuals. Individuals, it is believed, act impulsively and without external restraint in their decisions; thus, it is assumed that individuals are more extreme in their decisional behavior. But to the factors discussed so far—group size, membership composition, role structure, and conformity—we need to add another potential pathology: **group extremization.** As it turns out, although groups may not be more apt to take risks than isolated individual decision-makers, they are, on average, more *extreme* (either riskier or more cautious) in their decisions than private decision-makers. A group will tend to move away from the center, in either direction.

A corollary to this rule is the finding that not only are groups more extreme, but they are polarized in the same direction as the majority of individual predispositions. Group dynamics appear to intensify or magnify predominant group values. This is referred to as the **group polarization** phenomenon.

While there are a plethora of potential explanatory variables, two hypotheses stand out. First is the *interpersonal comparison hypothesis,* which stresses the social characteristics of the group. It assumes that people tend to perceive and present themselves favorably in relation to others. When the group discusses an issue, positions are revealed; in an attempt to maintain desirable self-perception, a person may shift his or her position after learning that others have the same proclivities, only more strongly. Essentially, group discussion "releases" the individual to intensify a personal position by shifting to what he or she perceives as the emerging group norm. According to the interpersonal comparison hypothesis, relevant arguments have little to do with moving the group. It is simply desirable to move in the direction of the perceived majority.

The second hypothesis, *informational influence,* suggests that during opening discussions, arguments are advanced that predominately favor the initially preferred alternative. Individuals learn the preferences of the majority and adopt it.

The amount of overlap between the interpersonal comparison and the informational influence hypothesis is significant. The first stresses social characteristics;

group extremization The propensity of a group to be even more extreme—either to risk or to caution—in their decision compared to the average of individual preferences of the group's members.

group polarization The group serves as a magnifier of predominant or existing individual values that exist in the group as a unit of decision.

the second stresses rational capacities. Both hypotheses, however, stress the importance of group norms as a strong catalyst for group polarization.

In principle, then, the composition of the foreign policy elite is presumably correlated with the level of response (bellicose or diplomatic) issued by a nation. Furthermore, the "who" represents not only the level-of-analysis, individual or small group, but also the *type* of individual or small group.

Individual versus Group: The Quality of Decision

Small groups are not always undesirable as decision-makers. The question of which unit of analysis—individual or small group—performs better during crisis situations depends upon many factors in addition to those outlined in this chapter. Social-psychological research indicates that each unit has particular assets and liabilities with respect to task accomplishment, data recall, and the quantity of options discussed. Some individuals are positively stimulated in the presence of others, some are negatively influenced, and still others remain unaffected. The group appears to be superior to the individual in the accomplishment of manual as compared to intellectual tasks. Groups also have a tendency to report fewer (but more accurate) facts than individuals, because of a group's willingness to merge with perceived group norms. Moreover, groups generally will recall more information than individuals, presumably, says Hare, "because of their greater capacity to store information" (1976, 43–44).

It is a matter for caution, though, that group processes do affect the decisional outcomes of a group. Janis reinforces this point by saying that

> a group whose members have properly defined roles, with traditional and standard operating procedures that facilitate critical inquiry, is probably capable of making better decisions than any individual in the group who works on the problem alone. And yet, the advantages of having decisions made by groups are often lost because of psychological pressures that arise when the members work closely together, share the same values, and above all face a crisis situation in which everybody is subjected to stresses that generate a strong need for affiliation. (Janis and Mann 1977, 25)

Alexander George and his colleagues stress that group interaction processes "include efforts to deal with the emotional needs and stress that can be aroused by the value complexity and uncertainty which . . . are often associated with foreign policy decision-making" (George et al 1975, 45)

We have already discussed the importance to group decision-making of group norms. Norms establish behavioral parameters for individuals acting both alone and in the context of social groups. Particularly in the latter case, norms influence such factors as cohesion, conformity, membership, composition, and task accomplishment. If the potential advantages of small-group decision-making are to be secured and decision-making pathologies based on norms are to be avoided, then it is necessary that (1) a differentiated role structure develop within the group so as to permit cogent contributions from all members, and (2) the processes of reaction, questioning, and suggestion-making within the group not be inhibited.

The quality of a decision depends, as does the functioning of the decision unit, on several organizationally related factors. If a small group is charged with responding to a crisis event, then norm-promoted factors such as size and cohesion play a crucial role in shaping the decision outcome. If, on the other hand, an individual in isolation must respond to the same crisis, factors such as belief systems, psychological tensions, and stress can play a large role in mapping a response. Of course, such factors are not restricted to only one particular unit of analysis. Both norms and stress, for instance, permeate all behavioral responses, both individual ones and those within the dynamic context of the small group. But by treating the attributes of the decisional unit as independent variables along with these other social-psychological factors, it is then possible to discover how the *quality* of the decisions reached may differ (see figure 5.1).

As we have shown, personality is *at times* a highly significant factor in the conduct of international affairs. Who is to say that World War II would not have occurred without Adolph Hitler, or that the Persian Gulf War of 1991 would not have occurred without Saddam Hussein? While studies of personality factors are important, they are by no means the sole means of unraveling the mystery of international politics.

Figure 5.1
Factors Influencing Decisional Quality
Stress on Decisional Units

Stress on Decisional Units	Decisional Quality and Group Norms				
	Small Group Dynamics →	(Poor) Information Processing →	Choice-Shift →	Behavioral Symptoms →	Foreign Policy Failures
I Reduced Attention Span Task & Information Overload Task & Role Conflicts *II Cognitive Rigidity* →					
Diminished Ability to Cope with Complexity	Perceptual Evaluation Begins	Cohesion/Solidarity Build Concurrence-	Decisional Extremization/ Polarization (Norm Enhanced)	Increased Risk-Taking	Post-decisional Regret
Rise of Dominant Percept	Less Differentiation of Tasks	Increases Poor Information		Aggression	Poor-Quality Decisions
Character Regression *III Attenuated Time Perspective*	Size Diminishes— Deviants Excluded	Processing Builds Sloganistic Thinking		Passivity Overly Cautious Behavior	
Premature Closure– Reduced Cue Awareness Simplified Spatial & Temporal Focus Bolstering/Value Complexity Simple Learning Enhanced/ Complex Learning Inhibited	Group Norms Surface	Excessive Optimism Lack of Vigilance Defensive Avoidance/ Hypervigilance "Groupthink Syndrome"			

Source: Minix 1982

State action is the action taken by those acting in the name of the state. In this chapter, we have investigated not only the *idiosyncratic,* or individual personal variables that can affect the behavior of a leader in taking state action, but also the interplay between individuals in a small-group setting—the environment in which most foreign policy decisions are made.

Summary

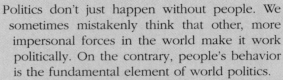

Politics don't just happen without people. We sometimes mistakenly think that other, more impersonal forces in the world make it work politically. On the contrary, people's behavior is the fundamental element of world politics.

Each human being has a unique personality. Moreover, each individual's personality is multifaceted, revealing itself differently in different settings, such as when working alone versus when working in a group setting. These variations in human behavior affect global decisions, just as they do smaller ones.

In this chapter, we have examined the interplay between the psychological and the sociological factors affecting a nation's foreign policy. This hybridization of the three disciplines of political science, psychology, and sociology produces a new subfield known as political social psychology.

Political social psychology examines group dynamics and the decisional quality of a nation's foreign policy decisions. Such a perspective analyzes such things as how decisions are made, by whom they are made, and the size and composition of the decisional unit, as well as group conformity, cohesion, and role structure.

We also have investigated the influence of stress upon national decision-makers: the degree to which stress contributes to group cohesion and possibly to groupthink, a highly dangerous syndrome yielding poor-quality decisions. Further, we have examined the degree to which groups are more extreme than individuals acting alone in terms of decision-making. The evidence suggests that groups make riskier or more cautious decisions than would individuals acting in isolation during crises.

Key Terms

Idiosyncratic

Social psychology

Political personality

Attitudes

Opinions

Beliefs

Belief system

Decisional quality

Psychological predispositions

Cognitions

Defensive avoidance

Bolstering

Hypervigilance

Decisional extremization

Crisis

Small groups

Group dynamics
Cohesion
Conformity
Norms

Groupthink
Stress
Group extremization
Group polarization

Thought Questions:

1. Which is more important, the psychological or the sociological set of variables upon policy outcomes?
2. How do group dynamics affect decisional quality?
3. What is decisional extremization?
4. What is groupthink?

References

Bales, R. *Interaction Process Analysis*. Reading: Addison-Wesley, 1950.

Bennett, S. "Modes of Resolution of a Belief Dilemma in the Ideology of the John Birch Society," *Journal of Conflict Resolution* 6 (1962), 244–54.

Cooper, C. *The Lost Crusade*. Greenwich: Fawcett, 1972.

Festinger, Leon, Henry W. Riechen, and Stanley Schachter. *When Prophecy Fails*. Minneapolis: University of Minnesota Press, 1956.

George, A. "The Case for Multiple Advocacy in Making Foreign Policy." *American Political Science Review* 66 (1972), 751–85.

George, Alexander, David K. Hall, Margaret G. Hermann, Charles F. Hermann, Robert Keohane, and Richard Smoke. *Appendices*. Commission on the Organization of the Government for the Conduct of Foreign Policy. Washington: GPO, 1975.

Guthman, Harold. *We Band of Brothers*. New York: Harper and Row, 1971.

Halberstam, D. *The Best and the Brightest*. Greenwich: Fawcett, 1972.

Hare, A. *Handbook of Small Group Research*. New York: Free Press, 1976.

Hermann, C., ed. *International Crises: Insights from Behavioral Research*. New York: Free Press, 1972.

Holsti, O. "The Belief System and National Images: A Case Study." *Journal of Conflict Resolution* 6, (1962), 244–52.

———. "Cognitive Process Approaches to Decision-Making: Foreign Policy Actors Viewed Psychologically." *American Behavioral Scientist* 20/1, 1976, 11–32.

Hoopes, T. *Limits of Intervention*. New York: David McKay, 1969.

Janis, I. *Victims of Groupthink*. New York: Houghton Mifflin, 1972.

Janis, I., and L. Mann. *Decision-Making*. New York: Free Press, 1977.

Kelman, H. *International Behavior*. New York: Holt, Rinehart, 1965.

Kennedy, R. F. *Thirteen Days*. New York: Norton, 1969.

Lenter, Howard, "The Concept of Crisis as Viewed by The United States Department of State," in Charles F. Hermann, *op cit*.

Lewin, Kurt. *Field Theory in Social Science*. New York: Harper, 1948.

Minix, Dean A. *Small Groups and Foreign Policy Decision-Making*. Washington, D. C.: 1982.

Omestad, Thomas, "Psychology and the CIA: Leaders on the Couch." *Foreign Policy* (Summer 1994), 105–122.

Paige, Glenn D. "Comparative Case Analysis of Crisis Decisions: Korea and Cuba," in Charles Hermann, *op cit.,* 4–55.

Robinson, James A. "Crisis: An Appraisal of Concepts and Theories," in Charles A. Hermann, *op. cit.,* 20–38.

Schachter, S. *The Psychology of Affiliation*. Stanford, Calif.: University of Stanford Press, 1959.

Schlesinger, A. *A Thousand Days*. Boston: Houghton Mifflin, 1965.

Shapiro, M., and G. Bonham. "Cognitive Processes and Foreign Policy Decisions." *International Studies Quarterly* 17 (1973), 147–74.

Sherif, M. *The Psychology of Social Norms*. New Yorker: Harper, 1936.

Snyder, Richard G., H. W. Bruck, and Burton Sapin. *Foreign Policy Decision-Making*. New York: Free Press, 1963.

Snyder, Richard C., and Glenn D. Paige. "The United States' Decision to Resist Aggression in Korea." *Administrative Science Quarterly*. Vol. 3, 34–78.

Sorenson, T. *Kennedy*. New York: Bantam, 1966.

Chapter 6

Ideas That Make the World Go 'Round

Introduction

ideology A finely honed belief system of how the world works or should work.

fascism A virulent form of ethnic nationalism most commonly associated with Mussolini's Italian regime of the same name during World War II.

Nazism A virulent form of ethnic nationalism commonly associated with the regime of Adolf Hitler's Germany during World War II.

liberal democracy The set of Jeffersonian political principles that allows for limited government, private property, majority rule, and minority rights.

capitalism Economic system based upon the precepts of private ownership of real property, profit maximization, and limited central government.

Maoism The Chinese variant of Marxism-Leninism that stipulates that the revolution is permanent, not subject to replacement in the dialectic process. Named after the first Chinese Communist leader Mao Tse-tung.

I deas matter, and so do ideologies. We will define **ideology** as a coherent system of beliefs and ideas that motivate individuals, groups, and nations. The folk wisdom found in proverbs reminds us that there is nothing more powerful than an idea whose time has come, and that the pen is mightier than the sword. In this century two major conflicts—World War II and the Cold War—have been to a large extent the result of the clash of ideas: of **fascism** and **Nazism** against **liberal democracy,** and of Marxism against liberal democracy. Even today many nations are organized in large part on the basis of ideas—the United States, for example, on the basis of liberal democracy and **capitalism,** and China on the basis of **Maoism**/Marxism.

The interplay of ideas and national interest shapes the conduct of international relations. The rising importance of both liberal democracy and capitalism around the world calls for our attention, as does the underlying Confucian system of much of East Asia. At the same time, religious fundamentalism in various guises leads to turmoil, conflict, and terrorism. Understanding these ideologies provides the student of international relations with important insight into value systems, goals, and even ethical dimensions of both individuals and nation-states. And such an understanding helps explain how the international system operates.

In this chapter we will examine a number of vitally important current ideologies—liberalism, capitalism, socialism, Marxism, Confucianism, and fundamentalism—as well as two once-discarded but now reemerging ideologies, fascism and Nazism. In so doing, we will attempt to understand the content and the effect, both current and potential, of each one on global politics and international relations.

Liberalism, Capitalism, and Democracy

These three major ideas and systems tend to accompany one another, so we will consider them in the same section. After dominating so much of Western European and American thought for the past two centuries, these vital ideas are now challenging and transforming the political landscape in regions as disparate as the former Soviet Union, China, and South Africa.

The Roots of Liberalism

Liberalism has its roots in the Renaissance, with its renewed emphasis on the role of the individual. The emergence of Protestantism reinforced this appreciation of the role of the individual and paved the way for the rise of liberalism.

As a coherent set of ideas, liberalism rose from the tumultuous history of seventeenth-century England. During that time, the rapidly growing Puritan middle class challenged the power of the aristocracy, and ultimately both the monarch and the idea that kings were divinely appointed. In the aftermath of a century of war, an English Puritan named John Locke articulated a revolutionary theory of government and of the nature of man. In his seminal work *Two Treatises on Civil Government,* Locke set forth most of the basic ideas of liberalism. He began with three fundamental propositions: first, that human beings are by nature rational and therefore capable of learning; second, that human beings hold a series of **natural rights,** that is, rights conferred by no king or earthly authority, but belonging to them from birth; and third, that in the holding of rights and

natural rights Inalienable rights innate to human beings; these are not given by government, and hence cannot be taken away by government.

John Locke is generally considered the founder of modern liberalism and perhaps the most important political philosopher since Aristotle.

rationality, human beings are essentially equal. The most important rights identified by Locke were life, liberty, and property—he was, after all, a representative of the middle class. He held that in a state of nature, that is, in some distant past, human beings had existed without government and generally respected one another's rights.

However, he believed, inevitable conflict arose at some point in history about the extent of these rights. Locke's view was that in order to deal with such conflict, and ultimately to protect their rights, men create government as their agent. Government is in effect the result of a contract between the people and the rulers. There are mutual responsibilities as well as mutual rights. For example, people must behave rationally, which means that they must obey the just laws created by government, recognizing that the goal of these laws is the protection of their own rights. Government in turn must behave reasonably, creating laws that are for the benefit of all, not just the few, and that fall equally on all. These laws must be open and fair. Locke particularly singled out Parliament as the guarantor or trustee of the people's rights. Because so much of the conflict between Parliament and King in the seventeenth century had turned on the power to tax, Locke lodged the power to tax with Parliament, in which the people were represented; the power to tax was, after all, the power to take away property, and only the people's representatives could be trusted to tamper with this natural right.

Even with these safeguards, Locke recognized, there were still dangers that governments would infringe upon the rights of the people, jeopardizing those very rights that it was created to protect. Should this happen, Locke wrote, the people had first to remonstrate with the government, to warn it that it was exceeding its authority and abusing its power. If this did not work, then the people had a final right and responsibility: they could overthrow the government that, after all, they had created, and replace it with a new government that would in fact respect and protect the rights of the people. The right of revolution, then, is inherent in the nature of government. Locke recognized that such a right was dangerous, but he argued that people, being rational, will do everything they can to avoid the mess and turmoil of revolution. Furthermore, if there were no right to revolution, then people would be condemned to tyranny.

Locke's ideas and assumptions should sound familiar to American students, for they lie at the very foundations of the American political system and were used by Thomas Jefferson in his eloquent defense of the American Revolution, the Declaration of Independence. It is worth noting a few features of this Lockean system. First, it is entirely a secular system. That is, despite Locke's Puritanism, God plays no direct part in the establishment of a government. Government is purely a civil and worldly institution. (Thus, the Puritans had not defied God's will when they had rebelled against the Stewart kings.) Second, Locke took a basically optimistic view of human nature: as a rational being, man can learn and can become better. This optimism was to permeate the eighteenth-century Enlightenment, which provided the conceptual framework for the American and French revolutions and for modern liberalism.

During the eighteenth century, when the intellectual life of Europe (and Europe's American colonies) was suffused with this optimism, further glosses upon liberalism emerged. The *Social Contract* theory, implicit in Locke, was developed by Jean-Jacques Rousseau; essentially a restatement of the Puritan concept of the covenanted society, the social contract theory posited a society composed of individuals pledged to one another. Other French *philosophes* elaborated on such ideas as the separation of powers (Montesquieu) and freedom of speech and separation of church and state (Voltaire).

Summing up much of the Age of Reason was the liberal humanism of Thomas Jefferson. Jefferson not only reaffirmed Locke's doctrine of the natural rights theory of government, but also gave it a typical Enlightenment touch by adding the pursuit of happiness to the list of natural rights. In addition, Jefferson expressed great faith in the wisdom of the common man, especially his idealized yeoman farmer, self-sufficient, attuned to the rhythms of nature, and beholden to no one. He also expressed misgivings about government too far removed from the people, and often said that local and state government should have more power than the national government. (As president, however, Jefferson would be willing to expand the powers of his office and of the national government when he felt it necessary—for example, when making the Louisiana Purchase.) Jefferson also endorsed the idea of revolution, at one point calling for a revolution every twenty years.

The Roots of Capitalist Theory

The Enlightenment, which was concurrent in England with the rise of the Industrial Revolution, also saw the emergence of new ideas about the nature of economic activity and the proper relationship between government and the economy.

Chief among those developing the new economic theories was Adam Smith, a Scots philosopher whose *Wealth of Nations* appeared in 1776. Much of what Smith had to say was a direct refutation of the prevailing economic philosophy, mercantilism. According to mercantilists, the state should direct all economic activities for its own ultimate benefit. The export of goods was desirable, since it would bring gold and silver into the nation, but the import of goods was to be prevented, since it would allow gold and silver to flow out of the nation.

Adam Smith's *The Wealth of Nations,* the first systematic presentation of capitalism, remains the foundation of capitalist thinking.

In *The Wealth of Nations,* Smith advocated severing relationships between the state and the economy and, as John Locke had, emphasized the role of the individual. This individual, making rational decisions about consumption—what to buy, how much to buy, and what he or she would or could pay for it—would essentially set the limits of economic activity. The decisions of thousands and thousands of rational individuals would create the demand for goods, and then manufacturers would supply the goods, in the quantity and at the price demanded by the consumers. No government role was necessary to regulate the activities of the economic marketplace; individual decisions aggregated together would operate as what Smith termed an "invisible hand," efficiently and rationally determining the functioning of the economy.

Smith also argued that foreign trade, both export and import, should be left to the individual manufacturers and merchants to determine on the basis of supply and demand. He advocated what are known as laissez-faire tactics: manufacturers and merchants should freely choose, on the basis of supply and demand, what to manufacture and to whom to sell it. To Smith, the freely competitive marketplace functioned like a machine (a favorite metaphor of the eighteenth century) to produce the greatest number of goods at the lowest prices.

It is important to note that both John Locke and Adam Smith, although they clearly recognized the importance of economic activity, the role of private property, and the accumulation of wealth, cautioned against too great accumulation of property and wealth. Like their Puritan ancestors, they believed that within a just society wealth would be fairly even distributed, so that no one had too great wealth and, conversely, no one was desperately poor. Both would probably have been appalled at the excesses of capitalism in the late nineteenth and twentieth centuries.

Additionally, both Locke and Smith saw the role of government as relatively small. According to Locke, the primary purpose of government was to adjudicate disputes among the members of society, that is, to deal with issues that arose when one individual's rights came into conflict with those of another. Government was to make laws, enforce them, protect the nation, and collect only the taxes necessary for these minimal functions. Adam Smith also limited the functions of government, denying that it had any role in ordering or regulating the economy. Instead, he believed that government's major responsibility was the maintenance of law and order within the state, so that the economy could function efficiently and individuals could act freely on their rational economic decisions.

Liberal Internationalism

Modern liberals tend to be idealistic, focusing more on the common human needs and dreams that they think unite the world's peoples than on the national boundaries that divide them. Liberals believe in the international rule of law and put a great deal of faith in international institutions like the United Nations. An orderly world is achievable, liberals believe, and all nations can and must ultimately submit to the rule of law and assume roles as law-abiding participants in the world. (This emphasis on common humanity, needs, and goals can sometimes lead to what conservatives deride and fear as "one-world-ism," the view that perhaps national differences can one day vanish and be replaced by a single world government. Most liberals do not actually foresee this happening, and few openly embrace the idea. However, liberals are fond of quoting astronauts, as we said in Chapter 1, that there are no borders or boundaries visible from space on the single, fragile globe we all inhabit.)

With their belief in a single "human community," liberals have tended to support international exchange programs that send individuals to study in foreign nations, hoping that such exchanges will emphasize the common characteristics of human beings in different political and economic systems and will lead to greater friendship and understanding. Cultural exchanges, such as traveling musical and theatrical groups, art exhibits, and overseas libraries, are also tools that modern liberals hope to use to promote international understanding and goodwill.

Expecting good faith, rationality, and decency in relations with other nations, liberals also tend to place great faith in treaties and in the ability of the world community (in fact, in the very existence of a world community) to order its affairs by negotiations and compromise. Liberals also tend to be at the forefront of such movements as international environmentalism, again emphasizing the common good and the common needs of humanity as a whole. Such optimism often leads to disappointment. Finally, modern liberals tend to emphasize the necessity of free trade. The present international economic regime is fundamentally a liberal structure.

Modern Capitalism

Contemporary capitalism embraces private property, the conduct of business for profit, the necessity of a government able to guarantee stability and to enforce contracts, and the marketplace rather than the government as the driving force behind economic decision-making. There are many variations of this—the Japanese government, for example, plays a far greater role in its economy through setting industrial policy than does the United States—but the fundamentals of capitalism are essentially constant. The accumulation of wealth by individuals as well as by corporations is the final sign of success within the capitalist economy, but all benefit from economic development; as John F. Kennedy remarked, "a rising tide lifts all boats."

The role of the entrepreneur, that is, the individual who begins a business or is primarily responsible for the development of a particular industry, is generally vital to the continued development of the capitalist economy as well. Among entrepreneurs are Andrew Carnegie and John D. Rockefeller in the early industrial economy, Steven Jobs and Steve Wozniak in the modern personal computer industry, and Akio Morita in today's personal electronics industry. This emphasis on the role of the individual and the immense wealth that such an individual can accumulate is often uncongenial in societies that tend to be more communitarian than individualistic. For example, in contemporary Russia, which is struggling to replace its old command economy with something on the order of a capitalist system, there is tremendous resentment against the handful of entrepreneurs who have become extremely rich. Much of this is culturally and historically based. According to a sardonic joke, if an American farmer sees his neighbor purchase a pedigreed bull, he will go out and buy a bull with a better pedigree. If a Russian peasant sees his neighbor buy a pedigreed bull, he will pray that it dies.

Democracy

"Democracy" is probably one of the most loosely used words in modern politics. It is used to refer to forms of government that range from republicanism to representative government to authoritarian regimes masquerading as democracies.

As it is used today, **democracy** refers to almost any system of government in which the people of the nation have some sort of say in the choice of lawmakers and leaders. It is, in effect, any kind of government that embodies the goals and philosophies of classical liberalism. Democracies are characterized by limitations on the powers of government and by the accountability, usually through the electoral process, of legislators and leaders to the people.

democracy System of government characterized by elections for lawmakers and a nation's leadership. Its philosophical foundation is classical liberalism.

The original democracy, that of Athens in the sixth and fifth centuries B.C., rested on direct and immediate participation by citizens in the setting of policy and the making of decisions, through a citizens' assembly. Such a system may have been suitable to a relatively small Greek city-state, but would clearly be impracticable in large modern states. Consequently, most governments that we refer to as democratic are actually representative governments, in which elected individuals exercise authority on behalf of the larger citizenry. Recently there have been suggestions that modern communications may make total democracy possible even in a large, sprawling modern state—presidential wanna-be Ross Perot floated such ideas in 1992—but there are still serious roadblocks in the way of such a plebiscitary system.

Despite conflicts over whether democracy is based on principle or on process, more than 120 governments in today's world bill themselves as democracies (see fig. 6.1), and the number is growing as the collapse of the Cold War continues. Before celebrating this too much, we must remember that the old Soviet Union called itself a democratic government, although the Communist Party was the only party, and the vast majority of citizens could only rubber-stamp candidates proposed and decisions reached by that party.

Whether or not the nations emerging from decades of communist control can truly make the transition to democracy, and whether nations still struggling to emerge from the shadow of colonialism will ever do so successfully, remain open questions today. In many of these nations, as noted elsewhere, some of the most important elements usually found in democracies are missing. For example, modern democracy emerged in conjunction with the rise of the Puritan middle class in England, and the success of democracy seems directly tied to the existence of a strong middle class. Education also seems to be a prerequisite for democracy, which calls upon individuals to make wise choices and to accept limitations on their own absolute rights in order to protect the rights of others. The question of whether democracy is possible in the absence of a middle class or an educated population is a vital one, for many of the emerging would-be democracies lack one or both of these vital components.

In addition, democracy and capitalism seem inextricably intertwined. The emphasis on the role and rights of the individual that makes democracy function is equally essential for capitalism, at least as it is presently constituted and understood. While this represents part of the lure of democracy for many—the possibility of simultaneously achieving individual liberty and economic prosperity is tremendously attractive—it also means that nations striving to make the transition

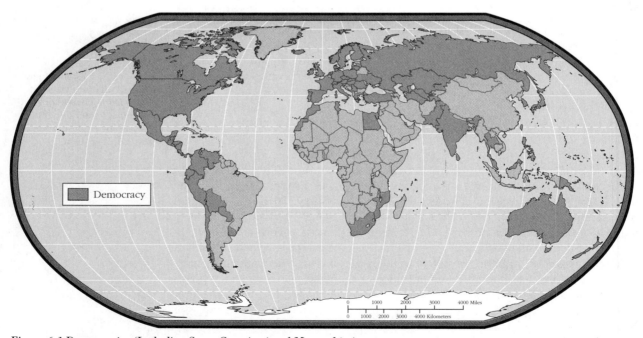

Figure 6.1 **Democracies (Including Some Constitutional Monarchies)**

to democracy must at the same time attempt to create, sometimes out of whole cloth, capitalist economies to accompany and support democracy.

Recently there has been a great deal of exultation about the "triumph" of liberal democracy and capitalism, but we suspect that much of this jubilation is premature, to say the least. Both systems, democracy and capitalism, not only offer great rewards for the individual but also place great demands upon the individual. It is not yet clear that many nations can make that transition, or that individuals long used to the constraints of nondemocratic systems and command economies will in fact be comfortable with the freewheeling democratic and capitalist systems so widespread in Western Europe and its North American offspring.

Consolidating Capitalism and Democracy

Stephan Haggard and Robert R. Kaufman point out that the process of democratization in many countries is entering a new phase and facing new problems of consolidation. The wave of democratization that crested in the 1980s, they maintain, often coincided with reforms towards market economies as well. The process of democratization and economic reform is now a fait accompli in southern Europe, central Europe, and most of the republics carved from the former Soviet Union, and parts of Asia; the question now is not whether these new democracies can initiate reform, "but how they will meet the new challenges likely to arise as economies are stabilized." The daunting issue today is consolidation, of both economic and democratic reforms (Haggard and Kaufman 1994).

Three key issues have emerged: the role of the state in achieving sustainable growth, the distributional consequences of reform and their implications for political conflict, and the need for accountability by leaders of the reform process. In the late 1980s and early 1990s, Haggard and Kaufman maintain, conditions were favorable for democratic and economic reform. The new regimes benefited from the collapse of the Soviet Union and the end of the Cold War and from the fact that the failed authoritarian regimes could be used as whipping boys by the new democratic leaders. Those times are gone, however, and the new democracies face new problems. Inflation and economic deterioration can have a corrosive impact on liberalization, as in Peru and Brazil. In former communist nations, there is a danger that ex-communists and right-wing movements will be able to tap into "a nostalgia for the old order." Consolidation of the new regimes both politically and economically is thus critical in order to preserve and enlarge democratic and capitalist gains (Haggard and Kaufman 1994).

First, the role of the state in the economic realm must be redefined, with recognition that the Anglo-Saxon model is not the only viable one. In fact, some economists have identified as many as seven different major styles of capitalism, defined by the role of government and the individual, different time scales, different self-images and self-definitions, and different leadership and career styles. The United States, Great Britain, Germany, Sweden, France, the Netherlands, and Japan represent successful but very different styles of capitalism, while the emerging "tigers" of Asia such as Singapore and Taiwan are synthesizing elements of the various styles (Hampden-Turner and Trompenaars 1993). Outsiders must always leave room for different styles, some of which will involve either greater or less state involvement than they are accustomed to, and they also must allow for the economic and political constraints under which the new systems have emerged. Many of these transitions, as Jeffrey Sachs points out, were in response to crisis, what he terms "life in the emergency room" (In Haggard and Kaufman 1994).

Second, the new regimes must deal successfully with issues of poverty and income inequality. Market reforms in particular have provided opportunities and windfalls for upper income groups, impoverishing many people who are already struggling and radically skewing income distribution. Those urging reform must always keep in mind that government efforts to reduce inequality and alleviate poverty are not only compatible with market reform but also may be the only route to democratic consolidation. Antipoverty programs to cushion the shocks of structural adjustment have worked well in Mexico, Bolivia, and Chile, for example, and may be needed in many new democracies (Haggard and Kaufman 1994).

Finally, Haggard and Kaufman argue that consolidating democracy may well require leaders to act autocratically: "the institution of reform usually requires a substantial concentration of discretionary political authority to surmount resistance" from interests threatened by reform. Eventually, however, in order to consolidate economic and democratic reforms, executive authority "must be depersonalized and integrated into a broader framework." Haggard and Kaufman suggest the possibility of a European-style corporatist framework in which policy agreements are directly negotiated by representatives of labor, business, and the state. A parliamentary system represents a second model for institutionalizing reform and encouraging stable decision- and policy-making procedures. By fusing legislative and executive authority, a parliamentary government provides stronger incentives for political cooperation than the presidential system. However, whether parliamentary or presidential systems dominate, the consolidation and institutionalization of reform also depends on the emergence of stable and well-defined political parties. Such changes are within reach of the fragile new democracies in developing countries; although their achievement will lack the exhilaration that marked earlier sweeping changes as the Cold War ended, they are vital. "The transformations taking place during [this next phase] are likely to be more incremental and less dramatic, but no less difficult or critical for the consolidation of stable capitalist democracies" (Haggard and Kaufman 1994).

Jeffrey Sachs, a Harvard economist who has served as advisor for economic transformation in Russia as well as many other countries, warns of great risk as well as great promise in the next decade. "The 1990s is one of the great watershed decades in economic history," he proclaims. The promise is that of consolidating a global capitalist world system "with profound benefits for both the rich and the poor countries." Such consolidation would benefit global security as much as global economics, he argues, since "with a few notable exceptions, the market revolution has gone hand in hand with a democratic revolution." The risk is that domestic pressures, particularly those in favor of protectionism, will lead the major capitalist trading states to shut down the open international trading system just as it is at the brink of its greatest triumph (Sachs 1995, 50).

According to Sachs, within the last decade nations with a combined population of approximately 3.5 billion people have embarked on reform programs designed to lead to capitalism. Although they have taken different paths, these core reforms include six common factors: open international trade, currency convertibility, private ownership as the "main engine of economic growth," corporate ownership as the "dominant form for large enterprises," openness to foreign investment, and membership in key international institutions such as the International Monetary Fund (IMF), the World Bank, and The General Agreement on Tarriffs and Trade/World Trade Organization (GATT/WTO). Although there are powerful culturally based distinctions among styles of capitalism, Sachs argues, advanced economies share core features—openness, private ownership, corporate governance—that offer "a relatively straightforward set of guideposts for the most fundamental reforms" (Sachs 1995, 51–52).

The "Capitalist Revolution of the 1990s" is unraveling the world system that existed for the last fifty years for one reason: "the alternatives proffered by the Second and Third worlds did not work." These models of state-led, autarkic development collapsed over the last decade, Sachs writes. "The most remarkable story . . . is not that successful economic institutions inexorably replace unsuccessful ones, but that unsuccessful ones can persist so long, often at the cost of unimaginable human suffering" (Sachs 1995, 53–59).

However, like Haggard and Kaufman, Sachs points out that backsliding is still possible. Three major challenges face the world today: the consolidation of market reform, the need for the developed countries to hold firm to their international commitments, and the necessity of deepening the system of international law in order to govern the emerging global economy. At this time, Sachs fears, "not only the Russian economy, but also Russian democracy, has been put recklessly at risk by Western neglect." There has been no firm intellectual understanding that the purpose of economic aid is political, "to support fragile democratic regimes attempting to implement more basic reforms." The sums of aid that the United States has offered to Russia have been "derisory," about .005 percent of the American gross domestic product. Finally, neither the Bush nor the Clinton administration has led a coordinated Western effort to aid Russia. Russia has been "within reach of successful market reform" since 1991, Sachs writes, but these Western, and American, failings have helped undermine Russian public support for reform and have played into the hands of extremist and military forces. The stakes involved are far too great to allow such failure (Sachs 1995, 59–61).

Sachs concludes that it is still possible to proceed with consolidation of both market and democratic reforms, but that the United States in particular must take a far more active, and far more internationalist, role than it seems poised to do. "If the United States can manage to stick with its abiding principles that have brought it to the brink of an integrated, law-bound world system, and if Americans in conjunction with the other advanced democracies can deliver aid with generosity and farsighted self-interest, this generation has the possibility to usher in an unprecedented period of peace and prosperity" (Sachs 1995, 64).

Challenges to Liberal Internationalism

Other voices warn of critical weaknesses within the liberal internationalist outlook and call for a thorough rethinking of it. "Communism is dead," writes Stanley Hoffman, "but is the other great postwar ideology, liberal internationalism, also dying?" (Hoffman 1995, 160)

Historically, liberal internationalism has sought a legitimate world order established by liberal states living in harmony. With the triumph of constitutional, representative governments, liberal internationalists believed, conflict would diminish, as states transferred their ideas of consent and rational discussion to the international arena. The emancipation of individuals and the resultant "world public opinion and . . . transnational economic society" would increasingly define cooperation and peace as the national interest. However, Hoffman writes, two questions were unanswered. First, how could this liberal vision be realized? Should liberal states use force to achieve their ideals? Second, how

Democracy in Russia?

Democracy is not an easy concept to define or even describe. Like many other concepts in political science, such as power, you simply know it when you see it. But there are some rather broad contours that outline the basic tenets of a democratic system. And we would like to attempt to determine whether democracy as we know it in the West can plant itself in Russia, a nation that historically lacks any of the conventional underpinnings we refer to as "democratic." To do so, we must posit two questions. First, what is a democracy? Second, can it happen in Russia?

Using the American political system as a benchmark, we can observe that a system of liberal democracy rests upon several shared presumptions and propositions. First, there is a belief in the *political equality* of all citizens, often summarized as "one person, one vote." Second, there is a belief in *majority rule, with the preservation of minority rights*. Third, there is a functional belief that the best way to conduct the business of government is through a *repub-*

GLOBAL PERSPECTIVES

lican form of government, in which citizens elect representatives for a set period of time to do the business of government for them. Instead of a direct, participatory government in which every citizen must decide what should be done on every issue, duly elected officials carry out the business of government until the next election. To get people to run for office and to convince the electorate to vote for them, American democracy has developed the organizational tool of the *political party*. A party helps stage elections, recruits candidates, and attempts to convince voters that its candidate is the best person for the job. Parties have proved to be an invaluable tool in making the American system of government run smoothly. Transferring the reins of government between parties is done in a rather routine, often "ho-hum" fashion. The combined notions that "all is well now that my party won" and that "we'll get them next time" afford the stability required for a functioning democracy. Running throughout this republican, democratic apparatus is the closely associated economic system of *free-market capitalism*. Capitalism is closely aligned

should liberalism deal with nationalism? Although national self-determination represented a deep-set liberal principle, it was not clear what kind of "self" was entitled to self-determination. What should be done about minorities within such states? What should be done about authoritarian nationalism? And how could liberals reconcile the inherent conflict between the rationalism of liberalism and the emotionalism of nationalism? (Hoffman 1995, 161–64)

Liberal internationalism, according to Hoffman, has been best at performing "negative tasks" such as removing economic barriers, opposing colonialism and imperialism, and containing communism. Today, however, the world appears to be dissolving into chaos, and Hoffman is not sure that liberal internationalism, at least as it is presently constituted, can meet that challenge. Liberal internationalism must reform itself in order to shake off chaos-induced paralysis, Hoffman argues. "Marxism is discredited. Realism promises only the perpetuation of the same old game and is no better equipped to face the politics of chaos than is liberalism." Hoffman continues, "Liberalism remains the only comprehensive and hopeful vision of world affairs, but it needs to be thoroughly reconstructed—and the task has not proceeded very far, [in] either . . . its domestic or its international dimensions." Hoffman leaves little doubt that if liberalism does not soon begin to solve its dilemmas, global chaos and anarchy remain real possibilities, despite the apparent triumph of liberalism (Hoffman 1995, 177).

to democracy as an economic system that accentuates individual liberties and private ownership by individuals or groups, with as little government regulation or control as possible. This is opposed to government ownership of the means of production, as in socialist or communist states.

With this as a thumbnail sketch of democracy (and implicitly its capitalistic economic system), the question remains: Can it happen in Russia? Will the seed of democracy fall into a fertile furrow in the largest state of the former Soviet Union?

Russian President Boris Yeltsin was asked in a recent *Time* magazine interview about the danger of Russia sliding back to its authoritarian past. Yelstin replied,

> Theoretically, such a danger exists. We are only beginning to build our new democratic state and new economy. Given our history, these are extremely hard tasks, and we are forced to pursue both goals at the same time. . . . A strong civil society, a middle class and a culture of law are basic conditions for a stable democracy in any country. But these preconditions are only taking shape in Russia. For these reasons, the danger of an authoritarian regime will exist here for some time yet. . . . Russia is not the country

it once was. Our free press is a safeguard for democracy. (*Time*, May 8, 1995)

The answer as to whether Russia will become a liberal, Western-style democracy will be told in time. But strong doubts linger in the West about the Russian political culture and its commitment to both democracy and capitalism. The controversy rages over how to create a liberal democracy from the ground up, so to speak. Should the nation have a strong decentralized liberal economy first, followed by the democratic trappings of a free press, political party competition, and republicanism? Or should these democratic underpinnings come first to provide a basis for a liberal capitalism? It is truly a chicken-and-egg situation. To be sure, it will not be a smooth, easy transition from a Marxist-Leninist-Stalinist totalitarian (or post-totalitarian) society to a free and open society of the West. One thing seems certain. Such a transition to a liberal democratic, capitalistic society cannot be imposed from outside. The desire for such a radical change from the past must be internally driven. And it is this internal desire that is still germinating in Russia. The question is this: Will the ground be ready?

The Next Ideology?

One scholar, Graham Fuller, cautions that the current apparent triumph of liberal internationalism, democracy, and capitalism may be simply a transitional stage toward the development of "the next ideology" (Fuller 1995, 145).

The fundamental principles upon which the essential Western vision rests—free-market capitalism, human rights, and the nation-state—"impose daunting and destabilizing strains upon Third World states and societies at large." These principles are not "quick fixes" for such societies, but may actually amplify their problems. "The 'next ideology' to emerge, then, will be [one of] opposition to Western challenges by Third World regimes that cannot cope with their effects." That ideology, Fuller writes, will be "an amalgam of opposition to its values and institutions." It will be a rejection of modernization and its political, social, and economic dislocation (Fuller 1995, 145).

Fuller argues that the core values of Western culture are in fact universal and ultimately will become widespread. However, he warns that different cultures will adopt varying forms of these values. Capitalism, democracy, and the nation-state all possess a "dark side," Fuller writes, and Western nations must become more aware of this dark side. The gap between rich and poor is growing worldwide, and capitalism can create crisis in fragile states "as it imposes a form of economic triage—some winners, but many losers." Further, democracy is revolutionary, introducing "broad-scale and often wrenching social reform." Finally, the idea of the sovereign nation-state can inflame rather than solve ethnic conflict, and democracy can be "explosive and fragmenting in character" (Fuller 1995, 149–52).

Additionally, Fuller warns, "the existence of native cultures is threatened by the general homogenization of world culture." Systems of international markets and communications create "freeways" for the importation of foreign cultural materials such as food, clothing, music, and even values. The cultural anxieties that rise from these drastic changes are welcome fuel to radical political groups that call for the protection of and return to traditionalism. Modern culture thus symbolizes the power of Western states over weak, traditional societies. "This 'civilizational clash' is not so much over Jesus Christ, Confucius, or the Prophet Mohammed as it is over the unequal distribution of world power, wealth, and influence, and the perceived historical lack of respect accorded to small states and peoples by larger ones" (Fuller 1995, 153–54).

To prevent the emergence of a catastrophic clash between traditional Western states and values and "the next ideology," Fuller warns that "the values of democracy and the free market [must] undergo a process of evolution and 'correction.'" These values must be not only fitted to Western states but also must prove their "suitability" for developing states. This is still possible, Fuller maintains, and is imperative if the universal values of Western culture are to be realized (Fuller 1995, 159).

Socialism

socialism Economic theory that denies for the most part the legitimacy of private property; socialism advocates a large role for the central government in policy and planning.

Socialism grew out of nineteenth-century utopian movements that saw private property as a source of trouble within society, since it encouraged acquisitiveness, greed, and inequality. The earliest socialists were men like Robert Owen of England, who had optimistic faith in the essential goodness of human nature and sought to create political and economic systems in which this goodness could flourish. This early socialism often led to communitarian experiments like Owen's New Harmony, set on the bucolic banks of the Wabash River in Indiana; here there was no private property, all individuals were equal and self-governing, work was to be apportioned to all, and goods were to be shared by all. Sadly, the New Harmony experiment lasted only a few years before internal strife tore it apart.

Others shared Owen's vision and began to proclaim that the best way to achieve the socialist ideal was to abolish private ownership of the means of production. Factories should belong to the people as a whole, or to the workers who toiled in the factories, or to the government as the trustee of the people, these late-nineteenth-century socialists proclaimed. Only by taking the ownership of the means of production out of private hands could equity within society, and fair treatment of workers, be guaranteed.

Modern socialism is wedged rather uneasily between capitalism and communism, and has lost much of its clear identity in the struggle to avoid being lumped with one or the other competing system. The twentieth century has witnessed a variety of socialist experiments in advanced industrial economies. Probably the most interesting has been in Great Britain, where the triumph of the Labour Party in elections immediately after World War II led to widespread nationalization of key industries such as railroads, steel, and coal mining. In addition, the socialist government of Great Britain created the National Health Service to provide basic medical care for the entire population. However, these experiments with socializing basic means of production were not entirely successful; the election of a Conservative government in the early 1980s meant privatization of most of the nationalized industries, although the National Health Service remained.

Today Great Britain, Germany, Sweden, and many other European nations have mixed economies, in which socialism generally refers not only to public ownership of means of production but also to extensive social welfare programs run by the state. Health care, subsidies for child rearing, mandatory vacations and paid leave for a variety of family problems, including the birth or adoption of a child as well as illness, and old-age pensions are major components of these social welfare programs. All obviously represent attempts to alleviate the worst problems created by rampant capitalism without threatening the capitalist system itself. Quite recently, however, several European nations, most particularly Germany, have begun questioning the enormous expense of this social welfare program, and there are signs that the "welfare state" is coming under serious attack in several European nations. It should be noted, however, that the long Conservative administration of Margaret Thatcher in Great Britain had no more success in seriously dismantling the social welfare system there than did the highly conservative eight-year administration of Ronald Reagan in the United States.

Socialism seems to offer special attractions to many developing nations, which define the term loosely, as a collective effort of the people and a cooperation between government and private industry for economic growth. Seen in this light, socialism appears to reinforce traditional communitarianism.

Marxism

The multiple sins of the nineteenth-century Industrial Revolution—the exploitation of workers, child labor, slums, poverty, and general misery—led to multiple attempts to figure out how to retain the benefits of industrialism while lessening its human costs. The most important of these attempts is **Marxism,** a set of economic and political beliefs based on the theoretical work of Karl Marx. A German by birth, Marx spent years of research in the National Library of Great Britain compiling statistics to bolster his denunciation of capitalism and support his "scientific" explication of history. His *opus magnum, Das Kapital* (1868), remains one of the most important texts in political and economic theory, although much of what Marx said has been modified and even distorted by twentieth-century practitioners of "Marxism." In this section we will first look at Marx's original ideas and then examine their adaptation by three major practitioners and theorists, Vladimir Ilyich Lenin and Joseph Stalin of the Soviet Union, and Mao Tse-tung of the People's Republic of China.

Marx began by fusing together two concepts: **dialecticism** and **economic determinism.** Dialecticism originated in the work of the German philosopher Georg Hegel in the late eighteenth century. Hegel believed that all of history is a dynamic process, constantly in the state of becoming rather than the state of being. The mechanism for this dynamic, according to Hegel, is the dialectic, a never-ending chain of change. The dialectical process begins with an idea or a fact, what Hegel terms a thesis. In turn, this thesis will generate its opposite, its antithesis. And then, from the struggle between thesis and antithesis, something entirely new emerges: the synthesis. The appearance of the synthesis is not the

Marxism The ideology named after Karl Marx, the nineteenth-century German philosopher. With Georg Hegel, Marx emphasized the dialectical progression of history—thesis, anti-thesis, synthesis—which, according to the theory, yielded a higher stage of human being, who is seen as merely an economic animal.

dialecticism A view of history that states that the progression of man is economically determined in stages of action and reaction to the existing order, bringing the political system to a higher state of perfection.

economic determinism A Marxist belief that all of the superstructure is caused or determined by the substructure; all politics is economically determined.

Second only to Locke in his influence on the twentieth century was Karl Marx, the founder of communism.

substructure In Marxist terms, the economic foundation of a society, which determines the superstructure.

superstructure In Marxist terms, the part of society that does not specifically deal with economics, e.g., the arts, sex, religion, etc., but that is determined by the substructure of economics.

end of the dialectical process, but merely the beginning of its next phase, for the synthesis takes on the characteristics of a thesis, generates its antithesis, and then leads to yet another synthesis. Thus change, and progress, occur as the result of the constant conflict between ideas and their opposites.

To this dialectical process Marx welded the idea of economic determinism, that is, the belief that the human being is fundamentally an economic animal and that economic **substructure** determines all the other characteristics—including ideas, philosophies, and political systems—of any given society. To understand the class structure—who is running things and how, and how any given ideology is used to justify the ruling class—all one must do is look at the economic substructure. Substructure determines **superstructure,** which is comprised of everything else in society—art, sex, literature, politics, etc.—and which the economic substructure determines. Marx had little time for man as a rational or even a good being; he was concerned almost completely with the economic nature of the human being.

With these ideas in place, Marx explained that all of history can be understood as a series of dialectical processes determined by the material conditions of each stage of historical development. In its earliest phase, human society consisted of a primitive utopian communist stage in which there was no private property and thus, at first, no greed. In this original society, all shared alike according to the formula that Marx foresaw as the end as well as the beginning of human development: "from each according to his ability, to each according to his need."

However, the dialectical process was at work even in that utopian society, and as a result, human society evolved into its next level, the slave society, in which people themselves became property and wealth was unevenly distributed. Through the dialectical process, the slave society then gave rise to the feudal state, which in turn led to capitalism. Capitalism in turn, Marx said, would inevitably give way to socialism, and lead eventually to the highest stage of human development, **communism:** the mature, ideal state in which all would share equally.

The mechanism for this dialectical change, according to Marx and his collaborator Friedrich Engels, was class conflict. Inevitably, at each stage of historical development the ruling class would cling to the existing system and defend it with everything it had, while the rising class would seek to overthrow the ruling class and create its own society in response to its own economic needs and system.

One of the most important elements of this change within the Marxist system is its inevitability. Change will come, and human history will move from stage to stage, as the result not of human will but of scientifically described historical processes. Class conflict, and the violence that such conflict will breed, is every bit as inevitable as the final triumph of the proletariat, the exploited working class of the capitalist system that will create the communist system out of its ruins. Marx in fact denied that his thought constituted an ideology, since he defined ideology as the rationale used by the dominant class to justify and retain its power. Instead, he saw dialectical materialism as the only scientific way to explain the workings of history and to predict its outcome.

communism An umbrella ideology based upon economic relations between the people and the state, originating with the writings of Karl Marx.

Leninism

Vladimir Ilyich Lenin, principal architect of the Bolshevik Revolution in 1917, made substantial changes in classical Marxist doctrine. Perhaps most important, he argued that it was possible to "leapfrog history." After all, if Marxism were rigidly interpreted, a Marxist revolution in Russia would be impossible, since Russia had by no means made the transition from feudalism to capitalism. Industrialization had progressed slowly in the sprawling Romanov empire, and in only a handful of cities, such as St. Petersburg and Moscow, was there anything approaching the proletariat that Marx had characterized as the vanguard of the revolution. Consequently, Lenin argued that it was not necessary to follow every step of the Marxist schema literally; instead, in Russia, the small proletariat, properly organized and controlled, could lead the entire state forward, leapfrogging history and going almost directly from the feudal state to communism. This theoretical adjustment to doctrinaire Marxism explained and legitimized the Bolshevik revolution.

Another important contribution of **Leninism** was organizational: the transformation of the proletarian revolution from the mass movement apparently envisioned by Marx and Engels into a much smaller, conspirational movement. Lenin recognized that a mass movement was simply not feasible, given the oppression of the tsarist regime and the comparatively small size of the Russian proletariat. Instead, Lenin organized the Bolshevik movement in Russia into a series of conspiratorial cells, each one operating independently from the others, its members not knowing members of other cells, so that even if that one cell were arrested, others would remain safe. In ironic contrast to classical Marxist theory and even to Lenin's adaptation of it, most of the leaders of the Bolshevik revolution were not genuine proletarians, still in short supply, but intellectuals like Lenin himself, who had never worked in a factory. These leaders were intoxicated by the "scientific" optimism of Marxism. Lenin also stressed what he called **democratic centralism,** that is, the idea that an essentially authoritarian system would reflect the democratic will of the people. He never did manage to explain how he would actually combine these two opposites, and during the period when he dominated Soviet politics "centralism" far outweighed "democracy."

Leninism The variant of Marxism that led to the ideological establishment of the USSR. Lenin saw the Communist Party as the principal organizing component of the ongoing revolution.

democratic centralism A decision-making system in which all participants agree publicly with the government's decision, regardless of whether they do so privately or not.

Vladimir I. Lenin adapted Marx's ideas to Russian realities in order to win the Bolshevik Revolution of 1917 and create the Soviet Union.

imperialism In Marxist terms, the highest stage of capitalism in which capitalist states subjugate other, usually poorer nations, for their own economic benefit.

A third major contribution that Lenin made to Marxist doctrine was his theory of imperialism, which proclaimed that **imperialism** was a necessary consequence of capitalism. In order to prevent their inevitable collapse, Lenin wrote, capitalist states had to become imperialist in order to secure markets for their surplus goods and access to natural resources. Thus, the rise of the Industrial Revolution and capitalism in the nineteenth century had triggered the great surge of imperialism in the latter part of that century that had brought much of the world under the control of the major capitalist nations. By stressing the link between capitalism and imperialism, Lenin made communism more attractive to those in Africa and Asia particularly, who could then see capitalism as the cause of their being incorporated into European empires, and thus look to communism as a way to free themselves from imperialism.

Lenin also emphasized that the communist state, such as the newly formed Soviet Union, was merely a stopping place on the journey to an ideal world in which there would be no governments and no nation-states. In this future, Lenin wrote, all states would "wither away," since the purpose of the state is to protect the interests of the ruling class. In a classless society, all would share equally, and thus there would be no need for government.

Stalinism

Joseph Stalin, Lenin's successor, also made significant changes in orthodox Marxist ideology. Perhaps his most important theoretical shift from Marx's thought was his insistence that it would be possible to build a communist state in a single country. Revolution need not be a worldwide phenomenon, Stalin argued, but could be successfully carried out in a single nation. This pitted Stalin against Leon

Building on Lenin's ideas, Josef Stalin created a brutally repressive regime in the Soviet Union.

Trotsky, his chief rival for power in the Soviet Union after Lenin's death. Trotsky advocated the classical position that a single communist state could not survive by itself, but must use its resources to promote worldwide revolution. Stalin not only argued that revolution in a single country was possible, but also aided other revolutionary movements only grudgingly, more to enhance the Soviet cause than to achieve genuine revolution. In China, for example, he insisted that the Chinese Communists slavishly follow him in promoting Soviet interests and following the Leninist model of using the urban proletariat as the vanguard of revolution, despite the minuscule size of China's urban proletariat. Under withering criticism from Trotsky, Stalin ultimately solved this controversy as he did many other problems: with violence. Trotsky fled the Soviet Union, but he could not flee Stalin; in 1940 he was murdered in Mexico by Stalinist agents.

Stalin's brutal and paranoid personality led him to turn to violence as a way of perpetuating his power and enforcing his interpretation of Marxism. The forced collectivization of agriculture in the Soviet Union, for example, cost the lives of as many as thirty million people, many of them by starvation. In establishing a totalitarian state in the USSR, Stalin used fear and brutality to guarantee his own rule. He often justified this in the name of efficiency and combating danger to the state.

Unlike Lenin, who had believed that the Soviet Union would have to proceed through at least a modified capitalist stage (embodied in his five-year NEP, or New Economic Plan), Stalin wanted to take the nation directly to socialism, and so instituted a highly centralized "command economy" to bring about rapid industrialization under the direction of an increasingly large and entrenched bureaucracy. Stalin's brutal forced collectivization of agriculture was one part of this

Stalinism The form of
totalitarianism that
occurred in the Soviet
Union during the reign of
Joseph Stalin (1925–1953).

Soviet surge toward socialism. Stalin would ultimately boast, despite the disagreement of many Marxist theorists, that the Soviet Union had in fact achieved socialism.

Another major feature of **Stalinism** was the cult of personality that surrounded the leader. Statues, portraits, sayings of Stalin—there was not a town square or empty wall anywhere in the Soviet Union safe from adornment with one or more of these. This cult of personality, combined with the brutality that lurked within that personality, transformed the Soviet Union into a terribly repressive totalitarian state, in which all authority resided in Stalin himself; his word alone was sufficient to send people to their death or to lifelong exile in the abysmal prison camps known collectively as the Gulag.

Total control over all aspects of cultural and artistic life was another major element of Stalinism in the Soviet Union. Art, literature, music, history, even science were impressed into service on behalf of the Soviet state and its leader. The glorification of the state and leader took precedence over any possibility of genuine artistic expression or scholarly research. "Socialist realism" resulted in gigantic murals glorifying muscles and machines, with human figures ("the new Soviet man and woman") of enormous musculature and faces lifted toward icons of Stalin in rapt adoration.

Stalinism thus embodied many of the most repressive features of modern totalitarianism under the rubric of Marxism: the cult of the leader, cultural repression, heavily bureaucratized command over the economy, indoctrination of youth into a series of Communist organizations, and official state repression of any deviation (under Stalin, for example, many dissidents were classified as insane and committed to asylums, from which they seldom emerged). Although apologists often cited the Soviet Union's tremendous advances in industrialization and its valiant defense against Hitler during World War II as justification for Stalinism, it nonetheless constituted one of the most brutal and repressive state systems in history.

Stalinism as an International Force

Historians still argue about whether Stalinist foreign policy rested on ideology or on Soviet national interest. The calculated cynicism of the 1939 nonaggression treaty with Nazi Germany certainly seems to indicate that national interest alone drove the decision to link up a major ideological enemy. Many attribute much of the responsibility for the Cold War to Stalin's relentless rhetorical defense of communism, and see the imposition of the Iron Curtain over Eastern Europe as a step in the worldwide expansion of communism. Others argue that in fact, Stalin's postwar policy was determined largely by his interpretation of Russian national interest, particularly the desire to control the western borderlands and marches through which both Napoleon's and Hitler's invasions had moved so easily. These historians argue that Stalin's foreign policy was essentially conservative; he did not encourage the Maoist revolution in China, for example, and as he had since the days of his violent disputes with Trotsky, he continued to focus on advancing communism in a single country rather than orchestrating a global revolution. In the opinion of these historians, generally known as "revisionists" because they challenge the orthodox interpretation of the roots of the Cold War, the struggle between the United States and the Soviet Union, although couched in the language of an ideological crusade, was fundamentally about power, about which of the two superpowers that emerged from World War II would achieve global domination.

Maoism

The third important variant of Marxism in the modern world came not from the industrial or industrializing nations, but from the nonindustrial state of China. Mao Tse-tung, leader of the Communist revolutionary forces in China and then leader of the People's Republic of China, made several important changes in orthodox Marxism in order to explain his vision for China's future and to achieve that vision.

First, early in his career, Mao identified the peasantry as a genuine revolutionary force in China. Despite orthodox Marxism's insistence on the primacy of the proletariat in the socialist revolution, Mao asserted that the peasants of China (not coincidentally far and away the largest segment of China's population) would spearhead the revolution. According to Mao, the peasantry constituted a blank slate upon which the revolution could be written and from which a new "revolutionary man" could be forged.

Second, Mao stressed the role of will, or what is sometimes called voluntarism, in the revolutionary process. While orthodox Marxism contends that history moves forward more or less autonomously and that in effect people conform to the tides of historical change and dialectical materialism, Mao stressed the role that the individual, alone or joined with others, can play. With enough will, nothing is impossible. To illustrate the power of individual will, Mao offered a Chinese allegory, "The Foolish Old Man and the Mountain." According to this tale, an elderly man found his view blocked by a huge mountain and decided to move the mountain. Although his neighbors derided him, he and his sons began to try to move the mountain, shovelful by shovelful. Finally, God saw what the "foolish old man" and his family were doing and one night, while everyone was fast asleep, God and the angels came down and moved the mountain. Thus, by

Mao Tse-tung's variations on Marxism included emphasis on a peasant revolution, the idea of continuing revolution, and the importance of will.

analogy, the Chinese people did not have to accept imperialism, poverty, or oppression, but could take control of their own lives and their own nation, and literally move themselves into the future.

A third major component of Maoism is its emphasis on **permanent revolution.** Unlike other Marxists, Mao did not believe that the dialectic would suddenly come to a screeching halt when socialism was achieved. Instead, revolution would and must continue. Without the constant renewal of revolutionary fervor, Mao believed, there would be too much backsliding; people would become complacent and forget their revolutionary roots, allowing their revolution to stop and then to collapse. In order to prevent this, Mao periodically launched the Chinese people on great bursts of revolutionary fervor designed to preserve the original purity of the revolution. Combining the emphasis on the role of the will with the necessity of revolutionary renewal, Mao initiated "The Great Leap Forward" in the 1950s, and then the "Great Proletarian Cultural Revolution" in the mid-1960s. Both exacted a terrible price from the Chinese people. The Great Leap led to starvation for hundreds of thousands, while the chaos and violence unleashed by the Cultural Revolution killed millions and plunged the Chinese economic and educational systems into a darkness from which they have only slowly recovered. Critics point out that these catastrophic events represented not just theory but also power politics, as Mao fought to maintain or regain his authority as absolute leader of China, and ultimately established a cult of personality as pervasive and overpowering as that of Stalin.

Mao also departed from orthodox Marxism by linking the Communist movement in China to renascent Chinese nationalism, particularly during the 1930s, when Japan's invasion of China presented both a threat and an easy target upon which to focus nationalism. Classical Marxist doctrine sees the state as the creation of the ruling class in order to perpetuate its power, and urges the workers of the world to ignore national boundaries and respond to class solidarity; Mao, on the other hand, fused nationalism with communism to produce a potent ideology that promised simultaneously China's redemption from imperialism and the Chinese peasantry's redemption from exploitation by feudal interests. This fusion of anti-imperialism and revolution was to make Maoism especially attractive in Africa, Asia, and Latin America.

The extent to which Maoism broke with classical Marxism, and perhaps even more significantly, with Leninism-Stalinism, would lead to one of the most important events of the Cold War period, the Sino-Soviet split. Although in theory they were linked by common ideology, in fact the two great nations had very different needs and perceptions of their national interests. In the 1920s Stalin had attempted to direct the Communist revolution in China, with lethal consequences for thousands of Chinese revolutionaries, and when the People's Republic of China was established in 1949, he treated the new communist state as a junior partner. The split between the two giant communist nations occurred in part as a result of Chinese resentment at this treatment, in part because of the ideological challenge that Maoism posed to European Marxism, and in part because the two great powers of China and Russian had long butted up against each other in Central Asia.

Contemporary Marxism

The collapse of the Soviet Union and its satellite system has radically undermined the position of communism throughout most of Europe. Although it will be

permanent revolution The primarily Maoist idea that the revolution is never-ending, a permanent stage in the dialectic process.

decades before the last traces of communism are eradicated in central and eastern Europe, and in the former Soviet Union itself, Marxism as an ideology has been fairly thoroughly discredited and renounced. Soviet-style command economies are now in transition to market economies throughout most of Europe, although in many cases the transition will be a perilous process. A handful of dedicated Marxists, like former Soviet president Mikhail Gorbachev, maintain that the collapse of the Soviet empire had little to do with flaws in Marxist ideology, since the Soviet Union was not yet a fully Marxist state. However, a vast majority of former adherents of Marxism in Europe have bailed out.

Eurocommunism

One of the most interesting developments in contemporary Marxism has been the scramble by Marxist parties in western Europe to increase their options. The result is **Eurocommunism,** a doctrine that maintains its ultimate Marxist faith but renounces the ideas of class struggle and violent revolution in favor of democratic participation within existing parliamentary systems. Whether these apparently contradictory beliefs and practices can be maintained will be one of the more interesting issues to follow in the next decade.

Eurocommunism A variant of communism marked by the belief that communism can evolve within the democratically controlled European state without violent revolution.

Neo-Maoism?

Despite the virtually complete collapse of Marxism in Europe, China, the world's largest nation, continues to bill itself as a Marxist-Maoist state. However, in the last ten years or so the Chinese government has vacillated between allowing experiments in market system economies and democratic procedures and ruthlessly suppressing what it views as "too much" democracy, as in the 1989 Tiananmen Square slaughter. Deng Xiaoping, still holding onto titular leadership, has moved away from Maoist ideological purity. Deng has long proclaimed that it doesn't matter what color a cat is, white or black, as long as it catches mice. This pragmatic, anti-ideological approach earned him years in exile, but more recently has

Kim Jung-Il and Fidel Castro preside over two of the remaining handful of communist regimes in today's world.

opened the way for limited free-market experiments in at least some areas of China. For China, the major question is whether a marketplace economy automatically will guarantee much greater democracy, or it will be possible to combine marketplace economics with some variant of the existing Marxist-Maoist system, and thus perpetuate the power of the current rulers.

Marxism Elsewhere

Other Marxist or quasi-Marxist systems are also in flux. In North Korea, the death of Kim Il Sung will surely have consequences we cannot begin to predict for the Marxist state there. Whether his son Kim Jung Il will be able to replace Kim Il Sung in an equally pervasive cult of personality is an open question. It also remains to be seen whether the younger Kim will be able to assert control over the elaborate bureaucracy that presently embodies the state. Vietnam, still tied in theory to Marxism, seems to be open to more and more market economy experiments, and is clearly ready to lure trade and manufacturing from the rest of the world. And in Cuba, Fidel Castro's Marxist regime seems to be tottering toward its end, although as of this writing it remains the only entrenched communist regime in the Western Hemisphere.

However, it may well be premature to write any sort of obituary for Marxism as a doctrine. These ideas have shown themselves to be both resilient and adaptive, and the ills of the capitalist system that Marxism was designed to cure have by no means vanished.

Fascism and Nazism

Linked together both historically and intellectually, the ideologies of fascism and Nazism emerged in the first quarter of the twentieth century and ensured that the second quarter of that century would be the bloodiest, at least in absolute numbers, in human history to date. Both rose from a kind of romantic irrationalism in the nineteenth century, both denied that man was either a rational or a moral being, and both glorified the state, the leader, and violence. One of the most powerful influences on both doctrines was the work of Friedrich Nietzsche, a nineteenth-century German philosopher who praised the irrational, painted religion and democratic politics as tools of the weak to control the strong, and exalted the "superman" who rose above traditional concepts of morality and behavior to create his own world and his own morality.

Fascism

Fascism, the older cousin of Nazism, originated in Italy with Benito Mussolini, a former newspaper editor who welded together a coalition of the discontented and dispossessed in the aftermath of World War I. Mussolini proclaimed that if the Italian people united behind him, he would in effect restore the glories of the long-departed Roman empire. He christened his ideas "fascism" after the *fasces,* the bundle of twigs held in the talons of the Roman eagle to symbolize the unity of the diverse groups within the empire. As Hitler would after him, Mussolini relied not only on the appeal of his ideas, but also on the fists of his followers, specifically on a paramilitary gang of thugs known as the Blackshirts who "took care" of opposition.

After achieving power in Italy in 1922, Mussolini began to implement and develop his ideas. Above all else, the Italian Fascists emphasized the primacy of the state; it was the nation that gave meaning to the individual, not vice versa, as liberalism proclaims. The individual discovered his or her identity by fusing it with the identities of all others and achieved fulfillment by becoming part of the greater whole. Since Mussolini insisted that the Fascist Party alone embodied the state, there was no room within the Fascist system for "legitimate opposition" parties of the sort that contend for power within liberal democracies. Any dissenter, any individual or party that opposed fascism, became something entirely new, an "enemy of the state." Thus political opponents found themselves political prisoners.

Under Mussolini, fascism also emphasized pageantry and ritual as ways of mobilizing people and bonding them to the will of the state. Just as the Fascist Party embodied this will of the state, the military embodied the strength of the state and transcended it. Mussolini blended this potent brew of nationalism and militarism with a heady dose of marches, rallies, flags and banners, and torchlight parades. These served as means both to mobilize the people and weld them into a single whole, and to mesmerize the people, transfixing them and distracting their attention from the brutality that underpinned much of the Fascist structure.

Industry and business constituted a major part of the Fascist state as well, and they, like individuals, were expected to submerge their individual good in the greater good of the state. This doctrine permitted far greater efficiency in the operation of some industries, and apologists for Mussolini often noted that "at least he made the trains run on time."

Fascism also glorified the military as one of the chief embodiments of the state, and also as the means for achieving the restoration of ancient glory. In virtually all his public appearances Mussolini wore a military uniform, and his rhetoric stressed military virtues such as courage, bravery, and conquest. By nature fascism is expansionist and aggressive, and thus an enormously destablizing doctrine. In the early 1930s Mussolini began to try to put fascist doctrine into practice with the invasion of Ethiopia, as his first step towards restoration of the Roman empire. Although the conquest of Ethiopia proved far more difficult than Mussolini and the Fascist government had assumed, the invasion marked the first major break in Europe's peace, and the beginning of the long downward slide to World War II.

Finally, fascism glorified the ultimate leader. Fascism went far beyond the cult of personality to portray the leader himself as the repository of all national virtue, the final arbiter of all national good, and the ultimate embodiment of national power and strength. Mussolini became known simply as *Il Duce,* "The Leader."

Nazism

As Hitler acknowledged early in his climb to power, **national socialism,** or Nazism, began as a "junior partner" to Mussolini's Fascist movement. However, with the addition of virulent racism to the already potent fascist brew, Nazism became a highly successful ideology that enabled Hitler to wield virtually unchallenged power for more than a decade, and to begin a ruinous war that ended with Germany's destruction.

The key difference between Fascism and National Socialism, or Nazism, was Nazism's intense racism. Blending German romanticism, particularly the glorification of an ancient *volkische* past, with an extreme Social Darwinism that emphasized the idea of "survival [and triumph] of the fittest," Nazism offered the German

national socialism A form of fascism found in Nazi Germany which glorified the state *(volk)* and used extreme racism to that end.

people explanations for their defeat in World War I and another, far greater, opportunity for achieving the greatness they deserved. German mythology particularly intrigued Hitler, with its emphasis on the special past of the Germanic peoples and their almost mystical links to one another. Nineteenth-century romanticism in Germany had glorified this mythical past and enshrined it in works such as Richard Wagner's great operatic epic, *The Ring Cycle (Die Valkyrie, Siegfried, Die Gotterdammerung,* and *Das Rheingold).* Hitler was fascinated by the mystical themes of greatness and the grandeur of destruction in these operas, and frequently attended performances of them.

While glorification of a mystical past greatness represented what might be called a positive side to Nazi ideology, there was a far darker, demonic side: a virulent racism linked to Social Darwinism. In the late nineteenth century, Social Darwinists had extrapolated Darwin's ideas of natural selection through competition for scarce resources into the idea of "survival of the fittest," and had then used these ideas to explain and justify the rise of modern industrialism and its often brutal exploitation of workers. Others had taken these ideas as justification for imperialism, a titanic struggle in which a fitter or superior nation imposed its will on a weaker or inferior nation. From these ideas it was not a very far stretch to the idea that some races were superior, others inferior, and that it was the destiny, even the mission, of the superior ones to enforce their wills on the inferior. Racism was nothing new, but Social Darwinism in effect added a scientific gloss to already-existing racist ideas.

Hitler proclaimed that the Germans were the superior race, a kind of national superman in the Nietzschean sense, and that it was their destiny, even their responsibility, to impose their will on lesser races and peoples. He particularly emphasized the dominance of the "Nordic" type—tall, muscular, blond-haired and blue-eyed, as the epitome of the superior race (ironically, Hitler himself was rather short, with brown hair and brown eyes). Poised against this superior race, and plotting to prevent it from achieving its destiny, were the inferior races, the worst of which were the Jews. Anti-Semitism, like its cousin racism, was nothing new in European history; for fifteen hundred years, Christian churches, both Catholic and Protestant, had condemned the Jews as a race for the death of Christ, and anti-Jewish laws and pogroms were common in eastern Europe and Russia during the nineteenth century. Nazism would ultimately carry this anti-Semitism to a new and lethal level, as the Nazi state in Germany first stripped Jews of all their rights and then moved toward what Hitler terms the "final solution," the complete destruction of all Jews.

In some ways, Hitler's twisting together of these ideas—the superiority of the German people and the evil inferiority of the Jews—was a brilliant blend, offering Germany the Jews as a scapegoat for their twentieth-century woes (the loss of World War I and the harsh conditions imposed on the defeated nation at Versailles), and simultaneously promising them a future in which their enemies would finally get what they deserved and the German people would take their rightful place as the rulers of a Europe cleansed of Jews and other inferiors. Hitler also proved himself a master of crowd psychology, holding audiences of a hundred thousand or more enthralled as he spoke, and a master of pageantry, manipulating mass ritual and ceremony brilliantly to enlist the emotions of the German people. Mass rallies such as one at Nuremberg in 1936 enabled Hitler to bind the masses of the German people to him and to the symbols of his political party: the swastika and the polished precision of a reborn German military.

Like fascism, Nazism glorified both the irrational in human beings—thus the emphasis on hatred and on the destruction of whatever was hated—and the military, both as a repository of traditional Germanic values (authority and obedience, courage, loyalty, bravery) and as the tool by which Germany would regain its rightful place. Rebuilding the German military became Hitler's first priority, because he recognized it both as an immense source of price for the German people and as the embodiment of the medieval virtues of warriorhood that he sought to restore and then use for conquest.

Conquest would become a major theme of Nazism, whether it was the conquest of the self to achieve immersion in the greater good of the race, the conquest of the inferior races within Germany, or ultimately the conquest of all of Europe, and perhaps the rest of the world, in the name of the superior German people. Nazism promoted a relentless imperialism in the name of national superiority, of nationalism less in the sense of the state per se than in the idea of the people as a nation. Aggression was legitimate if it meant the triumph of the German people and the fulfillment of their destiny. Violence and irrationality, directed against either inferior betrayers like the Jews or inferior nation-states like Russia, were praised as manifestations of superiority.

The intense emotionalism of Nazism, with its fervent exaltation of the "superior" race and its bitter condemnation of anything standing in the way of its triumph (Jews, communists, democracy) was enormously appealing, offering an explanation for past failure, a cathartic release of both guilt and responsibility, and a future limited only by weakness. Not surprisingly, among those most enthralled by Nazism were the young, who could find a new identity, or in fact bypass the dilemmas of identity-building completely, by submerging themselves in the Nazi movement, with its promise of a bright future for those proclaimed as superior simply by virtue of their race.

Like fascism, Nazism demanded that all elements of the state—industry, the military, the people—submit to the will of the state and set aside individual and thus dangerous desires for its good. Like fascism, Nazism was totalitarian, using all the tools of the modern state—police, secret police, communications and media, and education—to control the people, to enlist them in this new crusade, and to destroy those who refused to go along. Like fascism, Nazism also glorified the leader. Adolph Hitler became the embodiment of the *fuhrer prinzip,* the leadership principle, and as "Der Fuhrer" was the absolute and unquestioned leader of the German people. And finally, like fascism, Nazism launched its adherents on wars of conquest that led to their defeat and virtual destruction.

Fascism and Nazism in the Contemporary World

Although apparently discredited by their defeat in World War II and the revelations of the horrors that they had created, fascism and Nazism have recently enjoyed a resurgence in parts of Europe. The brew of racism, hatred, and hope remains potent.

In Italy, neofascists formed an important part of the coalition that won the 1994 elections. In Germany, neo-Nazis (primarily but not entirely alienated youths) have indulged their penchant for violence and their hatred of foreigners (the "inferior" races) by protesting against Turkish workers and by burning buildings housing these workers, resulting in a series of deaths. Anti-Semitism also has been observed recently in Germany, with the defacement of Jewish cemeteries.

Current German leaders have tried hard to erase remnants of Nazism, apologizing to the Jewish people and to the Polish people for the horrors of the Holocaust and the blitzkrieg, but they have had little success in stemming the violence of the neo-Nazis. Right-wing political movements perilously close to fascism and Nazism are currently prospering in France, while in the United States groups such as the Aryan Nation preach anti-Semitism and engage in paramilitary training; some of these groups are armed to the teeth.

Perhaps the most disturbing recent manifestation of fascism, or something that looks perilously close to fascism, has come in Russia. There, conditions in

From Superhighway to Superhateway?

Does the right to free speech stop when speech is hate-mongering? If so, what agency or group has the right to declare that speech wrong, and what can they do about it? Questions like these, which have been part of American society since the Bill of Rights was ratified, are now being asked about the Information Superhighway, as various hate groups have begun to discover that they, too, can benefit from the communications revolution.

More than 250 neo-Nazi and racist groups in the United States and Canada are now part of the communications revolution, using desktop publishing, FAX machines, computer bulletin boards, and even the Internet to spread their angry messages of white supremacy and hatred. In 1994 one enterprising young neo-Nazi, George Burdi, established his own media company, Resistance Inc., to ensure the spread of his ideas. Resistance Inc. publishes its own magazine, promotes its own rock band, and maintains an Internet site to promote its materials and tell people how to order them.

Former Ku Klux Klan member Don Black, who served two years in federal prison and learned to use computers there, has an Internet bulletin board, Stormfront, which he uses to promote what he calls a white rights movement. Black spends up to eight hours a day maintaining the Stormfront bulletin board and staying in contact with other white separatists.

The arrival of neo-Nazis and other hate groups on the Internet has raised serious concerns. Some fear that more sophisticated communications will make such groups more effective. Already, Burdi's Resistance media center has helped boost member-

GLOBAL PERSPECTIVES

ship in various skinhead neo-Nazi cells from a low of one thousand in 1987 to an estimated four thousand hard-core members today. Some students of such movements say that new technology, skillfully used, could produce a mass hate movement, and others maintain that there are even today clear signs of growing militancy in these hate movements that may well be related to the use of new technologies.

The question is what, if anything, can be done about this. Some people argue that free speech cannot be used as a cloak for hate messages and that such messages must be limited. Arguments have been made that information providers, such as Prodigy, America Online, and CompuServe, must be held responsible for overseeing what appears on their networks, and in fact these services do try to exercise some control over what they describe as offensive material. However, there is no governing agency per se overseeing the Internet, whose users tend to take pride in the generally anarchic character of the system. Most users of the Internet regard any attempt to regulate what goes on there with enormous suspicion. The very nature of the Internet makes attempts to establish control virtually impossible, and many argue that seven hate bulletin boards out of the thousands and thousands linked to the Internet represent a very small proportion.

Perhaps the most important conclusion to be reached about the current controversy over electronic hate-mongering is the recognition that the brave new world of global electronic communications may not be all that brave a new world after all, but simply a much faster version of the world within which it operates, neither a utopia nor a world of horrors. (Rozsa 1995; Schneider 1995)

many ways frighteningly similar to those that permitted the rise of fascism and Nazism in the 1920s seem to exist: a great nation humbled, its pride tattered, its economy shattered, its military in shambles. Striding onto the stage, a charismatic figure preaches hatred, particularly of Jews, and promises restoration of lost greatness. Whether Vladimir Zhirinovsky is a junior Hitler, as some fear, or merely a buffoon ·(as Hitler himself was at first portrayed) is still a matter for debate and controversy. Sadly, there is no controversy about the depth and virulence of anti-Semitism to which Zhirinovsky appeals. With his promises that Russian troops will occupy all the "lost territory" of the old Russian and more recent Soviet empires, that they will wet their boots in the Indian Ocean, Zhirinovsky has provoked fears among many that his neofascism will provide the vehicle for resurgent Russian power tied to aggression and imperialism, not in the name of international communism but on behalf of Russian nationalism and national superiority. A nuclear-armed neo-Hitler is a truly frightening prospect, but a possible one.

Confucianism

For more than two thousand years, **Confucianism** was the orthodox political and ethical belief system of a series of Chinese empires and of many of the states that drew their political systems from China, such as Japan, Korea, and Vietnam. It was based on the teachings of a philosopher in the sixth century B.C., Kung Fu-tze (Master Kung), known as Confucius to the West, who looked back to what he perceived as a golden past and attempted to apply principles gleaned from studying the past in order to produce a better present.

Confucius and most of his followers and advocates agreed that human nature was basically good; in the fourth century B.C. Mencius observed that just as water tends to run downhill, so human nature tends to be good. Education, especially education in rules of correct behavior drawn from study of the past, burnished that essential goodness. The ultimate goal of education, according to Confucianists, was the cultivation of *jen,* normally translated as virtue but expressed far more vividly by Arthur Waley as "human-heartedness"—that is, the finest qualities of the human being. Thus the scholar represented the most cultivated virtue, and also shouldered the greatest responsibilities. According to Confucianism, the educated man (women were locked out of the system) must serve government, in order to ensure just government and a harmonious society. In addition, the educated individual must always serve as an example for the uneducated, who would always be in the majority but who could cultivate their own virtue by watching proper behavior and ritual. To some degree, Confucianism argued that outward behavior, such as following correct ritual, could foster inner virtue. The generalist who was virtuous was far more valuable to society than the specialist who understood only a narrow area and had not cultivated virtue.

Government was thus conceived as the realm of the virtuous and educated, whose role was to serve the good of the people by advising the emperor, educating him in correct ritual, helping him cultivate his own virute, and chiding him when he strayed from the path of virtue (which could be a high-risk proposition). The emperor ruled, according to Confucian theory, because he held what was known as the Mandate of Heaven. The dynasty in power had seized the Mandate from a previous dynasty that had lost it because it had ceased to be virtuous in ceasing to rely upon the service of the scholar-officials. Confucianists envisioned history as a series of cycles, with each dynasty seizing the Mandate of Heaven

Confucianism Orthodox Chinese political and ethical belief system that viewed human nature as basically good.

from a failed predecessor, ruling according to Confucian virtue for a while, and then finally losing its grip on the Mandate as it began to deviate from the ways of virtue. It was part of the role of the virtuous educated officials to remonstrate with the emperor who seemed to be straying from Confucian virtue, and if that didn't work, to abandon ship and attach themselves to a new dynasty that promised to abide by Confucian traditions and rule by virtue. Dynasties would come and go, but the scholarly bureaucracy would remain.

Confucianists ranked society into four categories. At the top were the scholar-officials. Just below them were the farmers, the peasants who constituted 90 percent of China's population. Third came artisans and workers, and last were merchants and traders. Military men were not even part of this system. "One does not use good iron to make nails," goes the Chinese saying, "nor good men to make soldiers." Although this theoretical hierarchy did not necessarily reflect China's realities—China always supported a thriving commerce and manufacturing base as well as large armies—it did influence ultimate aspirations for success. John King Fairbanks, America's leading China scholar, put it brilliantly: in traditional China, the goal was not to build a better mousetrap, but to acquire the government monopoly on mice. The wealthy merchant educated his sons so that they could assume a place among the scholar-gentry, and large clans made sure that the bright sons of poor clansmen received an education for the same purpose. Ancestor tablets celebrating the virtues of the past listed those who were educated and who had become part of the imperial administration, not those who had become wealthy.

Confucianism also stressed the importance of a harmonious society, and emphasized the necessity of maintaining five key relationships in order to achieve that harmony. These relationships were emperor to subject, father to son, husband to wife, brother to brother, and friend to friend. As long as these relationships were in order, the harmony of society was assured. However, if there was strife and contention within society, the relationships had to be corrected by what was known as the "rectification of names," a term and practice that Mao Tse-tung later introduced into Chinese Communism.

At its worst, Confucianism could deteriorate into an empty series of rituals and prescribed behavior, performed by rote as if they alone could supply meaning. At its best, Confucianism brought about humanistic government and society in which the focus was not on what was best for the government but on what was needed to insure harmony, and thus stability and prosperity.

The Culture State

The Chinese traditionally used Confucianism to define the difference between civilized peoples (that is, those who followed Confucian practices) and barbarians who did not practice Confucianism. The Middle Kingdom was a culture-state, not a nation-state. There was no question of foreign relations as they were understood in the West, as equal sovereign states dealing with one another; instead, Confucian China related to other states only as a superior to inferiors. Emissaries from other states on China's fringes were always welcomed, for they brought "tribute" to China in the form of gifts and exotic products, and presumably had come to observe how a world should be arranged and run. The Chinese rewarded these "tribute missions" with bountiful gifts in return (sometimes representing little more than bribes to militaristic nomads who otherwise threatened China), but in no way considered them as equals. China would surely expand, but expansion would come as those surrounding China observed Confucianism in action and responded, as their own inward goodness guaranteed, by adopting first Chinese ways and then Confucianism itself. (The benevolent understanding of how China had grown did not, incidentally, prevent the Chinese from sending armies deep into the interior of Central Asia, or from spending nearly a thousand years suppressing Vietnamese independence.) The extent of the Confucian world at its height is shown in figure 6.2.

How much of Confucian culture remains in the contemporary world is hotly debated. Fairbanks saw many remnants of Confucianism in the People's Republic of China, even in the doctrines of Mao Tse-tung, and titled one of his most perceptive works on modern China *The People's Middle Kingdom.* In the Republic of China, on the island of Taiwan, Confucius's birthday is still an official holiday, and schools teach Confucianism; the students produced by these schools then play key roles in the thriving commercial and manufacturing economy of Taiwan. For more than fifteen hundred years, Japan also participated, at least in theory, in the Confucian cultural system, although the Japanese emphasis on feudal and military values clearly conflicted with Confucian ideas. Whether this Confucian underlay is at least partially responsible for Japan's remarkable economic success is debated, but clearly the Japanese stress on consensus and group harmony reflect in part traditional Confucian values.

Two things are clear in looking at Confucianism's legacy in modern Asia. First, the values of virtue, education, and harmony that permeate Confucianism persist to a considerable extent, and have continued to play a major role in

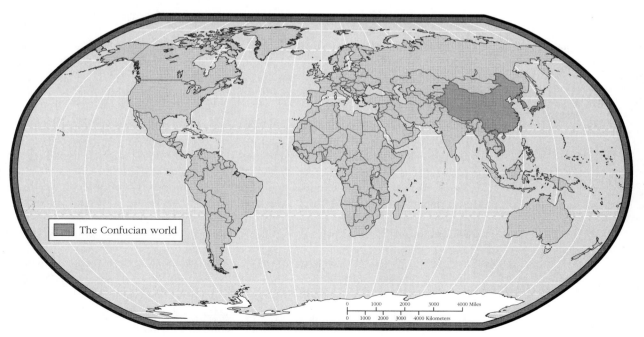

Figure 6.2 **The Confucian World**

ordering East Asian society. Second, the American view of Confucianists as "Asiatic Puritans" is a tremendous oversimplification of the similarities between two fundamentally different cultures, and attempts to view contemporary Confucianism as a kind of Protestant ethic lying at the root of East Asia's economic and political reinvigoration clearly create more problems than they explain. Nonetheless, Westerners would do well to study Confucianism in order to understand both traditional and contemporary value systems in East Asia.

Religious Fundamentalism

Religion has long been a major factor in international relations, from the conflicts between the ancient Israelites and their neighbors through the Christian-Islamic wars of the Crusades to the terrible bloodletting of Europe's Reformation period. In the contemporary world, while religion per se is still important, our concern is primarily with specific subsets of major religions, those that call for a return to a simpler past and to fundamental values as a means of regulating society. Fundamentalism is flourishing in at least three of the world's major religions, Christianity, Islam, and Hinduism, and has had a major impact on international relations.

As we stress throughout this book, our contemporary world is in a time of rapid, escalating, and often bewildering change. People living in the developed industrial nations often have trouble keeping up with, and accepting, the pace of change, and the problem is often worse for those in the nonindustrialized and developing portions of the globe. Modernization—in the form of secularism, materialism, accelerated trade and marketplace activity, global communications, and foreign television, books, and movies—often seems to threaten traditional values and traditional cultures. Not surprisingly, those who have had the greatest stake in traditional societies, in which religious rather than secular values counted most, often have led the attack on modernization in the name of religion, traditional values, and fundamentalism.

religious fundamentalism
A religious return to the basic values of various religions around the world, affecting the political action of the adherents.

Religious fundamentalism thus includes a call for a return to traditional values and an attack on secular, modernizing trends, in forms as diverse as different legal systems, clothing, religion, and television programs.

In the United States, religious fundamentalism to this point has had little if any effect on foreign policy and formal international relations, although it undoubtedly has spurred thousands of missionary efforts that carry American Protestantism not only into traditionally non-Christian areas of Africa and Asia, but also into Roman Catholic Latin America. However, religious fundamentalists are pursuing higher and higher levels of political activism in the contemporary United States; as more fundamentalists gain office, and as more officeholders have larger and larger numbers of fundamentalists in their constituency, we can expect greater demand for the values of traditional American Protestantism (and to a lesser extent, Catholicism) to be reflected in the United States' relations with the rest of the world.

Not surprisingly, religious fundamentalism is strongest not in the industrialized Christian world but in the industrializing non-Christian world, especially in the Middle East, North Africa, and the Indo-Pakistan subcontinent. (However, as the 1996 assassination of Israeli Prime Minister Yitzhak Rabin by a radical fundamentalist Jew reminds us, neither fundamentalism nor fanatacism are confined to developing nations).

Islamic Fundamentalism

The Shi'ites

Certainly the best-known and arguably most influential version of religious fundamentalism in the contemporary world can be found in Islam. Contemporary Islamic fundamentalism traces its roots almost to the very beginning of Islam itself, to a split within the Islamic community about the succession to the Prophet Mohammed. After the Prophet's death, fierce arguments erupted about who should become *caliph:* leader of the Islamic world, successor to Mohammed, and God's messenger on earth. A small group known as the Shi'at Ali (followers of Ali) claimed that the caliphate should descend through the family of the Prophet; as Mohammed had no sons, the succession should devolve upon his cousin and son-in-law, Ali. A much larger group within Islam, who became the dominant Sunnis, preferred a caliph chosen by the Prophet's associates or a council of religious scholars. The Shi'at Ali temporarily won their argument when Ali became the fourth caliph, but he was assassinated after less than five years' rule, and the succession then devolved as the Sunni preferred. Ali's followers, to become known as the Shi'a or Shi'ites, became a minority splinter group within Islam.

Nearly two decades after Ali's death, a group of Shi'ites led by Hosain, the son of Ali and Mohammed's daughter Fatima and thus grandson of the Prophet, rebelled against what they saw as the injustice of Sunni rule. Only seventy-two in number, including women and children, the rebels faced certain death, but

The Ayatollah Khomeini presided over the Shi'ite fundamentalist revolution in Iran that overthrew the Shah of Iran in 1979.

fervently believed that Islam demanded that its followers be willing to die on behalf of their beliefs rather than live with injustice. Revolt against perceived tyranny was a duty to God, and martyrdom an honor. Modern Shi'ites commemorate the death of Hosain and his followers in Karbala (now in southern Iraq) with reenactments of their martyrdom in an Islamic passion play during the festival of Ashura, much as fervent Christians carry a cross along the path followed by Jesus just before his crucifixion.

Thus today's Shi'ite community, estimated at 12 to 15 percent of Islam's 900 million followers worldwide, sees itself as the guardian of Hosain's tradition, as victims of authority and persecution specially entrusted to struggle against injustice and abuse of authority. Within the Shi'ite community, religious leaders, or mullahs, play major roles, often assuming what Europeans would call civic as well as religious authority and leadership. Shi'a calls for a return to the early Islamic world, when the Islamic community looked to its faith for guidance in all matters and saw it as a way of life. Islam includes laws governing politics, economics, and society in general, as well as spiritual beliefs. The *Shari'a,* or Islamic legal code, covers business, banking, hygiene, marriage and divorce, defense, taxes, punishments, and family relationships.

Today's Shi'ites combine absolute faith in the universality of Shari'a with a deep commitment to fight injustice, and challenge abuses of secular authority, and a long and honored tradition of martyrdom. Shi'ism enjoys a revolutionary potential because of the position of its mullahs, or religious leaders, who are expected to exercise their authority in civil matters as well. While Sunni clergy are primarily advisors to the faithful, Shi'ite theologians interpret religious law and duty for their followers, and in theory their word is law (Wright 1989, 46–48).

Nowhere is the linkage of religious and civil authority clearer and more potent than in Iran, where the Ayatollah Khomeini mobilized millions of Shi'ites to overthrow the modernizing and often abused authority of the Shah and to create a theocracy ruled according to Shari'a. Proclaiming that "Every day is Ashura and every place is Karbala," Khomeini made Shi'ism into a potent revolutionary force that drove out the Shah, overturned much of the modernization and Westernization that the Shah's regime had achieved, and then made Iran a center for revolutionary and often terrorist activity on behalf of Islam. As a Shi'ite state, Iran now is ruled by what is left of the original revolutionary coalition—the Islamic revolution, like so many others, tended to devour its creators—in the name of Islam. Religious and theological leaders dictate law and its application, rejecting what they see as the evils associated with the West, particularly the "Great Satan," the United States.

The triumph of Islamic fundamentalism in Iran has had profound effects on its international relations, and equally important consequences within the rest of the Islamic world. One of the most obvious results of the Iranian revolution has been the vastly increased influence of Islamic fundamentalism throughout the Muslim world. The Ayatollah Khomeini was a charismatic figure whose ability to galvanize those who saw themselves as victims of injustice and abuse of authority extended far beyond the borders of Iran. Today there are powerful fundamentalist movements in Islamic nations as disparate as Algeria, Egypt, and Pakistan. In Algeria, for example, military leaders canceled democratic elections when it became apparent that fundamentalists would probably win a majority of votes, and today Algeria teeters on the edge of explosive revolution. In Egypt, which has been one of the most modernizing nations in the Middle East, and which took the lead in making peace with Israel, fundamentalists have agitated against the secular civil government and particularly have railed against the relatively liberated position of women within Egyptian society. And in Pakistan, a confusing succession of military dictatorships interspersed with democratically elected governments has left room for the rise of a fundamentalist movement whose wrath is directed equally against Pakistani modernization (reflected in the leadership of a woman, Benazir Bhutto) and Hindu enemies in India.

Iraq, a source of considerable trouble in the Middle East and elsewhere, also has a substantial Shi'ite population, perhaps a numerical majority, that chafes under the rule of a Sunni minority and what Shi'ites (like many others) see as the abusive authoritarian dictatorship of Saddam Hussein. Hussein has used great brutality to suppress and control Shi'ism, especially in the vulnerable southern areas of Iraq that border both Iran and Kuwait; his aggressive foreign policy, with all the turmoil that it has caused, is motivated at least in part by the desire to enlist his followers against both Shi'a and other perceived enemies.

The most prominent international result of Islamic and particularly Shi'ite fundamentalism is the rise of terrorism directed against any target that represents the evils of modernization in any way. Thus Shi'ite terrorists have been especially active in the more modern Middle East and North Africa. In Egypt, for example, fundamentalist terrorists have carried out a series of attacks against tourists, in an attempt to undermine the authority of the secular government and to erode its economic base as well. Algeria also has seen an increasing level of terrorist violence, often directed against foreigners who both represent the hated contemporary Western values and are often obvious and easy targets. The role of fundamentalist terrorism in Lebanon is inextricably mixed with the convoluted politics of that nation, but there is little doubt that the rash of kidnappings and holding of hostages that took place in the 1980s in that besieged nation was a direct consequence of the Iranian revolution and took place at the urging of, and with the financial support of, the Iranian mullahs.

A series of Muslim dictators, including both Saddam Hussein and Moammar Qadafi of Libya, has attempted to climb on the fundamentalist bandwagon. Saddam, for example, presented his invasion of Kuwait and the subsequent Persian Gulf War as a *jihad,* or holy war; virtually no leaders in the Muslim community, Sunni or Shi'ite, accepted this. Qadafi, erratic and unstable, also senses the revolutionary power of Shi'ism, but to what extent he will be able to harness it is uncertain.

Islamic fundamentalism also has had widespread international repercussions because of its impact on traditional Western values, such as freedom of speech and freedom of ideas. Two prominent cases involve Islamic writers whose works are seen as violating traditional Muslim values: Salman Rushdie and Taslima Nasrin. The publication of Rushdie's book *Satanic Verses,* which satirizes the Prophet, set off a firestorm of protest in Iran and resulted ultimately in the Ayatollah Khomeini's issuance of a *fatwa,* or Islamic rule, calling for the death of Rushdie. Proclaiming Rushdie a blasphemer, Khomeini called on followers of Islam to execute not only him but also anyone else involved in the publication of *Satanic Verses.* Rushdie promptly went into hiding, from which he has emerged for only an occasional public appearance. Bookstores selling the book were bombed, and a prominent Muslim leader in Belgium who opposed the *fatwa* was assassinated. After a time the Iranian theocracy offered $2.6 million to anyone who could kill Rushdie, as well as a $1 million bonus if the "executioner" were Iranian.

Taslima Nasrin, a Bangladeshi feminist, incurred the wrath of Islamic fundamentalists by what she characterizes as a misquoted call to revise the Koran, the

Islamic holy book. Despite her protestations that she was misquoted, Nasrin also has called for substantial changes in the position of women within Islamic society, particularly the elimination of strict rules that limit many Bangladeshi women to childbearing and housekeeping. Charged by an Islamic court in Bangladesh with offending the religious sentiments of Muslims, Nasrin has fled to Sweden but has been pursued by threats. Bangladeshi fundamentalists have threatened also to topple the Bangladeshi government for allowing her to flee, although technically she has not violated any law.

Both Rushdie and Nasrin have become international symbols of the struggle between traditional values as asserted by Muslim fundamentalists and modernizing values such as freedom of speech and new roles for women. It is a struggle that promises to continue long into the future.

It is important to note that not all Islamic fundamentalism is driven by the revolutionary potential of Shi'ism. The Kingdom of Saudi Arabia, for example, follows an extremely conservative sect of Islam known as Wahabi, and Saudi law derives from the Shari'a. Thus, although the Saudi government practices what seem to many Westerners to be barbaric punishments—the cutting off of hands for theft, stoning to death for adultery—Shi'ites also see the Saudi government as wrong. First, it is a monarchy, and Shi'ites generally consider monarchy to be an abusive and dangerous form of government. Furthermore, Shi'ites deeply resent that the Saudis, with all their perceived flaws, have within their borders the holiest of Islamic holy places, Mecca, and thus control the *haj,* the pilgrimage to Mecca required of all devout Muslims. The Ayatollah Khomeini called repeatedly for the overthrow of the Saudi monarch, and the season of *haj* recently has seen Iranian pilgrims rioting against Saudi rule.

Whether this kind of internecine struggle between Shi'ites, Sunnis, and Wahabis will spill over into the already-complex politics of the Middle East and North Africa remains to be seen, but the possibility is both very real and very frightening. In this case outsiders may find themselves hoping that ethnic differences among the various Shi'ite factions—Algerians, Egyptians, Iraqis, and Saudis are Arabic, Iranians are Persian, and Pakistanis are Indo-European—will prevent a possible Shi'ite coalition that could stretch from the Atlantic Ocean to the Indian Ocean.

A Caveat

Islamic fundamentalism
Muslims who rely upon the ancient works of Islam, the Koran and the Sunna, to guide their lives.

A warning to exercise great care in discussing Islamic fundamentalism comes from Yahya M. Sadowski, a scholar of Islamic movements. According to Sadowski, there are actually four very different forms of "political Islam." These are illustrated in figure 6.3. **Islamic fundamentalism,** as defined by a group of French scholars studying political Islam, refers solely to those who believe that Muslims should draw upon only the most ancient works if Islam, the Qur'an (Koran) and the Sunna (the example of the Prophet Mohammed), and should reject any other traditions or non-Islamic values accumulated over the last fourteen hundred years. According to Sadowski, this doctrine of fundamentalism holds great appeal for urban elites who see it as affirmation of their values against the more popular views held by the lower classes. Politically, this fundamentalist view requires strict enforcement of the Shari'a, Islamic law. By this definition, there are two Islamic fundamentalist states, Saudi Arabia and Iran (one Sunni and the other Shi'a—Sadowski 1995, 10–11).

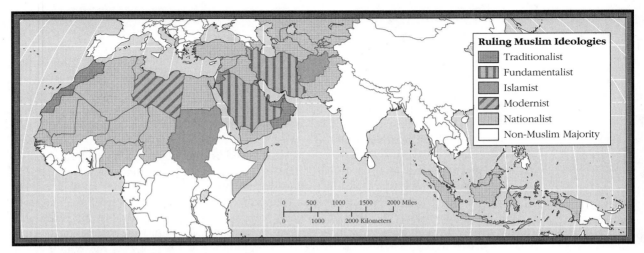

Figure 6.3 The Muslim World
Source: Based on Yahya M. Sadowski, "Bosnia's Muslims: A Fundamentalist Threat?" *The Brookings Review* (Winter 1995), 10–11.

Islamism, the second type of political Islam, is what Westerners often mistakenly refer to as "fundamentalism." Held largely by intellectuals and professionals with exposure to Western-style education and values, Islamism is what Sadowski terms a "post-modern" doctrine rising from rejection of modernity and modern values. It incorporates not only Islamic works but also antimodernist western philosophers such as Heidegger and Spengler. The Islamists, far from disdaining the urban poor as do the fundamentalists, have a broad following among this volatile constituency and thus hold great revolutionary potential. The Muslim Brotherhood, organized in Egypt in the 1930s and still active there, was the first Islamist group; Islamists have seized power in Afghanistan and Sudan in recent years, and are currently challenging authority in Egypt, Algeria, and among the Palestinians. In Egypt, however, the terrorists who have wreaked such havoc on the tourist trade in the last few years appear to be even more militant radicals who are challenging the Muslim Brotherhood (Sadowski 1995, 11; "Sad Dreams by the Nile" 1995, 35).

Islamism Post-modern Islamic doctrine that rejects modernity and incorporates some antimodernist western philosophers.

Traditionalism is the third distinct type of political Islam. It too hearkens back to the Prophet, but it is primarily the domain of the rural elites who "steadfastly follow traditional leaders out of a sense of religious obligation." Traditionalists call for the restoration of all aspects of traditional village life, economic and social as well as religious (Sadowski 1995, 11).

traditionalism Muslims who yearn for a return to traditional or old-fashioned values of village life and its economic, social, and religious beliefs.

The fourth distinct form of political Islam is **reformism,** whose central tenet is that truly moral behavior cannot be imposed by the state, but must come from the individual conscience. Thus reformists believe that it is necessary to stop introducing laws and begin instead to educate people. Reformists call for the creation of a "new Islamic intelligentsia" to inspire a cultural renaissance in the Islamic world. Not surprisingly, reformism is most widespread in areas in which Muslims are a minority, such as India and the Balkan peninsula (Sadowski 1995, 11–12).

reformism Muslims who believe that moral character stems from within, and cannot be imposed by the state.

One way to highlight the differences among these varieties of political Islam is to examine the way in which they view the Koran and the Shari'a.

Fundamentalists believe that the Shari'a is an infallible blueprint for a perfect society. Islamists, in contrast, believe that the Shari'a cannot provide guidance for all contingencies of modern life; still, they embrace it as a foundation on which legislation may be based. Reformists go still further to emphasize the spirit rather than the letter of the Koran and the Shari'a. They see Islam as a system of values rather than a set of social institutions, and argue that Muslims should never reject out of hand anything that makes the world a better place (Sadowski 1995, 13).

Sadowski warns that by lumping these various factions together under the heading "fundamentalists," the West runs the risk of making the same mistakes it made during the Cold War, when it viewed communism as a monolithic institution. At that time, he argues, the West missed great opportunities to exploit differences among communist nations, particularly the Sino-Soviet split; now, by ignoring the differences among Islamic factions, the West may well miss opportunities to exploit these differences. Sadowski concludes, "Rather than examining the diverse ways in which poverty, corruption, and autocracy combine to fuel war, we are circling our wagons in preparation for a global confrontation with 'ethnic' movements." But to succeed in the post–Cold War world, he stresses "we will have to discriminate among the sundry parties to the world's conflicts, to learn which are really threatening and which are not." The alternative, Sadowski writes, is the adoption of a "the only good Muslim is a dead Muslim" attitude (Sadowski 1995, 15).

Hindu Fundamentalism

Recent years have seen the phenomenon of fundamentalism emerging within Hinduism, the principal religion of India. Fundamentalist Hindus believe that their position, and the position of their religion, is threatened by two major non-Hindu groups within India, Muslims and Sikhs. The growth of Hindu extremism has been remarkable, particularly since unlike Islam or Christianity, Hinduism has no one sacred book, no single agreed-upon set of beliefs, and a wide-ranging pantheon of gods. Nor, unlike Islam, does Hinduism have a tradition of political activism or of attempting to translate religious values into civil law. However, Hindu priests in many parts of India recently have attempted to inject religion directly into Indian politics and even to rewrite the present democratic Indian constitution in order to make India officially a Hindu state, in effect disenfranchising the Muslims, Christians, Sikhs, Jains, Buddhists, and Jews who constitute nearly 20 percent of India's population.

A militant political party, the Bharatiya Janata Party (BJP), has emerged as the active embodiment of this new Hindu militancy, and has gained power in a number of Indian states. BJP leaders have called for and achieved the destruction of several Islamic mosques and are now raising a call for the establishment of "Rama Raiya," a sort of "God's Kingdom," throughout India. Although the BJP achieved a plurality in India's 1996 elections, the government it formed collapsed almost immediately. Like many other groups, the BJP may well find leading to be much more difficult than opposing.

Two minority religious groups in India, Muslims and Sikhs, have become the particular target of BJP and Hindu anger and violence, in part because of quasi-ethnic and historical factors. Sikhs, the religious majority in Punjab, a particularly sensitive area in northeastern India, have become more extremist and aggressive in the last few years. The Sikhs seek both religious and political separation from India, and their separatism has given rise to Indian government attempts to suppress them. In 1984 Prime Minister Indira Gandhi ordered an attack on the Golden Temple, the Sikhs' holiest shrine, and paid for it with her life when her Sikh bodyguards assassinated her. Since then the Indian Punjab has been under virtual military rule, and Indian Hindu troops have harshly suppressed the violent Sikh secessionist movement. One Indian-American writer observes that the Punjab has become "an Indian version of Northern Ireland." (Mehta 1994, 18)

The situation is equally volatile in Kashmir, in which there is a long history of Muslim dominance. Kashmir has been the site of violent contention between Muslim Pakistan and Hindu India since the partition of the Indian subcontinent in 1947. The hostility between India and Pakistan that emerged in 1947 has continued to rage in Kashmir since then, playing into the hands of both Islamic and Hindu fundamentalists. Today the Indian army has turned Kashmir into "a virtual police state," which unintentionally but inevitably has made the Islamic secessionist movement even stronger. (Mehta 1994, 20) Exacerbating the problem in India, and stoking the fires of Hindu extremism, has been the spilling of hundreds of thousands of Islamic refugees from desperately poor Bangladesh into the northeastern state of Assam. Hindus are now calling for the expulsion of these refugees.

There are nearly a hundred million Muslims scattered throughout India, and whether Pakistan will ultimately attempt to present itself as the protector of these Muslims remains unknown. Certainly, as Islamic fundamentalism becomes stronger in Pakistan, as well as in Kashmir, the odds of some sort of Pakistani action, whether merely rhetorical or military, are increasing. Making the whole situation far more dangerous, of course, is that fact that both India and Pakistan possess nuclear capability. Significant deterioration in the unity of India, the world's largest democracy, could substantially muddy global politics not only by inviting Pakistani intervention and thus raising the possibility of nuclear conflict, but also by opening the way for secessionist movements among a number of Indian states. Such instability also could raise temptations for China to take advantage of the situation along the northeastern frontier between the world's two largest nations, the site of major battles as recently as the 1960s.

Although Hindu fundamentalism is less well known than its Islamic counterpart, at least in part because it has been confined largely to India and has not yet spilled over into recognizable international terrorism, it raises frightening possibilities of increased and accelerated destablization in an already volatile area of the globe. It is not at all certain that if limited nuclear conflict erupted on the subcontinent, it could be contained. It is also possible that other states in the region—Russia, Iran, and China in particular—might find reasons to join in. And it is also possible that Muslim fundamentalists could react to Hindu fundamentalism in India by spreading terrorism there, as well as renewing terrorism throughout the Middle East, Europe, and even the United States.

As we can see from the discussion in this chapter, ideologies, both political and religious, have played and continue to play major and often disruptive roles in global politics. What seems only logical and reasonable to some often becomes a threat to others, and old hatreds that seem long buried find reinvigoration in the shape of evolving ideologies. While Marxism appears to be at low ebb today, major dangers to global stability and international peace are presented by resurgent fascism and even Nazism in Europe, militant Islamic fundamentalism, and Hindu extremism.

The clash of ideas on the global stage continues, despite the end of the Cold War confrontation between democracy and communism. What will be the result of the spread of both democracy and capitalism—if they are indeed capable of thriving in societies that lack both middle classes and traditions of respect for the individual? Is Michael Doyle correct in his speculation that liberal democracies will not go to war against one another? Are we in fact, as Francis Fukuyama proclaims, approaching "the end of history," a time in which liberal democratic ideas will prevail? If so, what will become of the Confucian tradition, or of resurgent ultra-nationalism, whether expressed as fascism and neo-Nazism in western Europe or as the Russian chauvinism of Zhirinovsky and his adherents? What new mix, if any, will emerge from the clash of Islamic fundamentalism and Western secularism in the Middle East and North Africa? Can the fragile democracy of India withstand the growth of fundamentalist Hinduism? Can a democratic-Confucianist fusion emerge and hold in China, or will the remnants of Maoism make that impossible and prevent China's full entry into the global marketplace?

And what about the ideas that seem to have "lost" the historical struggle? Fascism and Nazism should have been buried in the ruins of Italy and Germany when World War II ended, but there are still many who proclaim adherence to them. The numbers are small, but they are both vocal and occasionally active, as witness recent problems in Germany. With World War II now a half-century behind us, will the glittering attractions of these doctrines and their appeal to primordial emotions rise phoenixlike from their ashes and again bring tumult and destruction to the international scene? Communism as well seems to us in the West a discredited dogma ready to be consigned to the dustbin of history, but there are still many, including Mikhail Gorbachev, who argue that Marxism never really failed because it was never really tried. The Soviet system, defenders of Marxism argue, was not Marxist; thus, its collapse does not represent the failure of Marxism, but may be providing another opportunity to prove that Marxist ideas are in fact the real road to a better future for much of the world.

Summary

Nations usually are organized according to a set of general beliefs or principles that we call ideologies. Although these ideologies are largely concerned with domestic issues, such as the way the state should be organized or the correct relationship between the state and the individual, they also can have a profound influence on the way states and individuals act in the forum of international relations.

Liberalism, Capitalism, and Democracy: These interlinked concepts rest on a belief in the essential rationality and goodness of human nature, emphasizing individual rights and responsibilities. While liberalism tends to lead to the development of democratic states, it also appears to be closely tied to capitalism, which also emphasizes the power of the individual rather than the state. In the international realm, these beliefs usually lead states to emphasize law, trade, and a variety of means to achieve stability and justice.

Both democracy and capitalism appear to be developing in many states throughout the world, particularly those of the former Soviet bloc, although whether this development can be sustained is still an open question.

Marxism: The "scientific" study of history that predicts the ultimate fall of the state and the emergence of an egalitarian utopia, Marxism takes conflict among states for granted and emphasizes the importance of revolution and struggle. Such forms of Marxism as Leninism and Stalinism, which played a major role in the former Soviet Union, are now discredited and all but abandoned. However, other forms of Marxism, including Maoism and Eurocommunism, still remain powerful international forces.

Fascism and Nazism: These manifestations of ultranationalism, leavened with racism in the case of Nazism, drove international relations during the 1930s, culminating in World War II. Although discredited by the war, and apparently abandoned by Germany and Italy, fascism and Nazism still exist and still retain their potential to cause serious problems.

Confucianism: The dominant ideology of East Asia for more than two millennia, Confucianism stresses harmony within a society, to be achieved by the maintenance of a series of familial or family-style relationships. The extent to which Confucianism still endures as a major ideological force in Asia is open to debate.

Religious Fundamentalism: In many areas of the world, the transformation of global politics, with its challenges to traditional ways and traditional values, has led to attempts to reassert traditional values. In many cases religion drives this reassertion of traditional values. While fundamentalism can be found in many societies, this chapter focuses particularly on Islamic and Hindu fundamentalism and their implications for international relations, including terrorism and ethnic warfare.

Key Terms

Ideology	Communism
Fascism	Leninism
Nazism	Democratic centralism
Liberal democracy	Imperialism
Capitalism	Stalinism
Maoism	Permanent revolution
Natural rights	Eurocommunism
Democracy	National socialism
Socialism	Confucianism
Marxism	Religious fundamentalism
Dialecticism	Islamic fundamentalism
Economic determinism	Islamism
Substructure	Traditionalism
Superstructure	Reformism

Thought Questions

1. How are the systems of liberal democracy and capitalism related?
2. Analyze the prospects for the consolidation of democracy and capitalism within the next decade.
3. What factors account for the possible resurgence of fascism and Nazism?
4. In what key ways does Confucianism differ from liberal democracy and capitalism?
5. What is responsible for the rise of religious fundamentalism? What are some of the consequences, both present and potential, of religious fundamentalism?

References

Fuller, Graham. "The Next Ideology." *Foreign Policy* (Spring 1995).

Haggard, Stephan, and Robert R. Kaufman. "The Challenges of Consolidation." *Journal of Democracy* (October 1994). INTERNET. www Page at www.enews.com/magazines/democracy/current/100194.1.html. Downloaded March 12, 1996.

Hampden-Turner, Charles, and Alfons Trompenaars. *The Seven Cultures of Capitalism: Value Systems for Creating Wealth in the United States, Japan, Germany, France, Britain, Sweden, and the Netherlands*. New York: Doubleday, 1993.

Hoffman, Stanley. "The Crisis of Liberal Internationalism." *Foreign Policy* (Spring 1995).

Mehta, Ved. "The Mosque and the Temple: The Rise of Fundamentalism." *Foreign Affairs* (Spring 1994): 16–21.

Rozsa, Lori, "Computerized Hate Enters Superhighway." *Houston Chronicle*, March 18, 1995.

Sachs, Jeffrey D. "Consolidating Capitalism." *Foreign Policy* (Spring 1995).

"Sad Dreams by the Nile." *The Economist,* June 3, 1995.

Sadowski, Yahya M. "Bosnia's Muslims: A Fundamentalist Threat?" *The Brookings Review* (Winter 1995).

Schneider, Keith. "'90s Neo-Nazis Have Developed 'New Model for Purveying Hate." *Houston Chronicle,* March 19, 1995.

Wright, Robin. *In the Name of God: The Khomeini Decade*. New York: Simon and Schuster, 1989.

Part Three

How the Game
Is Played

Chapter 7

International Political Economy

Introduction

❝**I**nternational political economy"—it's a forbidding term, conjuring up visions of whirring computer networks, dour men in black suits and tight white collars hunched over ledger books, and grim-faced bankers sadly shaking their heads as they contemplate the balance sheets. Actually, those images *are* part of international political economics—but so are the Sony Walkman you wear while you're out jogging, the Honda or Mercedes that you and your family may drive, and the juicy grapes you snacked on this afternoon.

Probably nowhere in the field of international relations are the twin—and conflicting—themes of simultaneous integration and disintegration more important than in economics. Global integrative machines such as the General Agreement on Trade and Tariffs (GATT) are changing and strengthening at the same time that regional trade blocs such as the European Union (EU), the North American Free Trade Agreement (NAFTA), and a proposed but distant Pacific trade zone are threatening to divide the global economy along geographic lines. The Bretton Woods system, the global trading system devised at the end of World War II, finds itself under increasing pressure and in some areas, such as regulation of international currency, completely stripped of its former powers.

Amplifying the impact of these changes are two continuing transformations of the global economy: the emergence of information-driven, high-technology, post-industrial economies as industrialized nations begin to "deindustrialize," and the simultaneous shift of manufacturing to the developing nations. As the Cold War fades, many students of international relations expect that economic competition will replace military competition and perhaps even war itself as the primary determinant of relations among the world's nation-states.

In this chapter we will look primarily at trade and finance. This will lead us to examine, among other topics, the centripetal, or unifying, components of the Bretton Woods system and the implications of its transformation, as well as the centrifugal, or separating, tendencies of the European Union and NAFTA. In chapter 8 we will focus on issues affecting North-South relationships, such as development and the powerful changes restructuring the formerly centrally managed economies of the Eastern European nations. In both chapters we will try to examine not only what is going on now but the implications of these global changes for the future.

The Global Economy in Transition

To understand some of the fundamental shifts going on today, we must first look at the four sectors of the global economy. The primary sector deals with the production or the extraction of natural resources; it includes agriculture, fishing, forestry, mining, and oil, for example. The secondary sector is manufacturing, that is, transforming raw materials into finished goods for consumption or sale. The tertiary sector of the economy provides services to facilitate the distribution of finished goods; tertiary activities range from serving a meal at a restaurant to conducting a wide range of banking activities to providing transportation for manufactured products. Recently economists have added a fourth sector, the quaternary sector. Quaternary sector activities take advantage of advanced electronic communications and are not tied to a particular physical base. The communications revolution has brought the quaternary sector into being; banking and finance conducted through modern electronics are also part of the quaternary sector.

Right now the global economy is a mixture of all four sectors. In Latin America, Africa, and much of Asia, nations are struggling to make the transition from the primary to the secondary economy, with varying degrees of success. At this point, Asian nations seem the most successful and African the least. The advanced industrial nations of North America, Europe, and Japan are in transition from the tertiary to the quaternary economic sectors. This process is sometimes referred to as "deindustrialization," since it involves the shift of manufacturing plants and jobs to nations journeying from the primary to the secondary sector. This also means taking advantage of the cheap labor available in the primary-sector nations, as well as, in effect, exporting pollution to them. However, to be able to engage in quaternary-sector activities, nations must have highly educated work forces capable of performing the communications- and information-oriented jobs of that sector (Roet 1995; see also Drucker 1994 and Thurow 1993 for more on this topic).

International Trade

One of the most important aspects of the global economy, and thus of international political economics, is international trade, the exchange of goods among nations.

Contending Theories of International Trade

Not surprisingly, the nature and role of international trade have provoked controversy for the last two centuries. Three contending interpretations reach very different conclusions about the importance of such trade and the reasons it should exist. More recently, an amalgam of a couple of approaches known as "new trade theory" or "strategic trade" also has emerged.

Liberalism

Economic liberals generally follow the lead of Adam Smith (see chapter 6, "Ideas that Make the World Go 'Round," for a full discussion of Smith's ideas) in assuming that human beings are naturally economic animals and that the growth of trade is inevitable. Markets will evolve of themselves, with no need for government intervention or direction. Such markets inevitably will increase economic efficiency, maximize economic growth, and thus improve the general welfare of society. This is as true of international markets and trade as it is of domestic markets and trade. Generally, economic liberals believe that trade and other forms of economic intercourse among nations create peaceful relations among nations, that the mutual benefits of trade and expanding interdependence among national economies will promote cooperative relations and, in turn, international stability. As one economist writes, "a liberal international economy will have a moderating influence on international politics as it creates bonds of mutual interests and a commitment to the status quo" (Gilpin 1987, 31).

Economic Nationalism

economic nationalism
Belief that the economic interests of the nation are subordinate to the state.

In sharp contrast to this essentially optimistic liberal view of the role of trade in shaping international relations stands the point of view known as **economic nationalism.** Economic nationalists argue that all economic activities must be subordinate to the essential goal of state-building and the national interests of the state. These nationalists see the sovereign state as dominant in international matters and believe that national security interests must take precedence over trade; if necessary, military power rather than trade should play a dominant role in the organization and function of the international system. Economic nationalists in many ways hark back to the mercantilism against which Adam Smith argued in the eighteenth century. At its most pernicious, economic nationalism found expression in the policies of Nazi Germany, with its emphasis on industrialization and militarism; at its most benign, economic nationalism relies on tariffs and other less transparent trade barriers to give one nation an advantage over others. Economic nationalists also dispute the liberal assertion that trade can be mutually beneficial; they insist instead that if one nation benefits, it must necessarily be at the expense of another, and thus it is only prudent to protect the national interest by ensuring that one's own nation will hold the advantage.

Marxism

Marxist theorists, with their view that **capitalism** is an inherently exploitative economic system, have tended since the time of Lenin to view international trade among capitalist nations as essentially imperialistic, a desperate attempt to sustain a despicable and collapsing system. This system is inherently unstable—Lenin saw it as a major cause of World War I—and must inevitably lead to uneven international development, because the advanced industrial countries will seek to profit at the expense of the less developed areas of the world, and will hold such areas in colonial submission, either formally or informally. The purpose of international trade, then, is not to benefit the state, but to prop up a failing economic system, and in effect to export to the developing world the exploitation upon which capitalism rests. These ideas have been particularly important in shaping "dependency theory" among less developed countries, which we will discuss in chapter 8.

capitalism Economic system based upon the precepts of private ownership of real property, profit maximization, and limited central government.

Comparative Advantage

One of the most important theories underlying international trade is the concept of **comparative advantage,** which seeks to explain why goods are manufactured in some areas and traded to others. The theory of comparative advantage originated with the classical liberal economic thinker David Ricardo in the early nineteenth century. Ricardo argued that comparative advantage represented the fundamental rationale for free trade. He recognized that the industrial revolution had changed the nature of international trade; no longer did any nation hold an absolute advantage in the manufacture of goods or production of commodities. Instead, Ricardo said, all advantage is relative, or comparative. The international division of labor in an industrial world rests on comparative costs; countries will tend to specialize in producing those goods or commodities whose costs are comparatively lowest; that is, nations will produce what they can produce cheapest and thus most competitively. Such specialization works to the mutual advantage of all nations, since each can buy cheaply what it cannot produce cheaply, and at the same time, will sell what it can produce most efficiently. As Ricardo wrote, "Under a system of perfectly free commerce, each country naturally devotes its capital and labor to such employments as are most beneficial to each" (Ricardo 1817, 174).

Ricardo used the example of Portuguese wine and English cloth to drive home his idea of comparative advantage. Portugal can produce excellent wines

comparative advantage An economic principle stating that any two nations will benefit if each specializes in what it can produce best, and acquires through trade what it cannot produce.

because its soil and climate are well suited to viniculture; however, that soil and climate are poorly suited to the production of wool. Thus Portugal will be far better off if it concentrates on doing what it can do best, producing wine, and imports its cloth from England, which enjoys comparative advantage in cloth production. England gains by importing wine and specializing in the production of cloth, and Portugal gains by specializing in the production of wine and importing cloth. Thus international trade based on comparative advantage produces a system from which all can benefit mutually.

The H-O-S Theory

H-O-S model The Heckscher-Ohlin-Samuelson theory of international trade, also known as the neoclassical liberal theory of trade (*see* comparative advantage).

The principle of comparative advantage has been modified in the last century to include a number of other factors and to become more dynamic. This neoclassical liberal formulation is known as the Heckscher-Ohlin-Samuelson theory, or the **H-O-S model** of international trade, after its three chief authors, Eli F. Heckscher, Bertil Ohlin, and Paul Samuelson. The H-O-S model accepts Ricardo's underlying thesis, but includes such elements as capital, labor, resources, management, and technology when assessing comparative advantage. Thus, "a country will export . . . those commodities which are intensive in the use of its abundant . . . factor," and conversely will import those that are most intensive in terms of its scarcest resources (El-Agraa 1987, 175). Countries with bountiful land will produce wheat, while those with abundant labor will produce labor-intensive products like machinery. Thus, "countries . . . should capitalize upon those factors in which they ha[ve] a particular advantage in order to produce specialized products with a comparative advantage in world trade." (Isaak 1995, 119–20). Samuelson adds that eventually there will be equalization of factor prices in international trade, and thus virtually no need for migration from overpopulated to underpopulated nations (Isaak 1995, 120). Even more recent theories of comparative advantage have stressed the vital importance of technology and economies of scale, and most recently the educational level of the national workforce has been seen as a dynamic element in assessing comparative advantage (Thurow, 1993, 1996).

The "New Trade Theory"

new trade theory The impact of history and historical accident upon the comparative trade advantages of a nation.

In the late 1970s some economists began to question theories of comparative and absolute advantage. After all, they pointed out, most trade took place between advanced nations, which tended to have equivalently (highly) educated workforces, access to the same technologies, and increasing similarities in many other ways. According to these economists, developing what became known as the **"new trade theory,"** the possession of certain resources may influence what a country produces and trades, but history and historical accident also play major roles. For example, the United States and Germany are alike in possession of skilled engineering forces and in the resources available to them, but "time and chance have . . . caused the two countries to develop different competencies at a more detailed level [of trade], with America leading in aircraft, semiconductors, computers, and Germany leading in luxury automobiles, cameras, machine tools." Thus, although from a broad perspective the two economies look similar—with high technology and educated workforces—close up they are very different.

Within the U.S., the role of history and accident in determining where things are made is clearly illustrated in the carpet industry. Most of the carpets sold in the United States are made in or near the small town of Dalton, Georgia. This curious concentration began with a teen-age girl who made a tufted bedspread as a wedding gift in the late 1890s, starting a local handicraft industry. When tufted carpets replaced woven rugs as the most desirable floor covering after World War II, Dalton already had the specialized skills necessary. Carpetmakers clustered around Dalton; their numbers meant a large market for people with the specialized skills to make tufted carpets, and as the number of workers increased so did the number of companies. Second, the cluster of carpetmakers also meant virtually guaranteed success for businesses that provided support for the specialized workers. Finally, the clustering of similar manufacturers tends to promote the exchange of information, and thus the advance of technology (Krugman 1994, 224–34).

Strategic Trade. Recognizing this, a group of economists known as the "strategic traders" began to argue that it should be the role of national governments to promote certain concentrations of industry in order to give their nations better competitiveness in the international marketplace. In the early 1980s Canadian economist James Brander and Australian economist Barbara Spencer began to urge that national governments aggressively support certain domestic companies to give them a better international competitive position. According to the Brander-Spencer model, which incorporates the "new trade theory" and transforms it into "strategic trade policy," governments must support industries that otherwise would be roughly competitive with or even slightly less competitive than those of other nations. For example, when both Boeing, an American corporation, and Airbus, a European firm, were deciding whether or not to develop wide-bodied aircraft, Boeing had what seemed to be comparative advantages over Airbus, including an earlier start. However, a group of European governments promised to subsidize the Airbus, thereby overriding Boeing's advantages and causing Boeing ultimately to drop out of the race to build the wide-bodied aircraft. The European governments had given Airbus a strategic advantage, in the terms of the New Trade Theory, by pursuing a **strategic trade policy** of supporting their industry over that of another nation.

In this view, strategic trade policy seems to justify international trade policies that are both interventionist and confrontational. If international trade is defined as a competition with winners and losers, then the strategic trade policy is not only sensible but also absolutely necessary. Governments must develop economic strategies that make domestic producers superior to their international competitors; they must develop national industrial policies that maximize inherent advantages (Krugman 1994, 239). In other words, national governments must choose which domestic industries are the potential winners and then back them to the hilt.

Critique of Strategic Trade. Supporters of free trade, like Paul Krugman, point out major flaws in this emphasis on strategic trade. For one thing, seldom will there be only one manufacturer in a given sector; even if the government promotes that sector, competition among several manufacturers will tend to hold down both prices and profits. There will be no "global jackpot." Second, picking a "winner" is not as easy as strategic traders might like us to think; if it were, nobody would lose money on the stock market. Finally, as Krugman points out, "You can't promote all domestic industries; by subsidizing one, you help it bid capital and labor away from others." This other side of the coin is that strategic trade policy *for* one industry ends up as strategic trade policy *against* other industries (Krugman 1994, 241–42).

strategic trade policy
Usually a government's direct, positive involvement in the strategic advantage of a particular industry in that nation.

According to Krugman, the rise of strategic trade theory, and the prominent place it seems to play in the economic ideas of the Clinton administration, for example, pose two central problems. First, there is the risk that in the attempt to win global markets, the strategic traders will instead destroy them. Second, there is the danger that the acceptance of "a foolish ideology in one area" will lead to the acceptance of equally foolish ideologies in other areas, in an intellectual Gresham's Law. The confrontational nature of strategic trade, the idea that competition is paramount, will lead to trade wars, Krugman warns, and "a trade war is a conflict in which each country uses most of its ammunition to shoot itself in the foot." And this kind of ultracompetitive government-directed international economy would be inherently destabilizing politically. "It would not be surprising if a world of trade conflict among the big advanced countries was a world of political instability, and maybe growing anti-Western feeling, in smaller and poorer countries from Latin America to the former Soviet Republics" (Krugman 1994 287–88).

Other Issues in International Trade

However, as the title of this chapter implies, international trade is not just about economics; it is also about politics, and the politics of trade is often complex. International trade is complicated not just by the conflicting theories and definitions we have outlined, but also by the tendency of other issues to intrude into the question of trade.

Politicization

MFN status Most favored nation status: status granted by the U.S. government to foreign nations, who thereby receive tariff preferences.

Nations often attempt to attach political issues to trade policy. One of the most recent examples of this is the United States' dithering about whether or not to continue extending **Most Favored Nation (MFN) status** to China. One large group of Americans argued that American policy should link MFN status to an improved Chinese record on human rights; they argued that it was entirely legitimate to use trade policy as a way to induce change in China's behavior, specifically in its internal policies. A second group argued that the best way to bring about desired change in China's behavior was not to link trade issues to internal policies, but to grant China MFN status and then, having brought China more fully into the community of nations, continue to work for improved human rights policy in China. The controversy, which goes back to the 1980s, was temporarily resolved in favor of continuing MFN status for China. However, this clearly illustrates the temptation to link trade issues to other, more clearly political issues. It also illustrates the degree to which traditional liberal optimism still dominates the American view of international relations and international trade, in this case in the form of the assumption that more is to be gained by including than by excluding China. (We will explore the U.S.–China trade morass in more detail in chapter 8.)

The debate continues. In May 1995 Kent Wiedemann, Deputy Assistant Secretary of State for East Asian and Pacific Affairs, testified before a congressional subcommittee on current China policy. "The Administration believes that the U.S. national interest is served by developing and maintaining friendly relations with a China which is strong, stable, prosperous, and open." Wiedemann continued that "broad engagement between the U.S. and China offers the best way, over the long term, to promote the full range of U.S. interests with China, including our human rights, strategic, economic and commercial concerns." Wiedemann also linked trade with communications and democratization: "Through trade, U.S. concepts filter into the consciousness of all Chinese. Opening markets for America's ideas industries—movies, CDs, interactive software, television—and for products that make communications easier—such as fax machines and copiers—spread U.S. values and ideals" (Wiedemann 1995). Thus the Clinton administration, like the Bush administration before it, seems to accept the idea of the "global village" that we will discuss in Chapter 13, "The Web of Global Communications." Critics of current China policy have warned that it simply will not work. Writing on the anniversary of the Tiananmen Square massacre, one such critic tartly observed that the administration does "not seem to believe that governments are destined to behave internationally as they behave toward their own citizens. [They would have you believe that] Deng Xiaoping and company can behave responsibly and morally internationally even as they murder, torture and jail their own people for peacefully asking for democracy." The truth is, according to this writer, that "the world's governments should not fool themselves. Beijing will behave internationally in the same fashion [as at Tiananmen] if it decides it has something to gain" (Hoagland 1995).

Deficits

Another important illustration of the way international economic issues tend to become international political issues is the matter of trade deficits. Ideally, international trade would be so well balanced, with each nation utilizing its comparative advantage, that every nation would export roughly the same amount of goods as it imported. In fact, the balance of imports and exports between nations in the international marketplace can sometimes become seriously skewed, with major political as well as economic repercussions. Probably the best-known, and perhaps the most potentially dangerous, such imbalance exists today between the United States and Japan. Year after year over the last decade or more, the United States has imported a great deal more merchandise from Japan than it has exported to Japan; the result has been a growing imbalance in the U.S.–Japan trade and a blossoming trade deficit (difference between total exports and total imports) in Japan's favor that is now approaching $80 billion a year.

Some economists, however, point out that the rapid changes in the modern economy, with the growing importance of intellectual capital and the rise of the information age, have made traditional methods of calculating such things as the balance of trade obsolete. Walter B. Wriston, former CEO of Citibank, argues that until accountants and economists devise means of calculating the value of information, all statements about balances of trade and trade deficits should be treated with great skepticism (Wriston 1992).

Nonetheless, U.S. trade figures, however incompletely compiled, have been dismal in recent years. American political and economic leaders decry this imbalance and place the responsibility for it on what they see as unfair tactics employed by the Japanese, such as "dumping" goods on the American market (selling them at much lower prices than are charged within Japan itself). Defending themselves against accusations of unfair trading practices, the Japanese respond that the growing trade imbalance simply reflects higher Japanese standards of quality and greater efficiencies in manufacturing. By implication, the Japanese defense is this: "it's not our fault that our goods are both cheaper and better than your shoddy, overpriced stuff." At times the rhetoric has been extremely ugly, with the Japanese referring to the United States as a mongrel nation weakened by its multiracial society. Americans tend to respond to this by accusing the Japanese of being unfair and even racist in their criticisms of the United States.

So far the dispute between the two great Pacific nations has been confined to increasingly angry speeches, including one U.S. senator's invoking of images of Pearl Harbor and Hiroshima. However, there have been calls in the United States for retaliation against the Japanese, and threats from the Japanese of retaliation against any such retaliation. High-level trade talks between the two nations have dragged on for several years, with the United States threatening but not yet invoking a number of anti-Japanese trade laws, and the Japanese proclaiming that they are innocent victims of American discrimination and incompetence, that they are in effect being made the scapegoat for inefficient and noncompetitive declining American industries. There have even been warnings that should this trade imbalance and heated rhetoric continue, matters could escalate from competition through confrontation to conflict. One sign of such fears is a rather sensationalistic book called *The Coming War between the United States and Japan.*

Technology Export

A third area in which politics affects trade, and vice versa, concerns the question of which technologies a country will allow to be exported to which other nations. Clearly many modern technologies, ranging from computers to radar to aircraft, fall into the category of "dual-use" technology; that is, they can be used for essentially civilian and peaceful purposes, but they also have the potential to be converted to military use. In the United States, for example, the State Department must approve and license the trading of a wide range of potential dual-use technologies. Thus when a particular manufacturer proposes selling supercomputers to Russia or China, for example, the State Department must decide whether these marvelous machines will in fact be used for the civilian and peaceful purposes alleged by the potential buyers, or there is too great a risk that they will end up being used for the "wrong" purposes. In chapter 12, on weapons, we will see clearly the ways dual-use technologies in the hands of unscrupulous nations or individuals can present real dangers to the rest of the world. However, as American manufacturers increasingly shift to high-level technology in order to pursue their comparative advantage in the world marketplace, there will be greater and greater pressure to license the international marketing of high technology and dual-use technology to benefit the American economy. Correctly weighing economic benefits against potential political pitfalls is at best difficult and at worst impossible.

Cultural Economic Differences

A further complication of international trade rises from the very different natures of national economies. The general assumption is that trade between Europe, the United States, and Japan will be comparatively easy because all three are capitalist. But it has become glaringly obvious that not all capitalism is the same, that there are in fact different national "cultures" of capitalism. Although all capitalist nations agree on certain fundamentals—the importance of private property and the profit motive, for example—there are substantial differences in the way different nations actually implement their capitalist systems. Recent research reveals that the major capitalist nations, rather than being more or less identical, range along a spectrum that has a highly individualistic and competitive system at one extreme and a consensus-based, government-influenced system, at the other.

The United States and Great Britain represent the most extreme examples of individualistic, highly competitive capitalist systems. In the United States, not only is there no government involvement in what could be called either industrial or trade policy, there is also literally no room for cooperation among corporations in the same field, even should they want to cooperate rather than compete. Since the late nineteenth century, Americans generally have regarded any such attempts at cooperation as inherently dangerous; the Sherman Anti-Trust Act, passed in 1890, has existed as a potential (if not always a realized) means for punishing those that have attempted to cooperate. Although American manufacturers recently have begun to complain that anti-trust measures harm their international competitive position, and although presidential candidate Bill Clinton talked occasionally about establishing an American industrial policy, it seems unlikely that, at least in the near future, the United States will abandon its individualistic and competitive system, which in so many ways mirrors the larger United States culture.

Japanese culture, on the other hand, stresses cooperation and the necessity of reaching consensus; group rather than individual values are stressed, and American-style individualism is interpreted as selfishness and lack of regard for the greater good. Not surprisingly, these cultural values find ready expression in Japanese capitalism, where cooperation within various industries is stressed over competition, and where government historically has worked closely with specific industries.

At about the same time Americans afraid of the consequences of runaway monopolism were passing the Sherman act, the Japanese government was turning over to private hands government-developed industries, while still maintaining a close relationship with those industries. Until World War II, the Japanese industrial economy was controlled by a handful of extraordinarily powerful industrial barons, often descendants of powerful samurai clans, known as the *zaibatsu*. After World War II the *zaibatsu*, convicted of wartime collaboration with the aggressive Japanese military, were disbanded, but the tradition of intra-industry cooperation continued; today many Japanese industries are effectively controlled by industrial groups known as *keiretsu*. These *keiretsu* work closely with MITI, the Ministry of International Trade and Industry, to develop Japanese strategies for developing particular industries and then for penetrating foreign markets.

To Americans attempting to enter Japanese markets or compete with Japanese-manufactured goods, all of this smacks of collusion at levels that would land the perpetrators in American prisons. But to the Japanese this is a perfectly sensible, and time-tested, way of doing business; competition would be wasteful and in creating losers as well as winners would cause too many people to lose face, one of the worst of all fates in a society that places high value on harmony and conformity. Thus people on one side of the Pacific perceive those on the other as using grossly unfair and even illegal systems of organization, while people on the other side view their American counterparts as selfish and wasteful. (For further discussion, see Hampden-Turner and Trompenaars, 1993.)

Hegemony and the International Economic Order

Another vital concept in the international economic order is that of the **hegemon,** the great power that plays the major role in maintaining the existing order. According to many theorists, the stability of the liberal world economy demands

hegemon A regional or world economic and/or political-military power that seeks to impose the existing world order on others for the sake of its own stability.

a hegemon, a power able and willing to establish and maintain a liberal economic order. Without such a hegemonic power, they maintain, the liberal economic order tends to disintegrate into chaos. In essence, the hegemon is the key to the kind of liberal world economy envisioned in the Bretton Woods agreements.

The hegemonic power must be committed ideologically to the legitimacy of the liberal world order and must be willing to make sacrifices in order to maintain that order. For example, the hegemon must keep its markets open to goods from around the globe yet be willing to accept various levels of protectionism from its trading partners. The hegemon must be willing to provide stability in trade, willing to provide a stable currency to anchor the international system, and both willing and able to enforce the rules of the world trade regime. The hegemonic power must control raw materials, sources of capital, markets, and competitive advantages in production of highly desirable goods. In addition, the hegemon must possess a large domestic market capable of absorbing the imported goods that will flow into its economy because of its role as hegemon. Finally, the hegemonic power must be able to meet threats to the international economic system quickly and efficiently; it cannot focus only on the routine maintenance of the system, but must excel at crisis management. For example, the hegemon must be able to serve as "lender of last resort" in movements of financial crisis.

Historic Hegemons: Great Britain and the United States

In the past two centuries only two nations have met the qualifications of hegemon: Great Britain, which provided stability for the international liberal economic order from the end of the Napoleonic Wars until the outbreak of World War I, and the United States, which assumed the role of hegemon after World War II. In both cases, the hegemonic states were militarily powerful, but it was their economic power and their willingness to accept the responsibilities and occasional problems of hegemony that determined their role. In contrast, although Nazi Germany exercised great military power on the eve of World War II, and the Soviet Union was a superpower for most of the half-century after that war, neither could have served as hegemonic powers.

However, a number of theorists argue that the hegemonic system, designed to produce stability, is ultimately unstable. "For internal and external reasons, the hegemonic power loses its will and its ability to manage the system." According to Robert Gilpin, "the hegemon grows weary and frustrated with the free riders and the fact that its economic partners are gaining more from liberalized trade than it is." The military and economic costs of maintaining the system begin to weigh heavily on the hegemon, and it gradually can become unable as well as unwilling to meet the inevitable financial crises that arise in the world trading system. Other members of the system that have benefited from the hegemon's protection can become more and more competitive and undercut the hegemon's economic position. Over time the power of the hegemon, and its will to play the role of hegemon, erodes, and ultimately the system again becomes unstable. Theorists see the world's economic crisis between the two world wars as the result at least in part of the inability of Great Britain to act as hegemon, and there are multiple signs that the United States has slipped from its role as hegemon as well. As Gilpin expresses it, "the difficulties experienced by the United States during the closing decades of the twentieth century in adjusting to profound shifts in the global location of industry and the revolution in the price of energy have undermined its power and international position" (Gilpin 1987, 72–80).

Chapter 7 / International Political Economy ◆ 233

Hegemons, past, present, and future? American president George Bush (center) and British prime minister Margaret Thatcher (right) at a meeting of the G-7, accompanied by leaders of the other major industrialized nations that may, or may not, become future hegemons.

Is the Hegemonic System Dead?

One of today's leading economists, Lester Thurow, a professor at the Massachusetts Institute of Technology, foresees the hegemonic system giving way to an economic free-for-all pitting Japan, the European Community, and the United States against one another. Thurow argues in effect that the hegemonic system is over, and that the liberal trade regime of the twentieth century may well yield to a system of regional blocs. This is not necessarily all bad, Thurow maintains. Other economists argue that we may see the emergence of a tripolar hegemonic system, with Germany serving as the hegemon for Europe, the United States filling the same role for the Americas, and Japan doing so for the Asian-Pacific Rim.

Evolution of the World Economic System

Trade on a global scale can be traced to as far back as the Roman Empire in the West and the Han Dynasty in China, when camel caravans carrying precious silks and satins snaked their way across the Eurasian continent so that wealthy Romans could luxuriate in their fine textures. However, even two thousand years ago, this kind of international trade could generate problems. While the Romans delighted in Chinese silks, they had nothing that they could sell in turn to China, and thus the camel caravans that had carried silks and satins to Europe returned to Asia caring primarily Roman gold and silver. Today we would call this a serious trade imbalance. The Romans were not quite sure what to call it, but they did see the hemorrhage of gold from their empire as a danger, and ultimately responded by making it illegal to wear silk. (In modern terms, this would be akin to an American attempt to solve its trade imbalance with Japan by making it illegal to drive Hondas or Toyotas.)

The collapse of the Roman empire temporarily ended this global trade, although Arab traders kept sea routes to China and India open from the eighth century onward, but the gradual revival of Europe at the beginning of modern history stimulated such widespread trade once again. It was primarily the search for markets and products that drove Europeans outward from the edge of the

Eurasian continent to Africa and Asia, and it was in search of shorter routes to Asia that Christopher Columbus and John Cabot made their epochal fifteenth-century voyages to the Americas.

Imperialism

First the Spanish, Portuguese, and Dutch, then the English and French, and later the Germans, Italians, and Belgians established far-flung empires to advance their control of global trade. Although neither the United States nor Russia reached so far beyond their borders as these other nations, expansion propelled them both across great continents containing vast natural resources. The United States also acquired an "informal empire" by exerting dominance over Latin America, including the use of Marines to establish stability when deemed necessary, and acquired the Philippine Islands on the edge of the South China Sea, a jumping-off point for trade with China. One historian estimates that by 1914 European powers directly controlled 84 percent of the world's land (Kennedy 1989, 150), and presumably a commensurate proportion of its population.

However, while these global empires profited their European masters, they often victimized the colonial peoples. "The imperial powers typically pursued their various interests overseas in a blatantly aggressive fashion. Bloody, one-sided wars with local inhabitants of contested territories were commonplace; 'sporting wars,' [German leader Otto von] Bismarck called them" (Cohen 1995, 30). Proud empires like those in India and much of West Africa were absorbed into competing European imperial systems, and China's ancient domain was "carved up" by European powers eager to gain access to China's resources and population, but unwilling to take responsibility for dealing with the problems created by dynastic implosion and imperialist encroachment. In all of Asia, only Japan and Siam (modern Thailand) escaped some degree of imperialism, while in Africa virtually the entire continent was divided up among the European states. Ironically, Japan would "learn its lesson" from watching the systematic dismemberment of China and Southeast Asia; its Meiji Restoration, launched in 1867, was nothing more than an intensive economic and military modernization run from the top down. By the end of the nineteenth century, the rapidly modernizing Japan itself had become an imperialist power; it went to war against China in 1894 and against Russia in 1904, both times primarily over the right to expand into the rich Manchurian province of China, and also acquiring control of Formosa (modern Taiwan) and Korea.

The link between trade, imperialism, and politics became painfully clear in early nineteenth-century China. Year by year the trade imbalances grew. Ultimately, the Europeans found something they *could* sell, however illegally, to the Chinese: opium. When the Chinese protested the illegal trade, which was enormously disruptive to civil and social life in South China, Europeans ignored first their pleas and then their demands. Two brutal wars resulted from China's attempts to stem the opium trade, the First Opium War (1839–42) and the Second Opium War (1857–60). Among the results of the opium wars were the "unequal treaties" that granted European powers massive benefits in China and the opening of the great age of European imperialism in Asia, what the Chinese call the "Century of Humiliation." Ironically, although the opium wars desperately weakened the ruling Ch'ing dynasty, the European powers, once they had extracted the concessions they wanted from the Ch'ing, then propped it in place to protect *their* positions in China. This probably postponed the collapse of the Ch'ing and the rise of revolution in China for one or even two generations and thus altered China's future.

However exploitative of native peoples and native resources these European empires, both formal and informal, were, they did perform an important function in terms of global economics. They prevented formation of a truly global economy, instead dividing the world into a series of "currency zones" determined by their respective colonial masters. For example, the British Empire was the "sterling zone," in which only the British pound sterling was legal for trade, and from which all non-sterling nations (including the United States) were effectively barred. Although there was a thriving trade between the United States and the British Isles, American merchants were thwarted in their attempts to trade in Britain's overseas empire. Similar currency zones kept outsiders from trading in the French or Belgian or Italian empires. Thus the European empires imposed a structure, if not always a welcome one, on the global economy.

It was in part the conflict over empires and access to imperial trade that precipitated World War I, and in turn World War I fatally weakened the global imperial system. The German empire vanished completely, absorbed by the British, the French, and the Japanese, while all the other European imperialist nations, including Britain and France, were so weakened by the rigors of the struggle that the collapse of their empires became primarily a matter of time.

World War II would provide the *coup de grâce* to the European and Japanese empires, and to the order that these empires had provided for international political economics. While the vanquished—Germany and Japan particularly—found their industrial capacity virtually destroyed at war's end, their cities pulverized, and their economies in shambles, many of the victors faced almost equally serious problems. Great Britain and France were nearly bankrupt, with severe damage to parts of their industrial capacity, and the Soviet Union lay devastated, its industrial machinery destroyed, its economy in tatters, its cities and roads and bridges in ruins, and its population reduced by nearly 15 percent.

Of all the major combatants, only the United States had survived the war unscathed, its industrial economy not only intact but tremendously boosted by the demands of wartime production, and its population virtually untouched. When the war ended, the United States stood at a pinnacle of global economic dominance never before, and never since, achieved. Almost half of all industrial goods produced worldwide flowed from American factories; two of every three ships at sea had been made in the United States, and the American GNP had doubled in the three and a half years between Pearl Harbor and Nagasaki.

The Bretton Woods System

In order to establish a stable economic system for the postwar world and to promote economic recovery, the major Allied nations sent representatives to a conference at **Bretton Woods,** New Hampshire, in 1944. Two principal institutions designed to maintain international economic stability emerged from Bretton Woods; the World Bank and the International Monetary Fund (IMF). In the immediate postwar world, the General Agreement on Trade and Tariffs (GATT) and the **Marshall Plan** would supplement the Bretton Woods agreements and would dominate the Western bloc economy well into the 1970s. With vast amounts of American aid, the Japanese and West German economies would stage "economic miracles" that would bring both defeated nations to enormous economic power. In the Soviet Union and the Eastern bloc it dominated, the

Bretton Woods Agreements on rules, institutions, and procedures devised at the end of World War II at Bretton Woods, N.H., to facilitate global economic relations.

Marshall Plan The American plan to aid in the reconstruction of its European allies after World War II.

allocation of vast amounts of natural resources to wartime priorities and the bungling of centralized economic administration restricted growth, but nonetheless the Soviet bloc also achieved considerable economic advances. A number of circumstances would begin to unravel this interwoven global economy in the 1970s, but before we look at them we will examine more carefully the Bretton Woods system.

The International Monetary Fund

In order to stabilize currency and stimulate global trade by ensuring generally accepted exchange rates, or currency convertibility, the Bretton Woods conference first created the International Monetary Fund (IMF). The Bretton Woods participants agreed to peg their currencies to the United States dollar, which in turn was tied to gold at thirty-five dollars an ounce.

To ensure stability of individual currencies, each of the Bretton Woods participants established a "pegged rate" for its currency. That is, each nation declared a par value (or "peg") for its currency in the international market. If the currency drifted one percent above or below this par value, the nation was obligated to intervene in the exchange market, either buying or selling its own currency in order to "stabilize" it at the par value. However, each nation retained the right to alter its currency's par value in order to correct a "fundamental disequilibrium" in its balance of payments. Although this adjustment mechanism was key to the entire system established at Bretton Woods, its details were never spelled out in the Articles of Agreement. This omission would return to haunt members of the IMF in later years.

Then, to ensure that each country would enjoy an adequate system of monetary reserves—essential if the adjustable "pegged rates" scheme was to work—the Bretton Woods negotiators sought a way to establish a supplementary source of currency reserves. In essence, parties to the Bretton Woods agreement established a pool of national currencies and gold, with each country assigned a "quota" to contribute to the Fund according to a complicated formula intended roughly to reflect each country's relative importance in the world economy. These quotas or "subscriptions" were payable as follows: 25 percent in gold or currency convertible into gold, and 75 percent in the member's own currency. When short of the reserves necessary to intervene on the open market to stabilize its currency, the member nation could then "purchase" (i.e., borrow) foreign exchange from the IMF in return for equivalent amounts of its currency.

Leery of falling into the economic warfare that had characterized the 1920s and 1930s, the Bretton Woods participants drew up a framework of rules to guide international exchange adjustments. The purpose was to ensure that countries would remove their existing exchange controls and return to a system of multilateral payments based on currency convertibility. Governments generally were forbidden to engage in discriminatory currency practices or in exchange-control regulation.

In addition, the participants at Bretton Woods agreed to use the IMF as an institutional forum for consultation and cooperation on international monetary matters. No one wished to return to the economic anarchy of the 1930s; on the contrary, everyone welcomed the establishment of an established machinery of procedure for consultation. This was perhaps the most significant achievement of a remarkable conference. For the first time in history, governments formally committed themselves to the principle of collective responsibility for the management of the international monetary order.

Triffin's Dilemma and the Collapse of Bretton Woods. As one cynical student of this brave new world points out, "The Bretton Woods designers began with a cracked world and painted on it their own hyperrational construction, abstracted from the messy unreasonableness of ordinary living . . . . Their plan had no technical flaws. Unfortunately, the world had many" (Millman, 1995, 74).

The Achilles heel of the Bretton Woods system was identified by economist Robert Triffin, and is thus christened **"Triffin's dilemma."** In order to provide enough dollars to keep world markets working, the United States had to run a budget deficit. And gradually those deficits began to erode the dollar's value, so that the dollar came to be worth quite a bit less than the thirty-five dollars per ounce of gold that was its official price. What would happen if holders of increasingly lower-valued dollars decided, quite intelligently, to convert the greenbacks into solid gold? There was an easy answer: the United States could simply cut its deficits and stop spending more than it received. However, if the United States cut its deficits, it would also decrease the global money supply and trigger worldwide recession, or perhaps even a global depression. "Solving the deficit problem would have meant choking the world's monetary supply, but not solving the deficit problem meant further erosion of the gold price [and the value of the dollar]. Thus, Triffin's dilemma" (Millman 1995, 81–83, 294).

The exchange system began to flounder in the 1960s, when the growing American balance of payments deficit coupled with domestic American inflation began to erode confidence in all the American ability to continue as hegemon. Since the entire Bretton Woods monetary system rested on the assumption of a stabilizing U.S. economic policy, the erosion of confidence in the United States began to undermine the entire system. In 1971 President Richard Nixon, concerned that the overvaluation of the American dollar would continue to cause inflation and blossoming trade deficits, "closed the gold window" by announcing that the United States dollar was no longer convertible into gold. This cutting of the link between gold and the dollar left the dollar, and all other currencies, free to find their own level in an international exchange market. It also effectively ended the Bretton Woods monetary system, although the basic Bretton Woods institutions—the World Bank, the IMF, and GATT—remained in place. (For more on this topic, see Cohen 1995, 209–29.) Later in this chapter we will explore the international exchange markets and the "casino economy" that emerged from the ruins of the Bretton Woods system.

Triffin's dilemma Named after the economist Robert Triffin who discovered that the United States must run a budget deficit to bolster the world's economy.

The World Bank

Although the International Monetary Fund received most of the attention at Bretton Woods, and was probably considered its greatest accomplishment, in the long run the "stepsister" of the Bretton Woods conference may turn out to be far more important. The International Bank for Reconstruction and Development, better known as the World Bank, was established largely at the United States' urging and direction, to stabilize the international loan market and permit the reconstruction and development of Europe. Reflecting American preferences and an American vision of a new world order, the World Bank was designed to reduce the risk of foreign lending, to establish an international standard for sound loans through its

When the Shoe's on the Other Foot

GLOBAL PERSPECTIVES

For generations American investment overseas has been lauded as an economic benefit to all, an opportunity to advance American interests, and a humanitarian means to improve local conditions and pave the way for democracy, or at least stability. In the first twenty-five years after World War II, U.S. foreign direct investment (FDI) soared. However, as other national economies began to recover and then to pick up steam, FDI began to flow *into* as well as out of the United States. As the pace of foreign direct investment in the United States (FDIUS) accelerated, the U.S. has become the leading host nation for FDI. (It also remains the leading *source* nation for FDI.) In the 1980s especially, other nations embarked on what one economist calls an international shopping spree, snapping up U.S. businesses and other assets.

By 1990, FDIUS controlled approximately 10 percent of the American economy; foreign-controlled firms accounted for some 4.3 percent of nonbank U.S. employment, and 8.9 percent of the manufacturing workforce. Most of this FDI involved acquisi-

tion of existing assets rather than the construction of new facilities. Manufacturing represents the largest sector for FDIUS, followed in order by the wholesale and retail sectors, finance and insurance, petroleum, real estate, and banking. Although the last two areas are smaller in dollar terms, they are often the most visible. Some 20 percent of American bank assets are now owned by foreign investors (half of that amount by Japanese investors), and large chunks of real estate in major cities like Honolulu, Houston, and New York are also foreign owned.

This FDIUS has touched off an intense debate among American politicians and economists; some argue that FDIUS is essentially beneficial, while others raise alarms about potential dangers of FDIUS. Arguments both for and against FDIUS are summarized below.

The Case for FDIUS

1. Historically, the United States has always had a high rate of FDIUS. For example, one-third of the capital that built the American railroad system in the nineteenth century was foreign.

own practices, and to upgrade the available information about international investment opportunities.

The World Bank's equity consists of capital subscribed by its member countries, in effect its shareholders; today, these are 155 in number. Most of its operating funds (the money it can lend) come from the sale of securities to private investors and central banks, making the World Bank the largest nonsovereign borrower in the international capital market. There are also two major subsidiary organizations within the World Bank, established to give it greater latitude. In 1956 the International Finance Corporation (IFC) was created to make both loans and equity investments. Its major purpose is to promote the spread of private enterprise worldwide and to help developing countries secure venture capital. The IFC uses its own funds to generate financing for projects in order to pull in other investors through syndication, underwriting, and confinancing. The second major World Bank subsidiary, the International Development Association (IDA), was set up in 1960 to aid the poorest of the developing countries; the funds that it lends come entirely from donations given by wealthy countries, and go exclusively to nations that could not qualify for commercial financing.

In its earliest years, the World Bank directed its resources largely towards "hard-hat" projects: large-scale, capital-intensive projects designed to create the infrastructure needed for economic recovery and development, such as power

2. There is still far more American FDI overseas than FDIUS here.
3. Because of FDIUS, the United States is benefiting from technology transfer; the technology transfer into the U.S. through FDIUS is more than six times greater than the outflow of technology.
4. FDIUS permits more research and development in the United States; foreign-controlled companies spend almost twice as much on R&D than domestically owned companies.
5. FDIUS leads to job creation, often of higher-paying jobs than American-owned firms are creating.

The Arguments against FDIUS

1. No matter what its benefits, FDIUS leads to erosion of control over economic decision-making and thus of American autonomy.
2. There is not a level international playing field; it is much easier for FDI to enter the United States than for American firms to invest overseas.
3. FDIUS allows foreigners much greater access to American technology than Americans are allowed to foreign technology.

4. It is enormously dangerous to allow foreigners to control industries with national security implications, such as the aircraft and computer industries.
5. FDIUS really doesn't lead to much job creation; there is also a great deal of job destruction.
6. FDIUS permits foreigners to pick off their major American competitors and thus gain near-monopolies globally.
7. FDIUS opens the way for intensive lobbying by foreign interests at both the state and the national levels, potentially distorting American political decisions and the political process.

Clearly, the whole issue of FDIUS is enormously complex, and calls for much more than the knee-jerk nationalistic response that we don't want foreigners owning Rockefeller Center or our major motion picture studios. There are clear benefits as well as clear problems connected with FDIUS. Much of the debate turns on whether or not a national industrial policy should be formulated to deal with this as well as other American issues in a global economy.

(Choate 1993; Coughlin 1995; Omestad 1995)

plants, highways, port facilities, telecommunications, and so forth. The assumption was that once such infrastucture was in place, the individual state then could use laissez-faire principles to continue development. There was a strong emphasis on the role of the state in planning, particularly in the allocation of resources.

However, in the 1970s the World Bank began to shift its strategy away from investment in large infracture projects, which some criticized as an international version of "trickle-down economics" that benefited the wealthy while merely promising eventual benefits to the poor. Instead, under the guidance of former American Secretary of Defense Robert McNamara, who became its president in 1967, the World Bank began to invest heavily in projects intended to benefit the very poorest of the world's population. Rural development attracted massive funding from the bank, as did projects involving family planning, health, nutrition, water, sanitation, and attempts to aid the urban poor. The boxed feature in chapter 14 entitled "Villains in Pinstripes?" analyzes criticisms of the bank by environmentalists and others who feel that the consequences of World Bank funding have been diametrically opposite to what was intended.

The 1980s saw the Bank proclaim a new direction as it began to emphasize structural reforms in poor countries. This new strategy, in line with the resurgent free-market ideas of Margaret Thatcher and Ronald Reagan, stressed either privatizing state-owned enterprises or at least curbing their hold on the state economy, involving protected economies in international competition, reducing government intervention in all areas of economic activity, and creating an "enabling environment" for private domestic economic development. As the chapter 14 feature on the Bank makes clear, whether it has succeeded at these goals is still hotly debated.

GATT

The third major structural component of the postwar economic order, in addition to the IMF and the World Bank, is the General Agreement on Tariffs and Trade (GATT). Originally conceived as part of a third formal arm of the IMF/World Bank structure, to be known as the International Trade Organization (ITO), GATT found itself on its own when the United States Congress objected so strongly to the ITO that its charter was not even submitted for a vote. Thus GATT, essentially a treaty, emerged as the make-do substitute for a genuine international trade organization.

Basically a treaty that binds its signatories to certain rules of international trade, GATT was signed by an original twenty-plus countries in 1947. It incorporates a code of behaviors for nations in the international marketplace that is designed to increase world trade by decreasing barriers to trade. It particularly targets the tariff barriers established by nations to protect their domestic producers, whether agricultural or industrial. All nations within GATT are bound to give one another "most favored nation" (MFN) status, which means that any concession given to one nation must be given to all. The purpose of MFN status is to produce a "level playing field" in which no nation's products receive preferential treatment or face unusual barriers in international trade. The drafters of the treaty hoped that MFN would make free trade contagious. In addition, GATT provides a forum in which member nations can settle disputes or work out agreements on particularly sticky issues; the propensity of these negotiations to go on and on has led some participants to claim that GATT really means the "General Agreement to Talk and Talk." GATT also binds its signatories to reciprocity (that is, equal treatment), to nondiscrimination, and to **transparency,** so that all governments and producers can become aware of trade barriers (Isaak 1995, 124–25).

transparency GATT's mechanism to alert all nations to trade barriers imposed by some states.

GATT's Successes.   Conference diplomacy has given GATT greater successes. GATT has sponsored a series of multilateral trade negotiations intended to decrease world trade barriers and thus increase world trade and, in theory, world prosperity. In the 1950s and 1960s these talks, culminating in the so-called Kennedy Round, were particularly important in bringing Japan and western Europe into the world economy. In large part the success of these early rounds drew upon the willingness of the United States to accept asymmetry, that is, not to insist on reciprocal trade concessions by western Europe and Japan, and on its parallel willingness to accept "cheating" by other nations. American openness to do this rested primarily on American dominance of the world economy. After all, the United States could not continue its dominant world position unless it had trading partners, that is, other nations economically powerful enough to purchase products of the vast output of American factories.

GATT's Problems.   In international trade as in everything else, it seems that every success simply leads to new problems. GATT and its interminable "rounds" did succeed in reducing tariffs worldwide; the average tariff in industrial nations dropped from more than 40 percent in 1947 to less than 5 percent by 1990. But once nations could no longer rely on tariffs to create and implement national trade policy, they showed remarkable creativity in devising a wide array of other means to restrict trade: "nontariff barriers," or NTBs. Among the most important NTBs have been restrictive quotas, customs procedures, government procurement practices, health standards, and environmental protection requirements. Some of these restrictions are more or less legitimate results of national culture and concerns, while others clearly are directed at getting around MFN practices and tariff reduction in order to protect local products. Furthermore, agricultural protectionism (agriculture was specifically omitted from GATT) has led to deliberately inflated agricultural prices; the estimated worldwide costs to consumers and taxpayers from such projectionist measures was estimated at $300 billion in 1990 alone.

In the 1980s GATT began to encounter more and more problems, which in turn had a variety of sources. First, protectionist ideology became more widespread in the 1970s and 1980s, the product of the same forces that produced greater pressure for free-market practices in the World Bank and gave rise to the eras of Margaret Thatcher in Great Britain and Ronald Reagan in the United States. In addition, the successful reindustrialization of Japan created new dilemmas for the Western world, as did the rise of the so-called "Little Dragons" of Asia, such as South Korea, Taiwan, Hong Kong, and Singapore.

The Uruguay Round

The result of these changes and problems was the Uruguay Round of GATT negotiations, which opened in Punta del Este in 1986 and finally closed with proclaimed success in December 1993. On the Uruguay Round's ambitious agenda were, among other things, liberalized rules for trade in agricultural products, intellectual property rights (copyright protection, for example), NTBs, dumping, and services. This agenda reflects the rapidly changing world trade picture, with services like banking insurance, broadcasting, telecommunications, construction, and so forth now constituting a much larger part of the world economy than they once did. One hundred and eight nations participated in the Uruguay Round, and negotiations were divided up into fifteen distinct negotiating committees. Ironically, as protectionist sentiment rose in the United States, Britain, and much of the European community, new nations clamored to enter GATT, including many developing nations that previously had seen GATT as a private club operated for and by the industrialized countries, and a substantial number of former Soviet-bloc nations in the tumultuous process of shifting from centralized socialist regimes to market-oriented economies.

Among the major provisions of the final trade accord were an overall cut of more than 33 percent in tariffs worldwide, the phasing out of textile quotas by industrialized nations to open their markets to cheaper imports, tougher restrictions on "dumping" (exporting goods at below-cost prices), gradual reductions of tariffs on crops and on crop subsidies, and tougher protection for "intellectual property," which includes protecting copyrighted and patented material, as well as establishing more stringent rules against cheap "knock-offs" of designer products.

The WTO. Most important, the new Uruguay Round agreements created a completely new structure, the World Trade Organization (WTO), to administer GATT's provisions, replacing the weak and ill-defined authority of GATT with a permanent institution that will incorporate and enforce free-trade principles more efficiently. The very recently formed WTO is meant to be a new international institution, on a par with the IMF or the World Bank, "that will outline a framework for all areas of international trade and will have the legal authority to settle trade disputes." The WTO will have a permanent secretariat, but the ultimate decision-making body will be a biannual ministerial meeting. This WTO council will have subsidiary working groups that will hear charges of unfair practices and recommend settlement in specific areas of trade dispute, such as intellectual property, goods, and services. There will also be a permanent appellate council whose decisions will be binding. "The World Trade Organization will be akin to an International Court of Justice for world trade, with the institutional strength and legal mandate to ensure fair trade and global economic integration" (Pitroda 1995, 46–47). Or so the enthusiasts of the WTO proclaim. There are many who have feared this new organization.

Although it is intended to resolve disputes among trading nations more rapidly and efficiently than the cumbersome GATT machinery could; the WTO has become the target of attacks from many within the United States who fear that it represents an infringement on American sovereignty. Since each nation will have a single vote in the WTO, critics have maintained that it quickly will become just another version of the United Nations General Assembly, where "the developing nations [can] gang up on the First World." Additionally, in cases of disagreements, member nations will have to accept binding arbitration; consumer advocate Ralph Nader has warned that such arbitration would be used to erase state, local, and federal rules on the environment, safe working conditions, and food labeling. Advocates of the new WTO have pointed out that the United States always has retained the prerogative of withdrawing from the organization. These advocates also have predicted that the new trade rules will result in a $100 billion dollar per year increase to the American economy. After fierce debate of this kind, the U.S. Congress approved the new agreements, including American participation in the WTO; the new system went into effect on January 1, 1995 (Skidmore 1994; Roberts 1994; Martz 1995).

The Marshall Plan

The final component of the postwar planning for stabilization and development grew out of the desperate plight of the European nations at war's end, a plight underlined by the severe winter of 1946–47 and the disintegration of the great overseas empires, marked by Britain's early 1947 decision to withdraw from the eastern Mediterranean. A growing sense that Soviet expansion was merely a replay of Hitler's 1930s adventurism added to the sense that something needed to be done immediately. Politically, the American containment policy (see chapter 11, "War") resulted from this sense of urgency. Economically, the Marshall Plan, officially known as the European Recovery Plan, was its outcome. First introduced by Secretary of State George Marshall (wartime chief of staff of the United States Army) in a commencement address at Harvard University in May 1947, the Marshall Plan envisioned a series of grants and loans to be extended to European nations to enable them to rise from the ruins of their economies. Other goals of the Marshall Plan, unstated but clearly present, included stabilization of the Western economies to undermine any potential attractiveness of communism, and the revival of Europe's ability to absorb the output of American factories. The Soviet Union was invited to participate in the Marshall Plan but refused, claiming that it constituted an invitation to a new form of colonialism that would place all of Europe under the American thumb.

Ultimately, sixteen European nations accepted the American invitation to participate in this great scheme, which became the single largest foreign aid program in the history of the world. The United States contributed some thirteen billion dollars in the form of loans and grants to get the European nations back on their economic feet, in what Winston Churchill called the most selfless act in human history. (Skeptics have pointed out that the "selfless" nature of the Marshall Plan is open to question, since one of the main purposes of its creation was to ensure international markets for American goods.)

In the short term, the Marshall Plan succeeded spectacularly. By 1950 industrial recovery was well underway in the target nations, and world trade began to pick up. But in the long run, Americans may rue their embrace of the Marshall Plan. One of the requirements for participation in the Marshall Plan was that the Europeans were to develop an economic plan in which they would work together. From the initiation of the European Coal and Steel Community in 1950, this pattern of cooperation would accelerate, producing first the Common Market and ultimately the recently created European Community. This process of economic integration was accompanied by a form of military integration through the formation of the North Atlantic Treaty Organization, or NATO (again, originally intended to "contain" the communist threat), and may well lead to a much fuller European political integration as well. Ironically, the creation of the European Community in 1992 as the world's largest single trading bloc may prove to be an embarrassment to the United States in years to come. We will discuss this tendency to create trading blocs and its potential repercussions later in this chapter.

Finance

For the past several hundred years, ever since the rise of the great banking families during the Renaissance, international finance has played a major role in the international economy. Traditional private capital flow in the form of loans and investments in stocks and bonds now has been augmented by new sources of capital, including foreign direct investment, unilateral aid, and multilateral aid. In addition, new forms of international financial activity, including the Eurodollar market and the rise of computerized trading, have further transformed and complicated the international financial picture. As the financial system has grown more complicated, it has also grown more important. More than one student of international political economy would agree with Peter F. Drucker, a well-known economist, that "increasingly, world investment rather than world trade will be driving the international economy" (1994, 8).

At the heart of the international financial system is the need to transfer capital from regions with surplus capital, which generates relatively low returns, to regions that need capital, in which capital will achieve relatively high rates of return and thus be used most efficiently. At least in theory, lenders and borrowers alike benefit from this more efficient use of the world's investable capital. Thus the flow of capital, which will tend to be from more developed countries to less developed countries, benefits the entire international system. Lenders receive a higher rate of return on capital than they would otherwise, thus accumulating even more capital, and borrowers gain access to funds they need for development.

In addition, this flow of capital has major political impact. Far more than trade does, foreign direct investment, loans, and aid tend to create superior-subordinate relationships; the lender often will ask for or even demand substantial changes in the recipient nation's political and economic system in order to create greater stability and thus protect capital. In addition, bankers and stockholders sometimes have called upon their own nations to use diplomacy or force to protect their foreign investments. Recipients of investment, aid, and loans often have become resentful of the influence foreigners exercise in their economies as well as in their political and social policies.

However, interesting shifts in the perceived distribution of power often can occur in the relationship between lender and borrower. When the original negotiations about a loan are going on, the creditor is in the driver's seat and can exact highly favorable terms. But once the loan or investment has been made, the recipient or debtor can convert weakness into strength by demanding new, more favorable conditions of repayment, or threatening to default entirely unless the terms of the loan are changed. Thus what begins as an entirely financial arrangement can quickly take on political dimensions.

A Brief History of the International Financial System

Like the international trading system discussed earlier, the international financial system is best understood historically in terms of hegemonic powers. In other words, like the trading system, the financial system tends to be dominated by a single nation that acts as hegemon, controlling the system, directing the flow of capital, and acting as the lender of last resort. The hegemon is the primary source of capital for developing nations, and its currency is the basis for global financial relations. One of the hegemon's major roles, in addition to generally managing the international financial system, is to stabilize the system in time of crisis.

British Hegemony

The recent history of the world economy can be defined in terms of three periods: 1870–1914, 1920–39, and 1945–71. In the first era, Great Britain played the hegemonic role; all currencies were pegged to the pound sterling, and British institutions constituted the primary lenders on the international financial market. British funds financed a substantial part of the development of the United States, Canada, and Australia during this period. The Bank of England and the City of London stood at the very center of the world's financial system.

As the world struggled to emerge from the chaos of World War I, Britain found itself sharing hegemony with the United States, which had emerged from the war as the world's greatest creditor nation. The major European nations had been forced to liquidate many of their overseas investments in order to pay for the war, and American banks had advanced huge loans, particularly to Great Britain and France. But since the international currency system remained tied to the pound sterling, New York in effect competed with London for dominance. When the stock market crash of 1929 drove the United States into the Great Depression, the flow of American capital dried up. This in turn exported the Depression and in many ways the international financial system virtually collapsed. Economic disorder and political strife followed, both major contributors to World War II.

American Hegemony

After World War II, the United States emerged as the unchallenged hegemon, particularly when the Bretton Woods system tied international currency to the dollar. However, the postwar period saw some significant changes in the nature of international finance, with governments and international institutions such as the World Bank and the IMF joining private banks as major sources of capital. The success of the American-financed Marshall Plan opened the way for other nations to begin extending direct aid to developing economies, and the politics of the Cold War often turned this unilateral aid into simply an extension of the conflict between the United States and the Soviet Union. Such aid often has been highly controversial, in part because the recipients of the aid frequently have lacked the infrastruture to make good use of it. Other critics, particularly conservatives, fear that government-to-government aid encourages state intervention in developing economies and either retards or completely prevents the development of free-market economies. The strings often attached to such aid draw the wrath of nationalists in the recipient nations, who denounce such aid as simply a new variation on the old theme of imperialism. In fact, humanitarian concerns generally have played a minor role in determining who will receive how much aid; the establishment of spheres of influence, the bolstering of military alliances, and the rewarding of allies have tended to play much larger roles. Thus the current largest recipients of American foreign aid are Israel and Egypt, and something on the order of 85 percent of this aid is military, not developmental or humanitarian. Unilateral aid has in effect become an adjunct or an instrument of both foreign and commercial policy.

The World Bank

Multilateral aid has been provided by various international agencies: the World Bank, regional development banks, and the International Monetary Fund. Multilateral development banks (MDBs) are the largest source of aid to developing countries; they also provide development policy and technical assistance. The World Bank also has played an increasing role in providing development funds, while the debt crisis of the 1980s (see chapter 8) required that the IMF, in trying to provide the liquidity to solve that problem, become more involved in development, as well. Multilateral aid, like unilateral aid, generates substantial controversy. Critics charge that the MDBs and the World Bank make too many unwise loans that are squandered by corrupt governments and do little to aid development; the World Bank also has increasingly become a target for environmentalists, who charge that "development" too often simply means destruction of natural resources on a huge scale and the creation of major environmental and ecological problems.

Conditionality, the demand by lenders that borrowers meet certain conditions (reduction of budget deficits, for example, or greater respect for human rights) is highly controversial. Not surprisingly, lenders see conditionality as essential for both political and economic reasons, while borrowers see conditionality as interference with their sovereignty and imperialist intervention in their domestic affairs. "Soft" loans, made at very low interest rates or requiring no interest payments at all, generate still more controversy. Two World Bank agencies, the International Development Association and the International Finance Corporation, are

conditionality The demand by lenders that borrowers meet certain conditions.

are the chief sources of soft loans. While debtor nations propose a vast expansion of such loans, countries like the United States generally oppose soft loans completely for both budgetary and ideological reasons.

Control of the major multilateral lending agencies is another bone of contention; developing nations want to see the United Nations General Assembly assume jurisdiction over these institutions, while the developed nations shudder at the prospect. Developed nations believe that unilateral and multilateral aid should bring less developed nations to the point at which they can participate in an open, market-oriented international economy as quickly as possible. However, the developing nations place their greatest priority on economic development and political independence, with the development of market-oriented economies at a much lower level of priority.

The End of Hegemony

This third era of international finance began in 1971, with the "Nixon shock" taking the United States off the gold standard and allowing the dollar to "float," and ended in the astonishing transformation of the United States into a debtor nation in 1985 and the emergence of Japan as the world's largest creditor nation. Today, eight of the world's ten largest commercial banks are Japanese—the remaining two of the top ten are French—and the largest American bank ranks only twentieth on the international scene. However, the dollar still remains the major unit of currency for international transactions, by no means replaced by the yen, and it is not at all clear that the Japanese are ready or willing to assume the role and responsibilities of hegemony. How the loss of hegemony will affect the United States also remains unclear, and it is not completely certain that the world's largest economy will ever absolutely lose the hegemonic position. As mentioned earlier in this chapter, one possible evolution is the emergence of a trilateral hegemony reflecting the regionalization of world trade as well, with Japan, the United States and Germany as cohegemons. However, this would require much greater cooperation and coordination than has yet been evident among the three powers.

1985

Despite the dire predictions of George Orwell, 1985 rather than 1984 may well turn out to be a critical date in modern history. The final act in the collapse of the hegemonic system came in September 1985. Representatives of the G–5 (the United States, Japan, Germany, France, and Great Britain) met secretly in New York to decide what to do about the dollar, whose value had been steadily rising. By that time, the consensus was that "clearly, the dollar had gone too far." To bring the dollar back down to realistic levels, the G–5 announced its decision "to encourage appreciation of the non-dollar currencies." In other words, the dollar would float completely freely. This announcement started a stampede, as "suddenly, everyone was selling dollars, and the greenback went into free fall" (Millman 1995, 225–26).

Since 1985

In addition to the general problems and issues of international finance already discussed, three major new phenomena have emerged in the world of international finance: the Eurodollar market, the debt crisis, and the rise of "megabyte money." Separately, each of these represents a major change in world finance. Taken together, they represent a genuine revolution, shifting control of much of the world of finance from governments to often unruly market forces. "To a degree rarely seen before, bond traders and the currency markets are driving policy, rather than reacting to it. In the "90s, bankers don't matter; markets do" (Sanger 1995). The rather genteel and stately approach of central bankers and government regulators has been replaced by what one analyst calls "nuclear finance" and "vigilante markets." According to this point of view, "the breakdown of the Bretton Woods system, the invention of new financial markets, the discoveries of financial economists [the "number-crunchers" who live in the world of chaos and fractals]—all have turned finance into a science as esoteric and inscrutable as quantum mechanics" (Millman 1995, 223–24).

Eurodollars

Traditionally, national governments have had the power to determine the value of their money, both by regulating how much is printed and by buying or selling their own currency on international markets. However, in the 1950s and 1960s the United States gradually lost control of its own currency, as the result of what became known as the "Eurodollar market."

The roots of the Eurodollar market go back to the Russian Revolution of 1917. The newly formed Bolshevik government of the USSR held substantial amounts in American dollars that it wished to use for international trade, but it hesitated to deposit those dollars in American banks lest the U.S. government either seize or freeze those assets. Consequently, the Soviets deposited the dollars in European banks. By the 1950s and 1960s, both the Soviet Union and the People's Republic of China were keeping huge sums in dollars in European banks, safely out of the reach of American regulators (Isaak 1995, 88; Millman 1995, 84–85).

From the 1960s onward, large sums of American dollars have been deposited in European banks, outside the United States monetary system and thus beyond the control of American authorities. Then these "communist" dollars were joined by dollars from other depositors, primarily the OPEC nations that wanted to use the dollar as the basic currency for oil prices, and also to keep the dollar in fairly good shape, since such great proportions of their earnings were in dollars. It was cheaper to borrow dollars on the **Euromarket** than in the United States, both because of American currency regulations and because of reserve requirements. This, coupled with inflationary policies in the United States, has led to an exponential growth of the Euromarket, which now includes other currencies beyond the dollar. In 1973 the gross sum in Eurocurrency accounts worldwide amounted to $315 billion; today the Euromarket consists of well more than four trillion dollars. The distinguishing characteristic of the Euromarket is that the money is not in the official currency of the country in which the deposits are located. **Eurodollars** have been joined by Euroyens, Euromarks, and Eurofrancs, among other currencies. All this cash not only has generated many new kinds of investment instruments, but also has provided a huge loan pool not tied to the policies of any government or multilateral organization. Governments are not exactly thrilled to have lost almost complete control over their own currencies, and the volume and speed of trades and other financial transactions in the Euromarket has introduced a large element of instability into the international financial system.

Euromarket The market comprising the members of the European Community.

Eurodollars The common-fund currency of the European Union.

The "international casino" is in full swing at the Tokyo Stock Exchange, which has been on a wild roller-coaster ride in the past few years, at one point losing nearly 50 percent of its total value.

The International Casino

international casino Global computerized system in which money, seen as a commodity itself, is traded at superfast speeds (*see* derivatives).

derivatives Trading instruments not based directly on conditions, but tied to such things as options and futures; i.e., sophisticated bets on what could happen, not what actually is going on.

In some ways dwarfing the consequences of both the Eurodollar market and the debt crisis is the impact of computers and the information age upon international financial transactions, especially currency trading, through the formation of the **international casino.** John Maynard Keynes once warned that advanced technology could in effect turn money into a commodity itself, encourage speculation, and create what he called a "casino economy." Today his prediction seems to have come true. Trillions of dollars flow through the global financial network daily, with only about 10 percent of transactions actually tied to trade in goods and services; the rest is the highly volatile, highly speculative, and often highly profitable trade in money itself, whether in international currencies or in the huge varieties of derivatives now available. (**Derivatives** are trading instruments not based directly on conditions but tied to such things as options and futures, that is, sophisticated bets on what could happen, rather than what is actually going on.)

Electronic transfers of funds via globally integrated computer networks now operate on an around-the-clock basis, with electronic money speeding from trader to trader and nation to nation at almost the speed of light. Although electronic transfers account for only 2 percent of global buying and selling, they involve five out of every six dollars that move through the world economy.

One of the most important agents, and symbols, of the speed of change within the global financial markets is the computer network that ties nations and traders together, making possible near-instantaneous transactions that allow currency speculators, for example, to take advantage of ten-second "windows" in exchange rates. The ramifications of the global electronic financial network are staggering. For one thing, it has almost entirely divorced "money" from reality and made it into a symbol to be manipulated electronically. "Homeless money" and "megabyte money" are two terms used to refer to this development. The editor of the *Harvard Business Review* in fact refers to "the death of money," because of the way in which it has become almost entirely a commodity. The value of money is now determined not by the central bank or central bankers of any nation, but by the worldwide array of currency traders who buy and sell, gambling huge amounts on relatively tiny fluctuations in the value of one currency in terms of another.

In the 1970s the Chicago Commodities Exchange, which had long run "futures" markets on pork bellies and grains, began to experiment with "futures contracts" on the value of money. Essentially, such a contract allows a trader to hedge his or her bets on money value fluctuations by locking into a buy or sell agreement at a set price sometime in the future. By 1989 the Chicago Commodities Exchange alone listed more than 350 varieties of futures contracts, most of them in finance and derivatives, and more than seventy new exchanges devoted to futures contracts had sprung up around the world. These new markets have enormously increased the flow of money globally, aided by the truly remarkable electronic networks that have come into being. Enormous profits are being generated, and enormous risks taken. For example, Citibank, the largest American bank involved in the global casino economy, earns roughly $600 million a year just from profits in currency trading; a single British financier, George Soros, personally earned an estimated $1 billion in 1992 the same way.

CHIPS

GLOBAL PERSPECTIVES

One of the major consequences for global business of the international communications revolution has been the fantastic increase in the speed with which business transactions now occur. Both agent and symbol of this global acceleration is the Clearing House Interbank Payments System (CHIPS). Established by eleven major New York City banks, CHIPS has become a vital component of the global economy. Coded requests to make payments of millions and millions of dollars flow into CHIPS' two mainframe computers via 134 dedicated phone lines; after security measures to make sure that the orders are valid, the money is on its way. The entire process, from receipt of request to computerized international transfer of funds, takes less than *one second*. Over one trillion dollars flows through CHIPS every day (two billion dollars a minute)—more than the entire money supply of the United States! There are 122 banks on line to the CHIPS computers, which they pay only eighteen cents per payment order—less than that if their transactions exceed eighty thousand per month. This electronic superhighway for dollars, combined with the Federal Reserve's own, rather smaller national system,

pushes around $1.7 trillion a day, four-fifths of worldwide payments in dollars. And the pace of electronic transfer of funds is accelerating. In 1980 the flow of electronic money was roughly twelve times the balances held in accounts at the Federal Reserve; by 1991, the daily flow was 55 times this bank reserve (Passell 1992).

CHIPS in turn is tied to numerous other computerized trading networks, including SWIFT (Society for International Financial Telecommunications), a Belgian-based system that links together one thousand banks, a British equivalent called CHAPS, and a number of other similar systems.

Inevitably, the highly computerized electronic CHIPS system has created a whole new range of concerns about security—what would happen if both mainframes crashed or were crashed at the same time—and about the effects this speedup is having on the global economy.

CHIPS operators are confident about many aspects of security. Elaborate "black boxes" scan each incoming request to make sure that it is correctly coded. This "electronic authentication barrier"

(Continued on p. 250)

CHIPS
(continued from p. 249)

links the dollar amount of each transaction to the coding itself; thus, an order to move seven million dollars requires an entirely different code from an order to move seventy million. Furthermore, if the black boxes cannot authenticate an order, the phone line to the transmitting financial institution is automatically severed.

The mainframe computers receive their power from storage batteries fed by the city's power grid. The control room has a system that would flood the entire area with halon gas to snuff out any potential fire. And finally, there are two backup computers "somewhere in New Jersey" linked to an independent communications grid that can take over operations if necessary. The only time the system has been tested, when a hardware failure took out both New York computers in October 1991, less than five minutes of processing time was lost in transferring all operations to the New Jersey backups (Passell 1992, 66).

Nonetheless, the speed at which these international transfers of huge amounts of money occur raises concerns about the possibility of what is called monetary gridlock. One worst-case scenario envisions a CHIPS member bank unable to cover all of the day's transactions, thus invalidating all the other transfers made that day on the basis that the initial transfer had been valid. If this were to happen, then the entire day's transactions would have to be "unwound": every transaction involving the defaulting bank would have to be erased, and all other accounts completely redone to reflect these changes. Conceivably, this could lead to days or even weeks of gridlock, as banks sought to cover their shortfalls. Hundreds of billions of dollars in assets would have to be frozen, at least temporarily, and hundreds of corporations would have to scramble to borrow from other sources in order to meet daily payments. Within the United States the possibility of this happening is virtually eliminated by the Federal Reserve system, which covers such shortfalls with temporary loans. Once the Fed had to loan a large bank \$23.6 billion to cover transfer problems created by a software snafu. However, no such backup exists for the international system, and all concerned acknowledge that it is possible, although unlikely, that the pace of technological development could outstrip the system of control that CHIPS has set in place, and that "The Big One" could happen—however long the odds (Passell 1992, 66, 75).

---

hot money The speed that money is transferred in the electronic casino.

"Hot Money." The speed at which money moves in the international casino has led more than one analyst to refer to it as **"hot money,"** and to raise serious questions about the consequences of the speed at which the new markets operate. "Investors can now move money from Treasury bills to Mexican retail stocks to German government bond options just by picking up the phone." The whole idea of national currencies is now being questioned. "In this new market, money moves faster than ever, raising the possibility that billions can flow in or out of an economy in seconds." The new investors, who control perhaps two trillion dollars in assets and move that money with astonishing ease and speed, represent a quantum change from the "patient" banks and multilateral development agencies that provided the global capital supply only a decade ago. "So powerful has this force [of "hot money"] become that some observers now see the hot-money set becoming a sort of shadow world government—one that is irretrievably eroding the concept of the sovereign powers of a nation-state" (Glasgall 1995, 36).

Flouting the Law? A second consequence of the electronic transformation of global finance is that it has become much easier to "launder" money, that is, to take money from some illicit enterprise such as the drug trade. The speed and anonymity of the global money transfer system have made the process of transforming "dirty" money into "clean" more rapid, and much simpler, than it was in the past. Electronic transfers are secret, and sending funds to banking accounts out of a country, and thus beyond the reach of national police or tax collectors, does not even require speaking to a bank officer; a fax or modem will do the job perfectly. By 1990 banking officials estimated that worldwide drug profits had reached $300 billion a year, most of which flowed through the electronic financial network. Tiny nation-states that function as tax havens, "mostly islands featuring warm weather, good flight connections, and plenty of faxes" (Barnet and Cavanagh 1994, 389), are now linked to the global financial network through elaborate electronic systems. Grand Cayman, one of the busiest tax havens, supposedly boasts the highest concentration of fax machines in the world to service its 548 banking outposts, which hold assets valued at roughly $400 billion.

The Markets Ride High.   A third important result of the explosive growth of the electronic global financial network is that it has reduced nations to virtual impotence in critical areas such as the formulation and enforcement of economic and monetary policy. The world of high-speed money, like so many other international systems, is essentially anarchic and governments have basically lost control over their own money. In September 1992 a "feeding frenzy" of currency speculation pitted German deutschemarks, desirable because of the high interest rates within Germany, against the currencies of Finland, Italy, Spain, and Great Britain. The four nations whose currencies came under attack ultimately devalued their currencies, raised their interest rates, and spent twenty-four billion marks to prop up the lira and ten billion pounds to keep the British pound sterling afloat; the Bank of England desperately raised interest rates five percentage points, but not even that worked to defend the pound. The Bank of International Settlements estimates that currency exchange and speculation today ranges upwards of $800 billion every day, with not more than 10 percent of that sum tied directly to normal commercial transactions; almost $700 billion is simply currency exchange in the international casino. Even the hours during which most of these trades occur reflects some of the changes in the global economy: approximately 30 percent of all trading activities take place while the Asian markets are open, 45 percent while the European markets are up, and only 15 percent while American markets are open.

A "quiet but momentous revolution" has taken place in international finance as market forces have gradually replaced governments as the chief controllers of money and finance. This revolution has wrested control over money and finance from sovereign states and has "replaced the ordered despotism of bureaucrats with the chaotic, Darwinian democracy of the trading pits" (Millman 1995, 24, 96). In a somewhat overdramatic statement, one analyst notes that the markets' "vigilante economics knows no national border, bows to no regulatory authority, [and] accepts no rule but the rule of financial power" (Millman, 98). Another analyst notes less heatedly that "conventional concepts of state power are simply dwarfed by the awesome might of the new global financial markets." According to this source, global currency markets now trade $1.2 trillion every single day, almost as much as the entire *annual* budget of the United States. These markets "embody a power that transcends frontiers, commands an alternative allegiance from the citizens of individual states, and can humble governments and leaders." Even the most powerful economies in the world are vulnerable to the "tidal waves of global money" that wash around the world daily. The managers of these global markets, according to this analysis, "in their growing sovereignty over economic policy making, . . . present the biggest challenge to the authority of the nation-state since nation-states were first born" (Walker 1995).

Meltdown? Finally, the enormous volatility of this global casino market with money as its chief commodity creates all kinds of hair-raising possibilities for some kind of international meltdown. Experts believe that much of the $700 billion or so in non–"real world" currency trading is held in extremely short-term deals, lasting anywhere from a few hours to a maximum of a few weeks. These global networks are clearly vulnerable to hardware breakdowns, as well as software "glitches." They are vulnerable to attack by "hackers," who may attempt to break into systems for pleasure or for profit. And the global casino, with its tremendous volatility, is also implicated in stock market "crashes" like the one that affected nearly 25 percent of the U.S. New York Stock Exchange listings in October 1987. Fast financial footwork by the Federal Reserve and others prevented that drop from becoming a meltdown on the scale of the 1929 stock market crash, but it remains entirely possible that future electronic casino operations could easily lead to future meltdowns on several major stock exchanges—New York, London, and Tokyo, for example—simultaneously. Should that happen, it is not clear that there is any mechanism in place globally that could accomplish what the Federal Reserve did in 1987, that is, prevent complete disaster.

Will E-Cash Replace Money? In a recent article in *Business Week,* Kelley Holland and Amy Cortese raise the possibility of an entirely new form of money: digital or electronic money, called "E-cash." According to Holland and Cortese, **E-cash** is virtually inevitable, a logical outgrowth of an increasingly wired world. (See chapter 13, "The Web of Global Communications," for more on this phenomenon.) Holland and Cortese define E-cash as "money that moves along multiple channels largely outside the established network of banks, checks, and paper currency overseen by the Federal Reserve." However, while "regular" money is created at least in part by banks lending out more money than they actually have on deposit, any kind of nonbank money supplier could, at least in theory, issue E-cash by backing the digital cash with a fraction of its own regular cash. "Nonbanks, which are largely unregulated, could create money just as commercial banks do now." (Holland and Cortese 1995, 46).

e-cash Digital or electronic money.

Although E-cash will certainly make transactions over the Internet easier, and bring us much closer to the cashless world envisioned by legions of science fiction writers, it also raises some serious questions. Who can issue E-cash? Who can regulate it? How will you tax transactions in cyberspace, which transcends national boundaries? What kind of security can be provided for E-cash transactions? (Holland and Cortese 1995, 46).

Analysts of the E-cash world see momentous changes, not all of them good. For example, laundering money and evading taxes will become much, much easier. "E-money can be easily sent in and out of a country undetected, facilitating money laundering on a grand scale. Tax evasion could become a matter of pushing a buttom. And without foolproof cryptography, counterfeiters" could have a field day (Holland and Cortese 1995, 47).

Most important of all, E-cash could completely erode and destroy the present system of national currency. A pioneer in cyber-checking, David E. Saxton, observes that "digital cash is a threat to every government on the planet that wants to manage its currency." Among other problems, governments would lose the ability not only to create but also to monitor their own money supplies; in the United States, for example, the Federal Reserve probably would lose control over a significant portion of the American money supply. When more and more money originates outside the reach of traditional institutions responsible for regulating currency, such as the Bank of England or the German Bundesbank, money markets become more and more volatile; as we have seen already; even at this point their volatility is worrisome and perhaps even dangerous. "The effects of high-speed electronic trading have been painfully apparent in market crises over the past several years. Market swings could be magnified if consumers and businesses could send their money around the globe with the touch of a button on a PC" (Holland and Cortese 1995, 52).

E-cash is on its way, a variety of analysts conclude, and the world had better start getting ready for it and solving the problems we have mentioned. Some agencies, such as the Federal Reserve and the Financial Crimes Enforcement Network, are beginning to think about E-cash. "There's no going back," according to one official. "The genie's out of the bottle. The Internet doesn't have an off switch" (Holland and Cortese 1995, 52). And, as a recent commentator notes, the development of e-cash is logical. E-cash weighs nothing and moves at the speed of light. It is "money incarnated, finally, as pure information." That should come as no surprise, since "information is what money has always been about." Money, after all, is fundamentally information about wealth and value, and thus, like all information, can be easily digitized (Gleick 1996, 28).

The Rise of Regional Trading Blocs

Further complicating an already-complex international economic system is the rise of regional trading blocs that create economic unions among nations in physical proximity and at the same time exclude all others; such blocs of course represent major centrifugal forces competing against the centripetal forces of the interlocking international economy that is appearing.

The European Union

The first of the major regional blocs was the European Union (EU); prefigured as early as 1951 by the European Coal and Steel Community; the EU came into full being on January 1, 1992, with the dropping of all trade barriers and, supposedly, a move towards a single European currency. Since 1992, the EU has proceeded in fits and starts. The failure of Denmark and Sweden to ratify the Treaty of Maastricht, the instrument of economic unification, was a serious blow to unity, and continuing nationalistic pressures, especially on currency issues, are still impeding rapid movement toward full realization of the EU. Nonetheless, eastern European nations are clamoring for admission to the EU, and even Russia is exploring the possibility of a closure link with the EU. As of this writing, the EU comprises some 350 million people, having lost its "largest economic bloc" rank to the North American Free Trade Agreement (NAFTA). However, unlike NAFTA, the EU envisions political as well as economic integration.

NAFTA

The **North American Free Trade Agreement (NAFTA),** under negotiation for several years and finally ratified in 1993, brings together the United States, Canada, and Mexico into an integrated free trade zone of some 380 million people, with a combined economic product of $6.5 trillion. Critics, spurred on largely by economic nationalism, feared that NAFTA would mean the export of American jobs to Mexico, with its much cheaper labor. Ross Perot, one of the most vocal

NAFTA North American Free Trade Agreement: agreement that incorporates Canada, the U.S., and Mexico economically into a free-trade zone.

opponents of NAFTA, warned that American workers would hear "a giant suck-ing sound" as their jobs disappeared south of the border (see cartoon). Support-ers of NAFTA warned that the association was necessary in order to compete with the EU, and also claimed that the combination of American capital and technol-ogy, Mexican labor, and Canadian raw materials offered an almost ideal combi-nation, and that Mexican oil would permit the United States to ease its dangerous dependence on Middle Eastern petroleum. Defying the doom-sayers, all three nations ratified NAFTA in the fall of 1993. As of this writing, several other West-ern Hemisphere nations, including Chile, have lined up to join NAFTA, and there is serious discussion of incorporating both the Mercosur and the ANDEAN pact nations, who include most of the rest of the Americas, into NAFTA. The current American Secretary of State, Warren Christopher, has even suggested that NAFTA and the EU might consider developing economic links. However, the NAFTA agreement, unlike that of the EU, contains no intimations whatever of any kind of political integration.

APEC?

There is also, albeit on a much slower time-table, some movement toward creat-ing an Asian-Pacific free trade zone. In November 1994 the eighteen members of the Asia-Pacific Economic Cooperative (APEC) agreed to create a loosely knit

"I don't know what the hell happened—one minute I'm at work in Flint, Michigan, then there's a giant sucking sound and suddenly here I am in Mexico."

Source: Drawing by M. Stevens; © 1993 The New Yorker Magazine, Inc. Reprinted by permission of the publisher from *The New Yorker,* November 22, 1993, 88.

trade association that would span the Pacific. The APEC nations, which include the United States, China, and Japan, have agreed to scrap all tariff barriers by no later than 2020, which to many people seems like a long, long time from 1994. However, there will be serious problems of economic integration in the APEC area. Not only does the vastness of the Pacific make such integration more difficult to achieve, but so too do fears of both a resurgent Japan, whose World War II excesses have been neither forgotten nor forgiven, and a revitalized China, which traditionally has exerted hegemony over most of the East and Southeast Asian sphere. Nonetheless, the pressures to create an effective Asia-Pacific trade bloc will be enormous, particularly if the EU and NAFTA are anywhere nearly as successful as their proponents believe they will be.

Whether the centrifugal forces represented by these regional blocs, depicted in figure 7.1, will offset the centripetal forces of modern communications, multinational corporations, and an increasingly intertwined global and financial world remains to be seen; without a doubt, their very existence will make the opening years of the next century extremely interesting and challenging.

We have only skimmed the surface of the massive changes taking place in today's global economy. Some of these changes are integrative; that is, they tend to bring together nations into a truly global economy. Others, especially the rise of regional economic blocs, have disturbing disintegrative or centrifugal implications. Another extremely important question is where the rise of the information economy will take the world, and whether it will increase or decrease the gap between North and South. In the next chapter we will examine the major North-South issues and controversies, trying to shed still more light on the new course of the global economy.

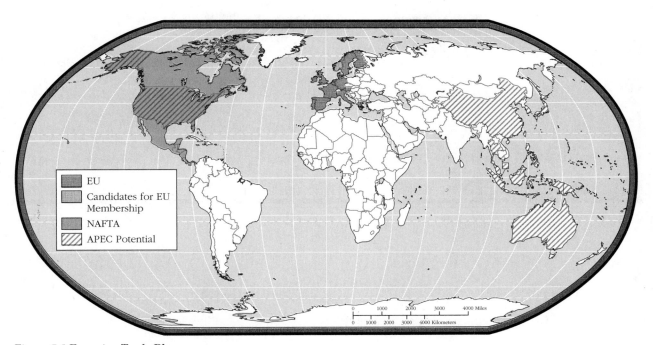

EU

Candidates for EU Membership

NAFTA

APEC Potential

Figure 7.1 **Emerging Trade Blocs**

Summary

International Trade: Three major theories dominate our understanding of international trade. The liberal view sees international trade as a positive good and wants a barrier-free world. Economic nationalists are leery of trade and want a protected domestic economy. Marxists see international trade as another manifestation of capitalist exploitation. An enormously complex issue, international trade raises questions about deficits, trade wars, the export of technology, and cultural differences between superficially similar economies. The last few years have seen the creation or prediction of major regional trading blocs—the EU, NAFTA, and the future APEC—that have the potential both to divide the world market and to effectively lock out nonmembers.

The Bretton Woods System: During World War II, the Allies attempted to construct a coherent and rational postwar international economic system that would encourage recovery, promote stability, and provide the means for developing nations to improve their position. The World Bank, the International Monetary Fund, and GATT were the three pillars of this system, and the U.S. dollar was the currency to which all others were pegged. By 1971 the Triffin dilemma—what was good for world trade was not necessarily good for the American economy—led the United States to cut the dollar loose from gold and in effect begin unraveling the Bretton Woods system. The weakening of the dollar that began in 1985 completed the process. No one is completely sure what, if anything, will replace the Bretton Woods system.

Finance: The Bretton Woods collapse has been very much tied to major changes in the world of finance, particularly the development of finance propelled by the communications revolution. The result has been the rise of the Eurodollar economy and what is called the "international casino" in currency trading. Both have undermined the ability of central governments to control the value and protect the stability of their own currencies in another assault on sovereignty.

Key Terms

Economic nationalism	MFN (most favored nation) status
Capitalism	Hegemon
Comparative advantage	Bretton Woods
H-O-S model	Marshall Plan
New trade theory	Triffin's dilemma
Strategic trade policy	Transparency

Conditionality
Euromarket
Eurodollars
International casino
Derivatives

"Hot money"
E-cash
North American Free Trade
    Agreement (NAFTA)

Thought Questions

1. Briefly outline the liberal, nationalist, Marxist, and "new trade theory" approaches to international commerce. What is the strength of each? The weakness of each?
2. Trace the rise of the Bretton Woods system and its principal components.
3. What was Triffin's dilemma? What was the result?
4. Why and how did Bretton Woods collapse?
5. What is GATT? How is the WTO supposed to work? Why do some people oppose both?
6. Analyze the impact of the electronics communication revolution on world economics, both trade and finance.
7. What problems might the rise of international trading blocs create? What might they solve?

References

Babai, Don. "General Agreement on Tariffs and Trade." In Joel Krieger, ed. *The Oxford Companion to Politics of the World*. New York: Oxford University Press, 1993.

Barnet, Richard J., and John Cavanagh. *Global Dreams: Imperial Corporations and the New World Order*. New York: Simon and Shuster, 1994.

Barnet, Richard J., and Ronald E. Muller. *Global Reach: The Power of the Multinational Corporations*. New York: Simon and Shuster, 1984.

Blustein, Paul. "U.S., Asia-Pacific Nations Move toward End of Trade Barriers." *Houston Chronicle,* November 13, 1994.

Choate, Pat. *Agents of Influence*. New York: Pantheon, 1993.

Cohen, Benjamin. "A Brief History of International Monetary Relations." In Jeffrey A. Frieden and David A. Lake, *International Political Economy: Perspectives on Global Wealth and Power,* 3d ed. New York: St. Martin's Press, 1995.

Coughlin, Cletus C. "Foreign-owned Companies in the United States: Malign or Benign?" In Jeffrey A. Friedan and David A. Lake, *International Political Economy: Perspectives on Global Wealth and Power,* 3rd ed. New York: St. Martin's Press, 1995.

Drucker, Peter. *Post-Capitalist Society*. New York: Harper Collins, 1994.

El-Agraa, Ali M. *The Theory of International Trade*. London: Croom and Helm, 1983. In Gilpin, *op.cit.*

Gilpin, Robert. *The Political Economy of International Relations*. Princeton, N.J.: Princeton University Press, 1987.

Glassgall, William. "Hot Money." *Business Week.* March 30, 1995.

Gleick, James. "Dead as a Dollar." *New York Times Magazine,* June 16, 1996.

Hampden-Turner, Charles, and Alfons Trompenaars, *The Seven Cultures of Capitalism*. New York: Doubleday, 1993.

Hoagland, Jim. "Everybody wins, except China's citizens." *Houston Chronicle.* Aug. 31, 1995.

Holland, Kelley, and Amy Cortese. "The Color of Cybermoney." *Business Week*. February 27, 1995.

Isaak, Robert, *Managing World Economic Change: International Political Economy*. Englewood Cliffs, N.J.: Prentice Hall, 1995.

Jenkins, Barbara. "Multinational Corporations." In Joel Krieger, ed., *Oxford Companion to Politics of the World*. New York: Oxford University Press, 1993.

Kennedy, Paul. *The Rise and Fall of the Great Powers*. New York: Vintage, 1989.

Krugman, Paul. *Peddling Prosperity: Economic Sense and Nonsense in the Age of Diminished Expectations*. New York: W.W. Norton, 1994.

Martz, Larry. "GATT Is a Turkey That Needs Killing." *Newsweek Interactive*, February 13, 1995.

Millman, Gregory J. *The Vandals' Crown: How Rebel Currency Traders Overthrew the World's Central Banks*. New York: The Free Press, 1995.

Omestad, Thomas. "Selling Off America." In Jeffrey A. Frieden and David A. Lake, *International Political Economy: Perspectives on Global Wealth and Power*, 3d ed. New York: St. Martin's Press, 1995.

Passall, Peter. "CHIPS." *New York Times Magazine*, October 18, 1992.

Pitroda, William. "From GATT to WTO." *Harvard International Review*. Spring 1995. 44–46.

Ricardo, David. *Principles of Political Economy and Taxation* (1817). In *The Works of David Ricardo*. London: John Murray, 1871. In Gilpin, op. cit.

Roberts, Craig. "Adam Smith would have loved GATT." *Houston Chronicle*. Dec. 9, 1994.

Roet, Jeff. "The Geopolitics of NAFTA and the Global Economy." Unpublished speech at San Jacinto College. Jan. 10, 1994.

Sanger, David E. "Do Fickle Markets Now Make Policy?" *New York Times*, March 19, 1995.

Silverman, Dwight, "Remote Meetings for Firms Turning into Virtual Reality." *Houston Chronicle*, January 9, 1994.

———."Digital Nation: Computer Networks Redefine Workplace", *Houston Chronicle*, February 7, 1995.

Skidmore, Dave. "Clinton, Dole Closer to Deal on Trade." *Houston Chronicle*, November 23, 1994.

Thurow, Lester. *Head to Head: The Coming Economic Battle among Japan, Europe, and America*. New York: Warner Books, 1993.

———.*The Future of Capitalism: How Today's Economic Forces Shape Tomorrow's World*. New York: William Morrow, 1996.

Tolchin, Martin, and Susan J. Tolchin. *Selling Our Security: The Erosion of America's Assets*. New York: Penguin, 1993.

Walker, Martin. "Priesthood of high finance overawes politicians," *Houston Chronicle*. June 21, 1995.

Wiedemann, Kent. Testimony before House Ways and Means Subcommittee on Trade. May 23, 1995. Internet download. gopher://dosfan.lib.uic.edu.70/of-1%A7013%3A95/05/23%20. Downloaded September 15, 1996.

Wilder, Clinton. "Making Borders Disappear: Citibank Asia Pushes Centralization from Turkey to Guam," *Informationweek*, February 27, 1995.

Wriston, Walter, *The Twilight of Sovereignty: How the Information Revolution is Transforming Our World*. New York: Charles Scribner's Sons, 1992.

Chapter 8

The Geoeconomics of Today: Integration and Disintegration

Introduction*

The end of the Cold War has produced many new, distinct political and economic developments. As we have indicated throughout this book, the world is simultaneously integrating and disintegrating, or as some prefer to term it, converging and diverging. There is no better place to inspect this phenomenon than in the realm of the North-South rivalry over geoeconomics.

In the words of Professor Jeffrey Roet, "accelerated by the end of the Cold War and agreements such as NAFTA, a profound transformation is re-configuring the world's economic and political geography. This structural evolution will be as significant as the Industrial Revolution was, so we all should know how global and far-reaching these economic reverberations will be" (Roet, 1995).

Development

The development of nations has traditionally been a topic of intense interest in the study of international relations. The state of development of a particular nation influences not only the everyday lives of its people, but also the political and economic contacts it has with the outside world. According to the World Bank,

> Development is the most important challenge facing the human race. Despite the vast opportunities created by the technological revolutions of the twentieth century, more than 1 billion people, one-fifth of the world's population, live on less than one dollar a day—a standard of living that Western Europe and the United States attained two hundred years ago. (World Bank 1991, 1)

Nearly three-fourths of all nation-states can be considered underdeveloped; these include primarily the developing countries of Africa, Latin America, and Asia, although some of the new republics spun off from the Soviet Union (and many say Russia itself) fall into this category as well. A variety of terms are used to describe these nations: underdeveloped, developing, Third World, or least developed countries. These words all express the same concept: the particular term used depends on the preference of the authors or on which term was in vogue when their research was being done. Underdeveloped or developing nations share several common characteristics: prevalent poverty, high rates of population growth, low literacy rates (see table 8.1, which is depicted graphically in figure 8.1), high fertility rates, low per capita income (see table 8.1), and a life expectancy about half that of industrialized or developed nations (again, see table 8.1). Furthermore, the gap between developed and developing nations is widening. Although some developing nations' economies are growing each year, the GNP of developed nations is growing much faster. Additionally, in most developing nations tremendous population growth has wiped out gains in overall GNP. In some cases, population growth has even resulted in a drop in per capita GNP; this is particularly true of some of the developing nations of sub-Saharan Africa, where population growth has been 3 percent or more per year.

Development, however, is not purely an economic process; most social scientists would agree that development must include economic, political, social,

---

*Dr. Dragan Stefanovic, Assistant Professor at Appalachian State University Department of Political Science and Criminal Justice, is co-author of this chapter.

Table 8.1

"Further Breakdown of Selected Nations According to HDI"

	Life expectancy at birth (years) '87	Adult literacy rate (%) '85	Real GDP per head (PPP-adj'd) '87, $	HDI	Rank by GNP per head	Rank by HDI
Niger	45	14	452	0.116	20	1
Mauritania	47	17	840	0.208	40	8
Malawi	48	42	476	0.250	7	14
Zaire	53	62	220	0.294	5	20
Togo	54	41	670	0.337	24	27
Madagascar	54	68	634	0.440	14	38
Egypt	62	45	1,357	0.501	49	45
Indonesia	57	74	1,660	0.591	41	54
Philippines	64	86	1,878	0.714	46	65
Iraq	65	89	2,400	0.759	96	76
Malaysia	70	74	3,849	0.800	80	85
Portugal	74	85	5,597	0.899	94	95
Singapore	73	86	12,790	0.899	110	96
Argentina	71	96	4,647	0.910	89	99
USA	76	96	17,615	0.961	129	112
Sweden	77	99	13,780	0.987	125	129
Japan	78	99	13,135	0.996	126	130

Source: Data from "The Human Condition," *The Economist,* May 26, 1990, pp. 80–81.

and even cultural factors. Thus some nations, Singapore for example, are economically developed but lag behind politically and socially. Moreover, development is a process that involves continuous change; historically, nations have not always advanced, but have sometimes regressed and even collapsed completely. No society meets all criteria for complete development. Even the United States, one of the most fully developed nations, still has problems such as homelessness, crime, and unemployment that must be resolved. To properly express development as a continuum rather than an absolute, we will use the terms less developed countries (LDCs) and most developed countries (MDCs).

Goals of Development

Before proceeding further, we need to examine what development is: how it is defined and what its goals are. We must thus examine development from economic, political, and social points of view, since each one of these areas has different, although intertwined, goals. The term **development** is best defined as *a process that takes a particular nation-state from a less to a more developed status,* or as a positive progression toward a particular development goal.

development A process that takes a nation from a less developed to a more developed status. Usually measured by a nation's GNP.

Economic Goals

Not surprisingly, there are several different views of what constitutes economic development. Perhaps the simplest view is that development is a continuous increase in a nation's gross national product (GNP), with the goal of matching or exceeding the GNP of the MDCs. This view assumes that the richer a nation is in general, the better off its individual citizens are. However, many scholars contend that GNP is a poor indicator of the economic status or the well-being of the population in general. Some who are concerned primarily with equality look at income distribution to determine how well the entire population is doing. These scholars examine the income of the wealthy and compare it to the income of the poor. If the gap between the incomes of these groups is too large or if this gap is increasing rather than shrinking, there is a problem of income inequality. Generally, nation-states with income inequality problems are viewed as underdeveloped; if the gap between rich and poor is increasing, the nation is classified as not developing. Finally, another group of scholars tries to ascertain how well the population's basic needs are being met and use that to measure development. They measure variables such as availability of food, shelter, and health care, as well as the level of safety and security that the state provides. As this discussion makes clear, there is as yet no firm consensus on exactly what constitutes economic development or how to measure it.

Political Goals

The goals of political development are better defined than those of economic development. Most non-Marxist scholars agree that the ultimate goal of political development is the establishment of a democratic government with a decentralized economy. (Orthodox Marxists have the establishment of a classless society with a centralized economy as their goal.) While most scholars may agree on the ultimate goal of a democratic government, there is considerable disagreement about the process required to establish democratic government and the timetable that needs to be observed. Some scholars believe that democratic government should be instituted immediately, by any means available. They believe that once democracy is established, development in all other areas follows almost automatically. Others assert that the process of establishing democracy must be more

These Rwandan refugees exemplify the compounded problems of development in the face of a low-level Human Development Index worsened by war and refugee status.

gradual, allowing a transitional phase during which the environment necessary for sustaining democracy can be established. According to this latter point of view, the most important condition in the early phases of development is political stability. Only with such stability can the people be united, state authority established and legitimate political institutions built, and the political culture of the country changed to accept and support democracy. Without such changes, these scholars argue, a democracy has no base on which to build; even if established, it cannot endure.

Social Goals

Social development at its most basic implies movement from a traditional to a modern society. In the traditional society, the family controls political, economic, social, and cultural life. Such a society has an ascriptive political system that is normally authoritarian, a subsistence economy, and almost no division of labor. Education as we know it is almost nonexistent, and literacy rates are extremely low. Infant mortality rates are high, with very low life expectancy for those who do survive infancy. The nomadic tribes of Africa and a number of Indian tribes within the Amazon jungle are typical examples of pure traditional societies. A modern society, on the other hand, is characterized by a political system based on merit and elections (usually staged with more than one political party), and a competitive industrial base with an advanced division of labor designed to produce both consumer and capital goods for profit. Such a society enjoys a high level of education and offers equality of opportunity to its citizens. Infant mortality is low, life expectancy high. (For worldwide life expectancy rates, see fig. 8.2.) There are obviously few societies that are either completely traditional or

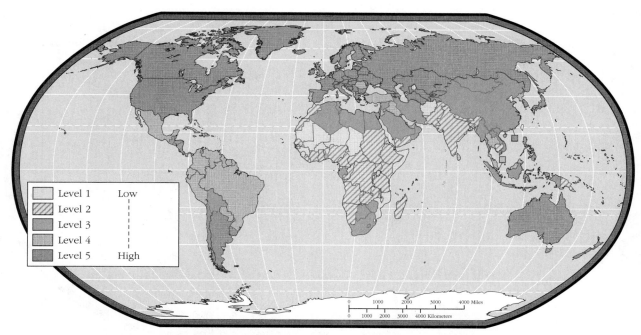

Figure 8.1 **Map of World According to Human Development Index**
Source: Data from "The Human Condition," *The Economist,* May 26, 1990, pp. 80–81.

transitional societies
Societies moving from less developed status to developed status.

completely modern; most fall on a continuum between these two extremes. These are called **transitional societies,** and can be identified readily by their mixture of traditional and modern elements. South Korea and Mexico are but two such examples.

To measure social development, scholars have examined such areas as education, health, and demographic patterns. Among the elements most closely scrutinized are literacy, average number of school years attended, infant mortality, life expectancy, average caloric intake, and patterns of urbanization. Some have constructed indices that cover more than one variable and permit comparison among nations. A well-known index of this kind is the **Physical Quality of Life Index (PQLI)** developed by Morris D. Morris. The index is computed by examining infant mortality, literacy, and life expectancy rates of national populations, and then converting and placing on scales ranging from 1 to 100 the values of these variables. To arrive at a single-number index, Morris gives each table, representing one of the three variables, equal weight, adds the three numbers, and divides by three. The resulting number is the PQLI for a particular country. Figure 8.1 shows the world according to the Human Development Index, a variant of the PQLI, while Figure 8.2 illustrates one of the most important factors determining PQLI, life expectancy at birth.

PQLI Physical Quality of Life Index: index used to rank nations according to life expectancy, infant mortality, and literacy rates, in the assessment of progress in terms of basic human needs.

Culture and Development

culture A pattern of beliefs, values, attitudes, customs, and behaviors that is learned by the individual from his or her family and society. It predisposes an individual to act in specific ways that are acceptable to society.

Although culture is difficult to define and conceptualize, we must do so in order to understand the complex processes by which culture influences development. Anthropologists and others who attempt to define and describe **culture** have posited a number of different definitions. According to Edward B. Taylor's classical definition,

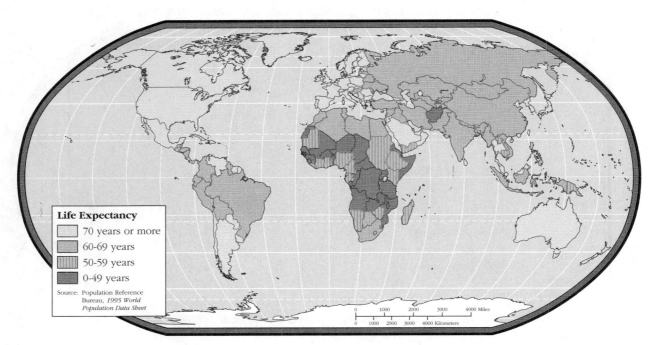

Life Expectancy
- 70 years or more
- 60-69 years
- 50-59 years
- 0-49 years

Source: Population Reference Bureau, *1995 World Population Data Sheet*

Figure 8.2 Life Expectancy

> Culture, or civilization, taken in its wide ethnographic sense, is that complex whole which includes knowledge, belief, art, morals, law, custom, and any other capabilities and habits acquired by man as a member of society. (Taylor 1924, 1)

It is important to note that culture as defined by Taylor and others is not inherited; it is learned behavior. This is vital, because any learned behavior can be modified with proper education and incorporated into development strategies. Although Taylor says that an individual acquires culture from society, it is also essential to recognize that the family plays the predominant role in teaching the individual culture.

Since we are interested here primarily in development and international relations, we will avoid overly broad definitions of culture and instead use the following definition:

> Culture is a pattern of beliefs, values, attitudes, customs, and behaviors that is learned by the individual from his or her family and society. It predisposes an individual to act in specific ways that are acceptable to society.

Students of development too often ignore the role played by culture at the individual and local level. Lawrence Harrison, a twenty-year veteran of the United States Agency for International Development (AID), writes, "I have been increasingly persuaded that, more than any other of the numerous factors that influence the development of countries, it is culture that principally explains, in most cases, why some countries develop more rapidly and equitably than others" (Harrison 1985, xvi). The great Swedish economist Gunnar Myrdal decried the manner in which economic planners routinely ignored the role of culture:

> A major part of the work on planning for development in South Asia has been hindered by the assumption that beginning analysis can be concentrated on economic conditions—output and incomes, conditions of production, and levels of living—plus those policies that affect only these conditions . . . . There is also the assumption that the chain of causes linking these economic conditions is not affected by attitudes and institutions. Instead it is often assumed that the latter will automatically be highly responsive to changes in the economic conditions. In reality, attitudes and institutions are stubborn and not easily changed, least of all indirectly. (Myrdal 1971, 433)

A number of social scientists have tried to determine the links between culture and economic development. A pioneer in the field, Max Weber, investigated the link between the Protestant work ethic and development, while more recently psychologist David McClelland correlated entrepreneurial activities and achievement motivation with development. Alex Inkeles, a social psychologist, studied individual modernity, and concluded that "a change in attitudes and values" constitutes "one of the most essential preconditions for substantial and effective functioning of those modern institutions which most of the more 'practical' programs of development hope to establish" (Inkeles 1974, 313).

Strategies for Development

Over the years a variety of economic development strategies have been created to help LDCs achieve more developed status. The earliest of these modernization strategies evolved from classical economics and were designed to resolve developmental problems by concentrating on local conditions and obstacles. Other strategies have been based primarily on what is known as dependency theory, which grows from Marxist analysis of the development of capitalism in nondeveloped nations; their proponents have looked at the international economic environment for their developmental solutions.

The Modernization School

Before World War II there was little research on development. Most of our contemporary LDCs in Africa and Asia were part of the European imperial system. As colonies, these African and Asia areas traded with their colonial masters, exporting natural resources to them and depending on them for most imported manufactured goods. Nation-states in Latin America had been independent for more than a century and had developed a modest industrial base that produced goods for local consumption, but depended on more developed countries for major capital goods and technology. To generate necessary foreign exchange, most LDCs exported either agricultural goods or raw materials (primary goods). At that time, development was seen to occur when countries used their comparative advantage to trade goods they were best positioned to produce. Since LDCs were best prepared to produce exotic agricultural goods and/or raw materials that the industrialized nations wanted or needed, little effort was made to diversify LDC economies by industrialization.

After World War II, the United States' experience in rebuilding Europe began to modify modernization strategies. Economist Walt W. Rostow developed a widely accepted theory of development based on what he defined as the five stages of growth any nation had to follow in order to become developed. In Rostow's progression, a nation would move from a traditional society through preconditions for take-off, take-off, and the drive to maturity, to a mature, high-mass-consumption economy. Fundamental to Rostow's schema were the accumulation of capital by increasing savings, investment in manufacturing, and the existence of favorable political institutions for economic growth (Rostow 1990). However, Rostow's stages of growth addressed only economic factors, neglecting the "necessary structural, institutional and attitudinal conditions" needed for development to occur (Todaro 1994, 73).

Structural change modernization models, as developed by W. Arthur Lewis and Hollis B. Chenery among others, concentrated on changing LDCs' traditional agriculture-based economies to ones based on industries and manufactured goods. However, these models did not deal with local social and cultural realities, since their originators believed that industrialization was the only necessary goal. In addition, they failed to take into consideration the international economic situation. Often, important factors such as regional and international competition, size of markets, quality of local labor, and technology needs were neglected when industrialization projects were designed and started.

A variety of other modernization strategies have been developed and used by LDCs in the last forty years. Some of the more popular approaches to development have included import substitution, which we will discuss in the section on dependency; **etatism;** export orientation; and, more recently, privatization and free markets.

Etatism (from *état,* the French word for "state") and its more modern form, export orientation, hinge on government involvement in the buildup of industry

etatism Government involvement in the building up of industry and the promotion of exports.

and the promotion of exports. Many of these schemes failed because the industry that was created depended on the importation of costly raw materials that the particular country lacked; on the availability of trained labor; and on the ability of the country to develop its own technology or to import it from other countries. Moreover, these strategies also failed to address political, social, and cultural factors of equal importance. With the exception of a handful of Asian states—especially Japan, South Korea, Taiwan, Hong Kong, and Singapore—these schemes failed to lead to development.

Finally, there are scholars who have recommended a mixture of other modernization approaches to deal with local problems. In the early 1960s Barbara Ward, for example, recommended investment in education, modernization of farming, and expansion of industry as the main factors necessary for development. In the late 1960s a handful of scholars concluded that industrialization was not the answer to development; instead, they advocated the encouragement of agriculture and the discouragement of both urbanization and population growth. In the 1970s, the emphasis in some development strategies shifted from macroeconomic growth goals to individual necessities, when it became clear that the condition of the poor was not improving as rapidly as expected, and that consequently something needed to be done for the masses. Consequently, the focus of studies turned toward fulfilling the basic needs of the populace and toward more equitable income distribution.

To finance most of the modernization projects mentioned, countries have received massive aid and monetary loans. In a large number of cases, because of endemic corruption, a substantial portion of these funds have found their way to private, individually held, Swiss bank accounts, rather than to the projects they were allocated for. Many of the undertakings for which these loans were earmarked have failed, for obvious reasons. As a result of these failures, LDCs could not generate the revenues expected from these projects in order to pay back the loans. Instead, they became debtor nations and had to devote large portions of their national incomes just to pay the *interest,* not even the principal, on these loans. Their problems were compounded because they now had to simultaneously overcome development problems and repay the loans. Since LDCs had been eager to borrow money to finance a variety of development projects, they had received substantial loans, especially in the second half of the 1970s; international banks had large amounts of money available and were eager to lend it. Much of this was Arab money deposited after the tremendous increase of oil prices in the early 1970s. In the 1980s the debt problems of the LDCs increased substantially as the money supply decreased and interest grew, requiring more and more of their national GNPs simply to make interest payments. Such is the case currently with the peso crisis in Mexico (see boxed feature).

The 1980s and early 1990s have witnessed a return to classical economics, as more and more LDCs have introduced free-market policies and encouraged the privatization of publicly owned industries. In addition, economic activities that produce exports have been encouraged and often subsidized. These policies have become more popular as countries have become aware of success stories in Asia and Latin America.

In Latin America the remarkable story has been the success of Chile in opening up its economy, privatizing industry, and improving its overall economic status. In addition, by privatizing a large number of its industries, Chile has been able to generate funds to service its large debt. Debt-ridden LDCs have seen this as an

Have We Got a Peso for You!

GLOBAL PERSPECTIVES

During the first week of January 1995, Mexico sent a shock wave to its two other North American partners: $40 billion of investments are on the verge of default and they need to be secured.

President Clinton had no choice, politically or economically, but to propose a bailout for his Mexican partners in NAFTA. What he proposed was a $40 billion rescue plan on top of an $18 billion international package.

Said Jorge Mariscal, director of Latin American stocks at Goldman Sachs, "a company like that has to have a new business plan" (quoted in Myerson 1995). "The NAFTA has lured many investors," said Allen R. Myerson in the *New York Times*, "into thinking that Mexico is just like Canada, only with palapas instead of permafrost" (1995).

In December 1993, a month after passage of NAFTA by the U.S. Congress, American investment in Mexico soared to $3.9 billion—a fourfold increase over that in the same month a year earlier. With the passage of NAFTA, many American companies began operating as if Mexico were merely an extension of the American Southwest. Automakers turned a swath of northern Mexico into Detroit South.

However, with the devaluation of the peso, buying power for Mexicans evaporated overnight. The earnings of many American corporations now doing business in Mexico suffered drastically. Mattel and Kimberly Clark are two examples of recently arrived American companies in Mexico that are now reeling from the decline in peso power. An international currency trader, Chemical Bank in New York, lost $70 million due to the decline in the purchasing power of the peso.

The current crisis is reminiscent of an earlier 1982 peso crisis, but this time Mexican officials have had to persuade more players than just the international banking community. "With the banks, you could restructure the loans with a few bankers," said Robert Hormatts, vice chairman of Goldman Sachs International. "Now you have to devise a mechanism that's persuasive to tens of thousands of stock and bond holders who can dump their holdings if they don't like what they see" (quoted in Myerson 1995).

---

extremely attractive policy to emulate. Chile is still developing, but its success to this point has made it a model for a number of nations.

The Dependency School

dependency An economic theory that states that the South is disadvantaged in a neocolonial sense, due to the rules of the international economic system allegedly imposed by the North.

In addition to those who advocate strictly local economic or political approaches to development, some scholars have concentrated on the international economic system and the role that development nations play in this system. These scholars are members of what is known as the **dependency** school of thought. Dependency theory was developed in Latin America in the mid-1960s by a group of neo-Marxist scholars who were dissatisfied with the results of the import substitution strategy espoused by the Economic Council for Latin America (ECLA), and with other modernization strategies. The apparent successes of the Chinese and Cuban revolutions, which had skipped the capitalist stage of development completely, made these scholars optimistic about their own ability to start a revolution. As neo-Marxists, these scholars saw industrial workers as an integral part of imperialism, not as possible revolutionaries, and they viewed both industrialization and urbanization with major misgivings. Seduced by the idea that they could emulate Cuba with its apparent (although heavily subsidized) development success, they wanted to start a socialist revolution.

Since the 1960s, dependency theory has gained worldwide adherents and has become known as the World Systems theory. Dependicists such as Amechi Okolo blame underdevelopment on the capitalist nations that "have collaborated in designing and perfecting an intricate and complex control network" designed to maintain the existing order, making it "virtually impossible for the new nation to extricate herself" and become developed (Okolo 1986, 309–10). Other dependency authors posit that world resources are finite, and therefore that for some nations to be rich, others must be poor. The poor nations are relegated to the periphery of the world economic system, while the rich industrial nations who do not want to share the resources occupy the core. Dependency authors have presented solutions ranging from recommendations that countries should break away from the international system to the development of a new economic order that would entail a massive redistribution of wealth from the rich to the poor nations.

Structuralism. Among the most important contributors to dependency theory were Raul Prebisch, an Argentinian economist whose views, articulated in his 1949 book *The Economic Development of Latin America,* played a major role in the development of the dependency school, and Hans Singer, whose 1950 article, "The Distribution of Gain between Lending and Borrowing Countries," complemented and expanded upon Prebisch's views (Love, 1993, 741–42). In their view, the basic problem of the developing nations was that the global trade system, including GATT, was structured against them. Thus these critics founded what is known as **structuralism.** According to Prebisch and the other structuralists, the world consists of two components, the core and the periphery. Despite liberal theories, there was no equitable international trading system through which all nations could benefit equally from pursuing their comparative advantage. Instead, the core nations, the industrialized powers, produced the manufactured goods that were consistently in high demand and therefore profitable, while the periphery or developing nations had to rely on the export of commodities such as agricultural products and minerals for which demand was lower, and profits consequently were much lower. Thus the world trade system permanently confines a periphery or developing nation to an inferior, essentially colonial dual role: that of provider of raw materials and consumer of imported manufactured goods, or perpetual market for the core nations.

Thus there exists a built-in, or structural, trade gap between core and periphery. Try as they might, developing nations can *never* earn enough through their commodity exports to pay for the manufactured goods on which their ability to industrialize depends. GATT provides relatively free trade in manufactured goods, but allows nations to protect their own agricultural sectors freely; this seems proof positive that the entire international trading system, for all its liberal claims of equity, is inherently tilted against the developing periphery. GATT is nothing but a "rich man's club" (Isaak 1995, 128–29; Love 1993 741–42; Gourevitch 1993, 718).

The early structuralists were uncertain how to deal with the problem. Despite the conventional wisdom that international trade would be the primary engine of development by increasing global wealth, structuralists like Prebisch were skeptical. After all, they argued, it was the *entire structure* that was skewed against the periphery. A rising tide might lift all boats, as John F. Kennedy once remarked, but if you started out with a large boat, you would end up with a large boat, and if you started out with a small boat, you would end up with a small boat, no matter how high the tide. Prebisch described this phenomenon as "immiserizing growth," or, growth that still left the poor, poor. (Haggard 1993, 414).

structuralism A neo-Marxist economic perspective on development that sees the world as divided between the core, or rich states, and the periphery, or poor states. Such a perspective believes that there is a built-in or structural trade gap between the core and the periphery.

**import substitution
strategy** Developing
alternatives at home for the
importation of goods and
services.

Economic Solutions.   Structuralists argued that periphery nations should pursue an **import substitution strategy (ISS).** Rather than relying on selling exports
to pay for imports, they should find a way to avoid the imports altogether by
erecting barriers against expensive foreign goods and replacing them with domestically manufactured products. Brazil, for example, embarked on a program to
produce automobile fuel from sugar cane, to substitute for expensive imports of
oil. A number of developing nations, including Mexico, Chile, Turkey, and a number of central and eastern European nations followed similar strategies of developing light manufacturing (Haggard 1993, 414–16; Isaak 1995, 128–29).

However, while light manufacturing (textiles, clothing, processed food) might
work for a time, ultimately development depends on heavier manufacturing
(durable goods and capital goods); this requires skilled labor, large capital investment, and advanced technology, none of which light manufacturing either
requires or produces. Thus, periphery nations pursuing import substitution strategies found themselves with two options: develop state-owned industries, or rely
on foreign investment, both through foreign direct investment and through multinational corporations. Either solution raised new questions and problems. ISS led
to domestic policies favoring urban areas over rural ones, depressing both wages
and commodity prices. Classical liberal economists argued that ISS was highly
inefficient, sacrificing the benefits of comparative advantage. Other critics pointed
out that ISS resulted in increased dependence on foreign MNCs, and led to
increased, sometimes staggering debt loads for governments that borrowed extensively to jump-start state-owned enterprises. (Later in this chapter, we discuss the
international debt crisis that resulted from this borrowing spree.) The manufactured goods produced through ISS could not be exported, and thus trade imbalances remained and trade deficits mushroomed. Further, critics argued, ISS tended
to promote political and economic corruption, with small groups of elites prospering while the majority of a nation's citizens remained mired in poverty.

By the late 1980s a number of countries, still economically lagging and under
intense political pressure to liberalize trade restrictions, began either to abandon
ISS or to leaven ISS policies with other tactics, such as greater emphasis on
exports and the development of international competitiveness, the building of
mixed industrial economies, and experimentation with innovative development
strategies (Haggard 1993, 414–15).

Political Strategies.   Decolonization and the resultant emergence of a large
cadre of developing nations increased pressure for a political response to the
problems articulated by the dependency theorists, as did world trade patterns,
which saw periphery nations' share of world trade fall from 41 percent in 1950 to
only 30 percent in 1960. As economic solutions thus appeared to lag, Raul
Prebisch led the push for political answers as well. He became the founding
secretary-general of the United Nations Conference on Trade and Development
(UNCTAD), which the General Assembly established in 1964 to provide a forum
for articulation and promotion of periphery nations' views, and to accelerate their
economic development. UNCTAD would be, Prebisch hoped, the "poor man's
club" that could offset GATT, the "rich man's club." Not surprisingly, industrialized
nations viewed UNCTAD, its structuralist origins, and its dependency school dog-
mas with intense skepticism. They distrusted UNCTAD's suspicions about the
innate unfairness of the Bretton Woods system, its contravention of free-market
principles by stressing the need for ISS and government intervention, its demands

for preferential access by periphery manufacturers to core markets, and, finally, its demands for free, or at least freer, access to Western technology. UNCTAD meets every four years in a general conference, and has a permanent professional staff of about four hundred. Its conferences focus on such issues as shipping, food problems, technology and technology transfer, export earnings, the "brain drain" from periphery to core, and environmental problems (Isaak 1995, 132–34; Rothstein 1993, 955–56).

Although critics quipped that UNCTAD stood for "Under No Conditions Take Any Decisions," others point to a number of positive consequences of UNCTAD pressure and lobbying. For one thing, UNCTAD was the midwife to the Group of 77 (G-77) in the UN General Assembly, which has transformed the way the UN operates (see chap. 4). UNCTAD also influenced GATT to create the Generalized System of Preferences in the early 1970s, eliminating tariffs on manufactured and semimanufactured goods from developing nations. Finally, UNCTAD has provided a forum in which developing nations can discuss mutual problems and promote general solutions. The New International Economic Order (NIEO), discussed later in this chapter, grew in part out of UNCTAD's work in the early 1970s. However, in the 1980s and 1990s, UNCTAD's influence has declined, although it still generates useful research, provides technical assistance for the poorest of developing nations, and promotes cooperation among the developing nations. As one scholar notes, UNCTAD is the principal author of its dilemma: "If UNCTAD were to change its principles and become less confrontational, it would probably seem redundant; if it were to continue to demand radical changes without successes, it would become irrelevant" (Rothstein 1993, 936).

At present, then, UNCTAD seems destined to remain a relatively minor player in the politics of global trade, although it will continue to provide a voice for the developing nations, or at least those that perceive themselves as periphery nations. (It is important to note that some developing nations—Taiwan, Korea, and Singapore, for example—have simply ignored dependency theory, structuralism, and UNCTAD, while becoming very successful—Rothstein 1993, 933–36; Isaak 1995, 132–34.)

The New International Economic Order (NIEO).   Despite various development strategies, per capita income in developing nations has continued to lag far behind that of the industrial nations. From 1952 to 1972, real per capita income in the industrial nations (in 1973 dollars) doubled from $2,000 to $4,000, while that of developing nations increased by barely 70 percent, from $175 to $350. And the income disparity doubled, from $1,828 to $3,700. OPEC's success at quintupling oil prices in 1973 stimulated hope in developing nations that they too could benefit from raising commodity prices. Thus, at the UN's Sixth Special Session, in 1974, developing nations issued a call for what they termed a New International Economic Order (NIEO) which would make development a global priority and restructure the world economy to allow greater participation and effectiveness by the developing nations. The NIEO also called for increased aid to developing nations.

NIEO has been criticized as simply a grab bag of existing structuralist and dependency school demands generated "by a shared sense of past and present grievances, by a new sense of power, and by the belief that the time had come for a radical restructuring of the old order" (Rothstein 1993, 628). NIEO achieved limited success in the negotiation of a series of agreements between the European Commission and the African, Caribbean, and Pacific states (ACP). In Africa, four

Lomé agreements (1975, 1979, 1984, and 1991) aimed at restructuring the economic patterns developed under imperialism; in fact, the convention built on an earlier series of agreements between France and some of its former African colonies. The Lomé agreements specified stabilization of commodity prices for twelve major ACP products. They also virtually eliminated European tariffs on ACP products and promised technical and financial aid. All signatories to Agenda 21 at the "Earth Summit" in Brazil in 1992, including the United States, agreed in principle to accept the Lomé conventions. However, the Lomé agreements have been only mildly successful and have fallen far short of their original goals: economic restructuring, transformation, and development. The fate of the Lomé conventions in the wake of the end of the Cold War and the advent of the European Union is uncertain (Isaak 1995, 181–84; Martin 1993, 548–49).

Much the same can be said of the NIEO. As one scholar observes, "The NIEO is a classic illustration of failed international reform" (Rothstein 1993, 628).

The problem with dependency theory is that on one hand it offers unrealizable utopian solutions and on the other it completely disregards existing problems at the local level, instead blaming underdevelopment on an international economic order "controlled" by more developed nations. As Tony Smith points out in his critique of dependency theory, it "serves a historically conditioned ideological function of bringing together Marxists and southern nationalists around certain categories of analysis that serve their respective interests. As a result, dependency theory is wedded to its bias of seeing local problems of development in terms of international forces in order to satisfy nationalist sentiments, just as it is committed to downplaying the realm of the political by virtue of its allegiance to Marxism" (Smith 1984, 144).

State of the Inquiry

It is evident from our discussion that after several decades of study by a variety of scholars, the question why some countries are less developed than others still remains unanswered. Scholarly studies have advanced our understanding of development and have clearly shown that the environment needed for development is influenced by the types of economic policies countries pursue, the types of political systems they have, the political cultures that exist, and the prevalence of cultural attitudes such as fatalism and a poor work ethic. Nevertheless, it is apparent that a number of factors that also play an important role in creating the proper environment for development remain to be identified and studied. Moreover, it is also evident from the numerous failures of developmental strategies that the models that have been used not only lack some important variables but also misunderstand the role of other important variables.

The accumulation of capital, for example, which plays a key role in modernization theories, is clearly an essential element in any developmental strategy; however, by itself it is not sufficient to permit development to occur. The sizable aid and loans that many LDCs have received have made capital available, but in many cases development simply has not occurred. Many projects assumed that capital by itself would create the necessary environment for development; they failed as a result, because they did not take into account the dynamic combination of economic, political, social, and cultural factors.

It is clear that strategies for development that do include social and cultural factors as well as political and economic ones are desperately needed in order to ensure global stability.

Finance

The International Debt Crisis

In the 1970s and early 1980s a number of factors combined to increase radically the debt load of a substantial number of developing nations. The enormous increase in world oil prices in 1973 and again in 1979 caused many developing nations to go heavily into debt simply in order to obtain the petroleum products they needed. The Eurodollar and later the Eurocurrency markets had huge surplus amounts of money available that the holders were willing to lend, often without much control or collateral, perhaps in the naive belief that nations could never go bankrupt. The establishment of the International Development Association (IDA) by the World Bank made available substantial amounts in "soft" loans with no strings attached, and developing nations lined up to receive such loans. Finally, the general growth of the international economy produced a sense of euphoria, a "boom" mentality that envisioned continued steady growth.

Reality was something else. By the mid-1980s the world economy had plunged into a major recession, with the resulting high interest rates making it more and more difficult for debtor nations to "roll over" their debt, that is, to borrow money to pay off the original debt. Furthermore, the higher interest rates in developed nations stimulated huge capital outflows from developing nations, much of that capital from the loans. Estimates are that from 1979 to 1985, $34 billion fled Mexico alone; other debtor nations, primarily Latin American ones, faced similar outflows. Total capital flight from the developing nations is estimated at $100 billion between 1979 and 1982. Furthermore, most of the loans of the late 1970s and early 1980s went to only a handful of nations; 80 percent of developing countries received less than 2 percent of the loans, while nearly 50 percent of all loans went to only five nations. By 1980 more than forty developing nations were in arrears and about to default on their loans. In 1982 the Mexican government announced that it could not pay what it owed, that it was in fact broke, and dozens of other governments followed suit. A lending spree had suddenly become a debt crisis.

Responses to the debt crisis were varied. Debtor nations claimed that they were victims of international banks and agencies that had made it far too easy for them to borrow far too much money; they had in effect been seduced into near-bankruptcy. Creditors, on the other hand, maintained that the inability of the debtor nations to make even their interest payments, much less to begin paying down the actual sums they owed, was the result of profligacy, poor judgment, and outright corruption. As is often the case, there was a substantial amount of accuracy in both sets of charges.

Collapse of the entire international finance system as a result of the debt crisis was a real danger. A temporary solution was found by allowing the International Monetary Fund (IMF) to extend highly conditional loans to the most indebted nations, to stave off bankruptcy temporarily. A general recovery in the late 1980s lowered interest rates internationally and opened markets for the debtor nations' exports. Finally, banks and financiers developed a number of creative ways to turn the debt crisis into a new series of financial instruments, buying and selling the debt of various nations in a profitable new international marketplace. However, by the end of the 1980s international indebtedness was still soaking up huge amounts of money from the debtor nations; developing nations in 1989 paid out $50 billion more to service, or to make interest payments on, their debts than they received in new loans. The chief victims of the international debt crisis continue to be the citizens of the debtor nations, squeezed by both internally as well as externally imposed austerity programs.

The Geoeconomics of the Post-Cold War Era

Integration of Forces

What we are witnessing at present is the convergence, or integration, of many different sectors of the world economy, to produce one globally integrated economy. Multinational corporations are doing business in every economy of the world, and these global economic giants are leading the way for such things as product and/or service availability to be universal. This economic integration is heavily reliant upon instantaneous global communication, access to markets and technology, and availability of natural resources.

In terms of communication, much of the global "talk" is carried by the telecommunications network known as the "information superhighway." English is the "standard" language of the world, in politics as well as economics. In fact, the English language is so pervasive that it has led to a global popular culture, as evidenced by the popularity of the cable news channel, CNN, with its international news focus (Roet 1995).

High technology is another facet of this global convergence. High technology is perhaps the most pervasive factor that drives global economic and political change, and it is one of the key reasons for the end of the Cold War. Centralized communistic economies could not compete globally with the sophisticated tentacles of the liberal, Western economies. These formerly centralized economies simply imploded under their own weight.

The dependence upon natural resources is a common thread holding the global economies together. Global trading—even among nations that are often politically hostile to one another—is the current bond of the contemporary world. The West does not agree with the ideology of Muslim fundamentalism; nor do the mullahs of Iran embrace what they see as Western decadence. But they both like trading oil for high-tech goods and services, and vice versa. Since all nations have a vested interest in natural resources because of global trade, there is a growing awareness and appreciation of common ecological problems. But while a global agenda for action concerning such problems exists (at least in fragmented form), there is no political resolve on the part of nations at this time to tackle such concerns on a global level.

Disintegration of Forces

The disintegration, or divergence, of sectors in the world is as visible and as ferocious as the forces that are pulling the world together and making it smaller. With the world being pushed together and pulled apart simultaneously, one has to wonder how long the global body politic can survive such tectonic forces. The socio-political-economic fabric of the world is malleable, but only to a certain degree.

The first of the divergence factors is nationalism. We have discussed this concept previously (see chap. 3); it is helpful here to look at what nationalism has done in a more economic sense. Ethnic nationalism, unleashed at Versailles, has spurred cultural groups that are part of larger nations into civil wars. The Balkans are the prime example. But not only in the Balkans, or in Africa, or in Asia is this a problem. Similar examples can be found in Canada, with the separatist sentiments of the French Quebecois. Such sentiment has been highlighted recently, in the extreme narrowness of the 1995 referendum vote by which the Quebecois agreed to stay in Canada—for now. "The renegotiation of NAFTA and the reaffirmation of the internationalization of the St. Lawrence Seaway are just two of many problems that [would] multiply with division" of Canada into two states (Roet 1995).

Ultranationalism on the part of any one state is likewise worrisome for the political economy of the world. Presently, the worst such threat is the presence of ultranationalism in Russia, which could hamper global convergence. The consequences of this phenomenon, should they occur, would send tremors unmeasurable on any political-economic Richter scale around the world.

Integration and Disintegration from North to South, East to West

In terms of Third World geoeconomics, the relationships between the LDCs and their former colonial masters still contain what some consider "exploitive" characteristics, while others have labeled the quality of such relationships **interdevelopmental symbiosis.** These relationships are said to be symbiotic, or mutually beneficial, because the cheap labor and raw materials of the South, coupled with their growing markets, are merged with the technology and financial markets of the North for mutual advantage (Roet 1995). From this perspective, all sides stand to prosper, albeit some with less expense or risk than others. The North gains access to raw materials and new markets; the South, by selling its primary goods, creates conditions for consumer demand, thus relieving pent-up political and economic pressure for consumer goods and services.

interdevelopmental symbiosis A mutually beneficial situation said to be existing between the South with its cheap labor and raw materials and the North with its markets and technology.

The geography of the post–Cold War world is very different from the landscape political analysts dealt with during the era after World War II. At that time, analysts divided the world into three (some may say four or even five—see fig. 8.3) sectors: the First World (Western and industrialized), the Second World (Communist and industrialized), and the Third World (in varying degrees of poverty and mostly unindustrialized, but *perhaps* salvageable over time with assistance). The fourth world has little chance of being salvaged, and the fifth world is generally considered to have none. The world is still seen as essentially tripolar, but in a different sense.

Issues such as the ones outlined above were generally discussed in a rich-versus-poor framework centering on the degree and diversity of national industry. And while that organizing scheme of development is still somewhat valid for certain parts of the world today (most of sub-Saharan Africa, for example), it is more important to look at the "interdevelopmental symbiosis" between the haves and the have-nots—or, as some call it, the political economy of inclusion with respect to the three geoeconomic poles.

The three centers of economic power today revolve around the European Union (EU), with its twelve countries and 350 million people, NAFTA, with its $6.5 trillion dollar market and 380 million consumers, and the Asian-Pacific rim, with its population of almost two billion people. The "rim" lacks formality and specificity, but has the potential for anchoring economically the remainder of the world.

The North American Free Trade Agreement (NAFTA)

To many, this is the ideal marriage of three partners (Canada, the U.S., and Mexico). The United States' role in this *ménage à trois* is to supply the capital and technology for cheap Mexican labor to use imported Canadian raw materials so that goods and services are produced. Mexico also offers a pent-up supply of consumer demand. In symbiotic fashion, the expected high Mexican economic growth rate is intended to stimulate the integrated North American economy. Of course, this is largely a symbiosis that can occur only if the perpetual peso crisis can be controlled. What is more, NAFTA allows the North American economies to lessen their reliance upon Middle Eastern oil. "NAFTA encourages Mexico to become an efficient, long-term energy source for the U.S. through downstream privatization, infrastructural modernization, and subcontracting drilling operations to boost exploration and production" (Roet 1995).

What does this mean for the United States? If the twentieth century has been the American century, then the U.S. is once more in a good position to maintain its leadership role into the twenty-first century. But in the next century, instead of using a single-lens trans-Atlantic telescope, America will undoubtedly look south and east. It will focus on Latin America and the Pacific rim, with an especially watchful eye toward China as an unparalleled emerging market. In addition, the concept of interdevelopmental symbiosis could mean inclusion in the NAFTA framework for the whole of the Western Hemisphere.

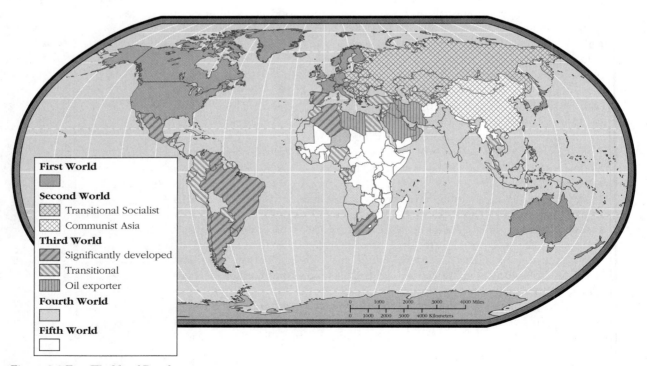

Figure 8.3 Five Worlds of Development

The European Union (EU)

Nowhere are the simultaneous concepts of integration and disintegration clearer than in Europe. The integrative forces of NATO and the EU itself provide a core around which further unification can occur. On the other hand, at least two other factors contribute to the disintegration of Europe: its geography and virulent nationalism.

NAFTA has kept the pressure on the Europeans to stay the course with respect to integration, which will extend to political as well as economic union. There is also pressure to continue the renegotiation of labor and other social welfare contracts in line with an evolving world standard. Monetary union with a single European currency, as provided for by the Maastricht Treaty, will eventually take place. NAFTA therefore becomes a challenge to the EU, not only in economic terms, but also politically. The Europeans are not sanguine about the prospects that their former trans-Atlantic partner, the U.S., will shift its attention to its own hemisphere and towards the East. On the other hand, the hot spots of nationalism that pock Europe add a large element of uncertainty to the long-range prospects of total European integration.

The Asian-Pacific Rim

The Asian-Pacific Rim suffers more from disintegration, or divergence, than do the two other poles. Formal integration is a long way off, and historical and cultural animosities are deep. The atrocities perpetrated by the Japanese upon the Chinese and the Koreans during World War II are still remembered, not to mention old behaviors by the Japanese towards its colonies in Asia. The Chinese, too, are victims of deep anti-Chinese sentiments in parts of Southeast Asia, which are aggravated by Chinese territorial claims within its traditional sphere of influence (Roet 1995). But it is likely that the pressure for integration brought to bear by the North Americans through NAFTA and the Europeans through the EU will force the Asian-Pacific Rim peoples toward integration. In a world that now defines economic competition only through unification, the East cannot remain economically or politically fragmented indefinitely.

A U.S.-China Trade War?

Headlines in the *Houston Post* on February 5, 1995 proclaimed, "U.S.-China Trade War Breaks Out: Standoff Leads to Exchanging of Stiff Tariffs."

The article states that the U.S. acted first and imposed 100 percent tariffs on $1.08 billion worth of Chinese products. The Chinese government retaliated by saying that it would raise tariffs 100 percent on American imports, including video games, compact discs, cigarettes, and alcohol.

From the American perspective, much of the problem centers around alleged Chinese piracy of

GLOBAL PERSPECTIVES

American products. A CD of Madonna or Michael Jackson sells for $1.75 or less, and such pirating has cost American companies one billion dollars in lost sales. And these pirated copies are sold not just in China, but internationally, thus undercutting American producers and copyright holders. U.S. officials contend that at least twenty-nine factories are hard at work copying licensed material illegally. In one case, pirated laser disc copies of the Walt Disney hit *The Lion King* were available in China before the legal version hit the U.S. markets.

Many textbooks written on international relations during the last decade or so speak of the gap between the North and the South in vivid, despairing economic terms. While this gap does exist and is growing larger, we have opted to look at the relationship between the traditional poles of rich and poor nations through the lenses of global integration and disintegration. Specifically, we have adopted the concept of "interdevelopmental symbiosis" to describe, explain, and to some degree predict what the relationship between the have and the have-not states is today.

While there are areas of the world that do not fit well into such a conceptualization, most do. Today's North-South rivalry may have assumed a different form. We see today a world that speaks less of the old concepts of economic penetration, counterpenetration, and dependency, and more of symbiosis, or mutually beneficial, albeit asymmetrical, relationships between parties. This is not to say, however, that the world has found harmony in its geoeconomic relations. Such a world has never and will never exist. But as the world moves from a geopolitical to a geoeconomic focus, new concepts are needed to describe, explain, and predict geoeconomics. Interdevelopmental symbiosis may play a part.

Summary

Development: Development is a broad term that generally includes social and political elements as well as economic ones; in fact, it is extremely difficult to separate these elements. A problem to date is that relatively little attention has been paid to the link between culture and development. Two major approaches to development are modernization, which can involve import substitution or a number of other economic tactics, and dependency, which sees underdevelopment as the result of imperialism and thus has primarily a political focus.

Finance: A major problem between developed and less developed countries in the past decade has been the debt crisis. As a result of overenthusiastic demands for loans in developing nations, and the willingness of developed nations to extend loans or sometimes even to pay off existing loans, many developing countries have found themselves terribly overextended economically. The resulting debt crisis threatened to unravel the international financial system until a series of compromises were achieved to alleviate the crisis, but many of the underlying problems still exist.

The Geo-Economics of the Post–Cold War World: Relations between the developed and developing nations (sometimes called the North-South split) are undergoing rapid transition. The optimist can see major integrative forces that should bring the two worlds much closer together, but it is equally easy for the pessimist to point out disintegrative forces pulling them apart. The development of major regional trading blocs such as NAFTA and the EU, and the potential APEC, threaten to isolate parts of the developing world not involved in such blocs and consign them to more or less permanent underdevelopment.

Key Terms

Development
Transitional societies
Physical Quality of Life Index (PQLI)
Culture
Etatism

Dependency
Structuralism
Import substitution strategy (ISS)
Interdevelopmental symbiosis

Thought Questions

1. Explain the key differences between the world view of liberal economists and that of structuralists.
2. Discuss the various strategies for development outlined in this chapter.
3. Why do some people consider geoeconomic issues more important today than geostrategic ones?
4. Discuss the relationships between UNCTAD, the G-77, NIEO, and ACP.

References

Coughlin, Cletus C. "Foreign-Owned Companies in the United States: Malign or Benign?" In Jeffrey A. Frieden and David A. Lake. *International Political Economy: Perspectives on Global Power and Wealth,* 3d ed. New York: St. Martin's Press, 1995.

Gourevitch, Peter A. "Political Economy." in Joel Krieger, ed. *The Oxford Companion to Politics of the World.* New York: Oxford University Press, 1993.

Haggard, Stephan. "Export-Led Growth." In Joel Krieger, ed. *The Oxford Companion to Politics of the World.* New York: Oxford University Press, 1993.

Harrison, Lawrence E. *Underdevelopment Is a State of Mind.* Lanham, Md.: University Press of America, 1985.

Inkeles, Alex, and David H. Smith. *Becoming Modern.* Cambridge, Mass.: Harvard University Press, 1974.

Isaak, Robert. *Managing World Economic Change: International Political Economy.* Englewood Cliffs, N.J.: Prentice Hall, 1995.

Love, Joseph L. "Raul Prebisch." in Joel Krieger, ed. *Oxford Companion to Politics of the World.* New York: Oxford University Press, 1993.

Martin, Guy. "Lomé Convention." In Joel Krieger, ed. *Oxford Companion to Politics of the World.* New York: Oxford University Press, 1993.

Myerson, Allen R. "Has the U.S. Got a Horse for You: Mexico." *New York Times,* January 22, 1995.

Myrdal, Gunnar. *Asian Drama: An Inquiry into the Poverty of Nations.* New York: Pantheon Books, 1971.

Okolo, Amechi. "Dependency: The Highest Stage of Capitalist Domination in Africa." In Ralph I. Onwuka and Olajide Aluko, eds. *The Future of Africa and the New International Order.* London: Macmillan Publishers, 1986.

Omestad, Thomas A. "Selling Off America." In Jeffrey A. Frieden and David A. Lake. *International Political Economy: Perspectives on Global Power and Wealth,* 3d ed. New York: St. Martin's Press, 1995.

Roet, Jeff. "The Geopolitics of NAFTA and The Global Economy," Unpublished Speech at San Jacinto College, Houston, TX, January 10, 1995, unpaginated.

Rostow, Walt W. *The Stages of Economic Growth.* 3d ed. New York: Cambridge University Press, 1990.

Rothstein, Robert L. "New International Economic Order." in Joel Kriegman, ed. *The Oxford Companion to Global Politics.* New York: Oxford University Press, 1993.

Smith, Tony. "Reiterating the Identity of the Peripheral State." In Mitchell A. Seligson, ed. *The Gap Between the Rich and the Poor: Contending Perspectives on the Political Economy of Development.* Boulder, Colo.: Westview Press, 1984.

Stefanovic, Dragan, *Culture and Development.* Unpublished dissertation. University of Tennessee, Knoxville, 1995.

Taylor, Edward B. *Primitive Culture.* New York: Brentano's, 1924.

Todaro, Michael P. *Economic Development,* 5th ed. New York: Longman, 1994.

Tolchin, Martin, and Susan J. Tolchin. *Selling Our Security: The Erosion of America's Assets.* New York: Penguin Books, 1992.

World Bank. *World Development Report 1991.* New York: Oxford University Press, 1991.

Chapter 9

Diplomacy and
International Law

Introduction

diplomacy The political craft of discussion and negotiation on a government-to-government level; the management of relations between states and other actors.

international law Rules governing state-to-state relations. Includes two sectors: public and private international law.

In many ways, **diplomacy** and **international law** are closely intertwined, with diplomats usually operating within parameters defined by international law, and international law being formed in large part by diplomatic negotiations and treaties. In this chapter we will examine these two facets of international relations separately, but we must always remember that they are closely linked and, when they are working best, reinforce each other.

Diplomacy

What Is Diplomacy?

Diplomacy, like war, is a means used by nations to achieve their desired goals. Diplomacy "is concerned with the management of relations between states and between states and other actors. From a state perspective diplomacy is concerned with advising, shaping and implementing foreign policy" (Barston 1993, i). It may involve multiple activities: face-to-face negotiations between belligerents or allies, economic deals between partners, or media posturing at international conferences. When Nikita Khrushchev pounded his shoe on the table at the United Nations, he was engaging in diplomacy every bit as much as Henry Kissinger was on his shuttle flights between Israel and the Arab states. The conduct of diplomacy may include correspondence, discussions, lobbying, diplomatic visits, consultations, treaties, and even coercion, but the goal is always the same: to achieve desired foreign policy goals.

Traditionally diplomacy has been primarily bilateral, conducted by a diplomat assigned by one nation to represent it in another state, usually in its capital. Today, however, supra-national organizations such as the United Nations and the European Union often conduct diplomacy as well, negotiating on behalf of their members and providing a forum for diplomacy of all sorts. The broadening of the spectrum of diplomatic actors is a recent development in the craft of diplomacy. In this chapter we will focus primarily on the interaction of states and nations as individual players in the game of diplomacy. We must remember, however, that in the contemporary world states seldom act unilaterally; it is far more common to see these traditional actors work in conjunction with other states via supranational organizations. For example, in carrying out Operation Desert Shield and Operation Desert Storm in the Persian Gulf, the United States did not move alone against Saddam Hussein's occupation of Kuwait. Instead, it formed a coalition with the Gulf Coast Council, the Arab League, the European Union, and the United Nations in order to oust the Iraqis.

To many, diplomacy is one side of a coin—war is the other. And in truth, when diplomacy fails, war is sometimes the result. However, war is only one end of the wide continuum on which diplomacy is located. States that are at peace with one another need diplomacy as much as those on the brink of war, and diplomacy is often most valuable in ending a war or winding down hostilities through a series of treaties that give all participants something of what they want. Diplomacy has two major definitions: "the art and practice of conducting negotiations among nations," and "skill in handling affairs without arousing hostility." Seldom can the first function be accomplished well without large doses of the second.

Ideally, diplomacy is the craft of managing to get what one's own nation wants from another nation or other nations without going to war—although the threat of war, sometimes referred to as "saber-rattling," can be an instrument of diplomacy. How do nations achieve their goals without war? And once conflict has erupted, how can nations achieve peace? For example, how can the Israeli government pursue its vital national interests with its Arab neighbors, which often have conflicting national interests? Can a peaceful, mutually agreeable settlement to disputes such as water rights along the Jordan River be achieved? If so, at what cost? What will the Israeli government give up in order to achieve its desired goal? Will this goal be worth the cost? To answer such questions, nations must above all else *communicate* with each other. To a great extent, then, diplomacy consists of communication directed by one nation or supranational organization towards another, in order to achieve a certain end result. This communication generally can take three different forms: signaling, negotiations, and public negotiations.

Signaling

Signaling is the least formal aspect of diplomacy, relying largely on nuance of either statement or action rather than on direct, face-to-face meeting between diplomats representing their respective nations. This indirect diplomacy may take many forms. For example, allowing direct media coverage of invasion exercises in 1994 was one way that the United States signaled the Haitian junta that American patience was exhausted and that coercion in the form of an invasion was the next step. Another instance occurred in 1967, when NATO placed its forces on a DefCon 1 alert during the Arab-Israeli war in order to signal the Soviet Union, quickly and forcefully, that the United States and its allies would not tolerate any Soviet intrusion into the conflict.

signaling Diplomacy by nuance or indirect communication, rather than face-to-face negotiation.

Signaling also can be a positive process; when President Richard Nixon referred to "The People's Republic of China" rather than using the usual American term "Communist China" in a 1971 speech, he was sending a clear signal that the unwavering American hostility toward the PRC was abating and that friendlier relations between the two nations were possible. Likewise, the granting of most favored nation trading status to China recently is a signal that the United States wants to continue present trading patterns and discussions with China, despite serious concerns about human rights issues in that state.

Signaling, then, is perhaps the most subtle form of diplomacy, and nations have learned to examine one another's behavior and public postures carefully in order to understand exactly what is being communicated.

Negotiations

Negotiations between or among nations represent another key point on the spectrum of diplomatic communications. We usually picture negotiation as a group of international lawyers and diplomats seated around a large table draped with fine linen and adorned with microphones and pitchers of (we assume) water. Behind each diplomat stands a bevy of interpreters and lesser diplomats serving as couriers to those at the table. Or we see photographs of the United States secretary of state seated on a brocade armchair next to the president of Syria, conducting peace negotiations in the Middle East. Although these two portraits are genuine, they are in fact not the norm.

negotiations Processes in which two or more parties interact in developing potential agreements to provide guidance for and regulation of their future behavior.

Negotiation is "a process through which two or more parties—be they individuals, groups, or larger social units—interact in developing potential agreements to provide guidance and regulation of their future behavior" (Sawyer and Guetzkow 1965, 466). Usually nations communicate or negotiate with each other through their embassy staffs, but sometimes they must rely on intermediaries. For many years the United States did not or would not negotiate directly with the People's Republic of China. However, since the two nations had issues over which they had to negotiate, the U.S. relied on the government of Poland to communicate its positions to the Chinese. The government of Switzerland in particular has long been known for using its "good offices" to promote peaceful negotiations in international disputes. Negotiation gives nations a way of conducting their business short of war. We will discuss various types of negotiations later in this chapter.

public negotiation; public diplomacy Intentional use of the world media to jockey for position or outcome in a diplomatic negotiation.

Public Negotiation

Public negotiation, or **public diplomacy,** uses the media in order to persuade both world and national public opinion that decisions reached by the two sides in a dispute are imminent, and to build public support for those positions. Such

The unplanned perils of public diplomacy—then-Soviet leader Nikita Khrushchev at the United Nations just prior to pounding his shoe (in front of him) on the desk and calling a Philippines delegate "a jerk."

public diplomacy often resembles **propaganda** or the "spin doctoring" of modern political campaigns, by attempting to present whatever decisions are reached in the most favorable possible light for the home audience, as well as for the global one.

The Diplomatic Game

Recognition

In order for traditional diplomacy to take place, there must be what is called **diplomatic recognition** between the nations involved. This simply means that one nation recognizes another as sovereign, and recognizes the existing government as the legitimate government of the nation. Although this process sounds dull and dry, it often involves complex issues. If a nation has broken away from another, should it be recognized? The decision to recognize or not to recognize such a newly formed nation can have enormous consequences. For example, during the American Civil War, the newly formed Confederate States of America had based much of their hope of winning independence on the assumption that Great Britain would recognize them, that is, extend formal diplomatic recognition, as a prelude to extending the economic and perhaps even military aid that would be necessary to their maintaining independence. Britain's refusal to extend formal diplomatic recognition to the Confederacy sealed its fate. More recently, Germany's decision to recognize the breakaway Croatian and Bosnian states was a major factor in provoking the Serbian attack on these two nations that had just proclaimed their independence from Yugoslavia.

Usually the decision to extend diplomatic recognition is *pro forma,* more or less automatic. However, particularly in the case of a revolutionary state, the decision can be difficult. Although most diplomatic theorists urge that the only consideration in deciding about extending recognition should be whether or not the government in question actually controls the nation, other factors often intervene. For example, after the Russian Revolution, President Woodrow Wilson refused to extend diplomatic recognition to the newly formed Union of Soviet Socialist Republics, primarily because of his distaste for the Bolshevik regime, but also because he was appalled at the assassination of the Tsar and his family. Not until 1933 did the United States officially recognize the Soviet Union, and then it was as much an economic decision as a political one: American businessmen simply found it terribly difficult to carry out normal commercial transactions without formal relations between the two states. Similarly, the United States refused to extend recognition to the People's Republic of China in 1949, largely as the result of Cold War politics, and continued to insist that the rump government of the Republic of China on Taiwan represented all of China. This refusal to deal with the reality of the communist victory in China distorted America's Far Eastern policy for nearly thirty years, and played a significant role in both the Korean War and the Vietnam War.

In the intricate game of nations, the decision to break diplomatic relations is often even more significant than the decision to establish them. Often the breaking of diplomatic relations between nations has been the last step prior to war, the final sign that diplomacy has not worked and force is now seen as a necessary step. Interestingly, the decision to break formal relations often serves as an impetus to finding some sort of peaceful solution instead of resorting to war; in "crisis diplomacy," breaking diplomatic relations can be a useful ploy.

propaganda The use of information (sometimes false) in an act of psychological warfare directed at an opponent.

diplomatic recognition The legal acknowledgment granted by one government to another to permit normal international intercourse.

Ambassadors

ambassador A diplomatic representative sent from the home country to a host country to represent the home nation's view and relay data about the host to the home country.

When nations do recognize each other, the first step is usually the exchange of **ambassadors,** individuals who represent their own nations in dealings with other nations. To be an ambassador is often thought of as a "cushy" job. Foreign travel, intrigue, adventure, glamour, parties, and receptions dominate an ambassador's life—at least as it is portrayed in movies and novels. The real work of a nation's representative is far more mundane.

An ambassador has three principal responsibilities: to observe what is happening in the host nation and report back to the home government, to convey to the host nation the desires of the home government, and to represent the home government in negotiations, meetings, and ceremonial occasions. The ambassador is in effect a middle man on the ground linking his or her government to that of the host nation—in other words, a transmission belt in the total communications process between nations. The world electronic media have partially eclipsed this aspect of ambassadorial functions, but the ambassador is still vital in personally connecting two nations. While the media do not cover with any regularity the non-crisis area of the world, informed foreign policy depends on knowledge both of what is happening and of what might happen; it is essential that a government have people in any nation who are in touch with local politics, customs, and events. The adage "if CNN does not cover it, it is not important" simply is not true.

However, modern communications have radically altered the functions of the contemporary ambassador. More rapid communication between national capitals has reduced the ambassador's role in immediate and direct negotiation; unlike the nineteenth-century representative, the modern ambassador is not a fundamentally independent or autonomous individual empowered to take whatever actions are necessary. The center for decision-making has shifted to the home national capital, because of both the speed of modern communications and leaders' inclinations to bend and shape foreign policy themselves.

It is important to understand that ambassadors are by no means the only diplomats. A national leader often may use "personal emissaries" or "unofficial ambassadors" to communicate with another nation, bypassing the ambassador completely. For example, although the United States had diplomatic personnel on the ground in Haiti, President Clinton sent personal emissaries to convince the Haitian junta that the threat of invasion was both real and imminent, and thus to achieve a solution to the crisis. Prominent individuals such as former presidents, close associates of the national leader, and successful businesspersons and even celebrities can be used as personal emissaries.

It is also important to keep in mind that ambassadors, especially those sent to major foreign capitals, are usually political appointees; who may know virtually nothing of the languages, histories, customs, and governments of the nations to which they are sent. The vital role of ongoing and more or less permanent observation and assessment of the host nation rests primarily with the professionals on an embassy staff. These trained diplomats deal with the details of diplomacy, from working out agreements for their ambassadors to sign, to aiding commercial transactions, issuing visas, or aiding tourists and travelers in distress. An embassy staff also often houses intelligence agents, officially labeled part of the staff but charged primarily with clandestine activities such as recruiting and supervising spies. In addition to the embassy, located in the host national capital, a home nation also often maintains consulates, which we could understand as "junior embassies," in important cities outside the capital, in order to conduct routine business. Ideally, the embassy and consular staffs speak the language of the nation, are familiar with its politics, history, and customs, and provide much of the basic information used to formulate foreign policy.

However, the rapidly changing nature of modern diplomacy is also tending to change the role of the ambassador and the embassy staff. Modern international relations involves a vast range of issues, many of them technical, social, or economic in nature. Two major consequences flow from this. First, the increasingly technical nature of much of international relations has shifted the brunt of negotiation from the ambassadorial level, or even the national leader level, to the level of the "experts" who must bring their technical expertise to bear on given issues. For example, few ambassadors or national leaders possess the technical knowledge, or the time, to hammer out the tedious details of treaties dealing with offshore oil and gas rights, or the mechanics of assuring destruction of specified nuclear weapons. Second, the broadening of the diplomatic agenda to include issues of technical, social, and economic nature has tended to blur the distinction between what was traditionally considered *foreign* and what was traditionally considered *domestic* policy. The distinction between the two has in many areas vanished forever.

Another major role of the ambassador and the embassy staff is to convey an official image of the home country. For many people in the host nation, the only available image of the home country comes from just two sources: the media, and the ambassador and his or her staff. Often, the ambassador and embassy serve propaganda purposes as well, presenting a benign face to an unpopular policy or feigning willingness to negotiate. Posturing can be an important diplomatic function.

The Evolution of Diplomacy and Diplomatic Immunity

Political entities throughout history, ranging from the Greek *polis* to ancient empires, have always used emissaries to deal with one another, but modern diplomacy emerged gradually with the rise of the Italian city-states of the Renaissance, and took its present form only in the past three hundred years.

During the Renaissance, the independent city-states of the Italian peninsula began the practice, which continues today, of exchanging representatives who enjoyed special status. Since all states are both "sending" and "receiving" states, each state has a responsibility to treat the ambassador of a foreign nation "with respect," because its own ambassador is similarly "at risk" in another country. In short, reciprocity is the goal that is sought. As such, the rules of **diplomatic immunity** are essential for the maintenance of international relations. Most of the rules pertaining to diplomatic immunity are contained in the Vienna Convention on Diplomatic Relations (1961); the convention seeks to codify customary law, and can be used against other states that are not party to the convention (Akehurst 1987, 114). Article 31(1) of the Vienna Convention provides as follows:

diplomatic immunity Legal status of foreign diplomats in a host nation exempting them from most of the laws of the host state.

> A diplomatic agent shall enjoy immunity from the criminal jurisdiction of the receiving state. He shall also enjoy immunity from its civil and administrative jurisdiction, except in the case of:
>
> **(a)** a real action relating to private immovable property situated in the territory of the receiving state, unless he holds it on behalf of the sending state for the purpose of the mission;

This vivid image of American diplomatic personnel blindfolded and bound after the seizure of the American embassy in Tehran is a reminder of how fragile such concepts as diplomatic immunity can be and how difficult it is to deal with the defiance of such international conventions.

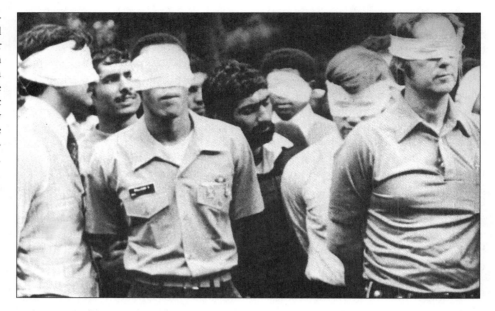

(b) an action relating to succession in which the diplomatic agent is involved . . . as a private person;

(c) an action relating to any professional or commercial activity exercised by the diplomatic agent in the receiving state outside his official function (Akehurst 1987, 116).

Article 29 of the Vienna Convention provides that diplomats shall not be liable to any form of arrest or detention, and that all appropriate steps must be taken to protect them from attack.

Sometimes diplomatic immunity is abused—residents of Washington, D.C., for example, resent the refusal of foreign diplomats to obey parking laws or to pay parking fines, and sometimes individuals accused of serious crimes are sheltered behind diplomatic immunity—but it remains an essential protection for the diplomat. Even after the Japanese attack upon Pearl Harbor, the United States and Japan arranged for the safe exchange of diplomats. When Iranian revolutionaries took American diplomats as hostages in 1989, there were virtually no mechanisms in place to deal with this serious violation of international convention, since diplomacy obviously could not work in a situation in which all diplomatic conventions had been shattered.

The rise of the modern nation-state, with its concept of equality among sovereign states, represented the next major step in the evolution of modern diplomacy. Heads of sovereign nation-states could negotiate with each other, as could their ambassadors and ministers. Because there were no effective multinational organizations, most diplomacy during the eighteenth and nineteenth centuries was bilateral, that is, between two states. Major international conferences like the Congress of Vienna, which ended the Napoleonic Wars and established the balance of power system on the continent of Europe, were relatively rare. In addition, most diplomatic negotiating took place in private, not in the glare of publicity, and many of the treaties signed between nations were secret—largely to keep information from national populations that might object to terms agreed upon by their diplomats. Although the system of behind-the-scenes negotiations and secret treaties came crashing to a halt with the Versailles conference and Woodrow Wilson's call for "open covenants openly arrived at," the failure of the League of Nations guaranteed the continuation of bilateral diplomacy as the most common form of interstate relations. After World War II, the polarization induced by the Cold War contributed to its continuation as well. Today, however, the end of the Cold War and the growing globalization of politics has begun to create a new diplomacy.

Case concerning United States Diplomatic and Consular Staff in Tehran

*O*n November 4, 1979, the U.S. embassy in Tehran, Iran, was overrun by several hundred of the three thousand Iranians who had been demonstrating at the embassy gates. They seized diplomats, consuls, and U.S. Marine personnel there and occupied the embassy premises. Two U.S. consulates in other cities in Iran were seized and closed the following day. The embassy personnel in Tehran were physically threatened and denied any communication with other U.S. officials or relatives.

Several hundred thousand demonstrators converged on the embassy on November 22, and the Iranian government made no effort to intervene or to assist the hostages. While some of the hostages were released, others were removed to unknown locations outside the embassy premises.

The United States instituted this suit against Iran in the International Court of Justice (ICJ), alleging that Iran breached the Vienna Convention on Diplomatic and Consular Relations, the Vienna Convention on the Prevention of Crimes against Internationally Protected Persons, and the 1955 U.S.–Iran Treaty of Amity.

The position of the Iranian government is contained in correspondence sent to the court. Iran refused to send lawyers to the court, file any official papers, or directly participate in the proceedings. The court nevertheless considered Iran's correspondence and included it in its judgment. The portion of the ICJ opinion that provides the historical context within which this controversy arose is set forth here (International Court of Justice 1980).

GLOBAL PERSPECTIVES

The Government of the Islamic Republic of Iran wishes to express its respect for the International Court of Justice, and for its distinguished Members, for what they have achieved in the quest for a just and equitable solution to legal conflicts between States, and respectfully draws the attention of the Court to the deep-rootedness and the character of the Islamic Revolution of Iran, a revolution of a whole oppressed nation against its oppressors and their masters, the examination of whose numerous repercussions is essentially and directly a matter within the national sovereignty of Iran.

The Government of the Islamic Republic of Iran considers that the Court cannot and should not take cognizance of the case which the Government of the United States of America has submitted to it, and in the most significant fashion, a case confined to what is called the question of the hostages of the American Embassy in Tehran.

For this question only represents a marginal and secondary aspect of an overall problem, one such that it cannot be studied separately, and which involves, *inter alia,* more than 25 years of continual interference by the United States in the internal affairs of Iran, the shameless exploitation of our country, and numerous crimes perpetrated against the Iranian people, contrary to and in conflict with all international and humanitarian norms.

The problem involved in the conflict between Iran and the United States is thus not one of the interpretation and the application of the treaties upon which the American Application is based, but results from an overall situation containing much more fundamental and more complex elements.

(continued on p. 290)

Case concerning United States Diplomatic and Consular Staff in Tehran

(Continued from p. 289)

Consequently, the Court cannot examine the American Application divorced from its proper context, namely the whole political dossier of the relations between Iran and the United States over the last 25 years. This dossier includes, *inter alia,* all the crimes perpetrated in Iran by the American Government, in particular the *coup d'etat* of 1953 stirred up and carried out by the CIA, the overthrow of the lawful national government of Dr. Mossadegh, the restoration of the Shah and of his regime which was under the control of American interests, and all the social, economic, cultural and political consequences of the direct interventions in our internal affairs, as well as grave, flagrant and continuous violations of all international norms, committed by the United States in Iran.

The ICJ opinion about Iran's conduct under international law follows. The paragraph numbers are those of the court.

The persons still held hostage in Iran include, according to the information furnished to the Court by the United States, at least 28 persons having the status, duly recognized by the Government of Iran, of "member of the diplomatic staff" within the meaning of the Vienna Convention of Diplomatic Relations of 1961; at least 20 persons having the status, similarly recognized, of "member of the administrative and technical staff" within the meaning of that Convention; and two other persons of United States nationality not possessing either diplomatic or consular status. Of the persons with the status of member of the diplomatic staff, four are members of the Consular Section of the Mission.

Allegations have been made by the Government of the United States of inhumane treatment of hostages; the militants and Iranian authorities have asserted that the hostages have been well treated, and have allowed special visits to the hostages by religious personalities and by representatives of the International Committee of the Red Cross. The specific allegations of ill-treatment have not however been refuted. Examples of such allegations, which are mentioned in some of the sworn declarations of hostages released in November 1979, are as follows: at the outset of the occupation of the Embassy some

were paraded bound and blindfolded before hostile and chanting crowds; at least during the initial period of their captivity, hostages were kept bound, and frequently blindfolded, denied mail or any communication with their government or with each other, subjected to interrogation, threatened with weapons.

Those archives and documents of the United States embassy which were not destroyed by the staff during the attack on 4 November have been ransacked by the militants. Documents purporting to come from this source have been disseminated by the militants and by the Government-controlled media.

36. The Court . . . . made it clear that the seizure of the United States Embassy and Consulates and the detention of internationally protected persons as hostages cannot be considered as something "secondary" or "marginal", having regard to the importance of the legal principles involved. It also referred to a statement of the Secretary-General of the United Nations, and to Security Council resolution 457 (1979), as evidencing the importance attached by the international community as a whole to the observance of those principles in the present case as well as its concern at the dangerous level of tension between Iran and the United States. The Court, at the same time, pointed out that no provision of the Statute or Rules [of the ICJ] contemplates that the Court should decline to take cognizance of one aspect of a dispute merely because that dispute has other aspects, however important.

[The court is able to hear this case because the] United States' claims herein concern alleged violations by Iran of its obligations under several articles of the Vienna Conventions of 1961 and 1963 with respect to the privileges and immunities of the personnel, the inviolability of the premises and archives, and the provision of facilities for the performance of the functions of the United States Embassy and Consulates in Iran. In so far as its claims relate to two private individuals held hostage in the Embassy, the situation of these individuals falls under the provisions of the Vienna Convention of 1961 guaranteeing the inviolability of the premises of embassies, and of Article 5 of the 1963 Convention concerning the consular functions of assisting nationals and protecting and safeguarding their interests. By their very nature all these claims concern the interpretation or application of one or other of the two Vienna Conventions.

The occupation of the United States Embassy by militants on 4 November 1979 and the detention of its personnel as hostages was an event of a kind to provoke an immediate protest from any government, as it did from the United States Government, which despatched a special emissary to Iran to deliver a formal protest.

It is clear that on that date there existed a dispute arising out of the interpretation or application of the Vienna Conventions and thus one falling within the scope of the Protocols . . . .

61. The conclusion just reached by the Court, that the initiation of the attack on the United States Embassy on 4 November 1979, and of the attacks on the Consulates at Tabriz and Shiraz the following day, cannot be considered as in itself imputable to the Iranian State does not mean that Iran is, in consequence, free of any responsibility in regard to those attacks; for its own conduct was in conflict with its international obligations. By a number of provisions of the Vienna Conventions of 1961 and 1963, Iran was placed under the most categorical obligations, as a receiving State, to take appropriate steps to ensure the protection of the United States Embassy and Consulates, their staffs, their archives, their means of communication and the freedom of movement of the members of these staffs.

62. Thus, after solemnly proclaiming the inviolability of the premises of a diplomatic mission, Article 22 of the 1961 Convention continues in paragraph 2:

"The receiving State is under a special duty to take all appropriate steps to protect the premises against any intrusion or damage and to prevent any disturbance of the peace of the mission or impairment of its dignity" [emphasis added by the Court].

So, too, after proclaiming that the person of a diplomatic agent shall be inviolable, and that he shall not be liable to any form of arrest or detention, Article 29 provides:

"The receiving State shall treat him with due respect and *shall take all appropriate steps to prevent any attack on his person, freedom or dignity"* [emphasis added by the Court].

The obligation of a receiving State to protect the inviolability of the archives and documents of a diplomatic mission is laid down in Article 24, which specifically provides that they are to be "inviolable at any time and wherever they may be". Under Article 25 it is required to "accord full facilities for the performance of the functions of the mission," under Article 26 to "ensure to all members of the mission freedom of movement and travel in its territory", and under Article 27 to "permit and protect free communication on the part of the mission for all official purposes". Analogous provisions are to be found in the 1963 Convention regarding the privileges and immunities of consular missions and their staffs (Art. 31, para. 3, Arts. 40, 33, 28, 34 and 35). In the view of the Court, the obligations of the Iranian Government here in question are not merely contractual obligations established by the Vienna Conventions of 1961 and 1963, but also obligations under general international law.

63. "The facts set out in paragraphs 14 to 27 above establish to the satisfaction of the Court that on 4 November 1979 the Iranian Government failed altogether to take any appropriate steps" to protect the premises, staff and archives of the United States' mission against attack by the militants, and to take any steps either to prevent this attack or to stop it before it reached its completion. They also show that on 5 November 1979 the Iranian Government similarly failed to take appropriate steps for the protection of the United States Consulates at Tabriz and Shiraz. In addition they show, in the opinion of the Court, that the failure of the Iranian Government to take such steps was due to more than mere negligence or lack of appropriate means.

. . .

77. In the first place, these facts constituted breaches additional to those already committed of paragraph 2 of Article 22 of the 1961 Vienna Convention on Diplomatic Relations which requires Iran to protect the premises of the mission against any intrusion or damage and to prevent any disturbance of its peace or impairment of its dignity. Paragraphs 1 and 3 of that Article have also been infringed, and continue to be infringed, since they forbid agents of a receiving State to enter the premises of a mission without consent or to undertake any search, requisition, attachment or like measure on the premises. Secondly, they constitute continuing breaches of Article 29 of the same Convention which forbids any

(continued on p. 292)

Case concerning United States Diplomatic and Consular Staff in Tehran

(Continued from p. 291)

arrest or detention of a diplomatic agent and any attack on his person, freedom or dignity. Thirdly, the Iranian authorities are without doubt in continuing breach of the provisions of Articles 25, 26 and 27 of the 1961 Vienna Convention and of pertinent provisions of the 1963 Vienna Convention concerning facilities for the performance of functions, freedom of movement and communications for diplomatic and consular staff, as well as of Article 24 of the former Convention and Article 33 of the latter, which provide for the absolute inviolability of the archives and documents of diplomatic missions and consulates. This particular violation has been made manifest to the world by repeated statements by the militants occupying the Embassy, who claim to be in possession of documents from the archives, and by various government authorities, purporting to specify the contents thereof. Finally, the continued detention as hostages of the two private individuals of United States nationality entails a renewed breach of the obligations of Iran under Article I 1, paragraph 4, of the 1955 Treaty of Amity, Economic Relations, and Consular Rights.

78. Inevitably, in considering the compatibility or otherwise of the conduct of the Iranian authorities with the requirements of the Vienna Conventions, the Court has focused its attention primarily on the occupation of the Embassy and the treatment of the United States diplomatic and consular personnel within the Embassy. It is however evident that the question of the compatibility of their conduct with the Vienna Conventions also arises in connection with the treatment of the United States Charge d'Affaires and two members of his staff in the Ministry of Foreign Affairs on 4 November 1979 and since that date. The facts of this case establish to the satisfaction of the Court that on 4 November 1979 and thereafter the Iranian authorities have withheld from the Charge d'Affaires and the two members of his staff the necessary protection and facilities to permit them to leave the Ministry in safety. Accordingly it appears to the Court that with respect to these three members of the United States' mission the Iranian authorities have committed a continuing breach of their obligations under Articles 26 and 29 of the 1961 Vienna Convention on Diplomatic Relations. It further appears to the Court that the continuation of that situation over a long period has, in the circumstances, amounted to detention in the Ministry.

79. The Court moreover cannot conclude its observations on the series of acts which it has found to be imputable to the Iranian State and to be patently inconsistent with its international obligations under the Vienna Conventions of 1961 and 1963 without mention also of another fact. This is that judicial authorities of the Islamic Republic of Iran and the Minister of Foreign Affairs have frequently voiced or associated themselves with a threat first announced by the militants, of having some of the hostages submitted to trial before a court or some other body. These threats may at present merely be acts in contemplation. But the Court considers it necessary here and now to stress that, if the intention to submit the hostages to any form of criminal trial or investigation were to be put into effect, that would constitute a grave breach by Iran of its obligations under Article 31, paragraph 1, of the 1961 Vienna Convention. This paragraph states in the most express terms: "A diplomatic agent shall enjoy immunity from the criminal jurisdiction of the receiving State." Again, if there were an attempt to compel the hostages to bear witness, a suggestion renewed at the time of the visit to Iran of the Secretary-General's Commission, Iran would without question be violating paragraph 2 of that same Article of the 1961 Vienna Convention which provides that: "A diplomatic agent is not obliged to give evidence as a witness."

. . .

83. In any case, even if the alleged criminal activities of the United States in Iran could be considered as having been established, the question would remain whether they could be regarded by the Court as constituting a justification of Iran's conduct and thus a defense to the United States' claims in the present case. The Court, however, is unable to accept that they can be so regarded. This is because diplomatic law itself provides the necessary means of defense against, and sanction for, illicit activities by members of diplomatic or consular missions.

84. The Vienna Conventions of 1961 and 1963 contain express provisions to meet the case when members of an embassy staff, under the cover of

diplomatic privileges and immunities, engage in such abuses of their functions as espionage or interference in the internal affairs of the receiving State. It is precisely with the possibility of such abuses in contemplation that Article 41, paragraph 1, of the Vienna Convention on Diplomatic Relations, and Article 55, paragraph 1, of the Vienna Convention on Consular Relations, provide

"Without prejudice to their privileges and immunities, it is the duty of all persons enjoying such privileges and immunities to respect the laws and regulations of the receiving State. They also have a duty not to interfere in the internal affairs of that State."

Paragraph 3 of Article 41 of the 1961 Convention further states: "The premises of the mission must not be used in any manner incompatible with the functions of the missions." An analogous provision with respect to consular premises is to be found in Article 55, paragraph 2, of the 1963 Convention.

. . .

85. Thus, it is for the very purpose of providing a remedy for such possible abuses of diplomatic functions that Article 9 of the 1961 Convention on Diplomatic Relations stipulates:

"1. The receiving State may at any time and without having to explain its decision, notify the sending State that the head of the mission or any member of the diplomatic staff of the mission is *persona non grata* or that any other member of the staff of the mission is not acceptable. In any such case, the sending State shall, as appropriate, either recall the person concerned or terminate his functions with the mission. A person may be declared *non grata* or not acceptable before arriving in the territory of the receiving State.

2. If the sending State refuses or fails within a reasonable period to carry out its obligations under paragraph 1 of this Article, the receiving State may refuse to recognize the person concerned as a member of the mission."

86. The rules of diplomatic law, in short, constitute a self-contained regime which, on the one hand, lays down the receiving State's obligations regarding the facilities, privileges and immunities to be accorded to diplomatic missions and, on the other, foresees their possible abuse by members of the mission and specifies the means at the disposal of the

receiving State to counter any such abuse. These means are, by their nature, entirely efficacious, for unless the sending State recalls the member of the mission objected to forthwith, the prospect of the almost immediate loss of his privileges and immunities, because of the withdrawal by the receiving State of his recognition as a member of the mission, will in practice compel that person, in his own interest, to depart at once. But the principle of the inviolability of the persons of diplomatic agents and the premises of diplomatic missions is one of the very foundations of this long-established regime, to the evolution of which the traditions of Islam made a substantial contribution. The fundamental character of the principle of inviolability is, moreover, strongly underlined by the provisions of Articles 44 and 45 of the Convention of 1961 (cf. also Articles 26 and 27 of the Convention of 1963). Even in the case of armed conflict or in the case of a breach in diplomatic relations those provisions require that both the inviolability of the members of a diplomatic mission and of the premises, property and archives of the mission must be respected by the receiving State. Naturally, the observance of this principle does not mean—and this the Applicant Government expressly acknowledges—that a diplomatic agent caught in the act of committing an assault or other offence may not, on occasion, be briefly arrested by the police of the receiving State in order to prevent the commission of the particular crime. But such eventualities bear no relation at all to what occurred in the present case.

87. In the present case, the Iranian Government did not break off diplomatic relations with the United States; and in response to a question put to him by a Member of the Court, the United States Agent informed the Court that at no time before the events of 4 November 1979 had the Iranian Government declared, or indicated any intention to declare, any member of the United States diplomatic or consular staff in Tehran *persona non grata*. The Iranian Government did not, therefore, employ the remedies placed at its disposal by diplomatic law specifically for dealing with activities of the kind of which it now complains. Instead, it allowed a group of militants to attack and occupy the United States Embassy by force, and to seize the diplomatic and

(continued on p. 294)

Case concerning United States Diplomatic and Consular Staff in Tehran
(Continued from p. 293)

consular staff as hostages; instead, it has endorsed that action of those militants and has deliberately maintained their occupation of the Embassy and detention of its staff as a means of coercing the sending State. It has, at the same time, refused alto-gether to discuss this situation with representatives of the United States. The Court, therefore, can only conclude that Iran did not have recourse to the normal and efficacious means at its disposal, but resorted to coercive action against the United States Embassy and its staff.

(Source: International Court of Justice, 1980, in Slomanson 1990, pp. 205–11)

The New Diplomacy

The new diplomacy is much larger in geographic scope. The number of sovereign nation-states has nearly doubled since 1960 as the result of decolonization, national self-determination, and zealous nationalism; today there are more than 180 nation-states, each staking its claim to a role in international politics and diplomacy. With the enormously increased number of actors, the spread of the diplomatic theater from Europe to include literally the entire globe, and the resultant complexity of issues on the diplomatic agenda, bilateral diplomacy has tended to become less important, while **multilateral diplomacy** (involving more than two states) has grown in importance. The various groupings of traditional international actors (nation-states), with the panoply of new transnational actors (NGOs, MNOs) have tremendously complicated the types, methods, amount, and tenor of diplomatic relations.

multilateral diplomacy Two or more nations banding together for some common diplomatic purpose.

The take-off stage for multilateral diplomacy was the signing of the Covenant of the League of Nations in 1919. Although the United States did not join the League, precedents were established for the United Nations.

Diplomacy has become an extremely complicated business in the late twentieth century. The number of players, the complexity of issues, the intensity with which these issues are debated, and the transnational character of our contemporary world have changed the ways in which diplomatic issues are addressed, resolved, and disseminated. And because of these factors, modern diplomacy has helped to transform the geopolitical landscape.

Multilateral diplomacy today is a result of many factors, but certainly the most important is the increased pluralism, or special interest nature, of global politics. Issues such as population, trade, environmental quality, and so forth have become so specialized that they are recognized as the domain of special interest groups formed to advance particular issue agendas. As a result, many low-level issues have a global context and can be addressed only multilaterally. High-level issues, those dealing with the grand designs of war and peace, are still largely in the realm of bilateral negotiations, although this is not so true today as it was before 1989.

Multilateral diplomacy is a common method of conducting contemporary negotiations, for several reasons. First, technology has made multilateralism much easier, since global communications are virtually instantaneous. Simply put, the greater the number of contacts a national actor experiences is, the greater is the likelihood that that actor will communicate in a multilateral fashion. Second, issues like the environment, which are becoming more and more important, are almost by definition global issues. Pollution produced by one nation is the problem of many neighboring states, and bilateral solutions simply will not work. Third, today the prevailing opinion is that multilateralism is a preferred, and probably safer, way for a nation's politicians to act. This has been especially true since 1989, as the sole remaining superpower, the United States, has often found itself incapable of acting, or unwilling to act, unilaterally. Operations Desert Shield and Desert Storm represent the culmination of late-twentieth-century multilateral diplomacy. These operations were orchestrated by the United States acting not as a single power, but in consultation and conjunction with the United Nations, the European Community, and the Arab League, among others. Without such a multilateral framework, Islamic states would have found it very difficult indeed to act against another Islamic nation such as Iraq.

Types of Diplomacy

Diplomacy today assumes multiple forms. One of the best-known kinds is *image* or *summit* diplomacy; usually attracting large amounts of media coverage, this leader-to-leader diplomacy is newsworthy and "sexy." Diplomacy also can be characterized as either *high-level* or *low-level* in terms of issues involved. High-level diplomacy deals with system change, while low-level diplomacy, which tends to dominate diplomatic activity on a daily basis, has to do with system maintenance and stability. Furthermore, diplomacy may be *direct* or *indirect, open* or *secret,* and either *separated* or *linked*. At times diplomacy can be characterized as *coercive diplomacy.* Finally, at the farthest and most dangerous extreme of the spectrum of diplomatic activity is *crisis diplomacy.*

Summitry and Image Diplomacy

Not surprisingly in an age of jet travel and instantaneous communications, diplomacy increasingly has become the special purview of leaders who want to polish their international image. For example, in the 1970s then Secretary of State Henry Kissinger engaged in what seemed to be a never-ending series of diplomatic flights to Middle Eastern capitals in pursuit of an elusive Middle Eastern peace. This so-called *shuttle diplomacy* made Kissinger a world celebrity. Heads of state also gravitate to the foreign policy arena in today's crowded agenda of political issues. Frequently domestic politics are so tightly controlled that the only way a head of state can capture the headlines and unite a quarrelsome population, however temporarily, is to engage in instant image-making by means of summit diplomacy.

Summitry also represents a way for leaders to come face to face with their counterparts. The Group of Seven (G-7) industrialized powers meets annually in a much-ballyhooed summit over international economic issues. Richard Nixon traveled to China and to the Soviet Union, as has virtually every president since then. The first "summit" took place in Vienna in 1956 between the American president, Dwight D. Eisenhower, and the newly emerging Soviet leader Nikita Khrushchev. Today summits have become elaborate affairs; thousands of minor diplomats, designated "sherpas" after the Tibetan and Nepalese porters and mountain-climbing guides, work for years beforehand to conclude agreements for the leaders to sign in order to make the summits appear meaningful beyond just the publicity they generate.

As one might imagine, there are enormous benefits, and enormous potential pitfalls, accompanying this personal, high-level diplomacy. One of the potential

summitry Negotiations between two or more heads of state.

United States President Jimmy Carter, Israeli Prime Minister Menachem Begin, and Egyptian President Anwar Sadat at their Camp David meeting, perhaps the most successful example of personal multilateral diplomacy.

benefits is that personal barriers may fade away and genuine friendships develop between formerly antagonistic leaders. There is no doubt, for example, that sincere personal feelings of considerable depth developed among President Jimmy Carter, Prime Minister Menachem Begin, and President Anwar Al-Sadat, feelings that enabled them to sign the Camp David accords in 1979. However, personal animosities may develop as well. One of these was evident in the tense first meeting in the Oval Office between Israeli Prime Minister Yitzhak Shamir and President George Bush, to discuss the issue of Israeli settlements in the Occupied Territories.

More traditional diplomats favor a cautious approach to summitry out of fear that presidents or others might "give away the store." Henry Kissinger, essentially an advocate of nineteenth-century diplomacy, wrote that "some of the debacles of our diplomatic history have been perpetrated by Presidents who fancied themselves negotiators." The former secretary of state also noted that the world's leaders almost always enjoy "a healthy dose of ego"; when two such healthy egos collide, "negotiations can rapidly deteriorate from intractability to confrontation" (Kissinger 1994, 142).

Additionally, personal meetings can either dispel or perpetuate misinformation and stereotypes. Boris Yeltsin's first trip to the United States in 1989 was a media disaster. Yeltsin was portrayed as a drunken, stumblebum political hack with nuclear warheads sprouting from his coat pockets. On his second visit in 1992 as president of Russia, Yeltsin redeemed his image and fashioned himself as a campaigning candidate, complete with baby-kissing and (American) flag-waving. And it seems clear that Nikita Khrushchev's impression of President John Kennedy as a weak and immature leader, gained at their 1961 Vienna summit, was a major factor both in Khrushchev's provoking the Berlin crisis by erecting the Berlin Wall that summer and in his beginning to put Soviet missiles into Cuba in 1962, thereby provoking the most dangerous crisis of the nuclear age.

Another drawback of summitry is that once heads of state are involved, they can disavow previous commitments carefully crafted by professional diplomats and cut quick deals. However, such deals have no fall-back position of authority, that is, no one to appeal to, and it is virtually impossible to retract an agreement, no matter how detrimental it is to the national interest, once a national leader has made a promise to another national leader.

Crisis and Coercive Diplomacy

Most foreign policy is routine and characterized by bureaucratic inertia. However, there is always the possibility of a diplomatic surprise. In 1980 presidential candidate Ronald Reagan was increasingly fearful of an "October surprise" involving the American hostages in Iran. Reagan feared that if President Carter made a diplomatic breakthrough and had the hostages released before the election, he could swing enough undecided votes to carry the election.

Although surprise is an element rarely discussed in the literature on diplomacy, it is important in both the military and the diplomatic components of a

Russian President Boris Yeltsin glad-handing American-style, and all but kissing babies, during his summit visit to the United States in 1992.

nation. Professor Michael Handel analyzes diplomacy as a continuum, running from routine or normal diplomacy on one end to surprise or revolutionary diplomacy on the other (see fig. 9.1).

On Handel's continuum, surprises can be of two different sorts: minor surprises and major, or revolutionary, surprises. "When a new initiative is not sufficient to bring about the desired change in the international environment, or in the relations between two states, a statesman may resort to the use of a *minor surprise* or even a *fait accompli*—something approaching a major surprise." There may even be times in the international system that immediate change can be achieved only by a diplomatic surprise or a *fait accompli* (what we in Texas would call a "done deal"). If change is desired and time is relevant, then surprises can be useful. President Sadat's 1977 peace initiative illustrates the value of surprise. "By going to Jerusalem, he circumvented the prolonged negotiations, cut short the formalities, and accelerated the chance of achieving peace in the Middle East—goals which would have taken years to accomplish at the scheduled Geneva Peace Conference" (Handel 1981, 3).

Of course, not all surprises are pleasant. In 1938 German dictator Adolf Hitler, eschewing even the appearance of negotiations, simply sent Nazi troops into Czechoslovakia, annexing a heavily German portion of that nation, and presented the rest of the world with a *fait accompli*. If the major European powers, Great Britain and France, chose not to accept this surprise, Hitler had left them with no room at all for diplomatic maneuver; their alternatives were to accept this act or to challenge it militarily. They accepted it, and Europe moved another step closer to World War II.

Crisis Management.   Surprise is a critical element of international crisis, and the management of crises is in turn of utmost importance in the conduct of diplomacy. High threat, short decisional time, and surprise are the distinguishing characteristics of crises. The crisis model postulates that crises are inherent in the international system and that for the most part they can be controlled and brought to satisfactory, peaceful resolution. Once a nation's security machinery kicks in, the theory runs, bureaucrats can master the situation in a controlled, responsive, diplomatic fashion. However, the opposite is more often the case. Crises do not necessarily produce the optimum conditions for diplomacy and negotiation.

The Cuban Missile Crisis (discussed in the boxed feature at the end of this chapter) is a case in point. This seminal crisis of the twentieth century, according to one of its closest students, "became something of a misleading 'model' of the foreign policy process" (Nathan 1975, 236). U.S. behavior during the Cuban Missile Crisis fell far short of the calm, deliberate, careful, conscientious decision-

Figure 9.1
The Diplomatic Continuum
Source: Michael L. Handel, *The Diplomacy of Surprise: Hitler, Nixon, and Sadat* (Cambridge, Mass.: Harvard University Press, 1981), 2.

Routine or Normal Diplomacy				Surprise Diplomacy
Little or no innovation	New diplomatic initiatives	Minor surprises	Faits Accomplis	Radical change

making and execution it often is presented as. Nonetheless, "Kennedy's apparent controlled and masterful way of forcing Khrushchev to withdraw the missiles in the thirteen-day crisis has become a paradigmatic example of the way force can be harnessed to a policy by an elaborate manipulation of threats and gambits, negotiation and intimidation" (Nathan 1975, 258).

Successful crisis management is something of a misnomer, as this example shows. Managing the equivalent of an international gorilla requires the manifest energies and maximum diplomatic skill of every player. But in the middle of an international hurricane, pulling out the charts is a tedious matter. How, asks Nathan, could quality decision-making have occurred if one of the Cuban Missile Crisis decision-makers was so fatigued and distressed that he drove into a tree at 4 A.M.? (Nathan 1975, 280)

The lesson learned from crisis management is that all the delicate and elaborate government plans for coping with the unexpected are often insufficient to bring a storm to resolution. The bromide, "Do what we did last time if it worked, and do just the opposite if it didn't" still seems to be the operative decisional scheme. The whole point of normal diplomacy, of course, is to ensure that there will be no crises.

Preventive Diplomacy

Preventive diplomacy—action to resolve, manage, or contain disputes before they escalate into violence—has become one of the watchwords of the post–Cold War era. More and more nations subscribe to the theory that almost any conflict can be kept below the threshold of violence, if not completely solved, if only there is early and determined intervention. Governments are proclaiming the importance of preventive diplomacy, institutions like the United Nations practice preventive diplomacy, and private foundations pour money into the study of preventive diplomacy (Stedman 1992–93, 46).

Former foreign policy maker and professor of international relations Lincoln Bloomfield points out that preventive diplomacy is highly desirable because "the best available strategy is to head off violations [of the international order] before they take place." The careful use of preventive diplomacy, he believes, could have averted most conflicts of the last fifteen years. The Falklands war between Britain and Argentina, Iraq's invasion of Iran, the Persian Gulf War, and even the Balkan wars were all preventable. Each one erupted either because preventive diplomacy was never tried or because when it was tried it was too little and too late (Bloomfield 1995, 155–60).

According to Bloomfield, three available approaches can strengthen and stabilize preventive diplomacy: publicity, deterrence, and peaceful change. In the world of modern communications, "publicity has already been a powerful diplomatic instrument," shaming or embarrassing nations into nonviolence. Deterrence, which has been effective in preventing nuclear war, must be used to prevent non-nuclear conflict by "a credible and timely threat of sanctions," and if necessary, by the dispatch of "conflict-prevention military units." Finally, the international community must establish procedures for solving disputes and facilitating peaceful change. The United Nations already has the machinery for prevention, deterrence, and enforcement; national leaders must be willing to use it (Bloomfield 1995, 155–60; see also Wendt 1995, 163–77).

Despite the high hopes of enthusiasts, skeptics abound. Stephen John Stedman, for example, maintains that preventive diplomacy has been oversold.

Successful preventive diplomacy requires foresight, the ability to predict where and when crisis can escalate to conflict. However, "the striking aspect of the performance of foreign policy experts over the last ten years has been their inability to predict the most important political changes." Successful preventive diplomacy also requires careful good judgment, a quality Stedman finds in short supply. The failure to calculate appropriate action, Stedman believes, could be costly; the case of Yugoslavia underlines the danger of miscalculation that escalates crisis into violence. "The urge to take preventive action—to do something, anything—can lead to ill-considered policies that lack strategic sense." Finally, Stedman points out that effective preventive diplomacy requires mobilization of public support "long before the pictures of violence show up on television"—not an easy task. Stedman thus concludes that preventive diplomacy is not the panacea its enthusiasts proclaim. "Absent well-defined interests, clear goals, and prudent judgment about acceptable costs and risks, policies of preventive diplomacy and conflict prevention simply mean that one founders early in a crisis rather than later" (Stedman 1992–93, 52).

Open versus Secret Diplomacy

Open or *public diplomacy* is a relatively recent phenomenon, largely the result of President Woodrow Wilson's initiatives at the Versailles peace conference in 1919. In setting forth his principle of "open covenants openly arrived at," Wilson was reacting to the commonly held belief that one of the major causes of the Great War was clandestine or secret diplomacy, which had failed to bring all issues and actors to the table. Wilson was in effect disavowing the Continental diplomacy established at the Congress of Vienna, a diplomacy marked by closed membership and diplomats who spoke only to one another, keeping the terms of treaties and agreements secret not only from potential foes but also from their own people.

Open diplomacy fit nicely with the concept of democracy, the newest form of government on the world stage in 1919. Secret diplomacy was seen less as a way of keeping secrets from one's adversary than as a means of keeping information from domestic enemies within the nation. Open diplomacy would, it was believed, eliminate this clandestine element and enlist the entire population in democratic support of national policy.

In fact, in many cases public or open diplomacy may indeed operate better than private or secret diplomacy. In South Africa's transition from apartheid to majority (black) rule, intense global media scrutiny of each step of the process, from the original agreements between the white government and leaders of the black majority through the jockeying for power of the African National Congress and its rivals to the actual passage of power from F. W. de Klerck to Nelson Mandela, may well have ensured a degree of stability in a highly volatile situation. Likewise, the openness of American attempts to force the Haitian junta to relinquish power, accompanied by open threats of force and mobilization of military might, was both an attempt to enlist the support of the American people for a fundamentally unpopular policy, and to hasten the departure of the colonels and generals.

Open diplomacy, however, will not work in all situations. While the bursting of flashbulbs and the whir of cameras may reduce misperceptions about what has been said, they also prohibit free and open discussion of issues. Only in private can negotiators freely express themselves and debate issues, or make the sorts of intricate compromises necessary to conclude agreements. Most practitioners as well as most pundits favor a free and open debate about policy issues, but private conduct of negotiations until terms are more or less ready to be revealed. It is extremely doubtful, for example, that former President Jimmy Carter, Senator Sam Nunn, and retired general Colin Powell would have been able to bring about a peaceful conclusion to the standoff between the United States and Haiti had they been forced to deal with the junta members in public; in private, they were able to work out a deal that both removed the dictators and permitted the unopposed landing of American troops to begin the process of restoring democracy. It is plain, then, that there are times and places for both public and private diplomacy.

Negotiations

At the heart of "normal" diplomacy, the day-to-day conduct of relations between and among nations, lies negotiation. An attempt to reach an agreed-upon solution prior to the use of threats or of force, negotiation is the most important tool in the diplomat's kit. Depending on the nature of the issue to be settled, negotiations usually are conducted at the ambassadorial level or below. Even closely orchestrated events like summits and major international conferences are the products of months and sometimes years of negotiating at the level of experts on a particular issue, even such a weighty one as arms control, not at the level of foreign ministers or secretaries of state, much less at the level of heads of state. The international Law of the Sea Treaty, for example, took ten years to complete and involved legions of diplomats. And a series of amendments to the General Agreement on Trade and Tariffs (GATT), the so-called Uruguay Round, consumed nearly eight years of tortuous negotiations involving specialists from 108 separate nations.

High-Level versus Low-Level Negotiations

Negotiations can be subdivided into many different categories. First, there are distinctions between *high-level* and *low-level* negotiations. Low-level negotiations, that is, those carried out below the level of ambassador, may be the highly technical work involved in producing agreement on issues as complex as the Law of the Sea or GATT. Or, they may be exploratory talks carried out at a low level in order to avoid premature publicity or outside interference at the beginning of what may be extremely delicate negotiations about volatile issues. High-level negotiations, on the other hand, take place at the ambassadorial level or above. Such negotiations are the official conduct of states; they often take place after an arduous series of low-level talks has laid the groundwork for agreement.

Direct versus Indirect Negotiations

Negotiations can be either *direct* or *indirect,* depending on the desire of the initiating country. Often, when negotiations are necessary with a nation or an entity not officially recognized by another, indirect negotiations represent the only real possibility. For example, the United States did not extend formal diplomatic recognition to the People's Republic of China until 1979, thirty years after the communist triumph in China. Nonetheless, there were a variety of issues between the two nations that required negotiation and resolution; consequently, they carried on indirect negotiations, using Polish officials as intermediaries to convey messages back and forth. The process was tedious, but probably better than the two nations' complete loss of contact with each other. Likewise, when Henry

Kissinger made his secret trip to China to open the way for Richard Nixon's epochal journey, the initial, indirect negotiations took place with the Pakistani government presenting the American case to China. Similarly, the United States did not formally recognize the Palestine Liberation Organization until 1991. Prior to that, all contact with the PLO was indirect, primarily through the intermediation of Arab states. Only after many secret and indirect sessions, in some cases lasting decades, could formal dialogue begin and formal diplomatic recognition ultimately come about.

Separate versus Linked Negotiations

Traditionally, issues under negotiation between states have been perceived as separate and distinct entities; thus, negotiations over water or fishing rights have had no direct bearing on disputes between the same nations over trade. Generally, this is still the case today. Nations can be at loggerheads over trade issues, but successfully negotiate water rights or immigration issues. Despite all the points of contention that may exist between two or more states, they may conduct successful diplomacy on some issues even while locking horns over other, seemingly intractable issues of deep concern.

linkage Tying your opponent so closely to you that he will not drag you into conflict.

However, in the 1970s the chief architect of American diplomacy at that point, Henry Kissinger, introduced the concept of **linkage** into the international arena. Kissinger believed that the United States, by linking the vital arms control negotiations then taking place on the SALT treaties to the behavior of the Soviet Union within the international system, could successfully control and even manipulate that behavior. If the United States could engage the Soviets in a series of trade and strategic arms negotiations, the Soviets would then be less likely to endanger their standing with the United States by international misbehavior in other areas, for example, by encouraging wars of national liberation. To Kissinger and American policy-makers, it was plain that all areas of Soviet behavior were linked together, and that exerting pressure in one area should produce favorable results in another. The Soviets, however, did not share this world view. They separated the issues and viewed them as discrete and independent of one another. Thus, negotiation in international arms limitations agreements did not, and in their view should not, preclude their fueling pro-communist efforts throughout the world. They denied that there was any linkage at all.

International Law

Why Study International Law?

The primary reason we study international law is that it is relevant to the conduct of relations between nation-states. States cannot function without constraints. If there were no constraints, anarchy would reign.

With the demise of the medieval feudal systems, some sort of system was needed to regulate the conduct of the world's new players, the nation-states. International law evolved over time to fill this void.

What happens when a nation's leaders decide to disregard international law? During the Chinese Cultural Revolution, from 1966 to 1976, all classes in international law were canceled, and all of the professors fired. As one Chinese writer stated, "in the Western capitalistic world, suppression of the weak by the strong and the eating of small fish by big fish are not only tacitly condoned by bourgeois international law but also are cloaked with a mantle of legality" (Slomanson 1990, 29). But when the Cultural Revolution ended in 1976, China's leaders decided that the nation must participate in the quest for world power. In 1982, the president of the Chinese International Law Society stated, "China's international lawyers must begin to work diligently to rebuild her science of international law which serves to promote world peace and truly represents the interests of the people the world over . . . . We also have the responsibility to train a new generation of specialists and scholars in international law" (Slomanson 1990, 29).

It took the Chinese government only a decade to learn the importance of international law; other nations have not been so quick to catch on. Nonetheless, international law is important: there are cases in which two nations, for example, have a legitimate disagreement, and adjudication is preferable to war.

The Origins and Evolution of International Law

Historically, war has been the hallmark of international relations in the age of nation-states. In order to achieve peaceful or "normal" relations among nations and to codify the rules governing state-to-state relations, a body of modern international law has been created through diplomatic means.

Operating under the general assumption that anarchy is the best way to describe international relations, some laypeople deny that international law exists. After all, there is no world congress to make such law, and no world government to enforce it. Trying to discuss international law within the context of statutory law as created by the United States Congress, for instance, is an exercise in futility. There is a corpus of law called international law, but in many ways it is

---

The Rights of States

A state is considered a "person" under international law, and hence is afforded certain privileges and rights arising from its international personality. The following is a list of the *inherent* rights of states—rights due them simply because they are states:

GLOBAL PERSPECTIVES

- **Right to exist:** This is a most difficult right to define. It is frequently defined as the right of each state to protect itself. The moment that a state comes into being, international law bestows certain benefits and burdens associated with its status as the political entity in control of a particular territory and populace.
- **Sovereignty:** State sovereignty is rooted in the European reformation and particularly in the Treaty of Westphalia, which established the nation-state system. Its twentieth-century formulation is manifested in international agreements using such phrases as "independence" or "territorial supremacy," which are synonymous with sovereignty.
- **Equality among Nations:** The first of many principles expressed in the UN Charter is that the UN "is based upon the principle of the sovereign equality of all its members." The OAS charter likewise stipulates that "states are juridically equal."
- **Self-Determination:** The principle of self-determination of nations has been expressed in many documents. U.S. President Wilson espoused this notion in his Fourteen Points address in 1918. The UN Charter and the General Assembly Resolution reaffirming the charter's principles both expressly refer to the "self-determination of peoples."

(Slomanson 1990, 48–49)

substantially different in both content and administration from what we normally think of as "law."

Much of what we have come to call international law today is law through *custom* and *convention:* in short, the "normal" precedent-establishing ways the business of international politics has been carried out historically.

These precedents often have been religious and ethical norms handed down by the Christian Church in Europe or by tribes in Indian, Chinese, and Islamic areas. However, it was in the Greek, Roman, and later-seventeenth-century European settings that a more codified system of laws, divorced from religion, was established.

Most of medieval European law developed as a result of the Church's incorporation of the ideas of natural law and order, adopted from the Roman empire. As K. J. Holsti states, "it was the Church, with its notions of hierarchy, authority and duty, and its ultimate sanction of excommunication, that had the largest impact in moderating the politics of the period" (Holsti 1995, 292). As an illustration of this, Holsti cites the Peace of God, declared by the Church in the tenth century, which attempted to impose restrictions on war, violence, and plundering. The Truce of God (1041), established by the Bishop of Arles and the Abbott of Cluny, was more successful: it did effectively limit the scope and degree of violence in certain parts of medieval Europe. For example, there was to be no fighting between Wednesday evening and Monday morning (Holsti 1995, 292). Later, the concept of *"just war"* was developed, including a set of rules of engagement to settle disputes (see the section on this concept later in this chapter).

The seven major legal systems in the modern world are depicted in figure 9.2. In many respects these systems are quite diverse. How, then, did international law develop? The modern premises of international law, sovereignty, territorial integrity, legal equality, and noninterference in the affairs of others developed

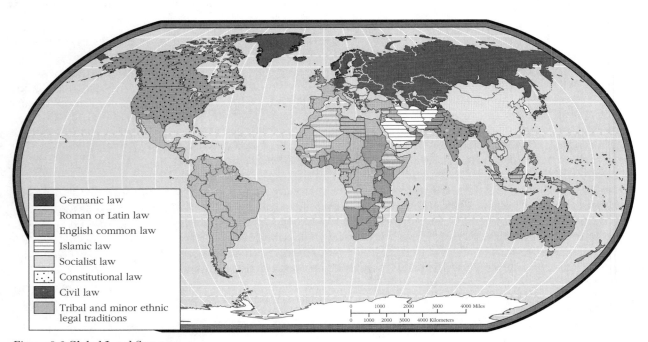

Legend:
- Germanic law
- Roman or Latin law
- English common law
- Islamic law
- Socialist law
- Constitutional law
- Civil law
- Tribal and minor ethnic legal traditions

Figure 9.2 **Global Legal Systems**

over time, and with a great deal of influence from commercial interests in Europe in the nineteenth century. Raw materials and markets in non-European areas of the world were but two of the reasons for the advancement of international law. "The greatest expansion of legal doctrines covered matters pertaining to the obligations of debtor states, sanctity of money, protection of commercial property during civil strife, and expropriation of private property" (Falk, Mendlovitz and De Visscher 1962, 133–34).

As early as 1625, Hugo Grotius attempted to codify international law in his monumental work *On the Law of War and Peace*. In many ways, the Treaty of Westphalia (1648) represented the first attempt at systematizing and implementing international law among the newly emerging nation-states. Since then, international law has evolved as a result of treaties, decisions made by international bodies such as the League of Nations and the United Nations, and even decisions by domestic courts that have affected international practices. However, there is still no single series of law books that encompasses all international law, no compendium such as the *Statutes of the United States* or *Decisions of the Supreme Court*. International law much more closely resembles the British constitution: it includes codified laws and treaties readily found in bound volumes mixed with equally important, unwritten custom and convention.

Nonetheless, despite the lack of centralized organization, an imposing body of international law has accumulated since Westphalia—law that governs, in normal times, almost every aspect of international commerce, contracts, communications, space, exploration and nuclear testing. Much of that law and convention has been created by such intergovernmental organizations as the United Nations, the International Postal Union, the International Court of Justice, the World Health Organization, and the World Trade Organization.

Two Types of International Law

We can divide international law into two distinct types, one familiar and the other less well known. The less-familiar type of international law, **private international law,** is basically routine and often hidden from public view. Private law is practiced when international lawyers deal with issues such as diplomatic immunity, passport violations, extradition of alleged criminals, the sharing of data across international borders, fishing rights, copyrights and patents, and so forth. Private international law deals with the details of daily life, and of so-called "low" politics. (See boxed feature for a discussion of private international law as it affects telecommunications.)

private international law A somewhat routine form of international law that deals with such issues as diplomatic immunity, passports, extradition, the sharing of data, fishing rights, etc.

Public international law, on the other hand, is what captures the attention of headline writers and television anchors. Public law deals with government-to-government relations on such issues as peace and national security. Although many remain skeptical about it—a former Israeli ambassador to the United Nations said that international law is that law which the wicked do not obey and the righteous do not enforce—there is a large and growing body of such law expressed in treaties, conventions, and customs. In this chapter we will focus primarily on the most significant area of international law, questions of war and peace.

public international law Government-to-government agreements covering relations on such issues as peace and national security.

Sources of International Law

There are five primary sources of international law, according to Article 38(1) of the International Court of Justice:

International Law and Telecommunications

While the Internet is largely self-governing, the other telecommunications media have come under some form of cooperative international regulation, almost from their inception. The first to do so was the telegraph industry, in which international communications created a series of problems involving common equipment, signals, and codes. In 1865 a number of nations met in Paris to discuss these problems. The result was the Telegraph Convention, which created the International Telegraph Union to deal with these issues. The ITU developed technical interconnection standards so that the various national telegraph services could link together, and established international Morse Code as the standard medium for transmission of messages. It also set up mechanisms for overseeing tariffs, sharing revenue for telegrams crossing international borders, using encryption, and assuring privacy (Fortner 1993, 13).

The development of radio created new kinds of problems, primarily issues of frequency allocation: how to prevent a massive airwave traffic jam with multiple stations transmitting on the same frequency.

GLOBAL PERSPECTIVES

In 1903 nine nations met in Berlin to head off chaos on the air. They began what is the continuing process of agreeing on which radio frequencies should be allocated for which purposes (marine radio, ship-to-ship, private and business, amateur radio, satellite, and broadcasting uses). From this meeting emerged an informal working group that became known as the International Radiotelegraphic Union, which organized subsequent conferences. In 1906 a second Berlin conference agreed that SOS should be the international distress signal. In 1912, in the aftermath of the *Titanic* disaster, the world's major nations signed an agreement that all ships have radio equipment in working order and at least one trained radio operator aboard. The first "modern" international conference, in 1927, saw more nations represented than had been at the great Versailles conference at the end of World War I. In 1932 the merger of the International Radiotelegraphic Union and the Telegraph Union created the most important modern international communications organization, the International Telecommunication Union (Hawley and Heil 1992; Fortner 1993, 11).

After World War II, and the enormous growth in technological development fostered by the war, the ITU became part of the United Nations, as a

(a) *international conventions* (i.e., treaties), whether general or particular, establishing rules expressly recognized by the contesting states;

(b) *international custom,* as evidence of a general practice accepted as law;

(c) the *general principles* of law recognized by civilized nations;

(d) . . . *judicial decisions* and the

(e) *teaching of the most highly qualified jurists* of the various nations, as subsidiary means for the determination of rules of law.

This extremely broad pronouncement is generally regarded by scholars as constituting the list of sources of international law.

International conventions are bilateral or multilateral treaties and agreements or treaties that commit the signatories to a certain behavior or set of standards. The Strategic Arms Limitation Treaty (SALT) signed by the United States and the former Soviet Union represents such an international convention, in which both parties agreed to engage in certain activities and not to engage in others.

International custom refers to a general standard of conduct agreed to by states over time. International customs may be traced as far back as Homer's *Iliad* and Thucydides' *Peloponnesian War,* in which warring parties accepted truces, heralds, and breaks for holidays and celebrations.

specialized agency under the General Secretariat. Today's ITU plays multiple roles: oversight of international legal agreements; promotion of the responsible use of telecommunications services; technical assistance to developing countries; coordination of space communications; registry of radio frequency assignments; encouragement of the lowest possible tariffs and rates; assisting in saving human lives through telecommunications services; and general administration, such as developing regulations and recommendations and collecting and publishing information on telecommunications issues (Hawley and Heil 1992; Frederick 1993, 102).

Typical of an ITU function is what is called a World Administrative Radio Conference (WARC), called every decade or two to deal with new technologies and refine use of the older technologies. The most recent WARC, which met in Torremolinos, Spain, early in 1992, brought together representatives of some 162 nations to deal with twenty-two specific items ranging from increased spectrum for high-frequency broadcasting through Low Earth Orbit satellite frequencies to the need for spectrum for Digital Audio Broadcasting. Even groups that had no formal agenda items organized to protect their interests. For example, the International Amateur Radio Union mobilized amateur radio operators worldwide to raise funds to study agenda proposals and ensure that the interests of amateur radio operators were respected. The chief United States amateur radio group, the American Radio Relay League, raised over $400,000 to fund this work. Official representation of the United States at this conference was carried out by the State Department, but the official U.S. delegation also included representatives of the Federal Communications Commission, the National Telecommunications and Information Administration, and the electronics and communications industry (Hawley and Heil 1992).

New technologies pose major problems of international regulation. An example of this is the attempt to regulate trans-border data flow (TBDF), or the international movement of computer-readable material. Although many governments want to protect individual privacy, or their own interests, by regulating the flow of information, there has been little success in negotiating any TBDF regulation. Businesses tend to view such regulation as a competitive burden, and the technical problems of encryption and decryption are enormous. Further, the idea of regulating TBDF also raises serious issues of freedom of speech; in most Western democracies, strong traditions of freedom of speech and press have set off alarms at the idea of government "tollbooths" along the information highway (Wriston 1992, 150–52).

General principles are more elusive to pin down than customs; the term refers to widely accepted standards of behavior, or simply to other forms of customary behavior. General principles would include, for example, the fair treatment of foreign nationals by other countries and the protection of personal property.

The phrase *subsidiary sources* cited by the International Court of Justice is even vaguer, but in general it refers to decisions made by the International Court of Justice, or to decisions affecting international law made by various other courts.

Given the splendid vagueness of the International Court of Justice, it is no wonder that the general public's perception of international law is at best fuzzy, and more often very dim. As well, the public's view of international law is probably quite different from the views of those diplomats, lawyers and merchants who deal with such law every day. The media and history books as well give considerable attention to high-profile elements of international law, such as the Kellogg-Briand Pact or the Covenant of the League of Nations. However, often such high-profile documents represent the headline failures of the international community to create and implement law. Since such elements were often of dubious merit to begin with or could not be enforced when violated, the public receives a negative view of all international law. But, despite such spectacular failures in the area of public international law, routine public and private international law governs daily relations among international actors.

In fact, private international law (governing such things as copyright provisions) tends to be more effective than public international law in regulating international behavior. Unlike domestic law, which works at least in part because the state possesses a monopoly on the use of force, public international law cannot be enforced readily; there is no central authority or enforcer within the international system (although the United Nations may be poised to begin playing such a role more efficiently). When international law works, it does so because of the community of interests and the distribution of power among the international actors. When there is no community of interests and the power distribution is unbalanced, international law tends to disintegrate into international anarchy.

Because of the primacy of the concept that individual states are sovereign, international law is dependent upon those states that wish to abide by and to enforce the rules of interstate, inter-actor behavior. By definition, sovereign states are ultimately responsible to themselves alone. As long as state sovereignty remains the paramount organizing principle of the international system, that system will always tend toward anarchy, with states deciding what the rules are and choosing which ones they will obey.

Such international legal anarchy has several causes. First, international law is not universally accepted. For most of its existence, the Soviet Union did not recognize international law, which it saw as a Western, capitalist construct that clashed with communist theory and the practice of both national and international politics. Second, many developing states see international law as status quo—oriented, directed to the interests of developed states. It props up the existing system of inequality in the distribution of wealth. To many in the developing world, such international law is inherently unjust. Finally, international law, with its ambiguities, can be manipulated too readily for propaganda purposes and used by governments to justify their policies or views.

International Law and War

Not surprisingly, given the contentious nature of states when issues such as boundaries, territory, and resources are involved, a great portion of the existing body of international law deals with war. As a tool of diplomacy, war has been steadily declining since 1815, as the world has shown, with the exception of a few notable spasms, increasing intolerance for war as a legitimate instrument of national policy. A repudiation of the use of force, or war, was included in the Covenant of the League of Nations in 1919; signatories to the Kellogg-Briand Pact of 1928 "outlawed" war and the use of force; and the Charter of the United Nations repudiates war or the threat of war and delegates to the Security Council the role of ensuring the collective security of its members. Today the majority of the world's states proclaim that they seek peaceful solutions to international tensions and renounce, in general, the use of war as an instrument of international policy. But certainly, war has not vanished.

And modern international law must cope with other forms of violence than war. International terrorism is an example. International law establishes guidelines for a state's reaction to acts of terrorism (we will discuss these later in this chapter). A primary principle is that reaction by one state against another one that sponsored an act of terrorism must be proportional. "Moreover, this right does not allow retaliation for past attacks. The response in self-defense to an armed attack must be necessary and proportional . . . and the victim of an act of terrorism will have to pursue other remedies against states it believes responsible and against the states that encourage, promote, condone, or tolerate terrorism or provide a haven to terrorists" (Henkin 1991, 47).

The Concept of "Just War"

For centuries, Western, Christian nations have wrestled with questions about when war is necessary or just, and how war should be conducted. The idea of a "just war" acceptable to Christianity dates to the writings of St. Augustine in the fifth century, but is most clearly associated with Grotius, the father of modern international law. According to Grotius, rulers and governments have to examine two separate but linked issues: *jus ad bellum* (the justice of war) and *jus in bello* (justice in war). The first question is whether war is just or permissible, and the second is how war should be conducted once it has been found justifiable. The "neo–just war" doctrine stipulates that peace is no longer of higher value than justice. The doctrine of *military necessity* justifies the use of "protective" military measures to guard national interests, but only when retaliatory force is absolutely necessary as a late recourse for defense, when all peaceful means have been exhausted. The modern view confines the just war to punishing aggression, deterring attack, protecting innocents, and maintaining the order of the international system. Sadly, states interpreting or ignoring such concepts have launched hundreds of small wars since 1945.

The Conduct of War and International Law

Just war theory always has distinguished between combatants and noncombatants, stressing the necessity of protecting noncombatants, or civilians. Neo–just war theory maintains this distinction and stipulates additional restrictions on the use of war. Among the limitations on war now specified in international law are these:

just war theory Doctrine of war concerned with when war is morally justified and how and against whom it should be conducted.

- no attacking of unarmed enemies
- no firing on undefended localities without military significance
- no poisoning streams or wells
- no pillaging
- no killing or wounding military personnel who have surrendered or are disabled by wounds or sickness
- no assassinating or hiring of assassins
- no ill-treating prisoners of war
- no aerial bombardment to terrorize or attack civilian populations
- no destroying civilian cultural objects and places of worship

(von Glahn 1992, 245–47)

Genocide. **Genocide** was defined by the United Nations (GA 96) on December 11, 1946 as

genocide The intentional destruction of a national, ethnic, racial, or religious group.

> acts committed with intent to destroy, in whole or in part, a national, ethnic, racial or religious group, as such:
>
> **a)** Killing members of the group;

b) Causing serious bodily or mental harm to members of the group;

c) Deliberately inflicting on the group conditions of life calculated to bring about its physical destruction in whole or in part;

d) Imposing measures intended to prevent births within the group;

e) Forcibly transferring children of the group to another group.

(von Glahn 1992, 256)

The same document labels genocide as "an odious scourge" that has occurred during all periods of recorded history.

The term *genocide* (derived from the Greek *genos,* meaning "race" or "tribe," and the Latin *-cide,* meaning "killing") came into use after World War II. It was coined by the jurist Raphael Lemkin, "whose remarkable achievement it was to initiate a one-man crusade for a genocide convention" (Kuper 1981, 22). Lempkin defined genocide as the destruction of a nation or ethnic group. Lempkin "explained that generally speaking genocide does not mean the immediate destruction of a nation, except when accomplished by mass killings of all members of a nation, but is intended rather to signify a coordinated plan of different actions aiming at the destruction of essential foundations of the life of national groups, with the aim of annihilating the groups themselves" (Kuper 1981, 22).

The crime of genocide as defined by the United Nations is wholly independent of crimes against peace and of war crimes. Recent atrocities in Bosnia involving the "ethnic cleansing" of the Bosnian Muslims at the hands of the Serbs, massacres of the Kurds and the Shi'ite majority in southern Iraq at the order of Saddam Hussein, mass murders by Pol Pot committed in the name of Kampuchean nationalism, Chechen deaths at the hands of Russians—this is but a short list of recent examples of genocide. What is intriguing is that under international law, state sovereignty may permit such "ethnic cleansing," or genocide.

Kuper (1981, 161) writes that the "sovereign state claims, as an integral part of its sovereignty, . . . the right to commit genocide, or engage in genocidal massacres, against peoples under its rule, and the United Nations, for all practical purposes, defends this right." Keeping in mind that the United Nations is an organization of states, not nations, and "since most states are, in fact, threatened by the claims of nations, it is little wonder that the UN is pro-state and anti-nation" (Pierre van den Berghe, quoted in Kuper 1981, 161).

The reader must decide which value is of greater importance: the value of state sovereignty, and implicitly, of the Wilsonian doctrine of noninterference in the internal affairs of others (even in matters of genocide), or the value of the sanctity of human life, wherever it exists.

Terrorism and International Law

terrorism Premeditated political violence perpetrated against a nation's noncombatants.

Terrorism is a common factor in the world today. It is a tool of groups—both nation-states and stateless groups—attempting to gain publicity for their cause (e.g., achieving statehood), or to disrupt normal processes within established nations for particular political ends. International terrorism is terrorism involving the citizens or the territory of more than one country.

In history, the term *terrorism* is relatively new. In 1798, the *Dictionnaire* of the Academie Francaise defined the term as *système, régime de la terreur* ("system, regime of terror"—Laqueur 1987, 11). The American Department of State defines terrorism as "premeditated, politically motivated violence perpetrated against noncombatants . . . [used as] targets by subnational groups or clandestine agents, usually intended to influence an audience" (United States Department of State, 1995). Numerous groups in the world with a variety of ideological or revolutionary axes to grind frequently resort to terrorism to advance their goals. Terror is a tool designed to outrage or inflame the innocents of a designated population; to gain media attention to the terrorists' cause(s), and ultimately perhaps to achieve some change in the state (either secession or creation).

To date, there are eleven international treaties and conventions that commit signatories to combat various terroristic crimes. For example, in December 1985, the Security Council of the United Nations unanimously adopted Resolution 579, which

- Condemns unequivocally all acts of hostage taking and abduction;
- Calls for the immediate safe release of all hostages and abducted persons wherever and by whomever they are being held;
- Affirms the obligation of all states in whose territory hostages or abducted persons are held urgently to take all appropriate measure to secure their safe release and to prevent the commission of acts of hostage taking and abduction in the future;
- Appeals to all states that have not yet done so to consider becoming parties to the International Convention on the Prevention and Punishment of Crimes against Internationally Protected Persons Including Diplomatic Agents adopted on 14 December 1973, the Convention for the Suppression of Unlawful Acts against the Safety of Civil Aviation adopted on 23 September 1971, the Convention for the Suppression of Unlawful Seizure of Aircraft adopted on 16 December 1970, and other relevant conventions;
- Urges the further development of international cooperation among states in devising and adopting effective measures which are in accordance with the rules of international law to facilitate the prevention, prosecution, and punishment of all acts of hostage taking and abduction as manifestations of international terrorism (UN Security Council, in Kegley 1990, 259–60).

Terrorism can be described as either *state-sponsored* terrorism (such as that carried out by Libya, Syria, and Iran), or that *sponsored by proto-state groups,* such as the Palestine Liberation Organization, the Kurds of Middle Eastern states, and secessionist organizations in Sri Lanka, the Punjab, the Basque region of Spain and France, and elsewhere. Governments that sponsor terrorists have given aid in the form of money, safe havens, strategy training, and so on. Such governments see terrorism merely as an extension of their own foreign and domestic policy goals, such as the furtherance of the Islamic or Marxist "revolutions" (see section on narco-terrorism later in this chapter).

In 1994, there were 321 international terrorist attacks in the world, compared to 431 in 1993. This represents a decline of 25 percent in one year (United States Department of State 1995). According to the U.S. Department of State (1995), the following is a list of *some* of the most notable state sponsors of terrorism and what they are currently engaged in:

Iran is still the most active state sponsor of international terrorism. Iranian terrorist operations concentrate on Iranian dissidents living outside Iran . . . . Iran continues to use terrorism as ruthlessly as it did under Khomeini and supports groups, such as Hizballah, that pose a threat to Americans.

Iraq provides safe haven and logistic support to several terrorist groups and individuals, including elements of the ANO, based in Lebanon; the

Mojadedin-e Khalq, which is opposed to the government in Tehran; Abu Abbas' Palestine Liberation Front; and notorious bomb-maker, Abu Ibrahim.

Cuba is no longer able to support armed struggle actively in Latin America and other parts of the world. In years past, Havana provided significant levels of military training, weapons, funds, and guidance to leftist subversives.

The People's Democratic Republic of Korea (North Korea) is not known to have sponsored any international terrorist attacks since 1987, when it conducted the midflight bombing of a KAL airliner. A North Korean spokesman in April 1993 condemned all forms of terrorism, including state terrorism, and said his country resolutely opposed the encouragement and support of terrorism.

Seemingly random acts of terrorist violence do not in fact occur without reason. Today's reasons, however, surge beyond the "mere" politics of the disaffected. We refer to this particular new and improved brand of state-sponsored terrorism as "narco-terrorism."

Narco-Terrorism and International Law

The link between narcotics, terrorism, and international law is relatively new. In short, drug dealing in the global arena is a way to subsidize international terrorist activities, which are proscribed by international covenants, conventions, and treaties, but which promote ideological causes for the sponsoring state(s).

narco-terrorism The use of drug trafficking to advance the aims of terrorist organizations.

Narco-terrorism, as we define it here, is the use of drug trafficking to advance the objectives of certain governments and terrorist organizations (Ehrenfeld, 1990, 1). The target of most narco-terrorists is the United States, and to a lesser extent, its Western European allies. According to Ehrenfeld (1990, 2), the reasons the United States is singled out as the recipient of drug trafficking are simple.

- Narco-terrorism is a state-sponsored terrorism that follows an anti-western, anti-capitalistic, pro-Marxist ideology;
- Drugs destabilize Western (e.g., primarily American) society;
- Results come at no cost to the narco-terrorists, since the whole enterprise is paid for by drug buyers in the U.S. and elsewhere.

Formulating a foreign policy to address this issue has not been easy for the American government. State-sponsored terrorism has involved states (such as Syria and the former Soviet Union) that have been key players in the American-sponsored Middle East peace process, as well as in the freeing of American hostages held in Lebanon. Muddying the waters with diplomatic maneuvers over state-sponsored terrorism could have unwound the peace process and made the extrication of hostages more difficult. Moreover, narco-terrorist activities have not been the focal point of the American intelligence community (primarily the CIA), but the purview of the Drug Enforcement Agency.

Peace and International Law

Modern international law was never intended to eliminate war. As we have seen, war or the use of force is viewed as justifiable under certain conditions and restrictions, although considered strictly a last resort. (We must add that not all members of the international system adhere to the prescription of war as a last resort.) The primary, fundamental principle of law, domestic or international, is the promotion of stability, not of justice. Justice is of secondary or tertiary value. However, international law has been and probably will continue to be an alternative to conflict for those who seek peaceful solutions. Legal and diplomatic procedures may be substituted for war from time to time, even though war itself will never disappear completely. And while international law will not, and does not seek to, eliminate war, it is available for those who seek nonviolent or less violent solutions to conflict. While international law is imperfect, failure to observe legal norms does not necessarily result from imperfections in the law (Holsti 1995, 296).

More often than not, international law is used as a justification for foreign policy actions already decided on. The U.S. action in the Cuban Missile Crisis is such a case study.

Diplomacy and International Law in the Future

As the world moves away (at least for now) from high-intensity conflicts such as World War I and World War II toward low-intensity conflict (see chap. 11) and

International Law and the Cuban Missile Crisis

GLOBAL PERSPECTIVES

The Government of the United States made a decision to *quarantine* (a legal term for "blockade") the island of Cuba in 1962 because of great alarm in the White House of President John Kennedy over the implantation of 42 Soviet MRBM (medium-range ballistic missiles), 12 launchers, 42 medium-range jet bombers, 144 SAM (surface-to-air missile) launchers, 42 MiG-21s (fighter aircraft), assorted missiles, and 22,000 Soviet troops. To the U.S. government, this act was a *crisis*. The question became how to defuse the crisis without starting World War III, which had all of the ingredients for being a nuclear war. After considerable Executive Committee (EXCOM) discussions, it was decided that a quarantine of the island nation would be put into effect to stop the Soviets from shipping further supplies, and to give the U.S. and Soviet governments some time. The American government acted in concert with the Organization of American States (OAS), seeking an authorizing resolution of force from, as well as the "good offices" of, the United Nations.

Although the American approach to this international crisis was, to be sure, anchored in politics, it was also undergirded by a strong sense of international law. There are varying views on American motives for this. Some analysts and people involved contend that international law was merely a justification for American foreign policy, or, at best, an afterthought; others, like Abraham Chayes, a lawyer for the U.S. Department of State, think differently. Chayes states, "the factual record is irrefutable . . . that the men responsible for decision did not ignore legal considerations. On the contrary, they made a considerable effort to integrate legal factors into their deliberations. The President and his advisers were properly concerned with the possibilities—for good or ill—in the situation they faced and in the course open to them. Law and legal institutions played a part in defining and shaping those possibilities" (1974, 100).

You may wish to do further reading on the Cuban Missile Crisis, then to decide for yourself what role international law played, and when.

heightened concern over global economic issues (see chap. 8), diplomatic negotiations probably will play an even larger role than they have to date. And diplomacy will certainly become more and more multilateral as global politics become more and more intertwined. The United Nations and other supranational organizations, such as the European Union, the Arab League, and the Organization of American States, will play larger roles in the struggle for diplomatic resolution of global conflicts. "Vest-pocket diplomacy" of the sort practiced by Henry Kissinger will be increasingly unfashionable, as democratic politicians stress the importance of "open covenants openly arrived at" and rely more and more on expanding global communications networks. In short, it will be increasingly difficult to conceal any diplomatic activity from the eyes and ears of the world press, with its enhanced ability to harvest news around the clock.

International law undoubtedly will become more important in the future. Private international law will remain paramount in terms of the daily regulation of international life, but the gap between private and public international law may close somewhat with the increased importance of multilateral public diplomacy. Public international law will begin to focus on such "low" issues as population growth and such "high" issues as world trade.

International anarchy may not vanish, but it will certainly diminish as nations, corporations, and individuals recognize both the dangers of global instability in an age of nuclear proliferation and the necessity of global stability in an age of global economics.

Summary

Diplomacy As we have discovered, diplomacy and international law are intricately intertwined. Diplomacy is a means by which nations achieve their desired goals. It is concerned with the management of relations between states and between states and other actors. The primary method of diplomatic contact is through negotiations. Negotiations, conducted by nations' representatives, are a short-hand way to stage peaceful resolutions to sticky international situations, be they trade issues, border disputes, or the cessation of hostilities. Negotiations are considered to be either secret or public, with several variations of each type. For example, negotiations can be direct or indirect, separate or linked, depending upon the desired outcome.

Traditional diplomacy has been bilateral, i.e., involving a relationship between two states. Former U.S. Secretary of State Henry Kissinger was famous for his "shuttle diplomacy" in various Middle Eastern capitals. Today, however, diplomacy has been given a much richer character by the introduction of other supranational actors, such as the United Nations. Operation Desert Storm is a good example of multilateral diplomacy: it included the Arab Gulf Coast Council, the Arab League, and the European Union, as well as the United Nations. A variation of public diplomacy, international summitry often is conducted by heads of state to provide their nations (and the world) with an open picture window on the conduct of diplomacy.

International Law   International law is another construct of diplomacy. It was created by nations to facilitate international codes of conduct. In short, international law is a constraint upon state behavior. Without such a constraint, anarchy would prevail. Under international law, a state is considered as a "person"; as such, a state has inherent rights. These are the right to exist, the right of sovereignty, equality among nations, and self-determination.

International law is either private or public. Private law, less well known to the general public, deals with the "low" politics of such things as copyrights, patents, fishing rights, etc. Public international law captures the attention of headline writers and television newspersons, and deals with treaties, conventions, and customs between nations.

The conduct of war intersects with international law in the concept of the "just war," which stipulates conditions or restraints upon the belligerents in a war. Today, it is important to note that genocide is prohibited by international law. In the same vein, terrorism has been outlawed by at least eleven different conventions or treaties. Terrorism assumes different forms: state-sponsored terrorism, acts by nationals against a nation or its peoples, and narco-terrorism.

In this high-tech age of instant diplomacy, and with an ever-increasing reliance by states upon multi-lateral diplomacy, international law will assume an even greater role in world politics than it did during the Cold War.

Key Terms

Diplomacy	Multilateral diplomacy
International law	Summitry
Signaling	Linkage
Negotiations	Private international law
Public negotiation	Public international law
Public diplomacy	Just war theory
Propaganda	Genocide
Diplomatic recognition	Terrorism
Ambassador	Narco-terrorism
Diplomatic immunity	

Thought Questions

1. Differentiate between public and private diplomacy.
2. Chronicle the evolution of the diplomatic art from Roman times to the present. What glaring changes have diplomats seen over time?
3. What is diplomatic immunity and why is it important?
4. Why study international law?
5. What is just war theory?
6. How do terrorists manipulate the media to further their causes?

References

Akehurst, Michael. *A Modern Introduction to International Law.* London: Unwin Hyman, 1987.

Anderson, M. S. *The Rise of Modern Diplomacy.* New York: Longman, 1993.

Barston, R. P. *Modern Diplomacy.* New York: Longman, 1993.

Bloomfield, Lincoln P. "The Premature Burial of Global Law and Order: Looking Beyond The Three Cases from Hell." *The Washington Quarterly,* Summer 1994.

Chayes, Abram. *The Cuban Missile Crisis: International Crises and the Role of Law.* New York: Oxford University Press, 1974.

Claude, Inis. *States and the Global System: Politics, Law, and Organization.* New York: St. Martin's Press, 1988.

Ehrenfeld, Rachel. *Narco Terrorism.* New York: Basic, 1990.

Fortner, Robert S. *International Communication: History, Conflict, and Control of the Global Metropolis.* Belmont, Cal.: Wadsworth Publishing, 1993.

Frederick, Howard H. *Global Communication & International Relations.* Belmont, Cal.: Wadsworth Publishing Co., 1993.

George, A. L. David K. Hall, and William R. Simmons. *The Limits of Coercive Diplomacy: Laos, Cuba, and Vietnam.* New York: Little, Brown, 1971.

Handel, Michael L. *The Diplomacy of Surprise: Hitler, Nixon, and Sadat.* Cambridge, Mass.: Harvard University Press, 1981.

Hawley, Sandra M., and James D. Heil. "WARC 1992." Update, Houston Amateur Radio Hotline, Jan. 15, 1992.

Henkin, Louis. "The Use of Force and U.S. Policy." In Stanley Hoffman *et al.* (eds.). *Right Versus Might: International Law and the Use of Force,* 2d ed. New York: Council on Foreign Relations, 1991, 37–69.

Hermann, Charles F., ed. *International Crises: Insights from Behavioral Research.* New York: Free Press, 1972.

Holsti, K. J. *International Politics: A Framework for Analysis.* Englewood Cliffs, N.J.: Prentice Hall, 1995.

Ikle, Fred. *Every War Must End.* New York: Columbia University Press, 1971.

International Court of Justice, 1980. *Case Concerning United States Diplomatic and Cousular Staff in Tehran,* 19 International League Materials 553 (1980).

Janis, Mark W. *An Introduction to International Law.* Boston: Little, Brown, 1988.

Kegley, Charles W. *International Terrorism: Characteristics, Causes, and Controls.* New York: St. Martins Press, 1990.

Kegley, Charles, and Gregory Raymond. *When Trust Breaks Down.* Columbia, S.C.: University of South Carolina Press, 1990.

Kissinger, Henry A. *A World Restored: Metternich, Castlereagh, and the Problems of Peace, 1812–1822.* New York: Houghton Mifflin, 1973.

———. *Diplomacy.* New York: Simon and Schuster, 1994.

Kuper, Leo. *Genocide: Its Political Use in the Twentieth Century.* New Haven: Yale University Press, 1981.

Lall, Arthur. *Modern International Negotiation: Principles and Practice.* New York: Columbia University Press, 1966.

Lockhart, Charles. *Bargaining in International Conflicts.* New York: Columbia University Press, 1979.

Mendlovitz, Saul H., and Charles De Visscher. *Theory and Reality in Public International Law.* Princeton: Princeton University Press, 1957.

Nathan, James A. "The Missile Crisis: His Finest Hour Now." *World Politics,* Summer 1975.

Sawyer, Jack, and Harold Guetzkow. "Bargaining and Negotiation in International Relations." In Herbert C. Kelman. *International Behavior: A Social Psychological Analysis.* New York: Holt, Rinehart, and Winston, 1965.

Slomanson, William R. *Fundamental Perspectives on International Law.* St. Paul: West Publishing Co., 1990.

Stedman, Stephen John. "The New Interventionists." "America and the World." *Foreign Affairs,* 1992–1993.

United States Department of State. *Patterns of Global Terrorism, 1994.* Washington: Department of State publication 10239, electronic version, April 1995. Gopher://Dosfan.Lib.uic.edu/of-1% 3A3080% 3A1994%20 Report.

von Glahn, Gerhard. *Law Among Nations,* 6th ed. New York: Macmillan, 1992.

Wendt, David. "The Peacemakers: Lessons of Conflict Resolution for the Post-Cold War World." *The Washington Quarterly,* Summer 1994.

Wriston, Walter. *The Twilight of Sovereignty: How the Information Revolution Is Transforming Our World.* New York: Charles Scribner's Sons, 1992.

Zartman, I. William, ed. *The Negotiation Process: Theories and Applications.* Beverly Hills, Calif.: Sage, 1978.

Part Four

Rules of the Game

Chapter 10

The Game of Nations: Intelligence and the Making of Policy

Introduction

What Is Intelligence?

The key ingredient in any kind of decision-making, whether it concerns what to wear on a given day or what policy to pursue in a given situation, is information—more specifically, information that has been carefully gathered and evaluated, or **intelligence.** One of the most enduring images of twentieth-century popular literature and culture has been the spy: the dashing behind-the-lines operative of World War II movies and James Bond novels, or the grim and deliberate chessplayer of John Le Carré's novels. While the romanticization of the spy and of **espionage** has caught and held the general imagination, intelligence is simultaneously more complicated and much more sophisticated than it is usually portrayed. In this chapter we will explore the "intelligence cycle"; the means used to gather, analyze, and evaluate intelligence; problems of intelligence operations, particularly within a democratic society; and possible futures of intelligence work.

As we implied in our opening sentence, intelligence includes but goes far beyond mere information. An encyclopedia contains a vast amount of information, but it would scarcely be adequate to provide intelligence to policy-makers trying to deal with a particularly knotty issue. Intelligence, strictly defined, is "the product resulting from the collection, evaluation, analysis, integration and interpretation of all available information which concerns one or more aspects of foreign nations or of areas of operation which is immediately or potentially significant for planning" (United States Departments of Army, Navy, and Air Force 1955, 53). Policy-makers in the political, the economic, or the military realm need facts of a certain kind: facts provided in context, which help answer certain questions or suggest certain patterns. In addition, intelligence in the modern state often includes two closely related concepts and fields that we will also consider: counterintelligence and **covert operations.**

In dealing with issues of intelligence in this chapter, we inevitably encounter large areas that are closed to public view, within both the United States and other nations. However, several major American congressional investigations into the Central Intelligence Agency, as well as various "kiss and tell" books by former CIA operatives, have cast some light into the dark shadows of intelligence operations. Consequently, much of what we say in this chapter will rely more on American than on other sources, and some of it will be more speculative than most of the rest of this text; it will be informed speculation, to be sure, but speculation nonetheless. (Although several of the newest books on intelligence are "kiss and tell" works by former, or self-described former, Soviet agents, one must exercise enormous skepticism in dealing with such works, which are not only self-serving but perhaps deliberately deceptive as well.) Keeping these caveats in mind, let us examine the "game of nations," modern intelligence work.

intelligence The gathering and analysis of information to be used in national policymaking.

espionage The gathering of national or commercial intelligence or data through various means of surveillance.

covert operations Undercover or covert intelligence-gathering.

The Intelligence Cycle

Intelligence does not exist in a vacuum; nations do not play the "game" for sheer fun, despite the romanticized view of intelligence. The primary purpose of intelligence is to provide vital information for policy-makers to consider before they make decisions that commit their governments and their nations to certain

intelligence cycle The process of taking information and turning it into useful data for policymakers of a nation. The steps involved are: planning and direction; collection; processing; analysis and production; and dissemination.

processes or decisions. Intelligence must always serve policy, or it is an expensive and useless luxury.

While there is no fixed or absolute pattern to the cycle of intelligence practiced by all major governments, international organizations, and corporations around the world, we can examine broadly the **intelligence cycle** followed by the United States. It is important to remember that this cycle can vary with particular governments or agencies, as well as with specific circumstances. A graphic depiction of the cycle and its role in policy-making is in figure 10.1.

Generally, the intelligence cycle includes five major steps: planning and direction; collection; processing; analysis and production; and dissemination. Each

Figure 10.1
The Intelligence Cycle

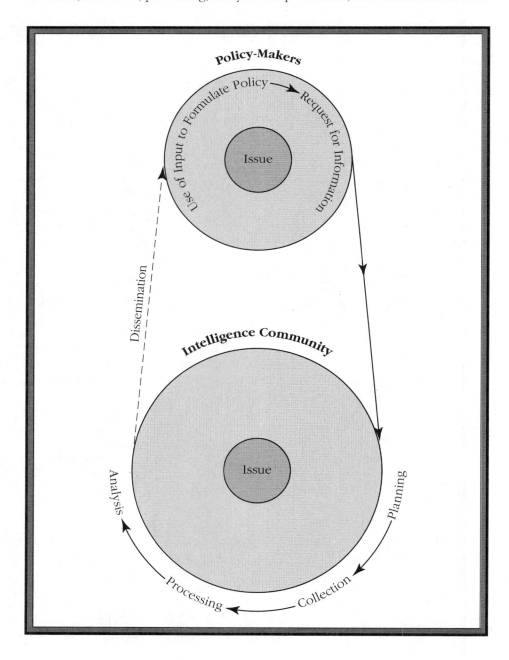

of these steps, independent but linked to the others, is vital (*1995 Factbook on Intelligence* 1995).

Planning and Direction

The first and most vital step of the intelligence cycle is planning and direction. What kind of information is needed? What are the most, and the least, important aspects of the information needed? What is the purpose of the information? What is the time frame for producing usable or useful intelligence?

Not surprisingly, the planning and direction process is often messy, since the acquisition of new intelligence often changes the direction of policy and produces an entirely new set of questions to be answered and issues to be dealt with. This constant feedback guarantees that policy-makers will have the best and freshest information they can acquire, but also creates a high decree of tension in both the intelligence service and the policy-making branch. As one student of intelligence observes, "the producers and consumers [of intelligence] often don't see eye to eye. The president often finds that the intelligence community does not provide him with useful information, while members of the intelligence community often get ambiguous and contradictory guidelines from their superior and the president" (Rosati 1993, 193).

Collection

Once the general outline of the intelligence desired has been determined, then the process of collecting the intelligence begins. This process may involve the use of agents and operatives to dig out information, the intense investigation of public sources to gather and collate information, or the use of technical means of intelligence-gathering, such as satellites.

Processing

Collected information intended for use as intelligence must be processed. Raw data is useless. Before it can play any role, raw information must be translated, decoded, sorted, and so forth. This "cleansing" readies the information for the next stage in the intelligence cycle, analysis and production.

Analysis and Production

The analysis of information and the actual production of usable intelligence is the next step in the intelligence cycle. Analysis of intelligence is an often painstaking process that involves collating recently collected information; comparing it to previous information to determine changes; putting the information within a context (political, economic, military, and cultural); checking and double-checking; and, in the most difficult and important stage of analysis, both reaching conclusions about the subject's capabilities—that is, what a particular nation or individual *can* do—and trying to ascertain what the subject intends to do. This often involves weighing contradictory information to reach informed assessments.

Production of intelligence is the next stage of the intelligence cycle. All that carefully gathered information and informed speculation does no good until it is put into usable form. This might mean producing daily intelligence estimates to be distributed to the highest-ranking officials of the government, background papers intended to provide analytical depth for decision-makers, or archival material to be stored for later use.

Dissemination

The last step of the intelligence cycle is the dissemination of the intelligence. Intelligence does no good at all if it simply languishes on an analyst's desk or in dust-collecting files. Those in charge of the entire intelligence operation must make sure that the intelligence gets into the hands of those who commissioned it and, more important, those who need it—whether they know they need it or not. Using this information, policy-makers come to decisions, decisions that may well carry with them the need for more intelligence, and thus trigger the intelligence cycle again.

The Utility of Intelligence

The gathering and dissemination of intelligence are part of a producer-consumer relationship; therefore, the utility of intelligence, that is, the extent to which intelligence aids decision- or policy-makers, is important. There are actually two separate questions: In what ways does intelligence aid decision-makers, and what attributes make intelligence useful? (Richelson 1989, 4)

While policy-makers establish the broad outlines of policy, intelligence frequently is used to make specific, narrow decisions. For example, policy-makers may be trying to determine whether Nation A should prepare for war on the basis of intelligence gathered about Nation B's military maneuvers. Is Nation B simply on a series of routine maneuvers in a defense-readiness posture? Is there a history of animosity between the two nations, or a pressing issue that has aroused hostility? These and other related questions need to be placed in some sort of intelligence framework to enhance the probability of *quality* decision-making. The Rockefeller Commission on the CIA concluded that "intelligence is information gathered for policy-makers which illuminates the range of choices available to them and enables them to exercise judgment. Good intelligence will not necessarily lead to wise policy choices. But without sound intelligence, national policy decisions and actions cannot effectively respond to actual conditions and reflect the best national interests to adequately protect national security" (quoted in Richelson 1989, 4).

Research and Development

Intelligence also provides much of the impetus for Research, Development, Testing, and Evaluation (RDT&E). For example, in 1968 U.S. intelligence monitored a Soviet submarine moving at a speed faster than the maximum speed conventional intelligence had estimated as possible. The new intelligence and the subsequent revision of thinking about the Soviet submarine fleet led to one of the largest construction programs in Navy history, the SSN668 attack submarine (Richelson 1989, 4–5).

War Plans

Other decisions in which sound intelligence is not just useful but mandatory include the development of nuclear war plans; issuance, resumption, or suspension of foreign aid; conflicts; crisis warning; and the monitoring of compliance to terms agreed upon by various nations.

Nuclear war plans—specifically, the Single Integrated Operational Plan (SIOP) developed by the United States—require a massive intelligence effort to locate potential targets and determine their importance, as well as their vulnerability to destruction. The intelligence input to the development of the SIOP is illustrated by the titles of a variety of documents from which the SIOP was drawn up: the "Nuclear Weapons Support Plan"; the "IOP Reconnaissance Plan"; and the "National Strategic Reconnaissance List", based on the "National Strategic Target List" (Richelson 1989, 5).

Foreign Aid

The issuance, resumption, or suspension of foreign aid also necessitates voluminous intelligence. Policy-makers need to know what the internal and external ramifications for both donor and recipient will be if their nation extends foreign aid to another. The same is true when the question is the resumption or the suspension of aid to another nation. Intelligence should provide evaluations of both the political and the economic repercussions of such action.

Conflict

Conflict and the potential for conflict, not surprisingly, generate the most intensive and extensive intelligence efforts. Nations, like people, desire to survive and to perpetuate themselves. In this sense, conflict includes not only military action but also a host of other perceived external threats. International trade and international negotiations are two prime examples of activities during which national decision-makers must be supplied with excellent intelligence in order to achieve the most favorable treaty terms possible.

In crises, situations that are closely akin to conflicts, nations demand high-quality intelligence. Providing *warning* is a key objective of national intelligence. During the Cuban Missile Crisis, for example, the United States relied heavily on intelligence estimates from the CIA and other sources to detect the shipment of Soviet missiles to Cuba. High-altitude U-2 reconnaissance aircraft first detected the implantation of missile silos on the island, and conducted daily overflights to provide information (not all accurate, it has been determined recently) on the progress of construction. Other data, such as how high or low Soviet ships rode in the water (a clue to the cargo they might be carrying), was also vital. From such intelligence the United States government made its plans to blockade the island of Cuba and prevent the installation and activation of Soviet missiles. Had adequate intelligence not been available, two equally disastrous scenarios would have been possible. Either the United States would not have been aware of the presence of Soviet missiles in Cuba until they were used as a direct threat to the American mainland, or the United States might have assumed that the missiles were already operational and launched a bloody invasion of the island that quickly could have accelerated to all-out nuclear war. In this case the availability of high-quality intelligence, despite the gaps it inevitably possessed, may well have averted global tragedy.

Verification

Checking compliance to international treaties also requires keen intelligence. When the United States and the then Soviet Union concluded the **Strategic Arms**

START Strategic Arms Reduction Treaty, 1991: agreement between the U.S. and the former USSR to reduce strategic forces.

Reduction Treaty (START), on-site verification was part of the bargain for both sides. If one side or the other were not living up to the letter, let alone the spirit, of the treaty, disaster was possible. Both nations possessed the ability to augment their intermittent on-site inspections with high-quality satellite reconnaissance intelligence; the possibilities of "cheating" were severely limited by the availability of such intelligence.

The Technological Capabilities Panel appointed by the Eisenhower administration concisely summarized the overall utility and value of intelligence, particularly in regard to military matters: "If intelligence can uncover a new military threat, we may take steps to meet it. If intelligence can reveal an opponent's specific weakness, we may prepare to exploit it. With good intelligence we can avoid wasting our resources by arming for the wrong danger at the wrong time. Beyond this, in the broadest sense, intelligence underlies our estimate of the enemy and thus helps guide our political strategy" (quoted in Richelson 1989, 6).

Timeliness

As we mentioned above, intelligence appearing too late in the hands of decision-makers is *not* intelligence. Intelligence demands both quality and timeliness. One analyst emphasizes the importance of the latter:

> The approval process for covert action can be time-consuming, exhausting, and nerve-wracking. One recent project was conceived of in May of one year but not carried out until February of the next. in another instance involving a terrorist hijacking of an airplane, a counter-terrorist team in a NATO country requested help from the CIA. The team sought expert advice from the United States on how to blow out the door of the airliner without harming passengers inside, a skill the CIA and one other Western intelligence agency had developed to a high degree. The CIA station in the NATO country cabled Headquarters for permission to help in this covert action. The hours passed. Finally, two days later, with still no decision from the United States, the NATO nation turned to another Western intelligence agency, which responded affirmatively over the telephone on the first call. Within a few hours, paramilitary commandos from this agency were enroute to the hijacked plane and soon successfully blew off the door for the counter-terrorist team. (Johnson 1989, 101–2)

Types of Intelligence

Just as intelligence has many different uses, it also takes many different forms. Among the most important are political, military, scientific and technical, sociological, economic, and ecological intelligence.

Political Intelligence

Understanding the domestic environment of other nations, friendly, neutral, or hostile, is vitally important to decision-making. In determining how to deal with another nation, the more decision-makers can know about its problems, such as internal domestic strife, civil war, economic dislocation, inflation, or depression, the more intelligent and far-sighted their thinking and decisions can be. Even the most simple and obvious pieces of intelligence, like election results or changes in the government, need to be reported and understood. Closed societies, such as the Soviet Union was and the People's Republic of China still is, present extraordinary challenges for the gathering of even basic information about such matters as who holds power within the government. Intelligence agencies often have spent enormous time considering who is standing next to whom in photographs, and perhaps even more important, who doesn't appear in the pictures, in order to track changes in domestic power alignments, and thus potentially in foreign policy. In open societies the problem is often quite the opposite: the deluge of information makes it difficult to extract important intelligence. Imagine the plight of the Russian analyst assigned to watch CNN, NBC, ABC, and CBS coverage of American elections in order to try to predict not only who will win but what it will all mean. It must give a term like "information overload" an entirely new meaning!

Military Intelligence

Military intelligence is necessary in order to design and implement national defense and security postures. Knowing where the opposition's missiles, ships, tanks, and armies are located; how many of each there are; what their capabilities are; what their state of readiness is; and so forth is essential for planning national security and the defense of the national interest. Even without the immediate threat of conflict, intelligence projects are necessary for defense planning and procurement.

It is important to collect and maintain military intelligence not only on one's likely adversaries but also on one's allies. Knowing your friends' weaknesses and strengths will aid your nation in deciding where to allocate defense dollars. And since alliances are not necessarily permanent—as a British prime minister tartly observed, "England has no permanent allies, only permanent interests"—prudence suggests that information on all sides should be as up to date as possible.

Scientific and Technical Intelligence

Scientific and technical intelligence includes information on both civilian and military developments. This area of intelligence is becoming steadily more important; the United States, for example, relied heavily on it during the Persian Gulf War. Knowing what the Iraqi government possessed in terms of chemical and bacteriological weaponry was vitally important. Atomic energy intelligence is likewise an important concern, especially regarding those nations holding nuclear arsenals. Knowing who is likely to join "the club" is of paramount importance. Certainly, the shipment of plutonium to a nation that contends it does not have nuclear capacity is a matter of, at the very least, extreme curiosity.

Sociological Intelligence

Sociological intelligence is closely related to political intelligence. Knowing which groups within a nation are politically active or docile, and why, is often vitally important. For example, knowing why the Serbs, Croats, and Bosnians are locked in deadly conflict requires detailed historical knowledge of their religious and ethnic feelings, within the context of current intelligence. Such knowledge could help analysts predict whether Russia might move away from the West to side with its Serbian cousins. They could then proceed to predict how this would affect

Western nations' policies with respect to Russia. A broad principle regarding sociological intelligence is that simple demographic data—average ages, percentage of males and females, educational levels, etc.—can provide valuable insight into a rival's or an ally's potential strengths and weaknesses.

Economic Intelligence

Economic intelligence is similarly essential. Import-export data, investment rates, employment and unemployment data, and so on are highly prized by any nation that simply wants to trade with another. Economic data are invaluable when nations are establishing trading blocs. In the establishment of NAFTA, for example, Canada, Mexico, and the United States all collected and maintained relevant economic data on themselves and on each other. Economic potential is also vitally important in gauging military capacity, given the close link between industrial capacity and military strength.

Ecological Intelligence

Finally, ecological, or environmental, intelligence is significant. Climate, weather forecasts, types of diseases, surface and subsurface ocean conditions, terrain, and gravitational pull are essential to agricultural and military planning, to name only two uses of such information.

"Static" and "Dynamic" Facts

One student of the intelligence process, Angelo Codevilla, divides intelligence into what he terms "static" and "dynamic" facts. Static facts change so slowly that they can be considered static, or in place over the long term: geography, climate, demography, culture, history, political and economic institutions, and the biographies of leaders. Dynamic facts, in contrast, are subject to constant change; these include the deployment of troops, the distribution of power within a closed political system, yearly harvests, and the intentions of the leadership of any given nation. Codevilla argues that in order for intelligence to be useful it must combine both the statics and the dynamics of any given situation. He points out further that "technical" facts—throw weight of missiles, range of artillery, "hardness" of armor—are also vital in some situations. The mix of all three kinds of facts, Codevilla argues, is essential in order to provide good intelligence that can be used for decision-making. Not all facts are equal, and in any given situation some facts are clearly much more important than others. What determines the importance of facts, Codevilla states, is the timeliness, volume, intelligibility, and inherent relevance of the information; thus, figures on grain harvests might be extremely valuable for trade negotiations but basically irrelevant for determining the purpose of a military buildup (Codevilla 1992, 4–14).

Collecting Information: The Sources of Intelligence

The sources of intelligence fall into two broad types: open, or public, sources and clandestine sources.

In an open society like the United States, a great deal of intelligence can be gathered by the simple process of reading and watching: through newsmagazines, professional and technical journals, computer networks, government documents, radio and television broadcasts, and publications by corporations, especially defense contractors. Even in a relatively closed society like the Soviet Union, professional journals and papers as well as books and memoirs often provided valuable insight for intelligence analysis. In many cases, public sources can provide 80 percent or more of the information that is required. One expert on modern intelligence estimates that the Soviet KGB was able to obtain anywhere from 75 to 90 percent of the information it desired through open or semi-open American sources. Another expert claimed that "if the Kremlin [were] forced to choose between subverting the national security adviser to the President [and purchasing] a subscription to the *New York Times,* it would take the *Times* because the Russians prefer a wide range of information to narrow, if high-level, stuff" (Knightley 1988, 383).

However, often the most valuable information is recognized as such by the guardians of national security, and therefore is secret, tightly held, and closely guarded. To collect such information, agencies must rely upon *clandestine* means and sources. This is the world of intrigue and secret intelligence so romanticized by screenwriters and novelists. Clandestine collection may rely upon either human sources (*HUMINT,* in the trade jargon) or electronic and signal sources (*ELINT* and *SIGINT*).

Human Intelligence

The spy is almost as old as history—certainly as old as the first organized group, be it family or tribe, that needed to find out what its neighbors were up to. Spies and spying have been at the center of the twentieth century's romanticization of intelligence work, in the personas of James Bond and "the spy who came in from the cold," and in reality, spies have often been supremely important in providing vital information.

Spies

Spies are found in astonishing variety: professional intelligence operatives, gifted amateurs, "walk-ins," double agents, and even triple agents. Virtually every nation has one or more agencies, dedicated to intelligence collection and analysis, that employ large numbers of human spies. Professional spies usually operate "under cover"; that is, they assume a job or a title that is legitimate in itself but intended to disguise their true mission and deflect suspicion away from the espionage they hope to commit. Embassies are common hunting grounds for spies placed as commercial or cultural attaches; the general assumption in the world of espionage is that military liaison officers are almost always spies as well. The purpose of this sort of spy is to collect intelligence first of all by observation and then, if possible, by dealing with nationals of the host country who can be "run" as spies. Enormous effort is put into recruiting potential spies from the academic and commercial worlds, effort that may range from offering cash to engaging in ruthless blackmail or even holding families hostage. Such recruits are carefully monitored, with the use of such "trade craft" as prearranged signals, safe houses, drop boxes for messages, and the use of microfilm. Codevilla stresses the importance of matching the agent to the intelligence to be gathered; for example, military intelligence should be collected by someone who has military experience or a military outlook, and engineers rather than poets should attempt to collect information about bridges or rockets (Codevilla 1992, 301–3).

Defectors

Two other kinds of spies are particularly desirable for an intelligence agency: the defector and the "plant," or "mole." Defectors may be motivated by ideology, money, or passion, but they have in common a formerly high enough rank or place or have given them useful information. The handling of defectors is always extremely delicate: is the defector genuine or a plant by the other side, and is the information genuine or a mix of the genuine and the deceptive? Often when a would-be defector approaches an agent about defecting, there is a concerted effort to convince the defector to stay in place rather than defect. In place, he or she can be a continuing source of information; once the defection has taken place, the information is instantly dated, although often useful.

Moles

mole Spy placed by one government or business within another to conduct espionage.

The plant, or the "mole," is one of the most useful, and most dangerous, kinds of spies. An intelligence service will attempt to recruit young men and women from another country, usually by stressing ideological ties, and then coach them to become involved in their own nation's intelligence service while remaining conduits of information for the other side. A **mole** may remain in place for many years, rising to greater and greater prominence within the home government, and doing enormous damage to that government's intelligence apparatus. Perhaps the most famous mole of the twentieth century is Kim Philby, a Cambridge graduate recruited by the Soviet Union in the 1930s; Philby became a high-ranking member of British intelligence, served as liaison between British intelligence and the CIA, and nearly attained the rank of head of British intelligence before he was finally rooted out. Warned that he had been discovered, Philby decamped to the Soviet Union, where he was treated as a hero, and lived out his life as an honored retiree in Moscow. The damage that Philby did to British and American intelligence during the tensest years of the Cold War—or, conversely, the good that he did for Soviet intelligence during this period—is incalculable. The dangers of having an enemy in place are threefold. The mole can provide the enemy with information about the home government's intelligence operations and agents, as well as providing the home agency with false information about the other side's operations and agents. In addition, once a mole has been uncovered, an intelligence agency can virtually disintegrate in a climate of suspicion and hostility, as once-burned, twice-wary agencies launch intensive "mole hunts" to track down and trap any other enemy agents in place.

They Are Expendable

Intelligence agents must always be aware that for the most part their employers consider them expendable. One of the most important principles of running agents is "deniability," that is, the ability of a government to deny any knowledge of an agent or the agent's activities. Very few agents are highly enough placed to be able to call on government resources for protection. A handful of spy exchanges have taken place, generally involving very highly placed agents who can be valuable to their own agencies, at least in part because they have been caught and interrogated, and thus can reveal a substantial amount about both the interests and the techniques of the other side. However, deniability does not always work, and when it doesn't the results can be embarrassing. In 1960, for example, President Dwight D. Eisenhower was about to hold a summit meeting with Soviet premier Nikita Khrushchev when the Soviet Union shot down a U-2 reconnaissance aircraft. The CIA, hoping that the pilot had taken the lethal cyanide capsule he carried in the event of capture, advised the president to deny any American connection with the aircraft. To Eisenhower's chagrin (and fury), the Soviets then trotted out pilot Francis Gary Powers, who had survived being shot down and was more than willing to tell the world that he was employed by the CIA. The summit meeting was summarily canceled, and the Cold War became for a while even icier.

Electronic or Signals Intelligence

With the coming of the information age, emphasis on gathering intelligence has tended to shift from the human to the electronic agent. As early as World War I, British intelligence enjoyed enormous success in intercepting and decoding German diplomatic traffic sent to the Western Hemisphere—albeit by what must seem incredibly primitive methods today. The British simply physically tapped into the transatlantic cable and copied every message sent by Germany to its New World diplomats! One of the most important results of this coup was the interception of the Zimmermann telegram, inviting Mexico to enter World War I as a German ally. The transmission of this explosive telegram to the American government and its publication provided the final impetus for the United States' entry into the war.

World War II saw several major advances in signals intelligence. Most important was the virtual duplication of both the German and Japanese code machines by British and American intelligence agencies. Interception of radio traffic was not the difficult part—there is no way to safeguard a radio frequency per se—but decoding intercepted messages presented enormous difficulties, as agencies switched from hand-encoded to machine-produced ciphers. The Ultra project in Britain and "Operation Magic" in the United States equipped the Allies to intercept and read vital enemy traffic. Although the interception of "hard" military intelligence was comparatively rare, interception of general traffic and diplomatic information was critical. (See Lewin 1978, and Prange 1981, for detailed information on the Ultra and Magic harvests.)

Today, with the proliferation of computers, satellites, and other high-technology toys, signals intelligence (SIGINT) has far outpaced other, more traditional methods of intelligence collection. For every dollar spent on traditional collection, one expert estimates, the United States alone spends seven dollars on sigint. The National Security Agency (NSA) and the National Reconnaissance Office have become in effect "electronic vacuum cleaners," constantly sweeping the electronic spectrum, not just radio transmissions, to intercept a variety of signals. Today signals intelligence can be broken down even further, into communications intelligence (COMINT), electronic intelligence (ELINT), and **foreign instrumentation signals intelligence (FISINT).**

COMINT includes primarily person-to-person communications, via telephone, radio, and satellite transmissions. NSA routinely monitors not only government-to-government communications, but also communications from designated individuals, trade missions, corporations, radical political groups, and

FISINT (Foreign Instrumentation Signals Intelligence) The monitoring of telemetry, or machine-to-people communications.

banks. According to one source, NSA's eleven acres of computers and super-computers can be linked to monitoring devices and programmed to hone in on certain key words selected by intelligence collectors in telex and cable traffic. These computers read the traffic at the rate of four million characters per second, "which means you can read the average daily newspaper before you could pronounce its title" (Knightley 1988, 370–71).

ELINT includes all sorts of electronic communications (radio, television, cellular telephones, and so forth). An important subelement of ELINT is FISINT, the monitoring of telemetry and other sorts of machine-to-people communications, which enables an intelligence agency to intercept data on such things as the performance of rockets and the operating characteristics of satellites. Such information possesses enormous importance in such processes as the verification of arms limitations treaties.

Photography and Satellite Intelligence

Another major area of sophisticated technological intelligence collection is photography, performed in rapid progression from World War II aircraft, then from high-flying secret reconnaissance aircraft such as the U-2 and the SR-71, and now from orbital satellites. Spacecraft such as the American shuttle and the Russian space station could soon be used as well, or may well be in use right now. Today reconnaissance can be conducted not only by traditional photographic methods, but also by radar imaging, with the development of laser imaging not far behind. In addition, both photography and radar imaging can be greatly sharpened and clarified by computer enhancement. Great claims have been made about satellite photography, including the (probably apocryphal) ability of the KH-11 satellite to "read" license plates in the Pentagon parking lot or the brand name of cigarettes in a Soviet officer's tunic. The truth is probably not quite so spectacular. (For details on satellite photography and imaging, see Burrows 1988.)

Intelligence Analysis

The Parameters of Analysis

Once information has been collected by any means, it must be turned into intelligence; it is at this point that the analyst enters the intelligence cycle. Since the purpose of intelligence is to give policy-makers the most accurate and up-to-date information possible, the analyst faces the enormous task of weaving together data and information from all the sources we have discussed in order to see the larger picture and attempt to understand both the current situation and the range of possible future ones. The intelligence analyst occupies the midpoint in the intelligence cycle, organizing material collected from all sources and putting it into usable forms. Although the analyst seldom has been the subject of novels and movies, his or her role is crucial. Analysis is necessary because there is never enough solid information. "There is not likely to be enough data to draw unchallengeable conclusions. After all, analysis is what you do when you don't know for sure" (Codevilla 1992, 16).

Several important factors govern the production of solid and useful intelligence. First, the analyst must understand the purpose of the intelligence, that is, the area of policy that will employ this intelligence. It would do little good, for

Although now obsolete, the U-2 represented a giant step forward in intelligence reconnaisance in the 1950s.

example, to present a detailed analysis of Country A's economy to a group of military planners. Second, the analyst must understand the limits of the information, and must ensure that the users of the intelligence are informed of the gaps, speculations, and assumptions built into the intelligence product. Almost by definition, intelligence must be limited in critical ways, particularly when it comes to issues of intention, and the end user must always be able to keep such limitations in mind. This is what Angelo Codevilla calls the "truth in labeling" problem (Codevilla 1992, 395).

In addition, the analyst must understand the cultures and political traditions of those who are being analyzed. There is no substitute for substantive knowledge in a particular field, from modern Russian to nuclear physics, if an analyst is to produce good analysis. The devil may well be in the details, but the analyst must know those details, possessing intricate understanding of the background (the statics) of what is being analyzed, if the dynamics are to make any sense. As Codevilla points out, "substantive knowledge is the intellectual key to good analysis." He continues, "There is no substitute for political analysts knowing details, for their distinguishing between the accidental and the underlying reality, and for their capacity to determine what is contingent on what" (Codevilla 1992, 387, 410).

The Pitfalls of Analysis

The intelligence analyst also must avoid a number of specific pitfalls.

Mirror Imaging

First is the danger of **mirror imaging,** or assuming that the subject of analysis will act in the same way that the analyst would. "Putting yourself in the other person's shoes" simply does not work, because the "other person" usually is operating in a different culture, with a set of working assumptions entirely different from those of the analyst. The simple fact that an American would react in a certain way does not mean that a Chinese or a Palestinian would do so. The danger of mirror imaging is particularly insidious because it is so natural.

mirror imaging The inclination of nations and people to view others as operating according to their own motivations or goals.

Stereotyping

stereotyping The regarding of all members of a certain group as identical in various attributes.

Allied to the danger of mirror imaging is the danger of **stereotyping,** or generalizing too much from specific known facts to general situations. For instance, although the Russians generally operate at a lower technological level than the Americans and the British, they don't always do so. Consequently, an analysis that assumes Russian technological capacity lags behind that of the United States in a specific situation may well be wrong. Not only is technological stereotyping dangerous; so are other sorts of stereotypes, such as social stereotyping. The images of the authoritarian and disciplined German or the unimaginative Russian may be generally true, but assuming that these images reflect reality at all times and in all cases will have disastrous consequences. Nonetheless, stereotyping is often difficult to avoid. It might be best if all intelligence-gathering and dissemination were conducted in a hermetically sealed environment free of stereotypes and national images, but this is impossible. In fact, stereotypes occur because they often furnish a convenient shorthand way of understanding a situation or a problem. The trick then must be to recognize the stereotype and be willing to move beyond it. Again, this calls upon the imagination and creativity of the analyst, the ability to "think beyond one's own skin."

"Blindness"

"Blindness" is a third major obstacle to sound essential analysis. Herman Kahn pointed out the existence in almost any field, of "educated incapacity," that is, the tendency of people trained in a certain discipline to think within accepted parameters and not to look beyond the assumptions that have defined these parameters, or "the inability of specialists to see things that are obvious to anyone who is not trained to ignore them." Analysts, many of whom are trained academicians in specific fields like economics, political science, or psychology, must be careful to try to look for the unexpected or the unexplained, literally to think beyond themselves. "Some people are so absorbed by an environment, or an idea, that they can see only within reality, or that they are educated *not* to see them." (quoted in Codevilla 1992, 387–89).

Overload

In today's world, the analyst must deal with the problem of overload, of simply having too much information. The sheer volume of information pouring into analysts' hands is overwhelming. As one analyst pointed out, American intelligence analysts in the 1980s had to sift through "an all-source glut: millions of words daily from foreign radio broadcasts, thousands of embassy and attache reports, a stream of communication intercepts, cartons of photographs, miles of recorded electronic transmissions" (Knightley 1988, 379). Merely sorting through this vast array of information is a nearly impossible task, and sorting through it in order to winnow out the most important and most timely material is all but impossible. This flood of information can make it more, not less, difficult to deal with the slipperiest part of analysis, understanding intention. Prior to the Falklands war between Argentina and Great Britain in the summer of 1982, for example, the United States collected enormous amounts of information, including photographs of the Argentinean buildup. However, the most important source of information about Argentinean intentions turned out to be *La Prensa,* the nation's leading newspaper, which as early as January 1982 was publishing front-page articles about the Argentinean intention to take the disputed Falkland islands by force should negotiations with Britain fail (Knightley, 379).

Timeliness

The analyst must make sure that analysis reaches the people who can use it, and who need to know not only the data but its implications, in a timely fashion. Probably the most striking recent example of the failure to accomplish this was on the eve of Pearl Harbor, when Operation Magic convinced its naval intelligence readers that a Japanese attack was imminent. However, by the time this conclusion was reached, it was Sunday morning in Washington, and it was virtually impossible to get the vital warning into the hands of the people who could do something about it. By the time a message raising the level of war-warning in the Pacific finally reached Pearl Harbor commanders, the Japanese raid was over, much of the pride of the Pacific fleet lay smoking and destroyed, and the United States was at war. (See Prange 1981 for more on this topic.)

Politicization

A major danger of the intelligence process is politicization, the tailoring of intelligence reports to fit the assumptions and even the prejudices of the decision-makers. It is tempting to tell policy-makers what they want to hear. This tendency is understandable; after all, policy-makers in all cultures and at all times have tended to reject what they didn't want to hear—any information that either contradicted their working assumptions or interfered with plans they had already hatched without much attention to intelligence sources. Hitler, for example, paid almost no attention to intelligence analysis that indicated the major Allied invasion of France would occur in the Calais area; he was sure that the Normandy landings constituted only a diversion (Codevilla 1992, 335).

Contradicting the leader is not the way to gain favor, money or power for any organization. During the late 1980s and early 1990s, accusations and counteraccusations flew through the corridors of the CIA and filled the columns of American newspapers, as lower-level analysts accused their superiors of tailoring analysis, especially of the Soviet Union, to fit the preconceptions of the Reagan administration. Human nature suggests that there is an inherent tendency to do just that—after all, no one wants to be the messenger who is shot—and the analyst must always guard against the danger. As Codevilla points out, the analyst, being only human, comes "fully equipped with . . . preference for pleasing over truth-telling" (1992, 16). The flip side of this, of course, is that consumers of intelligence always must guard against their own tendencies to shut out what they don't want to hear and to ignore or even fire the analyst who carries in unpopular messages.

Analysis and Collection

One further area of intelligence analysis that has undergone a good deal of reexamination recently is the relationship between the collector and the analyst. In the 1980s American officials expressed considerable concern that it was dangerous for analysts to be linked too closely to either operations or to collection of intelligence. Proposals were made that analysis should be completely separated from collection or from operations, in order to absolutely prevent any politicization of the process. Organizational changes proposed by Congress would have created completely separate and distinct agencies for each part of the intelligence process, but these changes were never implemented.

Today, however, members of the intelligence community are arguing for closer relationships between analysts and collectors. The former head of the CIA under the Clinton administration, James Woolsey, for example, argued that the relationship between collector and analyst must be closer. "I want to see the people who are engaged in intelligence collection working more closely with the analysts, particularly when they are going against some of the very difficult technical targets such as weapons proliferation." This closeness, Woolsey argued, should be literal as well as metaphorical: "I want the person in the CIA who best understands, for example, a particular Middle Eastern state's chemical program, and who may be an expert on chemical warfare, sitting in an office, very near the case officer and perhaps even going out with that officer to question the agent, who is, I hope, stealing secrets from that country's chemical warfare program. I want them to work as teammates, not to split up. Indeed, I'm even moving them into the same corridor at the CIA" (Woolsey 1994, 37).

Analysis and Policy-Making

There is also considerable concern that analysis be separated from the policy-making process. Observers of the intelligence process cite the necessity of keeping the two elements completely separate. As Codevilla points out, intelligence analysts should "stick to facts gained through special sources and methods." The role of the intelligence officer is to provide information for decision-makers, not to suggest policy or to attempt to influence decisions. Intelligence, Codevilla emphasizes, exists "in the service of policy. Intelligence, after all, never exists purely for its own sake" (Codevilla 1992, 391, 4). Woolsey points out that President-elect Clinton specifically directed him and the agency not to become involved in taking policy positions or in giving policy advice. Woolsey adds, "one of the main reasons you have an intelligence community is to provide information outside the policy fray" (Woolsey 1994, 37).

Counterintelligence

counterintelligence Intelligence that works against the activities of other nations' intelligence agencies.

One of the most important branches of intelligence work is **counterintelligence (CI):** literally, working to counter or go against the intelligence activities of other intelligence agencies. Counterintelligence includes the deception of other agencies, the encoding and transmissions of communications, and constant vigilance to ensure that one's own agency has not been penetrated. As Codevilla observes, "the objective of CI is to engage hostile intelligence, control what it knows, and if possible control also what it does." Counterintelligence is offensive in attempting to deceive the other side, and defensive in attempting to safeguard the integrity of the home operations. In effect, counterintelligence represents quality control over intelligence operations (Codevilla 1992, 31–32).

Deception

deception The art of subterfuge.

Deception is one of the most important tools in the CI bag. Its ultimate purpose is to leave enemy intelligence confused and misinformed about what is going on, to manipulate the other side's understanding and perception of reality. Deception is vital because "it can ensure that the enemy's strength is wasted, that your strength is matched against the enemy's weakness. . . . [Thus it] can make the weak strong and make the strong unchallengeable" (Codevilla 1992, 31–32).

Deception can be achieved in a number of ways. One of the most important is to feed false information to the other side, either by deliberately sending out false messages for the other side to pick up, or by using double agents who supposedly work for the opposition but actually are giving them information one wants them to have.

Another chief task of counterintelligence through deception is the protection of one's own information. Encryption, or encoding, of all national traffic, diplomatic, economic, or military, is one aspect of this protection. Thus the huge supercomputers at NSA generate thousands of codes each day, each one virtually unbreakable because it will be used only once, to safeguard the security of American communications traffic. So successful are modern encoding devices that the kinds of spectacular successes that Enigma and Magic made possible are probably gone forever. Cryptography expert David Kahn points out that "for the same amount of money as it spent five years ago, a nation can buy a cipher machine today with double the coding capacity" (In fact, as of this writing the rate of doubling of computer capacity has shrunk from five years to about eighteen months.) What this means is that on a regular basis, as the coding capacity doubles, the number of trials a cryptographer has to make to crack the code is squared. It then becomes virtually impossible to break the new code. Kahn observes that the number of nations whose codes the United States can break is constantly declining: "The window . . . through which NSA . . . and other code breaking agencies can look is constantly closing" (quoted in Knightley 1988, 375). And by implication, the possibilities of reading American codes also are steadily declining. In fact, in recent years the virtual impossibility of cracking codes has led to the use of analyzing both the volume and the flow or routes of opposition traffic as the principal means of attempting to understand what an opponent might be up to (Knightley, 375).

"A Wilderness of Mirrors"

Just as the collections branch of an intelligence service looks for every opportunity to plant agents in the other camp, the counterintelligence branch is on constant alert to discover and neutralize such agents. Anytime an intelligence operation is compromised, counterintelligence must investigate to find out what went wrong. Was it bad planning, was it just bad luck, or did someone give information to the other side? Counterintelligence involves virtually constant suspicion and surveillance of one's own people to safeguard against penetration and to ferret out moles, opposition agents planted within one's own service.

This constant vigilance requires that counterintelligence agents always be on guard and suspicious. The disruption of the other side's intelligence service can be achieved not only by planting a mole there, but also by playing into its suspicions, by inducing the other side to believe there is a mole and thus creating a "molehunt." When a full-scale molehunt is underway, suspicion reigns: everyone's motives, as well as actions, are under the microscope. Normal procedures are virtually impossible. If it gets out of hand, a molehunt can become what former CIA counterintelligence head James Angleton referred to as "a wilderness of mirrors," in which nothing is as it seems, or at least no one can afford to take anything for what it seems to be. This wilderness of mirrors easily generates a maze of paranoia that can paralyze an intelligence agency. In the aftermath of the Kim Philby discovery, British intelligence suffered years of partial paralysis as molehunters accused and counteraccused. Angleton's own extreme suspicion that there must be a highly placed mole in the CIA hobbled critical CIA activities.

A successful mole can be devastating to an agency, however. Kim Philby compromised both British and American intelligence operations at a critical juncture of the Cold War. Aldrich Ames, the recently unearthed CIA mole, is held responsible for the deaths of at least thirty-eight and possibly many more double agents recruited by the CIA from within Soviet and other agencies. While Philby acted from ideological convictions—he had been a convinced supporter of the Soviet Union from his university days onward—Ames apparently acted purely from greed, and was paid large sums of money by the Soviet Union. In addition to conviction and money, blackmail and threats also are used to recruit moles.

Because it can take such a long time for evidence of moles or deception to filter back into an intelligence agency, one intelligence expert suggests that whereas intelligence collectors need imagination, counterintelligence agents need long memories and an understanding of overall operations. "In short, CI people should be a very bright, dispassionate, monkish lot" (Codevilla 1992, 445). And counterintelligence people also must be able to question constantly what is going on in their own agency, constantly examining what they think they know and why they think they know it in order to uncover flaws. "A wilderness of mirrors" may well understate the intricate maze of charge and countercharge possible within the world of counterintelligence.

Covert Operations

One of the areas of intelligence activity that always has drawn a great deal of interest is covert operations, euphemistically called "special activities." The imagination immediately conjures up images of secret agents clad in black, their faces smudged with charcoal, skulking through darkened city streets or steaming jungles, on their way to blow up a vital bridge or hijack a train. An image born partly of World War II exploits and even more of novels, movies, and television, this view of covert operations contains only a grain of truth; the real business of covert operations is often grittier, and sometimes much duller, than this romanticized image.

In many ways, the inclusion of covert action, or special operations, within the realm of intelligence is a fairly recent development, although such activities are as old as human history. In the sense that all foreign policy aims to influence the behavior of another state or another government, covert operations are simply another tool of foreign policy. As Codevilla points out, covert operations will succeed only when they are informed by intelligent policy decisions and set in motion for clear and thoughtful policy reasons. The line between foreign policy relations and covert action is made clear by the term "covert," or "covered." While most diplomatic and foreign policy maneuvering takes place openly, covert activities by definition require a high level of secrecy in terms of their source. The activities themselves will be known—after all, if a foreign government becomes the target of subversion, it knows it—but the source or sponsor of these activities is to remain secret. "[U.S.] covert actions were meant to be *covered* by some stratagem so that they would not necessarily be attributed to the U.S. government [so that the U.S.] could avoid taking responsibility" (Codevilla 1992, 37). In general, foreign policy speaks to another nation's body politic *from the outside,* while the fundamental purpose of covert activities is *"to exercise influence from within—to exercise prerogatives which that body politic normally reserves for its own members"* (Codevilla 1992, 356; italics in original.) Table 10.1 shows at least part of the range of possible covert activities.

According to Codevilla, successful covert activities can enhance a nation's foreign policy: "Intrigue by well-placed agents can . . . reduce the price to be paid for hostile policies, gain allies, keep neutral a country that might otherwise enter a war as an enemy, or even make for deep cooperation beneath a cover of enmity" (Codevilla 1992, 40). Covert activities, then, can be a powerful instrument in the toolkit of international relations. Conversely, the consequences of failed covert operations can range from the embarrassing to the disastrous. And often even successful covert operations can generate unpredictable long-term consequences that ultimately may convert what first appears to be a successful covert operation into an ultimate failure.

Table 10.1
Covert Activities: Examples by Strategy

Military/Paramilitary

Sensitive intelligence collection
    Communications intercept
    Satellite reconnaissance
Indirect action
    Foreign military sales and grants
    Psychological operations
Direct Action
    Assassination
    Invasion

Economic

Sensitive intelligence collection
    Satellite reconnaissance
    Industrial espionage; of private parties and government entities by "friendly" and "unfriendly" actors
Currency destabilization

Ideological

Open broadcast (white) propaganda
False flag (black) propaganda
Disinformation

Diplomatic/Political

Overt intelligence collection
Sensitive intelligence collection
Indirect action
Direct action

Source: (Richelson, 1989)

Codevilla points out that often the success of covert operations is linked to the overall power of the sponsor. Although covert operations often are seen as more beneficial to weak than to strong states, this is not always the case. "Covert action works for the weak not insofar as they are weak but insofar as they are smart." Furthermore, Codevilla goes on, "it works even better for the strong than it does for the weak" (1992, 45).

Operations

Covert activities cover a wide spectrum of operations: one nation may attempt to influence another by propaganda, which can be particularly successful if the propaganda is apparently truthful material that appears in respected local media. Or covert agents may attempt to undermine confidence in a government by undertaking acts of sabotage or even assassination. Perhaps the ultimate act of covert operations is the coup d'etat, the overthrow of the leadership of another state and its replacement by new leadership that is deemed friendlier to the sponsor of the covert action.

During the Cold War, the leaders of the American CIA were particularly enamored of covert operations, seeing them as an effective way to deal with a ruthless foe, communism. Covert activities were "more forceful than diplomacy, less hideous than war." Within two years of its establishment in 1947, the CIA was sponsoring anti-Soviet activities in the Ukraine and Lithuania, attempting to overthrow the communist government of Albania, and spending millions to undermine the Communist Party in Italy. By 1960, according to one estimate, "there was hardly a country in the world . . . —friendly to the United States or otherwise—which did not knowingly or unwittingly play host to a CIA covert action operation" (Knightley 1988, 259). As Knightley points out, covert operations were both attractive and seductive. "The attractions of covert action—the freedom it gave people of ability to exercise power, money, secrecy, the appeal of patriotism, the front line of the Cold War—are greater than those of intelligence evaluation" (1988, 257). However, Knightley is also extremely skeptical about the overall value of covert actions: "Covert action, as a substitute for a coherent foreign policy, turned out to be little more than a gimmick, effective only when the internal forces were *already* moving in the direction that the CIA wished to push them" (1988, 253).

Problems of Covert Operations

The track record of the CIA in covert operations reveals both the difficulties of conducting such activities and the even greater difficulties of predicting their long-range consequences. (Because there is still so little access to Soviet records, and because British records are closed under the Official Secrets Act, we are again focusing on the American model, but we suspect that much of what we say is universally applicable.) For example, one of the CIA's greatest early successes in covert operations was helping to engineer the overthrow of Mohammed Mossadegh, a fervid nationalist Iranian prime minister who was popularly elected, but feared by the U.S. to be too nationalist and too radical in a state so close to the Soviet border and so vital to Western Cold War interests. In 1953 British and American intelligence collaborated to replace Mossadegh with Shah Mohammed Reza Pahlavi, whom Mossadegh had originally ousted. For many years this was presented as a major success. However, when the Shah was in turn overthrown again, this time by Islamic fundamentalists who reviled the United States as the "Great Satan," many inside and outside the American government began to have second thoughts about how successful the policy of subverting Mossadegh had been in the long run. In comparison to the Ayatollah Khomeini, Mossadegh began to look pretty good, at least in retrospect. Of course, the argument can be made that foreseeing the long-term effects of any foreign policy initiative, overt or covert, is often impossible. However, it does seem that covert activities, at least in part because they *are* covert, can more often do long-term damage to national policy.

A second major problem with covert activities is that all too often they tend to career out of control and to cross over boundaries of ethics and legality. As a student of modern intelligence points out, the founders and early operatives of the CIA "believed that they had embarked on a crusade but, ironically, like Marxists, they came to the conclusion that the nobility of their aims justified any means that came to hand." So-called "dirty tricks" became common. According to KGB analysis, "a lot of maniacs were allowed to go off every-which-way and do more or less as they liked. The dirty tricks multiplied. Naturally, if you think in terms of a global struggle, dirty tricks are inevitable, but without control and purpose they become incredibly wasteful and too often counter-productive" (quoted in Knightley 1988, 257). At least one student of the Cold War struggle concludes that in fact the KGB was far less active in covert operations than the United States. "Not a single major KGB covert action—comparable, say, to the Bay of Pigs or the Chile destabilization—has been uncovered. No intelligence service is that good or that lucky for 40 years on the trot, so one is forced to the conclusion that the KGB employs covert action sparingly, if at all" (quoted in Knightley 1988, 270). However, American covert operatives tended to behave as they thought the KGB and other Soviet or communist operatives were behaving. A special commission of the Hoover committee in 1955 claimed, "There are no rules in such a game. Hitherto accepted norms of human conduct do not apply. We must learn to subvert, sabotage, and destroy our enemies by more clever and more sophisticated, and more effective, methods than those used against us" (quoted in Knightley 1988, 270).

Thus, for example, the CIA plotted a variety of means, some of them approaching the loony tunes level, to assassinate Fidel Castro of Cuba. It participated in Operation Phoenix, the systemic assassination of as many as seventeen thousand suspect or not sufficiently loyal local officials in South Vietnam. The CIA also is accused of becoming involved in the international drug trade in Vietnam (see McCoy 1991), and of continuing its involvement in drug dealings in Latin America as part of its operations against the Sandinistas in Nicaragua (see Levine 1993). Certainly, there are hints that the KGB sponsored, if it did not directly engage in, similar activities, ranging from the attempted assassination of Pope John Paul II to the encouragement of the narcotics trade as a way of weakening American will.

The danger of all this, of course, is that in attempting to destroy an enemy by any means, an intelligence agency indulging in covert activities can become almost exactly like the enemy it is battling. According to Knightley, not only was covert activity often unsuccessful or even counterproductive during the Cold War;

worse, it threw away the United States' moral advantage over the Soviet Union. The United States had a reputation for respecting the sovereignty and the right to self-determination of other countries. The CIA's use of covert action led many to believe that there was little to choose between the United States and the

Soviet Union. In those countries, notably the Third World ones, where most CIA covert actions took place, people no longer distinguished between the CIA and the KGB; both were symbols of imperialism. Unwittingly, the American covert action operators had acquired the faces of their Soviet opponents. (Knightley 1988, 255–56)

A Caveat to the Student

This section on covert activities illustrates vividly the problem of attempting to discuss intelligence as part of foreign policy and international relations. By definition, most intelligence operations are shrouded in secrecy; consequently, we probably know a great deal more about the failures, whose consequences become all too visible, than about the successes, which often must remain secret if they are to continue to succeed. The wilderness of mirrors extends far beyond any single branch of intelligence work.

Intelligence Failures

Under close analysis, many of what are termed "intelligence failures," particularly in the related areas of analysis and policy-making, are less failures in the gathering and analysis of information than in its dissemination and use. Intelligence failures stem from three primary causes: failure in perspective, pathologies of communication, and paradoxes of perception (Betts 1977, 61–62).

According to Richard Betts, one of the best-known and most respected American scholars on intelligence, "Military disasters befall some states, no matter how informed their leaders are, because their capabilities are deficient. Weakness, not choice, is their primary problem. Powerful nations are not immune to calamity either, because their leaders may misperceive threats or miscalculate responses" (Betts 1977, 61). Betts continues,

> Optimal decisions in defense policy [author's note: in *all* policy] therefore depend on the use of strategic intelligence: the acquisition, analysis, and *appreciation* of relevant data. In the best known cases of intelligence failure, the most crucial mistakes have seldom been made by collectors of raw information, occasionally by professionals who produce finished analyses, but most often by the decision makers who consume the products of intelligence services. Policy premises constrict perception, and administrative workloads constrain reflection. Intelligence failure is political and psychological more often than organizational. (Betts 1977, 61)

Despite our understanding of the factors that result in perceived intelligence failure, we must remember that such failures can be catastrophic. If weather forecasts are correct 70 percent of the time, the weatherman is a hero. If an intelligence analyst's predictions are correct 70 percent of the time, the 30 percent failure rate could be disastrous in a nuclear world. Wars are caused by much smaller human errors—for example, the misperceptions that led to the outbreak of World War I.

As we have emphasized above, data transformed into intelligence is useless unless it reaches policy-makers *when they need it* (and all too often they needed it yesterday). This view of the problem, according to Betts, leaves room for optimism, because it implies that procedural curatives can eliminate the dynamics of error. For this reason, official post mortems of intelligence blunders inevitably produce recommendations for reorganization and changes in operating norms (Betts 1977, 63).

The term "paradox of perception" applied to intelligence failures might also be stated, "The more you try to fix something, the more goes wrong." Organizational reform produces additional layers of bureaucracy that inhibit the speed and quality of intelligence. Replacing new and untested systems with older systems whose flaws you now recognize is not necessarily a good answer. It might be best to do as President John Kennedy once said: "We won't repeat the mistakes of our predecessors. We'll make our own!"

Betts offers some sage, although not always reassuring, advice on intelligence failures. First, he writes, in the simplest situation, the intelligence system can avert policy failure by presenting relevant and undisputed facts to nonexpert principals who might otherwise make decisions in ignorance. Perhaps, he points out, it is not the answers that the intelligence community must bring to the table, but the important questions about the limitations of knowledge and the dangers of such ignorance (Betts 1977, 88). Second, Betts advises us to accept the fact that intelligence failures are natural and will occur again. Unlike our personal failures, intelligence failures can have global consequences, but we need to learn to live with them. In short, Betts writes, we must learn to tolerate disaster (1977, 63).

Global Intelligence Structures

Virtually every state has a national intelligence community of some sort. In this section we will briefly examine the intelligence structures of some of the major global players in order to provide some kind of insight into the actual application of the theories we have outlined above.

Great Britain

Until the early twentieth century, no state had permanent intelligence machinery. Great Britain was the first to establish such a structure in 1909, in response partly to perceived German threats and partly to the urging of a small body of individuals who mixed genuine intelligence concerns with overblown romantic visions evoked by a spy novelist.

Today the original British structure has evolved into two principal agencies, MI5 and MI6. MI5, charged with the conduct of domestic security, concentrated on counterintelligence for most of its existence, but with the end of the Cold War has now shifted its focus to terrorist threats. According to a recently released pamphlet from the agency, the Irish Republican Army and the threat it poses consume 44 percent of resources of the MI5, with surveillance of international terrorist threats accounting for another 26 percent. Employing some two thousand people, MI5 now works closely with Scotland Yard.

MI6 is concerned primarily with the gathering and analysis of foreign intelligence. The British are far more close-mouthed about their intelligence agencies than most other Western nations. Budgets are classified, with the details kept even from Parliament, and operations, both successful and failed, are shrouded behind laws, like the Official Secrets Act, that make it a crime to publish details about their activities. For several generations the British intelligence services have been "the most reclusive and monkish of the Western intelligence agencies, a closed and secret society of faceless bureaucrats, most of them men, toiling from drab and unmarked office buildings in deepest London." (Schmidt 1993) These details at least have begun to change. The head of MI5 is now a woman, Stella Rimington, and both MI5 and MI6 are moving into new quarters in London: a glossy new office building bristling with antennas for MI6 and a completely refurbished Edwardian building for MI5, at an estimated combined cost of $660 million. Clearly the British government foresees a bright and busy future for intelligence operations, despite the end of the Cold War (Schmidt 1993; Knightley 1988).

The United States

The United States' intelligence apparatus is both much newer and much more convoluted than Britain's. An early agency created to intercept and decode foreign cable traffic was shut down by the secretary of state in 1929 with the acerbic comment, "Gentlemen do not read one another's mail." That may be true, but intelligence has never been a gentleman's game. World War II and the Cold War convinced American leaders that a centralized intelligence community was necessary. One of the major reasons for the failure of intelligence to provide adequate and timely warning about Pearl Harbor, for example, was the scattering of material among several agencies. Consequently, as part of gearing up to the fight the Cold War, the American government established the Central Intelligence Agency (CIA) in 1947. Its director was simultaneously head of the agency and director of intelligence for the entire United States government. Initially, the CIA charter dealt only with the collection, analysis, and distribution of intelligence; however, agency leaders, still buoyant from their World War II experiences in secret operations under the OSS (Office of Strategic Services), quickly expanded CIA duties to include covert operations as well. The command responsibilities with the current CIA are shown in figure 10.2.

In addition to the CIA, not only do the American military services still have their own intelligence functions, but so do a number of government bureaucracies, such as the State Department and the Commerce Department. The Cold War also saw the creation of further agencies, such as the National Security Agency and the National Reconnaissance Office. Unlike the CIA, which has opened up to some extent (for example, for many years the exit from the George Washington Parkway to the CIA headquarters building in Washington was marked "BPR," or "Bureau of Public Roads;" today a sign proclaims "CIA"), but the NSA and the NRO remain highly secret. Known as the Puzzle Palace for its role in unlocking codes and encrypting American traffic, the NSA was established not by Congress, but by a secret presidential directive in 1952. For many years the U.S. government refused to acknowledge its existence, leading to jokes that "NSA " stood for "No Such Animal" and "Never Say Anything."

In theory, both the CIA and the NSA are barred from any sort of domestic operation, although it is widely believed that both have crossed that line in the past. Within the United States, the Federal Bureau of Investigation has jurisdiction over counterintelligence; that splitting of responsibilities has led to frequent and sometimes acrimonious conflict between the CIA and the FBI about jurisdiction and procedure.

The National Reconnaissance Office oversees the deployment, tracking, and analysis of spy satellites. In 1994 the NRO found itself in congressional hot water when legislators suddenly "discovered" that a huge office complex they thought

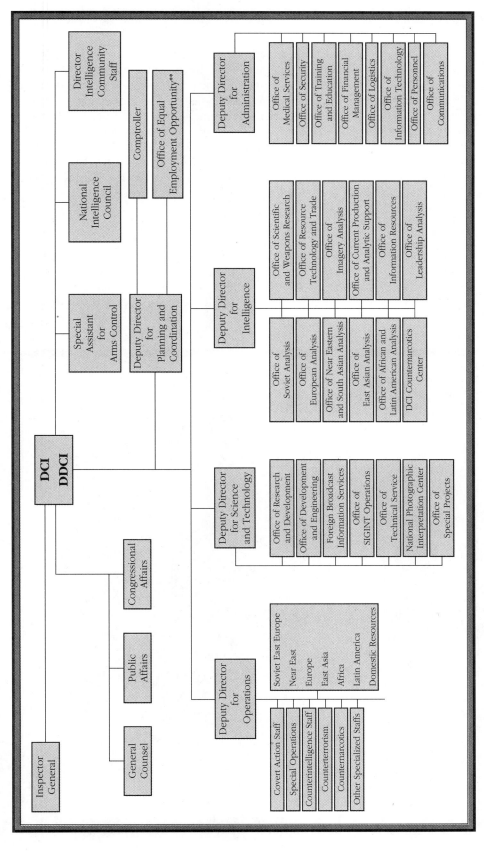

Figure 10.2 **Director of Central Intelligence Command Responsibilities***

Source: Ronald Kessler, *Inside the CIA* (New York: Pocket Books, 1992), xxxvi–xxxvii.

*DIC Counterintelligence Center; DCI Counterterrorist Center and DCI Counternarcotics Center

**Also serves as Special Assistant to the DCI for Affirmative Employment

was being built for Rockwell International was actually the NRO's posh new head-quarters. Members of Congress complained that they had not known that NRO was spending some $310 million or more to construct the "stealth" building. Virtually all intelligence spending is shrouded in secrecy as part of the Pentagon's "black" budget, but analysts of the intelligence community estimate that the United States spends roughly $28 to $30 billion annually on the collection of intelligence. The NRO, with its high-tech, high-cost satellite responsibility, is the largest single intelligence spender, at an estimated $6.5 billion, more than twice the CIA's budget (Kranish 1994; see also Bamford 1983, for more on American intelligence). Figure 10.3 illustrates the various agencies involved in U.S. intelligence.

Russia

It is more difficult to write about the Russian intelligence and security apparatus because, with the collapse of the Soviet Union, it is very much in a state of flux. The tradition of secret services and their role in domestic oppression goes far back into Russian history. As early as 1565, Ivan III (Ivan the Terrible) formed the

Figure 10.3
United States Intelligence Structure
Source: 1995 Factbook on Intelligence, Washington, D.C.: Central Intelligence Agency, 1995. Internet http://www.odci.gov/cia/publications/facttel/index.html (downloaded Feb. 16, 1996).

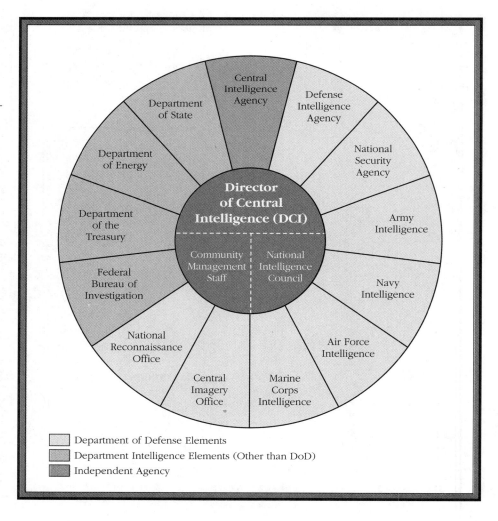

Central Intelligence Agency

Defense Intelligence Agency

Department of State

National Security Agency

Department of Energy

Army Intelligence

Director of Central Intelligence (DCI)

Department of the Treasury

Community Management Staff

National Intelligence Council

Navy Intelligence

Federal Bureau of Investigation

Air Force Intelligence

National Reconnaissance Office

Central Imagery Office

Marine Corps Intelligence

☐ Department of Defense Elements
☐ Department Intelligence Elements (Other than DoD)
☐ Independent Agency

Wired Spooks

In some ways CIA agents would seem to be the last people you would expect to find online. However, the CIA has recently gone online in a big way.

Surfers cruising the Internet can easily find the CIA Homepage, where the agency makes available two of its most important unclassified publications, *The World Fact Book* and *The Fact Book on Intelligence*. Its address, in case you haven't been there already, is HTTP://www.ic.gov.

However, the CIA also sponsors its own highly classified network, Intelink, modeled in many ways on the Internet. The bottleneck between the collection and analysis of data and the dissemination of intelligence to policy-makers has finally been broken. No longer must White House, Pentagon, or State Department officials wait for physical delivery of intelligence by the "pizza truck," which unfortunately had no immunity from Washington's infamous traffic jams.

Now anyone wired to the Intelink can simply call up the needed information, including real-time satellite photos. The Intelink hardware is staggering: two floors of mainframes at the agency's Langley headquarters, constituting a maze so complex that

GLOBAL PERSPECTIVES

numbers and letters are painted on the walls to ensure that technicians do not become hopelessly lost. Here are stored more than four trillion bytes of secret information—the equivalent of a stack of documents more than thirty miles high. Thirty-five separate intelligence agencies feed data into Intelink, but only three thousand users have access to the secret and top-secret files. State-of-the-art encryption and special telephone lines protect the security of the Intelink system, and the system itself is physically separate from the Internet link and its possible vulnerability to hackers.

Additionally, the CIA is discovering how to surf the Internet for information—even Russia is now publishing many of its economic statistics on the Net, for example, in order to attract investors. And electronic bulletin boards can prove to be unexpected treasure troves, as one computer security expert recently discovered. After posing a simple question about the efficacy of stealth technology on an electronic bulletin board for aerospace engineers, he received responses, and hard data, from more than a dozen engineers and scientists—and an Air Force officer. It was, the bemused questioner says, "more information than I ever thought I would ever need" (Waller 1995, 63–64).

Oprichnina, whose black-clad members carried out a reign of terror against anyone suspected of disloyalty to the new Tsar, massacring entire cities. Tsarist governments continued to maintain political police, with the Okhrana serving that function at the time of the 1917 revolution. Within a few weeks of the Bolshevik Revolution that year, Vladimir Ilyich Lenin established the new Soviet Union's first secret police, the Cheka. During the lifespan of the Soviet Union, the secret police would operate under a number of titles (GPU, OGPU, NVD, NKVD) before emerging as the KGB in 1954.

The **KGB** (Komitet Gosudarstvennoi Besopasnosti, or **Committee for State Security**) was charged with both domestic and international intelligence. At its largest the KGB employed more than seven hundred thousand people in a complex organization (see figure 10.4). Its internal operations made the KGB feared and often hated by the Soviet people, particularly since it dealt with political dissidents as well as spies and often went well beyond the theoretical limits of the Soviet constitution. With its wiretapping, bugging, and even urging of children to turn informant on their parents, the KGB "turned the entire Soviet Union into a sort of giant electronic ear." Over the decades, the KGB and its predecessors "hauled opponents of the regime off to prison camps, suppressed dissident writers,

KGB The former Soviet intelligence agency that paralleled the CIA of the United States.

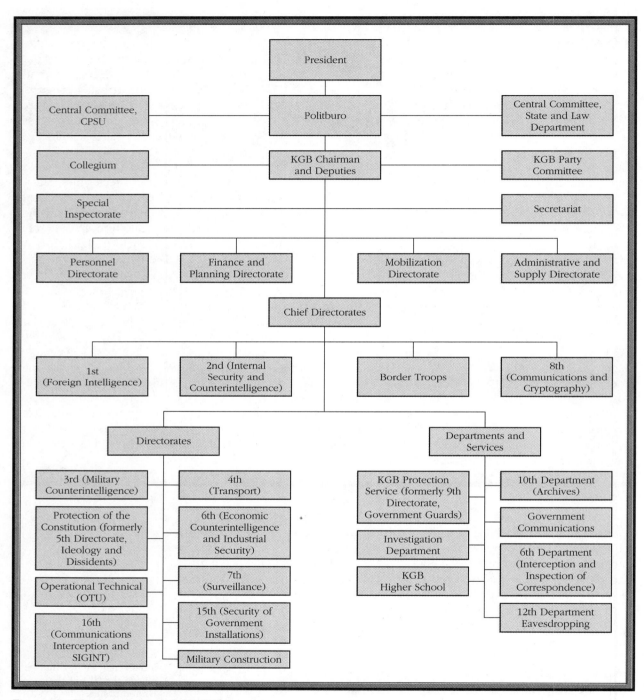

Figure 10.4 The Organization of the KGB
Source: Desmond Ball and Robert Windren. "Soviet Signals Intelligence (Sigint): Organisation and Management." *Intelligence and National Security.* vol. iv (1989), no. 4. and Gordievsky.

and . . . served as the secret police of a system that claimed millions of victims." It was "the jackboot on the stairs, the instrument of terror that could, in an instant, pluck people from the safety of their homes and send them to some Siberian gulag [prison camp]." Under Stalin particularly, the KGB earned and deserved the title

"Ministry of Fear" (Wise, 1992). The KGB was especially skillful at "disinformation," or black propaganda—the publishing of false articles to destroy confidence in Western leaders and institutions—and also at "running" second-hand intelligence operations such as using the Bulgarian intelligence agency to attempt to assassinate Pope John Paul II. Today the KGB has vanished along with the Soviet Union itself. In its place are two separate institutions, one charged primarily with foreign intelligence and the other with the maintenance of internal security.

The disbandment of the KGB has left thousands of trained agents looking for jobs in which they can employ their hard-gained skills. It is safe to assume that other nations have hired former KGB agents in large numbers. Former soviet republics, of course, would use these agents as the basis for their own intelligence services. As the acting director of the CIA ruefully observed in 1991, "There are at least three KGB's today, and perhaps as many as 18" (Wise in 1991, 68). In addition to contributing to this proliferation of intelligence agencies in newly created states, a number of KGB agents may well be offering their services for sale on the open market. Within the past four years there have been frequent press reports of advertisements in European newspapers supposedly placed by former KGB agents anxious to find work for either national or corporate employers.

Is the Russian intelligence apparatus up to its old tricks? In the spring of 1995 the Russian parliament passed, and President Boris Yeltsin ultimately signed, legislation giving the Federal Counterintelligence Agency broad new powers to conduct searches without warrants, to carry out electronic surveillance, and to resume gathering foreign intelligence. Critics immediately raised warning flags that this legislation represents a revival of the KGB and a major threat to human rights and privacy (Williams 1995).

The People's Republic of China

The importance of intelligence has long been acknowledged in China. In the fifth century B.C., the great military philosopher Sun Tzu wrote about the value of accurate and timely intelligence for both statecraft and military affairs. Thus, "even in ancient times China had developed and documented an understanding of intelligence needs and practices for military and diplomatic activities" (Eftimiades 1994, 3). Not surprisingly, the contemporary People's Republic of China also understands and appreciates the role of intelligence. However, in the PRC the intelligence process goes beyond simply "informing statecraft"; as Nicholas Eftimiades, the leading public scholar of Chinese intelligence practices, notes, the PRC's intelligence apparatus is "inextricably linked to the foreign policy decision-making process and internal methods of economic and political control" (Eftimiades, 4).

Contemporary China's most important civilian intelligence agency, the Ministry of State Security (MSS), came into being in 1983 as the result of combining intelligence and security functions from two other agencies, the Ministry of Public Security (MPS) and the Investigations Department of the Communist Party's central committee (Eftimiades 1994, 17). Figure 10.5 depicts the structure of the MSS. The MSS's most important goals are the acquisition of foreign high technology, the identification and influence of foreign policy trends, and the monitoring of dissidents, both domestic and external. (Eftimiades, 14).

Apparently completely separate from the civilian intelligence operations is military intelligence, centered in the Military Intelligence Department of the General Staff Department of the People's Liberation Army, also known as the Second Department (Eftimiades 1994, 75), In addition to attempting to gather information in standard categories (order of battle, biography, weapons, targeting, operational

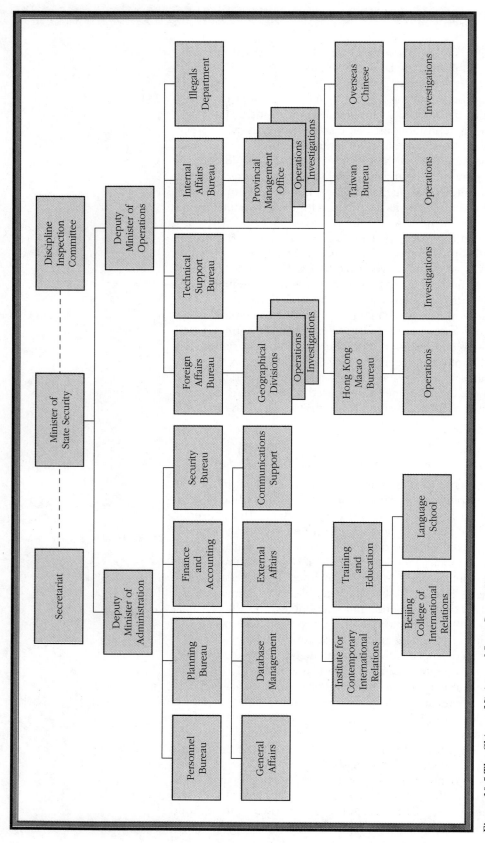

Figure 10.5 The Chinese Ministry of State Security

Source: Nicholas Eftimiades, *Chinese Intelligence Operations* (Annapolis, Md.: Naval Institute Press, 1994), 24.

plans), the MID is deeply involved (in fact, is considered by some to be China's dominant agency) in the field of high technology (Eftimiades, 76–77).

In addition to the two dominant intelligence structures, the MSS and the MID, China also possesses several more or less second-level organizations with at least some intelligence responsibilities. Among these organizations are the General Political Department of the People's Liberation Army, the Commission of Science, Technology, and Industry for National Defense, the Investigations Department of the Chinese Communist Party, the New China News Agency, and the Political Legal Leading Group of the Chinese Communist Party, which ostensibly is responsible for overall management of the Chinese intelligence community (Eftimiades 1994, 103–10).

Despite China's long tradition of emphasis on the importance of intelligence and the presence of multiple civilian and military intelligence agencies, Eftimiades presents a generally negative assessment of overall Chinese intelligence activities. "Like much of the PRC government, China's intelligence services just do not work—or at least very well." Reflecting problems in the general society, the intelligence community is bogged down in bureaucracy and red tape. The omnipresence of the Party, perceived as necessary for control, is a major impediment to efficient operations. Consequently, Eftimiades writes, "PRC intelligence operations in Western nations are characteristically poorly conceived and executed." Nonetheless, Eftimiades notes, several factors argue that China's success not only exists but also will increase. The sheer volume of Chinese intelligence activity virtually guarantees some successes. Additionally, the dismal ignorance in the West of Chinese language, history, and culture make any sort of counterintelligence activities difficult. They really need not be so difficult: Eftimiades points out that a peculiarity of Chinese government in general, and intelligence services in particular, is "their inability to keep most information secret." China's society consists of elaborate interlinked networks of family and friends, and information tends to flow freely along these conduits. "As a result, even the most closely guarded government secrets can be heard on the streets of Beijing." Americans tend to dismiss such second- and third-hand information as "rumors intelligence" *(RUMINT)*, when in fact close analysis and comparison of it could provide valuable insights.

Eftimiades reaches two general conclusions about the evolution of Chinese intelligence. First, it will become more sophisticated and more effective. And, second, Chinese intelligence services will continue to play a large and perhaps even expanded domestic political role in repressing political dissent and maintaining tight levels of control (Eftimiades 1994, 113–16).

Industrial Espionage: Wave of the Future?

One of the fastest-growing and most important areas of intelligence operations is the field known as **industrial espionage,** the theft of information about both business and technology. Given the current shift of international competition from the military to the economic playing field, no one should be surprised to discover that information on manufacturing computers or on the details of complex information systems is now as valuable as battle plans of armies.

industrial espionage Commercial spying for information on product/service development, data, sources, etc.

This industrial spying can take two distinct forms: public and private. Several governments, including those of France and Japan, are well known for conducting extensive industrial espionage activities. In 1993 the U.S. government revealed the existence of a twenty-one page document apparently issued by the French government targeting a number of American companies, especially in the aerospace industry. Top priority was given to companies that competed directly against French companies in the international marketplace (Jehl 1993). According to a former director of the CIA, Stansfield Turner, "The French are the most predatory [intelligence] service in the world now that the old Soviet Union is gone." And the French apparently see little reason to keep their industrial espionage efforts

Shocked, Simply Shocked

GLOBAL PERSPECTIVES

Abandoning the world of cloak-and-dagger espionage for a foray into economic and industrial espionage may not be quite as simple as it may have seemed for the CIA. In March 1995 the French government was shocked, simply shocked (*à la* Claude Rains' sly police chief in the classic film *Casablanca*) to discover that CIA agents had carried out extensive economic espionage in France. Five Americans, reportedly all CIA agents and including the former station chief, had apparently bribed civil servants to learn French negotiating postures and tried to buy technical secrets from workers for the state telecommunications company. In a major flap, directly related to problems in domestic French politics, the influential newspaper *Le Monde* published a series of counterintelligence documents detailing American activities.

Although the agency neither confirmed nor denied the truth of these allegations, many in the intelligence community were shocked, simply shocked that the French chose to go public with the accusations. For one thing, even allies routinely spy on one another; for another thing, the French secret service is especially notorious for industrial and economic espionage, including the ransacking of American businessmen's hotel rooms and the bugging of their seats on Air France. And the CIA has certainly made no bones about its shift from Cold War espionage to economic spying. While the American intelligence agency concentrates on gathering general information about trade policy and so forth, its French counterpart works on behalf of specific French companies—many of which are wholly or partially government-owned.

What *was* different—and shocking—about this episode was that the French chose to go very, very public about it, demanding that the five accused agents leave France. While the publicity seemed

clearly designed to deflect public attention from a scandal within the government that was highly embarrassing during an election year, it may have backfired.

At the same time the public flap has provided fuel for the current controversy raging in the U.S. about what the future of the CIA should be with the Cold War over. Agency officials have seized eagerly on the idea of economic espionage and claim to have saved American businesses several billion dollars already, but critics see this new emphasis as primarily a ploy to justify continued and even enlarged funding for an outmoded agency. First, these critics question whether operatives recruited and trained for the Cold War have the aptitude for economic espionage. Should "covert action spooks" now be out looking for French negotiating positions? Second, critics ask whether such espionage is in fact really profitable. "France's own experience shows that short-term commercial gain is not worth the moral and entrepreneurial costs involved," according to one observer, who continues, "Being unlike France has made America the world's greatest economic power." This critic goes on: "Most of what we need to know about France we can find out by buying *Le Monde*. Unfortunately, it turns out we learn a great deal we need to know about the CIA from *Le Monde* as well."

While the controversy in France has died down, in part because of Ambassador Patricia Harriman's haughty "let them eat cake" response to the French government, the controversy about the future role and utility of the CIA seems sure to continue. War may be hell, but it seems that peace doesn't rank very far behind, at least for some people. (For more details, see Burns 1995; "France Accuses Yanks of Spying" 1995; "France Investigates Spy Leak" 1995; "French Claim 5 Americans Were Spying" 1995; Hoagland 1995; Watson 1995.)

secret. Pierre Maríon, the former head of the Direction Générale de la Sécurité Extérieure (DGSE), the French equivalent of the CIA, minced no words when he said, "In the technological competition we are competitors. We are not allies." He also stated that in the early 1980s, while he ran the DGSE, he had established a special unit of some twenty-five agents to help the French aerospace, telecommunications, computer, and biotechnology industries, all of which are partially owned by the French government (Greve 1992). In the same vein, Japan's Ministry of International Trade and Industry (MITI) is widely suspected of extensive espionage operations, particularly through its subsidiary Japan External Trade Organization (Schweizer 1993, 80).

Estimates of the cost to the United States alone of such industrial espionage range from a low of $24 billion a year to a high of $100 billion a year (Lee, 1993; Schweizer 1993, 24). Actual costs may be much higher than these estimates; many companies are reluctant to report such incidents because reporting will reveal their own weaknesses and failures, information any organization is reluctant to make public. In any case, all experts agree that both the amount and the cost of industrial espionage will continue to rise.

Although governments are active in the area of industrial espionage, the field is also wide open to companies and individuals. For example, in the 1980s Japan's Hitachi conducted a sophisticated campaign against IBM in order to steal technology secrets (Schweizer 1993, 46–65). In less blatant attempts to gain valuable information about competitors, companies frequent "raid" their competitors' personnel to hire away those with inside knowledge of cutting-edge developments.

One of the most notorious cases of this in recent years was the defection of a high-level General Motors executive and seven of his closest associates to Volkswagen of Germany, and the concurrent attempt by VW to recruit at least forty other GM executives. At the center of this scandal stands Jose Ignacio ("Inaki") Lopez de Arriortua, GM's worldwide purchasing chief, known for his role in cost-cutting at GM. Lopez was about to be named head of GM's North American operations when he announced that he was leaving to join VW. Not only did Lopez and his associates carry with them detailed knowledge of GM's strategic planning, but they apparently also carried a huge cache of documents providing details about GM operations and plans. Volkswagen announced that all such sensitive documents had been destroyed, but German police discovered at least four cartons of GM documents in the apartment of a Lopez associate (Burger 1993; "Volkswagen Admits GM-Leak Possibility" 1993). Understandably, GM has remained silent about the potential or actual damage done by either Lopez's defection or the "destroyed" documents.

The recent increase in such industrial espionage should surprise no one. For one thing, industrial espionage is not exclusively a modern phenomenon. Nations and individuals have long used such espionage as a short-cut in industrial or economic development. In fact, one of the most spectacular and important of all examples of industrial espionage took place in the late eighteenth century. Recognizing that the United States lagged far behind England in the Industrial Revolution, American entrepreneurs tried to induce English persons with knowledge of such crucial areas as machine spinning and weaving to come to the United States. In fact, so serious was the threat that the English government clamped a lid on attempts by artisans to emigrate to the United States, and customs agents routinely searched baggage to ensure that no one was smuggling diagrams or blueprints out of the country. Offers of large cash rewards for such information finally paid off when a young Englishman named Samuel Slater, highly knowledgeable about the construction of textile factories, came to the United States armed with nothing but a keen memory. Slater's knowledge, combined with cash from an entrepreneur, not only provided the foundations for the American textile industry but also launched the young nation on the path of industrial development.

However, several factors make industrial espionage more prevalent, more difficult, and more profitable today than ever before. For one thing, the end of the Cold War seems to mean that international competition will be less focused on military affairs and far more intense in the economic area. Just as water seeks its own level, intelligence tends to move toward the most important and prominent targets. In addition, the communications revolution has left corporations vulnerable to espionage, through means from the interception of communications and the penetration of computer systems to the easy use of fax machines to send information from company offices to those of their competitors. Large numbers of surveillance devices developed for government intelligence work are now available on the open market, including listening devices, bugs, miniature and subminiature cameras, tiny TV cameras, and pocket-sized copying machines. However, at least one expert contends that the number of one method of industrial espionage in the United States today is far more low tech: rifling through

Although microwave relay systems such as the one pictured are at the heart of modern communications, they are vulnerable to interception and decryption by agencies like the National Security Agency.

garbage bins and dumpsters to find copies of vital documents. And this method is perfectly legal, according to a 1988 Supreme Court ruling (Lee 1993). A third important factor in the rise of industrial espionage is the surplus of well-trained intelligence agents whom the end of the Cold War has left unemployed. Not only do such agents possess the skills to carry out industrial espionage, but they may also be addicted to the thrill of intelligence work. According to one individual who made the transition from military to commercial intelligence, "The lifestyle is addictive. "It's like a venereal disease; once it gets in your blood you never get rid of it" (Marlowe 1993).

The executive director of a nonprofit organization called Business Espionage Controls and Countermeasures adds two other reasons for the proliferation of industrial espionage. Because of increased speed in product development and tougher international competition, he says, information has become much more valuable than it used to be. In addition, he cites lower ethical standards in business generally as technical innovation outpaces ethical guidelines (Lee 1993). Another factor undoubtedly is the attenuated loyalty to corporations that inevitably accompanies downsizing and the realization that no jobs are permanent and secure. A final factor in the rise and success of industrial espionage is that relatively few firms, at least in the United States, have been attuned to the possibilities of such espionage or have taken steps to prevent it.

It seems reasonable to conclude, then, that industrial espionage will continue to be a growth industry for governments, corporations, and individuals, and that it will probably spawn a second growth industry dedicated to the protection of proprietary secrets, projects under development, marketing campaigns, and corporate strategic planning.

Intelligence and Democracy

Innate Tension

The tension between intelligence operations and democracy is a continuous and serious problem. While democracy calls for, and thrives on, openness, intelligence operations demand secrecy, in both the safeguarding of one's own vital information and the safeguarding of operations against other nations' secrets. One analyst of intelligence operations puts it this way: "The problem of secrecy in American democracy is chronic. Intelligence . . . has been vital to the growth and preservation of the United States. At the same time, since intelligence requires secrecy to be effective and therefore limits openness, it has represented a threat to democratic society" (Ameringer 1990, xi).

Democracies have been perceiving and reacting to this threat for a long time. In England, the scales have been weighted on the side of secrecy, with the Official Secrets Act proscribing discussion of anything designated as secret. As one skeptic points out, this has permitted British intelligence to become "the custodians of an enormous warehouse of scandal." After all, "their files contain all that is most shameful in the national memory—assassination plots, lawbreaking, conspiracies against elected governments, and the full extent of Soviet penetration" (Greengrass 1988, vii). However, occasionally determined individuals have found ways to circumvent this secrecy: in one case, a former MI5 agent denied permission to publish his memoirs in England simply sent them to an Australian publisher not bound by the Official Secrets Act (Wright 1988, vi).

In the United States there is no Official Secrets Act, but the CIA and other agencies usually have been able to operate with great secrecy nonetheless. For example, anyone signing up to work for the CIA must agree to let the Agency read anything intended for publication and allow the CIA to delete anything it feels could compromise national security. This can reach the extremes of absurdity, as when the Agency refused to allow one retired director to quote from his own public speeches. Nonetheless, the Supreme Court has upheld the right of the CIA, and presumably of other American intelligence agencies, to tie agents to such clauses. In the relatively rare cases in which former agents have simply defied the CIA and published their work, the CIA has taken them to court. While it has not always been able to prevent publication, in one case it succeeded in having substantial areas of a book deleted; in another it ensured that the author could receive no profits from his work (see Snepp, 1977, for more on this topic). In many of these cases it is obvious that the fundamental purpose of the censorship is not to protect not national security but the reputation of the CIA, by preventing the revelation of embarrassing mistakes.

The United States has attempted to deal with the tension between democracy and intelligence work both by giving Congress oversight functions for the intelligence community and, when it seems that perhaps democracy has been violated through excess secrecy, by holding public hearings. In the 1970s a long series of hearings chaired by Senator Frank Church laid bare some of the CIA's most questionable activities, and in the 1980s another series of hearings chaired by Senator David Boren did the same. Nonetheless, serious concerns remain about "who will watch the watchers." Questions also have been raised about the use of "black budgets," that is, sections of the federal budget that are simply blanked out, as a means of financing intelligence activities. Several senators recently have questioned the constitutionality of such "black budgets," and it seems inevitable that the controversy will continue.

The potential conflict between democracy and intelligence work is most crucial not in long-established democracies like the United States and England, but in the democracies struggling to emerge in the former Soviet Union and much of the developing world. The KGB no longer exists, at least in theory—but Russia particularly has a tradition dating back to the sixteenth century, not only of intelligence agencies but also of secret police. Whether old habits can be broken and new ones substituted remains a crucial question. Admittedly, even before the collapse of the Soviet Union, the KGB had been attempting a new openness, even allowing limited tours of its headquarters, but how deeply that attitude of openness penetrated is, at least at this point, impossible to know.

Compounding the innate tensions between democracy and secret activity is the tendency for secrets to grow exponentially. Recent estimates are that throughout the United States government, as many as eighty thousand documents *per day* are being stamped "Confidential" or "Secret," or given much higher classifications. It appears that the reason for the floodtide of secret documents is less their content than the desire of individuals to enhance their own status and self-importance, by both classifying everything in sight and then having access to such "sensitive" material.

The "Clipper Chip"

One of the best illustrations of the continuing tensions between democratic openness and the needs of the intelligence community, not only for secrecy but also for the ability to intercept communications, is the controversy over the **clipper chip** that is raging right now. At the heart of this controversy is the federal demand that intelligence agencies be able to tap telephones despite tremendous advances in telephone encryption technology. In 1991 American Telephone and Telegraph announced that it was about to mass-market Surity 3600, a relatively cheap, compact scrambler for telephone messages. However, Surity 3600 was so good, making it (by estimate) sixteen million times more difficult for public agencies to break private encryption, that the federal government designed the "clipper chip" as a back door for decryption even of Surity 3600 messages (Rozansky, 1994). Afraid of the possibility that terrorists, organized crime, spies, and heaven knows who else would be able to shield their communications, the federal government has proposed the nationwide use of what is called the "clipper chip," a encoding device that would shield users from eavesdropping by everyone— except the federal government. (See fig. 10.6 for how the clipper chip would work.) Supposedly the "key" to the clipper chip would be held by the government, to be turned over to the CIA, FBI, or NSA only by a judge's warrant.

Civil libertarians, private businesses, and information revolutionaries violently oppose the clipper chip. Not only would it open the possibility for the government to "tap into every phone, fax, and computer transmission," severely undermining privacy rights, but it would also severely handicap American businesses in competition with foreign rivals (Elmer-DeWitt 1994). The clipper chip, writes

clipper chip A proposed encoding device that would shield against telephone eavesdropping by everyone except the U.S. federal government.

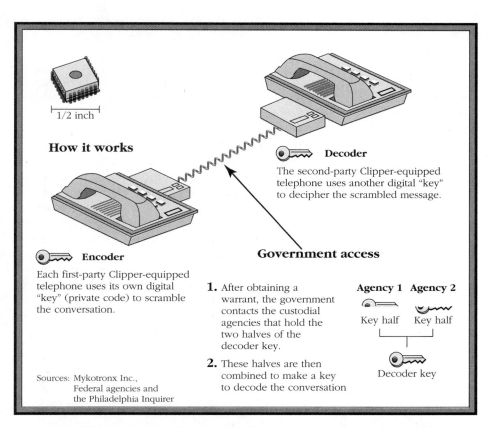

Figure 10.6
The Clipper Chip Controversy

Source: Adapted from the *Houston Chronicle,* July 31, 1994. Data from Mykotronx Inc., federal agencies, and the *Philadelphia Inquirer.*

columnist William Safire (not usually known to side with the American Civil Liberties Union), "would encode for federal perusal whenever a judge rubber-stamped a warrant, everything we say on a phone, everything we write on a computer, every order we give to a shopping network or bank or 800 or 900 number, every electronic note we leave our spouses or dictate to our personal-digital-assistant genies." In effect, he argues, the federal proposal "demands we turn over to Washington a duplicate set of keys to our homes, formerly our castles, where not even the king in olden days could go."

Safire and others point out that in fact the clipper chip probably would not work anyhow. Crooks and others could easily circumvent it by purchasing foreign-made equipment, and "the only people able to be tapped by American agents would be honest Americans—or those crooked Americans dopey enough to buy American equipment with the compromised American code" (Safire 1994).

Several bills have been introduced that would require the installation of the clipper chip in any American-made communications electronics, including telephones, faxes, and computers. The proposed Digital Telephone and Communications Privacy Improvement Act would allot up to half a billion dollars to federal agencies to enable them to monitor citizens' calling patterns and credit card transactions via telephone and, in the near future, via the two-way cable networks now being planned by telephone and television cable companies. Critics claim that such a network would constitute Big Brother surveillance of the American people and would be intolerable (Markoff 1994).

Another way in which the communications revolution is making it more and more difficult for agencies such as the FBI, the CIA, and the NSA to conduct surveillance is in the area of computer communication networks such as the Internet. New algorithms for encrypting computer communications, the so-called PGP ("pretty good privacy") developed—and given away—by a young programmer named Phil Zimmermann, have made it possible to transmit encoded computer traffic that is virtually impossible to break, even for sophisticated national agencies. Zimmermann is also working on a way to adapt his PGP program to shield voice communications (Elmer-DeWitt 1994).

All that seems certain at this point is that the debate will continue, pitting those concerned primarily about security and providing protection (including the vast network of national intelligence agencies) against those concerned primarily with the rights of privacy and leery of greater and greater government intrusion in both individual and business affairs. If this kind of controversy is going on in the United States with its long history of safeguards for privacy and speech, we can only wonder what kinds of issues may be going on behind in the scenes in emerging democracies with no such histories. Would democracy even be possible in a society in which a national government could tap into everything citizens said and monitor virtually everything they did? On the contrary, are the communications revolution and the perceived needs of intelligence and counterintelligence sending even well-established democracies reeling down the path toward Big Brother?

The Future of Intelligence

The end of the Cold War, coupled with revelations about CIA covert activities in Haiti and the Aldrich Ames scandal, has convinced a number of people that it is time for the United States to abolish the CIA and get out of the intelligence business. One American senator even introduced a bill to that effect. Interestingly, only in the United States has there been this kind of reaction, and we suspect that even there it will be extremely short-lived.

As CIA leaders have observed, the end of the Cold War does not mean the end of all external threats to the United States or to American security. The metaphor of one dragon being replaced by many snakes not only serves the interests of the CIA but also accurately expresses the changing world situation. During a time of transformation and flux such as we are now in, intelligence is even more necessary to keep track of multiple threats at multiple levels. If nothing else, Russia, with its twenty-seven thousand nuclear warheads, each of which can be retargeted at the United States in as little as fifteen minutes, demands constant surveillance, analysis, and informed policy decisions. And of course the United States is not the only nation faced with rapidly changing intelligence needs. Russia itself must be concerned, with fifteen newly independent nations on its borders, several of which still retain nuclear weapons. It also must watch carefully the actions of the United States and its NATO allies.

However, it seems certain that intelligence activities in the near future must expand beyond their traditional emphasis on political and military information. Clearly, economic information, in terms of both production statistics and business plans, will become more and more important. While some agencies, like the CIA, have proclaimed that they will not become actively involved in industrial espionage, others, probably including Russian intelligence, have set no such limits on themselves. And even the CIA has stated that while it will not engage in information-gathering, it will warn American corporations and industries when it discovers that they have become the targets of industrial espionage. This counter-intelligence link between public and private entities will represent a new experience for peacetime Americans, and it raises serious questions about issues of privacy and public intrusion into private spheres.

Another area in which intelligence-gathering has become even more important globally is terrorism. Although terrorism has ebbed in recent years, there is no guarantee that it will not flare up again, or that nations that up until now have been basically exempt from terrorist activities (including the United States), may well find themselves on the front line. Counterterrorism demands the same combination of infiltration, penetration, and covert action that more traditional intelligence activities have produced.

The war against global drug traffic and the allied rise of international criminal syndicates presents another major challenge to global intelligence agencies. So too does the attempt to prevent, slow, or at least keep track of the proliferation of weapons of mass destruction, including not only nuclear but also chemical and biological weapons.

The future probably will also see renewed emphasis on human intelligence. Although technology will continue to expand exponentially, the introduction of computers and sophisticated, complex computer programming probably has sounded the death knell for massive reliance on technical intelligence-gathering as the mainstay of national intelligence. In order to deal with terrorism and drugs, the use of human agents capable of penetrating terrorist and drug organizations, or the use of members of those very organizations recruited as sources, will become steadily more important.

We also can predict that the tension between the openness that characterizes a democracy and the secrecy that characterizes intelligence operations will continue to exist. However, it is important to recognize that such tension can have two very different outcomes. At its worst, tension can pull apart a society, shredding the important ties of trust that bind a society together, uniting citizens and government. At its best, tension can serve as a spur to personal and organizational creativity, if the society and government involved can respond to the fundamental issues raised by forging new and even better ways of doing things. Intelligence, the attempt to understand what nations and people have done, are doing, and plan to do, is as old as humanity itself, and there is little reason to expect that it will become obsolete or unnecessary at any foreseeable time in the future.

Summary

Intelligence plays a critical role in the formation of policy, but remains one of the areas treated least in the general study of international relations. The formulation of policy requires information, and information gathered and analyzed through the intelligence cycle can, and should, inform policy-makers.

Types of Intelligence: While policy-makers may emphasize different kinds of intelligence, depending, for example, on whether they are making primarily commercial, diplomatic, or military policy, intelligence must cover a wide range of areas in order to provide accurate and usable information. In addition to political and military intelligence, intelligence dealing with economies, science and technology, sociological information, and environmental issues is also critical. Both producers and users of intelligence also must be careful to distinguish between static and dynamic facts.

Sources of Intelligence: Although we usually think of secret agents and spies when we think about intelligence-gathering, this so-called human intelligence is only one of a triad of intelligence sources. Electronic or signals intelligence has become enormously significant in the age of computers, with vast sums of money devoted to intercepting and attempting to decode electronic signals. Additionally, visual surveillance performed by satellites and aircraft using photography, radar, and other forms of high-technology information-gathering has become vital as a source of intelligence.

Intelligence Analysis: Raw information is relatively useless. Only through the process of analysis can such information become useful, and then only if it is disseminated to those who need it, and in a timely fashion. Whether analysts are specialists in history, economics, linguistics, area studies, or technology, they all face pitfalls in the work of analysis. Mirror imaging, stereotyping, and politicization can distort intelligence analysis and mislead rather than inform policy-makers.

Counterintelligence: In this "world of mirrors," suspicion is epidemic. While penetration of intelligence agencies by "moles" is an extraordinarily dangerous problem, almost equally dangerous is the paralysis of an intelligence agency by the fear of moles. Deception and disinformation are important parts of the world of counterintelligence as well.

Covert Operations: Covert operations sometimes present great opportunities to influence a nation's policies or to undermine an unfriendly government, but the failures of covert operations have produced embarrassments and enormous problems for many nations. Additionally, what may seem to be a great coup at one point in history may have negative long-term consequences.

Global Intelligence Structures: Virtually every nation maintains some sort of intelligence service. We have examined four major services: those of Great Britain, the United States, Russia, and the People's Republic of China. Such examination reveals the way in which intelligence agencies often mirror cultural differences and assumptions. Particularly interesting is the way in which the two English-speaking nations attempt to separate domestic activities from the gathering of intelligence and the way in which the other two nations combine intelligence-gathering and domestic surveillance in the same agencies.

Industrial Espionage: The end of the Cold War may have brought many spies "in from the cold," but individual agents and national intelligence agencies are both finding new work in the field of industrial espionage, which promises to be a growth field well into the twenty-first century. This shift in the focus of intelligence-gathering reflects the global shift from military to economic competition.

Intelligence and Democracy: The stealth and deception endemic to intelligence work often conflicts with the openness and emphasis on individual rights that characterizes democratic society. Such innate tension between the perceived needs of intelligence agencies and the demands of democracy has frequently produced problems for the United States' intelligence apparatus, particularly the CIA. Another manifestation of this tension is the current controversy over the clipper chip: at issue is where the rights of the individual to privacy, even encryption, of personal communications, end and the needs of the state to monitor potential criminal activity, foreign or domestic, begin. As communications become more and more sophisticated and complex, we can expect more rather than fewer such controversies.

Key Terms

Intelligence

Espionage

Covert operations

Intelligence cycle

Strategic Arms Reduction Treaty
    (START)

Mole

Foreign Instrumentation Signals

Intelligence (FISINT)

Mirror imaging

Stereotyping

Counterintelligence

Deception

KGB (Committee for State Security)

Industrial espionage

Clipper chip

Thought Questions

1. What is the intelligence cycle?

2. Is "HUMINT" obsolete?

3. Compare and contrast the intelligence structures of Britain, the United States, Russia, and China.

4. What kinds of tensions are there between democracy and intelligence?

5. Do you believe that industrial espionage is the "wave of the future"? Why or why not?

References

Ameringer, Charles D. *U.S. Foreign Intelligence*. Lexington, Mass.: Lexington Books, 1990.

Andrew, Christopher, and Oleg Gordievsky. *KGB: The Inside Story*. New York: Harper Perennial, 1990.

Bamford, James. *The Puzzle Palace: Inside the National Security Agency, America's Most Secret Intelligence Organization*. New York: Penguin, 1983.

Betts, Richard. *Soldiers, Statesmen, and Cold War Crises*. Cambridge, Mass.: Harvard University Press, 1977.

Burger, William. "Inaki Lopez's Last Stand." *Newsweek*, August 2, 1993.

Burns, Robert. "Flap in France Adds Fuel to U.S. Debate over Future of CIA." *Houston Chronicle*, February 23, 1995.

Burrows, William E. *Deep Black: The Startling Truth Behind America's Top-Secret Spy Satellites*. New York: Berkeley Books, 1988.

Carr, Caleb. "Aldrich Ames and the Conduct of American Intelligence." *World Policy Journal* (Fall 1993), 19–28.

"Clinton Backs Federal Agencies on Need for Computer Snooping." *Houston Chronicle*, February 5, 1994.

Codevilla, Angelo. *Informing Statecraft: Intelligence for a New Century*. New York: The Free Press, 1992.

Dictionary of United States Military for Joint Usage. Washington, DC: Departments of Army, Navy, and Airforce, May 1995, p. 53.

Dobbs, Michael. "How Soviets Penetrated U.S. A-Bomb Secrets." *Houston Chronicle*, October 25, 1992.

Eftimiades, Nicholas. *Chinese Intelligence Operations*. (Annapolis, Md.: Naval Institute Press, 1994.

Elmer-DeWitt, Philip. "Who Should Keep the Keys?" *Newsweek*, March 14, 1994.

"France Accuses Yanks of Spying." Associated Press/Prodigy, February 23, 1995.

"France Investigates Spy Leak." Associated Press/Prodigy, February 23, 1995.

"French Claim 5 Americans Were Spying." *Houston Chronicle*, February 23, 1995.

Greve, Frank. "Intelligence Officials Say French Spies Pose Threat to U.S. Industry." *Houston Chronicle*, October 25, 1992.

Hoagland, Jim. "Don't Ask CIA to Spy on French Trade." *Houston Chronicle*, February 25, 1995.

Jeffreys-Jones, Rhodri. *The CIA and American Democracy*. New Haven, Conn.: Yale University Press, 1988.

Jehl, Douglas. "List Prompts Efforts to Thwart French Spying at U.S. Firms." *Houston Chronicle*, April 30, 1993.

Johnson, Loch. 1989. "Covert Action and Accountability: Decision-Making for America's Secret Foreign Policy," *International Studies Quarterly,* March 1989, 33, 81–109.

Kahn, David. *The Code-Breakers: The Story of Secret Writing.* New York: New American Library, 1973.

Kessler, Ronald. *Inside the CIA.* New York: Pocket Books, 1992.

Knightley, Phillip. *The Second Oldest Profession: Spies and Spying in the Twentieth Century.* New York: Penguin, 1988.

Kranish, Michael. "'Black Budget' Programs Likely to Get More Attention." *Houston Chronicle,* August 14, 1994.

Lacayo, Richard. "Nowhere to Hide: Using Computers, High-Tech Gadgets and Mountains of Data, an Army of Snoops Is Assaulting our Privacy." *Time,* November 11, 1991.

Lee, Moon. "The Rise of the Company Spy." *Christian Science Monitor,* July 12, 1993.

Lewin, Ronald. *Ultra Goes to War.* New York: McGraw-Hill, 1978.

Levine, Michael. *The Big White Lie: The CIA and the Cocaine/Crack Epidemic.* New York: Thunder's Mouth Press, 1993.

Markoff, John. "New Technology Sought for Surveillance: Software Would Aid Crime Fight, Officials Say." *Houston Chronicle,* February 28, 1994.

Marlowe, Gene. "Coming In from the Cold War: Industrial Espionage Takes Off as Spies Work for U.S. Firms." *Houston Chronicle,* June 13, 1993.

McCoy, Alfred W. *The Politics of Heroin: CIA Complicity in the Global Drug Trade.* Brooklyn, N.Y.: Lawrence Hill Books, 1991.

1995 Factbook on Intelligence. Washington, DC: Central Intelligence Agency, 1995. Internet http://www.odci.gov/cia/publications/facttel/index.html. Downloaded Feb. 16, 1996.

Prados, John. *Keeper of the Keys.* New York: William Morrow, 1991.

Prange, Gordon W. *At Dawn We Slept.* New York: Penguin, 1981

Ranelagh, John. *The Agency: The Rise and Decline of the CIA.* New York: Simon & Schuster Touchstone, 1987.

Raviv, Dan, and Yossi Melman. *Every Spy a Prince: The Complete History of Israel's Intelligence Community.* Boston: Houghton Mifflin, 1990.

Richelson, Jeffrey. *The U.S. Intelligence Community.* Cambridge, Mass.: Ballinger, 1989.

Rosati, Jerel. *The Politics of United States Foreign Policy.* Ft. Worth, TX: Harcourt, Brace, Jovanovich, 1993.

Rozansky, Michael L. "Taking a Byte out of Crime: Clipper Chip Stirs Protest over Eavesdropping." *Houston Chronicle,* July 31, 1994.

Safire, William. "Sink Clipper Chip—Don't Turn Over to Government the Keys to Our Castles." *Houston Chronicle,* February 16, 1994.

Schmidt, William E. "Britain's Spy Agencies Begin to Come Out From the Cold." *The New York Times,* August 8, 1993.

Schweizer, Peter. *Friendly Spies: How America's Allies Are Using Economic Espionage to Steal Our Secrets.* New York: Atlantic Monthly Press, 1993.

Snepp, Frank. *Decent Interval.* New York: Random House, 1977.

Snow, Donald M., and Eugene Brown. *Puzzle Palaces and Foggy Bottom: U.S. Foreign and Defense Policy-Making in the 1990s.* New York: St. Martin's Press, 1994.

Tuchman, Barbara. *The Zimmermann Telegram.* New York: Bantam, 1971.

Valentine, Douglas. *The Phoenix Program.* New York: Avon, 1990.

"Volkswagen Admits GM-Leak Possibility." *Houston Chronicle,* August 9, 1993.

Waller, Douglas. "Spies in Cyberspace." *Time,* March 20, 1995.

Watson, Russell. "Trade Spies: The CIA Takes Off the Gloves." *Newsweek Interactive/*Prodigy, February 26, 1995.

Weiner, Tim. *Blank Check: The Pentagon's Black Budget.* New York: Warner Books, 1991.

Williams, Carol J. "KGB Revisited?" *Houston Chronicle,* April 7, 1995.

Wise, David. "Closing Down the KGB." *New York Times Magazine,* November 24, 1991.

———*Molehunt: How the Search for a Phantom Traitor Shattered the CIA.* New York: Avon, 1992.

———"Was Oswald a Spy, and Other Cold War Mysteries." *New York Times Magazine,* December 6, 1992.

Woolsey, James. "Intelligence Quotient: The Mission of the CIA in a New World." *Harvard International Review* (Fall 1994).

Wright, Peter. *Spycatcher: The Candid Autobiography of a Senior Intelligence Officer.* New York: Dell, 1988.

Chapter 11

War: Its Types, Culture, and Causes

Introduction

The Four Horsemen of the Apocalypse—Death, Famine, Plague, and War—have traced a bloody course of sorrow, destruction, and devastation through human history. In the twentieth century alone Famine and Plague have claimed countless millions of victims, while War has taken at least one hundred million lives.

Technology has now made it frequently possible to overcome two of the dreaded horsemen, Plague and Famine, although political will sometimes make it difficult to do so. Encounters with the third Horseman, Death, have been postponed by that same technology; in the United States, for example, average life expectancy at birth has risen from forty-eight years at the beginning of this century to seventy-six as we near its end.

Ironically, while technology has blunted the impact of these three Horsemen, it has made all the more dreadful the ravages of the Fourth Horseman, War. As the century opened, the most deadly weapon faced on the battlefield was the machine gun. For the first time in history, thousands upon thousands could be killed in a single day's battle. During World War I, the butcher's bill on battlefields dominated by the machine gun was horrific: 60,000 dead in an hour at Verdun,

200,000 dead in a week at Passchendaele, 400,000 dead in two weeks at the Somme. But these numbers pale in comparison to those produced by today's deadliest technology. Nuclear and thermonuclear weapons raise the spectre of death tolls in *minutes* of war to be counted not in the thousands or even millions, but in the hundreds of millions. Experts predicting the cost of all-out nuclear exchange between the United States and the then Soviet Union estimated at least 140,000,000 dead in the United States and as many as 180,000,000 dead in the Soviet Union. Other experts gloomily forecast the death of the entire planet and its five billion human inhabitants within two or three years of a nuclear war, as the result of fallout, radiation, and "nuclear winter." (For further discussion, see Sagan 1989 and Schell 1982)

Despite its terrible costs, war seems to be a human habit. Researchers at the University of Oslo and the Norwegian Academy of Sciences calculated that in the 5,584 years since 3600 B.C. the world has seen 14,531 wars. There were no wars at all in only 292 years of the 5,584 studied—that is, in less than 5 percent of the total years in recorded history. As an expert cynically noted, "These rare instances of peace are probably due to inadequate historical records." The Norwegians estimated that 3.6 billion people had died in those fourteen thousand wars (Dunnigan and Nofi 1990, 419). Other experts add that since 1945, during the Cold War era sometimes referred to as the "Long Peace," there have been well over one hundred wars, which have taken the lives of as many as fifty million people (Dunnigan and Nofi, 382). Depending on how one counts these things, there are somewhere between forty and one hundred wars going on right now. One expert observes cynically that "one could argue that there are twenty wars going on in Lebanon and as many as a dozen in Burma [Myanmar]." Virtually all of these are either low-intensity conflicts or internal (or mostly internal) wars, like that now ravaging Bosnia (Dunnigan and Nofi, 454). Figure 11.1 depicts all wars going on at the time of this book's publication.

Ironically, the absolute deadliness of nuclear technology, and the increasing deadliness of non-nuclear technology, such as poison gases and "smart" bombs, may also be moving us in the direction of ending war altogether. A handful of students of war now suggest that major wars involving the largest and most powerful nations in direct confrontation with one another may indeed be a thing of the past, made impossible by the lethalness of weaponry and by a natural instinct for survival.

In this chapter we will examine war from a number of different points of view. First we will look at the anatomy and types of war, and then at the links between war and culture. Finally, after examining the causes of war, we will discuss the future.

The Anatomy of War

Wars can range in scope and intensity from small, localized conflicts to global struggles that directly or indirectly involve most of the earth's population. The Joint Chiefs of Staff of the United States see war as part of a continuum that includes four major segments: peaceful competition, peacetime competition, (both characterized as low-intensity conflict), conflict, and war (Gallagher 1991, 1). Figure 11.1 illustrates this operational continuum. Notice that "low-intensity conflict" (LIC) can occur during both peacetime competition and conflict, while war itself occupies an entire section of this continuum and includes limited,

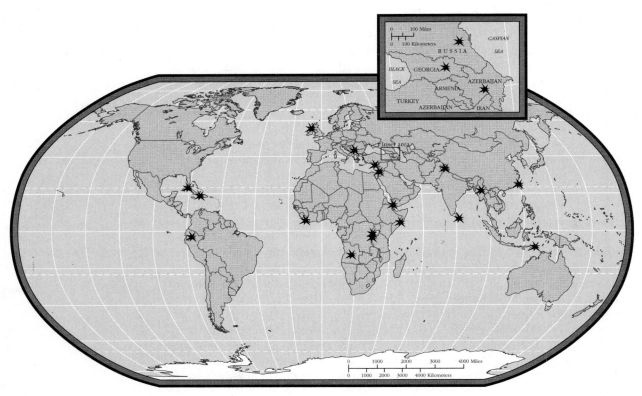

Figure 11.1 **Current Conflicts**

general, nuclear, and strategic war. In this section we will include a discussion of the most intense form of low-intensity conflict—guerrilla war—and then examine both limited and general war. We will deal with nuclear and strategic or global nuclear war in chapter 12, "Weapons: The Technology of Death."

Definitions of War

war The conduct of armed hostilities between states or within states.

Not surprisingly, **war** has several different definitions. A broad definition sees war as an "armed contest between two independent political units, by means of organized military force, in the pursuit of a tribal or national policy." A narrower definition characterizes international war as "a substantial armed conflict between the organized military forces of independent political units" (Kugler 1993, 962).

Civil Wars and International Relations

We must recognize also that civil wars, that is, wars between groups contending for power within a nation or struggling to become independent political units, can have important consequences for international relations as well. The most common way in which a civil war can affect international relations is by drawing in a major power on the side of one of the two major antagonists. It has not been unusual throughout history for combatants in a civil war to try to gain support from a strong outside power. For example, the South entered the American Civil

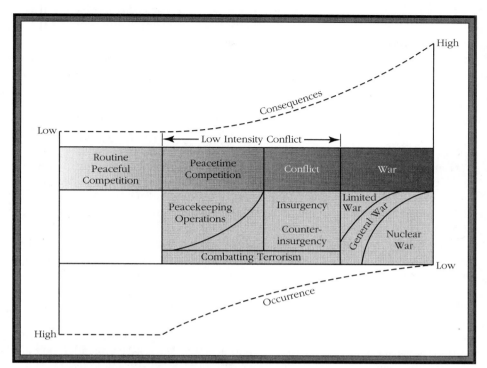

Figure 11.2
Operational Continuum
The U.S. Joint Chiefs of
Staff have developed this
operational continuum to
show the various types of
war and how they tend to
shade into one another.
The broken lines at the top
of the diagram show how
consequences of various
conflicts could range from
low to extremely high in
either general or nuclear
war. The broken line at the
bottom of the diagram
shows how frequently the
various types of war have
taken place or might take
place.
Source: Based on CSM James J.
Gallagher, USA (ret). *Low
Intensity Conflict: A Guide for
Tactics, Techniques, and Procedures.* (Harrisburg, Penn:
Stackpole Books, 1991).

War convinced that Great Britain, heavily dependent on Southern cotton, would come to the aid of the Confederacy. The British government did in fact toy with the idea of entering the Civil War on the side of the South, and did provide considerable aid for the Confederacy, particularly in the construction of ships. But Great Britain's ultimate decision to remain neutral sealed the South's fate.

In the years leading up to World War II, the Spanish Civil War became essentially a "sneak preview" of the great war to follow, as the fascist powers of Italy and Germany provided massive technological support to the Spanish fascists led by Francisco Franco. The legitimate Spanish Republic under attack by the fascists received minimal support from the democracies, although individuals from the democracies fought in units such as the Abraham Lincoln brigade, composed almost entirely of United States citizens. The communist government of the Soviet Union, which perceived fascism as a major threat, did provide aid to the beleaguered Republicans. Franco's 1939 victory was a major factor convincing Adolf Hitler to plunge Europe into war, since to him it proved the weakness and vulnerability of the democracies, unwilling and unable to prevent a fascist triumph.

This perception of civil wars not as isolated and discrete but as part of much larger struggles was present in a number of civil wars during the half-century of the Cold War, as either the United States or the Soviet Union perceived one side in a civil war as its friend and the other side as a friend of its rival. A frequent scenario was that one or the other superpower increased both the intensity and the duration of a civil war by pouring support into a nation, to counter supposed advances by friends or allies of the other superpower. This became a formal part of American foreign policy as the Truman Doctrine, through which the United States pledged to support any reasonably democratic government against internal subversion, in large part on the assumption that such subversion would be communist-initiated, or at least communist-supported.

The Angolan Example

Angola provides a classic modern study of foreign intervention in a civil war. A Portuguese colony since the late fifteenth century, Angola began its armed struggle for independence in the 1960s as part of the great wave of anticolonialism and decolonization that swept over Africa during this period. Ultimately the Angolan liberation movement split into three factions, reflecting both tribal and ideological divisions, as well as the ambitions of their leaders. The MPLA (Movimento Popular de Liberacao de Angola) advocated a nonracial, nonethnic, socialist approach to Angolan independence and development. The FNLA (Frente Nacional para a Liberacao de Angola) was both antisocialist and opposed to the involvement of white and mestizo (mixed-race) Angolans in the liberation movement. UNITA (Uniao Nacional para a Independencia Total de Angola) shared FNLA's opposition to the white and mestizo participation and, after a brief flirtation with Maoism, was also antisocialist.

As Portuguese rule drew to a close in 1975, civil war erupted in Angola. South Africa, Zaire, France, and the United States (primarily through the Central Intelligence Agency) gave substantial military and economic support to FNLA and UNITA; in turn, MPLA relied on such support from the Soviet Union and Cuba. Substantial numbers of Cuban troops were deployed in Angola to support MPLA, stopping the advance of UNITA, FNLA, South African, and Zairian troops and forcing them to retreat. MPLA proclaimed the People's Republic of Angola, a one-party socialist state, in November 1975 and adopted Marxist-Leninist ideology and Leninist "democratic centralist" structures. The new Angolan regime has been recognized by many governments (not including the United States) and is also a member of the International Monetary Fund.

The current scaling back of the Cold War certainly has reduced the possibility of superpower intervention in civil wars, particularly since one of the two superpowers has in effect vanished, but the danger still exists that civil wars can draw in great powers.

Conventional and Unconventional Wars

War generally is defined as an organized combat between opposing sides, but in fact the degree of organization involved in wars can vary widely. Highly organized wars fought between major units of opposing armies using battlefield weapons but neither nuclear nor chemical/biological agents are known generally as "conventional" wars. Wars that find one or both sides relying heavily on irregular forces, that is, forces that shift chameleon-like between military and civilian enterprises, are known as "guerrilla" wars, from the Spanish for "little war." We will examine guerrilla war briefly before looking at conventional war and distinguishing among types of conventional war. Recently, the term **low-intensity conflict (LIC)** has come into vogue to characterize guerrilla warfare.

Guerrilla War

Historically, **guerrilla war** has been the tool of smaller and weaker forces against much larger and stronger foes. As a student of guerrilla warfare writes, "For a number of reasons guerrilla warfare has evolved into an ideal instrument for the realization of social-political-economic aspirations of underprivileged peoples. This is so patently true as to allow one to suggest that we may be witnessing a transition to a new era in warfare" (Asprey 1994, x). Guerrilla forces are quite lit-

low-intensity conflict Warfare ranging from guerrilla war to low-level conventional war between modern armies, but never including the use of nuclear weapons. Under United States doctrine, low-intensity conflict includes: counterinsurgency; proinsurgency; peacetime contingency operations; and military "shows of force."

guerrilla war Low-intensity, unconventional war, usually fought by an insurgency of irregulars against much stronger forces.

These two youthful Vietcong guerrillas are holding "homebrewed" weapons, assembled from spare parts and handmade components. Such ability to improvise is a major factor in guerrillas's success.

erally fighting a different kind of war than their better-trained, better-equipped, and better-armed enemies. The guerrilla fighters are "irregular" forces for the most part, possessing neither the weapons nor the training to carry on conventional war. Unlike conventional armies, which tend to maneuver for direct face-to-face battles and seek decisive victory, guerrilla warfare is indirect, with its participants generally planning to wage "protracted" war rather than win immediate, large-scale victories. Often in guerrilla warfare the mismatch that occurs between the army of the larger and stronger power, attempting to fight a conventional war, and the guerrillas, waging a very different, "unconventional" war, gives guerrilla forces considerable advantage. The guerrillas' type of warfare is much cheaper to conduct and generally controls the tempo of fighting, since they choose when and where they wish to strike. According to one student of war in the twentieth century, this might well be termed the "century of the guerrilla," since, by his count, guerrillas have defeated conventional forces in two out of every three encounters (Keeley 1996, 80, 211–212).

Guerrilla tactics have been employed by many peoples throughout history. For example, the first few years of the American Revolution saw guerrilla warfare; the so-called Continental Army was composed largely of volunteer units or militia, "citizen soldiers" completely untrained in the tactics of eighteenth-century conventional warfare, with its emphasis on close-order drill and volleys of musket fire. Of necessity American commanders like Washington watched militia employ "irregular" tactics, often fighting in what was termed "Indian style." The militia "made it impossible to control the country without occupying it . . . [and] thwarted pacification yet refused to stand in the open and fight . . . . The militia, maligned and misunderstood, was the safety net of the Revolution. So long as it responded to Washington's calls, the war would go on" (Perret 1990, 25–26. See also Asprey 1994, 48–72).

In this century, the most common appearance of guerrilla forces has been in **wars of national liberation,** that is, wars conducted by native people to win their freedom from colonial masters. The wars of liberation in Indochina, Angola, and Indonesia all began with guerrilla tactics, and all resulted in decisions by the larger and stronger powers to withdraw from the nations and in effect concede defeat. However, many other instances of guerrilla war are essentially a form of civil war, with one group attempting to overthrow a government in power. The most important example of this form of insurgency is the long guerrilla war waged by the Chinese Communist forces under Mao Tse-tung against the government of Chiang Kai-shek from the early 1930s to 1949.

wars of national liberation Wars to gain or restore independence, often fought by small numbers of unconventional forces motivated by revolutionary ideology as well as a desire for independence.

Maoist Guerrilla Warfare.　Mao Tse-tung blended his own version of communist ideology (see chap. 6) with classic Chinese military ideas (see "The Chinese Paradox," later in this chapter, for a discussion of Sun Tzu) and sheer necessity. In so doing, he formulated a series of guerrilla doctrines that appealed to insurgents worldwide. Mao urged that guerrillas be what he termed a "people's army"; when his Red Army forces were not fighting, they were conducting literacy campaigns, providing medical care, helping with both planting and harvesting, and generally working with the people of the area in which they operated. Mao established strict rules for the conduct of his forces and clearly understood the tactics of protracted war. A famous poem he wrote summarizes these tactics:

> The enemy advances, we retreat.
> The enemy halts and encamps, we harass.
> The enemy seeks to avoid battle, we attack.
> The enemy retreats, we pursue.

Mao's eight points for his guerrilla forces to obey clearly set forth his new principles for fighting:

1. Put back the doors you have taken down for bed-boards;
2. Put back the straw you use for bedding;
3. Speak politely;
4. Pay fairly for what you consume;
5. Return everything you borrow;
6. Pay for everything you damage;
7. Don't battle within sight of women; and
8. Don't search the pockets of captives.
   (Wilson 1980, 134–35)

Nowhere were the possibilities of Maoist guerrilla tactics and strategy more strikingly demonstrated than in the long war waged by Vietnamese guerrillas against first the French and then the Americans, and nowhere was the difficulty of winning a war from an enemy who was conducting an entirely different sort of struggle made clearer.

Conventional War

The term **conventional war** refers to the engagement of large, well-equipped units in large-scale combat against similarly trained and equipped forces. Obviously, conventional warfare in the eighteenth century was substantially different from what we would call conventional warfare in the twentieth century; however, in all conventional war the opposing forces are fighting essentially the same kind of war according to commonly accepted ideas of warfare.

Today, at the end of the twentieth century, conventional war means war fought by infantry, artillery, aircraft, and naval forces. World War I, World War II, and the Gulf War were all conventional wars.

For much of the period from the early Middle Ages until the late nineteenth century, conventional war was generally confined to the battlefield, and the only legitimate targets were those wearing uniforms. Armies—which usually were composed of professional soldiers and mercenaries—attempted to avoid actions that would endanger civilians. Consequently, the death tolls in these conventional wars remained comparatively small. However, developing technology and changing definitions of war, both largely the result of the Industrial Revolution, began to make it more and more difficult to differentiate between civilian and military targets. The result was the emergence of a new and far more lethal form of conventional warfare, called "total war."

conventional war War conducted without the use of nuclear weapons.

Total War

In many ways, the American Civil War can lay claim to being the first **total war** of the modern era. It was certainly the first large-scale war in which emerging technologies—iron production, the railroads, superior manufacturing techniques for weapons, the telegraph—began to make an impact. The Civil War showed clearly that the effectiveness of an army in the industrial era depended not only on the quality of its soldiers and generals, but also on the amount of weapons, ammunition, and equipment that the state could get to the army, and the ease with which the army could move, using the rail system. Consequently, commanders began to see the opposition army not as an entity independent of anything else in the state, but as part of a continuum that stretched from farms providing food to factories producing weapons, munitions, and clothing for the army and then to railroads carrying troops and matériel. (See Reston 1984 for more on this topic.)

Total war became more devastating during World War I, during which some ten million soldiers died. The machine gun perfected by Hiram Maxim could fire six hundred rounds a minute, as much firepower as one hundred infantrymen had produced in the Civil War. However, because of trench warfare as well as use of the machine gun, most of the World War I fighting was confined to the battlefields.

total war Modern form of conventional war in which older distinctions between military and civilian targets no longer exist.

Mobilizing a Democracy. In one way, however, World War I did serve very much as a forerunner of later wars. World War I was the first war fought by enormous armies composed largely of volunteers or conscripts. The millions of men mobilized to fight dwarfed the numbers who had fought in the American Civil

War. And in the Western democracies of England, France, and the United States especially, World War I showed how the need to energize an entire population, as well as to enlist a substantial part of the male population of military age, could lead to enormously exaggerated rhetoric. World War I consequently was portrayed by its participants not just as a war for territorial or economic gain, but as an apocalyptic battle in which nothing less than the fate of civilization itself was at stake. Attempting to mobilize a reluctant American people, President Woodrow Wilson had to convey the idea that this conflict was a "war to end all wars" and a "war to make the world safe for democracy." With this type of heated rhetoric, it became more and more difficult to see the opposing side as human, and simultaneously it became much easier to think of total destruction as what this inhuman enemy deserved.

Democracies may in fact have little choice but to fight total wars, since the mobilization of a democratic people is so difficult. Only by painting the war as a conflict between good and evil, with the absolute destruction of the enemy as the primary goal, can the leaders of a democracy rally the population behind them. And with this level of rhetoric, unconditional surrender becomes the only acceptable conclusion of war; World War II is a good example of this. Certainly, when the Persian Gulf War ended with Saddam Hussein still alive and Iraq in most ways still intact, many Americans were bitterly disappointed.

In fact, the Gulf War provides a good model of this process of demonization that has accompanied the rise of modern warfare. The rallying behind a cause of the whole society took place as President George Bush characterized Saddam Hussein as another Hitler. Certainly, as repulsive and evil as Saddam appeared to many in the West, he in no way paralleled the total evil and power of Adolf Hitler. Despite his pretensions, he posted relatively little threat to the general population of Europe. But in order to galvanize the American people to fight Saddam, the president and his advisors apparently decided that they would have to paint the direst possible picture of Saddam.

On the other side of the coin is a similar process; portraying your ally as larger, and generally much better, than life. Thus President Ronald Reagan, trying to garner American public opinion in support of the "Contra" rebels in Nicaragua, called the Contras "the moral equivalent of the [American] founding fathers." Few others had seen much resemblance between the Contras, many of them holdovers from former dictator Somoza's National Police Force, and men such as Washington, Jefferson, and Adams. However, their canonization by the Reagan administration then became the justification for the entire Iran-Contra Affair, with its widespread lawbreaking and contempt for law and legal processes. Likewise, during the Vietnam War, a series of American leaders idealized a series of South Vietnamese leaders, most of whom had done little to deserve such high praise. As one student of military history has pointed out, "You can look forward to this year's wars being promoted as effectively as the latest consumer products" (Keegan 1993, 357).

World War II.   During World War II, rapid technological development enabled both sides to carry out full-scale total war: not just a war of words and demonology, but one of widespread destruction, in which civilian populations became "legitimate" targets. Most important, the development of high-altitude bombers permitted the opponents to carry the war deep behind the battlefields and into enemy territory, striking at cities and towns as well as industrial facilities. The "Blitz" against London and other English cities lasted barely more than two months, but it virtually destroyed the City of London, severely damaged Whitehall and Westminster, including the chamber of the House of Commons, and accounted for over thirteen thousand civilian deaths in London alone. British aircraft retaliated by bombing German cities from 1940 onward.

In 1942 the British abandoned their policy of bombing only identifiable military targets and instead adopted "area bombing," under the philosophy that operations should be focused on the morale of the enemy population, and particularly that of enemy workers. This so-called strategic bombing was something entirely new in warfare, and certainly an abandonment of traditional military principles of protecting civilian populations. By the spring of 1945, in the Pacific War, American penetration of the Japanese imperial sphere was sufficient to enable massive high-level bombing raids to be launched from recently seized islands against the Japanese home islands themselves. Japanese cities, built largely of wood and paper, became ideal targets for incendiary weapons. Under the direction of General Curtis LeMay, implementing his tactics of strategic bombing, much of Japan would burn.

The final and most devastating act of World War II involved the most advanced technology of total war, the atomic bomb. Debate still rages today about whether the use of this new weapon, a quantum leap in the destructive capacity of humanity, was either necessary or justified. Despite strong arguments on the part of those who considered use of the bomb unnecessary, it was probably inevitable, given the general escalation of violence, the acceptance of total war, and the American desire to use technology rather than American lives to defeat the enemy. We may never know the total death toll at Hiroshima and Nagasaki, the two Japanese cities hit by atomic bombs, but photographs of those cities and the testimony of survivors reveal the devastating impact of a single bomb. The devastation of German cities like Berlin was almost as great as that of Hiroshima and Negasaki, but while the death toll in Berlin stopped rising the day the war ended, the death toll from the Hiroshima and Nagasaki bombs continues to rise even now, as individuals succumb to radiation-induced cancers and leukemias (see Rhodes 1986 for a history of the atomic bomb).

Lethality and Casualties. Conventional warfare today is far more lethal even than it was in World War II. Technology has produced an incredible increase in the general deadliness of weapons. One military historian, Colonel Trevor N. Dupuy (U.S. Army Ret.), has developed a formula showing how great the increase in what he terms "theoretical killing capacity" has been (see fig. 11.3). Dupuy's "theoretical lethality index" shows that the killing capacity of weapons systems grew more or less gradually and arithmetically from the use of hand-to-hand weapons through the introduction of gunpowder and the rise of the Industrial Revolution. But then, lethality increased geometrically. The least lethal weapon he examines, the early firearm known as the arquebus, had a theoretical lethal index of 10, while the most lethal weapon he deals with, a one-megaton thermonuclear bomb, has a theoretical lethality index of 695,385,000 (Dupuy 1984, 92).

A 1980 United States Army estimate concluded that non-nuclear conventional war had become from 400 to 700 percent more lethal than it had been during World War II. For example, the "casualty effect" of modern artillery has increased by 400 percent, its range by 60 percent, and its "zone of destruction" by 350 percent. Rockets have changed the equations of war as well. For example, a single Russian infantry battalion firing only 18 rocket launchers can place 35 *tons* of explosive rockets on targets up to 17 miles away in just 30 seconds. A single U.S.

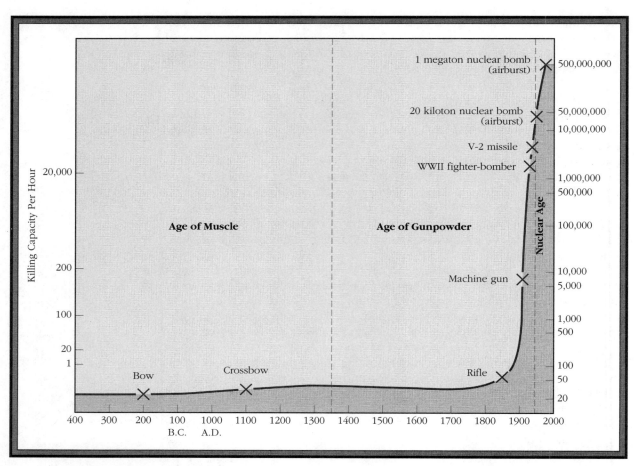

Figure 11.3 **Historical Increase of Weapons Lethality**
This diagram illustrates the increased killing capacity of weapons as we have moved from the Age of Muscle to the Age of Gunpowder to the nuclear age. Note how sharply the curve begins to rise about the time of the American Civil War, and how fast it rises thereafter.
Source: Based on Colonel Trevor N. Dupuy, U.S. Army (Ret.), *The Evolution of Weapons and Warfare* (New York: Da Capo Press, 1984), 288–89.

M-163 Vulcan cannon, used for air defense, can fire 3,000 rounds of explosive 20-millimeter shot per minute with nearly 100 percent accuracy within two miles of the gun position. The Gulf War demonstrated the effectiveness of much of this new technology, with cruise missiles, stealth aircraft, and "smart" bombs obliterating a large proportion of their targets. In addition, modern conventional warfare is much more intense than that of World War II. During World War II, heavy combat meant two to four "combat pulses" per day. Today's combat divisions are configured and trained to deliver twelve to fourteen combat pulses a day in around-the-clock operations (Gabriel and Metz 1991, 100–101).

Civilians rather than soldiers have been the primary casualties of these phenomenal increases in the lethality of weapons. Dupuy notes that combat troops in modern conventional warfare are much more widely dispersed on the battlefield than they were during World War II, and thus while the lethality of weapons has increased, the actual casualty rate has diminished (Dupuy 1984, 307–18). Table 11.1 shows the gradual decrease in casualty rates, from the near-total anni-

Table 11.1

Battle Mortality from Antiquity to Korean War

PERSONNEL INVOLVED	Total	Died	% Mortality
"Iliad"			
All casualties	213	192	90.0
Close range	147	138	93.5
Long-range	66	54	82.2
"Aeneid"			
All casualties	180	164	91.0
Close range	120	115	96.0
Long-range	60	49	81.6
Crimea			
British Army	26,083	5,498	21.5
World War I			
Canadians	122,672	51,678	42.2
British Army	2,216,976	573,507	25.8
World War II			
Australians	2,637	516	19.5
Normandy Troops	2,452	962	39.3
Korea			
U.S.A.	142,091	30,928	21.7
Commonwealth	6,080	1,263	20.9
British			
all casualties	1,337	216	16.2
gunshot wounds	694	127	18.2

Source: P. B. Adamson, "A Comparison of Ancient and Modern Weapons In The Effectiveness of Producing Battle Casualties," *Journal of The Royal Army Medical Corps,* Vol. 23 (1977), 97. From Richard A. Gabriel and Karen S. Metz, *A Short History of War: The Evolution of Warfare and Weapons,* Professional Readings in Military Strategy, no. 5 (Harrisburg, Penn: Strategic Studies Institute, U.S. Army War College, 1991).

hilation of units in the Homeric wars to casualty rates of approximately 20 percent in the Korean War.

The other side of this picture of reduced battlefield and military casualties, however, is a soaring rate of civilian casualties. Technology has made war "civilianized." In World War I, approximately twenty soldiers died for every civilian; by World War II, the ratio was about even, one to one; in Korea, there were five civilian deaths for every military death; and in Vietnam, thirteen civilians died for every soldier. Nuclear war would see hundreds or even thousands of civilian deaths for every military death (Dunnigan and Nofi 1990, 381). Figure 11.4 illustrates the shift in the ratio of civilian to military casualties.

Limited War

The concept of **limited war** could not exist until total war had appeared. Prior to total war, all wars had in effect been "limited" by the participants' decision not to attack civilians or noncombatants. The concept of limited war implies that the limitations on warmaking derive not from limitations of the participants' abilities or weaponry, but from a conscious decision *not* to use the full range of available weapons or to attack any and all potential enemy sites. The implication is always that limited war could be transformed into total war, that at least one side in the

limited war War in which participants decided not to use their full range of weapons or to attack any and all potential enemy sites.

Figure 11.4
**Military to Civilian Deaths,
Twentieth Century
Major Wars**
Source: Data from James F.
Dunningan and Albert A. Nofi,
*Dirty Little Secrets: Military
Information You're Not Sup-
posed to Know* (New York:
William Morrow, 1990), 199.

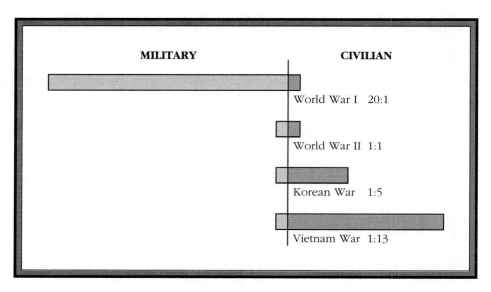

war has the ability to conduct total war, but chooses not to. Since World War II,
limited wars generally have taken place within the context of the Cold War rivalry
between the United States and the Soviet Union; a major factor limiting war has
been the fear that if one power were to cross a well-defined but theoretical line,
limited war could escalate to total war and then to nuclear war.

Korea.   The first limited war was fought in Korea, beginning in 1950. The
Korean peninsula, under Japanese control from 1910 to the end of World War II,
had been divided between a pro-American South Korean government and a pro-
Soviet North Korean government. Soviet and American troops had occupied the
split peninsula temporarily, but both had substantially withdrawn in 1948. Korea
was supposed to be reunited as a single state, as it had been historically, but the
Cold War prevented that from happening immediately. Instead, both the Americans and the Soviets created client states, each of which claimed the right to rule
the entire peninsula. Given the tensions of the Cold War, both Koreas were armed
and trained by their superpower "protectors." The two opposing Korean armies
occupied virtually face-to-face positions along the thirty-eighth parallel, which
divided North from South Korea, and often feinted attack.

Then in June 1950, the North Korean army actually attacked South Korea,
pouring across the thirty-eighth parallel and driving the South Korean forces, out-
numbered and caught off guard, almost to the tip of the peninsula. Americans
immediately perceived the North Korean attack as part of an overall Soviet-
directed plot (this interpretation is still controversial). President Harry Truman
committed American forces to the defense of South Korea and, thanks largely to
a Russian walkout, convinced the United Nations to take nominal control of the
war effort under the rubric of collective security.

During the three years of war in Korea, the United States chose to avoid use
of its most powerful and most dangerous weapon, the atomic bomb, and to
attempt to keep war confined to combatants. During the Korean War there was
virtually no bombing of North Korean cities. In part this was because North Korea
had little industrial capacity and therefore presented few targets. But it also
stemmed from a conscious and deliberate decision to limit the scope of this war.

However, both Presidents Harry Truman and Dwight Eisenhower did in fact "rattle the nuclear saber."

The United States would fight two more major limited wars in the remaining years of the Cold War: the Vietnam War and the Persian Gulf War. Although they were in many ways very different—certainly the Vietnam War was much longer and much costlier than the Gulf War—in both cases the United States chose to limit its use of weapons and its choice of targets, and not to expand the wars.

Vietnam presented a particularly difficult version of limited war, because it lasted so long—basically, from 1965 to 1973—and because its frustrating nature brought calls for tougher and tougher means of fighting from military leaders. A bitterly divided American public did not give its full, unconditional support to this war; by contrast, the public had reluctantly supported the war in Korea, and would enthusiastically support the Persian Gulf War in the future.

Democracies and Limited War. As we have mentioned, limited wars, especially limited wars fought thousands of miles from home for essentially murky purposes, are enormously difficult for democracies to support. One of the most important students of recent military strategy and of war in general, U.S. Colonel Harry Summers, concludes that wars, even limited wars, can be won only if public support is effectively mustered. Summers concludes that a major reason for the American defeat in Vietnam was the failure of civilian leaders to mobilize popular support for the effort. "Factoring the American people out of the strategic equation," Summers argues, "was one of the most consequential and far-reaching mistakes of the Vietnam war." Summers quotes then Secretary of State Dean Rusk: "Since we wanted to limit the war, we deliberately refrained from creating a war psychology in the United States . . . . We tried to do in cold blood perhaps what can only be done in hot blood, when sacrifices of this order are involved" (Summers 1992, 7–19).

Other Characteristics of Limited War. We must note two or three things about the concept of limited war. First, what is a limited war for one or more combatants may not be a limited war for *all* combatants. In Korea, for example, both the United States and China fought limited wars, and neither suffered severe damage on its own territory. For the Koreans, however, the war was hardly limited, and there was tremendous exertion and equally great suffering on both sides of the thirty-eighth parallel.

Second, the definition of "limited" war can be stretched almost infinitely by the side that has proclaimed it is limiting its actions. For example, in 1970 President Richard Nixon, while still proclaiming that the United States was fighting a limited war, ordered secret and illegal bombing of Cambodia, whose ruler, Prince Norodom Sihanouk, was renowned as the best diplomatic tightrope walker in Southeast Asia for having kept Cambodia out of the war. There seems little debate that the American decisions first to bomb Cambodia and then to invade it played a major role in motivating the Cambodian communists, the Khmer Rouge, to escalate their insurgency and ultimately led to the tragedy of Cambodia in 1973–75, when at least one million and perhaps as many as three million Cambodians were uprooted, driven into the countryside, worked to death, or simply executed. America's limited war became total war and near-annihilation for the Cambodian people.

Third, "limited" war is not necessarily much less violent than total war. In Vietnam, for example, although the United States refrained from the use of nuclear weapons, it unleashed virtually every weapon in its conventional arsenal: carpet bombing by B-52s, napalm, high-explosive shells, undersea mines, and so forth. The United States; dropped three times as much high explosive over *South Vietnam* alone as all participants had used in all of World War II. In addition to carpet bombing in both the North and the South, and in Cambodia and Laos as well, the United States deployed vast amounts of ordinance, including and enormous array of chemicals, against the Vietnamese foe. In order to be able to operate better in triple-canopy jungle, the United States made massive airdrops of defoliants, herbicides intended to kill all vegetation and thus remove cover from the Viet Cong and the North Vietnamese.

"Limited war," then, is itself a limited term. While it implies a decision to use some measure of restraint, at least on the part of the major power involved, it can still lead to incredible levels of violence and high casualty rates among civilians.

War and Culture

There are clear links between particular cultures and the ways they approach and fight wars. In this section we will briefly examine links between culture and war in three major modern societies: Western Europe, the Islamic world, and China.

Western Europe

Although war has always characterized Western European society, there have frequently been painful moral conflicts between war itself and the Western Christian ideals of being peacemakers, turning the other cheek, and not killing. The first serious attempts to link Christianity and war came at the start of the Crusades, when leaders of the Roman Catholic Church, at that time the only church in Western Europe, developed the idea of a "holy war"—in this case, a war to redeem the holy sites of Christianity from a non-Christian foe. However, this idea of "holy war" held only if the enemy was non-Christian, and Christian ethicists struggled to develop ideas that would justify war even between or among Christians. The result was the doctrine of "just war" that evolved in the Middle Ages and early modern period.

Just War

just war Doctrine of war concerned with when war is morally justified and how and against whom it should be conducted.

The modern concept of **just war** rests on seven basic principles. First, there must be what is termed a *just cause;* that is, war must be waged as self-defense against an aggressor. A purely aggressive war could not be a just war. It is debatable whether a "preventive war" begun in order to prevent attack from an aggressor nation, like Israel's 1967 pre-emptive war against the Arabs, could constitute just war under this definition.

Second, *a legitimate authority must make the decision to go to war.* In other words, the leaders of a nation, not leaders of lower-level military units, should make such a decision. Third, the warring nation must observe *proportionality* between means and ends. To use an analogy often heard during the American involvement in Vietnam, one should not use a hand grenade to kill a mosquito. Fourth, a just war requires that there be *a reasonable chance of attaining legitimate objectives through the use of force.* In other words, a just war cannot be waged just for revenge or for impossible results. Just war must be realistic. Fifth, just war can happen only when *all other means of achieving the nation's goods have been exhausted.* It must be the last, not the first, resort, taken only when all peaceful means have been exhausted and have failed.

Sixth, *participants in a just war must not use immoral weapons,* that is, weapons that are indiscriminate or that cause needless suffering. This is one of the most difficult precepts of just war, particularly since, as we have discussed above, the thrust of military technology in the twentieth century has been for the development on less and less discriminating weapons. A one-ton "blockbuster" bomb is considerably less discriminating than a hand grenade, a machine gun is much less discriminating than a rifle, chemical weapons are much less discriminating than "a whiff of grapeshot," and nuclear weapons almost by definition are nondiscriminating. A number of contemporary thinkers on military problems have concluded that given these factors, modern warfare may in fact be incapable of being defined as "just."

Finally, and in some ways most important, *decisions to go to war and conduct war must be made for moral and legal purposes.* That is, one cannot go to war for essentially illegal or immoral purposes and then claim that one is conducting a just war because weapons are limited and civilian casualties are avoided (Viotti: 1993, pp. 306–7; see also Walzer 1992). Much of the history of international law and treaties is concerned with putting the principles of just war into general effect. (See chap. 9, "Diplomacy and International Law," for an extended discussion of just war in internatonal law.)

Gradually there emerged other links between Christianity and warfare. During the Reformation, for example, Protestant and Catholic Christians cheerfully battled and slew one another, secure in the belief that they were doing what God wanted. Warfare on behalf of the "correct" version of Christianity blasted across western Europe for nearly two centuries and accounted for hundreds of thousands, if not millions, of deaths, both of combatants in battle and of noncombatants as victims of the array of diseases that accompanied the armies. The most devastating of all these wars erupted in the Holy Roman Empire, a loose coalition of German-speaking peoples that included what would become modern Germany and Austria. As a result of this war (1618–48), known as the Thirty Years' War, much of the Holy Roman Empire was left a wasteland, with cities destroyed, villages emptied, and wolves prowling the streets of towns. The creation of a unified German state was set back by nearly two and a half centuries, and much of nineteenth- and twentieth-century European history has been shaped by newcomer Germany's attempt to assume its "rightful" place. Ironically, at the end of this incredibly destructive war, the solution to the religious issues was essentially to restore the status quo, that is, to allow the ruler of any given area to determine whether the official, and exclusive, religion of the area would be Catholic or Protestant.

The Western tradition has thus been to justify war, even by a Christian society and even against other Christians, and to view war as more or less rational and perhaps even inevitable. Perhaps the best example of this view of war is the work of the nineteenth-century Prussian strategist, **Karl von Clausewitz,** whose text *On War* is in many ways still at the heart of Western thinking. To Clausewitz, war was essentially part of a spectrum along which international politics could be conducted; it was, in his famous dictum, "a continuation of politics by other means." Drawing on the Napoleonic wars particularly, Clausewitz also emphasized the importance of the "decisive battle," that is, the one major battle that can bring war to an end by making one side the clear victor and the other the clear loser.

Clausewitz, Karl von
A nineteenth-century German military thinker of the realist school of thought.

Waterloo, the battle at which Napoleon was finally defeated and his dreams were shattered, is the perfect example of the decisive battle in the Clausewitzian view.

In this Western tradition, emphasis is placed on two major goals: destruction of the enemy's forces and control of the enemy's territory. In many ways, chess is an excellent analogy for the Western style of war, with its direct confrontational style and its emphasis on putting the rival player's pieces out of commission.

The Islamic World

War also has been a major component in the Islamic tradition. The society in which Islam rose, on the Arabian peninsula of the seventh century, was a society in which conflict was endemic. The Prophet Mohammed himself had been a warrior, and the warrior tradition is very much respected within the Islamic culture. According to Islam, the world is divided into two parts: the House of Islam and the House of War. All who submit to the will of Allah (and therefore all Muslims) are within the House of Islam. All other people belong to the House of War, and are subject to conquest and conversion. In fact, in the early centuries of Islam, Muslims (literally, "those who submit to the will of Allah") fought a long series of wars of expansion and conquest to impose the new religion on as many as possible. From the Arabian peninsula, armies bearing the new religion exploded across North Africa and even into western Europe, where Islamic control of Christian Spain lasted nearly eight hundred years, and into the Middle East, which became the heart of the great Islamic empire known as the Caliphate, ruled first from Damascus and then from Baghdad.

Ultimately, the Islamic wars of expansion would carry Islam across the Middle East and into the Indian subcontinent, and from there along the Malay peninsula and into the Spice Islands (modern Indonesia) and the southernmost tip of the Phillippines. Unlike Christians, who struggled to reach a theory of justified war, followers of Islam were driven by an incredibly powerful idea: the idea of Islam and the right of all believers to take arms against any who opposed them. Thus, in a sense, Islam anticipated some of the bloodiest wars of the modern world by stating that an idea, and particularly a religion, was well worth fighting for (Keegan 1993, 192–93).

jihad According to Islamic faith, a holy war against infidels (nonbelievers).

Another part of the Islamic tradition of war is the concept of **jihad.** In its original form, *jihad* (literally, a "holy war") referred to the concept of war against the infidel, which must be proclaimed by the religious leaders of the community. It was guaranteed that anyone killed carrying out *jihad* would be taken immediately to heaven. Consequently, followers of Islam fought with tremendous ferocity in the assurance of eternal life in heaven. In modern times there has been in some places a rethinking of the concept of *jihad,* and many Islamic theologians now view *jihad* not as a literal war of conquest against the infidels, but instead as the constant striving of the individual for perfection in Islam. The war implied in *jihad,* in other words, is seen not as a war between peoples but as a war within the individual—literally, a war for his or her own soul (Gilsevan, 1993, 491–92).

Nonetheless, various Islamic leaders recently have attempted to proclaim *jihad* on their own. In the 1991 Persian Gulf War, for example, Iraq's Saddam Hussein called for *jihad* against the United States and the other nations leagued together to drive his forces out of Kuwait. However, no other Islamic state responded to his call, and it is not clear whether the concept was of any use to Saddam in motivating his own forces. Given the speed with which the allied coalition swept into Kuwait and through Iraq, and the high rate of surrender among

Iraqi forces, it seems unlikely that the vast majority of Iraqis were inspired to action by a *jihad* proclaimed not by a spiritual leader but by a military dictator.

The Chinese Paradox

China presents a different, much more paradoxical picture. Traditional Chinese society drew its values from the teachings of the sage known as Confucius in the West, and Kung Fu-tze in Asia. His teachings, recorded by disciples after his death in the sixth century B.C., have shaped Chinese ideas of the nature of society and the place of war and the warrior within society for two and a half millennia. Confucius taught that the ideal society was one ruled by educated men, those in whom education had distilled the essence of "human-heartedness," the finest principles of human nature. Not only should the emperor possess such virtue; so too should his advisors and those whom he chose to direct his government. Thus the traditional imperial government was staffed by "scholar-officials," educated individuals who had passed an elaborate series of examinations on Confucian theory and were thus considered best suited to rule the empire. The scholar's real claim to influence and rule was not his education, but the moral superiority with which that education had in theory endowed him. A series of fundamental relationships (ruler to subject, father to son, etc.) was devised with the understanding that as long as these relationships were rightly ordered, harmony would prevail and society would be stable. (See chap. 6, "Ideas That Make the World Go Round," for a fuller discussion of Confucianism.)

Under the Confucian system, society was divided into four basic classes of people, in descending order of their value; scholars, peasants, artisans and workers, and merchants. Soldiers were not mentioned. "One does not use good iron to make nails," a Chinese proverb says, "nor does one use good men to make soldiers." British military historian John Keegan points out that "the Confucian ideal of rationality, continuity, and maintenance of institutions led them to seek means of subordinating the warrior impulse to the constraints of law and custom." Thus, Keegan continues, "the most persistent feature of Chinese military life was moderation, designed to preserve cultural forms rather than serve imperatives of foreign conquest or internal revolution" (Keegan 1993, 388).

Nonetheless, China also possesses a long history of warfare; an empire so vast always has had borders to defend, internal rebellions to quell, and potential enemies to defeat. For centuries the various dynasties maintained huge armies, especially in the vast central Asian region known as China's Inner Asian Frontier, potentially most vulnerable because of the presence of barbarians just beyond the areas of Chinese settlement. And issues of dynastic succession often were settled by war. However, any dynasty that conquered China invariably discovered that it had to adopt the Confucian system in order to rule the empire. As the ancient proverb says, "China may be conquered by the sword, but it must be ruled by the writing brush." Even "barbarian" dynasties, like the Mongol Yuan and the Manchu Ch'ing, relied heavily on Confucian scholars to staff their administrations, and the conquerors, even the emperors, found themselves becoming scholars simply to be able to rule.

Yet classical China produced one of the great theorists of war, Sun Tzu, as early as the fifth century B.C. It was Sun Tzu who first articulated the concept of protracted war, although he began his work on war with the statement that going to war was essentially an admission of failure, because peaceful means were always to be preferred as a way of solving differences. Sun Tzu's principles of war, in direct contrast to the Western emphasis on the decisive battle, emphasize the importance of evasion, delay, and indirectness (Sun Tzu 1963).

In contemporary China, Mao Tse-tung has stressed the importance of military power, beginning with his statement that "power grows from the barrel of a gun." Mao emphasized that military power and political power were closely interlinked, and used the army as a means of dealing with civilian issues, even such things as literacy and health care. At the same time, Mao also emphasized the importance of moral force, which he linked to successful use of military force, and of human will, which he believed was capable of overcoming all kinds of material and military shortcomings.

The Causes of War

Just as war itself is a complex series of events, so too the causes of war are often difficult to unravel. Explanations for why war occurs can be essentially theological (original sin and human nature), economic (lust for someone else's property), or behavioral (war as a learned behavior). In this section we will examine the major theories of the causality of war.

In his great work *History of the Peloponnesian War,* the fifth-century-B.C. Greek author Thucydides literally invented analytical history, briefly outlining earlier conflicts among the Greeks and succinctly presenting each party's stated reasons for going to war. However, Thucydides himself was unconvinced by these arguments, stating, "The real reason for the war is, in my opinion, most likely to be disguised by such an argument." The actual causes of the Peloponnesian war were both far more important to understand and far simpler to express. "What made war inevitable was the growth of Athenian power and the fear which this caused in Sparta" (Thucydides 1972, 49). That's it—short, succinct, and inclusive. In Thucydides' brief sentence are summed up the causes of war most commonly identified even today: the economic dilemma of Athenian expansion, the potential if not real imbalance of power between two major states, and Sparta's psychological reaction to that economic and power imbalance. As classical scholar Donald Kagan summarizes Thucydides, war grew from three mainsprings: honor, fear, and interest (Kagan 1995, 8). The following discussions will expand on Thucydides, but it is doubtful that we, or anybody else, can improve upon him.

Economic Theories of War

Liberal economists of the nineteenth century, like many at the end of the twentieth century, optimistically believed that free, unfettered trade among nations would quite automatically result in peace and mutual prosperity. The more nations traded with one another, buying, selling, and using one another's goods, the more international calm and peace could prevail. There might be minor skirmishes, but never again would the European continent be ravaged by warfare on the Napoleonic scale.

However, during the latter nineteenth century and early twentieth century, other analysts stood this logic on its head. They argued that economics was the underlying cause of war. War happened when nations in search of new markets, cheap labor, and raw materials collided with one another. The persistence of this belief is reflected in the United Nations' call for a literal re-formation of global economics to eliminate inequities, the New International Economic Order (NIEO), passed by the General Assembly in 1974. The underlying assumption of the NIEO was that once economic inequities among nations were eliminated, or even moderated, the root causes of war in the modern world would be likewise eliminated. However, the industrialized nations did not react enthusiastically to what was in effect a call for global redistribution of wealth—*their* wealth—and the dreams of the NIEO have faded gradually, replaced by renewed emphasis on development and aid from industrial to developing nations, or from the industrialized North to the nonindustrialized South.

Marx

Perhaps the most influential proponents of the economic view of war have been Karl Marx and his disciples, for whom everything was economic. (See chap. 6, "Ideas That Make the World Go Round," for a fuller discussion of Marxism.) According to Marx and his followers, economics controls all aspects of society, and the economic substructure dictates political, social, moral, and legal systems—both those within and those that link nations. Conflict is inevitable within any state, as history works its way from the original utopian state, which has been corrupted by the acquisition of private property, the dominance of one class over another, and class warfare. The violence that would be found in class warfare might well spill over into relations between and among states as well.

Hobson

The first influential theorist to apply Marxist economic analysis to warfare was John A. Hobson, an Oxford-educated journalist. Hobson began to formulate his theories of what he called economic imperialism while covering the Boer War at the very beginning of the twentieth century. This war saw a small group of Boers, descendants of the original Dutch settlers of South Africa, pitted against Englishmen intent on claiming this strategically vital territory for the British Empire. In his dispatches Hobson focused less on the war itself, or on the issue of British imperial interests, than on the role played by diamond monopolists and other wealthy capitalists, like Cecil Rhodes, who were clearly more interested in the opportunity to exploit South African resources than in protecting and extending the interests of the British Empire.

Hobson's theory of **economic imperialism** began with the assumption that some capitalists had amassed a large surplus of wealth by suppressing wages of their workers. Laborers were barely able to provide the essentials of life for themselves and their families, and certainly could not spent anything on what they perceived as luxuries. Thus capitalist societies faced a dilemma: workers could not consume enough of a nation's industrial output because of their low wages (underconsumption), and consequently capitalists had to find other places to invest their money to achieve an even larger return on their investments (overproduction). Hobson characterized such investment abroad by venture capitalists seeking to deepen their pockets as imperialism. Imperialism thus was not a political matter, but an economic one, "the endeavors of the great controllers of industry to broaden the channel for the flow of their surplus wealth by seeking foreign markets and foreign investments to take off the goods and capital they [could] not sell or use at home" (Hobson 1965, 85).

Hobson thus saw business as controlling the state, or, in a more contemporary formulation, the flag as following trade. However, what was good for British

economic imperialism Transference of one's economic system or products abroad, displacing the existing system or products produced.

shipbuilders was not necessarily good for all of Britain. A handful of merchants and manufacturers profited, not the nation itself. In fact, according to Hobson, imperialism involved Britain in conflicts at cross-purposes with its true national interests. "Finance capitalism manipulates the patriotic forces which politicians, soldiers, philanthropists, and traders generate; the enthusiasm for expansion which issues from these sources, though strong and genuine, is irregular and blind; the financial interest has those qualities of concentration and clearsighted calculation which are needed to set imperialism at work" (Hobson 1965, 132). While Hobson did not believe that every war was economically motivated, he believed that certain capitalists would take every opportunity to exact profit and gain from any foreign war. Wars created profits, and profits were good for those who sold munitions.

Lenin

Vladimir Ilyich Lenin, who directed the Bolshevik Revolution in Russia in 1917 and founded and led the Union of Soviet Socialist Republics until his death in 1924, carried the Marxist analysis of economic causes of warfare even further.

Deeply influenced not only by Marxist theory but also by World War I, which he saw as a capitalist-orchestrated conflict that the working class should steer clear of, Lenin wrote an influential treatise, *Imperialism: The Highest Stage of Capitalism,* in 1919. Lenin wrote that capitalism must inevitably lead to imperialism. The development of monopolies—trusts, combines, syndicates, and cartels— would concentrate the forces of production and would intensify the competition for raw materials. This in turn would be augmented by the equally inevitable development of banking oligarchies. The struggle to find easily accessible, cheap raw materials would combine with the equally important struggle to develop markets. Finally, capitalism would transform the older colonial policies into a struggle for spheres of economic interests in which the powerful capitalist nations could more successfully exploit the weaker ones. Finance capitalism, the advanced stage of industrial capitalism epitomized by the early-twentieth-century European powers like Britain, France, and Germany, inevitably led to imperialism, and imperialism inevitably led to war among the imperialists.

In Lenin's view, then, while war itself might be complex, the causes of war were simple. There was, in fact, a single cause of war: capitalism. Consequently there would also be an easy way—at least for Marxists—to end all wars and achieve enduring peace: overthrow capitalism and establish the proletarian state. Peace would finally occur when all capitalist states had been abolished and the worldwide workers' state had begun to wither away with the arrival of a totally harmonious society in which all economic causes of conflict had been removed.

Problems with Economic Cause Theories

The first and most obvious problem with this Marxist and quasi-Marxist analysis of the causes of war is that it oversimplifies. War is such a complex event, and wars have resulted from so many different causes, that to attempt to narrow everything to a single cause seems bound to fail from the very beginning. Although Thucydides would have agreed in part with the Marxist analysis—he did, after all, see Athenian imperialism as a major cause of the Peloponnesian War—he also added other dimensions, such as power considerations and psychological factors.

Quincy Wright, author of one of the most important studies of modern war, claims that contrary to Marxist theory, "capitalistic societies have been the most peaceful forms of societies yet developed" (Wright 1970, 302). In fact, Wright says, agrarian and socialist states have initiated far more modern wars than capitalistic ones. For example, he states that the Prussian Junkers, with their great agrarian estates in eastern Germany, were the spearhead of German militarism in 1914, rather than the Rhineland industrial capitalists. In 1939 it was the National Socialists, not the capitalists of France and England, who initiated war. Japanese militarism "sprang from the peasantry and the army, not from the bankers, merchants, and industrialists." British imperialism, Wright maintains, drew its chief support from the conservative landed aristocracy, not from the liberal merchants and industrialists. Over and over, Wright says, "businessmen, bankers, and investors have generally urged peaceful policies in time of crisis. Dominantly agrarian countries like Russia and the Balkans were more ready to spring to arms during the 19th century than were the industrialized states" (Wright 1970, 303).

Behavioral Theories of War

In this century a number of social scientists, both within and outside the field of political science, have attempted to examine behavioral theories to see whether they can adequately explain why wars occur. Many of these behavioral scientists have used both paleoanthropology and recent studies of human behavior to try to determine whether war is inevitable.

Aggression

Much of this approach to the causes of war revolves around the study of **aggression.** Is aggression instinctive or learned? If individuals are inherently aggressive, can the same be said of nations? In the late 1950s and 1960s (at the height of Cold War tensions and openly debated possibilities of nuclear war), a number of people began to write about the innate tendency of human beings toward aggression and thus toward war.

Konrad Lorenz, a Nobel Prize–winning scientist, based his analysis of human aggression primarily on observation of animal aggression. His studies showed, he said, that aggression "is an instinct like any other and in natural conditions it helps just as much as any other to insure the survival of the individual and the species" (Lorenz 1967, x). Lorenz also links aggression to species that form love bonds, like the human being. Bonding protects males and females from each other, he proclaims, protects their territory, and preserves their young. Thus in animal species, he writes, aggression is perpetrated primarily by males against "intruder" males who covet both the female and the territory. However, Lorenz maintains, there are important differences between aggression in the wild and aggression in human beings. In the natural state, animals have developed means of "turning off" aggression, largely by behaviors such as retreating or displaying signs of submission. Thus the wolf that rolls on its back, opening its vital organs to its opponent in a sign of absolute submission, triggers a response that shuts down aggression in the victor and permits the survival of the vanquished. Lorenz argues, however, that while humans originally had such a mechanism, the submissive response has largely "atrophied" because of the development of weapons. The use of weapons—the throwing stick, the axe, the bow and arrow—"distanced" aggressor

aggression An instinct that in natural conditions helps to insure the survival of the individual and the species.

from victim and gradually extinguished the instinct that allowed a defeated foe to survive. In this way, Lorenz argues, "man [was] . . . transformed from a subsistence hunter of other species into an aggressive killer of his own" (quoted in Keegan 1994, 85).

Journalist Robert Ardrey carried Lorenz's work much farther. His best-seller *The Territorial Imperative* (1967) was based on recent anthropological studies that showed very early proto-human habitats littered with cracked skulls and broken bones. Ardrey concluded that the proximity of human hearths and cracked human skulls meant that our earliest ancestors were not only innately aggressive creatures, making the first tools into weapons with which to kill both prey and potential rivals, but also cannibals who cracked thighbones to suck out the marrow. Building on that fairly slight base, Ardrey derived a picture of the earliest humans as aggressors, almost constantly at war with their environment and with one another. This darkly pessimistic view served both to justify contemporary bellicosity—after all, it was only natural for humans to be warlike—and to imply that peaceful behavior among human beings, and thus among states, was all but impossible.

These views of human beings as biologically and culturally inclined to aggression, to the destruction of their own species, seemed to fit well into the Cold War and the aftermath of World War II. After all, the scores of millions who had died in World War II and the hundreds of millions who might well die should Cold War explode into nuclear war could be seen easily as victims and potential victims of human nature. These theories in effect absolved persons of responsibility for their violent behavior and shifted that responsibility to nature itself, much as earlier religious theorists had seen war as an inevitable result of the Fall of Adam and Eve.

The Critics

This severely determinist view of aggression and war soon found many critics. A number of anthropologists pointed out that there were many primitive societies that led entirely peaceful existences, like the Zuni of the American Southwest. Those who believe that man is not naturally violent, and that war thus can ultimately be eliminated, have responded to the aggression theorists with heavy artillery.

For example, neurobiologists have attempted to explore the brain itself to discover whether there is an innate "seat of aggression" and whether human aggression is inevitable and uncontrollable, as Lorenz, Ardrey, and their followers would believe. In fact, scientists have discovered deep within the human brain what they call "the seat of aggression," the limbic system in the lower brain. However, these same neurobiologists have established that although aggression is indeed lodged in the lower brain, it is controlled by the frontal lobes. There may be a tendency toward aggression, but it is controllable by the upper brain: the rational faculty of the eighteenth-century Enlightenment (Keegan 1993, 81–82).

Further damage to the "human being as natural killer" school of thought has been done by more recent anthropological studies, which seem to indicate that the necessities of functioning within a social group have been far more important in the development of human behavior than aggression. The work of Don Johanson, discoverer of "Lucy" and her family, indicates that as long as five million years ago our earliest known anthropoid (humanlike) ancestors lived in families and apparently shared food and responsibilities (Johanson and Edey 1981; Johanson and Shreeve 1989). Other recent anthropological work shows that the supposedly primitive and barbarian Neanderthal man, which flourished one hundred thousand or more years ago, not only lived in family groups but also apparently cared for the older or disabled members of the family who could not take care of themselves. Neanderthal sites show remains, for example, of "elderly" Neanderthals crippled by severe arthritis or by broken bones; these people, unable to care for themselves, had apparently been nurtured, in some cases for years, by their fellows.

These anthropological findings of the 1980s seemed to fit much better into the "kinder, gentler" world that was being extolled during that decade, the age of the "sensitive, caring man." Certainly this far more optimistic view of human beings as not after all innately aggressive gave cause for the belief that further war was not inevitable and that humans indeed might not be living on the eve of destruction.

However, no matter how rosy these scenarios are, there does seem to be some validity to the idea that there are innately aggressive individuals. The front pages of daily newspapers graphically detail aggressive behavior translated into criminal activity at what sometimes seems an accelerating pace. Even if we grant that many people may have aggressive tendencies although well controlled or suppressed almost completely, this still leaves us confronting another question. How does aggressive behavior among individuals translate into aggressive behavior at a national level? To deal with this, we will shift to a different level of analysis, to look at the role played by individual nations and by the international system itself in war.

A recent attempt to place the origins of war within an evolutionary context suggests that it is not innate aggression but historical development that leads to war. Robert L. O'Connell, a military historian and intelligence analyst, traces the origins of war to the rise of settled agricultural societies and urban centers. These urban centers, such as Sumer, were inherently unstable, vulnerable to disease, overpopulation, and famine. Within the context of such instability, O'Connell maintains, war originated as a balancing mechanism. War permitted the seizure of land and resources, expansion, and, in times of pestilence, refreshment of the labor pool by allowing the use of captives. (O'Connell 1995, 95–96) "War did all these things, not elegantly but directly and effectively" (O'Connell 1995, 100). War as an organized institution, O'Connell maintains, originated relatively late in the evolution of humanity: "humankind was not born to war but came to it late in our existence and as the result of fundamental shifts in subsistence patterns" (O'Connell 1995, 225). War then was not an innate human condition, but a response to particular demographic patterns, those of the large urban center dependent on agriculture, caught in the "plant trap."

State and System Theories of War

People behave differently in groups than they do as individuals. Nations also behave differently from any of their citizens. This is a major assumption of political scientists, international relations scholars, sociologists, and anthropologists. These social scientists tend to view conflict as normal, whereas psychologists, dealing primarily with individuals, view conflict as abnormal and dysfunctional. However, this doesn't mean that political scientists view conflict as beneficial. It could be normal for a person to be chronically ill; that doesn't mean that being ill is good for that person. However, some modern theorists see conflict as potentially beneficial to a state because of its integrative effects.

Scapegoating

Coser-Simmel thesis Concept used in conjunction with conflict literature that asserts that a nation might seek relief from internal problems by initiating a conflict with a foreign nation to alleviate pressure internally.

scapegoat theory The theory that a nation starts a war to divert attention from its internal turmoils.

Political scientists are fascinated with the relationship between *internal* and *external* political conflict. If a nation is experiencing turmoil within its boundaries, does this mean trouble for one or more of its neighbors? Might rulers facing trouble at home look beyond their boundaries for relief by galvanizing their people against an objective, foreign enemy? This idea is formally known as the **Coser-Simmel thesis:** external threat = internal cohesion. In other words, if you have internal strife, alleviate it by creating an external threat.

This **scapegoat theory** of war is discredited by Geoffrey Blainey (1972) and others. Blainey questions the premise that if a nation is in trouble at home, it is "cheaper" or "easier" to pick on an external foe than to suppress the internal dissidents. Moreover, says Blainey, if a foe recognizes that a nation is internally weak, might not the foe initiate the war? Modern empirical theorists like Rudolph Rummel (1963) and Raymond Tanter (1969) both support Blainey's contention. They find little correlation between internal turmoil and external aggression. Thus, as intriguing and intuitively appealing as the scapegoat theory may be, internal turmoil is probably only a minor part of the theory of international conflict. In fact, as the United States discovered during the Vietnam War, external conflict may in fact produce or exacerbate internal turmoil.

System Failures

The failure of international systems can also be a major factor in the eruption of war. For example, the interlocking treaties that the major powers had agreed to late in the nineteenth and early in the twentieth centuries had been intended to restore the balance of power system disrupted by the emergence of Bismarck's militaristic Germany. However, instead of restoring the balance of power, these treaties tied nations to one another in such a way that the irresponsible actions of small and weak nations ultimately dragged the larger powers into the cataclysm of war. The fuse for World War I was lit in the Balkans, where Serbia, assured of support from the Russian Empire, pursued a reckless policy that led to confrontation with the much larger Austro-Hungarian Empire. In turn, the Austro-Hungarian leaders pursued reckless policies because they were sure of unconditional support from Germany. Thus Balkan politics tugged at the system of treaties, and like dominoes falling, nation after nation moved to fulfill treaty obligations, driving the next player to even more extreme measures, and finally pulling all of Europe, most of the Middle East, and much of the rest of the world as well over the cliff.

This ability of small powers to drag larger powers into war loomed large again during the Cold War, as both the United States and the Soviet Union linked their fortunes to those of their client states and interpreted virtually every facet of international relations as directly related to their own interests, rather than assuming that perhaps the smaller nations had interests of their own. While this left some room for smaller nations to maneuver by playing the superpowers off against each other—Anwar Sadat of Egypt proved particularly masterful at this—it also carried the high risk that miscalculation would precipitate direct confrontation between the superpowers (as it did during the Cuban Missile Crisis), and that such direct confrontation could easily escalate into nuclear war (as it luckily did not during the Cuban Missile Crisis).

The collapse of the international system at the outset of World War I led to almost desperate attempts to create an even stronger, "foolproof" international system after the war. The League of Nations was intended to provide an alternative to a world of nations linked to one another by treaties: an international congress where problems could be worked out, and a mutual security system that could contain and suppress violence if it should erupt. However, lacking two of the most important powers, the United States and the Soviet Union, the League of Nations was virtually impotent from the moment it first convened. By the 1930s, a combination of the inherent weaknesses of the League, the lack of major players in it, and a lassitude induced by memories of the Great War and the problems of the Great Depression had all but incapacitated it. As the world careened toward war, aggressor nations like Italy, Japan, and Germany withdrew from the League and ignored both its warnings and its pleadings.

The failure of the League of Nations led to yet another attempt after World War II to erect a global structure capable of sustaining peace; the United Nations. This time both the United States and the Soviet Union participated in the global structure—which may not have been a blessing. While the League of Nations had been partially hamstrung by the absence of these two powers, the United Nations was completely hamstrung because of their presence. The Cold War meant that at least for a decade or more, members of the General Assembly, and the Security Council as well, tended to side with one or another of the Cold War antagonists. The United Nations became more of an arena for confrontation between the two sets of allies than a forum for discussion and solution of problems. The result was that the United Nations became essentially a shield for American actions during the Korean conflict, and in some ways all but ceased to function on the global, superpower level from then on. (In chap. 4, "The Galaxy of Global Actors," we have considered these institutions in greater detail.)

There also has been a concerted effort for the last century to create treaties and other forms of international law in order to provide a stable international system that will prevent or contain war. Such agreements as the various Hague and Geneva conventions, the **Kellogg-Briand Pact,** and the charters of both the League of Nations and the United Nations all represent attempts to use law itself to create a system that makes war impossible. Sadly, a look at any morning paper or fifteen minutes with "CNN Cable News" all too quickly confirms that such efforts still leave a great deal to be desired. On the other hand, the international cooperation attained during the Gulf War of 1990–91 at least holds out hope that future cooperation to stem war will be possible now that the Cold War has ceased to provide the basic framework for international relations.

Kellogg-Briand Pact
A treaty (1928) that sought to outlaw war as an instrument of national policy.

Leadership: The Nexus of State and Individual

One of the most perceptive contemporary writers on the causes of war, John Stoessinger, focuses on the intersection point between states and individuals, the leaders, in presenting case studies of seven major wars in this century. Stoessinger sees two principal and intertwining causal factors: the personalities of the leaders, and the perceptions—or more often, misperceptions—of the leaders. He rejects the mechanistic or fatalistic view that war is inevitable, that it occurs when events pass beyond human control: "Such a view is wrong; mortal men made these decisions. They made them in fear and in trembling, but they made them nonetheless. In most cases they were not evil men bent on destruction but frightened men entrapped by self-delusion. They based their policies on fears, not facts, and were singularly devoid of empathy. Misperception, rather than conscious evil designs, seems to have been the leading villian in the drama" (Stoessinger 1993, 2).

In the conclusion to his outstanding book, Stoessinger draws a number of lessons about the causes and beginnings of wars. First, he points out that no nation that began a major war in this century emerged as a winner. His second point is that in the nuclear age, war between nuclear powers is clearly suicidal; wars between small countries with big friends are likely to be inconclusive and interminable. Thus, only small and nearly impotent nations can hope to fight decisive wars. Stoessinger goes on to observe that in the twentieth century, a "victor's peace" is seldom lasting unless the vanquished state is completely destroyed. Thus the Allied victors' peace at Versailles merely paved the way for another round of general war, and the Israeli victor's peace over the Arabs in 1967 led within a few years to renewed war.

Stoessinger stresses as well the importance of leaders' personalities in the outbreak of war. "The case studies indicate the crucial importance of the personalities of the leaders." Stoessinger finds that larger, abstract forces like militarism, nationalism, and economics are far less important than the personalities of the leaders, which "have often been decisive." In terms of World War I, Stoessinger finds what he calls "the relentless mediocrity of the leading personalities on all sides" to be a critical factor. The personality of Hitler was, in Stoessinger's opinion, the crucial factor in precipitating World War II, while the hubris of General Douglas MacArthur and the egos of Presidents Johnson and Nixon played key roles in prolonging the agonies of the Korean and Vietnamese wars.

However, Stoessinger continues, "the most important single precipitating factor in the outbreak of war is misperception." Distortions appear in four key ways, he explains: in a leader's image of himself; a leader's image of his adversary; a leader's view of his adversary's intentions; and a leader's view of his adversary's capabilities and power. Stoessinger points out as well that virtually all leaders on the eve of war confidently expect to win a short war. The problem is, Stoessinger writes, that "this common belief in a short, decisive war is usually the overflow from a reservoir of self-delusions held by the leadership about both itself and the nation." The quintessential cause of war, he continues, is the leader's misperception of his adversary's power. This perception is far more important than any reality: "It is not the actual distribution of power that precipitates a war; it is the way in which a leader thinks that power is distributed." Stoessinger goes on to say, "Thus, on the eve of each war, at least one nation misperceives another's power. In that sense, the beginning of each war is a misperception or an accident" (Stoessinger 1993, 209–18). In "The Game of Nations" (chap. 10), we have discussed the function of intelligence-gathering and its role in the making of policy—and the ways that even the finest intelligence can go astray.

"Crazy States"

A related problem in the consideration of leadership and war is what is sometimes called the "crazy state," that is, the state whose leader does not conform to generally expected norms of conduct or decision-making. The classic example of a "crazy state" was Nazi Germany under Hitler, but modern nations such as Moammar

"Hot Lines"

More than ever, the maintenance of peace depends on accurate and rapid communications. For example, most contemporary American missiles are characterized as "Launch on Warning" (LOW) systems. That is, they are to be launched as soon as there is information that other missiles have been launched against the United States, instead of waiting until those missiles have landed. In 1984 alone there were 256 "serious" LOW errors (Frederick 1993, 11). Miscommunication or noncommunication can be hazardous to the world's health.

Certainly the most dramatic illustration of the necessity for direct and rapid international communication was the Cuban Missile Crisis of October 1962. The first (as far as we know, the only) direct superpower confrontation that threatened to escalate into nuclear war, the missile crisis demonstrated how vulnerable the entire world was to any failure in communications. The crisis began to unfold when satellite reconnaissance photographs clearly showed that the Soviet Union had begun placement of offensive nuclear missiles in Cuba, which the United States interpreted as a direct and immediate threat to its own territory as well as a skewing of the balance of power. After a series of tense White House meetings, the administration of President John F. Kennedy decided against air strikes to take out the missile sites. Instead, the United States proclaimed a quarantine of Cuba and demanded that the Soviet Union withdraw the missiles. Initially, Soviet Premier Nikita Khrushchev responded belligerently, rattling Soviet missiles. Nuclear war seemed possible, if not yet imminent, and the world faced its first direct nuclear threat. Messages moved back and forth between Kennedy and Khrushchev by a variety of uncertain channels: traditional diplomatic routes, with their cumbersome encoding, transmission, and decoding; personal messages carried by a number of individuals, including a television reporter; and finally, over-the-air broadcasts indicating that the Soviet premier was backing down and was ready to remove the missiles from Cuba. The American government received too letters from Khrushchev, one belligerent and the other conciliatory; it decided to act upon the conciliatory message

GLOBAL PERSPECTIVES

and ignore the belligerent one. The crisis was defused and virtually everyone worldwide breathed a deep sigh of relief.

However, the multiple communications problems encountered during the Cuban Missile Crisis starkly illustrated the dangers of relying upon uncertain and sometimes indirect communications systems. In 1989 Anatoly Dobrynin, who had been Soviet ambassador to the United States during the missile crisis, recalled that he had sent critical messages to his own government via Western Union bicycle messengers, "who may have stopped for lunch or to chat with friends, completely oblivious to the world-shaking messages they were carrying" (Brugioni 1991, 565).

In the aftermath of the missile crisis, analyses focused in part on the dangers posed by slow and indirect communications. As President Kennedy himself concluded, "In a nuclear age, speed is very desirable. So we are hoping that out of this present conversation we can get instantaneous communication" (quoted in Brugioni, 565).

Such instantaneous communication took the shape of the "hot line" between Washington and Moscow, formally approved in June of 1963. The initial hot line, which became operational on August 30, 1963, was a teletype system capable of transmitting coded messages at the rate of one page every three minutes. The communications revolution has produced a far more modern system of computers and fax machines, linked together by two satellite systems and an undersea cable to provide virtually instantaneous communications.

The American hot line originates from the Pentagon, inside the windowless complex known as the National Military Command Center, which can relay messages to the president by a variety of means. Twelve translators remain ready day and night, and every hour on the hour they send and receive test messages to ensure that the hot line is working. Despite movie and television dramatizations, the leaders do not actually talk directly to each other. Written messages avoid any possibility of misunderstanding because of simultaneous translation, and allow leaders time to consult with their advisers and prepare well-thought-out responses (Drew 1993).

(continued on p. 394)

"Hot Lines"
(Continued from p. 393)

Although it has never been used in a nuclear crisis, the hot line has seen use in a number of lesser crises. During the six days of the Arab-Israeli War of 1967, President Lyndon Johnson and Soviet Premier Aleksei Kosygin exchanged more than twenty messages over the hot line to make sure that the superpowers did not become entangled in the conflict, and then to bring about a cease-fire. President Richard M. Nixon used the hot line to confer with his Soviet counterpart during the India-Pakistan War of 1971 and the Yom Kippur Arab-Israeli War of 1973, and President Jimmy Carter employed the hot line to try to develop greater rapport with Soviet premier Leonid Brezhnev and to register American anger at the Soviet invasion of Afghanistan in 1979. The winding down of the Cold War in the late 1980s and early 1990s has allowed Soviet, Russian, and American leaders to communicate directly via the telephone, but the hot line remains ready just in case, as "the nuclear age's equivalent of dialing 911." Since its installation, it has been, as one writer reports, the embodiment of hope, "the idea that if the two leaders could just communicate, common sense would prevail, no matter how late the hour" (Drew 1993).

Quadafi's Libya and Saddam Hussein's Iraq also may be viewed as "crazy states." While some of the international difficulties in comprehending what Quadafi or Saddam might do next stem from cultural differences, they, like Hitler, often take risks that seem far too great by normative standards of acceptable levels of risk. Additionally, "crazy state" leaders do not accept normal diplomatic processes; Hitler's consistent use of the "big lie" confounded the diplomatic community of the 1930s. Nor do they seem to make "rational decisions," often relying on intuition that makes predicting, and therefore planning to deal with, their actions virtually impossible. This leads to the phenomenon of "the rationality of irrationality": irrational behavior may give the "crazy state" and its leader enormous advantages in dealing with rational states and leaders expecting rational behavior. Students of "crazy states" emphasize that normal diplomacy and normal decision-making is generally inadequate to deal with the "crazy state," particularly the one with a charismatic leader, and that strategies such as deterrence may in fact be counterproductive. Devising strategies to deal with "crazy states," especially ones equipped with nuclear or chemical/biological weapons, will have to be a major focus of both diplomatic and strategic planning in the future (Jablonsky 1991).

The Future of War—Or, Does War Have a Future?

The Cold War is clearly over. The nearly fifty-year conflict between the United States and the Soviet Union has vanished, as has the Soviet Union itself. The major question facing those involved in international relations today is this: What will replace it? We can be more specific to this chapter: Does the end of the Cold War mean the end of all wars among the major powers, or does it mean that with the constraints of nuclear terror and superpower whim removed, war will become more widespread?

As you might expect, experts are split more or less down the middle on this question. A substantial group argues that future major wars are unlikely, if not outright impossible, while another group argues that we will see not only more "small" wars, but also a heightened possibility of wars involving major powers.

The "No More Wars" Proponents

The End of History?

One of the most interesting approaches to the question of the future of war has been advanced by historian Francis Fukuyama. In an interesting and controversial article followed by a book, Fukuyama argues that in effect history has ended (Fukuyama 1992). Interpreting history as a clash of ideas, with the competition between Marxism and liberal democracy as its most recent stage, Fukuyama argues that the end of the Cold War and the collapse of communism represents the end of history as we have experienced it for the past two hundred years. Liberal democracy and its companion capitalism have triumphed, Fukuyama argues, and their triumph virtually eliminates the possibility of future major wars. "There [will] . . . still be a high and perhaps rising level of ethnic and nationalist violence . . . [T]errorism and wars of national liberation will continue to be an important item on the international agenda. But large-scale conflict must involve large states still caught in the grip of history, and they are what appear to be passing from the scene" (Fukuyama 1992, 17). These ideas have evoked an enormous amount of controversy and criticism, including the obvious one that history involves much more than simply the clash of ideas.

No Wars between Liberal Democracies?

Another scholar, Michael Doyle, has concluded that there is little likelihood of war between liberal democracies, and that the growing number of such democracies, or at least of self-proclaimed democracies, is thus reducing the probability of war. In a 1986 article, building on the analysis of Immanuel Kant, Doyle distinguishes a number of reasons that democracies are unlikely to fight one another. One reason is the very nature of democracy. Voters do not like war, for which they must pay in both blood and taxes, and are likely to view war with another democracy as illegitimate. Further, because leaders serve limited terms in democracies, personal animosities among democratic leaders are unlikely to cause war. Further, democracies tend to respect international law and use diplomacy to solve conflicts. Because they respect not only law but one another, liberal democracies will expect cooperation. There is an "expectation of amity" that may well be self-fulfilling. Finally, the interaction of liberal democracies "adds material incentives to moral commitments." Since trade and the prosperity associated with it can function best in peacetime, with open markets, democracies will tend to avoid war in order to continue enjoying prosperity. And because this trade takes place within the marketplace, states do not have direct responsibility for it and thus "states can stand aside from, and to some degree above, these contentious market relations and be ready to step in to resolve crises" (Doyle 1986, 1151–67).

A recent attempt by Bruce Russett and his colleagues to empirically test Doyle's thesis that liberal democracies don't go to war against one another has supported Doyle's basic ideas. According to this group, a number of factors support this idea. For example, democratic leaders accustomed to peaceful resolution of domestic conflict will tend to follow similar methods internationally and will expect their counterparts to do the same. Consequently, stable democracies will allow democratic norms to guide their international behavior and peace usually will result. These researchers also conclude that violence between democracies probably will occur only if one of them is unstable (Russett, Antholis, C. Ember, M. Ember, and Maoz 1993, 35).

The Skeptics: Not surprisingly, the optimistic view that conflicts between or among democracies will be scarce has been challenged. In a recent article, Christopher Layne examines four cases of near-war between democracies, and concludes that democratic peace theory did little to predict the outcomes of the four test cases (1994). He concludes that realism provided better means for such prediction. Consequently, Layne suggests that the empirical evidence purporting to support democratic peace theory should also be revisited. Doyle rebuts by emphasizing that by no means has there been enough testing of what he sees as the two potential models contesting liberal democratic theory: realism and Marxism. "In short, before we can truly engage in a debate over a general theory in international politics, other traditions will need to catch up" to the work already done on liberal democratic theory (Doyle 1995).

The "Lesson Learned" Perspective

Others who agree with Fukuyama's conclusion that there is small likelihood of future wars among the major powers reach this conclusion from a very different perspective. For example, John Mueller argues that just as institutions like slavery and dueling once seemed perfectly sensible and logical to societies and nations, in time people came to see them as wrong, costly, and immoral, and thus eliminated both of them. Mueller points out that "an accepted, time-honored institution that serves an urgent social purpose can be obsolescent and then die out because a lot of people come to find it obnoxious" (Mueller 1994, 24). He continues, "If war, like dueling, [came] to be viewed as a thoroughly undesirable, even ridiculous, policy, and if it [could] no longer promise gains or if potential combatants no longer value[d] the things it [could] gain for them, then war would fade away. . . . Like dueling, it could become unfashionable and then obsolete" (Mueller, 27). The physical and psychic costs of war are enormous, Mueller says, and people seem to be catching on to that fact. "War does not appear to be one of life's necessities. . . . One can live without it, quite well in fact. War may be a social affliction, but in important respects it is also a social affectation that can be shrugged off" (Mueller, 29).

Interestingly, two of the major students of war, its history, and its causes both agree that war is over, at least in its most destructive form, total war. Both John Stoessinger and John Keegan agree that there will be no major wars in the foreseeable future. Stoessinger argues that war is a sickness that, like other murderous sicknesses that have plagued human history, can be conquered. He also draws a clear distinction between aggression and war. "Whereas aggression may be inherent," he writes, "war is learned behavior and as such can be unlearned and ultimately selected out." Human nature can be changed, Stoessinger argues; therefore, "like slavery and cannibalism, war too can be eliminated from humanity's arsenal of horrors." Stoessinger writes that he takes heart from the end of the Cold War and the collapse of the Soviet Union. Not only has tyranny collapsed, but also nations are now abandoning tyranny and optimg for democracy. On a triumphant note, Stoessinger concludes, "There has been a slow dawning of compassion and of global consciousness over humanity's bleak skies in recent years. It is this dawn of global consciousness that is our greatest hope. From this new hope we shall forge the weapons against war. For we have built both cathedrals and concentration camps. . . . We are not burdened with original sin alone; we also have the gift of original innocence" (Stoessinger 1993, 209–27).

British military historian John Keegan, whose *History of Warfare* (1993) is one of the most recent attempts to fashion a grand and coherent picture of war, somewhat surprisingly argues that war may be coming to an end: "Mankind, wherever it has the option, is distancing itself from the institution of warfare." Keegan bases his opinion on his observation of war—"a lifetime of reading about the subject, mingling with men of war, visiting the sites of war and observing its effects"—and his belief that rational people may finally be recognizing that war is counterproductive. "War . . . may well be ceasing to recommend itself to human beings as a desirable or productive, let alone rational, means of reconciling their discontents." After all, Keegan writes, "mankind does have the capacity to correlate the costs of and benefits of large and universal undertakings." For much of human history, he argues, war appeared to "work": its benefits outweighed or at least appeared to outweigh its costs. Today, however, the costs clearly outweigh the potential benefits of war. Just the cost of weapons development has distorted and strained the budgets of even the wealthiest nations, while poor nations can afford to fight neither the larger states nor one another. "War truly has become a scourge," Keegan writes, just as disease long has been one. The scourge of disease has been virtually eliminated, he argues, and war can and may well be eliminated in the same way. Keegan acknowledges that eliminating war, turning away from this crucial element of the human past, demands unprecedented changes. "There is no precedent, however, for the menace with which future war now confronts the world" (Keegan 1993, 59–60).

The development of nuclear weapons, "the logical culmination of the technological trend in the Western way of warfare," Keegan writes, represents "the ultimate denial of the proposition that war was, or might be, a continuation of politics by other means." Clausewitz is obsolete in a war of nuclear weapons. "Politics must continue; war cannot." Keegan advocates that the Western powers learn from other military cultures, like those of Asia and of some primitive societies. "There is a wisdom in the principles of intellectual restraint and even of symbolic ritual. . . . There is an even greater wisdom in the denial that politics and war belong within the same continuum. Unless we insist on denying it, our future . . . may belong to the men with the bloodied hands" (Keegan 391–92).

The Evolutionary Perspective

Robert O'Connell, who argues that war was the product of a specific stage of human development, consequently argues that as human society has evolved beyond that point, it may well have evolved beyond the need for war as well. With the rise of industrial societies that have moved beyond the "plant trap" in which the earlier urban agriculture-based societies were enmeshed, O'Connell writes, has also come the rise of individualism and participatory democracy, and with them, O'Connell believes, has come the end of war. The overall direction of history, the building momentum of development and democracy, may well presage the end of war. Democracy is toxic to war. Humans learned to wage war, O'Connell writes, because it made sense in the kinds of societies we lived in. "However, as societies have changed, and basic patterns of human relationships have changed, war now makes less and less sense. It will be hard, and war will always remain a threat, but humanity can only hope that the path of history will continue to lead us away from [war's] carnage and despair" (O'Connell 1995, 238–43).

The "It Ain't Over 'til It's Over" School

endism Theory that humanity has reached the end of history in terms of ideological struggles.

One of the most important critics of those who feel that major war, and perhaps eventually all war, has ended is Samuel P. Huntington. In a cogent essay entitled "The Errors of Endism," Huntington argues that two basic fallacies undergird **endism.** First, he writes, "endism overemphasizes the predictability of history and the permanence of the moment." Current trends may well not continue into the future, he writes, and social scientists have proven notoriously wrong in their past predictions. "Given the limitations of human foresight, endist predictions of the end of war and ideological conflict deserve a heavy dose of skepticism." Even more important, Huntington writes, "endism tends to ignore the weakness and irrationality of human nature." The endists assume that people will behave rationally and focus on such issues as cost-benefits ratios in making decisions about war. "Human beings are at times rational, generous, creative, and wise, but they are also often stupid, selfish, cruel, and sinful." Out of a deeply pessimistic view of human nature, Huntington writes that "the struggle that is history began with the eating of the forbidden fruit and is rooted in human nature . . . . So long as human beings exist, there is no exit from the traumas of history." Consequently, Huntington concludes, "To hope for the benign end of history is human. To expect it to happen is unrealistic. To plan on it happening is disastrous" (Huntington 1994, 43).

An even more pessimistic view of human nature and the possibility of future wars comes from John J. Mearsheimer in his 1994 essay "Why We Will Soon Miss the Cold War." Mearsheimer argues that "the prospect of major crises, even wars, in Europe is likely to increase dramatically now that the Cold War is receding into history." This view rests on Mearsheimer's realist perspective that the "distribution of military power among states is the root cause of war and peace." With the end of the Cold War, he argues, Europe now is reverting to "a state system that created powerful incentives for aggression in the past." The collapse of bipolarity has given rise to the possibility of multipolarity once again, a condition that Mearsheimer sees as essentially unstable, creating the possibility of small wars than can easily escalate into larger ones in the fashion of World War I. Furthermore, the collapse of the Cold War has unleashed the hypernationalism that led to past European wars, and may well do so again. There is little evidence that Europeans have concluded rationally that war is too costly or obsolete, he argues.

Furthermore, those who argue that war has become economically too costly, or unlikely because nations are now interdependent on one another in international trade, overlook the fact that states are "not primarily motivated by the desire to achieve prosperity." States must operate both in an international political and an international economic environment, and whenever the two conflict with one another, political considerations are far more important. "Survival in an anarchic international political system is the highest goal a state can have" (Mearsheimer 1994, 55).

Mearsheimer also knocks down the widely bruited idea that the apparent triumph of democracy worldwide lessens the possibility of war, because democracies generally do not fight one another. "The historical record shows that democracies are every bit as likely to fight wars as are authoritarian states," Mearsheimer writes, although perhaps not against each other. In addition, "mass publics, whether in a democracy or not, can become deeply imbued with nationalistic or religious fervor, making them prone to support aggression and quite indifferent to costs" (Mearsheimer 1994, 57).

To counteract what he sees as the natural tendency of states to go to war in pursuit of their own interests, Mearsheimer proposes three policies. First, he advocates what he calls the "controlled proliferation" of nuclear weapons to counter the withdrawal of Soviet nuclear forces from central and eastern Europe. Second, he stresses that the United States and Great Britain must become the "balancers" in the emerging multipolar state system. And third, he warns that "hypernationalism" must be kept under control, particularly in eastern Europe. "States that teach a dishonestly self-exculpating or self-glorifying history should be publicly criticized and sanctioned." But Mearsheimer warns that even if these policies are implemented (which he doubts will happen), Europe will probably never again enjoy the stability of the past forty-five years. (Mearsheimer 1994, 60–61).

Classical scholar Donald Kagan's *On the Origins of War* also takes a pessimistic view of the future of war. After discussing the various reasons some scholars have concluded that future wars are unlikely, he points out, "This is not the first time that new conditions and ideas have led many to believe that a unique prospect of lasting peace was at hand." However, this belief clearly has not been borne out by history. New weapons, new technologies, new international systems—none of these have been able to foreclose war as a human option. "Over the past two centuries the optimists and pessimists, each predicting the end of war for different reasons, have been proven wrong," Kagan writes. "Believing in and hoping for progress, they forgot that war has been a persistent part of human experience since before the birth of civilization" (Kagan 1995, 1–5).

Martin van Creveldt argues that there will be future wars, but that they will no longer follow the Clausewitzian model of **trinitarian war:** war as a function of the government, the military, and the people. For one thing, van Creveldt argues, nuclear weapons have made such wars impossible. Second, low-intensity conflict carried out by **partisans** with neither government nor uniforms has become accepted. Although nuclear wars have not occurred, this low-intensity conflict carried out by guerrillas or partisans has toppled empires and governments worldwide. This trend will continue, van Creveldt predicts: while general war is unlikely, low-intensity conflict will continue to erupt into the foreseeable future (van Creveldt, cited in "Defence Technology" 1995).

trinitarian war War supported totally by the triad of the people, government, and the military against an enemy.

partisans Those who fight usually within their nations, sometimes without the tacit support of their government.

As is so often the case in wrestling with complex issues, your authors suspect that the answer to the question "Does war have a future?" is a less-than-resounding "Yes, sort of." We think that the possibility of global nuclear war has diminished, although perhaps not forever. There is always the possibility of an accidental nuclear exchange, or of a large nuclear war triggered by a smaller one. However, since the Soviet Union has ceased to exist, there really does not seem to be much chance of a full-blown nuclear war.

Flashpoints

Unfortunately, there probably will continue to be both conventional wars and low-intensity conflicts well into the future. There are still multiple hotspots around the world where war either exists already or could easily erupt in the near future. Some of these "flashpoints" represent small, poor nations that will receive virtually no global attention, no CNN coverage, unless a terrible humanitarian cataclysm grows out of their war, as it did in Somalia. Others are states on the periphery of the global enterprise, in which there is relatively little interest or about which there is virtually no concern. Their wars will not run the risk of involving larger powers, and thus will make only a very small blip on the international radar. In fact, the argument has been made that in the future, major powers simply may christen such war zones "wild places" and leave them to their mutual destruction (Roet 1995).

The potential wars (shown in fig. 11.5) about which there is great concern are, for obvious reasons, those involving larger and more powerful states, or those involving states that could potentially drag in one or more of the major powers. In a study of such potential wars, one American strategist concluded that there were at least twenty wars waiting to happen, and that ten of them would involve states that might imperil or at least involve the interests of larger states. Among the "future wars" this strategist foresees are the sixth Arab-Israeli War, the fourth India-Pakistani War, the Third Gulf War (between Iran and Iraq), the Second Korean War, the Hungarian-Romanian War over Transylvania, and the Sino-Russian Conflict (Dupuy, 1993). Optimistically, Dupuy writes that none of these future wars will involve the use of nuclear weapons, and most of them will end quite quickly, sometimes through the intervention of the United Nations and sometimes through quick victory by one side.

There is little doubt that such flashpoints exist (see Wright and McManus 1991), and that consequently there is still a high possibility, if not probability, of future wars. Nonetheless, although we do believe that there will be such wars (see fig. 11.5 for their possible locations), we also believe that they will most likely remain subnuclear, that is, never escalate to the level of using nuclear weapons. Furthermore, the conventional wars that may occur at such flashpoints may well be less important geopolitically than the continued occurrence of low-intensity

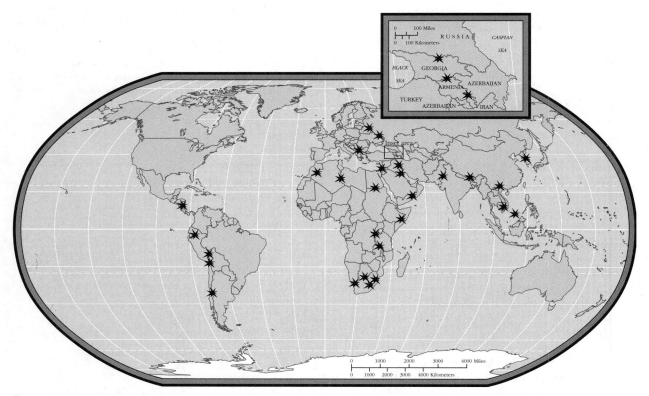

Figure 11.5 **Global Flashpoints**

wars, the protracted conflicts of the sort that have been rampant throughout sub-Saharan Africa and much of Latin America in the past fifteen years. One keen student of military affairs counts at least one hundred nations that soon may find themselves at war, either internally or externally (Dunnigan and Bay 1991, 556; see also Nye 1996).

Even if war is not an innate part of the human condition—and the authors are not completely sure that it is not—stupidity is. Consequently, wars at some level seem probable well into the foreseeable future. Some of these wars may involve exotic weapons, but they are more likely to feature conventional artillery and tanks than the guided missiles or robotic equipment that the major powers either have or are developing. Unfortunately, one of the most probable of these future weapons is *plastique,* a shapable explosive, still a weapon of major importance to terrorists, who view themselves as warriors, despite the reluctance of others to assign them this role.

The spectre of large-scale nuclear war has receded, although the danger of "small" nuclear wars probably is accelerating. The danger of even a small nuclear war and the enormously enhanced violence of conventional war both argue that humankind must "unlearn" the habit of making war, must use its intelligence to control its instincts, and must recognize that there are better ways to continue politics than war. However, we must admit that we see these possibilities, however necessary, as somewhat unlikely. There are too many "warlovers" like Saddam Hussein, too many fanatics willing to sacrifice their own lives and those of hundreds or thousands of others for their cause, to permit us much optimism.

Summary

One of humankind's oldest scourges, war has taken well over one hundred million lives in the twentieth century alone. Attempting to eradicate this scourge will be one of humankind's greatest tasks in the twenty-first century.

The Anatomy of War: War can take many forms, ranging from civil war to global war, and from limited war to total war. The spectrum of conflict intensity ranges from low-intensity (such as guerrilla) war, through conventional war and ultimately to nuclear war. While the probability of nuclear war is receding, the globe is seeing more and more low-intensity conflicts, and probably will continue to do so.

War and Culture: Like all human enterprises, war reflects human society and culture. Western Europe has expended great amounts of intellectual energy developing theories of "just war" to reconcile war with Christian principles. While war appears to enjoy a higher place within Islam, particularly under the concept of *jihad,* many scholars maintain that this term refers not to literal war but to spiritual warfare within the individual. In classical China, the scholar-gentry who ran the bureaucracy looked upon war and soldiers with disdain; paradoxically, classical China also produced one of the greatest theorists of war, Sun-Tzu, whose work is widely studied today.

The Causes of War: Since war is usually so destructive, and often proves nothing except that "God is on the side of the biggest battalions," scholars have long tried to understand the causes of war in the hope that such understanding can lead to ways to prevent war. Theories about the causes of war fall into four general categories: economic theories, behavioral theories, state and system theories, and theories based on leadership or the failure thereof.

The Future of War: A fierce debate is going on today about what kind of future, if any, war has. A number of scholars of war believe that war has become obsolete because weapons have become so lethal that they will never be used. On the other side, an equal or even larger number of scholars argue that war never will disappear completely, although they generally acknowledge that global wars may in fact be obsolete. One of the most important debates in contemporary international relations hinges on whether or not liberal democratic states will go to war with one another; so far the issue remains undecided.

Key Terms

War	*Jihad*
Low-intensity conflict	Economic imperialism
Guerrilla war	Aggression
Wars of national liberation	Coser-Simmel thesis
Conventional war	Scapegoat theory
Total war	Kellogg-Briand Pact
Limited war	Endism
Just war	Trinitarian war
Karl von Clausewitz	Partisans

Thought Questions

1. What are the differences between conventional and unconventional war?
2. Why do people consider low-intensity conflict the conflict of tomorrow?
3. Explain the theories of the causes of war. Which of these explanations do you believe does the best job of explaining conflict in this century? Why?
4. Discuss the theory that democracies do not fight one another.

References

Ardrey, Robert W. *African Genesis: A Personal Investigation into the animal origins and nature of man.* London: Collins, 1961.

Asprey, Robert B. *War in the Shadows: The Guerrilla in History.* New York: William Morrow, 1994.

Bhagavan, M. R. "Angola." In Joel Krieger. *The Oxford Companion to Politics of the World*. New York: Oxford, 1993.

Blainey, Geoffrey. *The Causes of War.* 3rd Ed. New York: Free Press, 1988.

Brugioni, Dino. *Eyeball to Eyeball: The Inside Story of the Cuban Missile Crisis*. New York: Random House, 1991.

"Defence Technology." *The Economist,* June 10, 1995.

Dinstein, Yoram. "Rules of War." In Joel Krieger. *The Oxford Companion to Politics of the World*. New York: Oxford, 1993.

Doyle, Michael. "Liberalism and World Politics." *American Political Science Review* (December 1986).

Drew, Christopher, "After 30 years, hot line stays in readiness for world crises," *Houston Chronicle,* July 25, 1993.

————"To the Editors." *International Security* (Spring 1995).

Dunnigan, James F. *How to Make War: A Comprehensive Guide to Modern Warfare for the Post—Cold War Era*. New York: William Morrow, 1993.

Dunnigan, James F., and Austin Bay. *A Quick and Dirty Guide to War: Briefings on Present and Potential Wars*. New York: William Morrow, 1991.

Dunnigan, James F., and Albert A. Nofi. *Dirty Little Secrets: Military Information You're Not Supposed to Know*. New York: William Morrow, 1990.

Dupuy, Colonel Trevor N., U.S. Army (Ref.). *The Evolution of Weapons and Warfare*. New York: Da Capo Press, 1984.

————*Future Wars: the World's Most Dangerous Flashpoints*. New York: Warner Books, 1993.

Frederick, Howard H. *Global Communications & International Relations*. Belmont, Cal. Wadsworth Publishing, 1993.

Fukuyama, Francis. *The End of History and the Last Man*. New York: Avon, 1992.

Gabriel, Richard A., and Karen S. Metz. *A Short History of War: The Evolution of Warfare and Weapons*. Professional Readings in Military Strategy, no. 5. Harrisburg, Penn.: Strategic Studies Institute, U.S. Army War College, 1991.

Gaddis, John Lewis. "The Long Peace." In Michael J. Hogan, ed. *The End of the Cold War: Its Meaning and Implications*. New York: Cambridge University Press, 1992.

Gallagher, CSM James J., U.S. Army (Ret.). *Low Intensity Conflict: A Guide for Tactics, Techniques, and Procedures*. Harrisburg, Penn.: Stackpole Books, 1991.

Gilsevan, Michael. "Jihad." In Joel Krieger. *The Oxford Companion to Politics of the World*. New York: Oxford, 1993.

Hobson, J. A. *Imperialism: A Study*. Ann Arbor, Mich.: University of Michigan 1965.

Hoyt, Edwin P. *Japan's War: The Great Pacific Conflict*. New York: Da Capo, 1986.

Huntington, Samuel P. "The Errors of Endism." In Richard K. Betts, ed., *Conflict after the Cold War: Arguments on Causes of War and Peace*. New York: Macmillan, 1994.

Jablonsky, David. *Strategic Rationality Is Not Enough: Hitler and the Concept of Crazy States*. Carlisle Barracks, Penn.: Strategic Studies Institute, U.S. Army War College, 1991.

Johanson, Donald, and Maitland Edey. *Lucy: The Beginnings of Humankind*. New York: Simon and Schuster, 1981.

Johanson, Donald, and James Shreeve. *Lucy's Child: The Discovery of a Human Ancestor*. New York: Avon Books, 1989.

Kagan, Donald. *On the Origins of War and the Preservation of Peace*. New York: Doubleday, 1995.

Keegan, John. *A History of Warfare.* New York: Alfred A. Knopf, 1994.

Keeley, Laurence H. *War Before Civilization: The Myth of the Peaceful Savage.* New York: Oxford University Press, 1996.

Kugler, Jacek. "War." in Joel Krieger. *The Oxford Companion to Politics of the World.* New York: Oxford, 1993.

Layne, Christopher. "Kant or Cant: The Myth of the Democratic Peace." *International Security* (Fall 1994).

Lorenz, Konrad. *On Aggression.* New York: Bantam, 1967.

Mearsheimer, John J. "Why We Will Soon Miss the Cold War." In Richard K. Betts, ed. *Conflict after the Cold War: Arguments on Causes of War and Peace.* New York: Macmillan,1994.

Minter, William. "Angolan Conflict." In Joel Krieger. *The Oxford Companion to Politics of the World.* New York: Oxford, 1993.

Mueller, John. "The Obsolescence of Major War." In Richard K. Betts, ed. *Conflict after the Cold War: Arguments on Causes of War and Peace.* New York: Macmillan, 1994.

Musashi, Miyamoto. *The Book of Five Rings: The Real Art of Japanese Management.* New York: Bantam, 1982.

Nye, Joseph. "Conflicts after the Cold War." *Washington Quarterly,* Winter 1996.

O'Connell, Robert L. *Ride of the Second Horseman: The Birth and Death of War.* New York: Oxford University Press, 1995.

Perret, Geoffrey. *A Country Made by War: From the Revolution to Vietnam—The Story of America's Rise to Power.* New York: Vintage, 1990.

Reston, James, Jr. *Sherman's March and Vietnam.* New York: Macmillan, 1984.

Rhodes, Richard. *The Making of the Atomic Bomb.* New York: Simon and Schuster, 1986.

Roet, Jeff. "The Geopolitics of NAFTA and the Global Economy." Unpublished Speech at San Jacinto College, Houston, TX, January 10, 1995. unpaginated.

Rummel, R. J., *Applied Factor Analysis,* Evanston, IL: Northwestern University Press, 1970.

Russett, Bruce, with William Antholis, Carol B. Ember, Melvin Ember, and Zeev Maoz. *Grasping the Democratic Peace: Principles for a Post-Cold War World.* Princeton, N.J.: Princeton University Press, 1993.

Sagan, Carl. "Nuclear War and Climatic Catastrophe." In Charles W. Kegley, Jr., and Eugene Witkopf. *The Nuclear Reader: Strategy, Weapons, and War.* New York: St. Martin's Press, 1989.

Schell, Jonathan. *The Fate of the Earth.* New York: Alfred A. Knopf, 1982.

Spector, Ronald. *Eagle against the Sun: The American War with Japan.* New York: Vintage Books, 1985.

Stoessinger, John G. *Why Nations Go to War,* 6th ed. New York: St. Martin's Press, 1993.

Summers, Colonel Harry G., Jr. (Ret.). *On Strategy II: A Critical Analysis of the Gulf War.* New York: Dell, 1992.

Sun Tzu. *The Art of War.* Translated by Samuel B. Griffith. New York: Oxford University Press, 1963.

Tanter, Raymond. "Dimensions of Conflict Behavior Within and Between Nations, 1958–1960." *Journal of Conflict Resolution,* March 1966.

Thucydides. *The Peloponnesian War.* Benjamin Jowett, tran. New York: Bantam, 1960.

Varley, H. Paul. *Samurai.* New York: Dell, 1970.

Viotti, Paul. "Use of Force." In Joel Krieger. *The Oxford Companion to Politics of the World.* New York: Oxford. 1993.

Walzer, Michael. *Just and Unjust Wars: A Moral Argument with Historical Illustrations.* New York: Basic Books, 1977.

Wilson, Dick. *The People's Emperor: A Biography of Mao Tse-tung.* Garden City, N.Y.: Doubleday, 1980.

Wright, Quincy. *A Study of War.* 2nd ed. Chicago: University of Chicago Press, 1965.

Wright, Robin, and Doyle McManus. *Flashpoints: Promise and Peril in a New World.* New York: Alfred A. Knopf, 1991.

Chapter 12

Weapons: The Technology of Death

Introduction

Political scientists disagree among themselves about whether or not arms races—attempts by competing powers to acquire ever larger arsenals of ever more sophisticated and lethal weapons—prevent wars, cause wars, or simply make wars more deadly once they do erupt. Few, however, would disagree with the observation that today we live in a world armed to the teeth, in which staggering sums of money are spent on weapons development and weapons acquisition. It is virtually impossible to compile completely accurate statistics on the world's armaments: largely for reasons of national security, most governments are understandably reluctant to make such information public. But even a cursory survey of what is known reveals genuinely frightening levels of weapons held by governments around the world.

In this chapter we will look first at conventional weapons and then focus on the international arms trade: we will also examine issues of weapons development and problems of weapons sales. Then we will look briefly at the world of CBW—chemical and biological weapons–which is becoming increasingly large and terrifying. Next, we will focus on the development of nuclear weapons; in addition to tracing the history of nuclear weapons, we will look at theories of how such weapons function in the modern world (specifically, deterrence theories), and then examine the problem of proliferation, the spread of nuclear weapons into the hands of more and more nations. Finally, we will examine the problems of disarmament and the twentieth-century treaties that have tried to stem the flood of weapons of all sorts.

Classifications of Weapons

The two broadest classifications of weapons are **conventional weapons** and weapons of mass destruction (WMD). Conventional weapons are in turn subdivided into heavy weapons—tanks, aircraft, heavy artillery, ship—and light weapons, such as rifles, sidearms, and shoulder-held missiles that can be transported easily by one or two men. The term "weapons of mass destruction" is pretty much self-defining; it includes nuclear weapons as well as chemical and biological weapons (CBW).

conventional weapons
Nonnuclear arms.

Conventional Weapons

As we have noted, exact figures on the numbers of conventional weapons are enormously difficult to obtain. Recent estimates by experts, however, give some general idea of how heavily armed our planet is. These estimates, for example, place the number of main battle tanks worldwide at 160,000; of fixed-wing combat aircraft at 43,000; and of combat ships at approximately 3,100. (Dunnigan and Nofi 1990, 45, 132, 175). Not surprisingly, the majority of this lethal force was in the hands of the two superpowers, the United States and the Soviet Union, until the end of the Cold War and the collapse of the Soviet Union. As figure 12.1 illustrates, the preponderance of conventional weapons remain in the hands of the superpowers and their successors. The rough numerical balance of military power that characterized the later years of the Cold War is reflected in the combined 30 percent of total conventional weapons in the arsenals of the former USSR and

Figure 12.1
**Distribution of
Conventional Weapons**

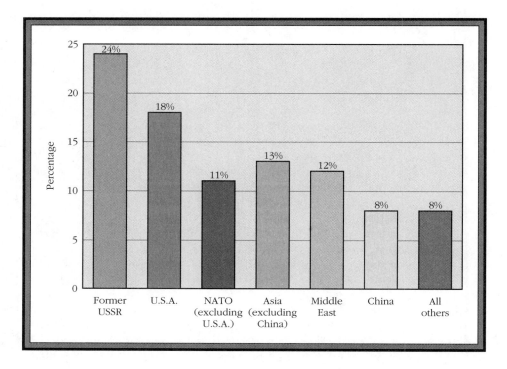

Figure 12.1
**Distribution of
Conventional Weapons**

Warsaw Pact nations, matched by the 29 percent held by the United States and the NATO allies. The end of the Cold War and the collapse of the Soviet Union probably altered this basic equation very little. However, with both Eastern Europe and even Russia itself looking for ties with NATO, the geopolitics, as opposed to the sheer numbers, of the two sides of the equation are immensely different.

Another way to gauge the number of weapons a particular nation possesses is to look at its military expenditures, both aggregate and per capita. The United States is far and away the largest spender on military materiel. Although the figures for Russia are suspect, since it is almost as difficult to obtain accurate figures for post-Soviet Russia as it was for the Soviet Union, analysts generally agree that Russian spending on military equipment has plummeted, and that the Russian defense industry right now is basically in free fall. However, even using these shaky figures, it is easy to see that American military spending dwarfs those of all other states. The United States spends at least 300 percent more than Russia on military equipment (this includes nuclear as well as conventional weapons). Germany's military spending is only 12 percent as much as that of the U.S., France's is barely 10 percent as much, Japan's 7.5 percent as much, and China's approximately 4 percent as much.

The International Arms Trade

international arms trade
The sale of conventional
arms by one nation to
another for profit and/or
geopolitical favor.

For many nations unable to support a large military-industrial complex, the key to defense is the **international arms trade,** a global enterprise involving the transfer of weapons ranging from the handguns to potential components for nuclear bombs. The global arms trade has involved as much as forty to fifty billion dollars a year, helping to create the world armed to the teeth in which we live.

This international trade thrives for a variety of reasons. Suppliers of arms in the international weapons bazaar have a complex series of reasons, both political/military and economic, for their participation. These suppliers, for example, want to provide their allies with enough firepower to enhance their own defenses. Not only does this increase (at least in theory) the amount of loyalty the ally owes the supplier; it also decreases the likelihood that the supplier will have to go to the defense of its ally, which is fully capable of fending for itself. In addition, providing weapons to allies guarantees that the supplier state and its allies, if they ever do go to war, will have few logistics problems, since they will all share the same basic weapons and use the same types of ammunition. Supplying weapons to an ally also can be a way to repay a past favor, to pave the way for a future favor (stationing listening posts on the ally's soil, for example, or gaining use of port and airfield facilities), or to show that the recipient nation is indeed an ally or a friend. Supplier nations also generally hope that by providing weapons to an ally, a friend, or a potential friend, they can gain some measure of influence over that nation's policies, either positively, by encouraging certain kinds of behaviors by the ally or friend, or negatively, by punishing the recipient by withholding weapons, ammunition, or spare parts. This is often the least attainable of the goals of the supplier nation (Klare 1994, 138).

The economic reasons nations engage in the international weapons bazaar are twofold. First, there is a purely commercial motive: by selling weapons, the nation can make money for itself, either to offset original research and development costs or to provide seed money for future weapons development. Second, export sales of weapons systems can extend the life of the original system, which may be obsolescent in the supplier's arsenal. This means a lower per unit cost for

---

Uncle Sam, Arms Merchant

Psssst! Wanna buy a weapon? How about some tanks? Step right up to the American arms bazaar.

Today the United States is far and away the world's leading arms merchant. Although as late as 1986 the U.S. sold a paltry 13 percent of the world's armaments, in 1993 U.S. arms transfer payments were nearly ten times greater than those of the runner-up, Russia: $22.3 billion to $2.8 billion. Since the Cold War ended in 1989, the United States has sold $82.4 billion worth of weapons worldwide, while the rest of the world's nations combined have sold only $66.8 billion worth.

This staggering American surge in arms sales stems from several factors. Obviously, the collapse of the Russian economy has been a major factor. So too has the performance of high-tech American weapons in the Persian Gulf War. Continuing and even escalating regional tensions also make for a seller's market:

GLOBAL PERSPECTIVES

one authority estimates that American-made weapons are being used in thirty-nine of the world's forty-eight ongoing conflicts.

Another reason for the great upswing in U.S. arms sales is that the Clinton administration has adopted an actively sales-oriented policy. Secretary of Commerce Ron Brown told U.S. weapons makers in 1993, "We will work with you to help you find buyers for your products in the world marketplace, and then we will help you close the deal." Both political and economic motives have shaped this policy. "People can say it's disgusting," says one U.S. manufacturer, "but foreign arms sales provide jobs, help maintain the industrial base, and . . . give us power and influence in international relations." (Rosenfield 1995)

A number of ploys help boost U.S. sales. The Pentagon, spurred by massive cuts in defense

(continued on p. 410)

Uncle Sam, Arms Merchant
(Continued from p. 409)

spending, sells used weapons to poorer countries and uses the profits to finance new, high-tech aircraft. It also distributes obsolete (by American standards) weapons free of charge. American companies employ creative advertising and rig complicated deals. For example, McDonnell Douglas currently is helping Kuwait peddle "old-generation" attack planes in hopes that Kuwait will use its profits to buy F-18 jets and AH-64 attack helicopters—made, of course, by McDonnell Douglas.

Critics find multiple flaws in this marketing surge. Massive weapons sales heighten tensions in the developing world, which is the recipient of 66 percent of all U.S. arms exports; endanger fragile governments; and cause massive casualties. Additionally, critics charge, in their zeal to sell arms, American companies are selling American technology as well. South Korea has recently purchased 120 F-16 jets, but only the first twelve will be made in the USA. The remaining jets will be built in

Korea—not by Lockheed, but by Samsung Aerospace Industries. Critics also worry about the danger of American troops sent into future missions in which they will face sophisticated American weapons. Citing increased dangers in the Panama, Somalia, and Haiti missions because their military forces had U.S. weapons, U.S. technology, or U.S. training, a Navy intelligence report recently warned that U.S. troops run an increasing danger of having to face "regional powers with relatively sophisticated weapons" (Thompson 1994; Rosenfield 1995).

In the summer of 1996 an advisory panel appointed by President Bill Clinton echoed fears that the booming arms trade may well threaten U.S. security and suggested that Washington and its allies all exercise greater restraint in selling sophisticated conventional weapons. The panel's report also warned that pushing arms sales in order to prop up American defense firms was short-sighted and wrong; national security interests must be the sole criteria for deciding arms sales, not economics. (Smith 1996).

---

weapons and also extends the production life of the weapon or weapons system, providing continued employment within the supplier's domestic economy (Klare 1994, 138).

Purchasers usually have their own reasons for acquisition of weapons and weapons systems. First, they may feel threatened by either internal or external enemies and thus wish to arm themselves as fully as possible. Second, a purchaser may believe that in acquiring weapons from a major supplier it is also acquiring at least an implicit guarantee of support and protection from the supplier, enough to deter a potential enemy that might be willing to attack a relatively small or weak power but would hesitate at the prospect that the small power's "big friend" might intervene. This reasoning probably had greater rational basis during the Cold War than it does now, in the far more fluid and confused post–Cold War era (Klare 1994, 138–39; Segal 1991, 116). Finally, the acquisition of weapons may be largely a matter of "showing the flag," that is, of trying to keep up with the big boys. A squadron of fighter jets can serve as a rite-of-passage purchase by a newly emerging nation, or can be used by a shaky civilian government "to satisfy the armed forces who like new toys (as happens in many Latin American states which face no real enemy, except possibly those at home)"—Klare 1994, 138–39.

Trends in the Arms Trade

The end of the Cold War has brought major changes in the international arms trade. No longer are the opposing superpowers bidding for influence and support with bargain basement prices. Instead, the contemporary arms trade is driven far more by local tensions and by the urgent needs of arms manufacturers to find

The Paris Air Show has historically provided the world's weapon makers a showcase for their wares; note the Concorde to the left of the photo and the Russian missiles to the right, all on display at the 1995 show.

buyers. Since peaking in the late 1980s, the international arms trade has been spiralling downward. In 1987, arms sales worldwide reached a high of $48 billion; by 1992 they had plummeted to $19 billion, an almost 60 percent drop (Spear 1994/95, 8–9). After a brief rise, aggregate military expenditure fell again in 1994, largely as the result of major cuts in procurement by the United States and Russia. Global arms expenditures are calculated at $27.725 billion in constant (1990) U.S. dollars (Anthony, Wezeman, and Wezeman, 1995).

The result of this is ferocious competition among arms sellers for a greater share of a shrinking market. Among the consequences of this competition are increasing pressures to sell weapons to "rogue" or "pariah" states like Libya or Iran, and a trend of bundling technology with weapons so that arms transfer increasingly implies technology transfer as well. Additionally, many sales are not weapons per se, but upgrades, or "force multipliers." Thus a nation that already has high-performance jet fighter aircraft will buy precision-guided munitions that greatly increase the aircraft's capabilities—at a much cheaper cost than that incurred by buying all new aircraft (Spear 1994/95, 8–9).

The Technology Push

However, two factors may well lead to a rapid and dangerous upswing in the arms trade. The first is a **technology push** as a result of what is called the **military technological revolution (MTR)** (see Global Perspectives on p. 412). The development of the kinds of "smart" weapons demonstrated in the Gulf War and their successor "brilliant" weapons, in which computers remove the human element from operations, has increased enormously the lethal potential of modern weapons. So too has the addition of even more sophisticated computers, often in combination with electronic and laser technology. The MTR has the potential to set off a new and deadly acceleration of the arms race. Even people become part of the MTR, as nations compete for the services of the highly trained personnel necessary to operate and maintain the new generations of weapons (Spear 1994/95, 10–11).

technology push The phenomenon that occurs with the advent of technological advances in military weaponry development. One new invention or advancement spurs another in a spiraling effect.

military technological revolution (MTR) The revolution that has occurred since the advent of "smart" weapons which eliminate the direct human element from field operations.

The Tension Pull

tension pull The pressure on smaller nations to acquire arms as a result of the demise of the Cold War; these nations rush to fill the void created by the loss of the superpower rivalry in weapons production.

The second factor that may contribute to the acceleration of the arms trade is the **tension pull.** With the constraints on local conflict imposed by the Cold War now removed, as we discussed earlier, governments that no longer can depend upon superpower rivalry to guarantee them both weapons and stability are increasing their weapons purchases. East Asia and the Middle East are emerging as the largest purchasers of weapons; many East Asian nations as well are rapidly developing their own weapons production capacities, as part of their industrialization programs (Spear 1994/95, 11). China in particular has become a major player in the international arms trade, with many of its sales going to a series of rogue states, including Myanmar (Burma), Iran, Syria, and North Korea (Pierre and Conway-Lanz, 1994/95, 71).

The Military Technological Revolution

GLOBAL PERSPECTIVES

Ironically, even as the Pentagon is developing nonlethal weapons, it also is pushing for deeper and deeper U.S. involvement in the military technological revolution (MTR) now unfolding. Proponents of continued U.S. involvement and leadership in the MTR argue that the four weapons that have dominated warfare for the last fifty years—the tank, the submarine, the airplane, and the carrier—are now "a technological dead end as obsolete as the cavalry charge." The microprocessor, "now being translated into a dizzying array of military applications," will shape the future and transform combat from "blood-and-guts" close combat into a "chess contest" between automated weapons systems fighting hundreds of miles apart.

The Gulf War was simply a curtain-opener, with its relatively crude stealth bombers and cruise missiles. Thanks to the MTR, "smart bombs" will yield to "brilliant missiles" guided by computer-linked satellites, able to fly scores of miles and select their own targets. Sophisticated surveillance systems will enable other missiles to destroy enemy tanks from distances of up to two hundreds miles. Some of these technologies are now under development; others are still on the drawing board.

A battle currently is raging in the U.S. military (and probably others as well) about whether to allocate increasingly scarce defense dollars to building more and upgraded traditional systems, or to accel-

erating the MTR. No matter what decision is made—to go slowly or quickly into the MTR—a new arms race and an even more frenetic international arms bazaar seem inevitable (Barry 1995).

Making the MTR even more dangerous, and perhaps more imperative, is the fact that much of the technology driving the MTR has derived from civilian rather than military research, reversing the historical process in which military research has gradually influenced civilian products. However, several of the chief components of the MTR—computers, micro-electronics, and genetic engineering—have been essentially developed within the civilian sector of the economy and are only now being adapted to military use. Consequently participation in the MTR will not require the kind of massive military research establishment that traditionally have been run by the great powers. The result, many fear, will be a free-for-all in which any state with a reasonably advanced industrial economy will be able to "leapfrog" over the large military powers with relative ease. David Shukman, military correspondent for the BBC who has studied the MTR, warns that this means that "however distasteful the suggestion, there may be no option but to stay in the [arms] race." Even as the nuclear arms race may be, to a considerable extent, coming under control, the arms race of the future may well be spiraling out of control (Shukman 1996).

(For further information, see Waller 1995 and "The Softwar Revolution" 1995).

The Light Arms Trade

Although sales of conventional heavy weapons have dwindled, there has been no such downswing in the sale of light arms. In fact, the sales of low-tech light arms may well be on the increase, because of their importance in the guerrilla fighting that characterizes civil strife and other low-intensity conflict. Although the sums involved in the light arms trade are substantially smaller than those involved in the heavy arms trade, small sums can buy large numbers of weapons. For example, a single modern jet fighter sells for as much as five hundred million dollars; a single modern assault gun sells for approximately one hundred and fifty dollars. In other words, a government (or a rebel group) can purchase either one jet or nearly three and a half million assault weapons for the same amount.

Among the largest purchasers of light arms are governments facing insurgencies. In the last three years Myanmar has spent nearly one billion dollars on light arms for operations against the Kachins, Karens, and other ethnic minorities seeking autonomy. Insurgent groups, ethnic minorities, sectarian militias, and narcotics traffickers are also among the largest purchasers of small arms (Klare 1995, 24–25).

Shifts in Purchasing Trends

Just as there have been shifts in the patterns of arms transfers, there also have been changes in the nature of the arms transfers: the kinds of weapons or weapons systems that are being purchased. In the early 1980s much of the arms trade consisted of what are known as "major front-line systems": main battle tanks, fighter and fighter-bomber aircraft, and warships. According to one analyst, Third World buyers concentrated on modernizing all components of their military forces at the same time. Consequently, between 1980 and 1993, Third World arsenals increased by 7,889 tanks and self-propelled guns, 2,258 supersonic aircraft, 83 major surface warships, and 1,300 helicopters. Since all of these represent "big ticket" items, the dollar value of international arms transfers soared to forty-seven billion dollars in the mid-1980s.

However, by the later 1980s a combination of global recession and the rising costs of individual weapons and systems, as well as the end of the Iran-Iraq war, led to cutbacks by Third World countries in the purchase of major front-line systems, and thus to a decline in the overall dollar value of the international arms trade. By 1989 it had fallen to "only" thirty-five billion dollars. However, a substantial portion of that amount was in the form not of new systems, but of "upgrade kits": advanced-propulsion, fire-control, and armament systems designed to increase the life cycles of already-purchased materiel by permitting the owners to update the various weapons and systems they already possessed. Thus, for a relatively modest investment, nations have been able to enhance the value of what they already possess and postpone having to buy even more weapons (Klare 1994, 143).

The Lure of High Technology

The apparently stunning success of high-technology American weapons during the Gulf War, and the daily CNN coverage that let viewers around the world see those weapons in action from aircraft cockpits, the decks of aircraft carriers, and sometimes even Baghdad itself, created an enormous demand for these sophisticated weapons. Precision-guided bombs and missiles, anti-missile missiles,

Patriot missile batteries, such as those shown (right), are one of the most popular new technologies, and one of the most desirable.

multi-role strike aircraft, and all-weather reconnaissance systems became extremely "sexy," desired by many nations willing to pay high prices for entry into the future of weapons. The Kingdom of Saudi Arabia, its vulnerability made all too evident by the Iraqi invasion of next-door neighbor Kuwait, has spent more money on imported weapons in the 1990s than any other nation, stocking up on F-15 multi-role aircraft, Patriot antimissile missiles, air-to-ground missiles, AWACS radar aircraft, and antitank missiles. From 1990 to 1992 alone, the Saudis ordered

This damage inflicted in Saudi Arabia during the Gulf War may have been from an Iraqi Scud missile—or perhaps from a Patriot missile that broke up the Scud.

$27.5 billion worth of American weapons, and Kuwait ordered another $6.8 billion; Egypt, Israel, Turkey, and the United Arab Emirates also purchased substantial amounts of high-tech American weapons. Iran and Syria placed similar orders with the Soviet Union, but it is doubtful that these orders ever will be filled (Klare 1994, 144–45).

"The Yard Sale at the End of History"

The collapse of the Soviet Union and the desperate attempts by many Russians to stay alive has triggered what one analyst refers to (with Fukuyama's essay clearly in mind) as "the yard sale at the end of history." What some Russians euphemistically call the "privatization" of the former Soviet army has seen Soviet arms of all levels, up to but not yet including nuclear weapons, for sale in a grand scramble to raise funds. President Boris Yeltsin has charged that officials in the Ministry of Defense have stolen and sold entire ammunition depots. Other weapons have ended up in the hands of private citizens, warring ethnic factions, and, apparently, organized crime (Bogert 1993).

As Russian troops pulled back from the Baltic states, large amounts of weapons apparently were put on the auction block. One Lithuanian reported he had been offered a brand-new heavy infantry flamethrower, capable of incinerating everything within 150 yards, for $1,300. In other parts of the former Soviet Union as well, the disintegrating Russian forces sometimes simply left large caches of ammunition behind them. For example, when Russian troops withdrew from the ethnic enclave of Chechnya, they abandoned thirteen thousand firearms and thousands of grenades, many of which ended up on the black market.

Most of the weapons with which the former Soviet Union intended to fight the United States and NATO or China now are surplus, available for a price to any state, be it a former ally, a former foe, or even one of the "pariah" states, like Libya. How this availability of cheap weapons on an enormous scale will affect both future arms trade and international security is not yet clear (Bogert 1993, 50–51; Burrows and Windrem 1994, 232–71).

In one especially convoluted transaction; the Pentagon actually acquired, at yard sale prices, the components to Russia's S-300, the equivalent of the American Patriot antimissile system. The end buyer was the Defense Intelligence Agency; the broker, BMD International, an arms trader chaired by Frank Carlucci, former Secretary of Defense and National Security Adviser; and the site of the purchase, the former (now independent) Soviet republic of Belarus. DIA will use its copy of the sophisticated Russian technology to evaluate the S-300 system and design ways for American pilots and weapons to evade it. Since the breakup of the Soviet Union in 1991, DIA and presumably other American intelligence agencies have cast wide nets to trawl the latest Russian military technology, as both Russia and the former Soviet republics sell off the crown jewels of the Soviet military system (Gerth 1994).

Missiles

One of the most ominous developments in the Middle East has been the apparent beginning of an arms race in middle-range ballistic missiles. Substantial quantities of such missiles were used during the Iran-Iraq war, with each side targeting the enemy's capital city and civilian population. Iran and Iraq both employed the Scud missile, a direct lineal descendant of the V-2 developed and used by

Germany during World War II; the modern version was capable of carrying a 2,000-pound explosive warhead with considerable accuracy over a distance of 300 kilometers. Iraq began using the missiles against Iran as early as 1982, but Iran could not retaliate in kind until acquiring missiles from Libya, Syria, and North Korea in 1985. In total, the warring states fired 963 ballistic missiles at each other, many of them reaching their targets in the capitals of Baghdad and Tehran. At least fifty thousand casualties are attributed to the Scud attacks, which cost the participants roughly one billion dollars (Dunnigan and Nofi 1990, 105–6).

Recent students of weapons proliferation count sixteen Third World nations with ballistic missile capability, including both North and South Korea, India and Pakistan, Libya, Serbia, Brazil, and Argentina, as well as several of the new nations that emerged from the rubble of the Soviet Union. Several of these nations also have either CBW or nuclear capability, which makes the blossoming of missile capability even more frightening (Burrows and Windrem 1994, 508).

This proliferation of ballistic missiles is all the more disheartening because it has taken place against the backdrop of the Missile Technology Control Regime, a serious attempt by industrialized nations to halt the spread of ballistic missile technology.

In April 1987 seven industrialized Western states agreed not to spread ballistic missile technology for weapons with a range of more than 300 kilometers or a payload of more than 500 kilograms. By 1991 the regime had fifteen formal adherents and had added cruise missiles to its list of prohibited weapons (Segal 1991, 117). However, as Saddam Hussein's use of Scud missiles against targets in Israel and Saudi Arabia during the Persian Gulf War vividly demonstrated, the technology to build such missiles is quite portable, and it probably will be impossible to halt the spread of either technology or missiles.

Attempts to Control the Arms Trade

Within the regular channels of arms transfers, analysts foresee several important patterns emerging to dominate the 1990s. First will be a reaction to the resurgence of the arms trade in the Middle East, as oil states like Saudi Arabia, Kuwait, and Bahrain, shocked and shaken by Iraq's invasion of Kuwait, seek to arm themselves. Immediately after the Persian Gulf War, the United States took the lead in attempting to orchestrate an agreement to limit arms sales in the volatile Middle East. In July 1991, representatives of the five permanent members of the United Nations Security Council began a round of meetings in Paris to work out details of a system that would reduce the flow of weapons to the Middle East. In October 1991, representatives of these five nations met again, this time in London, and adopted a set of draft guidelines on conventional arms export. Among other things, the guidelines specified that the signatories would consult with one another about major arms sales and avoid transfers that would prolong any existing conflict or could be used for any purpose except the legitimate security needs of the recipients. However, in less than a year, the United States announced the sale of 150 F-16 fighters valued at $150 billion to Taiwan; as a result, China announced that it was withdrawing from the talks, and any progress on limiting arms sales to the Middle East ground to a halt. There have been no further attempts at international limiting of Middle Eastern arms sales (Klare 1994, 135–36).

In a recent article, an arms trade analyst proclaims that the United States is on the brink of obtaining a monopoly in the international arms market. Ethan

Kapstein argues that inefficient and terribly expensive arms production will disappear gradually from many countries, as it is already beginning to disappear from Russia, leaving the United States, with its efficient, state-of-the-art military-industrial complex, unchallenged as chief supplier of arms to the world. As weapons become more and more expensive (and high technology virtually guarantees that this will happen), fewer and fewer countries will be able to afford the research and development costs, Kapstein asserts. In 1990 alone the U.S. government spent nearly $40 billion on defense-related research, development, training, and evaluation. World arms exports peaked at $64 billion in 1984 and U.S. analysts expect the market to stabilize at approximately $40 billion per year for the rest of the century.

Kapstein concludes, "Once the United States becomes the virtual monopoly supplier of advanced conventional weapons, the small sales that will remain available to other countries will hardly be sufficient to maintain increasingly costly domestic arms industries" (Kapstein 1994, 15). The spectacular success of American weapons during the Persian Gulf War, combined with the end of the Cold War, with its superpower-imposed restraints on who could buy what from whom, has opened the way for a tremendous surge of American arms sales, Kapstein argues. Kapstein also optimistically concludes that the coming American monopoly will generally act as a force for peace and stability by enabling the United States to shape world events. He also warns, however, that should conventional weapons become too expensive, other nations might feel forced to develop alternate sources of weapons, no matter how great the expense, or that they might forsake conventional weapons completely and instead concentrate on weapons of mass destruction: chemical, biological, and nuclear weapons. But his final prediction is more hopeful: that an American monopoly, by forcing other nations to close their inefficient and costly weapons productions facilities, will allow these "governments . . . to put scant resources to more productive pursuits" (Kapstein 1994, 13–19).

Another recent attempt at getting some kind of handle on the global arms trade, again spurred by the Persian Gulf War, was the establishment of the United Nations Conventional Arms Register, intended to produce greater openness in the weapons trade. By mid-1993, some seventy nations, including the six largest arms trading states, had accounted to the United Nations for their sales and purchases. Submission of information to the register is voluntary, and there is no way of knowing how complete or accurate the reports are, but analysts believe that the register could be a beginning in the process of monitoring the global arms trade (Hanley, 1993).

Consequences of the Global Arms Trade

This global arms trade has several serious consequences for international relations. First, it seems that the ready availability of weapons may well be directly related to more frequent regional conflicts. There is a high correlation between the diffusion of modern weapons and the increased tempo of global violence. "As the global flow of arms has expanded, there has been a corresponding increase in the number of major conflicts under way at any given time" (Klare 1994, 147).

Additionally, the increased availability of modern weapons generally has meant that once combat begins, it will be very intense and often quite protracted. The Iran-Iraq War, for example, lasted eight years, consumed $55 billion worth of imported arms and ammunition, and resulted in approximately 1.25 million casualties. The ten-year struggle in Afghanistan, in which guerrilla fighters enjoyed the use of shoulder-held Stinger missile launchers, produced perhaps five hundred thousand deaths and three million refugees (Klare 1994, 147). Bloody fighting in the Balkans and in Rwanda has exacted death tolls in the hundreds of thousands' and despite a Balkan cease-fire and a lull in Rwanda, still could flare up again at virtually any moment.

In addition, there are serious fears that the escalation of violence in regional conflicts could easily become an escalation to nuclear exchange in areas, like South Asia, where large states can inflict tremendous conventional destruction on one another.

Nonlethal Weapons

Ironically, at a time when violence through the use of conventional weapons seems to be accelerating, there is also considerable research on the development of nonlethal weapons. The U.S. Pentagon is in the process of developing a wide array of nonlethal weapons that could be used to control mobs, subdue gunmen and terrorists, and defeat enemies while avoiding civilian casualties. The catalog of weapons now under development reads like a cross between Star Trek and Buck Rogers: a laser rifle that could be set to kill or to stun; high-power noise generators; a riot gun that would fire beanbags rather than rubber bullets; chemical compounds ("slick'ems and stick'ems") that would make pavement either too slick or too sticky to move on; and foams that would harden into toffee-like glue or produce an avalanche of dense soaplike bubbles that left anyone caught in them unable to move, speak, or hear, but still breathing ("Soon, 'Phasers on Stun'" 1994).

However, a critic of "nonlethal" weapons points out that many should in fact be called "prelethal," since they are part of a continuum that can escalate from nonlethal to lethal. This critic, Stephen Aftergood, maintains that the development of nonlethal weapons has also been both very expensive and often repetitive, since tight security means that no one knows what anyone else is doing. Aftergood warns that "the hazards of unaccountable government, from secret wars to secret radiation experiments, are well known" (Aftergood 1994, 40–45). Furthermore, the development of such nonlethal technologies may well constitute a violation of four separate treaties, according to Aftergood: the Biological Weapons Convention, the Chemical Weapons Convention, the Geneva Protocols, and the Inhumane Weapons Convention. As one scientist reflects, "regardless of the level of injury inflicted [which could range from temporary or permanent blindness to severe pain, dizziness, and the disruption of internal organ functions], the use of many nonlethal weapons is likely to violate international humanitarian law on the basis of superfluous suffering and/or indiscriminate effects" (Rosenberg 1994, 44–45).

The Cost of Military Spending

Analysts estimate current military and defense spending, both on domestic production of weapons and in the global arms bazaar, at roughly one trillion dollars a year (nearly three-fourths of the total Third World debt). Were those funds transferred to the civilian sector, great advances in many fields might be possible. For example, for the price of a single new nuclear-attack submarine, somewhere between 5 and 7.5 million Third World children could be sent to school. The amount spent worldwide on defense in just two and a half hours, $300 million, was enough to eradicate smallpox worldwide in the late 1970s. The money spent on a single B-1 bomber, about $285 million, could provide basic immunizations to 575 million children worldwide, saving about 2.5 million lives annually. Every forty hours the world spends enough on defense, $4.6 billion, to provide sanitary water for everyone on earth who still lacks it. A single Stinger missile, at $40 thousand, exceeds the average income of an American family and nearly doubles the income of an average African-American family. Two thousand rounds of 7.62-mm rifle or machine-gun ammunition costs $480—more than the average Social Security beneficiary receives every month (Dunnigan and Nofi 1990, 372–73). While there are no guarantees that decreased worldwide military spending would be channeled into programs like immunizations, safe water, or education, it is clear that as long as the world's nations continue to expend such vast amounts on weapons, whether offensive or defensive, other vital needs will continue to go unmet.

Chemical and Biological Warfare (CBW)

Chemical and **biological weapons,** as well as nuclear weapons, are classified as *Weapons of Mass Destruction (WMD).* Like nuclear weapons, they seldom have been used in modern warfare, and like that of nuclear weapons, their very existence raises difficult questions.

chemical weapons Military weapons that are classified as weapons of mass destruction because of their chemical composition, e.g. mustard gas.

biological weapons Military weapons that are classified as weapons of mass destruction because of the biological nature of their composition, e.g. anthrax disease.

Biological Weapons

Disease always has accompanied war and often has served as a conqueror's greatest ally. Ancient armies threw decayed corpses into their enemies' water supplies. The smallpox that accompanied Spanish *conquistadores* to the New World became the Europeans' most successful weapon against the Aztec and Inca empires; with the virus carried by Indian traders, epidemics swept through the two empires, leaving them devastated, years before the *conquistadores* actually arrived. Farther to the north, Puritans often gave blankets taken from victims of smallpox, blankets still laden with vomit, pus, and the accompanying viruses, to Indians—lethal "gifts" indeed.

The twentieth century has not yet seen widespread use of biological warfare although there is intense suspicion that Saddam Hussein's Iraq may have "field-tested" typhoid fever as a biological agent against the Kurds (Dunnigan and Nofi 1990, 254). Besides typhoid, the principal agents considered for biological warfare include anthrax, bubonic plague, and dengue hemorrhagic fever.

Like its cousin chemical warfare, biological warfare at first glance appears attractive because it is relatively cheap. However, there are many negatives attached to the idea of using bio-weapons, even beyond any moral repulsion against such weapons. First, "offensive use of biological weapons may actually be highly counterproductive." Germs cannot tell friend from foe, and there is almost no way to be sure that sudden wind shifts will not bring the lethal agents back into one's own lines. Further, a nation under serious biological attack might well decide that it must retaliate either with its own bio-agents or with nuclear weapons (Dunnigan and Nofi 1990, 253). According to one analyst, "What makes biological warfare so frightful is that no one has actually tried it yet in modern times" (Dunnigan 1993, 415). Biological warfare is "too easy to start and too difficult to stop." Further, "germs and viruses are not as disciplined as soldiers and will attack any vulnerable victim they can reach" (Dunnigan and Nofi 1990, 254).

To perfect a biological weapon, first a nation would have to "invent" a new disease, probably a variant of an existing one, that would spread rapidly and be extremely debilitating. Then the nation would have to immunize all its own troops and, if the war were being conducted close to home, all its own population as well. It is hard to imagine that such widescale programs could be kept secret. Further, unlike nerve gases, biological weapons do not take effect immediately; even the most virulent fevers have an incubation period of at least a few days. This lag time might well allow the enemy to retaliate, with either its own bio-agents or nuclear agents. The winners might not survive (Dunnigan 1993, 415).

Of course, bio-agents might not be aimed at human populations. One could wreak considerable havoc on an opposing nation by spreading anthrax or some other equally lethal disease among its livestock (Dunnigan 1993, 415).

The Biological Weapons Convention

So appalling were the possibilities of biological warfare that in 1972 some seventy nations drew up and signed the Biological Weapons Convention (BWC). This convention prohibits the development, production, and stockpiling of bacteriological and toxin weapons and specifies that existing stockpiles are to be destroyed. Parties to the convention agree not to develop, produce, stockpile, or acquire biological agents or toxins in amounts or types "that have no justification for prophylactic, protective, and other peaceful purposes." They also agree not to develop delivery systems for such agents. The convention became effective in March 1975; to this point, 109 nations have signed the treaty (NATO 1994; Clark 1995).

Continuing Research

Although the United States destroyed its stockpiles of biological agents during the 1970s, and the presumption is that other signatories to the convention have done the same, research on biological agents continues. Justification for such nonoffensive research is threefold. First, research on biological weapons can be defensive, to allow a nation to develop defenses against possible biological weapons. Second, such research can allow a nation to learn how its armies can continue to operate in places where lethal diseases are widespread, the result not of bio-warfare but of local conditions. And, finally, bio-research can lead to breakthroughs in preventive medicine. For example, American researchers have conducted experiments in China to study various hemorrhagic fevers common there and in Korea. They also have gone to Argentina to study the value of vaccines for various diseases endemic to South America. Other experiments have involved working with Lassa fever, dengue hemorrhagic fever, anthrax, and other diseases common in the developing world. (For a more complete discussion of these diseases, see Chap. 14, "Global Issues.") Such research can have its risks, of course. In a 1979 accident in Sverdlovsk in the then Soviet Union, an accident at a biological warfare laboratory resulted in the deaths of more than one thousand people from anthrax. Even the U.S. Army's major site for bio-weapons research in Fort Dietrick, Maryland has had several "close calls" (Dunnigan and Nofi 1990, 254).

Despite the risk of accidents, and despite the ease with which such "defensive" research still could produce offensive results easily, other nations beyond the U.S. and Russia currently are conducting such research, according to U.S. officials. Among those suspected of being engaged in biological warfare research are Libya and Iraq (although one of the results of the Gulf War was the destruction of as much as possible of the Iraqi capacity to produce any weapons of mass destruction—Dunnigan and Nofi 1990, 254). And the fact that the purely "defensive" weapons being developed and tested could with little difficulty be converted to offensive uses remains troubling.

Chemical Warfare

Unlike biological weapons, chemical weapons already have appeared on twentieth-century battlefields. In April 1915 the German army inaugurated the use of chemical warfare by releasing chlorine gas to drift into the French and British lines. The Allies quickly developed both protective gear and their own chlorine gas, and the Germans then upped the ante by producing mustard gas and a number of other toxic substances. Tens of thousands died from these attacks; additional tens of thousands were left to die slow and ugly deaths from the lingering effects of the gases.

In a poignant scene, a man lies dead, his arm still around the small child he had tried to shield, in the Kurdish town of Halabja, the target of a poison gas attack by Saddam Hussein.

During World War II neither side used poison gas on the battlefield, primarily from fear of retaliation in kind by the other side. However, the Germans developed a large and lethal arsenal of chemical weapons; while most were stockpiled and not used on the battlefield, tons of toxic chemicals were used to annihilate millions of civilians in the death camps during the Holocaust.

During the Iraq-Iran war, Iraq made use of chemical weapons delivered by artillery shells or in canisters dropped from aircraft. Saddam Hussein of Iraq showed himself more than willing to use chemical weapons against the Kurdish population of northern Iraq, as well as his Iranian enemies. And many veterans of the Persian Gulf War are reporting strange and debilitating symptoms that they feel are the result of chemical weapons during that war. "Gulf War Syndrome" is still hotly debated and a cause for concern.

During the Cold War both superpowers developed huge stockpiles of chemical weapons. The United States and NATO countries, according to one estimate, held as much as forty thousand tons of chemical weapons, while the Soviet Union and its allies held nearly two hundred thousand tons. Despite attempts to limit the spread of chemical weapons, at least twenty nations today are suspected to have such weapons, and the recent use of sarin nerve gas by a Japanese religious cult underlines the relative ease with which such weapons can be built and used (Dunnigan 1993, 412).

Types of Chemical Weapons

Until recently, chemical weapons were defined broadly to include smoke, flares, incendiaries, flamethrowers, and napalm, but now the term *chemical warfare* is limited to the use of toxic agents on the battlefield (Clark 1995). Today chemical weapons generally include only two categories: blistering and blood agents, and nerve gases.

Blistering and Blood Agents.   The purpose of blistering agents is to kill or maim. Generally when one of these agents comes into contact with any sort of tissue, the result is terrible burning pain and destruction of tissue. Inhaled, these agents can kill immediately or produce terrible damage to the lungs that will cause a slow death; in some cases the agony has dragged out for twenty years or more. Blindness results from any contact with the eyes, and skin exposed to these agents will become so painful that people have been known to gouge out their own flesh to stop the pain. Phosgene, chlorine, and mustard gas are among the chief blistering agents. Blood agents are intended to cause severe damage and massive hemorrhaging to internal organs such as the kidney and liver. Protection against both consists of gas masks and protective clothing (Dunnigan 1993, 414).

Nerve Gases.   The various nerve gases are intended to attack victims' central nervous systems directly, usually producing respiratory paralysis and quick death. One analyst notes that nerve gas "hasn't been used that much because, in practice, it is tricky to manufacture in truly effective forms, difficult to store and deliver, and often not as effective as predicted." There are also antidotes to many of the more common nerve gases, usually some form of atropine. The person who has come into contact with nerve gas has about one minute to administer an injection of atropine. During the Persian Gulf War, when there was considerable fear that Saddam Hussein might use nerve gas against allied troops, there was serious discussion of mixing a tranquilizer such as Valium into the atropine injection to prevent the soldier from being paralyzed not by nerve gas, but by fear (Dunnigan 1993, 411). An unprotected population exposed to a nerve gas attack would suffer an 80 percent casualty rate, with half of those fatal, while an attack against troops prepared for it would inflict a 10 to 30 percent casualty rate, with 25 percent of those being fatalities (Dunnigan and Nofi 1990, 366; Dunnigan 1993, 412).

There is also a gray area involving the use of chemicals that are intended to be nonlethal. For example, during the Vietnam War the United States made widespread use of various sorts of tear and pepper gases, originally developed for use by police forces in riot control. Huge amounts of these gases were pumped into caves where Viet Cong or North Vietnamese forces were presumed to be. There were indeed fatalities, primarily among children hiding in these caves with their families. Additionally, the United States, in Operation Ranch-hand (whose motto was "Remember, only you can prevent forests,") dumped hundreds of thousands of tons of herbicides, including the infamous Agent Orange, over Vietnamese forests in order to destroy the canopy of leaves and reveal Viet Cong and North Vietnamese troops. Some of these herbicides contained known carcinogens such as dioxin. Today there are thousands of Vietnam War veterans suffering from various forms of cancer and other debilities who blame Agent Orange for their troubles, and for the health problems suffered by their children. There are many tens of thousands more Vietnamese suffering health problems that they believe can be traced back to the herbicides. Widespread use of napalm during the Vietnam War also led to questions about whether it should be included in the list of chemicals covered by international treaties.

A final, truly disturbing aspect of nerve gases is that their manufacture can be relatively simple. The sarin used by a Japanese religious cult to attack subway riders and sew panic and confusion was made by combining easily obtainable chemicals that the sect had purchased in large quantities. Another potent nerve gas, rysin, also can be made from "everyday" materials. The ease with which these deadly gases can be produced raises the possibility that they will be used extensively, either for blackmail or in reality, by terrorist groups.

Attempts to Limit Chemical Weapons

As early as 1899 the Hague Convention attempted to limit the use of chemical agents in war. After World War I, the Geneva Protocol of 1925 banned first use of asphyxiating, poisonous, or any other gas, and all similar liquids, materials, and devices. Not until 1975 did the United States actually sign the Geneva Protocol of 1925, but it had stopped producing chemical agents as early as 1969. In 1987 the Soviet Union announced that it had halted production of chemical weapons—but at almost the same time the United States announced that it had resumed production of such agents. This fact, combined with the use of chemical weapons by Iraq, intensified attempts to obtain a global agreement against the production and use of such weapons (Clark 1995).

In June 1990 the United States and the Soviet Union signed a pact pledging to stop producing chemical weapons immediately and to begin cutting back their stockpiles (Clark 1995). This led finally to the Chemical Weapons Convention (CWC), drafted in 1993. Under its terms, thirty-nine nations agreed to ban chemical weapons worldwide and to destroy their existing stockpiles (NATO 1994). The original plan was for the CWC to become effective in January 1995; however, not until November 1996 did the necessary number of nations actually ratify the CWC. It will go into effect in May 1997 (Crossette 1996).

However, even after ratification of the CWC, problems will remain. Five major challenges have been identified: implementation and verification of the CWC, destruction of chemical weapons in an environmentally safe and technically reliable manner, the problems posed by old chemical munitions and toxic armament wastes, countering proliferation of chemical and biological weapons, and strengthening the existing Biological Weapons Convention (Stock 1995). As one analyst ruefully observes, "Chemical warfare isn't going away, it's just getting more complicated" (Dunnigan 1993, 421).

Nuclear Weapons

The Development of Nuclear Weapons

Ironically, a great pacifist paved the way for the possibility of nuclear weapons at the very start of this century. When Albert Einstein published his landmark paper on the special theory of relativity in 1905, it contained the fateful equation $E=mc^2$; this equation implies that all matter can be converted to energy explosively. Clearly, such a mass-to-energy conversion could release vast amounts of destructive energy. In the early 1930s, atomic fission actually took place under controlled conditions, providing proof that the vision conjured up by Einstein's equation could become reality.

A Hungarian refugee scientist who had sought refuge from Hitler in England, Leo Szilard, actually devised a workable atomic bomb in his head in 1937 and patented his ideas (in patents that immediately were made secret by the British government). Szilard and other refugee scientists crossed the Atlantic in the late 1930s and began to talk among themselves about the horrible possibility that Nazi Germany, where the first actual splitting of the atom had taken place, might be able to develop an atomic bomb. In late 1939 these refugee scientists convinced Einstein to sign a letter to President Franklin Delano Roosevelt warning of the lethal possibilities of such a weapon in Nazi hands and urging that the United States develop its own bomb. Roosevelt authorized such work in 1940, but full-scale development began only in early 1942, when the United States Army took control of what became known as the **Manhattan District Project.** By the summer of 1945 an atomic device had been successfully tested. With the war against Japan still going on, President Harry Truman authorized use of this new weapon against Japanese targets. On August 6, 1945, the first atomic bomb was dropped over the city of Hiroshima, crowded with refugees; the death toll reached perhaps 145,000 by the end of the year, and is still climbing every year. Three days later, on August 9, 1945, the second American atomic bomb was used against the city of Nagasaki; by the end of 1945 the Nagasaki death toll had reached 130,000. Like that of Hiroshima, it is still rising.

Use of the two atomic bombs has been a source of controversy ever since. Critics charge that the devastation of both Hiroshima and Nagasaki was completely unnecessary: the Japanese were already defeated, they maintain, and had for months been sending out "peace feelers." Furthermore, critics allege, the bombs seem to have been targeted at least as much against the Soviet Union as against Japan. Truman and his advisers clearly hoped to end the Pacific war quickly to keep the Soviets from entering it, and they also saw the atomic bomb

Manhattan District Project U.S. project that developed the atomic bomb and launched the atomic (later nuclear) age in weaponry.

The devastation caused by the first atomic bomb is apparent in this photograph of Hiroshima, taken about a month after the bomb was dropped. In terms of today's arsenals, the Hiroshima bomb was a firecracker.

quickly to keep the Soviets from entering it, and they also saw the atomic bomb as the key to postwar American supremacy and domination of the Soviet Union.

Supporters of Truman agree with him that use of the bombs was justified if it resulted in saving even one American life, and that the effect of the bomb was in fact to save millions of lives, by ending the war before invasion of the Japanese home islands was necessary. In addition, the very fact that the weapon existed created a kind of momentum that implied it would then be used. After all, nearly two billion dollars had been spent in order to create the weapon, and not using it was thus all but unthinkable. How very much alive this controversy remains became apparent in the battle that raged through 1994 and 1995 about how the Smithsonian Institution's National Air and Space Museum would display the *Enola Gay,* the airplane from which the Hiroshima bomb was dropped, and what kind of commentary should accompany the exhibit.

The Arms Race

In the immediate aftermath of the war, there were abortive attempts to internationalize atomic weapons, but these attempts failed because the United States did not wish to yield its nuclear monopoly and the Soviet Union did not want to relinquish its opportunity to become a nuclear power as well. The result was an arms race that consumed some five trillion dollars on the part of the United States alone over the next forty-five years. In 1949 the Soviet Union exploded its first atomic bomb, on a timetable years ahead of what American leaders had believed possible; the United States then decided that it would have to develop a much more destructive weapon, the hydrogen bomb, whose power came not from nuclear fission but from nuclear fusion, the same force that fuels the furnaces of all stars. Within a year the Soviet Union had its own hydrogen bomb, and by 1960 there were five atomic powers: the United States, the Soviet Union, Great Britain, France, and China. By that time the primary focus of the arms race had shifted from the development of weapons to the development of delivery systems less vulnerable than aircraft.

This new, equally dangerous phase of the arms race began in the late 1950s with the launching of powerful rockets by the Soviet Union, rockets capable of orbiting satellites like the Sputnik series, or, many feared, perhaps of hurling nuclear warheads thousands of miles to land on targets in the United States. The Soviet Union built its first intercontinental ballistic missile (ICBM), the SS-7, in 1961, and the United States acquired its first ICBM, the Titan II, the same year. In 1961 the United States also acquired its first submarine-launched ballistic missile (SLBM), the Polaris; a very early and not particularly trustworthy Soviet SLBM, the SSN4, had been declared operational as early as 1953.

A dangerous phase of the arms race began in 1964 with the appearance of the Polaris III missile, which had multiple independently targetable reentry vehicles (MIRVs); in the jargon, Polaris III was the first MIRVed missile. The high-technology development of the MIRVed missiles meant that as many as ten or even twenty warheads could be fitted on the same missile, each one programmed to detach from the missile on a different course, aimed at a different target. Thus a single launch vehicle or missile could do the work of a dozen or more single-warhead missiles. By 1975 the Soviet Union had its owned MIRVed missile, the SS-17 (Chaliana and Rageau 1992, 218). Within a few years both superpowers had thousands of nuclear missiles—ICBMs, SLBMS, and intermediate-range ballistic missiles (IRBMs)—added to the arsenals of nuclear bombs in the holds of American B-52s and Soviet Tu-50s. At the greatest tension point of the arms race, the United States and the Soviet Union each possessed an arsenal of strategic nuclear weapons capable of killing every person in the world at least a dozen times over.

Theories of Deterrence

MAD

deterrence **A primarily psychological approach to defense based on the goal of avoiding damage to oneself and on the perception of the retaliatory capability of the enemy.**

The proliferation of nuclear weapons and the creation of powerful delivery systems spawned new theories of warfare and its avoidance that were geared specifically to the nuclear arms race. American and Western European theorists at "think tanks" like RAND created what is known as the theory of **deterrence:** the belief that if each superpower possessed the capacity to destroy the other, neither side would use its nuclear weapons, because this would in effect guarantee its own destruction as well. The widely used acronym for this theory, MAD, stood for Mutual Assured Destruction. MAD introduced a longer period of what has been called the "Balance of Terror": a world held in thrall by the fear of nuclear war and hopefully prevented from using nuclear weapons because of that fear. In effect, the people of each superpower became hostages to the other superpower.

This theory of deterrence perhaps overlooked one of history's most important lessons: what may look like a deterrent to one side often looks more like a threat to the other side, and the result of deterrence is not always what was intended. For example, in 1907 President Theodore Roosevelt sent the newly completed all-steel U.S. Navy's Great White Fleet to Japan, partly to "show the flag" and partly to deter Japan from imperialistic behavior in Asia. However, instead of interpreting the visit of the Great White Fleet as something that should deter them, that is, make them cautious and conservative, the Japanese saw the Great White Fleet as a threat. They concluded that they must themselves accelerate their naval building program and enter the great arms race of the early twentieth century. This deterrence/threat paradox has fueled more than one arms race in this century.

NUTS

The effectiveness of MAD depended on the belief by both sides that nuclear war was both unwinnable and unthinkable. Casualties on both sides, the thinking ran, would be so terrible that neither superpower could possibly survive intact. It would be, as Einstein said, a world in which the living would envy the dead. However, in the late 1970s a new school of theorists began to claim that nuclear war was "survivable," and thus "thinkable." This led to what became known as Nuclear Utilization Theory—a term critics gleefully reduced to NUTs in order to complement MAD. NUTs proponents believe that MAD relies too heavily on rationality, a commodity that may be in short supply should a nation be pushed to the brink of destruction. Consequently, it could be suicidal to assume that deterrence will work. Instead, NUTs proponents believe that a nation must be prepared to fight, survive, and win a nuclear war. Only by becoming capable of withstanding nuclear attack, NUTs theorists argue, can a nation truly deter its opponent from launching a first-strike nuclear attack.

This means that the United States, for example, should concentrate on civil defense measures and on ways to stop enemy missiles before they can hit. During Ronald Reagan's administration, from 1981 to 1989, officials argued that nuclear war could be made survivable relatively easily. Since a layer of dirt only three feet thick could shield people from the immediate effects of radiation and blast, they argued, "with enough shovels" nuclear war was survivable. This view actually was expressed by the head of the Civil Defense Agency, to the amusement of some and the consternation of many (Scheer, 1983).

Star Wars

Another Reagan-era spinoff the NUTs position was the decision to try to construct an antimissile defense system. The result was the Strategic Defense Initiative, (SDI), or **Star Wars,** as it was somewhat derisively known. President Reagan and his advisers envisioned a high-technology system capable of hitting Soviet ICBMs while they were still in space, using a variety of technologies ranging from lasers through particle-beam weapons to "brilliant pebbles." In his starry-eyed speech introducing the SDI program, President Reagan claimed that it would make nuclear war less threatening because the United States would be able to destroy virtually all of the other side's nuclear weapons in the air. So convinced was the president that Star Wars would work that he even offered to share the technology, once developed, with the Soviet Union so that both superpowers could enjoy ultimate deterrence.

Star Wars A proposed anti-ballistic missile system using laser technology.

Howls of disbelief and anger rose in the wake of the Star Wars speech. Critics charged that such a program was technologically all but impossible and economically so expensive that it would bankrupt the United States long before it could near completion. Conservative estimates are that a minimum of fifty-five billion dollars would be needed simply to implement a very limited first phase of SDI, and perhaps trillions more to establish a full-scale SDI system. Furthermore, the critics (primarily proponents of MAD) said that even beginning work on Star Wars would destabilize the existing nuclear standoff. If there was even a possibility that one side could erect a successful shield against the other side's missiles, they claimed, the other side might well decide to deliver a full-fledged nuclear strike before the shield could be completed. Otherwise, despite Reagan's optimistic promise of sharing such technology, one superpower would possess both nuclear weapons and an invulnerable shield, and the other side would possess nuclear weapons but no shield at all. Critics also pointed out that the installation of such a program, based largely on orbiting satellite systems, would "militarize" space itself, something that the world has so far avoided. There were also serious concerns that such a system could induce a false sense of confidence and lead to reduced efforts at arms control and at lessening superpower tensions.

In some ways much of the Star Wars debate has been rendered obsolete by the collapse of the Soviet Union and the end of the Cold War, but there is still some research taking place on SDI.

The Nuclear Freeze Movement

There are also those, of course, who view both MAD and NUTs as essentially insane, and argue that the only way to prevent nuclear war is to do away with nuclear weapons completely. The major antinuclear movement began in the 1950s, supported by such luminaries as Bertrand Russell, British philosopher and mathematician. Marches and rallies, as well as copious publications detailing the effects of nuclear war, expressed genuine fear at the prospect of nuclear weapons and the potential of nuclear war. In the 1980s the most prominent manifestation of this antinuclear sentiment was the nuclear freeze movement, which called not for the immediate abolition of all nuclear weapons, but for the stopping of construction on all new weapons, and then the gradual destruction of existing ones. The freeze movement had considerable success on college campuses in the United States, and even succeeded in having antinuclear referenda placed on ballots and passed in several states.

Nuclear Scenarios

Political and military strategists today can see two possible varieties of nuclear war: limited nuclear war and total nuclear war.

Limited Nuclear War

Limited nuclear war could occur in two fashions. First, the major powers could decide to use their nuclear weapons, but with limits. For example, if war were to erupt in Europe, such a war might involve the use of so-called tactical nuclear weapons. These are small, low-yield nuclear devices designed to be used on the battlefield itself. There are several shoulder-held bazooka-based warheads, for example, that could be fired several miles and explode without endangering one's own troops. At least, that's the theory. Such battlefield weapons never have been used in actual combat.

A second sort of limited nuclear war—the more likely type, at this writing—could take place between combatants that had developed nuclear weapons, probably atomic bombs but not hydrogen bombs, but that lacked sophisticated delivery systems and would use either short-range missiles like the Scud or fighter-bomber aircraft. The current proliferation of nuclear weapons among nations that are just joining, or just about to join, the nuclear club makes this possibility highly probable.

Both India and Pakistan possess nuclear weapons, for example, as well as old and festering anger against each other. There already have been several Indo-

Pakistani wars, luckily all fought before either side acquired nuclear capacity, but the underlying tensions that led to these earlier wars still remain. Should another Indo-Pakistani war erupt, then, we should not be surprised to see one or both sides brandish and then perhaps use comparatively small nuclear weapons. (Of course, the bombs that did such terrible damage to Hiroshima and Nagasaki also are considered "small" bombs by today's standards.)

Iran and Iraq also either have or are very close to having nuclear weapons, although the Persian Gulf War has probably set back Iraq's development of such weapons substantially. There is little question that Israel also possesses nuclear capacity, and little doubt that should another major Arab-Israeli war drive the Israeli government to desperation, it would use its nuclear capacity. In the case of Israel and the Arab states, recent developments seem to point in the direction of ultimate peace, although getting there is probably going to be a long-drawn-out and often painful process; in the case of Iran and Iraq, neither state has softened its belligerence.

Total Nuclear War

Total nuclear war today seems far less likely than it did even five years ago, thanks largely to the end of the Cold War and the unraveling of the Soviet Union. Russia, the heart of the old Soviet Union, still possesses a substantial nuclear arsenal; General Colin Powell, former chairman of the Joint Chiefs of Staff, observed, "I am still concerned about Russia because it is the only nation in the world that still possesses the power to destroy the United States." Although recently concluded agreements on the retargeting of existing Russian missiles so that they are not aimed directly at American targets seems a good sign, cynics point out that retargeting the warheads again would take only a few minutes. But recent Russo-American agreements to begin destroying nuclear missiles and converting their warheads to peaceful purposes also offer far greater hope of a non-nuclear future than most would have dared to dream of a decade ago.

Should total nuclear war erupt, the consequences would be devastating. Just before the Cold War began to unwind, the Soviet Union possessed a total of 28,000 nuclear warheads, and the United States 24,000. Great Britain possessed (independently of NATO weapons on British soil) some 525 warheads; France, 475; and China, an estimated 325. In addition, an estimated 50 warheads of various sorts have been lost in military accidents, generally the sinking of nuclear-powered submarines (Kidron and Smith 1991, 60–61). The lethality of these warheads has a wide range. In sheer killing power, a 20-kiloton weapon (just slightly larger than those used on Hiroshima and Nagasaki) could potentially take up to forty-one million lives; a 25-megaton warhead could account for upwards of ten billion lives, at least in theory. We say "in theory" because the population of the earth at this point is only some five billion; our killing capacity has outgrown our population (Kidron and Smith 1991, 53). Also at the end of the Cold War, the United States had just over 2,000 launch platforms, while the Soviet Union had some 2,500 launch platforms (Chaliand & Rageau 1992, 210). A single U.S. Trident submarine carries approximately eight times the destructive power used by all nations during World War II.

Scientists have spent hundreds of hours of computer time to try to understand what would happen in the event of nuclear war. Their conclusions are frightening. In his classic *Fate of the Earth* (1982), Jonathan Schell painted a devastating picture of what nuclear war would mean in concrete terms. The bomb

What Would You Do?

GLOBAL PERSPECTIVES

Suppose that you are president of the United States. Your secretary of defense comes into the Oval Office and solemnly informs you that he has absolute information that a first strike has been launched against the United States. There are thousands of warheads about to descend on American cities, defense sites, and industrial sites, and there is absolutely nothing that can be done to prevent it. Well over a hundred million Americans, probably including yourself, will die within the next few hours. However, if you order a retaliatory strike, it not only will kill more than a hundred and fifty million Russians in the next hour, but also will in all likelihood bring on the catastrophic nuclear winter that scientists have been warning of. Thus your retaliation will cause the death of the entire planet and its five billion inhabitants. And it will accomplish nothing to save American lives. In fact, by retaliating you will virtually guarantee the death of any Americans, not to mention Europeans, Africans, and Asians, who survive the initial strike.

If actually faced with this dilemma, would you order the retaliation, as all current nuclear thinking calls for? Or would you do nothing, allowing the Russian missiles to obliterate the United States without retaliation? It would be an excruciating moral dilemma. The entire theory of deterrence rests on the assumption that an American president, or Russian counterpart if the situation were reversed, would go ahead more or less blindly and order the counterstrike, even though it would accomplish little more than an instant of revenge and an eternity of death. It is certainly something worth thinking about.

most likely to be used against any major American city would be a gigantic 20-megaton bomb (one with 1,600 times the destructive power of those used against Hiroshima and Nagasaki). A 20-megaton bomb airburst over the Capital Building in Washington, D.C. would generate a 100 percent destruction blast wave with a radius of twelve miles. Everything inside the Washington Beltway would be leveled: the Capitol, the White House, the monuments, the Pentagon, the nearby Virginia and Maryland suburbs. The zone of heavy destruction would extend 21.5 miles from Ground Zero, reaching the Civil War battlefield at Manassas and flattening Mount Vernon, extending north to the Baltimore suburbs. The thermal pulse and its attendant fireball, nearly four and a half miles in diameter, would burn to death any person caught in the open for up to twenty-three miles from Ground Zero, and the searing heat would last for twenty seconds. A seventy-mile-wide mushroom cloud would engulf everything from the Civil War battlefield at Fredericksburg, Virginia, to the United States Naval Academy at Annapolis, Maryland. Depending on wind conditions, the "footprint" of lethal radioactivity could extend as far north as New York City and as far south as Charleston, South Carolina. People within a radius of several hundred miles would be temporarily blinded, sometimes with permanent eye damage, if they looked at the fireball.

A groundburst 20-megaton bomb with the Capitol as Ground Zero would produce less severe blast damage, but its fireball would engulf everything within a ten-mile radius, instantly killing everyone and everything within that range, from Silver Spring and Wheaton, Maryland, to Alexandria and Arlington, Virginia. Most matter within the fireball's immediate range would simply vanish, evaporated by the intense heat. Individuals up to fifty miles from Ground Zero would suffer lethal third-degree burns. However, much of the groundburst's killing effect would come from the enormous cloud of deadly radioactive material it would create. Ash and debris, much of it coming from a crater three miles in diameter and perhaps four to five hundred feet in depth, would swirl upward in a mushroom cloud and then descend back to earth in a storm of radioactive material. A worst-case scenario, positing prevailing southeast winds, puts the lethal area of the radioactive footprint up to eight hundred miles from Ground Zero. Consequently, a single 20-megaton bomb could not only reduce the national capital to a smoking radioactive hole in the ground, but could also kill perhaps twenty million people, nearly 10 percent of the country's total population.

Before its breakup, the Soviet Union was believed to possess more than one hundred such 20-megaton bombs. Contemplating the result of a total nuclear war, Jonathan Schell writes that the human population of the world would disappear and all that would remain would be "a **republic of insects**," the only survivors (Schell 1982).

republic of insects What some scientists believe to be the only surviving creatures after a nuclear exchange.

"Nuclear Winter"

According to scientists, nuclear war at levels less immediately catastrophic than those posited by Schell would be equally devastating. Reporting on a conference of scientists in Cambridge, Massachusetts in 1983, Pulitzer Prize–winning astronomer Carl Sagan developed the idea of **"nuclear winter."** Nuclear war would lead to dense clouds of smoke in the troposphere, equally dense clouds of dust in the stratosphere, the fallout of radioactive debris, and the partial destruction of the ozone layer. In much of the Northern Hemisphere, sunlight would be unable to penetrate the clouds of dust and smoke; twilight gloom or even total darkness could last as long as a week after nuclear war. Plants would not receive enough light to permit photosynthesis. Temperatures would drop precipitously, as much as thirty to forty degrees centigrade. (A twelve- to fifteen-degree drop would be enough to wipe out all wheat and corn production in the United States, Canada, and Russia. During the Ice Ages that covered much of Europe and North America in sheets of ice hundreds of miles thick and lowered the average sea level approximately 270 feet, the typical long-term temperature decline is estimated to have been only ten degrees.) Masses of people, inhabitants of not only those countries but also those around the world that depend heavily on imported food (Japan, for example, must import 75 percent of its food) would starve to death. The ground would freeze to depths of a yard or more; crops could not be sown, nor bodies buried. Disease would multiply, as people in the cold and dark, on the brink of starvation, became increasingly vulnerable. Water of any sort would become scarce or unavailable. The ecosystem would come under enormous stress, with many varieties of plant and animal life, both on dry ground and in the lakes, seas, and oceans, becoming extinct (Sagan 1989).

"nuclear winter" The freezing and desolate aftermath of hypothetical global nuclear exchange.

Other scientific evidence seems to support the general conclusions of the "nuclear winter" theory. For example, scientists are now fairly sure that the sudden extinction of dinosaurs some 165 million years ago resulted from the collision of a large asteroid with the earth. This theory proclaims that the dust and smoke caused by the explosive force of the collision dropped the ambient temperature by only a few degrees, which was enough to doom the hundreds of varieties of dinosaurs that "ruled" the earth at that time. The explosion of the great Krakatoa volcano in 1885 threw so much debris into the atmosphere that temperatures fell around the world: it snowed in Boston on the Fourth of July that year, and spectacular sunsets for several years were a happy legacy of the Krakatoa explosion. More recently, clouds of smoke and ash from massive forest fires in the western United States in 1988 so effectively blocked sunlight in Northern California that temperatures there fell to as much as thirty-six degrees below normal for more than a week (Dunnigan and Nofi 1990, 417). In 1992 the Pentagon announced that it had basically accepted the premises of the "nuclear winter" theory.

The American poet Robert Frost wrote, perhaps prophetically:

> Some say the world will end in fire,
> Some say in ice.
> From what I've tasted of desire
> I hold with those who favor fire.
> But if it had to perish twice,
> I think I know enough of hate
> To say that for destruction ice
> Is also great
> And would suffice.
> (quoted in Bartlett, 1955)

Other Nuclear Issues

One of the most important, and most interesting, of the issues that swirl around the question of nuclear weapons is the matter of control and decision. Whose finger, ultimately, is on the nuclear trigger? And under what circumstances will that individual decide to pull the trigger?

Are Accidental Wars Possible?

Most of us are familiar with movies and novels based on the premise that a lone lunatic somehow has seized control of the American or the Russian nuclear arsenal. One of the most memorable movies of the nuclear age, Stanley Kubrick's *Dr. Strangelove; Or, How I Learned to Stop Worrying and Love the Bomb,* dealt with this possibility. Another nightmare scenario, so far confined to the movies as well, is the danger of some sort of miscommunication that leads to the use of nuclear weapons, or to the brink of that abyss. A movie of the 1950s, *Three Days in May,* raised the idea of an American nuclear bomber headed for Moscow and a desperate American president ordering a nuclear attack on New York City in order to convince the Soviet leadership that it was all the result of accident. More recently, the possibility of tampering with computer systems and starting the countdown to nuclear war was the central theme of a highly popular movie, *War Games.*

From the beginning of the nuclear era, American leaders have reassured their population that such events could happen only in the movies, that American weapons are far too closely safeguarded for these to be realistic scenarios. We are all familiar with photographs and television news footage showing an American president shadowed by a military officer carrying a small suitcase-like bag. This is the "football," as it is called, that contains the codes and orders that any president would need to begin a nuclear war. Not only must a presidential order be given, but there is also an elaborate series of codes and other procedures to follow. For example, even after receiving a presidential order, an ICBM can be launched only if two officers separately verify the codes and then separately turn keys to begin the ignition process. Presumably this would prevent a single insane individual from independently launching such a missile. A similar situation prevails regarding nuclear submarines. And we presume that such a system, or a variant on it, is in place in Russia to prevent any accidental or lunatic launch of nuclear weapons. Although all of this appears reasonable, it is sometimes a good idea to remember the old proverb: "For every foolproof system built, a better fool is created."

There is also the dilemma of what to do if the president and members of the cabinet are either killed or rendered incommunicado by an electromagnetic pulse (EMP) capable of disrupting communications continentwide. Where then does the authority reside to order the launch of weapons? In some cases, such as in the use of tactical nukes, the ultimate authority may reside with a battlefield commander, who would have enormous discretion in choosing when and whether to use the available short-range nuclear arsenal. However, attempting to cover all possibilities, the Pentagon supposedly has prepared a hierarchical list of those who have the authority to authorize a strategic launch should the president not be able to do so. This list extends down some forty-two levels, to an assistant secretary of defense for research.

When to Pull the Trigger?

Another issue involving the launching of nuclear weapons is when and under what circumstances they should be used. The Soviet Union formally stated that it would never be the first to use nuclear weapons, and although the United States has not made such a formal pledge, it is generally understood that it too would never initiate nuclear war. However, both nations bristle with radar arrays aimed over the North Pole to give the earliest possible warning of an enemy nuclear launch. These systems are not necessarily perfect—there have been nuclear alerts for flocks of geese and the rising of the moon, for example—but they presumably will provide some sort of warning that missiles are on the way. There is, however, no such early warning system for submarine-launched missiles. While land-based missiles launched over the polar ice cap may take anywhere from fifteen to seventeen minutes to reach their targets, missiles launched from a submarine sitting one hundred or so miles off the American coast could begin striking seaboard targets within five to seven minutes.

Even assuming that there is some sort of effective warning, there still remains the question of when to launch nuclear weapons in response. Essentially, there are three possibilities: you can launch your missiles when you think the enemy has done so (launch on warning, or LOW); you can launch your missiles when you verify that you are under attack but before enemy missiles actually hit (launch under attack, or LUA); or you may wait until actual strikes from enemy missiles have been verified (launch on impact, or LOI).

There is fierce debate about which is the best method. Proponents of LOI say that it is the best way to avoid an accidental war, perhaps triggered by false radar readings or a cascading sequence of such readings and computer glitches. Critics of LOI point out that if enemy weapons had already detonated, much of the American ICBM arsenal would probably be out of commission because of the EMP. These critics, who tend to be of the NUTs school, argue that essentially it is a case of "use 'em or lose 'em." That is, if we do not launch weapons at least while under attack, or perhaps even after some kind of warning has been received, we will never be able to launch them. Opponents of the "use 'em or lose 'em" school, who tend to accept the MAD doctrine, warn that this hair-trigger approach could all too easily lead to an unwanted and unwarranted nuclear holocaust.

Targeting

One other important issue in dealing with the concept of nuclear war is the question of what kind of target nuclear planners should choose, assuming a relatively limited amount of warheads available. Basically, this choice breaks down into two very different opportunities: **countervalue targeting,** and **counterforce targeting.**

countervalue targeting
Nuclear targeting of the enemy's civilian population centers, in addition to its military-industrial centers.

counterforce targeting
Nuclear targeting of the enemy's military-industrial components.

Countervalue targeting focuses on the enemy's cities and infrastructure; its use is at the heart of the MAD approach, bearing as it does the assurance that if enemy warheads took out major American cities, our warheads would take out major enemy cities. In 1979 Secretary of Defense Harold Brown warned that under MAD, the United States would destroy two hundred major Russian cities, taking out 62 percent of Russian industrial capacity (and incidentally, 34 percent of the Russian population). The United States has specifically foresworn any targeting of Russian civilians, stating that it would instead target the Russian industrial complex; however, such targeting, given blast patterns, fallout footprints, and so forth, inevitably would cause vast numbers of civilian deaths. Presumably the civilians would never know that they were merely incidental casualties, and that the major target had been the petrochemical complex a few miles away.

Counterforce targeting, urged basically by the NUTs theorists, places far greater emphasis on the enemy's command and communications centers and its strategic nuclear forces as primary targets. The idea is not to punish the enemy for attacking you, but to remove the enemy's capacity to do so. Although civilian casualties would be far fewer under the counterforce doctrine than under the countervalue doctrine, the main problem is that for counterforce to work effectively, it would have to be a first-strike decision. That is, to make counterforce work and eliminate the possibility of a punishing enemy response, the United States would have to be the first to launch its weapons, and it would also have to hope that the enemy did not have an LOW posture.

The counterforce doctrine thus raises not only disturbing moral questions, but also important military ones as well. For example, if you have destroyed the enemy's command centers, how can the enemy then surrender? Or how can enemy submarine commanders be prevented from launching their missiles once they realize that all communications have been lost, most likely from a nuclear attack? And if the enemy has a launch on warning doctrine, the first use of missiles, even though not directed at civilian targets, would only provoke an all-out retaliation against American targets, thus leading to the total nuclear holocaust that the counterforce doctrine is at least in theory designed to prevent.

Arsenals and Proliferation in the Modern World

Proliferation

One of the most important concerns about nuclear weapons, particularly now that the end of the Cold War has reduced the likelihood of global nuclear war, is the possibility (in fact, the high probability), of the spread or proliferation of nuclear weapons beyond the major powers that have held them for the past thirty to fifty years. The original "nuclear club" had a membership of one—the United States—but by the early 1960s it had expanded to include five members: the U.S., the

Soviet Union, Great Britain, France, and China. Fears that the continuing spread of nuclear weapons could lead to nuclear war, nuclear accidents, or even nuclear terrorism led to the Nuclear Nonproliferation Treaty (NPT), which was signed by fifteen nations as it became operational in 1970. By 1990 the NPT had 140 signatories. However, both China and France remained outside the NPT until 1992.

Under the terms of the NPT, powers possessing nuclear weapons agreed not to transfer such devices to any non-nuclear state, and non-nuclear states agreed not to acquire nuclear weapons. In addition, non-nuclear states agreed to allow inspectors from the United Nations' International Atomic Energy Agency (IAEA) to monitor their nuclear facilities and to accept IAEA safeguards. But simply signing the NPT does not mean that a nation will not pursue nuclear weapons; North Korea signed the agreement in 1985 but has been aggressively pursuing an atomic bomb, and stonewalling IAEA inspectors, ever since. As well, Saddam Hussein's Iraq was very close to nuclear capacity when the Persian Gulf War began, despite Iraq's having signed the NPT (Davis 1994, 109; Segal 1991, 107–8).

In April 1995, at the end of the treaty's first twenty-five-year term, a global review conference of 178 nations decided to extend the NPT permanently. Under the terms of the treaty, only five nations—the United States, Russia, Great Britain, France, and China—are legitimate nuclear powers; these five are pledged to work "in good faith" to reduce their nuclear arsenals. Although the nuclear powers hailed the treaty's extension as the beginning of "a better future for our children and the generations to come," representatives from many non-nuclear nations saw it as nuclear "carte blanche" for the nuclear powers. And ominously, several states known to possess nuclear weapons—Israel, Pakistan, and India—still have not signed the NPT ("U.N. Permanently Renews N-Treaty" 1995). Known and possible "nuclear club" members, and other information on global nuclear weapons and reactors, are depicted in figure 12.2.

Is Nonproliferation Necessarily Good?

There is some debate about whether nonproliferation is necessary or even a good idea. John Mearsheimer, for example, argues that what he calls "managed proliferation," which would spread nuclear weapons gradually to major European powers like Germany, might well be the continent's best guarantee of future stability. Mearsheimer also would tolerate the spread of nuclear weapons into eastern Europe if the current nuclear powers could channel such proliferation into safe channels. However, he is pessimistic about whether proliferation could be controlled, and concludes that "proliferation is likely to occur under international conditions that virtually ensure it will be mismanaged" (Mearsheimer 1994, 52–53).

A second analyst of proliferation, Kenneth N. Waltz, argues that the spread of nuclear weapons throughout the world could well become a stabilizing force in a multilateral world. Waltz argues that nuclear weapons have helped maintain peace among the superpowers by raising the stakes of nuclear war so high that it has not happened, and that nuclear weapons might serve the same role in bilateral non-superpower relations as well. He also states that the Western fear of proliferation in the non-Western world is shaped as much by ethnocentrism as by realistic analysis. For example, he argues, it is unlikely that any Arab nation would attack Israel as long as both had nuclear weapons. "Rulers want to have a country that they can continue to rule. Some Arab country might wish that some other Arab country would risk its own destruction for the sake of destroying Israel, but there is no reason to think that any Arab country would do so." Waltz concludes

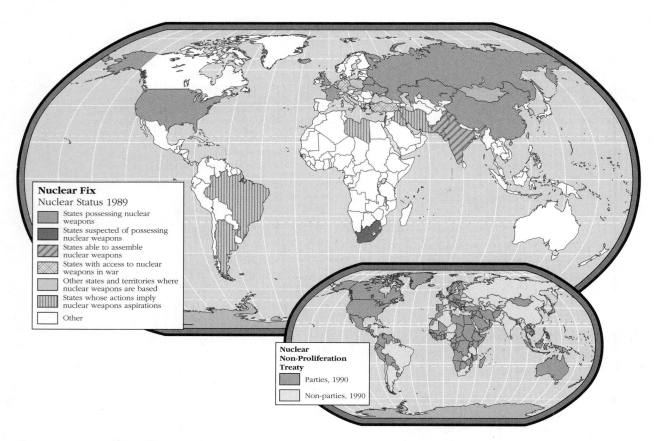

Figure 12.2 **Nuclear Club Members and Possible Members**
There are five declared nuclear weapon states, a sixth which has nuclear weapons but has not acknowledged it, a seventh which probably has nuclear weapons and two more states which can assemble them very quickly. Over 50 nuclear weapons and 7 military nuclear reactors have been lost at sea.

that the emergence of new nuclear states might not be so bad after all, since regional bilateral deterrence would be stabilizing rather than destabilizing, and since nations possessing nuclear arms might well spend less money on conventional arms. In fact, Waltz believes that "conventional arms races will wither if countries shift emphasis from conventional defense to nuclear deterrence" (Waltz 1994, 371–82).

Despite such viewpoints, the majority of analysts and scholars still consider **nuclear proliferation** to be extremely dangerous. As the *New York Times* tartly observes, "For some messianic fundamentalists in the Middle East, Mutual Assured Destruction is not a deterrent but a temptation" (quoted in Burrows and Windrem 1994, 120). Unfortunately, nuclear proliferation is no longer a mere possibility, but a fact of life.

nuclear proliferation The spread of nuclear weapons beyond the original holders to underdeveloped nations.

New Members of the Nuclear Club

The most recent major work on proliferation calculates that eight so-called Third World nations possess nuclear weapons: Belarus, China, Ukraine, Kazakhstan, India, Pakistan, Israel, and North Korea. In addition, four other nations, three of them "pariah states," are actively pursuing the acquisition of nuclear weapons:

Libya, Iran, Iraq, and Algeria. According to these sources, four additional nations have "quiescent" nuclear programs, that is, once active programs that have now been shut down: Brazil, Argentina, South Africa, and South Korea. Two further nations are on the "watchlist" for the development of nuclear weapons: Egypt and Indonesia (Burrows and Windrem 1994, 507).

This proliferation of nuclear weapons has occurred in a number of different ways. Despite safeguards against the transferral of nuclear technology, companies in a large number of industrialized nations, including the United States, France, and Germany, have sold large amounts of sophisticated technology to these nuclear wannabes. Although much of that technology was clearly adaptable to nuclear weapons research and development, a lot of it also was "dual-use" technology, that is, machinery and computers that could be used either for peaceful purposes or for the production of weapons. Even the transfer of uranium could be either for peaceful purposes, that is, for use as fuel for nuclear reactors to produce electric power, or diverted to the production of nuclear weapons.

In addition, much of the development of nuclear weapons outside the non-proliferation regime has been less the result of technology transfer than of hard work by citizens of the individual nations involved. Certainly nations like China, Iraq, Pakistan, India, and Israel have produced significant numbers of high-quality nuclear physicists fully capable of understanding the mechanics of producing fissionable material and assembling nuclear bombs. Ironically, many of the scientists involved in the production of nuclear weapons outside the NPT received much of their training in the United States and enjoyed access to American nuclear facilities for training and research. The nuclear outsiders also discovered that they could cooperate with one another, pooling their resources for research and development. Probably the most interesting example of this pooling of resources was between Israel and South Africa, which shared technology and resources and are assumed to have exploded a nuclear device over the South Atlantic in 1979. In 1993 South Africa's president F. W. de Klerk admitted that his nation had built, and then scrapped, six nuclear devices. Israel is assumed to have between fifty and three hundred nuclear weapons, perhaps including hydrogen bombs (Davis 110–21; Burrows and Windrem 1994, 275–313).

"Loose Nukes"?

Complicating an already-tangled nuclear proliferation scene is the collapse of the Soviet Union and the question of what will become both of its existing nuclear weapons and, perhaps even more important, of the scientists capable of building nuclear weapons and the materials with which they can do it. "The yard sale at the end of history" (discussed earlier in this chapter) represents a malignant joker in the deck. Even before the death of the Soviet Union, its accelerating collapse and the terrible economic problems that both produced and intensified that collapse had led to the creation in December 1990 of the International Chetek Corporation (from the Russian *Chelovek, Tecknologia, Kapital,* or "Man, Technology, Capital"). Some twenty major research centers, nuclear institutes, and nuclear production facilities, all led by nuclear weapons scientists, formed Chetek as a consortium to raise startup capital, pool their resources, and become a moneymaking venture. Chetek leaders published plans for a constructing Global Space System orbiting satellite and for reprocessing aluminum, copper, and magnesium strips, producing industrial diamonds, and performing a long string of other tasks, including genetic engineering. However, the most chilling Chetek proposal was

"loose nukes" Nuclear weapons that have found their way into the hands of renegade nations and militant groups as a result of the dissolution of the former Soviet Union.

the use of underground nuclear explosions to dispose of toxic waste materials. Although Chetek saw this proposal as a way of providing employment for otherwise unemployable nuclear physicists, as well as a solution to terrible environmental problems, many outside Chetek viewed with alarm the possibility of **"loose nukes"** in Chetek's hands that could slip into the hands of other, far less responsible individuals or could cause enormous environmental damage (Burrows and Windrem 1994, 233–41).

A Lutheran minister in the then East Germany claims that a young Russian lieutenant in the Special Troops of the Soviet General Staff offered to sell the international environmental group Greenpeace a Soviet warhead for $320,000. Although the sale was never consummated, perhaps because of the August 1991 coup and its aftermath, both the minister, who had researched and written about nuclear weapons, and Greenpeace took the lieutenant's offer seriously. The possibility of such "loose nukes" floating around Europe or, more catastrophically, slipping into the hands of Saddam Hussein or the mullahs who rule Iran, is terrifying. Defense Secretary Richard Cheney observed that the Soviet Union, with a nuclear arsenal of forty-five thousand warheads (according to Mikhail Gorbachev) could do a Herculean job of keeping control of these warheads, but that even if the Russians were "ninety-nine percent successful, that would mean you could still have as many as [450] that they were not able to control." To make matters worse, many of these warheads are small; about one-third of the weapons in the Soviet arsenal were small enough to be handled by only three men, and one-sixth of them, nearly 7,500 nuclear warheads, could be carried by a single individual (Burrows and Windrem 1994, 246–51).

Equally perplexing—and dangerous—are the 125 metric tons of weapons-grade plutonium stored in the Soviet Union, enough to make more than fifteen thousand nuclear weapons. Added to this is one thousand metric tons of highly enriched (bomb-grade) uranium, which is capable of being processed into forty-five thousand more bombs. Like Russia's arsenal of warheads, this store of potential bombs is scattered around the nation and perhaps vulnerable to pilferage. Russia also has been selling millions of pounds of uranium ore in the United States and elsewhere in the world, apparently beginning the process of liquidating a stockpile worth more than a billion dollars. Given the fact that the most difficult part of producing nuclear weapons is the production of fissionable material, either plutonium or enriched uranium, the possibility that even a small part of the Russian stockpile will reach the open market or the black market is the stuff of nightmares for those who fear nuclear proliferation (Burrows and Windrem 1994, 252–53; Robbins 1992, 40–51). In the summer of 1994 German authorities seized several small amounts of both enriched uranium and plutonium that apparently had originated in Russia, and in December 1994 Czech authorities seized six pounds of enriched bomb-grade uranium being smuggled in a car trunk ("Seized Material Is Enriched Uranium" 1994; see also Whitney, 1994).

In addition, within the former Soviet Union there are approximately two thousand scientists who could design nuclear weapons, perhaps five thousand capable of designing and operating uranium and plutonium processing facilities, and up to a total of one million weapons scientists of all sorts. In an attempt to stem a "brain drain" that would turn these highly knowledgeable scientists loose in non-nuclear nations, in 1991 and 1992 the United States appropriated nearly $800 million to cover the dismantling of weapons and to provide research opportunities—or just plain jobs—for this pool of nuclear talent. However, by the summer of 1993 less than $30 million actually had been spent (Burrows and Windrem 1994, 261–63).

Finally, the breakup of the Soviet Union led not only to the "yard sale at the end of history," but also to the distribution of the Soviet nuclear arsenal among four successor states of the Soviet Union: Russia, Ukraine, Belarus, and Kazakhstan. While most of the vast arsenal remained within the boundaries of Russia, or was brought back to Russia from the Baltic republics and elsewhere, the other three nuclear successor-states inherited enormous destructive capacities. Ukraine inherited nearly 200 ICBMs, 38 heavy bombers, and almost 4,500 total warheads; Belarus gained 72 ICBMs and 1,222 nuclear warheads; and Kazakhstan received 104 ICBMs and 1,690 warheads. Former Soviet commanders claimed that these weapons posed no problem because the launch codes necessary to activate the ICBMs had been taken back to Russia, but such a large number of nuclear weapons in the hands of new and precariously unstable nations made many people extremely nervous. In the spring of 1992, Ukraine, Belarus, and Kazakhstan all agreed to turn these nuclear weapons back over to Russia, but the Ukrainian parliament then balked, apparently figuring that possession of the nuclear arsenal would constitute a guarantee against Russian nationalist adventurism. However, following a visit by President Bill Clinton in the spring of 1994, the Ukrainian president repeated his pledge to make Ukraine a nuclear-free zone. In November 1994 the Ukrainian parliament finally agreed to join NPT and surrender its nuclear weapons (Burrows and Windrem 1994, 252–56; Church 1991, 40–41; Lemonick 1991, 45–46; Nelan 1993, 36–39; Mycio and Efron 1994).

Operation Sapphire

GLOBAL PERSPECTIVES

Thirteen hundred pounds of highly enriched uranium—enough to make at least thirty-six atomic bombs. Just sitting there, on the windswept plains of Central Asia, inviting theft or a quick and highly profitable sale to a rogue state. A newly formed government anxious to get rid of the stuff. A team of American experts, flown in secretly to get the uranium out of the country to safety in the U.S. And a deadline of six weeks in which to get it all done—in absolute secrecy—before the harsh Central Asian winter blasts across the steppes to shut down all local airfields.

These sound like the ingredients for a new Tom Clancy high-tech superthriller. They were, however, not fiction, but the facts of a real-life secret operation, christened "Sapphire," that unfolded in the fall of 1994. The collapse of the Soviet Union had left some 1,300 pounds of highly enriched uranium stranded in the new Central Asian republic of Kazakhstan. Originally intended to provide fuel rods for nuclear submarines, the cache of uranium provided a tempting target for clandestine sales or even outright theft. The Kazakh government, pledged to get rid of its leftover nuclear missiles, did not want the fuel and could not afford to guard it.

American scientists who visited the site in February 1994 were astonished to discover this cache of aging containers stuffed with the prized uranium. By early summer U.S. and Kazakh officials had agreed that the uranium would be spirited out of Kazakhstan to much greater safety in the U.S. American officials promised to pay about $100 million for the uranium, in part to keep it out of the hands of Saddam Hussein. Moscow signed off on the deal—it has plenty of enriched uranium—and the stage was set for a lead-lined cloak-and-dagger drama on the high steppes.

Thirty-one Americans, primarily scientists and technicians, flew into Kazakhstan aboard three huge C-5 transports and began working feverishly to repack the "hot" fuel into new, secure stainless steel drums. Tucked away in the cavernous hold of the C-5 was a complete chemical laboratory so that the scientists could test the enriched uranium and, if

(continued on p. 440)

Operation Sapphire
(Continued from p. 439)

necessary, bake it to remove moisture and make it safe for transport.

Operating in a specially secured area of the Kazakh plant, arriving before dawn and leaving after dark to avoid being seen, rehearsing their cover story (they were to say that they were from the International Atomic Energy Agency), the Americans worked fourteen hours a day, six days a week, to get all the material packed before winter made air transportation dicey. In just six weeks they completed a six-month task.

Loaded with more than half a ton of enriched uranium, the C-5s finally took off in late November. Extra flight crews and aerial refueling allowed the C-5s to remain airborne all the way home (a twenty-hour trip almost halfway around the globe), until they touched down at Dover Air Force Base in Delaware. Four heavily guarded truck convoys carried the potentially lethal material to Oak Ridge, Tennessee, for safekeeping until it could be reprocessed into low-grade commercial reactor fuel.

Exhilarated scientists and technicians happily celebrated their foray into James Bond territory, and U.S. officials publicly rejoiced at the removal of the uranium from the reach of terrorists and rogue states.

Meanwhile, spy fiction writers gnashed their teeth that real life had beaten them to the punch for a grand high-tech, high-adventure story line. Tom Clancy, eat your heart out! (Thompson 1994a)

To the Brink?

Even before the collapse of the Soviet Union and the accelerating dangers of proliferation, a number of nuclear confrontations that raised serious possibilities of nuclear war have taken place. Not surprisingly, most happened in the Middle East. According to two serious students of the area, as early as June 1967 Israeli officials armed two nuclear weapons after an Egyptian overflight of Dimona, Israel's main site for nuclear research and bomb production. These sources also say that during the early phases of the Yom Kippur war, when things were going sour for Israel, Israel put its nuclear arsenal on alert for possible use against Syrian and Egyptian military headquarters. And during the Persian Gulf War, when Iraqi Scud missiles rained down in Israeli cities, the Israeli government again went on nuclear alert; there was, many analysts say, a strong possibility of nuclear retaliation had the Iraqi missiles carried chemical warheads.

South Asia provided the other site for brink-of-war theatrics. In January 1987, with India and Pakistan almost coming to war, both sides quietly rattled their nuclear sabers. Pakistan cold-tested a nuclear device to assure that it would work against India, and India in turn put its nuclear forces on full alert. Burrows and Windrem claim (although others dispute them), that in May 1990, with India and Pakistan once more on the brink of war, Pakistan assembled its first two nuclear weapons and India again puts it nuclear forces on alert. According to these analysts, it took American intervention and armtwisting to prevent the South Asian conflict over Kashmir from going nuclear at that point (Burrows and Windrem 1994, 349–377, 506).

What Next?

Experts disagree among themselves about the exact number of nuclear warheads in the possession of any given nation, or the exact points at which quarrels nearly accelerated into nuclear war, but they tend to agree on one major point: the NPT and the IAEA generally have failed in their stated mission of preventing the spread of nuclear weapons. These purely technical solutions are too easily circumvented, through the sale of dual-use technology, deception and stalling on required IAEA inspections, lack of any adequate way to punish a state that violates the NPT, and the plain fact that nuclear weapons, at least the simplest but still highly destructive versions, are frighteningly easy to make. According to one expert, "The NPT's major success is in helping create a climate hostile to open proliferation" (Segal 1991, 110). Another analyst urges a more aggressive approach by the IAEA: a multilayered approach, including disarmament agreements and regional security regimes (Davis 1994, 129). And still others argue that just as war is considered to be a continuation of politics, so too must the construction and proliferation of nuclear weapons be considered not a military but a political problem. "Mutual trust must therefore replace mutual assured destruction everywhere, just as it has between the old cold war antagonists, or a cataclysm must sooner or later follow. This is no longer utopian idealism. It is a matter of life and death" (Burrows and Windrem 1994, 505).

Disarmament, Arms Control, and Arms Limitation

Almost since organized warfare began, people have thought that limiting or eliminating arms altogether would be the most effective way to prevent war and the destruction that accompanies it. The biblical admonition "Beat your swords into plowshares" expresses this hopeful attitude. Arms races have been believed responsible, at least in part, for wars, and thus the curbing or ending of arms races is a logical way to avoid wars. (However, there are theorists who question the presumed link between arms races and wars, asserting that it is not verifiable.)

Thus a major focus of international relations in the twentieth century has been the search for ways to limit, control, or eliminate arms. Although we tend to use terms like arms control, arms limitation, and disarmament more or less interchangeably, there are important differences. **Arms control** simply means an attempt to manage existing weapons and weapons systems: to reduce the number, type, design, production, distribution, and transfer of arms. **Arms limitation** refers in contrast to *capping* the number and types of arms a nation may possess. And **disarmament** implies the actual reduction of existing weapons. All three types of attempts to deal with the problems of arms races and proliferations are almost always bilateral or multilateral, the result of carefully negotiated treaties or executive agreements; it would be a very brave, or perhaps a very foolhardy, nation that would disarm itself in the face of armed enemies.

Three principal objectives have driven the movement for arms control or limitation and disarmament since World War II. First is the hope of reducing tension in the international arena and thus decreasing the likelihood of war. Second is the belief that arms control or limitation can reduce the destruction that could occur should war break out despite efforts at disarmament. For example, if nuclear weapons were eliminated completely, conventional wars, although terribly destructive, could never approach the levels of total devastation envisioned should strategic nuclear war erupt. The third and very important argument is that limiting or eliminating weapons can save nations vast amounts of money. That money could be used to improve the quality of life for a nation's citizens by building better roads, schools, health care systems, and so on. The hundreds of billions

arms control The overarching concept of weapons control in terms of number, type, and deployment. It includes arms limitation, reduction, and elimination.

arms limitation The setting of a cap or limit on the number, type, and deployment of weapons systems.

disarmament A process that would remove the possibility of nuclear war by abolishing nuclear weapons altogether. Today, the term is used primarily in conjunction with nuclear weapons.

of dollars spent each year on weapons systems and armies, navies, and air forces could buy a lot of goods and services for any nation—and could reduce taxes for hundreds of millions of people as well.

The Background of Arms Control

The idea of reducing expenditures on weapons and the dangers attendant on arms races are nothing new—the Greeks, Romans, Mesopotamians, and Han dynasty Chinese all negotiated such agreements with their foes—and the dream of limiting armaments has shaped much of twentieth-century diplomacy. On the eve of the century, the first Hague Conference (1899) began the long search for effective arms control and disarmament. When the devastation of World War I showed what modern weapons technology was capable of, the search for viable arms control accelerated: the Washington Naval Conference (1921–22), the London Naval Conference (1930), and the Geneva Conferences (1932–37) were all major, although ultimately failed, attempts to prevent another major war.

However, the introduction of nuclear weapons during World War II and the accelerating tensions between the United States and the Soviet Union that culminated in the Cold War lent a new urgency to the search for ways to limit weapons and decrease the likelihood of war. Early attempts at nuclear limitation, the Baruch Plan (1946) and President Dwight Eisenhower's Atoms for Peace and

War's Leftovers

GLOBAL PERSPECTIVES

One of the little-discussed but enormously important consequences of the weapons buildup of the twentieth century, and of the wars that have punctuated the century, is the vast array of unexploded munitions that still litter the world's former battlefields. Although the wars for which these munitions originally were intended may have ended three or four generations ago, they still are creating casualties. World War I munitions continue to kill farmers in France and children in Belgium; as recently as 1987, a large cache of phosgene gas was discovered at an old ammunition dump in Britain. Luckily, its containers were still intact.

Belgium, which was the scene of much of the most intense fighting of World War I and World War II, is a small country, but its fields routinely yield vast amounts of unexploded munitions. As late as the early 1990s, more than two hundred tons of unexploded bombs and shells were being discovered each year; about 10 percent of these shells contains poison gas, often the lethal mustard gas.

Several dozen bomb-disposal workers have been killed since the end of World War II in Belgium alone. In the early 1990s Belgium began spending about four million dollars to build a special facility to dispose of the seventy-year-old chemical weapons (Dunnigan and Nofi 1990, 418). World War II mines and bombs still litter other parts of Europe as well: an estimated 2,150 tons of unexploded munitions are discovered every year in Germany, and an equal amount in German areas annexed by Poland and Russia after the war.

The land mine constitutes one of the most commonly used, and still one of the most lethal, weapons of the modern arsenal. The United Nations estimates that there are more than one hundred million unexploded land mines in sixty-two countries. The result is that "like a deadly disease long absent and assumed conquered, the land mine . . . has reemerged on a scale unimagined and with hideous, unanticipated consequences" (Boutros-Ghali 1994, 9). The result is a humanitarian disaster.

In the 1982 Anglo-Argentine War, the Argentines scattered some fifteen thousand land mines on the

Open Skies proposals (1954–57), fell victim to the tensions that dominated both superpowers' foreign policies in the early Cold War. However, with the gradual attainment of rough parity—that is, possession by each superpower of approximately the same destructive capacity as its rival—serious arms control negotiations became possible. The general shudder over "what could have been" in the aftermath of the Cuban Missile Crisis, the most serious nuclear confrontation of the Cold War, added greater urgency to the search for arms reduction, and from 1963 to 1993 there was a fairly steady succession of major treaties limiting arms.

Negotiations on arms control or disarmament since World War II have reflected four major concerns. First is the desire to limit or outlaw particularly dangerous and horrific weapons: the weapons of mass destruction, such as chemical, biological, and nuclear weapons. Second has been the desire to stabilize deterrence by restricting the development of "provocative" weapons or forces that could increase the risk of war. Among these "provocative" weapons might be first-strike weapons that could win a war, defense systems that could undermine another nation's deterrence abilities, highly offensively oriented conventional forces, and command and control systems extremely vulnerable to attack. A third major objective of negotiations and treaties has been the attempt to prevent accidental or unauthorized use of weapons by either terrorists or lunatics, and to prevent mechanical failure or accident. Finally, as we have discussed above, there has been a great desire to limit nuclear proliferation.

Falkland Islands; there have been no known human casualties, but a fairly high number of sheep have been killed (Dunnigan and Nofi 1990, 366–67). During their war in Afghanistan, the Soviets placed more than twenty million mines on the ground. Most of these were small, camouflaged mines known as "footbusters," since their purpose was largely to maim by blowing off feet and legs rather than to kill outright. Since many of these were scattered widely in airdrops, they are often difficult to locate. The mines were designed to self-destruct after a few days, but slipshod quality control means that about 10 percent of the footbusters, that is, about two million mines, are still active. Interestingly, in attempting to clear the Falkland Islands of mines, the British developed special eight-pound boots to protect mine-clearing troops from such small mines. It is unclear whether or when this protective gear will become available for the Afghani mine-clearing effort, which now depends largely on sharp-eyed, and sure-footed, individuals walking carefully through mined areas and spotting mines before they detonate them (Dunnigan and Nofi 397–98). NATO forces deployed in Bosnia are at least as concerned about unexploded mines as about snipers.

Mines, sad to say, are relatively cheap to lay down—some cost as little as three dollars apiece—and terribly expensive to clear. One State Department expert estimates that the cost of cleaning up the presently existing minefields will run to approximately $300 billion—and another five hundred thousand to one million new mines are being laid every year (Boutros-Ghali 1994; Webster 1994; Ragano 1994). Until the task of minefield clearance is completed, countries in which wars have been fought can expect to contain substantial populations of legless or one-legged persons, ranging in age from very young children to elderly men and women, all victims of the land mine plague (see further Webster 1992).

Responding to concerns about land mines, the United States Army has begun to reconsider its long-standing policy of opposition to banning the use of these weapons. Nearly a dozen nations have already banned the use of land mines, and General John Shalikashvili, Chairman of the Joint Chiefs of Staff, has said that he was "inclined to eliminate all anti-personnel land mines." There are great hopes that other nations would follow America's lead in such a ban (Bonner 1996).

Problems of Arms Control and Disarmament

Can Enemies Agree?

However great the motives for limiting or eliminating weapons might be, there are several major obstacles confronting any negotiation process. First, almost by definition, such negotiations must take place between states that are at the least rivals and at the worst outright enemies. Even beginning the process of negotiation requires a willingness to deal with each other that is nearly impossible to attain in a climate of mutual suspicion and hostility. Overcoming high levels of distrust is extraordinarily difficult, and in fact there was little willingness by the superpowers to deal with each other on any basis of equality or trust until the close call of the Cuban Missile Crisis made it clear that the peoples of both nations were in fact mutual hostages, and that the risk of continuing at the same level was becoming increasingly great. As on analyst tartly observes, "a case can be made that arms control is really possible mainly when it is unnecessary" (Morgan 1993, 53).

Verification

Verification presents another major obstacle in the process of arms control and treaties. Naturally enough, each power wants the ability to make sure that the other side is abiding by terms of the agreement, and simultaneously wants to limit the other side's access to sensitive sites of its own as much as possible. Consequently, issues of verification tend to become delicate dances, as each side presses the other for what it is reluctant to concede itself. President Ronald Reagan's frequently repeated statement, "Trust but verify," concisely summarizes the dilemma of verification.

Domestic Drawbacks

Finally, each state contains constituencies that are highly skeptical of the entire process of arms control or that have a vested interest in the continuing development of weapons and weapons systems. Arms control agreements must involve an array of people ready to distrust the motives of the other side and determined to defend what they see as the national security interest (which often coincides quite neatly with their own self-interest). As a result, several important arms control agreements have been signed but never ratified; governments have simply abided by their terms and never run the risk of presenting the delicately negotiated agreements to perceived hostile audiences. For example, both the SALT II and the START II agreements have never been ratified, but both the United States and the Soviet Union (later Russia) generally have behaved as if the treaties are binding.

The "Law of Unintended Consequences"

Historically, arms control and disarmament treaties often have seemed to prove the "law of unintended consequences." Charles H. Fairbanks, Jr., and Abram N. Shulsky (1994) point out that past international agreements sometimes have generated as many problems as they have solved. For example, they argue that participants in arms control negotiations or agreements seldom worry about what they will do if a treaty is violated. Thus, when Germany began to rearm (against the provisions of several treaties) in the mid-1930s, the French and British were essentially caught flatfooted. "Any British or French effort at enforcing German disarmament demanded an effort vaguely comparable to that of war," (363) and the desire to avoid war was the reason the treaties had been created in the first place.

In addition, Fairbanks and Shulsky argue that disarmament or arms limitation can ultimately be destabilizing in two ways. First, if armaments are kept at artificially low levels by treaties, any break from the agreement will appear all the more dangerous and destabilizing, because it will represent a very large increase from a very low base. In addition, limitations on one type of arms often channel national research and weapons development into new directions, thus actually intensifying the race for new technology and sometimes even making it easier for nations to scrap obsolete systems they might otherwise have cherished and held on to. For example, the limitations on battleships achieved in the 1920s and 1930s actually led to accelerated development of aircraft and aircraft carriers. "The [Washington Naval] Treaty undoubtedly hurried an evolution away from a weapon whose era was waning, the battleship, and toward the air power weapon of the future. But from the standpoint of arms control, this was a step backward."

Also, Fairbanks and Shulsky contend, limitations on specific weapons tend to encourage attempts to extract unforeseen advantages from the treaty or, at the extreme, to encourage cheating. "This sort of behavior creates in turn new uncertainty, which [it] is precisely one of the great aims of arms limitation agreements to avoid." Finally, they argue that once political conditions have deteriorated so much that such treaties no longer matter, necessarily rigid arms control agreements will tend to snap apart. "The cost may be heavy; after an arms limitation treaty not renewed, as after a divorce, one cannot return to the starting point" (Fairbanks and Shulsky 1994, 358–70).

Arms Agreements

Despite all the possible pitfalls, the superpowers have negotiated, often with great difficulty, an important series of arms limitations and disarmament agreements. Those treaties successfully negotiated despite these obstacles generally fall into two categories: treaties or agreements that deal with specific regions, and treaties or agreements that are applied to specific types of weapons. We will briefly examine some of the most important of each type of treaty.

Area-Specific Treaties

A regional treaty generally is designed either to completely demilitarize an area not under the control of a single nation or to create a (usually) nuclear-free zone in a particular region. Among the most important general demilitarization treaties are the Antarctic Treaty (1959), which internationalizes and demilitarizes the entire continent, and the Outer Space Treaty (1967), which does the same for space, the moon, the planets, and other celestial bodies. The Seabed Arms Control Treaty bans the placing of nuclear weapons on the seabed, although it does not limit the passage of nuclear-weapon-carrying ships or submarines through the waters above the seabed. More limited in their goals are the Treaty of Tlatelolco (1967), which bans nuclear weapons in all of Latin America, and the South Pacific Nuclear Free Zone Treaty (1985), which does the same for the entire South Pacific. The

CFE   Conventional Forces Europe (popular name for the Paris Treaty on Conventional Forces Europe): treaty that limited deployment of troops in Europe and opened the way for agreement to widespread destruction of nuclear weapons in the START talks.

Paris Treaty on Conventional Forces in Europe (1990), generally known as the **CFE,** limits deployment of troops in Europe; this treaty opened the way for widespread destruction of nuclear weapons in the START talks (discussed later in this chapter). All of these treaties are multilateral, many of them negotiated under the auspices of the United Nations.

Weapon-Specific Treaties

Chemical and Biological Weapons

The drafting and signing of treaties that deal with specific categories of weapons predates World War II; probably the most important prewar treaty is the **Geneva Protocol** (1925), which, in reaction to the carnage of World War I, banned the use of chemical weapons. This has been one of the most successful of all international treaties, with all parties respecting it (as much from fear of the consequences of using such weapons as from any scruples about breaking treaties) during World War II and most of the hundreds of wars that have raged since World War II. The Geneva Protocol, which is not a treaty, was reinforced by the Biological Weapons Convention (1972), which banned the deployment or use of biological weapons and ordered the destruction of existing biological weapons. There is strong evidence that most nations, including the United States and Russia, have continued to develop both chemical and biological weapons—several serious outbreaks of anthrax and other epidemics in Russia seem to confirm this—but the argument is made that these weapons are made primarily so that antidotes or preventatives can be developed. Saddam Hussein of Iraq has intensified his status as an international pariah by his use of chemical weapons within his own nation against Iraqi Kurds; however, he seems not to have resorted to the use of chemical weapons during the Persian Gulf War. Finally, in the aftermath of the Gulf War, some 130 nations have signed the Chemical Weapons Convention (CWC) banning the possession of any sort of chemical weapons after 2005. Figure 12.3 depicts the possession, development, and use of chemical weapons as of 1990.

Geneva Protocol, 1925 International agreement that called for the decent treatment of prisoners of war and the sick and wounded. It also banned the use of chemical weapons.

Nuclear Weapons

The attempt to put the nuclear genie back in the bottle, or at least tie it down somewhat, began with limits on the testing of nuclear weapons. Although less flashy than limits on the production of these weapons, test bans are critically important because of their role in the development of new weapons and the necessity of occasionally testing existing weapons. Consequently, the first test ban treaty, signed in 1963, represented a major breakthrough in both the process and the conceptualization of nuclear arms control. Although it concerned only atmospheric, space, and underwater testing, the Limited Test Ban Treaty (LTBT) represented the first attempt by the superpowers to cooperate with each other. This treaty also was an early attempt to try to deal with environmental issues of the nuclear age, since aboveground testing already had produced substantial radioactive fallout and fears of its consequences. It would be followed by the Threshold Test Ban (1974), which limited underground testing to devices of 150 kilotons or less.

The successful test ban agreements gave rise to far more difficult attempts to limit strategic weapons with two Strategic Arms Limitation Treaties (SALT I and SALT II). SALT I (1972) actually had two components: an agreement to limit the total number of intercontinental ballistic missiles and submarine-launched ballis-

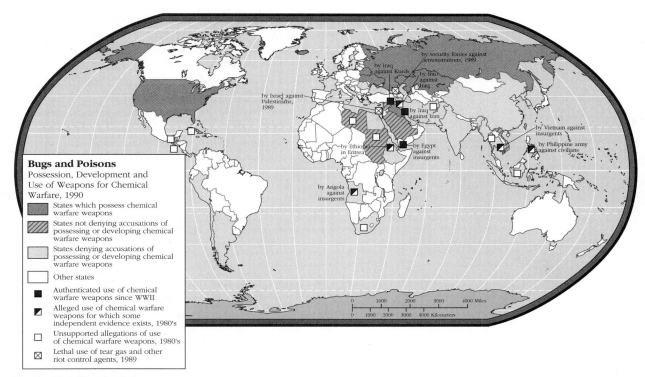

Figure 12.3 **Chemical Weapons**
The USA, USSR and Iraq are known to possess weapons for chemical warfare. Other states are suspected of having or developing them, but more is feared than known. There have been many allegations about their use but few proven cases. A single droplet of nerve gas on the skin is enough to kill.
Source: Adapted from Michael Kidren and Dan Smith, *The New State of War and Peace: An International Atlas* (New York: Simon & Schuster, 1995), 62–63.

tic missiles, and an even more important agreement to limit attempts by both superpowers to build defensive, antiballistic missile systems that might make a first attack more feasible. A major reason that President Ronald Reagan's Strategic Defense Initiative caused so much controversy was that it appeared to contravene the 1972 ABM treaty and thus to destabilize superpower nuclear relations. SALT II (1979), which was never ratified but which both superpowers generally observed, limited the number of strategic bombers and missiles each superpower had and also limited the number of warheads that any launch vehicle could carry.

An important step towards controlling nuclear weapons in general was the signing of the Intermediate Nuclear Forces Treaty (INF) in 1987; this treaty banned future development and deployment of ballistic and land-based cruise missiles with ranges of from 300 to 3,400 miles. INF also ordered destruction of all intermediate-range missiles in Soviet, U.S., and West German arsenals. So far it has led to the elimination of nearly three thousand missiles.

A second round of superpower negotiations on strategic nuclear weapons led in the mid-1980s to the Strategic Arms Reduction Talks (START), which reached fruition in the early 1990s. In the START I treaty (1991), both sides agreed to reduce their strategic nuclear delivery systems by approximately 40 percent and their total numbers of warheads by about 30 percent. When fully implemented, START I would reduce the number of Russian strategic nuclear weapons to 3,000 (down from 12,000) and the number of American strategic nuclear weapons to 3,500 (down from 10,000). After the collapse of the Soviet Union, the former Soviet states of Russia, Kazakhstan, Belarus, and Ukraine all agreed to abide by the START I terms. START II (1993) mandated even further reduction of strategic nuclear weapons, but in many ways the treaty has been overtaken by the pace of events, as both American and Russian leaders, especially President George Bush, President Mikhail Gorbachev, and President Boris Yeltsin, have seemed to compete with one another to announce unilateral (but quickly matched) arms reductions.

Strategic arms reduction entered a new dimension when Russian president Boris Yeltsin dramatically announced that he was ordering Russian missiles to be aimed *away from* the United States. President Bill Clinton responded in kind by announcing that American ICBMs would be retargeted to far-off reaches of the open seas. Although, as cynics noted, these missiles could be retargeted in less than fifteen minutes, the symbolic importance of these gestures is enormous.

The Future

Deterrence in the 1990s is far more complicated than it was at the height of the Cold War. Paradoxically, as the level of superpower contentions has ratcheted down, the level of regional power tensions has ratcheted up. Instead of two nuclear superpowers, there is now only one nuclear superpower, but a rapidly increasing number of nuclear powers. In the words of an American official, the Soviet dragon has been replaced by a bewildering variety of poisonous snakes. This multiplies the complexity of the deterrence equation, with its underlying assumptions of rationality and the motivations of the competing nations. What types of deterrence systems, if any, are applicable in this strange new world?

If the globe is to achieve some degree of stability or tranquility, greater emphasis will have to be placed on ways of controlling, reducing, or abandoning existing weapons systems. However, such a goal is achievable only by nations that desire it. Given the rampant fevered pitch of nationalism, religious reinvigoration, and resumed ethnic quarrels around the globe, as well as long-abiding regional conflicts, it is difficult to be terribly optimistic about the prospects for stabilization and tranquility below the level of the major powers.

Summary

Despite the end of the Cold War, nations around the world continue to spend huge amounts of money on weapons of all sorts, from small arms to chemical, biological, and nuclear weapons of mass destruction.

The International Arms Trade: Within the past few years there has been a decided shift in the international arms trade. Traffic in larger weapons and weapons systems has tended to diminish, but traffic in small arms has increased, as has the trade in "upgrades" intended to make existing systems more lethal. Ironically, the United

States has become far and away the world's largest supplier of arms. Further, the collapse of the Soviet Union has led to the dumping of enormous numbers of weapons onto the international marketplace by newly independent republics strapped for cash. Attempts to control the arms trade have so far proven ineffective, and the trade now seems to have expanded to include missiles.

Chemical and Biological Warfare: Although chemical weapons have not been used in a major war since 1918, and biological weapons never have had widespread use in a major war either, both are still being developed. Treaties supposedly limit their use, but research for defensive purposes is allowed under such treaties, and this work is going on even now. The Biological Weapons Convention has been ratified and put into effect; the Chemical Warfare Convention has not yet been ratified by enough nations for it to take effect. Both sorts of weapons present both frightening possibilities and terrible difficulties for the future.

Nuclear Weapons: From 1945 until 1990 the United States and the Soviet Union engaged in a massive buildup of nuclear weapons and the systems to deliver them, primarily ICBMs. Explaining and justifying the arms race were two major theories of deterrence, MAD and NUTS. While some theorists maintain that nuclear war is "survivable," others believe that even a relatively small-scale nuclear war could lead to "nuclear winter" and the virtual disappearance of life on earth. Controversy continues even today about such issues as targeting—counterforce or countervalue—the prevention of accidental nuclear wars, and the time at which missiles should be launched.

Proliferation and Arms Control: Today the problems created by the existence of nuclear weapons are multiplying, as more and more nations acquire the ability to produce these weapons. Despite the attempts of the "nuclear club" to stop proliferation, the technology is spreading, as is missile technology. This is particularly dangerous at flashpoints such as the Indo-Pakistani region and the Middle East. To stop such proliferation, treaties such as the Nuclear Nonproliferation Treaty have been drafted. In addition, arms control negotiations have produced a series of treaties limiting nuclear weapons and even leading to the destruction of existing weapons. There are also treaties banning chemical and biological weapons. The extent to which such treaties are enforceable, or will be observed by the signatories, is still an open question—and many of the nations most likely to use such weapons, such as Saddam Hussein's Iraq, have not signed the treaties. While the threat of global nuclear war seems to have receded, the spectre of limited nuclear war or even nuclear terrorism seems to loom even larger.

Key Terms

Conventional weapons	Chemical weapons
International arms trade	Biological weapons
Technology push	Manhattan District Project
Military technological revolution (MTR)	Deterrence
Tension pull	Star Wars

Republic of insects	Arms control
"Nuclear winter"	Arms limitation
Countervalue targeting	Disarmament
Counterforce targeting	Paris Treaty on Conventional Forces in
Nuclear proliferation	Europe (CFE)
"Loose nukes"	Geneva Protocol

Thought Questions

1. What forces drive the arms trade? What has accounted for the dramatic shrinking of the arms trade in recent years?
2. Define and explain the differences between conventional weapons and weapons of mass destruction. Give examples of each. Define and explain the differences between conventional weapons and small arms. Give examples of each.
3. Which do you consider the greater danger for the future, nuclear weapons or chemical and biological weapons? Why?
4. What are the major obstacles to the negotiation of arms limitations or arms control agreements? How have the few successes been achieved?

References

Achen, Christopher H., and Duncan Snidal. "Rational Deterrence: Theory and Comparative Case Studies." *World Politics* (January 1989).

Aftergood, Stephen. "The Soft-Kill Fallacy." *Bulletin of Atomic Scientists* (September/October 1994).

Anthony, Ian, Pieter D. Wezeman, and Siemon T. Wezeman. "The Trade in Major Conventional Weapons." *SIPRI Yearbook 1995.* Internet.http://www.sipri.se/pubs/yb95ch14.html, downloaded 5/18/96.

Barry, John. "The Battle over Warfare: Will the GOP Stall the Military's High-Tech Revolution?" *Newsweek,* February 13, 1995.

Bartlett, John. *Familiar Quotations.* Boston: Little, Brown, 1955.

Bogert, Carroll. "Selling Off Big Red." *Newsweek,* March 1, 1993.

Bonner, Raymond. "Pentagon Reconsiders Stand Against Ban on Land Mines." *New York Times,* March 17, 1996. Internet Download March 17 1996. Http://www.nytimes.com/3/17/96/intl/mines.html.

Boutros-Ghali, Boutros. "The Land Mine Crisis: A Humanitarian Disaster." *Foreign Affairs* (September/October 1994) 8–13.

Bundy, McGeorge. *Danger and Survival: Choices about the Bomb in the First Fifty Years.* New York: Vintage, 1990.

Burrows, William E., and Robert Windrem. *Critical Mass: The Dangerous Race for Superweapons in a Fragmenting World.* New York: Simon and Schuster, 1994.

Chaliand, Gerard, and Jean-Pierre Rageau. *Strategic Atlas: A Comparative Geopolitics of the World's Powers.* New York: Harper Collins, 1992.

Church, George J. "Proliferation: Soviet Nukes on the Loose." *Time,* December 16, 1991.

Clark, Jeffrey J. "Chemical and Biological Warfare." *Grolier's Online Encyclopedia.* Prodigy, 1995.

Crossette, Barbara. "A Global Ban on Chemical Weapons Is Set for Spring." *New York Times,* November 3, 1996.

Davis, "Defence Technology: The Software Revolution." *The Economist.* June 10, 1995. Special Survey Insert.

Downs, George W. "Arms Race." In *Oxford Companion to Politics of the World.* New York: Oxford, 1993.

————. "The Rational Deterrence Debate." *World Politics* (January 1989).

Dunnigan, James F. *How To Make War.* New York: William Morrow, 1993.

Dunnigan, James F., and Albert A. Nofi. *Dirty Little Secrets: Military Information You're Not Supposed to Know.* New York: William Morrow, 1990.

Fairbanks, Charles H., Jr., and Abram N. Shulsky. "Arms Control: The Historical Experience." in Richard K. Betts. *Conflict after the Cold War: Arguments on Causes of War and Peace.* New York: Macmillan, 1994.

George, Alexander L., and Richard Smoke. "Deterrence and Foreign Policy." *World Politics* (January 1989).

Gerth, Jeff. "U.S. Buys Russian Arms in Furtive, Frantic Market." *New York Times,* December 26, 1994.

Goodby, James E., Shannon Kile, and Harald Muller. "Nuclear Arms Control." *SIPRI Yearbook 1995.* Stockholm: Stockholm International Peace Research Institute, 1995.

Hanley, Charles J. "Seventy Nations Make Public Their Global Arms Deals." *Houston Chronicle,* July 30, 1993.

Hersh, Seymour M. *The Samson Option: Israel's Nuclear Arsenal and American Foreign Policy.* New York: Vintage, 1993.

Hoagland, Jim. "Ukraine Moving to Nuclear Showdown." *Houston Chronicle,* May 29, 1993.

Jervis, Robert. "Rational Deterrence: Theory and Evidence." *World Politics* (January 1989).

Kidron, Michael, and Dan Smith. *The New State of War and Peace: An International Atlas.* New York: Simon and Schuster, 1991.

Kidron, Michael, and Ronald Segal. *The New State of the World Atlas.* New York: Simon and Schuster, 1991.

————*The State of the World Atlas.* New York: Penguin, 1995.

"Kinder, Gentler Pentagon Turns to Nonlethal Weapons." *Newsweek,* February 17, 1994, 36.

Klare, Michael. "Adding Fuel to the Fire: The Conventional Arms Trade in the 1990s." In Michael Klare and Daniel C. Thomas, eds. *World Security: Challenges for a New Century.* New York: St. Martin's Press, 1994.

————"Awash in Armaments: Implications of the Trade in Light Weapons." *Harvard International Review* (Winter 1994/1995).

Lebow, Richard, and Janice Gross Stein. "Rational Deterrence Theory: I Think, Therefore I Deter." *World Politics* (January 1989).

Lemonick, Michael. "What About the Nukes?" *Time,* September 9, 1991.

Maoz, Ze'ev. "Power Capabilities, and Paradoxical Conflict Outcomes." *World Politics* (January 1989).

McNamara, Robert S. "The Military Role of Nuclear Weapons: Perceptions and Misperceptions." In Charles W. Kegley, Jr., and Eugene R. Wittkopf. *The Nuclear Reader: Strategy, Weapons, and War.* New York: St. Martin's Press, 1989.

Mearshimer, John. "Why We Will Soon Miss the Cold War," in Richard K. Betts, ed. *Conflict After the Cold War: Arguments on Causes of War and Peace.* New York: MacMillan Publishing Company, 1994.

Morgan, Patrick M. "Arms Control." In *Oxford Companion to International Politics.* New York: Oxford, 1993.

Morgenthau, Tom. "The Future of the Bomb." *Newsweek,* October 7, 1991.

Mycio, Mary, and Sonni Efron. "Ukraine Signs Treaty to Surrender Nuclear Arms." *Houston Chronicle,* November 17, 1994.

NATO. "Chronology of Key Arms Control Treaties and Agreements (1963–1994). Basic Fact Sheet No. 7. NATO Office of Information, April 1994. Internet.http://www.nato.int/docu/facts/home.html. Downloaded Feb. 24, 1996.

Nelan, Bruce W. "Fighting Off Doomsday." *Time,* June 21, 1993.

Pierre, Andrew, and Sahr Conway-Lanz. "Desperate Measures: Arms Producers in a Buyer's Market." *Harvard International Review* (Winter 1994/1995).

Ragano, Frank P. "Operation Desert Sweep Ousts Battlefield Waste." *National Defense* (March 1994).

Robbins, Carla Anne. "The Nuclear Epidemic." *U.S. News & World Report,* March 16, 1992.

Rosenberg, Barbara Hatch. "'Non-lethal' Weapons May Violate Treaties." *Bulletin of Atomic Scientists* (September/October 1994).

Rosenfield, Stephen E. "U.S. Arms Sales Are Good for Business but Thousands Are Killed as a Result." *Houston Chronicle,* March 1, 1995.

Russett, Bruce. "Deterrence." In *Oxford Companion to International Politics.* New York: Oxford, 1993.

Sagan, Carl. "Nuclear War and Climatic Catastrophe." In Charles W. Kegley, Jr., and Eugene Wittkopf. *The Nuclear Reader: Strategy, Weapons, and War.* New York: St. Martin's Press, 1989.

Scheer, Robert. *With Enough Shovels: Reagan, Bush and Nuclear War.* New York: Vintage, 1983.

Schell, Jonathan. *The Fate of the Earth.* New York: Alfred A. Knopf, 1982.

Segal, Gerald. *The World Affairs Companion.* New York: Simon and Schuster, 1991.

"Seized Material is Enriched Uranium." *Houston Chronicle,* December 21, 1994.

Shukman, David. *Tomorrow's War: the Threat of High-Technology Weapons.* New York: Harcourt Brace, 1996.

Skons, Elisabeth, and Ksenia Gonchar. "Arms Production." *SIPRI Yearbook 1995.* Stockholm: Stockholm International Peace Research Institute, 1995.

"The Software Revolution." *The Economist,* June 10, 1995.

Smith, R. Jeffrey. "Arms sales bring words of warning: security of U.S. may be at stake." *Houston Chronicle,* June 25, 1996.

"Soon, 'Phasers on Stun'." *Newsweek,* February 7, 1994. 24

Spear, Joanna. "Beyond the Cold War: Changes in the International Arms Trade." *Harvard International Review* (Winter 1994/1995).

Stock, Thomas. "Chemical and Biological Warfare." *SIPRI Yearbook 1995.* Internet.http://www.sipri.se/pubs/yb95in.html. Downloaded June 20, 1995.

Stock, Thomas, Erhard Geissler, and Tim Trevan. "Chemical and Biological Arms Control." *SIPRI Yearbook 1995.* Stockholm: Stockholm International Peace Research Institute, 1995. Internet. www.sipri.se/pubs/yb95in.html. Downloaded Feb. 20, 1996.

Stockholm International Peace Research Institute (SIPRI). "CWC Convention." Internet. Gopher://gopher.sipri.se:70/00/Project%20oh%the%20Effective%20. Downloaded Feb. 2, 1996.

Thompson, Mark. "Sapphire's Hot Glow: A Clandestine Operation Funnels Nuclear Material Out of Central Asia for Safekeeping in Tennessee." *Time,* December 5, 1994.

———. "Going Up in Arms: To Buttress Industry at Home and Policy Abroad, The U.S. Becomes the Arms Merchant to the World." *Time,* December 12, 1994.

"U.N. Permanently Renews N-Treaty." *Houston Chronicle,* May 12, 1995.

Waller, Douglas. "Onward Cybersoldiers." *Time,* August 21, 1995.

Waltz, Kenneth N. "The Spread of Nuclear Weapons: More May Be Better." In Richard K. Betts, ed., *Conflict After the Cold War: Arguments on Causes of War and Peace.* New York: Macmillan, 1994.

Webster, Donovan. "One Leg, One Life at a Time." *New York Times Sunday Magazine,* January 23, 1994.

———"The soldiers moved on. The war moved on. The bombs stayed.'" *Smithsonian,* June 1992, 26–36.

Whitney, Craig R. "Who Will Buy? Plutonium for Sale. Call 1-800-TERROR." *New York Times,* Sept. 21, 1994.

Part Five

New Problems,
New Players

Chapter 13

The Web of Global Communications

Introduction

Astudent in Nebraska sits down at her computer, logs onto the Internet, and accesses databases in Switzerland and Australia. A businessman in New York City picks up his telephone to talk to a client in Singapore. A grandmother in Scotland smiles at the tape-recorded sounds of baby talk from Bangkok. Chinese students in Boston fax copies of news stories to friends demonstrating at Tiananmen Square in Beijing. And politicians, diplomats, generals, and citizens around the world tune in to CNN to see cruise missiles streaking through Iraqi skies, tanks rumbling toward the Russian parliament building, or the smoldering remains of Kobe. The vice president of the United States touts the arrival of an "information superhighway," and the speaker of the house suggests that the poor be provided with laptop computers and modems.

As never before in human history, the world is linked together in a series of complex communications networks that provide often instantaneous transmission of information at all levels. From events as globally vital as those shaking Iraq or Russia to those as intensely personal as a grandchild's first words, people around the world have enormous amounts of information literally at their fingertips.

This is the Information Revolution, one of the chief agents of global transformation and integration. It has changed not only what people know or understand, and how quickly, but also how people, businesses, and governments conduct their affairs. In this chapter we examine the Information Revolution itself and then look at how it has affected all levels of human society around the globe. Among the major issues we will consider are the uses of this vast communications network, the enormous disparity in the extent and impact of the communications revolution on various societies, the degree to which the communications revolution has eroded traditional ideas of sovereignty, the consequences of this erosion, and the ways governments, businesses, and individuals use international communications.

Many of the dislocations currently playing havoc with the international economy rise from this information revolution, as nations struggle to enter the information age and then to cope with its consequences. Experts say that world knowledge doubles every eighteen months to five years, depending on the field (Frederick 1993, 8). In other words, by the time you complete a four-year degree, there will be nearly twice as much information available as there was when you began work on that degree! At the beginning of this century, over half of the workers in the United States toiled in the agricultural economy. By 1950, nearly half of the American workforce could be found in the industrial economy, involved in manufacturing steel and automobiles and consumer goods. Today, 50 percent of the American workforce is employed in areas directly related to information and communications (Schement, Belay, and Jeong 1993, 425).

This information and communications revolution inevitably has had a major impact on the way the world works at many different levels. For example, American popular entertainment has saturated a worldwide market. And American communications networks like CNN have brought world events into our living rooms with breathtaking immediacy. What are the implications of this?

Every day parts of the world face the real danger of information overload. About six hundred million newspapers are printed daily. Eighty thousand broadcasting stations transmit information and programs to one billion viewers and two billion listeners. More than a hundred news agencies produce forty million words of news stories in hundreds of languages. Seven hundred million telephones transmit voices, data, and pictures through hundreds of thousands of miles of cable and over a hundred communications satellites (Frederick 1993, 10). Such mind-boggling statistics begin to give us an idea of the scope of the information revolution and the potential for communications, that is, the transmission of information, to alter world events.

Today we tend to take such communications miracles for common. We can pick up the telephone to talk to people all over the world, send fax transmissions to Singapore or Australia, watch the beginning of the Persian Gulf War *live* in our own homes, or connect via computer to databases in Europe and Asia. And the communications revolution, only a few hundred years old, is still accelerating at an incredible pace.

The Communications Revolution

The Printed Word

Pinning down the exact beginning of the communications and information revolution is maddeningly difficult. In many ways it began more than five hundred years ago when Johannes Gutenberg perfected movable type and the printing press. Printed books could be reproduced in large numbers, contained vast amounts of information, and were portable, easily carried across borders or even oceans. Books still constitute one of the most important links in the modern communications network; nearly a million titles appear every year, in literally hundreds of millions of copies (Frederick 1993, 65). The thousands upon thousands of magazines that appear globally swell the number of printed words to staggering levels.

Telegraphy

As the Industrial Revolution progressed, the communications revolution also began to accelerate. In the early 1830s a homesick American artist studying in Europe, Samuel F. B. Morse, began to wonder how to use the newly evolving technology of electricity to speed international communications; within a decade he had perfected the telegraph. By the 1860s, thousands of miles of telegraph wire stretched across the eastern United States and across much of Europe as well. As early as 1851, British technicians laid the world's first underwater telegraph cable under the English Channel, and in 1858 an American, Cyrus Field, laid down the first transatlantic cable. Although that cable link lasted only a few weeks before snapping, the late 1860s saw the transatlantic cable repaired. By the end of the century, cables circled the globe. In 1903 American president Theodore Roosevelt, "dee-lighted" as usual by the new technology, demonstrated just how far the communications revolution had progressed by sending a message around the world in just nine minutes (Hawley and Heil 1990; Frederick 1993, 34–35; Fortner 1993, 80).

Telephones

In 1876 the American inventor Alexander Graham Bell introduced the first telephone, capable of transmitting not just coded messages but actual voices by wire. At first it was used almost exclusively for business, but this changed rapidly: by

1885 Europeans had more than one thousand switching centers and had made 92 million local calls and five million long-distance calls. Not surprisingly, the nation with the largest industrial economy, the United States, dominated telephone communications; by the turn of the century, Americans owned two-thirds of the world's telephones and made two-thirds of the world's phone calls. Nonetheless, the first transatlantic telephone cable was not laid until 1956; until then, telephone calls were sent across the ocean by high-frequency radio transmission. However, by the mid-1980s more than 150 thousand transoceanic voice circuits carried hundreds of millions of conversations; the advent of fiber-optic technology is expected to increase the number of available voice circuits to as many as two million by the start of the twenty-first century. The telephone is today the world's most frequently used means of global communication; by the year 2000, the average number of telephone calls made per hour is expected to reach 300 million (Fortner 1993, 17, 49, 83–84; Frederick 1993, 35–36; Wriston 1992, 44).

Radio

Both the telephone and the telegraph suffered one major limitation: they required thousands and thousands of miles of cable and wire in order to work. At the end of the nineteenth century an Italian inventor freed communications from wire and set the stage for modern global and even spaceborne communications. In the 1890s, Guglielmo Marconi recognized that the recently discovered electromagnetic waves could be used for wireless communications; by 1894 he was sending Morse code radio signals over distances of up to three kilometers, and by 1899 he had succeeded in sending radio signals between ships at sea and across the English Channel. In December 1901, Marconi transmitted the first transatlantic message, from Cornwall, England, to St. John's, Newfoundland, Canada. In 1906 a Canadian physicist, Ronald Fessenden, used radio waves for the first time to broadcast sound, both music and the human voice (Frederick 1993, 37; Fortner 1993, 84).

Technological innovation enabled radio to develop quickly in several applications: seaborne and other emergency communications, commercial broadcasting, government-controlled broadcasting, and amateur radio. As early as 1917 President Woodrow Wilson used this new means of communication to broadcast his momentous Fourteen Points address, outlining to Europe the American agenda for a postwar world. However, so few people had radio receivers that most Europeans learned of Wilson's ideas through the newspapers. The first commercial radio broadcasting station, KDKA in Pittsburgh, Pennsylvania, went on the air in 1920, and the first commercial radio network, NBC, emerged in 1927. Today there are nearly thirty-eight thousand radio transmitting stations worldwide—two-thirds of these in the industrialized nations—along with nearly two billion radio receivers. The distribution of these receivers is extremely important, since radio is probably the cheapest and most democratic of all contemporary media. Receiving information by radio requires no literacy, only access to relatively cheap transistorized technology (Frederick 1993, 67–68).

Radio also provides one of the most widely used personal technologies, with some 2.5 million amateur radio operators worldwide transmitting on a broad range of frequencies. These amateur radio operators not only engage in direct international communication but also serve vital roles in times of political turmoil and natural disaster. For example, during the August 1991 attempted coup in Russia, an amateur broadcasting station was established in the Russian "White House" and used to ensure that even if land lines were cut, communications with the outside world would be possible. Often amateur operators served as the primary source of information for the horrors that were happening in isolated Bosnian towns.

Television

Like radio, television is in many ways a democratic medium, since literacy is not required—but unlike radios, television receivers are expensive and thus limited in availability, particularly in nonindustrialized states. Although the cathode ray tube appeared in 1897, television became a dominant broadcast medium only after World War II. Its growth and impact have been enormous. Americans, for example, had one million television receivers in 1949, ten million in 1951, and more than a hundred million by 1975. Large-scale use of color television receivers in the United States began in 1964.

While the worldwide impact of radio largely depends on the direct reception of broadcast signals, the worldwide impact of television rises in part from the fact that televised shows can be filmed or taped and then sent to other stations around the world for rebroadcast. The proliferation of videocassette recorders (VCRs) and videocassettes also has had enormous consequences.

Satellites

The next step in developing communication was made in the form of the communications satellite, essentially an orbiting repeater that receives and retransmits signals. Appropriately enough, a science fiction writer, Arthur Clarke, first envisioned the possibility of satellite communications. In the October 1945 issue of *Wireless World,* Clarke set out the idea that a satellite orbiting at 22,300 miles above the earth would be geosynchronous; that is, its orbit would match exactly that of the earth, so that it would appear to be stationary above a particular point along the equator. Such satellites, Clarke said, would provide unbelievable communications possibilities.

In the late 1950s the United States began to experiment with communications satellites, progressing rapidly from the army's single-voice-channel Score, launched in December 1958, to Telstar and Relay, each with the capacity of one television channel or several hundred voice channels, in 1962. The first geosynchronous satellite, SYNCOM 2, was launched in 1963.

In February 1963, the Communications Satellite Corporation (COMSAT) was incorporated to establish a commercial communications satellite system in conjunction with other nations. Twelve nations joined to establish INTELSAT (the International Telecommunications Satellite Consortium) in mid-1964. "Early Bird" (INTELSAT I), launched in April 1965, provided 240 telephone channels across the North Atlantic. Today, INTELSAT has over 110 member nations, and 170 nations use INTELSAT satellites. From "Early Bird," with its 240 voice circuits, INTELSAT has advanced satellite technology to the point that its present satellites can carry as many as one hundred thousand voice channels or multiple television channels. Figure 13.1 shows how it would be possible, at least theoretically, to provide communications to virtually the entire globe by using only three satellites in equatorial orbit at 22,000 miles.

Given Cold War tensions, we should not be surprised to note that the Soviet Union established its own satellite system, Intersputnik, in 1968, to provide satel-

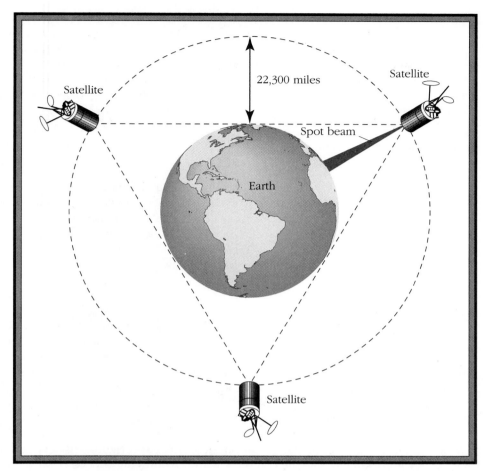

Figure 13.1
Footprint of Global Satellites
Hypothetically, three communication satellites positioned at equidistant points on a circle above the earth's equator, 35,000 kilometers in space, would be able to relay signals to the entire globe.
Source: Frederick 1993, 123.

lite links to its own territory, the Eastern European client states, and Cuba. In 1985 a consortium of Arab League nations launched two Arabsat communications satellites to provide Arab-language programs throughout the Middle East. Many nations also have their own domestic satellite systems, like the United States' COMSAT or Indonesia's Papelsat.

One hundred and eighty-four communications satellites presently orbit the earth. INTELSAT accounts for 26 of these satellites, while the United States and Russia have 54 and 45 geosynchronous satellites respectively (Fortner 1993, 169–70; Frederick 1993, 71–72, 91–93).

Computers

Perhaps the most important part of the communications and information revolution, the computer revolution took place in two phases: the development of the mainframe, and the arrival of the personal computer. Both have transformed communications in ways inconceivable at the very beginning of the computer age, during World War II.

Speed in making calculations has been a goal of research for several thousand years. For more than two thousand years Chinese and other Asian people have used the abacus to do rapid calculations. The mechanical calculator appeared in the West as early as 1642, when mathematician-philosopher Blaise Pascal built a digital calculating machine to help his father, a tax collector—but this machine basically stayed in the family, never widely used. One hundred and fifty years later an English mathematician and professor, Charles Babbage, took the first steps toward modern computing with his designs for a "difference engine" (1812) and an "analytical engine" (the 1830s). Still, the emergence of the computer did not occur until the eve of World War II.

Mainframes

In 1939 a group of American engineers and scientists produced the first electro-magnetic computer, Mark I. Dependent on punched-paper-tape instructions, Mark I required a full three to five seconds to complete a single multiplication—but it was automatic, and could complete long calculations without human intervention. The war provided the impetus for further computer development: the military desperately needed elaborate tables for artillery and torpedo trajectories, for example, and later for bomb trajectories as well. New weapons systems, coming on line rapidly, demanded rapid calculations of huge numbers. To provide them, engineers and mathematicians at the University of Pennsylvania built the first high-speed electronic computer, ENIAC (Electrical Numerical Integrator and Calculator). A thousand times faster than Mark I, ENIAC used 18,000 vacuum tubes, occupied 1,800 square feet of floor space, consumed 180,000 watts of electrical power, and produced enormous amounts of heat that had to be bled off. Moreover, ENIAC was not programmable, but had to be literally rewired, by hand, for every different problem it was set to do, and its vacuum tubes burned out with alarming frequency. Nonetheless, this first electronic digital computer was used for nearly a decade, from 1946 to 1955.

The next major step in computer development was theoretical. By 1947 a Hungarian-born American mathematical physicist, John Von Neumann, devised a way to store programs so that the computer could perform high-speed operations without human intervention. Computers using this architecture were both much smaller than ENIAC—about the size of a grand piano—and far more reliable, because they used only 2,500 small electron tubes. By the early 1950s the advent of the transistor, replacing vacuum tubes, and of magnetic-core memory ushered in the modern mainframe computer, increasingly smaller and faster.

The PC Revolution

The most important development in computers since the introduction of the transistor was the appearance of the personal computer, small enough to fit on a desk, and inexpensive enough for an average American college student to acquire. The first small personal computers, sold as kits, appeared in late 1974, but their appeal was largely confined to the relative few who could both assemble and program them. The first off-the-shelf personal computers appeared in 1977, when two legends in the computer world, Steven Jobs and Steve Wozniak, began building these small, comparatively cheap machines—in a garage. Other companies quickly began selling the small computers, and in 1982 IBM endorsed the PC revolution by marketing its first PC.

Since the mid-1970s the price of personal computers has fallen dramatically, while their capacity has increased even more dramatically. Computer enthusiasts claim that if automobiles had evolved the same way computers did, a Rolls-Royce would cost three dollars, get two hundred miles to the gallon, and reach speeds of four hundred miles an hour! There are now millions of personal computers in use in business offices, academic environments, and private homes worldwide.

The Internet

Computer communications have developed almost as rapidly as computers themselves. A business now can link together an internal computer network that allows a division in one state to send data or information instantaneously to a division in another state or even another nation. Linking together computers, or forming networks, has multiplied enormously both the communications possibilities and the problems of the new information society.

Origins and Growth.   One of the most interesting examples of a computer network, and a vivid illustration of how the communications revolution is continuing to grow, is the global network known as the **Internet.** The Internet traces its origin to the experimental network, ARPAnet, designed in the early 1970s by the U.S. Defense Department to support military research. One of the purposes of ARPAnet was to develop computer networks that could function in the event of bomb attacks and other military catastrophes. Consequently, the ARPAnet scientists developed a simple way for computers to send messages to one another over a large network. Because of this Cold War design, a writer on technology observes, "You couldn't destroy [the Internet] if you tried" (Krol 1995, 11–12; Elmer-DeWitt 1993, 62).

> **internet** Global computer network that constitutes one part of the information superhighway.

For almost a decade, access to this growing network was confined to researchers in computer science, government employees, and government contractors. Then, in the late 1980s, the National Science Foundation, looking for ways to link together its five newly created supercomputer centers, created a series of regional university networks and then linked these networks to each other and to the supercomputer centers. The Internet went public. The NSF promoted universal education access by funding campus connections for any campuses that had plans to become access centers themselves.

The Internet created by the NSF has expanded exponentially. In 1981 approximately two hundred computers were linked together on the proto-Internet; by 1991 that number had grown to three hundred thousand, and in just four years, by 1995 some *3.2 million* computers were linked to the Internet. This number does not include many military computers designed to remain "invisible" and is increasing at an astonishing rate ("Getting Wired to the Internet" 1995). Today virtually all American universities and most four-year colleges are connected to the Internet, and gradually secondary and primary schools are gaining access as well (Krol 1995, 12–13). Estimates are that worldwide, nearly twenty million people have access to the Internet (some authorities say the number may be as high as fifty million), and that number is growing every day. The Internet today links together approximately thirty thousand individual networks originally created by government agencies, researchers, and universities ("A Business Interest in Internet" 1993; Edwards 1995). The Internet presently is growing at an estimated rate of 15 percent per month, and now is thought to provide access to more than 1.5 million bulletin boards and databases. By the end of this decade, at least according to the most optimistic estimates, more than two hundred million people will be connected to the Internet.

The Internet Today.   The Internet reaches directly into more than ninety nations, including most of the western European countries; some of the eastern

European nations (including Poland, Russia, and Yugoslavia); several Asian nations (Japan, Korea, Singapore); parts of Latin and South America (Mexico and Brazil); a handful of Arab and African nations (Tunisia, South Africa); and India. Even in China, which is still in many ways an extremely closed society, more and more individuals are gaining access to electronic mail (e-mail). Most of these nations also are tied into other international networks, like BITNET, a primarily educational service; some nations, like Saudi Arabia, Turkey, and Russia, have BITNET but not Internet connections (Krol 1995, 350–52; "When Words Are the Best Weapon" 1995). The spread of the Internet into eastern Europe, Africa, Latin and South America, and much of Asia has been slowed by the lack of reliable telephone lines capable of the accurate transmission of digital data. While the rapid growth of fiber-optic networks in the developed world will increase connectivity and thus digital communications, the technical difficulties and huge economic costs of fiber-optic networks will probably impede the spread of the Internet into the partially industrialized and nonindustrialized worlds.

Although much of the cost of connecting to the Internet is borne by government funding, the network recently has seen more and more commercial use; private services intended to provide Internet connections for individuals also have sprung up. One recent researcher estimates that nearly 60 percent of the Internet's traffic is commercial rather than private or research-connected ("A Business Interest in Internet" 1993, 46). One market research analyst estimates that as the Internet's exponential growth continues, consumer markets on the Net could exceed $200 billion by the year 2000. In the United States, commercial services provide Internet connectivity at rates that range from three dollars an hour to a flat thirty dollars a month (Silverman 1993). Institutions participating in the Internet can spend as little as one thousand dollars per month for access for an unlimited number of users (Kantrowitz 1993, 43).

The range and amount of information available via the Internet is overwhelming. Using the Internet, an individual may access thousands of databases, scan library holdings globally, send messages anywhere in the world that the Internet connects to, and glean information from the Network News sections, an almost infinite series of electronic bulletin boards dealing with computer science, hobbies and recreational activities, science, social issues, and countless other topics. A recent check of the News section of the Internet listed more than thirteen thousand newsgroups (Krol 1995, 127–29). Although English is the primary language of the Internet, there are also technical, recreational, and social discussions in both German and Japanese (Krol 1995, 131). In addition, some news groups publish scientific articles electronically months before they will be available in printed journals, and also serve as forums for discussing the merits of research and discovery claims. For example, in 1989 the Internet served as a major means of communication about claims that cold fusion had been achieved, and in 1993 it played a major role in spreading the information, and confirmation, that a Princeton mathematician had proved Fermat's Last Theorem, a proof that other mathematicians had been in search of for almost three hundred years (Kantrowitz et al., 46). And when the Ebola virus erupted in Zaire in the spring of 1995, there was an Ebola page on the Net within a week, complete with medical papers, interviews with specialists in virology and in Ebola, and wire service news articles.

To this point, the Internet is a loosely governed organization many of whose participants pride themselves on the individualism and occasional near-anarchy of the Net. No single individual is in charge of the Internet. Instead, the ultimate authority for what happens on the Internet rests with a voluntary membership organization called the Internet Society, or ISOC. The ISOC in turn appoints a group of "invited volunteers" to serve on the Internet Architectural Board, which essentially deals with the approval of new standards for communication and allocation of network resources. Operational and short-term technical problems are handled by another volunteer organization, the Internet Engineering Task Force (Krol 1995, 14). Clearly, the successful operation of the Internet depends primarily on the willingness of the individuals and networks involved to work together cooperatively and with goodwill.

What the Future Holds.   Change in the Internet is inevitable. Like virtually all other modern communications technology, it is both expanding and evolving. One set of potential changes already has been alluded to: the growing commercialization and even privatization of the network. As more and more individuals acquire access to the Internet, new questions about funding will arise, especially since so much of the present Internet connectivity is largely or partially funded by governments (Krol 1995, 16–17). The NSF already has begun phasing out its funding of the Internet.

The other impending major change in the Internet and potentially all other computer network systems is the arrival of the **information superhighway,** more formally known in the United States as the National Information Infrastructure: a combined computer-television-telephone net that will allow access to the Internet, show first-run movies on home televisions, connect to a library, or tap into a video archive for reruns of *Mr. Ed* or *Masterpiece Theatre.* In theory, this information superhighway could provide interactive games, long-distance telephone service, direct access to United Press or to a stockbroker, and online shopping as well. In the United States alone, such an information superhighway could prove an economic bonanza. Former Apple Computers chairman John Scully estimates that worldwide revenues from such an interconnected global "infobahn" could reach $3.5 trillion with the next ten years—more than half of the entire U.S. gross national product. (Elmer-DeWitt 1993, 50–52). Several major American telecommunications companies already have begun planning the information superhighway. Pacific Bell has announced that it will spend $16 billion to build a data superhighway in California, and US West has invested $2.5 billion in Time Warner's cable and entertainment division ("Pacific Bell Plans Data Superhighway" 1993). Although the Clinton administration has seemed enthusiastic in its support of the information superhighway, enormous technical, legal, and political work remains before it can be realized.

> **information superhighway** The National Information Infrastructure, a combined computer-television-telephone net that will allow access to the Internet, viewing of movies, connections to libraries, and other services.

The Communications Gap

Almost as important as the very existence of the communications revolution is its uneven distribution: there is an enormous communications gap between the industrialized and the nonindustrialized nations, with serious implications for the future.

As tables 13.1 and 13.2 show, there is an enormous discrepancy in communications and information density, that is, the access to communications and information enjoyed by citizens of the two worlds. In every category of communications, residents of the industrialized world have roughly a ten-to-one advantage over residents of the nonindustrialized world. In the most sophisticated communications, the advantage is far greater. For example, the industrialized

Table 13.1

The Communication Gap Comparative Distribution of Key Means of Communication, Developed v. Developing Worlds

Category	Developed World	Developing World
Newspapers printed daily (per thousand people)	337	43
Book titles published annually (per million people)	507	57
Radio receivers (per thousand people)	1006	173
Television sets (per thousand people)	485	44
Radio transmitters (% of global total)	70%	30%
Television transmitters (% of global total)	84%	16%

Caption: Note that there is generally a 10:0 ratio in favor of the industrialized world. Only in radio transmitters does the gap narrow, and even there the ratio is more than 2:1.
Source: Based on data in Howard W. Frederick, *Global Communication and International Relations.* Belmont, Calif.: Wadsworth Publishing Company. 1993. pp. 64–79.

world, with approximately 25 percent of the globe's population, has more than 95 percent of its computers. In satellite communications, the disparities are even greater. The United States and Russia, with a combined 15 percent of the world's population, use 50 percent of the available geosynchronous orbit, while all non-industrial nations combined use less than 10 percent (Fortner 1993, 169–70; Fred-

Table 13.2

The Communications Gap: Selective Comparative Distribution of Means of Communication by Nation or Region

Category	Developed World	Developing World
Radio receivers (per thousand people)	North America 2000	Non-Arab Africa 142
Television sets (per thousand people)	North America 790	Non-Arab Africa 14
Personal computers (percentage of global total)	90%	Non-Arab Africa 0.5%
Personal Computers (per thousand people)	United States 384	Bolivia .00000153
Post Offices (ratio of post offices to people)	United States 1:5768	Burundi 1:266,088
Telephone lines (per thousand people)	United States 850	Non-Arab Africa 0.1

Caption: The disparities between the developed and developing worlds become even more vivid when one examines specific regions or nations.
Source: Based on data in Howard W. Frederick, *Global Communications and International Relations.* Belmont, Calif.: Wadsworth Publishing Company, 1993. pp. 64–79.

erick 1993, 71–72, 91–93). Even within the industrialized world, there are large disparities; for example, within Russia there is approximately one personal computer for every forty-eight workers, while in Germany there is one PC for every two workers. And the wretched quality of the Russian telephone system has made it virtually impossible for Russians to become part of the Internet or any other global net. On the average, only one out of every ten international telephone calls attempted in Russia is completed ("Even in Computing, It's Soviet Disunion" 1993, 46; "Russia's Nyet-Works" 1993, 90).

Literacy differentials and economic conditions accentuate and worsen these gaps in access to communications. For example, while the industrial nations all claim literacy rates of 90 percent or more, these rates fall rapidly outside the industrial world. Among the nonindustrialized areas, Latin America has the highest literacy rate, roughly 75 percent, while Asia has a literacy rate of 60 percent and Africa one of only 40 percent (Frederick 1993, 65). Given the rapid population increases in these areas and the enormous difficulty of allocating scarce national resources to provide education for rapidly increasing numbers of children, literacy rates can be expected to suffer in the next generation. Although the absolute numbers may increase, the relative numbers will continue to fall, and an ever-increasing percentage of the world's poorest people will be condemned to continuing poverty because of lack of access to information (see fig. 13.2). Economics also plays an important role in limiting individuals' access to communications and information. In the United States, for example, a full year's subscription to a newspaper will cost less than one day's wages for the average teacher; in India, Thailand, and the Phillippines, that same annual subscription will cost from eleven to twenty days' wages for a teacher (Frederick, pp. 64–65).

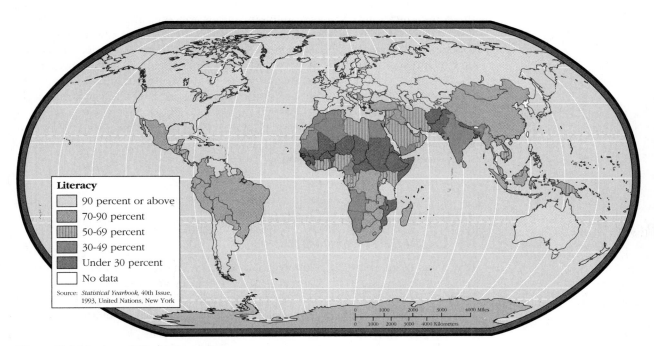

Figure 13.2 **Literacy of World Population**

The skewed distribution of literacy rates heightens the importance of radio and television communications; as we mentioned earlier, radio particularly is "democratic," in that it is relatively cheap technology and requires no literacy. Television of course does not require literacy, but the cost of a television set is hundreds of times higher than that of a radio set. Here again, however, the numbers starkly show the problems facing the nonindustrialized world in any attempt to enter the communications and information revolution, which it must do in order to have any hope of significant industrialization.

While table 13.2 shows the overall disparity in the distribution of radio sets, it does not tell the entire story. In the United States, for example, there are 2000 radio sets for every thousand people: two sets per person. In Haiti, there are only 40 radios per thousand people; in Burkina Faso (formerly Upper Volta), one of Africa's poorest countries, only 25 per thousand—and there are ten other countries with fewer than 50 radios per thousand people. The United States has 785 televisions per thousand people, while non-Arab Africa has only 14 TV sets per thousand people. Thirty-six nations have fewer than 10 sets per thousand people, and thirteen have fewer than 3 sets per thousand people. In a similar fashion, the industrialized nations, especially the United States, produce a wildly disproportionate share of global programming. Two-thirds of all television programs come from the United States! The United States imports almost none of its television programming (roughly 2 percent), while Latin America, Europe, and Africa import as much as 67 to 83 percent of the total broadcast content. Eighty-four percent of the world's television transmitters are in the industrialized nations, and 70 percent of the world's radio transmitters (Frederick 1993, 65–69).

The issues raised by this skewed communications distribution are profound, with serious implications for future international relations. For one thing, it seems virtually impossible that most of the nonindustrial nations will be able to overcome the communications gap. And in a world in which information is increasingly the single most valuable commodity, that bodes ill for the future. Additionally, the communications gap has resulted in serious concerns about cultural imperialism (which we will discuss later in this chapter). Perhaps the one bright spot in this situation is that urbanization in the nonindustrial world is accelerating yearly, with as much as two-thirds of the world's population expected to be crowded into urban centers within the next twenty years or so. While the implications of this urbanization for quality of life are disturbing, there remains the optimistic possibility that urbanized populations will almost by default have greater access to communications and thus to information than rural populations. But whether this greater access will lead to progress or to bitter resentment, anger, and political unrest is an unanswered question.

International Regulation of Communications

Few areas of international relations have presented more opportunity, or in some ways more necessity, for international cooperation and the development of a body of international law than communications. The electromagnetic spectrum has had to be carefully parceled out, regulations governing international mail, telephone, and telegraph messages have had to be developed, and the use of satellites and computer networks in particular now is requiring international cooperation. There is certainly much yet to be done—protection of intellectual material, for example, remains a major issue—but a great deal already has been accomplished.

The ITU

While the Internet is largely self-governing, the other telecommunications media whose development we have traced have come under some form of cooperative international regulation almost from their inception. The first to do so was the telegraph industry, in which international communications created a series of problems involving common equipment, signals, and codes. In 1865 a number of nations met in Paris to discuss these problems. The result was the Telegraph Convention, which created the International Telegraph Union to deal with these issues. The ITU developed technical interconnection standards so that the various national telegraph services could link together, and established international Morse code as the standard medium for transmission of messages. It also set up mechanisms for overseeing tariffs, sharing revenue for telegrams crossing international borders, using encryption, and assuring privacy (Fortner 1993, 13).

The development of radio created new kinds of problems, primarily issues of frequency allocation: how to prevent massive airwave traffic jams with multiple stations transmitting on the same frequencies. In 1903 nine nations met in Berlin to head off chaos on the air. They began what is a continuing process of agreeing which radio frequencies should be allocated for which purposes (marine radio, ship-to-ship, private and business, amateur radio, satellite, and broadcasting uses). From this meeting emerged an informal working group that became known as the International Radiotelegraphic Union, which organized subsequent conferences. In 1906 a second Berlin conference agreed that SOS should be the international distress signal. In 1912, in the aftermath of the *Titanic* disaster, the world's major nations signed an agreement that all ships have radio equipment in working order and at least one trained radio operator aboard. The first "modern" international conference, in 1927, saw more nations represented than had been at the great Versailles conference at the end of World War I. In 1932 the merger of the International Radiotelegraphic Union and the Telegraph Union created the most important modern international communications organization, the International Telecommunications Union (Hawley and Heil 1992; Fortner 1993, 11).

After World War II, and the enormous growth in technological development fostered by the war, the ITU became part of the United Nations, as a specialized agency under the General Secretariat. Today's ITU plays multiple roles: oversight of international legal agreements; promotion of the responsible use of telecommunications services; technical assistance to developing countries; coordination of space communications; registry of radio frequency assignments; encouragement of the lowest possible tariffs and rates; assisting in saving human lives through telecommunications services; and general administration, such as developing regulations and recommendations and collecting and publishing information on telecommunications issues (Hawley and Heil 1992; Frederick 1993, 102).

However, new technologies pose major problems of international regulation. An example of this is the attempt to regulate trans-border data flow (TBDF), the international movement of computer-readable material. Although many governments want to protect individual privacy or their own interests by regulating the flow of information, there has been little success in negotiating any TBDF regulation. Businesses tend to view such regulation as a competitive burden, and the technical problems of encryption and decryption are enormous. Further, the idea of regulating TBDF also raises serious issues of freedom of speech; in most Western democracies, strong traditions of freedom of speech and press have set off alarms at the idea of government "tollbooths" along the information highway (Wriston 1992, 150–52).

UNESCO

In addition to the ITU, twenty-four other United Nations agencies are concerned either directly or indirectly with international communications issues. Of these, the most visible and the most controversial is the United Nations Educational, Scientific, and Cultural Organization (UNESCO). UNESCO's basic purpose is to promote peace by increasing understanding among nations through the promotion of education and research; its preamble says, "Since war begins in the minds of men, it is in the minds of men that the defences of peace must be constructed." A major element of UNESCO's mandate is the promotion of the communications capacities of nations and the free and balanced flow of information (Frederick 1993, 100–101).

Perhaps the most controversial expression of UNESCO's involvement in international communications was the publication of *Many Voices, One World* (1980). In 1976 the biennial UNESCO conference at Geneva created the International Commission for the Study of Communications Problems under the chairmanship of Sean MacBride; consequently, the commission's report is generally known as the MacBride report. Although many of its recommendations seemed unremarkable—the report called for freedom of the press and for the elimination of obstacles to a free flow of information, both internally and internationally—some of its statements seemed inflammatory and dangerous to Western nations.

The report called for the creation of a New World Information and Communication Order, modeled after the New International Economic Order demanded by developing nations in the UN General Assembly (see chap. 4 and chap. 8). The MacBride report also called for greater involvement by national governments in news-gathering and news dissemination, and for greater responsibility on the part of journalists. Many industrialized nations interpreted this as opening the way for government-controlled media and, if not censorship, at least retaliation against journalists whose reporting contradicted official government views. UNESCO's calls for a balanced flow of information and the right of reply for those who felt unfairly treated by the media caused grave concern in the industrial democracies, which viewed these ideas as part of a larger attack on democratic culture and institutions by Third-World demagogues.

Ultimately, under the conservative Reagan administration, the United States withdrew from UNESCO in 1984; Great Britain followed suit in 1985. The controversy over the MacBride report and UNESCO continues today with no particular resolution—and no implementation of the MacBride report's recommendations in sight (Frederick 1993, 166–79).

Business and International Communications

The communications revolution has transformed international business as it has transformed virtually every other aspect of modern life. Entire new industries have sprung up to manufacture the new technologies and explore even newer frontiers of technology. Existing businesses have expanded and have faced cutthroat competition from both new and established companies. In many ways the new communications technologies have enabled us to enter a world without borders, with around-the-clock around-the-world news available to increasing numbers of nations and peoples.

In this section we will examine closely two major ways in which business has been affected by, and has been bringing about, the communications revolution. First we will look at the impact of global communications on the conduct of business worldwide, the so-called "borderless economy." Then we will look at the way various business enterprises are shaping the communications revolution through broadcasting, news agencies, and other means of developing and disseminating information.

The Global Economy

As Paul Kennedy points out in his book *Preparing for the Twenty-First Century,* the communications revolution already has created a borderless economy, especially in matters of finance and currency trading, and is rapidly heading that way in terms of production and marketing of goods as well. Already, thanks to global communications, trading in stock and currency goes on twenty-four hours a day. As the Asian exchanges are shutting down, their day done, the European exchanges are just beginning to operate; by the time the European exchanges are nearly finished with their day, the American exchanges are gearing up. Daily foreign exchange flows, says Kennedy, amount to one trillion dollars a day, far beyond the amounts either employed to purchase goods and services or invested. By the late 1980s, Kennedy states, more than 90 percent of the around-the-clock trading in the world's foreign exchanges was completely unrelated to trade or to capital investment (Kennedy 1993, 47–64).

Twenty-four-hour electronic global trading networks gradually are becoming a reality. In 1992 Globex, a twenty-four-hour electronic trading system created by the Chicago Mercantile Exchange, the Chicago Board of Trade, and Reuters Plc, went into operation. And the New York Mercantile Exchange launched Access, a proprietary after-hours system, in the summer of 1993. Within the next decade such proprietary systems may well evolve into a single global system linked to individual national systems, like that in Chile, to create a twenty-four-hour network. The electronic market unquestionably will spread and develop. As Leo Malemed, the driving force behind Globex and a champion of electronic trading, points out, "You can't ignore the technological advances occurring around us" ("The Future of Electronic Trading" 1993, 64–65). We have explored other aspects of the computer-driven international business network in chapters 5, 8, and 9.

The communications revolution also has changed radically the way businesses actually do business. Students of the information revolution like Peter Drucker and Walter B. Wriston argue that in our modern society information has become the primary capital of the industrial economy, and that it is the addition of knowledge to all phases of work that accounts for profit. Also, the communications aspect of the information revolution largely has decentralized information and thus perhaps power within the corporate or government structure. Further, with the links provided by modern communications, businesses are far more able to spread out globally because they can remain linked together via fax, modem, telephone, and satellite (Drucker 1994; Wriston 1992).

Broadcasting

Inevitably, the broadcasting and entertainment industry has provided some of the most dramatic examples of both the possibilities and the problems of the information revolution. As people around the globe tune into or are plugged into popular communications and popular culture, a "global culture market" is beginning to emerge. With the proliferation of VCRs, tape recorders, and international satellites, the same culture is available over much of the globe. "Tens of millions of Chinese and Indians, Frenchmen and Malays, are watching 'Dallas' and the 'Honeymooners,' which in their way may be more subversive to sovereign authority than CNN" (Wriston 1992, 46). According to at least one expert, "this market, of billions of plugged in 'culture traders,' is now the most powerful social and political force in the world" (Wriston 1992, 47). By watching the same programs and seeing the same desirable goods, people worldwide are in effect "voting" for free markets, consumerism, and modernism. Former Indian prime minister Indira Gandhi supposedly said that a revolution could be started in the Third World when a peasant watching a TV sitcom saw a modern refrigerator! (Wriston 1992, 45–46) This globalization of culture also raises serious issues about what is called "cultural imperialism," the fear that a global culture (largely American) will sweep away traditional cultures and traditional values; we will discuss this more fully below.

The internationalization of the communications industry is clear in the recent development of multinational communications networks. For example, in late summer 1993 an Australian-based corporation, the News Corporation, owned by Rupert Murdoch, spent $525 million to acquire a two-thirds interest in Satellite Television Asia Region (STAR), which uses a geosynchronous satellite to transmit television programming to virtually all of Asia. Murdoch already controls a vast international communications net, including the Fox network in the United States, and will use STAR to retransmit programs that Fox has created (like *The Simpsons*), or that are stored in the enormous film and television library Fox controls (like *M*A*S*H* and *Home Alone*). At present STAR has a limited market—an estimated seventeen million viewers by the end of this year—but the potential market is the world's largest, some three billion people. STAR already transmits Western television programming—BBC programs, MTV, and *Lifestyles of the Rich and Famous*—to Asia, and the Murdoch library will enormously enlarge its programming capacity. Other international communications companies, such as Time Warner, Turner Broadcasting, and Capital Cities/ABC, also are reported to be exploring the possibility of entering the potentially huge Asian market (McCarroll 1993, 53).

The commercial broadcasting network with the largest impact worldwide is Turner Broadcasting, whose CNN (Cable News Network) was seen in 132 countries as of the summer of 1992. Founded in 1980 as the world's first twenty-four-hour news network, CNN has become the United States' largest television news-gathering organization. Today it employs some 1,900 people in the United States and at nineteen news bureaus worldwide; in addition, some 150 broadcasters in 120 countries provide other news programming for CNN. CNN began to become an international medium in 1985 when it created CNN International (CNNI) to broadcast to Europe. In 1988 it expanded CNNI coverage to include Africa, the Middle East, and South and Southeast Asia; in 1991 CNNI replaced CNN in Asia and Latin America. Interestingly, CNN used a Soviet satellite for its first African, Middle Eastern, and Asian transmissions. In August 1989, CNN reached the Soviet

CNN, whose newsroom is shown in the photograph to the left, has clearly had an impact on the conduct of international relations and global politics. However, a major debate still rages on the nature and extent of that impact.

Union itself for the first time, when a single Soviet hotel began to receive CNN transmissions. There is also a Spanish-language CNN offshoot, Noticiero Telemundo-CNN, which reaches nineteen Central and South American nations as well as thirty-eight United States cities (CNN Press Kit 1992).

News-Gathering and Dissemination

Another major commercial aspect of international communications consists of the multiple news-gathering and news-distributing agencies that exist worldwide. More than one hundred news agencies exist worldwide. Not surprisingly, the five largest news agencies are all from the industrialized democracies: Associated Press and United Press International of the United States, Reuters of Great Britain, Agence France Presse of France, and TASS of Russia. These agencies perform prodigious feats of news-gathering and transmission. For example, AP transmits two million words daily to fifteen thousand separate outlets, using 1.3 million kilometers of leased wire, cable, and telephone lines, as well as radio and satellite transmission (Frederick 1993, 108).

In addition to these global giants, regional news agencies are becoming increasingly important in international communication and the dissemination of information. For example, there are three major Latin American news agencies operating almost exclusively in Spanish, and an English-language Caribbean news agency. In 1975, the Non-Aligned News Agencies Pool was established under the auspices of UNESCO. Today its chief organ, the Telegrafska Agencija Nova Jugoslavia (TANJUG), with fifty participating news agencies, collects and disseminates news from more than ninety (mostly government-run) news agencies. With ten distribution centers in Asia, Africa, Europe, and Latin America, TANJUG transmits about one hundred thousand words daily (Frederick 1993, 108–9).

Newspapers and broadcasters often subscribe to several of these agencies as well as maintaining their own reportorial corps. The Kyodo agency of Japan, for example, receives six hundred thousand words a day of foreign coverage from its own correspondents as well as from UPI, AP, and Reuters (Frederick 1993, 126).

Governments and International Communications

Governments both rely upon and manipulate international communications for a wide variety of purposes: to communicate with one another, to communicate with their overseas emissaries, and to present their points of view (either the truth or propaganda) to the world at large or to specific groups. In this section we will examine each of the ways governments use and depend upon the growing global communications network, including "Rolodex diplomacy" and public diplomacy.

"Rolodex Diplomacy"

One of the potentially most significant changes in the way nations relate to one another is the arrival of "Rolodex diplomacy," the ability of national leaders simply to pick up a telephone and talk directly to other national leaders around the world. President George Bush was particularly known for his love of the telephone. While such interaction among world leaders may well be beneficial if friendship and knowledge of one another is a critical factor in the conduct of diplomacy—an assumption that remains very much open to debate—there are two serious problems raised by such methods of conducting foreign policy. First, there is a great difference between what a president might say in the midst of a freewheeling telephone conversation and what diplomats might craft in months or even years of meticulous work. As we have discussed in chapter 9, particularly where highly technical subjects such as weapons control are concerned, presidential freelancing is not necessarily a good idea. Second, the increasing reliance on the telephone leaves no written record, thus creating present potential conflict about what actually has been said or promised, and also depriving future historians of ways of understanding what happened—or what went wrong.

Because of the communications revolution, the rules of diplomacy are still being written, but in this as in many other areas, it is clear that technology is altering politics (Wriston 1992, 174).

Government Broadcasting

Radio broadcasting was in some ways international almost from its very beginning; for example, Reginald Fessenden's 1906 transmission from Massachusetts was heard even in the West Indies. In March 1914, Belgium began to broadcast "grand concerts" to Europe in general, but World War I stopped this early attempt at international broadcasting (Fortner 1993, 91).

The decade after World War I saw the rapid maturation of radio technology and the decision by many governments to use this new medium. The Soviet Union had made radio appeals to workers in Western Europe and the United States as early as 1919, but the first continuous international radio service was established by Holland in 1927. By the mid-1930s Germany, Britain, France, Luxembourg, and Japan had joined the ranks of governments sponsoring international radio broadcasts. The Vatican, seat of the Roman Catholic Church, established its own international broadcasting service, Radio Vatican, in 1932. In addition, the American commercial networks, NBC and CBS, both experimented with international short-wave broadcasting throughout the 1930s (Fortner 1993, 104–5).

Propaganda

One of the major functions to which governments quickly devoted their international communications ability was propaganda, that is, the use of these communications channels to present their points of view, often highly biased ones, of current events. The revolutionary government of the Soviet Union established Radio Moscow in 1929 and almost immediately began broadcasting propaganda calling for revolution in several languages (Fortner 1993, 129). In the 1920s and 1930s, Benito Mussolini in Italy and Adolf Hitler in Germany became masters of propaganda. As one historian notes, "Both of these dictators were able to turn radio to their own political advantage, disseminating ideologies, creating and sustaining myths, castigating scapegoats, and building personality cults, all to mass audiences enamored with this new means of communication" (Fortner 1993, 123). Mussolini and Hitler quickly discovered that they could use mass communications not only to control their own populations, but also to spread their ideas beyond

Joseph Goebbels, Hitler's chief of propaganda, demonstrated the effectiveness of using media to conduct propaganda campaigns.

their borders, addressing other peoples in their own languages. By the mid-1930s, international communications had shifted from a problem to be solved to a danger to be contained (Fortner 1993, 123–24).

World War II

The British reaction to German and Italian propaganda broadcasts showed another way that governments could use radio: to present the objective truth. In 1937 Parliament authorized the British Broadcasting Corporation to begin foreign-language broadcasting, in part to counteract Nazi and fascist propaganda; the BBC inaugurated this foreign-language service in January 1938. From the beginning of its foreign-language broadcasts, the BBC decided that it would not use the "big lie" technique that had proved so successful for its adversaries, but instead would broadcast the "unvarnished truth" (at least as perceived by Britain) as the best antidote to propaganda. In short order the BBC became generally trusted and respected throughout the world for its commitment to truth—although, as several writers have pointed out, the truth itself often could be a form of propaganda (Fortner 1993, 130–36).

Although the Axis-British rivalry dominated the propaganda conflict during World War II, the United States and the Soviet Union also began to emerge as major players during this period. While most American broadcasting continued to be commercial, in 1942 the government forged a network of privately owned shortwave broadcast stations into the Voice of America. Later that same year the government created the Office of War Information (OWI), which became the most important part of the U.S. propaganda effort during World War II. However, OWI continued to rely on privately owned stations to transmit its messages. Like the BBC, both VOA and OWI tended to operate on the understanding that "truth is the only effective basis for American foreign information," and to attempt to transmit objective news broadcasts—many of which, of course, had the impact of propaganda in nations, like Italy and Germany, which long had been denied access to relatively truthful information (Fortner 1993, 136–39).

The Cold War

As the Cold War followed on the heels of World War II, both the U.S. and the USSR continued and even escalated their propaganda campaigns. In 1948 the U.S. Congress created a permanent international information agency and provided permanent funding for VOA. In August 1953 the United States Information Agency was created to coordinate U.S. information activities overseas. VOA is the "official" voice of the United States, although in fact its programming never has been beamed within the United States. According to its charter, VOA was established to serve as a source of reliable information, to represent all sectors of American society, and to present the policies of the United States clearly and effectively (Fortner 1993, 161–62).

The United States went beyond VOA to establish other radio services with a clear propaganda purpose: Radio Free Europe and Radio Liberty. These two services used native speakers to broadcast into Soviet-controlled areas like the Baltic states and Eastern and Central Europe, as well as the Soviet Union itself. Ostensibly private, these services were in fact primarily funded by the Central Intelligence Agency as part of its psychological warfare operations against the Soviet bloc. Much later, Radio Marti was beamed at Cuba with the same purpose.

The danger of such propaganda broadcasting, often directed at "rolling back" or at least destabilizing communism in Central and Eastern Europe, was vividly demonstrated in 1956, when RFE broadcasts may well have contributed to the doomed Hungarian uprising against the Soviet Union. Students of international propaganda have concluded that although RFE did not directly urge Hungarians to take to the streets—a futile and widely fatal gesture against the tanks the Soviet Union deployed to stop the uprising—RFE broadcasts before and during the uprising were often inflammatory and even conflagrational (Fortner 1993, 162–63).

The Soviet Union also sponsored a substantial number of international broadcasting networks, including Radio Moscow, Radio Peace and Progress, and Radio Kiev; these concentrated on providing propaganda to the nonaligned nations as well as to nations within the Soviet bloc. Both the United States and the Soviet Union encouraged and often underwrote broadcasts by services in their allied or client states as well (Fortner 1993, 164–65).

In addition to countering American and American-sponsored broadcasts with their own internal broadcasting, the Soviet Union and China (another major target of American efforts) interfered with such broadcasts by what is known as "jamming," that is, broadcasting either other programming or just plain "noise" on the same frequencies as the offensive broadcasts to prevent their reception. By 1962, for example, the Soviet Union had more than two thousand transmitters used exclusively for jamming, and its Soviet-bloc states in Eastern and Central Europe contributed another one thousand jamming transmitters. Trying to gauge the effectiveness of jamming, an international monitoring program estimated that in June 1986 between 95 percent and 100 percent of VOA, RFE, RL, and other international services into the Soviet Union were jammed. In 1989, the People's Republic of China engaged in extensive jamming of BBC and VOA broadcasts to prevent students from judging how their Tiananmen protests were being received in other Chinese cities from which those services broadcast. Even today, Cuba routinely jams both Radio Marti and Television Marti. All of this jamming takes and has taken place despite the fact that jamming is at least technically illegal under international law (Fortner 1993, 165–66).

After the Cold War

With the end of the Cold War, the role of both RFE and VOA began to change radically. Both were downsized, RFE dropped broadcasts in a number of languages, and the Clinton administration began to work on merging the two agencies, despite their very different functions. And there even have been negotiations about privatizing RFE archives and research operations (Binder 1993; Whitney 1994; "Radio Free Europe Will Drop Seven Languages" 1993). In the spring of 1995, RFE began relocating all its facilities from Munich to Prague, once a target of its broadcasts, in a cost-cutting maneuver.

Public Diplomacy

A major use of international communications since the end of World War II has been what is known as "public diplomacy": the attempt to influence the policy of other nations by direct appeals to their citizens through public communications. Leaders of nations often have tried to bypass traditional diplomatic channels in order to create more favorable opinions of themselves, of their nations' policies, and of their nation itself. Among the vehicles of public diplomacy are books and

Low Tech and the Ayatollah

GLOBAL PERSPECTIVES

One of the least understood aspects of the communications revolution is that communications technology does not have to be particularly complex in order to make a difference. We in the United States tend to be enthralled by the latest "bells and whistles," and to assume that the more sophisticated the technology is, the greater its impact will be. This is not necessarily so.

In 1964 the Ayatollah Ruhollah Khomeini was expelled from Iran because of the virulence of his preaching against the reign and attempted modernizations of Shah Mohammad Reza Pahlavi. Gradually the Shah grew uneasy at the Ayatollah's proximity to Iran, and in 1978 the Ayatalloh was expelled from Iraq, but with the Shah's consent, allowed to move to Paris.

The Shah assumed that once he was far from Iran, the Ayatollah's power would diminish. However, simple modern communications technology made the Ayatollah a threat to the Shah no matter where he was. In Paris, the Ayatollah simply made tape recordings of his anti-Shah sermons, and the tape recordings were distributed by his followers throughout Iran. No elaborate technology was needed, and the small tape recorders necessary to hear the Ayatollah were both cheap and widely available. Thus the Ayatollah was able to conquer distance with a cheap and simple technology and remain in direct and impassioned communication with his followers.

Furthermore, by being in a modern communications center like Paris, the Ayatollah gained access to the modern information networks and soon was gaining worldwide credibility and prominence in the international press. Young Western-educated aides to the Ayatollah orchestrated a brilliant propaganda campaign pitched to educated elites at the same time that the Ayatollah was repeating his strident message to the Iranian people.

No bells, no whistles, no complex technology. Just a telephone line from Paris to Tehran, cheap tape recorders, and easily reproduced tape cassettes. And the result? A revolution that has made Iran one of the most dangerous states in the contemporary world. And a valuable lesson in how to employ modern communications technology (Shawcross 1988, 117; see also Armstrong, 1991).

---

magazines, student exchange programs, tours by cultural or entertainment groups, and propaganda.

Two other means of conducting public diplomacy have been especially important during the information and communications revolution. One is the use of international radio and television broadcasting. The other is the staging of "pseudo-events" such as summit meetings, press conferences, and other sorts of international meetings—less to decide any particular issue (at many of these events the "final statements" are drafted before the date is set) than to present a global forum for various leaders to explain their policies and attempt to charm foreign audiences (Fortner 1993, 279–80).

Summitry

Although there have long been meetings between international leaders, the modern summit conference emerged during the 1950s when American president Dwight David Eisenhower and Soviet premier Nikita Khrushchev carried out a series of public meetings. In theory, such meetings were designed to give the leaders a chance to assess each other and to work out mutual problems; in fact, they quickly became highly ritualized affairs in which relatively little work happened. Certainly, anyone who saw Khrushchev stalking through Iowa cornfields, pounding his shoe on the podium at the United Nations, or touring Disneyland had a different opinion of the Soviet leader than before. Perhaps the last summit conference that had any kind of real impact was the Vienna meeting between Khrushchev and another American president, John F. Kennedy, in the summer of 1961. Khrushchev apparently emerged from that summit with a perception that Kennedy was weak and that the United States consequently could be pushed around. The result was a series of Cold War confrontations, first over Berlin and then over Cuba, that came perilously close to pushing the two nuclear superpowers into a global war.

Since that time, with one exception, made by Mikhail Gorbachev, that we will discuss shortly, summit meetings have become highly ritualized affairs with virtually all details settled in advance. The host country provides a media center with all available technology and other forms of aid to enable reporters from around the world to file their stories. The leaders are photographed posing together, usually smiling and in animated conversation. There is a final press conference (recently, almost always a joint press conference) at which the leaders explain their points of view and defend their policies.

The December 1987 summit in Washington, D.C. between American president Ronald Reagan and Soviet president Mikhail Gorbachev drew nearly two thousand journalists to Washington, in addition to the thousands who work there daily. In the two weeks bracketing the summit, major international broadcasters (including VOA, Radio Moscow, and the BBC) published more than 250 news stories on the summit and devoted more than seven hundred minutes (of an available total of seventeen hundred minutes) of news time to the summit. It was an all-out media blitz (Fortner 1993, 280). The Soviet Union dispatched its own spokespeople (Vladimir Pozner, for example) to the United States well ahead of the summit in order to try to shape American public opinion.

Yet the December 1987 summit, although it is a classical illustration of public diplomacy, also vividly illustrates the limits of public diplomacy. Most Americans, if questioned about what they remember of that particular summit, would probably be completely unable to remember any details of what the two leaders said, or even what the major issues discussed were. Yet large numbers of Americans probably could recount their astonishment at Mikhail Gorbachev's apparently spontaneous decision to order his motorcade to stop as it sped along Washington's main streets so that he could get out of his limousine and walk among large crowds of Americans, shaking their hands and smiling at them. Gorbachev's "walkabout" represented a major public relations coup and was public diplomacy at its finest.

Individuals and International Communications

It is extraordinarily difficult to assess how this information and communications revolution affects individuals. Clearly, there are two separate ways in which the individual relates to international communications: as an active participant in the flow of communications, and as a passive recipient of the enormous amounts of information generated by international communications.

Active Participation

We tend to take for granted that individuals will be participants in the global communications flow, but this is not necessarily true. For example, one of the most common forms of international communications, letter-writing, assumes literacy on the part of both the sender and the receiver. However, low literacy rates in many areas of the world bar as much as two-thirds of the population in many of the poorer, nonindustrialized nations from participation in so basic a form of communication.

Passive Reception

Skewed access also characterizes even the passive reception of the global flow of communications. Literacy rates are far from the only restriction on access. Consequently, while people in the developed countries of Europe, North America, and Japan have virtual media saturation, even the most developed nonindustrial nations are relatively media-poor. In most cases, in the developing world, media access is confined largely if not entirely to urban areas. The communications and information revolution have had wildly uneven impacts on individuals.

The Debate over the Impact of Media on International Relations

One of the most controversial areas of discussion and research on communications is what kind of effect the communications revolution is having and will have on the conduct of international relations in general, and on war in particular. Two very different points of view have emerged: first, the view that communications and media have a major impact on international relations, and second, the opposing view that the effect of media upon international relations is relatively limited. In the next few years we can expect to see a great deal more research, and, we suspect, controversy on this critical topic.

The CNN Effect

On the one side is the "CNN effect" on the setting of the U.S. agenda. According to the American ambassador to the United Nations, Madeleine Albright, "aggression and atrocities are beamed into our living rooms with astonishing immediacy. No civilized human being can learn of these horrid acts occurring on a daily basis and stand aloof from them" (quoted in Vita 1993). Proponents of the CNN effect believe, for example, that television coverage of dying children played a major role in President George Bush's decision to send U.S. troops to Somalia to help alleviate the famine there, and also played a significant role in pushing the United States toward intervention in Bosnia (Vita 1993). As one observer of the media impact points out, "We live in a world where Yasir Arafat works with a media consultant; where Mohammed Abbas, who hijacked the *Achille Lauro* and murdered an old man in cold blood, appears on American network television even [while] . . . a fugitive from justice . . .; where the Iranians stage marches for the cameras; and where Soviet [spokespersons] appear regularly on American TV" (Wriston 1992, 144). Wriston concludes that "the international agendas of nations are increasingly being set not by some grand government plan but by the media" (Wriston, 144).

Deeply respected international leaders worry publicly about the CNN effect. United Nations Secretary-General Boutros Boutros-Ghali pointed out recently that "when one crisis is in the spotlight, other equally serious situations are left in the dark." He noted that more people died in a single day in the Angolan capital of Luanda during Angola's civil war than died in months in Sarajevo, Bosnia's capital, but that virtually no one paid any attention to the former situation because television did not broadcast the Angolan suffering. Roughly the same number of people—an appalling five hundred thousand—died of starvation in Sudan as in Somalia, yet Somalia received television coverage, and international aid, while Sudan has been virtually ignored. "Why is the UN deeply involved in one crisis and not in another?" Boutros-Ghali asked. "One of the reasons is media attention. The interaction of television coverage and political interest is powerful and hard to predict" (quoted in Vita 1993).

Senior American statesman George Kennan wrote in a letter to the *New York Times,* "No one would deny . . . that without the preceding television coverage of the situation in Somalia, the support for the [dispatch of American troops] in Congress and the public would not have been what it was." Having acknowledged the CNN effect, Kennan went on to deplore it. "Fleeting, disjointed, visual glimpses of reality, flickering on and off the screen, here today and gone tomorrow, are not the 'information' on which sound judgments on complicated international problems are to be formed." After all, Kennan continues, television is a superficial medium unable to "consult the rich voice of prior experience . . . outline probable consequences, or define alternatives, or express the nuances of the arguments pro and con" (Kennan 1993).

War and the Media

Most of those who agree that the CNN effect exists also believe that the media will have an inhibiting effect on the conduct of future wars. In a thoughtful and important book, *The Living Room War,* Michael Arlen speculated on the role daily coverage of tragedy in Vietnam played in inspiring public criticism of American participation in that war and even wondered whether future large-scale wars would be possible when people realized the horrors caused by it (Arlen 1969). Television coverage of the Vietnam War shaped public opinion in other ways as well. For example, when highly respected CBS anchorman and commentator Walter Cronkite came out against continued American participation in the war in 1968, President Lyndon Johnson fretted, "If I've lost Walter Cronkite, I've lost the American middle-class" (Karnow 1983). A final example of the impact that television coverage could have on public opinion was the 1968 Tet offensive launched by the Viet Cong throughout South Vietnam; although militarily the offensive was a disaster from which the Viet Cong never fully recovered, it was perceived as a U.S. defeat by the American people when they saw televised pictures of Viet Cong fighters inside the United States embassy in Saigon. This perception played a significant role in eroding public support for the Vietnam War (Oberdorfer 1971). "Knowing in a general way that war produces violent death is one thing," Walter Wriston concludes, "but watching the carnage of a battle or the body bags being unloaded at Dover Air Force Base on your living room television set is quite another" (Wriston 1992, 13).

Conservative supporters of the Vietnam War as well as liberal critics agree that television changed American participation. Highly respected conservative columnist George Will, for example, writes "had there been television at Antietam on America's bloodiest day," when twenty thousand soldiers died in a monumental Civil War battle, Americans "might have preferred disunion to the price of union, had they seen the price, in color in their homes in the evening" (quoted in Cumings 1992, 84). Richard Nixon once observed of the Vietnam War coverage that "more than ever before, television showed the terrible human suffering and sacrifice of war. . . . The result was a serious demoralization of the home front, raising the question whether America would ever again be able to fight an enemy abroad with unity and strength of purpose at home" (quoted in Cumings, 84).

Recently, however, some dissenting voices have been raised. An October 1994 study by Douglas V. Johnson II cautions that not enough serious studies have been done to warrant the conclusion that the media have a great impact upon international relations. Johnson points out that while the TV effect can be overwhelming, it is usually transient. Thus, despite the near-saturation coverage of the Tiananmen democracy demonstrations in China in June 1989, and the general outrage at the brutality with which the Chinese government suppressed the demonstrations, neither the Bush administration then in power nor its successor Clinton administration actually brought any substantive sanctions against the Chinese government (Johnson, 1994 15 [pagination as downloaded from Army War College bulletin board, January 28, 1995]). Johnson cites Colonel Harry Summers, author of a classic study on Vietnam, and CBS anchor Dan Rather, in their (unaccustomed) agreement that while television may report the news, it does not and cannot create or drive public opinion (Johnson, 20). Additionally, Johnson points out that a strong and focused administration can drive public opinion, or, if necessary, ignore it while carrying out predetermined policy: "A working hypothesis might be that a mature administration can manage even the worst news about national security issues because the people naturally give the lead to the president in such matters" (Johnson, 15).

Johnson cites a number of other factors that, in his view, tend to reduce the impact of media, even television with its graphic and vivid images, on public policy and national security affairs. For example, he maintains that a "fatigue factor" sets in after events have dominated media coverage for an extended period of time. "At some point, any news story grows stale. . . . The networks are profit driven to keep the public attention, and a dip in ratings will result in an automatic shift of news to more dramatic events regardless of the apparent importance of the first event" (Johnson 1994, 25). Furthermore, "the media street is two way." A "savvy president" can use the media in order to shape public opinion and gain support for policies probably more effectively than others can manipulate media to shape policy (Johnson, 16).

Johnson concludes finally that while much more research is needed, several things seem fairly certain. The media impact on policy-making is complex. In part it is dependent on the popularity and skill of the current administration, since a president traditionally has been granted broad leeway in national security issues and in international relations in general. Although media images are often vivid and can attract the attention of the American people "if there is a clear humanitarian theme or a clear and present threat to U.S. national security," such images are only a small part of an enormously complex process of shaping policy and often have only transient effect. In national security matters especially, Johnson writes, "the government has the advantage of secrecy and a horde of salesmen should it choose to attempt to sell an issue." A president who truly leads, he believes, will be followed no matter what images flicker across television screens (Johnson 1994, 29–31).

Dissenting from the belief that television has made war all but obsolete in the United States and other media-dense democracies is Bruce Cumings. A scholar of the Korean War who draws in part on his own experiences in creating a documentary for television, Cumings believes that the Vietnam War was an anomaly, a period when government had not yet learned to control the media. In the Vietnam War, he points out, television coverage of the war was generally very favorable in its early years; television began to question the war only when American society was itself deeply divided, from 1968 to 1973. "Television [then] brought into the home not the carnage of war, but the yawning fissure in the American consensus that underpinned this war in the previous period. . . . [It did this] because ruling elites fell out over the war" (Cumings 1992, 84). Vietnam was not truly our "first television war," as so many assume, but simply a war fought "before the state understood how the medium could control the message."

America's first real television war, according to Cumings, was the 1991 Persian Gulf War, when the government had "perfected the full capacities of television for fighting, packaging, and selling warfare" (Cumings 1992, 1). By the time of the Gulf War, Cumings writes, "government studies of the role of the press in the Vietnam War had prepared the way . . . for herding journalists through 'new-type warfare' that would be too messy and violent for the uninitiates of the press" (Cumings, 114). Although television had stimulated debate before the war actually erupted, Cumings writes, "Gulf coverage . . . served the state once the storm broke" (Cumings, 105). The result was a carefully staged and managed war in which the press was kept as far as possible from the real battle while the Pentagon manipulated, censored, and massaged images of the war. The result was that

Live coverage from Baghdad, such as Peter Arnett's work for CNN, made the Gulf War much more immediate to television viewers.

television produced "a radically distanced, technically controlled, eminently 'cool' postmodern optic which, in the doing, became an instrument of the war itself" (Cumings, 103). It was, Cumings concludes, far more an exercise in manipulation than one in the subversive potential of television: "You could watch this war movie and be assured a happy ending" (Cumings, 117).

Adding her voice to the debate on the impact of television and the modern media revolution on international affairs is Johanna Neuman, foreign editor of *USA Today* and an instructor in international affairs. Neuman puts this debate into historical perspective by pointing out that virtually every new medium from the printing press to the Internet has alternately been hailed and feared, and that television is really no different. According to Neuman, "each generation is mesmerized by the innovations of its times, sure that no other generation has experienced the emotional upheaval that comes of technological change" (Neuman 1996, 23). As the French would say, "plus ça change, plus c'est la même chose," or "the more things change, the more things stay the same." "The marvelous thing about media history is its consistency. Whenever a new media invention intersects with the worlds of diplomacy and journalism, the same pattern recurs. The enthusiasts boast that the new medium will revolutionize the world. The critics lament that it already has. Neither is exactly wrong, nor completely right" (Neuman 1996, 277).

Journalists taking advantage of new technologies can influence public opinion, Neuman argues, but political leaders are primarily responsible for shaping both public opinion and national policy, not journalists. Frustrated diplomats or political leaders may try to blame journalists for policies that have failed, but it is leaders who shape such policy, and no matter how much impact the media may have, it is leaders who hold the ultimate responsibility. Technology may play a role—it unquestionably did, Neuman writes, in the collapse of the Soviet system—but people play more important roles. If media technology by itself shaped policy, she argues, then the Chinese students in Tiananmen square would have been every bit as successful as the German students who effectively tore down the Berlin Wall; the difference was not media technology, but how the leaders reacted. "To credit the media for fomenting revolution, even in places where it may have encouraged dissent, is to minimize the courage of individuals, and of individualism" (Newman 1996, 198). Leadership, the use of the "bully pulpit," is what usually determines policy, not media technology. "In every age from the French Revolution of 1789 to the Soviet coup of 1991, media technology is a partner to change, not its instigator. In cyberspace, too, it will fall to leaders to steer the technology" (Neuman 1996, 265).

Major Issues in International Communications

The communications revolution, while solving age-old problems of communications, has created new areas of concern. There are serious questions about the security of much of this global network, especially the telephone/computer link. There are equally serious questions about what the consequences of this rapid change are and will be. Has the communications revolution achieved a global village in which understanding leads to harmony? Or has it simply enhanced the existing divisions among nations and between the haves and the have-nots? Are human beings in fact capable of receiving and understanding the vast array of information now available, or are we in danger of communications overload and some sort of psychological or intellectual meltdown?

Global Village?

Early students of the information and communications revolutions, especially a Canadian scholar named Marshall McLuhan, optimistically predicted that it would lead to a worldwide version of the village, a community linked together by aural (speaking and listening) communications. The intimacy of this "global village" would have profound effects on such issues as war and peace. The world would become an interconnected unity, McLuhan wrote, in which social, racial, and ethnic barriers vanished. The communications network would "make of the entire globe, and of the human family, a single consciousness" (quoted in Frederick 1993, 119).

However, more recent scholars have concluded that the global village is the wrong metaphor for what the communications revolution has created. McLuhan has been demoted from a prophet to a purveyor of "zany . . . media metaphysics" (Frederick 1993, 119). Instead of a global village, McLuhan's critics maintain, what has emerged is a global metropolis, a system in which there is virtually no evidence of the intimate web of relationships that defines village life. A metropolis, according to these theorists, is instead a collection of villages and groups; within each there may be intimate connections, but among them there is relatively little communication. In the metropolis, people tend to be caught up in their own affairs and those of their local group, and thus pay little attention to, and have even less concern for the affairs of other groups. Some groups, especially the elites, may be better known than others, because their affairs receive greater publicity, but what will generally catch the attention of the metropolis is the spectacular event: a particularly terrible crime, a ghastly fire, or some other violent or bizarre event. "Information flow among segments of the metropolitan population is unequal; the population at large knows more about elites than about other members of the community. Intimacy is thus restricted and often artificial" (Fortner 1993, 24). In fact, there is some evidence that communications actually may be working differently on different levels: on a global level, modern communications is uniting a global elite that has access to media and communications. On a national level, the disparity between communications access among elites and urban dwellers on one hand and impoverished rural dwellers on the other seems to be leading to widening gaps within individual nations. Thus elites and urban dwellers are becoming alienated from their own countrymen at the same time that they are discovering they have a great deal in common culturally with elites and urban dwellers in other nations. The residents of Nairobi, Cairo, and Warsaw are part of the same global conversation and culture market, but the peasants of Kenya, Egypt, and Poland are alienated from the global conversation. Thus communications is simultaneously accelerating and intensifying both centrifugal and centripetal forces worldwide.

Unfortunately, the metaphor of the global metropolis does indeed seem to be more accurate. The disparities in access to communications and the ability to generate communications and information that we have examined earlier in this chapter seem to reinforce the concept of the global metropolis and to refute the somewhat optimistic, even utopian, view of the global village. Paul Kennedy points out that it is every bit as logical for groups exposed to images of affluence and materialism to nurture anger and resentment about the maldistribution of global wealth as it is for such images to inspire impoverished peoples to strive for a democratic society and marketplace economy (Kennedy 1993, 72).

Does the Truth Make You Free?

An underlying assumption that has guided the communications revolution and shaped Western attitudes toward freedom of communication is the belief that given accurate information, people will more or less automatically become more democratic and their societies more open. This has been an article of faith in Western thinking as far back as the beginning of the Christian era, when John the evangelist wrote, "You shall know the truth, and the truth shall make you free" (John 8:32). Western liberalism has seen "information as an antidote for error, truth as a goal best achieved by allowing free play in the 'marketplace of ideas,' and humankind as sharing a fundamental right to freedom of expression" (Fortner 1993, 195). These ideas reached their fullest expression during the eighteenth century, when Enlightenment thinkers such as Voltaire linked freedom of speech to such fundamentals as freedom of thought and human dignity itself. "I may disagree with what you say," Voltaire wrote, "but I will defend to my death your right to say it." And, of course, this view is enshrined in the First Amendment to the Constitution of the United States as well.

Consequently, the modern Western democracies have pressed for as much freedom of information as possible, and for an open flow of communications between both countries and peoples. In 1946 the United Nations General Assembly declared that "freedom of information is a fundamental human right and is the touchstone of all the freedoms to which the United Nations is consecrated." Two years later, in 1948, the Universal Declaration of Human Rights stated, "Everyone has the right to freedom of opinion and expression" (both quoted in Fortner 1993, 157). Article 19 of the same declaration goes on to proclaim that "this right includes freedom to . . . receive and impart information and ideas through any media and regardless of frontiers" (quoted in Frederick 1993, 248).

Even international businesses and broadcast networks use the value of information to justify their work. CNN, for example, proclaims that in its international news service it reaches the peoples of the world and provides them with the information that will promote democracy. "From Greece to Japan, from Pakistan to Mexico, the people upon whom democracy ultimately depends are following world events as they unfold on CNN. No longer dependent on day-old news . . . these viewers can be true participants in the immediacy of the information age." CNN goes on to claim, "Information equals power in this new age. A fair and balanced 24-hour global news network, available not just to governments and other elites, but to a broad spectrum of the world's population, may well turn out to be one of the most important guarantors of democracy in the 21st century" ("CNN Press Kit" 1992).

Despite all the optimism with which the communications revolution began, we must admit that so far the results have been mixed. There is a great deal more information available worldwide, but it does not yet seem to have lessened international hatreds or eliminated wars.

Information and the Collapse of the Soviet Union

One of the most recent studies of the collapse of the Soviet Union in the late 1980s, Scott Shane's *Dismantling Utopia* stresses the importance of the sudden and intoxicating availability of both communications and information to the Soviet people in bringing about the collapse of the Soviet system.

Soviet leaders had long recognized the importance of controlling communications and information: Lenin had said, "Ideas are much more fatal things than guns" (Shane 1994, 50). To control ideas and limit information, the Soviet Union persistently had jammed Russian-language broadcasts from Radio Free Europe and Voice of America and had kept communications technology tightly restricted. In addition to the miserable phone system we have already discussed, access to technologies taken for granted in the West—photocopying machines, for example—was tightly restricted. Censorship of newspapers, magazines, news broadcasts, and books was rigid, and many writers who dared criticize the Soviet system or leaders were exiled or otherwise punished. To ensure that citizens heard only the "correct" information, the Soviet government blanketed the country with television—including, according to Shane, even the most miserable rural village, accessible only by mud roads, composed of small wooden houses with no plumbing, heated only by wood fires. "Yet sprouting from the roof of even the humblest cottages was a TV antenna, linking this Tolstoyan world with the biggest television transmission system in the world." Asking why the government had invested so much in television and so little in plumbing, Shane answered his own question: "The Soviet leadership had recognized the importance of television as a medium for propaganda and political control." To exploit this medium, the Soviet government, even as its centralized economy was collapsing around it, erected an expensive satellite system and a series of nearly nine thousand broadcasting and retransmitting stations that reached 96 percent of the Soviet population (Shane 1994, 152).

Shane points out that two major historical changes within the Soviet Union prepared the way for the information-fed collapse: the enormous increase in the number of people completing secondary and college education, and the urbanization of the population. In the thirty years from 1950 to 1980, the number of people finishing secondary school more than quintupled and the number who finished higher education quadrupled. And by the mid-1980s, almost two-thirds of the USSR population lived in cities, with their much greater access to information. The Soviet Union had acquired an urbanized, educated population "ready for information" (Shane 1994, 26). Both *samizdat,* (the illicit copying of printed material, or self-publishing), and *magnitizdat* (the illicit copying of audiocassettes), began to flourish.

Given these basic changes within the structure of Soviet society, it became clear that "information remained the weapon to which the system was most vulnerable" (Shane 1994, 113). Even as Mikhail Gorbachev began to pursue his policy of *glasnost,* or openness, hoping that the new information and communications would undermine opponents of his *perestroika* ("restructuring"), dissidents began to use information to undermine the system itself. The information and communications revolution "swept across Soviet existence, touching every nook of daily life, battering hoary myths and lies, and ultimately eroding the foundations of Soviet power" (Shane, 4–5). Finally, "information slew the totalitarian giant" (Shane, 7).

Shane also points out that any technology is essentially neutral, capable of being used for good or bad. While communications technology and information played a major role in undermining the Soviet Union and its empire, it is also capable of being used as a medium of oppression by totalitarian governments. Indeed, Shane writes, to this point the role of communications and information in the Soviet Union has been largely negative. In the Soviet case, "information demonstrated an awesome capacity for destruction of the old order—but no equivalent capacity for creation. . . . It is the nature of information to undermine authority" (Shane, 280). For an even grimmer view of the uses of communications technology, see the accompanying special feature on George Orwell's *1984*.

Conflicts between Communications and Sovereignty

Given the potential impact of the communications revolution, and the disparities in communications abilities between the industrial and the developing nations, neither every government nor every nation has hailed the communications revolution. Many nations regard the permeability of their borders to the flow of information and communication as highly threatening. First among the concerns that these nations raise are issues of national sovereignty. As we discussed in chapter 3 on nationalism, the concept of sovereignty—that any sovereign nation is independent and autonomous, and that other nations may not interfere with its internal functions—led to the idea that national borders should be impermeable. However, no border is truly impermeable in the age of modern electronic communication, and that has created problems for those nations (generally not democracies) that want to exercise firm control over their populations' access to

Big Brother Is Watching You

GLOBAL PERSPECTIVES

Perhaps the most chilling phrase in modern literature, "Big Brother Is Watching You" constitutes an early warning that all may not be as it seems in the communications revolution. George Orwell's classic *1984* is one of the first attempts to peer into the emerging communications future; what Orwell saw was not the optimistic picture presented by most theorists, but a grim vision of modern communications controlled by a totalitarian leadership and used to manipulate an entire society.

Looming over the frightening world of *1984* is the telescreen, a two-way system that enables the rulers to watch everyone, a gigantic cyclopean policeman, an interactive future gone mad. No activity, from daily morning exercises to furtive lovemaking, is safe from the view of the telescreen and Big Brother. Among other results, the telescreen virtually eliminates the possibility of political dissent.

Powerful though it is, the telescreen is not the only weapon in Big Brother's arsenal. Orwell's protagonist, Winston Smith, is a very small cog in the very large machinery of the Ministry of Truth, which constantly rewrites history in order to make it con-

form to the current—and constantly shifting—policy line. People disappear, wars are rearranged, and the past becomes whatever Big Brother needs to justify the present or control the future. Apparently contradictory slogans—WAR IS PEACE, FREEDOM IS SLAVERY, IGNORANCE IS STRENGTH—are plastered everywhere, and language itself is twisted into "Newspeak," the twisted English in which traditional terms have lost all meaning except that assigned by Big Brother.

Orwell's anti-utopia clearly is a warning about the dangers inherent in advanced communications—the way such communications potentially can become an instrument of control rather than a means of liberation through information. Much of the debate that swirls around contemporary communications, concerning both practice and law, echoes Orwellian fears about a communications system that distorts rather than reveals and enslaves rather than liberates. In this century, the year 1984 has come and gone without the realization of Orwell's worst fears—but only continued vigilance can ensure that the modern communications age will not in fact become *1984*.

information and ideas. For example, although the then Soviet government with-held information about the nuclear accident at Chernobyl for several days, a French commercial satellite took pictures of the unfolding disaster that were quickly transmitted all over the world—including to the Soviet Union itself. (Kennedy 1993, 52).

We already have discussed how nations have attempted to jam radio and television signals originating from outside their borders. However, other forms of electronic communications, like the computer and the fax machine, may prove even more difficult to stop. The Chinese government, for example, protested vig-orously against television coverage of the Tiananmen protests. Since Chinese stu-dents demonstrating in Tiananmen Square were listening to VOA and BBC broadcasts to measure how much support they had in the rest of the world, the Chinese government ultimately began to jam these radio signals. However, the Tiananmen students were able to continue monitoring world public opinion by receiving fax transmissions of newspaper stories and editorials from their friends and relatives overseas, especially at American schools and universities. The Chi-nese government saw the transmission of faxes as well as the radio broadcasts as violations of its sovereignty, that is, its right to control its own internal affairs. However, people in other nations, such as the United States, saw the transmission of such information into China both as both an inalienable human right and an aid to democracy.

More recently, China's struggles with issues of Internet communications have illustrated the difficulties of a tightly-closed society attempting to enter the mod-ern world. China has had commercial Internet access only since July 1995, and estimates are that only between fifty thousand and one hundred thousand peo-ple, out of a population of 1.2 billion, actually use the Net. Nonetheless, the pos-sibility that these individuals will gain access to material published by dissidents overseas has apparently moved the Chinese government to clamp down on Inter-net access and content. The Chinese government suspended all new Internet sub-scriptions in January 1996. Regulations issued in February 1996 will probably lead to an end to this suspension but at the same time will attempt to limit what mate-rial can travel via the Internet to China (Faison 1996). The new regulations put all computer networks under the supervision of a government agency and ban all obscene or pornographic materials. Perhaps more chillingly, given China's politi-cal climate, they ban any sort of activity "at the expense of state security." That includes "producing, retrieving, duplicating or spreading information that may hinder public order"—in other words, anything that the government doesn't want ("Controlling the Internet, Chinese Style," 1996).

During the Cold War, the United States and the Soviet Union waged a war of words about the rights of information and communication. The United States gov-ernment defended the VOA, RFE, and other broadcasts it beamed into the Soviet Union and its satellite nations as part of a guaranteed free flow of information. "Limitations of freedom of information existing in the Soviet Union and its area of political and military hegemony . . . merit extraordinary concern," a presidential commission stated in 1973. The head of the United States Information Agency dur-ing the Reagan Administration, Charles Zwick, stated that "under Article 19 of the Declaration of Human Rights of the United Nations . . . there is a prohibition against any hindrance of a free flow of information across international bound-aries. So, the stated policy of multilateral signatories does not inhibit the free flow of information." However, the Soviet Union objected that "Western radio propa-ganda tries to exert constant pressure on the socialist countries" in order to shake and to undermine the Soviet system and to destabilize the nation (all quoted in Fortner 1993, 41).

Walter B. Wriston, former president of Citibank and himself a pioneer in international communications, has gone so far as to write about what he terms "the twilight of sovereignty." Wriston points out that "all new technology tends to erode the influence of existing power structures," and that the communications and information revolutions are particularly subversive to existing power structure because they decentralize control of information (Wriston 1992, 136). Since the concept of sovereignty, as we have seen in chapter 3, includes impermeable borders wrapped around territory and the right of a state to act on its citizens without interference, Wriston argues that modern communications are eroding traditional concepts of sovereignty. "Borders are no longer barriers to information. And where there are no effective borders, the concept of what constitutes sovereignty begins, by necessity, to alter" (Wriston 141). Within its own territory, the power of the state is diminishing: "as the information revolution makes the assertion of territorial control more difficult in certain ways and less relevant in others, the nature and significance of sovereignty are bound to change" (Wriston, 84).

Optimistically, Wriston concludes that the transformation of the idea of sovereignty is intertwined with the "virus" of democracy, which is rapidly being spread by the communications revolution. Furthermore, he writes, this is essentially an irreversible process. He quotes Michael J. O'Neill: "Today's world cannot be remodeled with yesterday's memories; there are no U-turns on the road to the future" (Wriston 1992, xii–xiii).

Cultural Imperialism

Although the Cold War has wound down, and the levels of international propaganda have dropped significantly, there remain other reasons that nations object to and even fear the communications revolution. Other than political dangers— and there are still nations that see these as omnipresent—some people, particularly cultural and intellectual leaders, are deeply concerned about what is called **cultural imperialism.** The dominance of a handful of nations, and an even smaller handful of languages, in international communications has made many people, both in the non-Western world and in the non-English-speaking Western world, concerned that their native cultures and native languages may well be swamped by the tremendous flow of communications in English in the form of radio and television broadcasts, movies, and music. The level of concern is highest in nations most concerned with preserving and promulgating particular traditions—the fundamentalist Islamic nations and peoples, for example—but it exists in many other places as well. The government of Saudi Arabia, a traditionalist Islamic state, recently banned television satellite receivers, although there are an estimated 150,000 in this relatively affluent nation. The penalty for violating the ban is $130,000. And even more recently, the government of Iran also banned satellite dishes, despite the fact that earlier bans on videocassettes and camcorders have been ineffective ("When Words Are the Best Weapons, 1995").

Even some people in the Western democracies have expressed serious concerns about cultural imperialism. For example, in the 1960s a French intellectual, Jean Jacques Servan-Schreiber, sounded the alarm about what he termed the "Coca-colonization" of Europe by the United States (Servan-Schreiber, 1968). In the recent negotiations on the General Agreement on Trade and Tariffs (GATT), an attempt to loosen restrictions on global trade, one of the major sticking points

cultural imperialism
Transference of one culture abroad, displacing the existing culture; usually accomplished via technological means such as television, movies, etc.

as the negotiations reached their conclusion was the determination by the French government to continue protecting its domestic film industry by limiting the importation of foreign, particularly American, films, and by subsidizing the French film industry through taxes on imported films. American film producers, needless to say, presented the problem as an issue of free speech, but the French industry and government remained adamant. Ultimately, the Americans and the French, in the interest of concluding GATT, simply agreed to continue to disagree. In a further instance of France's fight for cultural sovereignty, the French government, still seeing French culture as threatened despite myriad laws banning foreign expressions in advertising or official documents, has moved toward the creation of a national foundation to protect French culture. To be called the Heritage Foundation, this foundation will protect or manage the smaller artifacts of French culture—mills, chapels, markets, country inns, and landscapes—not already protected by the government. Parliament is expected to pass the enabling legislation by the summer of 1996 (Simons 1996).

It appears unlikely that there will be any quick resolution of these concerns. There are legitimate ideas on both sides of the debate. Western democracies generally believe that such concerns must be decided in what they term the international marketplace of ideas; that is, they feel that in free competition superior ideas, much like superior products in the economic marketplace, will triumph, and that such mechanisms guarantee continued improvement in the world of ideas, and continued progress toward universal freedom. These beliefs spring from fundamental understandings of human nature and the nature of democracy, and it will be very difficult for liberal democracies to accept any kind of limitation on freedom of communications. At the same time, many of those who protest against cultural imperialism fear that the power of modern technologies may well mean that indigenous cultures in the developing nations have virtually no hope of competing against the seduction of Western ideas and materialism. As these peoples are still in the process of nation-building, a sense of national identity based on these indigenous cultures is, in their view, vital to any chance of creating viable nation-states. And they also see values and traditions within their indigenous cultures that ought to be preserved.

Furthermore, the rising chorus of protest against control of the free flow of communications by industrialized democracies also takes root in concerns—shared by many in the industrial nations as well—that modern technologies may well lead to far too great a concentration of such control in the hands of a few multinational corporations, which will be motivated less by concerns about democracy, freedom, or cultural survival than by profit. Such concerns are legitimate, and reflect larger questions about the concentration of economic power that characterizes the emerging global economy.

Canada and "Ken and Barbie"

The very nature of the modern international communications environment makes it virtually impossible for nations to stem the flow of information through their borders, no matter how great their concerns for sovereignty or cultural imperialism. A recent series of events in Canada illustrates clearly the difficulties any government will encounter in attempting to prevent information from reaching its citizens. The "Ken and Barbie murders," as they are known, involved an attractive young married couple accused of gruesome murders involving the torture and mutilation of at least two young girls. In July 1993 the judge at the wife's trial banned all Canadian press coverage of the trial because he feared that such coverage, bound to be explosively sensational, would make it almost impossible to find unbiased jurors for the husband's trial.

Although the Canadian press abided by the judge's decision, American newspapers and television and radio stations began publishing accounts of the wife's trial, along with gruesome details of the murders. The result was a stream of Canadians across the border into the United States to purchase copies of the newspapers. Canadian customs officials responded by allowing each individual to carry only one copy of any American newspaper back into Canada, and hundreds of copies of American papers like *The New York Times* and *The Washington Post* piled up at border stations.

Although Canadian cable companies blocked out American news channels carrying coverage of the testimony, the Canadian government could do nothing about the thousands of satellite dishes owned by Canadian citizens; nor could it jam the American radio stations and television stations along the Canadian border. One Detroit, Michigan radio station, dubbing itself "Radio Free Windsor" (for the Canadian city just across the border from Detroit), featured hour-long broadcasts of the text of the *Washington Post* article. An Internet bulletin board carrying news about and details of the trial quickly sprang up, and officials of at least three Canadian universities blocked student access to that section of the Internet. However, it is clear that the vast majority of Canadians could find out what they wanted to about the grisly murders via fax, computer modem, television, radio, or newspapers, and that there was very little indeed that the Canadian government could do to shut down the flow of information (Watson 1995; Epperson and Scott 1993).

As an American newsmagazine article concluded, "In the age of the global village, no democratic society can wall itself off entirely, even from a story that most people wish they had never head about" (Watson 1995, 36). Once the husband's trial began in May 1995, the Canadian government lifted its generally ineffectual ban.

Information Overload, Information Anxiety

As the information and communications revolutions unfold, we are beginning to realize that they do not in and of themselves represent solutions to any of the world's problems. For one thing, the sheer volume of information available to the average citizen in an industrialized nation threatens to overwhelm any person's ability to absorb and make sense of the flow of information. Data themselves do not constitute information, and making sure that the data stream is transformed into comprehensible information presents a daunting task. With television cable companies developing the ability to offer hundreds of channels, with computer networks capable of spanning the globe and tapping millions of databases and other sources of information, with news flooding radio and television networks, people are beginning to fear that they will drown in a sea of facts. Just as data do not equal information, information itself is not the same as knowledge. Furthermore, available information is often jumbled, particularly when on-the-spot news coverage inundates the viewer with unedited and thus unorganized facts, with no way of filtering out false or misleading information and making sense of the larger picture. Information is often not available at the right time, or may be available in theory but unlocatable in practice. A recent book by Richard Saul Wurman, *Information Anxiety: What to Do When Information Doesn't Tell You What You Need to Know* (1990), raises fascinating questions about whether the information and communications revolution will enlighten or merely confuse individuals.

Adding his voice to the debate, Scott Shane asks whether information overload is responsible for what he characterizes as the frequent failure of the public to react to a glut of information about serious problems such as public education. He concludes that it is not a lack of any sense of moral urgency that leads to apathy, but "the very volume of information Americans are exposed to, which can make all the competing problems seem overwhelming, permanent, and insoluble." Communications and information played such a vital role in undermining the Soviet Union, he writes, because the very fact of information was new. "Facts in the Soviet Union had political power because of their novelty, which by definition could not last" (Shane 1994, 284).

Security Issues

There are major concerns about security rising from the communications and information revolutions. Not only do nations of the world devote billions of dollars to interception and reading of one another's most secret communications, but most of the means of communications available to the public and commercial sectors are terribly vulnerable to lapses of security. We have considered the issue of national security and communications in chapter 10, on intelligence, since signals intelligence is a major sector of contemporary intelligence operations. In this section we will look briefly at major issues in what are often considered private or protected communications: the telephone and the computer system.

Telephone communications are extremely vulnerable to interception. In foreign nations, for example, businesses often assume that their telephone lines are tapped and that anything they saw via telephone will be made available to the government and perhaps to the businesses of that nation. In the United States itself, there are laws against wiretapping without authorization, but new technology is already raising new concerns about security. As telephone companies are beginning to develop digitized communications capability, the major federal government agencies are becoming concerned that such communications will be virtually impossible to intercept. Both the Federal Bureau of Investigation and the National Security Agency already have aired their concerns that digitized communications could prevent domestic law enforcement agencies and international intelligence agencies from intercepting telephone conversations.

Computers and computer networks are vulnerable to security lapses in part because of their dependence on telephone lines, but also because of their very nature. Computer systems depend on well-known architecture (commands and so forth) that can be "hacked" by experts who specialize in breaking into systems, sometimes for the purpose of stealing information and often just for the sheer excitement of it. One of the best-known recent examples of this sort of break-in occurred when a German national was able, using international telephone lines, to break into a major American defense network by using various universities as ways of getting into the system, and stole a large amount of valuable classified information before finally being noticed and tracked down by a California computer professor (Stoll, 1990).

The Internet also has shown itself to be vulnerable to all kinds of mischief that can scramble or destroy data. One of the most famous examples of Internet security problems was the famous "Internet worm." A graduate computer student at Cornell University discovered "bugs" or flaws in the UNIX operating system that allowed him to gain unauthorized access to the Internet and thus to hundreds of thousands of computers around the world. The student, Robert Morris, wrote a program called a "worm." This program replicated itself in seconds on every computer it could gain access to. On November 2, 1988, Morris released his worm into the Internet system, where it immediately began to spread and then to replicate itself on individual machines. Within a few hours virtually every VAX and Sun unit on the Internet (two of the major computer systems linked through the network) had been brought to its knees. Morris probably intended his worm as a joke, but a programming error allowed it to get out of control and incapacitate the Internet virtually around the world. Ironically, Morris's father, a security expert at NSA, had written a classic article on breaking passwords that the son probably used to gain access to supposedly secure computers (Tanenbaum 1992, 182–83).

Computer viruses, that is, programs that are transmitted by networks and infiltrate individual machines connected to the network, are another major problem. Some viruses are simply jokes or attempts to prove that "their talented originators can do it", but others are malicious attempts to destroy data that sometimes can inflict physical damage on hard drives. Hundreds of viruses have been detected, and the prudent computer user installs a virus detection program that checks all new programs for any appearance by any virus. Entire sections of textbooks on operating systems and programs are now devoted to these issues of security. There is also an intense debate within the computer world about whether it is prudent to hire confessed hackers who have broken into computer systems in order to figure out how to protect those same systems from other hackers.

One expert on computer security warns that what he terms "information warfare," which extends beyond the simple theft of data into the "electronic anarchy" of **cyberspace,** is already costing the United States alone something between $100 billion and $300 billion a year; additionally, he warns, "almost 5% of our GNP slithers through the global network out of control." The solution is the development of a national information policy that will permit far greater protection of data and communications of all sorts (Schwartau 1994, 16).

The ingenuity of the "cyberburglars" is astonishing. In December 1994 thieves struck at the Internet, in effect hijacking data traveling along the information superhighway. Ironically, the target of the "cybertheft" was an authority on electronic security at the San Diego Supercomputer Center. A recently formed, government-sponsored group, the Computer Emergency Response Team, revealed the theft in notes posted on the Internet in late January 1995 and urged a series of protective measures to thwart the hijackers. Other networks and many companies have been struck by the cyberthieves as well. A recent survey of more than 1,200 companies discovered that more than half had reported financial losses from security breaches and digital theft in the previous two years. The actual number affected may be far higher, since many companies do not report such losses—and many may not even realize that they have incurred them! One company alone believes that it lost a $900 million contract when a competitor hacked into its computers and discovered its bid.

Unfortunately, the law has lagged behind the pace of communications development. In a recent case, a student at the Massachusetts Institute of Technology was accused of running a "pirate" bulletin board that allowed people to download more than one million dollars' worth of illicit software. However, when federal authorities charged him with wire fraud, a federal judge dismissed the case because "laws crafted during the telegraph era couldn't possibly cope with the

cyberspace The theory of communication and control through space.

abuses of the information age." What is true at the national level is even more true at the international level (Markoff 1995; Meyer, 1995).

"Cyber-Attack"?

GLOBAL PERSPECTIVES

Automatic teller machines shut down—or begin spewing out cash. Telephone lines reel out of order, and air traffic controllers suddenly lose the ability to contact airliners speeding cross-country. A power black-out plunges most of the East Coast into darkness. And the Pentagon discovers it cannot order the deployment of American troops.

According to a recent study by the RAND Corporation, a Santa Monica think tank originally established by the U.S. Air Force, the United States military is vulnerable to "cyber-attack" in the event of crisis or war. Positing an attack on Saudi Arabia as the focal point of a crisis, the RAND study showed that determined cyber-terrorists could shut down much of the U.S. information and transportation, virtually crippling the ability of the government and military to transmit orders.

In the RAND scenario, the cyber-terrorists were able to disrupt the national power grid, banking system, air traffic control, and oil and gas supplies. Nearly two hundred government, military, intelligence, and business officials participated in the mock crisis scenario, and, according to the leader of the research work, "nobody was able to tell reassuring stories about how this problem is going to get fixed."

The very nature of the U.S. communications grid, with its dependence on interconnectivity, makes it vulnerable to cyber-terrorism. Even the American military relies heavily on commercial communications channels. Although the present system may well survive a nuclear attack, it would be limited to transmission of brief messages and would not allow two-way communications.

At least one expert on communications security, David Banisar of the Electronic Privacy Information Group, maintains that relatively simple measures could solve much of the current problem. "There are lots of computers out there—and lots of military computers—where they have not done standard, simple security practices." Changing old passwords and using more cryptography (coded computer messages) would make great strides toward meeting the security problems uncovered by the RAND study, according to Banisar. At the same time, he cautions that the National Security Agency would probably become even more adamant in its demands to have the key to communications, such as the Clipper Chip; "frankly," Banisar says, "we don't think that's appropriate."

For now, the RAND study has galvanized each major branch of the military into studies of how to protect itself from cyberwar—and how to conduct it against potential American enemies. A group of high-level executives from the telecommunications industry has formed a presidential advisory committee to study the problem, and the RAND report recommends formation of a new office within the White House to coordinate response to the threat of cyber-warfare (Yeager 1996; see further Thompson, 1995).

Warning that "the electron is the ultimate precision-guided weapon," John Deutch, director of central intelligence, announced in June 1996 that the United States was creating a cyberwar center at the National Security Agency in order to prevent "an electronic Pearl Harbor." According to Deutch, cyberwar will pose a threat to American security in the twenty-first century second only to that posed by weapons of mass destruction. Although the United States cannot be brought to its knees by "a madman with a modem," Deutch said, it is vulnerable to "very, very large" attacks on the computers that run major Department of Defense installations as well as infrastructure such as power plants, telephone systems, air traffic control centers, and international financial transfers. Whether the threat comes from foreign governments, terrorist groups, or teenage hackers, the United States must take steps to reduce its vulnerability, Deutch warned. We can assume that other nations are taking the same steps (Weiner 1996).

Toward an Unpredictable Future

Discussion of the communications and information revolutions usually is not found in texts on international relations, but the scope of the ongoing revolution and its impact on society at the national and global levels demands greater and greater consideration of such issues. In this chapter we have raised many issues and asked far more questions than we can answer. This new technological revolution still is accelerating, and its long-term impact remains difficult to project. As Nathan Rosenberg, an economist studying political change, points out, few people if any have forecast correctly the results of any of the major technological shifts in the twentieth century. Guglielmo Marconi believed that his radio would be used mainly for ship-to-ship and ship-to-shore communications; the birth of the transistor, which made so much of the communications revolution possible, rated only a brief mention in a weekly column in *The New York Times;* in 1949 IBM thought that the number of orders for its computer would, with luck, reach ten or fifteen. New technologies, according to Rosenberg, "come into the world in a very primitive condition, with not all of their properties and characteristics understood." As we prepare to start paving the information superhighway, Rosenberg warns, "history should encourage us to maintain a healthy skepticism about the ability of governments or individuals to 'pick winners' among new technologies," or even to begin to grasp where those technologies will take us (quoted in Edwards 1994b).

The technologies are emerging and blending worldwide, altering irrevocably the shape of the globe and the way its residents relate to one another at all levels of analysis, and as students of international relations we must pay closer and closer attention to both the phenomena and the potential results.

Summary

One of the most important forces transforming international relations is the explosive growth of communications. From the first communications revolution, the advent of the printed word, to the most recent, the electronics explosion, individuals, businesses, and governments have been caught in an ever-accelerating world of communications that continuously has been transforming their lives and their world.

The Communications Revolution: We are now in the midst of the third communications revolution, the transition to computers and satellites. This literally has shrunk the world and changed the way people and governments deal with one another. One of the most important symbols and agents of this revolution is the Internet, tying together more than twenty million users worldwide.

The Communications Gap: It is important to recognize how uneven communications density is worldwide. Many of the simplest communications devices that we in the developed world take for granted, such as the letter, are not available to much of the developing world, not to mention more sophisticated systems such as computers and computer networks.

International Regulation of Communications: International cooperation on communications has existed since the mid-nineteenth century, but the electronics communication explosion has created new problems and concerns for regulators. UNESCO, the arm of the United Nations most concerned with culture and communications, has drawn the wrath of many developed nations with its demand for a New World Information Order, but these demands voice the concerns of developing nations that fear being overwhelmed by "outside forces."

Business, Governments, and International Communications: The communications revolution is affecting both the way businesses operate generally and the specific businesses that are involved directly in communications, particularly broadcasters and news organizations. Communications are creating a truly borderless world in which transactions can be instantaneous, while satellite broadcasting is bringing television and television news to larger and larger populations. Governments have seen the transformation of diplomacy since the communications revolution, with "Rolodex diplomacy," public diplomacy, and summitry playing more and more important roles. In addition, governments have taken advantage of broadcasting to both disseminate their points of view and spread propaganda, although the end of the Cold War seems to endanger such agents of propaganda as the Voice of America.

Individuals: Although some individuals are active participants in the communications revolution, through means such as computer networks and amateur radio, the majority of individuals worldwide remain so far passive recipients of communications, rather than active participants.

Media and International Relations: Although the extent of the influence is hotly debated, it is clear that the communications revolution has major implications for the conduct of international relations. The "CNN effect," by focusing attention on specific problems, may influence how the world reacts to various problems. At the same time, some scholars believe that media attention will make international relations, particularly by democracies, more difficult to conduct. Others believe that the future simply holds greater effectiveness by governments in manipulating the media during wartime.

Major Issues: The communications revolution raises major questions for international relations. Will the result be a global village or a series of global neighborhoods, with urban elites separated by thousands of miles but having more in common with one another than with their rural neighbors? What role will communications play in spreading democracy? Will the assumption that the truth will make you free hold up? Issues such as the conflict between sovereignty, with its concept of impermeable borders, and modern communications, to which any border is permeable, also will become increasingly important. Developing nations fear the impact of cultural imperialism, while both individuals and societies face the danger of information overload. Finally, major security problems confront international communications systems.

Key Terms

Internet	Cultural imperialism
Information superhighway	Cyberspace

Thought Questions

1. Everything new or different today is "revolutionary." To what extent is the field of communications genuinely revolutionary in terms of world politics?
2. What is the impact of instantaneous global communication on the ability of states to wage war in the modern world? To what extent are there differences between democracies and other forms of government?
3. How does the modern communications web affect state sovereignty?
4. Does the truth make you free?

References

Arlen, Michael. *The Living-Room War.* New York: Viking, 1969.

Armstrong, Karen. *Holy War: The Crusades and Their Impact on Today's World.* New York: Doubleday, 1991.

Bagdikian, Ben. *The Media Monopoly.* Boston: Beacon, 1983.

Binder, David. "Cold War Broadcasting Alters Its Programming." *New York Times,* June 27, 1993.

Brugioni, Dino A. *Eyeball to Eyeball: The Inside Story of the Cuban Missile Crisis.* New York: Random House, 1991.

"A Business Interest in Internet," *Houston Chronicle,* May 16, 1993.

Cioffi-Revilla, Claudio, Richard L. Merritt, and Dina A. Zinnes. *Communication and Interaction in Global Affairs.* Beverly Hills, Cal: Sage Publications, 1987.

"CNN Press Kit." Atlanta, Ga.: Turner Broadcasting System, Inc., 1992.

"Controlling the Internet, Chinese Style." *New York Times.,* Internet. http://www.nytimes.com/96/2/5/front/china-internet/html. Downloaded February 5, 1996.

Cumings, Bruce. *War and Television* London: Verso, 1992.

De Pompa, Barbara, and Mary E. Thyfault. "A Business Interest in Internet." *Information Week,* August 15, 1993, 46.

Drew, Christopher. "After 30 Years, Hot Line Stays in Readiness for World Crises." *Houston Chronicle,* July 25, 1993.

Drucker, Peter F. *Post-Capitalist Society.* New York: HarperCollins, 1994.

Edwards, John. "Business Eyes the Internet." Prodigy, April 25, 1994.

———. "The Clouded Crystal Ball." Prodigy, July 4, 1994.

———. "Internet: Home to 200 Million by 2000." Prodigy, January 30, 1995.

Elmer-DeWitt, Philip. "Take a Trip into the Future on the Electronic Superhighway." *Time,* April 12, 1993.

———. "First Nation in Cyberspace." *Time,* December 6, 1993.

Epperson, Sharon, and Gavin Scott. "Uncandid Canada." *Time*/America on Line, December 5, 1993.

"Even in Computing, It's Soviet Disunion." *Information Week,* August 2, 1993.

Faison, Seth. "China Issues Rules to Control Internet." *New York Times,* February 5, 1996. Internet. http://www.nytimes.com/96/2/5/front/china-censor/html. Downloaded February 5, 1996.

Fortner, Robert S. *International Communication: History, Conflict, and Control of the Global Metropolis.* Belmont, Calif.: Wadworth, 1993.

Frederick, Howard H. *Global Communication and International Relations.* Belmont, Calif.: Wadsworth, 1993.

"The Future of Electronic Trading." *Information Week,* June 21, 1993.

"Getting Wired to the Internet." *Houston Chronicle,* March 15, 1995.

Hafner, Katie, and John Markoff. *Cyberpunk: Outlaws and Hackers on the Computer Frontier.* New York: Simon and Schuster, 1991.

Hawley, Sandra, and James D. Heil. "Meet Mr. Morse." *QST: The Magazine of Amateur Radio,* April 1990.

———. "WARC 1992." Update, Houston Amateur Radio Helpline, January 1992.

Johnson, Douglas V. II. *Media: The Impact of the Media on National Security Policy Decision Making.* Carlisle, Pa.: Army War College, 1994. Army War College Bulletin Board. Downloaded Jan. 28, 1995.

Kantrowitz, Barbara. "Live Wires." *Newsweek,* September 6, 1993.

Karow, Stanley. *Vietnam: A History.* New York: Viking, 1983.

Kennan, George F. "If TV Drives Foreign Policy, We're in Trouble." *New York Times,* October 24, 1993.

Kennedy, Paul. *Preparing for the Twenty-First Century.* New York: Random House, 1993.

Krol, Ed. *The Whole Internet: User's Guide and Catalog.* 2nd Ed. Sebastopol, Calif.: O'Reilly and Associates, 1995.

Markoff, John. "Detour to the Data Superhighway." *Houston Chronicle,* November 1, 1993.

———. "Cyberburglars Are Using New Methods." *Houston Chronicle,* January 23, 1995.

McCarroll, Thomas. "New Star over Asia." *Time,* August 9, 1993.

Merritt, Richard. *Communication in International Politics.* Chicago: University of Illinois Press, 1972.

Meyer, Michael. "Stop! Cyberthief! Don't Be Alarmed, but the Law Can't Cope with Computer Crime." *Newsweek,* January 29, 1995.

Neuman, Johanna. *Lights, Camera, War: Is Media Technology Driving International Politics?* New York: St. Martin's, 1996.

Oberdorfer, Don. *Tet: The Story of a Battle and Its Historic Aftermath.* Garden City, New York: Doubleday, 1971.

"Pacific Bell Plans Data Superhighway." *Houston Chronicle,* November 12, 1993.

Passell, Peter. "Fast Money." *New York Times Magazine.* October 18, 1992.

"Radio Free Europe Will Drop Seven Languages." *New York Times,* June 23, 1993.

"Russia's Nyet-Works." *Information Week,* June 21, 1993, 90.

Samovar, Larry A., and Richard E. Porter. *Intercultural Communications: A Reader.* Belmont, Calif.: Wadsworth, 1988.

Schement, Jorge Reina, Gerner Belay, and Dong Youl Jeong. "Information Society." In Joel Krieger, ed. *The Oxford Companion to Politics of the World.* New York: Oxford University Press, 1993.

Schwartau, Winn. *Information Warfare: Chaos on the Electronic Superhighway.* New York: Thunder's Mouth Press, 1994.

Servan-Schreiber, Jean-Jacques. *The American Challenge.* New York: Atheneum, 1968.

Shane, Scott, *Dismantling Utopia: How Information Ended the Soviet Union.* Chicago: Ivan R. Dee, 1994.

Shawcross, William. *The Shah's Last Ride: The Fate of an Ally.* New York: Simon and Schuster, 1988.

Silverman, Dwight. "Fighting On-Line Civilization." *Houston Chronicle,* October 23, 1993.

Simons, Marlise. "France seeking to keep things French." *Houston Chronicle.* February 26, 1996.

Stoll, Cliff. *The Cuckoo's Egg: Tracking a Spy through the Maze of Computer Espionage.* New York: Pocket Books, 1990.

Tanenbaum, Andrew S. *Modern Operating Systems.* Englewood Cliffs, N.J.: Prentice Hall, 1992.

Thompson, Mark. "If War Comes Home." *Time.* August 21, 1995.

Tuchman, Barbara W. *The Zimmerman Telegram.* New York: Bantam Books, 1971.

Vita, Matthew C. "The CNN Effect." *Houston Chronicle,* May 7, 1993.

Watson, Russell. "Sex, Death, and Videotape." *Newsweek.* May 29, 1995.

Watson, Russell, and Linda Kay. "The Barbie-Ken Murders." *Time,* December 6, 1993, 36.

Weiner, Tim. "CIA Plans Center to Counter 'Cyberwar' Threat." *New York Times,* June 26, 1996. Downloaded June 26, 1996. http://www.nytimes.com/library/cyber/week/0626spy.html.

"When Words Are the Best Weapon." *Newsweek Interactive.* Prodigy. Downloaded Feb. 20, 1995.

Whitney, Craig R. "Radio Free Europe Seeking Partial Privatization." *New York Times,* March 20, 1994.

Wriston, Walter B. *The Twilight of Sovereignty: How the Information Revolution Is Transforming Our World.* New York: Charles Scribner's Sons, 1992.

Wurman, Richard Saul. *Information Anxiety: What to Do When Information Doesn't Tell You What You Need to Know.* New York: Bantam Books, 1990.

Yeager, Holly. "U.S. vulnerable to 'cyber-attack'." *Houston Chronicle.* March 17, 1996.

Chapter 14

Global Issues

Introduction

Nowhere is the growing interconnectedness of the world made clearer—and nowhere are the problems created and amplified by that interconnectedness more obvious—than in the three major global issues we consider in this chapter: population, environment, and disease. These three issues are closely related, in terms of both their potential for enormous global harm and the necessity of devising global strategies to cope with them. The ability of the world's nations and peoples to work cooperatively to deal with these problems will have as much to do with shaping the next century as economics or politics.

Population

One of the most fiercely debated of these global issues is population. While there is general agreement on current numbers and on some of the dilemmas created by those numbers, there is little agreement either on projected numbers or on whether the rapid growth of human population represents a major problem or a major opportunity. Issues of population are related to questions of women's rights, traditional cultural values, and religious forces. Because of this, attempts to cope with population growth are infinitely complex, arousing intense emotions that make it very difficult to deal with the question, much less the answer.

Battle of the bulge

Source: Drawing by Chris Riddell, from *The Economist,* September 3, 1994. Reprinted by permission.

Malthus

Virtually all modern concern about population traces back to an eighteenth-century clergyman named Thomas Malthus. In 1798 Malthus became alarmed at what he saw as the growing disparity between growth of the food supply and growth of the population. While the food supply grew arithmetically, he claimed, the population was growing geometrically. In other words, the growth of the food supply could be expressed as increasing in this progression: 1, 2, 3, 4, etc. In contrast, the growth of the population must be expressed as increasing thus: 1, 2, 4, 8, 16, etc. If the population continued to grow unchecked, and the food supply continued to expand much more slowly, the obvious consequence, Malthus wrote, would be fierce struggle for diminishing resources, a truly Hobbesian war of all against all. If human beings could not control the growth of their numbers, nature would, and in brutal ways: through famine, disease, and war.

Since Malthus sounded the alarm nearly two centuries ago, only some of his dire predictions have come true. Population has in fact continued to increase almost geometrically—but the food supply has managed to keep pace with population growth (see figs. 14.1 and 14.2). However, the debate that Malthus

Thomas Malthus began the debate about population with his gloomy eighteenth-century predictions of disaster; despite the failure of disaster to arrive so far, the debate continues.

Figure 14.1
The Theory . . .
Source: Adapted from *The Economist,* September 3, 1994. Data from United Nations Food and Agriculture Organization.

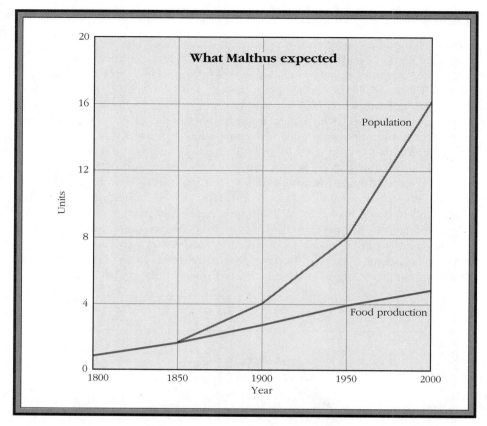

touched off continues to rage, and the issue of population growth and control is one of the most divisive in modern international politics.

The Numbers to Date

As we have said, in the debate on population there is little room for argument about the numbers to date. Population has in fact increased dramatically since Malthus's warning, and its rate of growth continues to increase as well. For most of human history, population growth has been relatively slow, with high mortality rates virtually canceling out high birth rates. Demographers and population biologists estimate that as recently as nine thousand years ago, just before the beginning of the agricultural revolution, global human population was roughly five million people. With the greatly increased food supply that agriculture made possible, global population began to increase, reaching perhaps 250 million by the year 1 A.D. For the next millennium and a half, population continued to grow, reaching roughly five hundred million by 1650. Around the midpoint of the seventeenth century, the growth curve began to rise sharply—the result, at least in part, of the discovery of the New World and the vast increase in global food supplies that such New World crops as the potato and corn made possible. Global population reached the one-billion mark by the end of the eighteenth century, when Malthus published his warnings, but did not reach two billion until roughly 1930. Then, acceleration set in: global population reached three billion in 1960, four billion in 1975, and five billion in 1986. It is estimated to have reached six

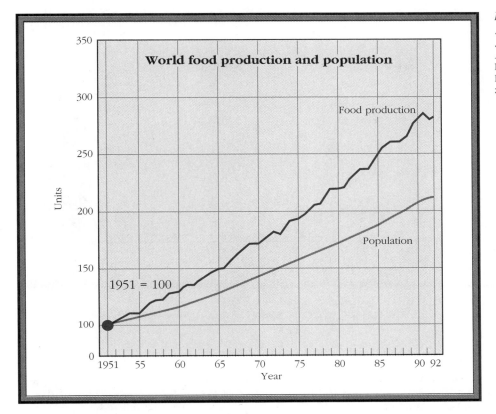

Figure 14.2
... the Reality
Source: Adapted from *The Economist,* September 3, 1994. Data from United Nations Food and Agriculture Organization.

billion by the end of 1995 (Semones 1990; Ehrlich 1990; Moffett 1994). This recent rapid increase is evident in figure 14.3

Another way to look at population growth is this: the global population took eighteen centuries after the birth of Christ to reach its first billion, less than a century and a half to reach its second billion, less than half a century to reach its third billion, only fifteen years to reach its fourth billion, barely a decade to reach its fifth billion, and probably less than a decade to reach its sixth billion! As U.S. president Bill Clinton pointed out, humanity took ten thousand generations to reach the first two-billion-people population mark, but the next two billion came within the lifespan of an average individual (fifty years), and the third two billion will have been added in the time it takes an individual to grow from infancy to early adulthood, a mere twenty years (Moffett 1994, 7).

We also can examine global population growth in terms of doubling time. The doubling from 250 to 500 million took 1,600 years; from 500 million to a billion, 150 years; from one to two billion, 130 years; and from two to four billion, *forty-five years!* It is not just the raw increase, but the rate of increase that demographers, individuals who study population issues, find so potentially distressing. Today, the global population increases by approximately ninety-six million people each year, the equivalent of a new Mexico or four new Canadas each year. Every ninety-six hours the planet gains another million people: a new Boston every two days, a new Houston every four days, a new Germany every eight months, a new Africa and Latin America combined during the decade of the 1990s (Moffett 1994, 7).

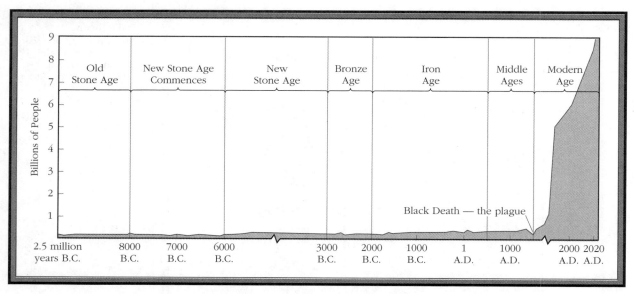

Figure 14.3 World Population Growth through History
Source: George F. Hepner and Jesse O. McKee: *World Regional Geography: A Global Approach* (St. Paul: West, 1992).

fertility rate The number of births per thousand women of childbearing age, i.e., 15–44 years of age.

replacement fertility rate The fertility rate that would not result in overall population growth in any particular group while simply maintaining current numbers.

population momentum The continuing growth of the population long after replacement fertility has been achieved.

To understand the continuing debate about what these numbers mean, and what they may mean in the future, we must first define some important demographic terms. **Fertility rate** refers to the number of births per thousand women of childbearing age, defined as from fifteen to forty-four years; the higher the fertility rate is, the more children women are having and the more rapidly population is growing. **Replacement fertility rate** is the fertility rate that would not result in overall population growth in any particular group, but simply would maintain current numbers. **Population momentum** is a way to describe the continuing growth of the population long after replacement fertility has been achieved, because there still will be large numbers of girl children entering their childbearing years. For example, Japan reached replacement fertility in 1957, but will not reach zero population growth until 2006. And if Mexico, with a large relative number of young women just entering the childbearing years, were suddenly to achieve only replacement fertility, Mexico's population would continue growing for the next fifty years simply because of the population momentum. More figures on population growth in specific nations are in table 14.1 As demographers point out, population momentum is somewhat like a speeding freight train: the brakes have to go on a long way before the proposed stop (Moffett 1994, 8; Semones 1990, 356–57).

The Debate: Growth Projections

The first arena for the debate about population is future numbers. What are the projected population growth rates for the planet? In 1992 the United Nations attempted to provide both best-case (or lowest) and worse-case (or highest) projected growth rates. According to the UN, if fertility rates drop below replacement levels, global population could level off at approximately six billion. Should fertility rates remain high, the world could be looking at a population of as many as

Table 14.1
Population Size, Fertility Rate, and Doubling Time, 20 Largest Countries, 1993

COUNTRY	Population (millions)	Fertility Rate (average number of children per woman)	Doubling Time (years)
Italy	58	1.3	3466
Germany	81	1.4	*
Japan	125	1.5	217
United Kingdom	58	1.8	267
France	58	1.8	169
Russia	149	1.7	990
United States	258	2.0	92
China	1,178	1.9	60
Thailand	57	2.4	49
Indonesia	188	3.0	42
Brazil	152	2.6	46
Turkey	61	3.6	32
Mexico	90	3.4	30
India	97	3.9	34
Viet Nam	72	4.0	31
Philippines	5	4.1	28
Egypt	8	4.6	30
Pakistan	122	6.7	23
Nigeria	5	6.6	23
Iran	3	6.6	20

*At its current mortality rate, Germany's population is shrinking and at this fertility rate will never double.
Source: Population Reference Bureau, *1993 World Population Data Sheet* (Washington, D.C.: 1993).

twenty-one billion people by the early twenty-second century. If population rates gradually level off, albeit at different times in different countries, in a scenario the UN defines as the most likely, global population probably will reach ten billion by the middle of the next century and then gradually level off at 11.5 billion in the twenty-second century. And if fertility rates remained at today's level (a highly unlikely possibility), the population might reach seven hundred billion by the middle of the twenty-second century (Moffett 1994, 9). Since fertility rates vary widely from nation to nation, and since they reflect hundreds of millions of individual decisions every day, there really is no way to tell who is correct in this part of the debate—the pessimists, who foresee a virtually unbearable population glut, or the optimists, who predict relatively slow growth.

Another aspect of population growth that many find particularly unnerving is that well into the foreseeable future, it will largely take place in the world's poorer countries, which will be far less able to absorb the impact of sharply increasing numbers.

Urbanization

Another characteristic of present and future population growth is that much of this growth is taking place in cities. In the twenty-first century the world will be host

In December 1992, air pollution in Mexico City reached emergency levels; the picture above shows how little success the sun had in penetrating the smog. Such pollution—and the United Nations already rates Mexico City's air quality as the worst in the world—will only become worse as the growth rate for Mexico City continues to soar.

urbanization The concentration of humanity in cities around the world.

to a dozen or more "megacities," in which tens of millions of people will be crowded together in intolerable conditions. In fact, even now the world is on the brink of a historic turning point. By the end of this century, demographers predict, more than half the world's population will be packed into huge cities. This degree of **urbanization** is unprecedented throughout all of human history. By the end of the next century, it is calculated, more than 70 percent of the world's population will live in cities that will occupy less than 2 percent of the earth's surface (Moffett 1994, 29). According to a United Nations report, just between 1990 and 1995 320 million people were added to the world's urban population—the equivalent of eighteen New York Cities. UN experts foresee that by the year 2000, there will be twenty-eight megacities (those with populations of eight million or more); twenty-two of these will be in the developing world. The turn of the century also will see the existence of at least six "hypercities" of fifteen million people or more. Mexico City alone will have a population equal to half that of Canada. If the UN projections hold, the ten largest cities will have a combined population of 163 million people—equal to that of the world's twenty-six smallest nations (Moffett 1994, 31). Figure 14.4 shows the projected growth rates for the world's largest cities.

This rapid urban growth has far outdistanced the ability of cities to provide necessary housing, sanitation, roads, and other aspects of infrastructure. The result is that in Cairo, for example, nearly half a million people now live in the City of the Dead, an ancient cemetery lacking running water, sewers, or electricity, in which entire families huddle in eight-foot-square crypts. In Brazil's Rio de Janeiro and Sao Paolo, hundreds of thousands of people exist in *favelas,* tin and cardboard shantytowns on the cities' outskirts, often perched precariously on hillsides and vulnerable to mudslides. In Mexico City, thousands of families spend their days digging through enormous garbage dumps searching for food, clothing, fur-

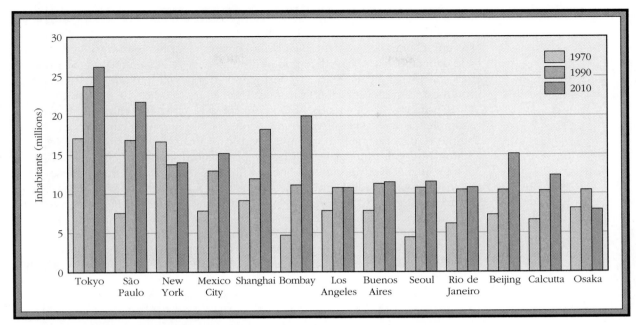

Figure 14.4 **The Largest Urban Agglomerations in the World**
Source: Adapted from George D. Moffett, *Global Population Growth: Twenty-First Century Chal-lenges* (New York: Foreign Policy Association Headline Series, 1993), 24. Data from United Nations Population Division.

niture—anything that more affluent people may have discarded; the air they breathe ranks with the most polluted in the world.

Historian Paul Kennedy notes that this mushrooming urban growth is changing the very idea of cities. For thousands of years, he writes, great cities such as Rome, Paris, Vienna, and London have been associated with wealth, creativity, culture, and economic opportunity. "By contrast," he continues, "Asian, Latin American, and Central American mega-cities of 20 million inhabitants have become increasingly centers of poverty and social collapse" (Kennedy 1993, 26).

The Debate: So What?

As we might expect, there are widely varying attitudes toward the entire issue of population growth, ranging basically from an appalled look at an unlivable future to a rosy "we can cope" view.

Leading those appalled by the prospect of steadily rising numbers is a group of neo-Malthusian population biologists led by Paul Ehrlich, whose *The Population Bomb* (1968) began the modern debate and whose *The Population Explosion,* written with his wife Anne, (1990) continued to sound the alarm. The Ehrlichs present two negative scenarios describing what continued unchecked population growth could lead to. The first possibility, they write, is "The Bang," a nuclear holocaust triggered by tensions created as "growing and already overpopulated nations struggle to divide up dwindling resources in a deteriorating global environment." The end of the Cold War has dramatically decreased that possibility (although it has certainly not eliminated it). Therefore, a far more likely prospect in the

Ehrlichs' view is "The Whimper." An earth stretched far beyond its carrying capacity will deteriorate; famines will eradicate large numbers of people; epidemics will sweep uncontrolled across the globe; an environment into which too many toxins and dangerous gases have been poured simply will give up; transportation systems will collapse and cities starve to death; and society will implode, returning at the very best to the level of the Dark Ages (Ehrlich and Ehrlich 1990, 174–80).

Those on the other side of the debate tend to be economists. Karl Marx, for example, disputed Malthus's gloomy conclusions, saying such an outcome would be the result of capitalism; do away with capitalism, achieve an equitable distribution of goods, and there will be no population problem, Marx argued. Technology aligned with good economics will solve it. Many other economists, most of them notably non-Marxist conservatives and even libertarians, echo Marx's argument. Probably the best known is Julian Simon; in *The Ultimate Resource* and a number of other important articles and books, Simon has argued that people constitute the earth's greatest resource; rather than causing resource depletion and environmental degradation, population growth actually will have positive results. First, population growth will stimulate demand for goods and services, thus increasing markets and leading to economic growth. Second, "the ultimate resource," says Simon, is human ingenuity and genius, which will discover new technologies and new ways of coping with increased populations. The enlargement of the population simply will produce that many more Mozarts and Michelangelos and Norman Borlaugs (the "father of the green revolution," which increased the world food supply enormously—Moffett 1994, 112–13).

While Simon views Paul Ehrlich and other alarmed population biologists as Cassandras who ignore hard data in pursuit of their dark nightmares, Ehrlich dismisses Simon as "an economist specializing in mail-order marketing" who stumbled into the population debate devoid of any real understanding of the issue. Ehrlich also points out that the drive for population growth is in fact built into our genes and our culture; "that's one reason so many otherwise bright and humane people behave like fools when confronted by demographic issues" (Ehrlich and Ehrlich 1990, 21).

Nathan Keyfitz, a well-known demographer, believes that in some ways the biologists and economists are using the same logic but different words—and then reaching very different conclusions. "What biologists call the struggle for survival," he says, "economists call the free market." He concludes, however, that those who believe population growth is not an immediate problem, but a potential problem that can be solved when it occurs, are simply wrong. "The preponderance of data and common sense insist that decisive and effective action be taken [now] to address the population dilemma" (Keyfitz 1994, 10).

The Debate: Other Voices, Other Issues

As if the debate between biologists and economists weren't enough, the population debate also sweeps in religious arguments, cultural traditions, and a whole range of women's issues.

The Religious Opposition to Population Control

Because it deals with some of the most fundamental aspects of humanity and morality—sexuality, family, individual choices—the debate about population growth inevitably has engaged various religious groups with various points of view. The Roman Catholic Church, governed by an elaborate hierarchy, presents a cohesive point of view, both chronologically and logically, although the extent to which it influences individuals is highly debatable. The Islamic faith, lacking a central authority such as the Vatican, presents no unified point of view.

Historically, the Catholic Church has taught that sexual activity must take place within marriage and must be for the purpose of procreation; contraception of any sort is immoral because it opposes that purpose. Also immoral are all forms of sexual behavior that could not possibly lead to conception (masturbation, oral and anal sex, coitus interruptus). As more and more forms of contraception have become available in the twentieth century, and as more and more people have become convinced that population growth must be limited, the church has remained adamant in its ban upon contraception. In 1930 Pope Pius X wrote, "Any use whatsoever of matrimony exercised in such a way that the act is frustrated in its natural power to guarantee life is an offense against the law of God and nature, and those who indulge in such are branded with the guilt of grave sin." It is the responsibility of a Christian couple "to raise up . . . members of God's household, that the worshipers of God and of Our Savior may daily increase." As recently as 1993, Pope John Paul II reaffirmed the Catholic Church's ban on artificial contraception, arguing that the "irrational control of births [prevents] the access of new mouths at the banquet of the Lord." The goal, he wrote, is not to decrease the number of guests at the banquet, but to increase the amount of food. In this, the Catholic Church has moved closer to the point of view that the real problem is not population control, but inequitable distribution of food and other resources. In addition, there is little doubt that many church leaders see the battle against population control as simply another element in their ongoing struggle against materialism, secularism, and sexual permissiveness (Moffett 1994, 241–46).

Interestingly, a great deal of research, as well as anecdotal evidence, shows that larger and larger numbers of Catholics are simply ignoring their hierarchy's position on artificial contraception (Moffett 1994, 241). However, the Catholic hierarchy remains rigidly and consistently against artificial contraception, although adamantly ignored by much of the laity. By contrast, the Islamic world, including its leadership, is split.

According to Mohammed Sayyid Tantavi, an Egyptian *mufti,* or keeper of doctrine, within the 850-million-member Sunni sect, "Islam provides no opposition to controlling birth . . . . the Shari'a of Islam does not forbid family planning as long as the couple sees that there is a necessity for it." But since there is no specific hierarchy within the *umma,* or Muslim community, there is no set position on family planning. Islamic tradition, based on Mohammed's injunction "to marry and have children" and the belief that children are the gift of God, has encouraged large families. Even today Muslim birthrates are among the highest in the world. At the same time, however, the Koran counsels parents to have only as many children as they can provide for, both physically and economically. The Prophet Mohammed is also quoted as saying, "The most grueling trial is to have plenty of children with no adequate means" (Moffett 1994, 248–50). Thus Muslim theologians easily can justify family planning, which is not in any way specifically contravened in the Koran.

However, because there is no strict hierarchy, many clerics at the local level continue to insist that the Koran opposes family planning. And with the rise of fundamentalism in the Islamic world, many more officials, both clerical and governmental, insist that family planning is simply an imperialist device to weaken Islam by keeping Muslim nations underpopulated (Moffett, 1994, 251). Consequently, birthrates in much of the Islamic world remain sky-high.

One of the most interesting sidelights of the 1994 Cairo Conference on Population, Women, and Development was the alliance forged between the Roman Catholic Church and a number of Islamic states, including fundamentalist Iran. And as the Cairo conference also demonstrated, the opposition of the Catholic Church to artificial contraception may be more important because of its political influence—its ability to force governments to curtail or cancel family planning—than because of its direct spiritual impact upon individual Catholics.

Cultural Traditions

Family planning and any attempts to limit population size also meet opposition in the cultural traditions of many peoples, cultural traditions that often have their roots in social and economic realities. The two most important features of cultural tradition that clash with family planning are the emphasis on large families and the role of women.

Large families generally are viewed as a necessity in preindustrial cultures; during the colonial period in the United States, for example, eight children were the norm, and it might not be unusual for a family to consist of ten to twelve children. Johann Sebastian Bach, the great eighteenth-century composer, was the father of twenty-one children.

Economic, Social, and Medical Pressures for Large Families.   Three realities, one economic, one social, and one medical, drive the demand for large families in preindustrial societies. Economically, large families are beneficial for peasants and small farmers; within a few years of their birth, children can begin taking part in the endless work of tilling the average peasant's small plot. Children become an essential part of the agricultural labor force quickly, and the more children a family can produce, the more "free" labor it can mobilize.

Socially, the more children a family has, the greater is the chance that these children will be able to support and care for their elderly parents in societies that have virtually no "safety net." In fact, even where old-age pensions or some kind of "social security" are available, the agricultural population often is excluded because its members to do not work for a wage. Having as many children as possible serves to guarantee, as much as possible, a comfortable old age for the parents.

Medically, the high infant mortality rates common in preindustrial societies mean that a couple must have large numbers of children in the hope that enough will survive to augment the family labor force and live to adulthood to provide support for their aging parents. Even today, many developing nations have excruciatingly high infant mortality rates; while Japan has an infant mortality rate of 5.3 infant deaths per thousand children under the age of one, and the United States has an overall infant mortality rate of 10.5 (although the figure soars much higher in slums and other poverty-ridden areas and is lower in higher socioeconomic areas with good prenatal care), the infant mortality rate in India is 101; in Nigeria, 124; in Ethiopia, 152; and in Afghanistan, 182 (Semones 1990, 341). Childhood mortality rates remain high in those nations with high infant mortality rates; thus, a large number of children serves basically as insurance for the family.

Thus, in many traditional or nonindustrial societies, the decision to have a large family is a rational one, given the economic, social, and medical realities of these societies. Perhaps as population even in many industrializing societies becomes more and more urban, the facts of urban life such as overcrowding, high prices, and high cost of education will cause more and more decisions to lower family size.

Preference for Male Children and Large Families. Part of the pressure for large families comes as well from the desire for male children and the determination to continue having children until there are sufficient males. Cultural tradition in many societies—in China and India, for example—stresses the necessity of male children who will become heirs, maintain the family name and family lineage, and stay within the family. Girl children will marry and join another family, in effect "wasting" all the time, effort, and money that goes into their rearing. Only boys remain part of the family. In China, in fact, it is not unusual for a childless or boyless couple to adopt a young male cousin or nephew in order to ensure perpetuation of the family. Given China's traditional emphasis on the importance of family, this is not surprising. However, it can have tragic results.

In traditional China, female infanticide was practiced fairly widely; even in contemporary China, it continues to exist. With the national policy of only one child per family as the result of China's desperate attempt to control its population growth, it is a widespread practice for a family to choose to abort female fetuses and not to bring a pregnancy to term until tests show that the developing fetus is a boy. The use of abortion as a tool of gender selection is widely deplored, and equally widely practiced—and not only in China. In a single clinic in Bombay, India, in one year eight thousand abortions were performed; according to an Indian government study, 7,999 of the aborted fetuses were female (Moffett 1994, 217).

One recent demographic study found that worldwide, some sixty million women are "missing"; that is, given the normal distribution of gender within the population, the world should have sixty million more females than it has! In developed countries, the ratio of females to males is approximately 105 to 100; in Africa and Latin America, the ratio is roughly equal, 100 to 100. However, United Nations statistics show that in China the ratio is 94.3 to 100; in India, 93.5 to 100; and in Pakistan, 92.1 to 100. One must suspect that such ratios are not accidental, but reflect the cultural preference for males. One demographer estimates that China should have twenty-nine million more women than it has, and India twenty-three million more, simply given normal statistical distribution (Sege 1992).

Traditional Women's Roles and Large Families. In many traditional societies, including several that are modernizing rapidly, part of the emphasis on large families derives from the desire to maintain the traditional status of women, generally an inferior one. Historically, in such societies there has been no role for women beyond that of wife and mother; the tradition of patriarchy is extremely strong. However, women have in fact gained some status within such societies through their role as mothers; often, the more children a women could have, the higher her status has been, and the greater has been her importance within the family. Additionally, in such patriarchal societies, men have made all decisions, including those concerning family size, usually without consulting their wives. Women have been, and often still are, powerless. This patriarchal tradition, with its downgrading of women's role and often of women themselves, remains extremely strong in much of the world today, and the idea that women might have a voice in vital decisions constitutes anathema.

Since limiting family size would change the role of women, traditional societies tend to resist such limits; consequently, in many areas of the world fertility rates remain extremely high.

The Feminist Perspective on the Population Debate

Not surprisingly, feminists bring their own perspective to the debate about population control and family planning. The main thread of argument that emerges from the feminist position is that family planning and the use of contraception to lower family size is not enough; instead of being the goal of government or global policy, family planning ought to be simply the first step in raising the status of women in general and dealing with women's health issues in particular. Many women disagree with the idea that lowering population must be the focus of dealing with women's issues and with reproduction in general. They argue that quality health care, education, and economic opportunities for women are far more important than simply limiting family size, and that only by tackling all of these issues can governments or agencies make any genuine progress toward empowering women and raising their status. Women must be valued in and of themselves, these women leaders insist, and must not be treated simply as the object of family planning. Critics of both the population reduction movement and the groups that oppose contraception and family planning assert that "neither takes the interests and rights of the individual woman as their starting point. Both . . . attempt to control women, instead of letting women control their bodies themselves" (Moffett 1994, 189). A woman deeply involved with the links between population control and women's rights says, "Programs that put demographic objectives ahead of women's rights . . . not only [have] failed to alleviate pervasive economic and environmental problems, but by diminishing the status of women . . . have further perpetuated the very problems family planning agencies have set out to solve. You can never help women out of the population trap unless you help them out of the poverty trap, and you will never help them out of the poverty trap until you take steps to equalize access to resources" (quoted in Moffett 1994, 193).

The issue of women's empowerment, that is, permitting women not only to take control of their bodies but also to begin to shuck their restricted traditional roles, is at the heart of the feminist critique of the population control movement. In fact, the evidence shows clearly that as women's education levels rise, their fertility rate drops (see fig. 14.5). However, current controversies over changes in women's status hold some promise of betterment of women's condition in the future.

The Global Environment

A second complex, controversial, and critical issue is the state of the global environment. As with the issue of population, the debate over the environment is taking place in an arena in which the lines of controversy are sharply drawn, even as there is comparatively little disagreement over the essential facts. In this section we will briefly examine some of the main global issues raised by environmentalists and look at the debate over those issues. As one author notes, the

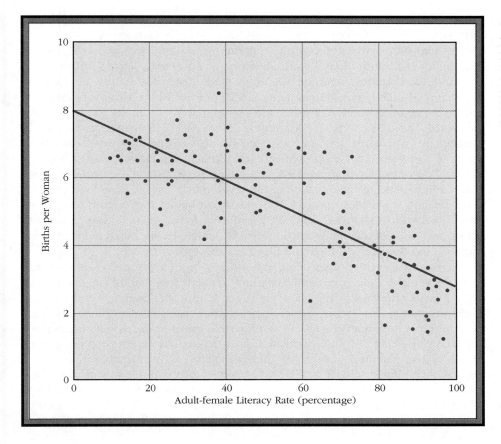

Figure 14.5
**A Little Learning:
Fertility Rate and Female
Literacy, 1990**
Source: Redrawn from *The
Economist,* September 3, 1994.
Data from World Population
Institute (based on 93 coun-
tries).

positions taken by the environmentalists on one hand and their critics, particularly economists, on the other are so very different that "it is as if the two sides, which have access to the very same data, are talking about different subjects" (Moffett 1994, 116).

Food Supply

Clearly, one of the most critical issues facing the planet is how the human race can feed itself. Food has significance far beyond mere sustenance; it is a major commodity in the international marketplace, and too often in the past the lack of food has led not only to famine but also to riot and revolution.

The past fifty years have witnessed an astonishing revolution in food production, often called the **green revolution.** Careful breeding of new strains of cereal crops, particularly rice, wheat, and corn, and extensive use of chemical fertilizers have enormously increased the world food supply. From 1950 to 1984, the world food supply increased at an annual rate of nearly 3 percent a year, easily outstripping population growth. However, after 1984 these increases began to level out, and in the late 1980s grain production slipped nearly 10 percent. Today there is enough grain available to feed the global population, if everyone were satisfied with a vegetarian diet. However, to provide a diet with 15 percent of its calories from animal products (meat, milk, butter), the world has enough food for only four billion people. That would leave 1.6 billion people with nothing at all

**green revolution The
increase in food production
due to disease- and drought-
resistant hybrid strains of
grain coupled with the use
of chemical fertilizers.**

to eat. Assuming a diet roughly comparable to the current American food pattern, with 35 percent of its calories from animal products, the earth could feed 2.5 billion people—less than half the world's current population. Because of the uneven distribution of food in today's world, a billion or so people, largely in the developed industrial nations, consume a more-than-adequate diet; among other things, these favored billion, constituting less than 20 percent of the world's population, consume almost 35 percent of the world's grain, much of it in the form of fodder for animals. At the same time, the poorest billion people on earth have a terribly inadequate diet; nearly four hundred million are so undernourished that their health is threatened or their growth stunted (Ehrlich and Ehrlich, 1990, 67–68).

Biologists and environmentalists argue that the world will be unable to continue even producing food at the current level, much less increase food production to match population growth. The green revolution, they argue, has run its course; soils are exhausted; chemical fertilizers have reached their maximum return; and "the bill is coming due, in terms of depleted soils, salted fields, drained aquifers, and the like" (Ehrlich and Ehrlich, 1990, 69).

Economists, on the other hand, argue that world food supply is almost infinitely expandable, given enough ingenuity, enough free-market operation, and enough work (Budiansky 1994, 57). However, it appears that many of the results of the revolution in genetic engineering that give economists so much hope for the future may well not be available at affordable prices to the developing nations that face 95 percent of future population growth. Genetic engineering companies already have patented several of the potentially most valuable "improved" species, including sweeter fruits, disease-resistant plants using specific enzymes, and plants engineered to resist insects. More patent applications are being filed. While the companies that have invested large sums of money in the research to produce genetically engineered plants argue that patents will guarantee them fair return on their investments and ensure further research, critics fear that such patents will lead to high prices and possible monopolies, particularly since many of the patents are broadly written ("Crop Patents Raise Concerns" 1994; see also Bailey 1995 and Easterbrook 1995).

Water

Even though much of the planet's surface—five-sixths of it—is water, environmentalists argue that most of this is salt water and thus generally unusable, and that the fresh water upon which humanity depends not only for drinking but also for agriculture is rapidly diminishing. Worldwide, they write, aquifers (huge underwater freshwater supplies) are being drained far faster than they can replenish themselves. Furthermore, intensive irrigation tends to build up salt deposits that eventually make further agriculture impossible. Pollution of lakes and rivers continues almost unabated in many areas of the world; in Russia, for example, the world's largest freshwater lake, Lake Baikal, once sparkling blue and pure, is now a cesspool; in large portions of the lake, life is no longer supported. Today at least 350 million people live in water-stressed or water-scarce areas (Moffett 1994, 126; Ehrlich and Ehrlich 1990, 70). The worldwide water supply predicted for the year 2000 is shown in figure 14.6.

The marine life that is such an important part of the human food supply is threatened as well. Because of pollution and overfishing, the Black Sea catch of edible fish has nosedived from a high of eight hundred thousand tons as recently as 1988 to a low of one hundred thousand tons in 1993, with even smaller catches

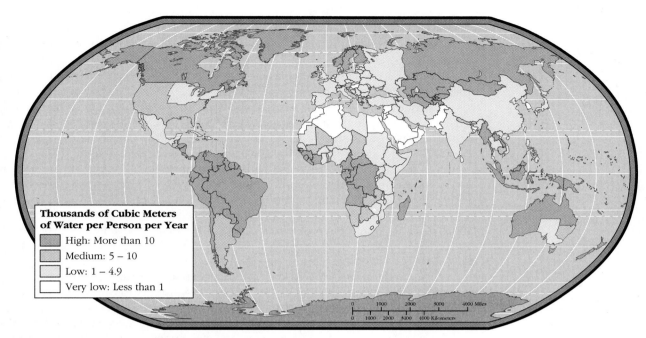

Figure 14.6 Per Capita Water Availability in the Year 2000
Source: Based on Council on Environmental Quality, *Global 2000 Report* (Washington, D. C.: U.S. Government Printing Office, 1981).

predicted for the future. Within that harvest, the proportion of desirable eating fish to low-value fish such as sprat and anchovies has shifted radically: in 1950 the desired, and thus profitable, fish accounted for more than two-thirds of the catch, while today they account for less than one-fourth. Many of the most desirable fish—bluefish, mackerel, and bonito—are not even caught today, the apparent victims of terrible overfishing (Montalbano 1994). This seems to be a global trend.

Misjudgment and mismanagement of water resources is another major source of concern. For example, the Aral Sea in the former Soviet Union was once the fourth-largest inland sea in the world and the site of a rich fishing industry. Today, because so much of the water that once fed the sea was diverted in an attempt to irrigate cotton growing in the nearby desert, the lake itself has become largely a desert. Its shoreline has now receded some twenty-five miles, and despite desperate efforts to dig a canal, most of its fishing fleet now lies stranded in glistening fields of salty sands once covered by blue waters (Gore 1993, 100).

United States Vice President Al Gore, who consulted with a "Who's Who" group of environmentalists to write his *Earth in the Balance* (1993), identified a series of what he termed "strategic," or global, long-range threats to the world's water supply. The five major problems that he discusses are the possible redistribution of the world's relatively small freshwater supplies because of global warming; the rise of sea levels with its concomitant threat to human and wildlife habitats; changes in land use patterns, especially deforestation, that threaten both the "filtering" of water and the hydrologic pattern of clouds and rain; industrial and chemical pollution; and the rapid population growth that puts increasing pressure on often fragile water supplies (Gore 1993, 100–112).

Rainforests

Deforestation, particularly destruction of the world's rainforests, is also viewed as a major global ecological problem. Rainforests play a major role in the global environment, absorbing large amounts of carbon dioxide and releasing vast amounts of oxygen to replenish the earth's supply. Excess carbon dioxide, of course, is one of the major suspected culprits in the "greenhouse effect" that may well be increasing the earth's average temperatures, with all kinds of problematic consequences (see discussion later in this chapter). All three major areas of tropical rainforest in the world (see fig. 14.7) are being destroyed today.

It is not surprising that these shrinking rainforests are found in areas of rapidly increasing population and often severe poverty. There seems little doubt that the major factor leading to rainforest destruction is the growth of population and the need of people at the very margin of subsistence to bring more and more land into cultivation. The problem is that despite their appearance of lushness, rainforests actually grow in very poor soil. Once the dense cover of the rainforest is removed, often by burning, the land exposed to both tropical deluge and tropical sun undergoes a process known as laterization: essentially, it is baked into something closely resembling a brick, absolutely worthless for farming and prohibitively expensive to reconvert to useful soil. In addition, the burning of the rainforest, the quickest and most convenient way to clear the land, also throws enormous amounts of carbon dioxide into the atmosphere—and large parts of the rainforest are no longer there to convert the potentially harmful carbon dioxide into much-needed oxygen. It is estimated that the great rainforest of Brazil's Amazon Basin produces as much as 20 percent of the world's oxygen supply—and that rainforest is vanishing at the rate of thousands of acres a day. The destruc-

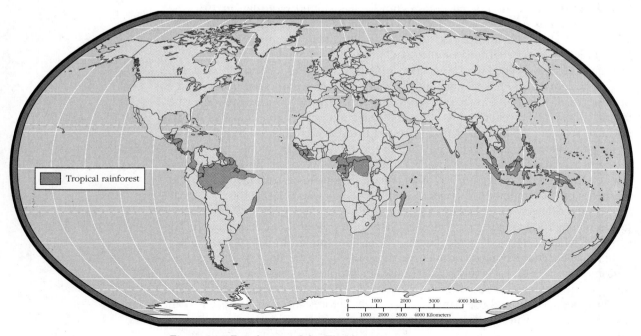

Tropical rainforest

Figure 14.7 **Rainforests of the World**
Source: Adapted from George F. Hepner and Jesse O. McKee, *World Regional Geography: A Global Approach* (St. Paul: West, 1992), 32–33.

tion of the rainforest is having two other major environmental consequences: first, the threat of extinction to thousands of species and the resultant blow to biodiversity, and second, the possibility, perhaps even probability, of the unleashing of deadly new diseases that have remained quiescent in forest reservoirs for thousands of years. We will discuss both of these in some detail later in this chapter.

The pace at which rainforests are disappearing increases every year. The best estimate is that by 1980 the annual rate of deforestation in the tropics, which involved rainforest almost entirely, was 28.2 million acres a year. By the early 1990s, the annual toll of tropical rainforests was an estimated 20.4 million acres— approximately the size of Panama (Kennedy 1993, 91). Central America provides several dramatic examples of deforestation. Since 1950, more than half of Nicaragua's forests have disappeared; El Salvador has less than 2 percent of its original forest left. Honduras, despite some forest reserves, faces the possibility that the current rate of deforestation will leave the country a desert by 2020. Guatemala, which shares with Belize the largest tropical rainforest in the Western Hemisphere outside the Amazon Basin, has lost 31 percent of its rainforest since 1988. One positive note is that while vast expanses of Costa Rica's original rainforest were felled to make room for banana plantations, its three remaining swatches of rainforest are at the heart of a thriving tourist industry, and tourism has replaced bananas as Costa Rica's top industry (Trotta 1995).

In the debate over deforestation, the lines between industrializing and industrialized nations are clearly drawn. Industrialized nations have been quick to criticize policies in industrializing nations that encourage the clearing of rainforest and the resettlement of thousands upon thousands of people. Leaders of the industrial nations decry the elimination of habitat, the diminished capacity of the atmosphere to absorb carbon dioxide and release oxygen, and the laterization of fragile soils that result from the destruction of rainforests and ask, or often demand, that this destruction stop. But leaders of the industrializing nations in which the rainforest largely is located point out that, from their point of view, they have little choice. Rapidly growing populations need land to live on and to cultivate; rainforest products—teak and mahogany—as well as the minerals hidden beneath rainforest canopies provide vital sources of national income; and debt

This area of logged out rainforest in Acre state, Brazil, may represent the future—and a terrible danger to human life.

burdens are pressing and demand repayment. Logging and mining offer quick and comparatively easy answers.

As in so many complex issues, both sides are partially correct. From a global perspective, destruction of the rainforest is a major issue and a terrible problem; from the perspective of an industrializing nation struggling to feed its population and repay huge international loans, destruction of the rainforest is rational. A possible solution to part of this problem, as some have suggested, is for the World Bank and other lending institutions to cancel certain portions of unpaid debt in return for cessation of deforestation.

A Southern Perspective

Alvaro Soto, A Colombian anthropologist, has written a provocative analysis of the environmental problem from a South American perspective. From the Southern point of view, he writes, environmental problems pale in significance in comparison to the problems of poverty. "Air pollution, carbon dioxide emissions, and the loss of biological diversity have little meaning for people who see their children die of malnutrition and who lack even the most basic health care" (Soto 1995, 301). According to Soto, the real problem is that issues such as poverty have become "decoupled" from environmental questions. While the North is concerned about "sustainability" in physical terms, the South sees social and economic issues as far more important. The problem is that the North, with its high-consumption habits, has become "overdeveloped."

Additionally, he writes, Northerners have lost sight of the "global commons," areas not held by any nation-state but shared by all, such as Antarctica, the atmosphere, the deep oceans, and outer space. Treaties now protect these global commons, but Soto believes that the concept of commons should be extended to nationally based resources as well. The natural resources of the world are in effect a common patrimony to be shared by humanity, not divided up on the basis of artificial boundary lines found on a map but not in nature. Southerners, Soto maintains, still recognize the concept of common property and share land and resources within their particular groups, but Northerners are too preoccupied with the idea of the individual and individual rights to recognize the importance of "commons." Thus they have attempted to establish ownership of common areas in order to exploit their resources. Treaties with this purpose have threatened "the right of the Third World to benefit economically from indigenous resources." The Northern motto seems to be, according to Soto, "What's mine is mine, and what's yours is mine" (Soto 1995, 310).

Northern solutions, such as swapping debt for social equity, "merely give the illusion of progress." According to Soto, "in the end . . . a solution to the socio-ecological crisis the world faces comes down to collective action for change taken by people working together." The earth's peoples must learn to communicate with one another in order to foster a truly global community. Only transnational exchange of ideas, cultures, and knowledge will end the present era of cultural isolation and permit the development of strategies for sustainable development (Soto 1995, 316–17).

Ozone

High in the earth's atmosphere, a thin layer of ozone filters the sun's rays, taking out much of the ultraviolet radiation that could be so harmful if it were to strike the earth and its inhabitants directly and unfiltered. However, recent scientific studies have identified two major problems in the earth's ozone layer: a perceptible thinning of the layer, and an actual hole in the ozone layer itself, a substantial area in which there is no ozone at all.

In the Southern Hemisphere, the consequences of the thinning ozone layer are already becoming apparent: Australian children are required by law to wear hats and neckscarves to protect them from ultraviolet radiation; an estimated three-fourths of all citizens over the age of sixty-five in the Australian province of Queensland have some form of skin cancer; in Patagonia, at the very southernmost tip of South America, hunters trap blind rabbits, their eyes overgrown with cataracts, and fishermen catch blind salmon. In the Northern Hemisphere, the ozone layer in winter and early spring is now some 10 percent thinner than it was just forty years ago. Every 1 percent depletion of the ozone shield results in a 2 percent higher exposure to ultraviolet radiation and a 4 percent increase in the incidence of skin cancer. Additionally, ultraviolet radiation is implicated in the suppression of the immune system. Scientists and doctors now advise people in both the United States and Europe to avoid prolonged exposure to the sun, to wear sunscreen lotions, and in effect to change their styles of life in order to prevent skin cancers and unforeseen other problems (Gore 1993, 85–88).

The ozone hole is a recent discovery, but in the decade or so since it was first measured it has grown larger every year. Today it covers an area roughly three times the size of the continental United States, and is still growing. The hole appears during the Southern Hemisphere's spring, in September and October, and has now enlarged to include at least one city, Ushuaia, in Argentina. The Argentinean government now urges all citizens of Ushuaia to avoid being out of doors for two months in order to minimize damage from ultraviolet radiation (Gore 1993, 86–88).

In addition to the direct damage that a thinning ozone layer and an ozone hole can cause to the human population, these two phenomena also are implicated in global warming and in decreased oxidation potential. Long-term effects of increased ultraviolet radiation on genetics, both animal and plant, are unclear—but many scientists warn that they do exist, and that they will be bad.

Ironically, the scientific community in general agrees on the primary cause of these ozone problems: airborne chemicals, particularly chlorofluorocarbons (CFCs) and other chlorine compounds. Chlorines actually bond with ozone molecules to produce new compounds. However, CFCs have been used widely in a variety of industrial processes, and as refrigerants and aerosol propellants as well. In 1987 an international agreement on lessening the use of CFCs was reached, and when it became apparent that the ozone depletion was becoming more rapid, the agreement was modified in 1989. Some eighty nations agreed to stop both production and use of CFCs by 2000, and to establish a fund to help poor nations develop viable alternatives. As Paul and Anne Ehrlich point out, these agreements could well serve as models for dealing with the many other global environmental issues (Ehrlich and Ehrlich 1990, 125–26).

In late 1995 and early 1996, reports by the World Meteorological Organization and by the United States' Climate Monitoring and Diagnostic Laboratory indicated that the ozone layer was continuing to shrink and the hole in the ozone layer had doubled between 1994 and 1995. According to UN scientists, the ozone layer today has diminshed over Antarctica by 35 percent since 1957, and over North America and Europe by 15 percent. Despite the Montreal Protocol of 1987, these scientists say that the depletion of the ozone layer will probably continue

"What would you recommend for the ozone hole?"

Source: Drawing by Weber, ©1992 The New Yorker Magazine, Inc. Reprinted by permission of the publisher.

to accelerate for the next ten years and will not begin to reverse itself until 2040 at the earliest. Not until 2050 to 2070 will ozone levels rise to what they had been in the 1950s, according to the scientists—"if everyone sticks to the rules" (Henson 1995; "New data support fears of a shrinking ozone layer" 1996).

Global Warming: The Greenhouse Effect

greenhouse effect Carbon dioxide and other gases that trap the warmth of the sun's rays on the earth, thus creating the effect of a global greenhouse.

Another major area of concern for ecologists and environmentalists is what is called the **greenhouse effect:** the global production of vast amounts of carbon dioxide and other compounds that trap the warmth created by the sun's rays beneath a blanket of gases, just as a greenhouse traps warmth beneath layers of glass. Over time, according to a number of scientists, the result is a gradual increase in the globe's temperature, or global warming. Humanity's reliance on fossil fuels and wood for energy causes vast amounts of carbon dioxide to be thrown into the atmosphere, and the amount of carbon dioxide is increasing yearly (see fig. 14.8).

Within the past hundred years there has been a measurable increase in the ambient global temperature (see fig. 14.9); however, scientists debate heatedly whether such an increase has any real meaning, given the long-term cycling of warming and cooling trends that have characterized the earth's history. A substantial number of scientists argue that we simply do not know whether global warming is a reality or not; they also argue that the earth possesses a self-correcting homeostatic system, like that of the human being, and that the earth itself will counteract any sort of global warming. Other scientists argue that too little is known about either the possibility or the consequences of global warming to warrant any kind of concerted action. Some scientists also point out that there are relatively few alternatives to fossil fuels, and that some of these alternatives, such as nuclear energy, may well create as many problems as the fossil fuels do. All these scientists, although they come at the question of global warming from different points of view, agree that the problem is not yet clear enough to justify the spending of large amounts of money.

Those scientists who fear global warming, on the other hand, argue that although the problem may be long-term, it is now, in the short term, that the world must take action to head off further global warming before it becomes irreversible. For example, roughly one-third of the entire global population lives along coastal areas on land that would simply disappear should global warming raise ocean temperatures just a few degrees and melt the huge ice blanket that now holds much of the world's water. Those who feel that something must be done now about global warming also argue that simply to pass on such a problem to future generations is morally and ethically suspect. In the issue of global warming, as in so many other of the issues we consider in this chapter, the interface between science and politics has produced an entirely new kind of battleground, in which information is both the best weapon and the most difficult to acquire.

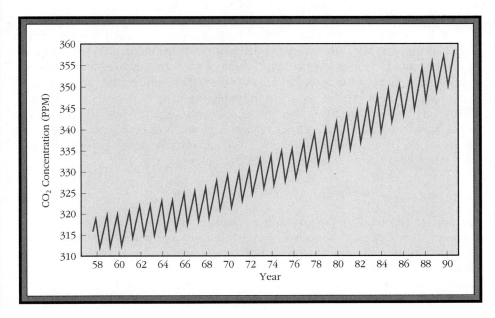

Figure 14.8
Monthly Average Carbon Dioxide Concentration (Mauna Loa Observatory, Hawaii)
Source: Redrawn from Al Gore, *Earth in the Balance: Ecology and the Human Spirit* (New York: Plume/Penguin, 1993), 5.

Figure 14.9
Global Temperature,
1880–1987
Source: Redrawn from Paul R. Ehrlich and Anne H. Ehrlich, *The Population Explosion* (New York: Simon and Schuster, 1990), 78. Data from NASA.

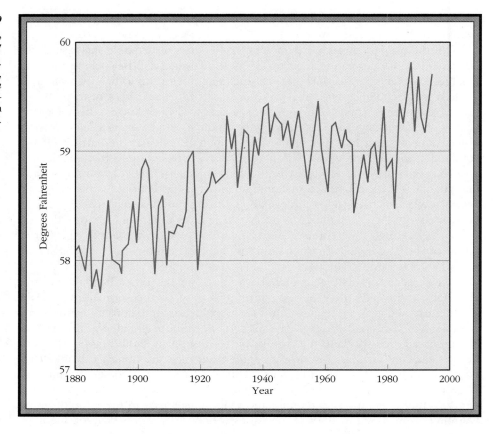

Al Gore points out that the most substantial danger of global warming is not the potential rise of coastal waters, washing away vast numbers of cities, but the potential long-term effect on the climate. He states that "the real danger from global warming is not that the temperature will go up a few degrees, it is that the whole global climate system is likely to be thrown out of whack" (Gore 1993, 97).

In the summer of 1996 a new United Nations report warned that serious public health threats—not only increased deaths from heat but also the exposure of more and more people to "tropical" diseases such as malaria—are imminent because of global warming. The report noted that virtually no industrialized nation will meet its goal of reducing the emission of greenhouse gases to their 1990 levels by the year 2000. The UN scientists wrote that while predictions on global warming are fraught with uncertainty and much more research is needed, the risks of a "wait-and-see" approach are dangerous since the potential consequences of inaction are so severe (Cushman 1996).

Extinction and Biodiversity

The surface of our planet teems with millions of different life forms, while millions more live beneath the soils or flourish in river and ocean waters. This biodiversity represents one of the great sources of planetary resilience, but many of these life forms today are threatened by population pressures, deforestation, pollution, global warming, and multiple other woes. Some of these forms we value simply because they exist—lions and elephants, for example. Some, such as the spotted owl, we value because they serve as "indexes" to warn when environmental catastrophe threatens. And many others we are not even aware of. Nonetheless, the rapidly increasing pace of extinction of both plants and animals raises serious concerns for the future.

Extinction itself is a perfectly natural process. In the Darwinian struggle for survival, extinction will always be the fate of a species, as soon as a better-adapted variant of that species appears. Biologists refer to the "background rate" of extinction to describe this expected, and absorbable, yearly loss of species. The planet also has been subject to periodic "great extinctions," such as the sudden disappearance of the dinosaurs about sixty-five million years ago. However, in the last century and a half the pace of extinction has begun to accelerate dramatically (see fig. 14.10), and the mounting destruction of the rainforests has multiplied this rate incredibly. Extinction may be a perfectly natural phenomenon, but more and more, human beings are providing the "first strike" that sets even populous and well-established species on the path to extinction (Raup 1991, 192–93). The main issue is whether this rapidly increasing pace of extinction poses a major threat to humanity, and if so, of what kind.

The "Genetic Library"

Scientists concerned about the rate of extinction and the threat that it poses to biodiversity point out that nature in effect serves as a "genetic library," preserving species of both plants and animals that are not presently used by human beings to any great extent but remain available. Since so much modern agriculture consists of monoculture, that is, the extensive cultivation of a single crop, our entire food supply is vulnerable to a disease or blight that can wipe out that single crop.

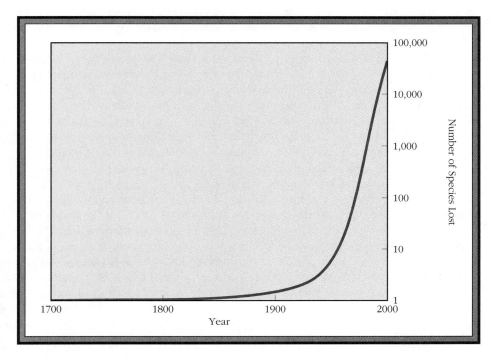

Figure 14.10
Accelerating Extinction Rate
Source: Adapted from Al Gore, *Earth in the Balance: Ecology and the Human Spirit* (New York: Plume/Penguin, 1993), 24.

The most dramatic example of this occurred in Ireland in the middle of the 1800s, when blight wiped out most of the potato crop upon which virtually all Irish people depended for basic sustenance. Half of the population of Ireland died of starvation or of diseases that took advantage of the weakness induced by malnutrition, and half of the remainder were forced to emigrate from Ireland.

Aware of the problems of monoculture and of too great a dependence upon only a handful of specific plants, for a long time scientists have been creating genetic banks: they have deliberately stored seeds or plants closely akin to those being cultivated, so that a major crop threatened by disease could be reinforced quickly by crossbred new strains resistant to that particular disease. Russian geneticist Nikolai Ivanovich Vavilov concluded that just twelve genetic homelands account for virtually all of the food plants consumed. Today, geneticists comb through these homelands trying to find genetic relatives of present crops in order to guard against future disaster. Scientists hold their task as guardians of genetic diversity in such high regard that during World War II, Russian scientists in Leningrad actually starved to death while safeguarding substantial supplies of grains that they were saving as part of the world's genetic bank (Gore 1993, 85).

However, no matter how carefully such genetic banks are maintained, nature itself is the most generous source of unexploited genetic material, and much of this genetic bonanza has a specific environment: the rainforest that is being so profligately destroyed. Estimates are, for example, that three out of every four bird species live in the rainforest, and that as much as 90 percent of the planet's total genetic pool lies within the rainforest. One-third of all modern medicines trace their origins to rainforest plants and shrubs, and scientists fear that the destruction of the rainforest potentially wipes out thousands of drugs that could combat cancer or any of the other lethal diseases still confronting us. Scientists argue that as many as 25 percent of the total number of species that existed in 1985 will be extinct by 2015 if the present trend of deforestation continues (Miller, Reid, and Barber 1991, 79). Fewer than 10 percent of the plants that now exist in the rainforest have been screened to discover whether they contain lifesaving compounds, and many are disappearing so rapidly that we may well never know (Chadwick 1994, 154).

There has in fact been some progress in dealing with this issue of biodiversity. For example, international efforts have begun to explore the possibility of using "old" plants to serve new purposes, such as planting the amaranth grain of the American Indians, which is significantly higher in protein than wheat or other "European" grains. While only twenty-five varieties of potato now are cultivated commercially, the Potato Institute just outside Lima, Peru maintains more than 3,500 varieties of potatoes. The International Rice Institute in the Philippines not only nurtured the green revolution of the 1970s but also preserves tens of thousands of genetically different strains of rice.

In addition, treaties now limit the annual fishing catch, as scientists estimate that world fisheries have virtually reached the point of no return. Whales of all sorts are protected by international treaties, although enforcement of such treaties is at best difficult. Large animal species threatened by extinction have come under the protection of several agreements, including a vital Convention on International Trade in Endangered Species of Wild Fauna and Flora (CITES) agreement that bans trade in such goods as elephant ivory, leopard pelts, and rhinoceros horn. Individual nations such as the United States have enacted endangered species laws. However, such laws are coming under increased attack by workers who consider themselves "endangered species" and by property owners who regard them as interferences with their property rights. Given various pressing economic motives, particularly the steadily rising demand for more cropland, more grazing land, and more land for human habitation, the balance between mankind and all other species continues to tilt toward mankind, at the price of steadily increasing extinctions.

In a recent study of biodiversity and extinction, noted paleoanthropologist and conservationist Richard Leakey argues against the purely economic view for the preservation of biodiversity; instead, he argues in favor of maximum effort to preserve biodiversity on the grounds of both aesthetics and ethics. We simply enjoy plant and animal life, Leakey maintains, not because of its utilitarian or economic value but because it pleases us; that alone is sufficient reason for careful conservation. Far more important, however, in Leakey's view, is the ethical argument in favor of preserving biodiversity. Earth's biota—its total of lifeforms—is an integrated and interactive whole, and humanity is a part of it. We are not, Leakey writes, "a privileged species that can exploit [the biota] with impunity." Instead, "the recognition that we are rooted in life itself demands that we respect other species, not trample them in blind pursuit of our own ends" (Leakey 1996, 253).

Admittedly, extinction occurs all the time, Leakey writes; there have been, as far as paleozoologists can determine, five great mass extinctions in earth's history. However, in today's world, humans are responsible for some 30,000 species going extinct each year—roughly the same rate of extinction that characterized the five mass extinctions. "The fact that one day *homo sapiens* will have disappeared from the face of the earch does not give us license to do whatever we choose while we are here." In fact, Leakey points out, at the rate species are disappearing today, we may well become both engineers and victims of the sixth great extinction (Leakey 1996, 253).

International Problems

Despite a handful of positive strides forward—most notably the 1992 Earth Summit held at Rio de Janeiro, Brazil—humankind continues to exert enormous pressure on what we only gradually are coming to recognize as a fundamentally fragile, and inextricably intertwined, global ecosystem. As George Moffett observes, "When population growth was slow and other frontiers remained to be conquered, the latitude for bad judgment and bad policy was broad. With populations high, the latitude is shrinking. In the past, the planet forgave [humankind's] mistakes, except in local settings. With over 5 billion people on the earth, it is considerably less forgiving. It is likely to be still less so as the world presses on toward its next 5 billion" (Moffett 1994, 135).

Perhaps the most confounding part of the environmental crisis is how easily these problems leap international borders. Industrial pollution in Switzerland fouls the Rhine estuary in Holland. Acid rain from the American Great Lakes area causes the death of fish in Canadian lakes. Radiation from the Chernobyl accident drifts from Ukraine across all of Europe. And degradation of the rainforests with their tremendous biodiversity and oxygen production will have effects far beyond the borders of the tropical nations that contain them. Clearly, international cooperation, perhaps at the cost of somewhat diminished sovereignty, will be vital. Existing treaties must be expanded and new ones concluded in order to meet these problems.

Disease

Throughout history, disease in all its complex and hideous array has shaped the fate of individuals, of nations, and of civilizations. The plague, often called the "Black Death," eradicated possibly two-thirds of medieval Europe. A savage influenza outbreak that raged from 1918 to 1920 killed more than twenty million people worldwide, a death toll almost three times greater than that of the World War I battlefields. Tuberculosis, the "white plague," once carried off tens of thousands of individuals each year. Smallpox demoralized and decimated the Native Americans, easing the process of Spanish conquest.

In the past few decades the wonders of modern science and medicine have seemed to "conquer" disease: antibiotics and insecticides have attacked microbes and their chief means of spreading, while vaccines have protected individuals against most of the ancient scourges—smallpox, yellow fever, and polio—and dramatically lowered the childhood toll of measles, mumps, and chickenpox. In this century, death rates have plummeted, longevity expectations soared. For a brief time in the 1980s, scientists and doctors congratulated themselves on virtually having eliminated infectious disease, at least in the industrialized nations, and confidently assumed that within a few years they would be able to accomplish the same magic in the developing world.

However, history tends to have teeth, and during the past decade those teeth have taken an enormous chunk out of such confident—some might even say arrogant—self-congratulation. While some ancient diseases have in fact vanished, others are now appearing in more virulent form, many resistant to the pharmacists' toolkit of antibiotics. Perhaps even more frightening is the discovery that as environmental destruction continues, and as a swelling population pushes into rainforests and jungles, new and terrifying diseases have begun to appear.

In this section we will examine three main topics: the eradication of smallpox and other major victories in the global battle against disease, the resurgence of diseases once thought "defeated," and the emergence of new and potentially devastating infectious diseases, such as AIDS, Marburg fever, Lassa fever, and Ebola fever.

Global Triumphs

Great cholera epidemics that swept across Europe in the late nineteenth century led to the formation in 1907 of the Office International d'Hygiène Publique, the first attempt at international cooperation on health issues. When the League of Nations was formed in 1919, it folded this organization into its health organization, and when the United Nations became established in 1946 it in turn almost immediately incorporated its predecessor into the World Health Organization (WHO), established in 1948. The goal of WHO is the attainment by all peoples of the highest possible level of health. To achieve this, it maintains a headquarters in Geneva, Switzerland, and six regional offices. Although it has been criticized for being too technology and drug oriented in its efforts, WHO has made some major steps in improving world health levels (Turshen 1993, 986–87).

Smallpox

WHO's greatest triumph, and one of the great success stories of modern medicine, has been the complete elimination of smallpox from the world. For nearly two millennia after its appearance around 50 A.D., smallpox ravaged populations and changed politics throughout the world. A fifteen-year smallpox epidemic burned its way across the Roman empire from 165 to 180 A.D., killing as much as 35 percent of the population in some areas and seriously weakening the empire. Smallpox carried by Spanish *conquistadores* raced ahead of them in the years after Columbus's first voyage, carried by infected Indians. The two mighty Indian empires that the Spanish faced, the Aztecs of Mexico and the Incas of Peru, felt the force of smallpox years before the Spanish arrived in person. When the Spanish did arrive, they discovered societies ravaged by disease—death rates from smallpox in some Aztec villages ran as high as 50 to 90 percent—and vulnerable to conquest. As many as fifty million Indians died of smallpox and other European diseases in the first century of contact between the Old and the New Worlds (Garrett 1994, 41; Crosby 1972, 35–63).

By the eighteenth century Europeans had discovered primitive vaccines against smallpox, and by the twentieth century smallpox virtually had disappeared in Europe and the Americas. However, it continued as a scourge throughout much of Africa and Asia. In 1958 the Soviet Union proposed a global campaign to eradicate the disease, and the campaign began in earnest in 1967. Teams of intrepid young doctors fanned out across Asia and Africa, seeking regional smallpox epidemics and vaccinating entire populations, sometimes forcibly. In 1977 the last known victim of smallpox on the face of the globe was cured: Ali Maow Maalin of Merka, Somalia. In May 1980 WHO triumphantly proclaimed victory: "the World and all its peoples have won freedom from smallpox." Total victory had cost only three hundred million dollars (Garrett 1994, 40–47).

Today, nearly two decades later, smallpox is still gone. The only samples of the smallpox virus on the face of the earth are confined to a series of test tubes, one set held by the United States Centers for Disease Control and Prevention in Atlanta, Georgia, and the other in Moscow under Russian control. For several years the fate of these vials has been the center of controversy, with some scientists urging that the virus be completely destroyed in order to prevent any accidental (or deliberate) release of the virus against an unprepared human population, and others arguing that the virus must be preserved in case it could be used to understand and prevent future epidemics, not just of smallpox but of similar diseases. As of this writing, the vials containing the virus are scheduled to be destroyed in the summer of 1996, although the scientific debate continues (Siebert 1994).

Global Failures

The successful campaign against smallpox was not duplicated against other major diseases, and in recent years there has been a resurgence of such diseases as malaria, tuberculosis, and a range of sexually transmitted diseases. Dealing with such diseases is extraordinarily difficult today because so many of them are now resistant to the antibiotics that WHO and national medical authorities have relied upon so long.

Malaria

WHO's global campaign against malaria rested on two pillars: the eradication of malaria-carrying mosquitoes through intensive use of pesticides, and the use of drug therapy to eliminate malaria from the bloodstreams of millions of victims.

With the United States as the chief proponent, the malaria eradication campaign began in the mid-1950s with great hope and confidence; Harvard Medical School even eliminated its curriculum on malaria control. However, by 1963, the self-imposed deadline set by world scientific leaders, malaria had been sharply reduced but not eradicated, and enthusiasm for malaria eradication plummeted—along with American funding. Harvard put malaria control back into its medical curriculum. Pesticide-resistant mosquitoes began to appear in large numbers, due at least in part to the Green Revolution with its heavy use of pesticides. And, most ominously, the major drugs used to treat malaria began to lose their effectiveness. By 1975, the worldwide incidence of malaria was two and a half times greater than it had been in 1961, at the highpoint of the antimalaria campaign (Garrett 1994, 47–52).

Malaria now has returned as perhaps an even greater scourge than it was before the global eradication campaign, and has largely transmuted into what doctors refer to as an *iatrogenic disease*: a disease caused by medical treatment. As Laurie Garrett, a careful student of global disease patterns, has observed, "In its well-meaning zeal to treat the world's malaria scourge, humanity had created a new epidemic" (Garrett 1994, 52). In 1990 far more people died of malaria-associated ailments than had in 1960. in 1990 WHO calculated that malaria appeared in more than three hundred million people each year, killing at least 3.5 million and seriously compromising the health of millions more. Transfusions to children suffering from malaria-induced anemia, especially in Africa, became a major means of the transmission of AIDS (which we will discuss later in this chapter). In some African nations the economic toll of malaria mounted to nearly two billion dollars a year. A new strain of malaria, multiply resistant to the entire arsenal of antimalaria drugs, has appeared in Cambodia, and threatens to spread to the rest of Southeast Asia, South Asia, and perhaps even Africa. The economic and human toll of malaria continues to escalate. Moreover, the United States in 1993 slashed its expenditures on malaria control outside of the country (Garrett 1994, 440–56).

Tuberculosis

Another ancient scourge that has made an astonishing comeback in recent years is tuberculosis (TB). The figures are staggering. WHO estimates that in 1993 alone 8.1 million people became infected with TB, and 2.7 million died of the disease; TB is now the world's number one killer among infectious or communicable diseases. According to WHO, approximately one-third of the world's population has been infected by the disease but not yet developed it. The death toll is expected to continue to rise; in the 1990s alone TB is projected to kill some thirty million people. Most cases of tuberculosis are relatively easy to treat with combinations of drugs, but two major problems seem to ensure that TB will become an even more deadly killer in the future. First, 95 percent of all tuberculosis cases today occur in the developing world, where both detection and treatment are difficult. Second, if individuals do not scrupulously adhere to a six- to eight-month regimen, the odds are very high that their tuberculosis will become drug resistant and perhaps even untreatable. However, as one expert writes, "the growing TB epidemic is a classic case of a public health crisis that could be headed off easily and inexpensively. . . . If we ignore the extraordinary opportunity that exists now to fight the epidemic, we will pay a high price in lives and extensive health care costs later" (Platt 1994, 31–34; see also Garrett 1994, 512–28).

Other Diseases

Other multiply resistant strains of bacteria are appearing as well, although they have not yet begun to take on the characteristics of a global epidemic. Nonetheless, the appearance of resistant strains of both streptococcus and staphylococcus germs does not augur well for the future. And the appearance of "flesh-eating bacteria" in several nations is not only gruesome but also frightening.

A number of older diseases also are making new appearances, their arrival underlining the interconnectedness of today's globe and the special problems that it poses. Perhaps most frightening was the outbreak of pneumonic plague, a close relative of the Black Death, in India in 1995. Within a few days of reports of its initial outbreak in one city, at least four other Indian cities, some of them hundreds of miles away, were also reporting cases of the plague. Clearly, the disease had spread so rapidly because of the relative ease of transportation between India's large cities. Indian scientists eventually concluded that this was pneumonic plague, far more virulent than the bubonic plague known as the Black Death; unlike bubonic plague, which is spread only by bites from infected fleas, pneumonic plague is airborne and spreads very rapidly. More than one thousand people were infected in the city of Surat, and at least fifty-six died (Hazarike 1995; "India Plague: It Was Pneumonic" 1995). In an apparently unrelated outbreak, several hundred cases of bubonic plague, causing at least twenty-two deaths, had occurred in Zimbabwe in the fall of 1994 ("Plague Kills Twenty-Two in Zimbabwe" 1994).

Newly Emerging Diseases

As if the catalogue of revitalized diseases were not dismaying enough, we today confront an entirely new array of diseases, most having appeared within the last twenty years and many incredibly deadly. Some of these are depicted in figure 14.11. In this section we will look at one specific disease, AIDs, and at a series of other diseases of terrible virulence, the hemorrhagic fevers that have emerged in Africa.

AIDS

The Past.   The story of the early history of AIDs is fairly familiar, so we will simply recapitulate it briefly here. In the late 1970s and early 1980s doctors worldwide began seeing the blossoming of what had been relatively rare diseases like Kaposi's sarcoma and pneumocystic pneumonia. As they investigated further, they discovered that these diseases were occurring in patients whose immune systems had virtually disappeared. However, in the United States and Europe, these strange symptoms initially were confined to homosexuals, intravenous drug abusers, and hemophiliacs infected through blood and clotting factor transfusion. By 1983, as doctors were beginning to identify the link between infection by the human immunodeficiency virus (HIV) and the outbreak of full-blown acquired immunodeficiency syndrome (AIDS) in the United States and France, a similar outbreak of the disease was beginning to sweep across Central Africa. Known as "Slim" or "the slimming disease" because of the extreme emaciation of its victims, this African version of the disease occurred in heterosexuals and in children. By the mid-1980s, several frightening aspects of the disease were obvious: although

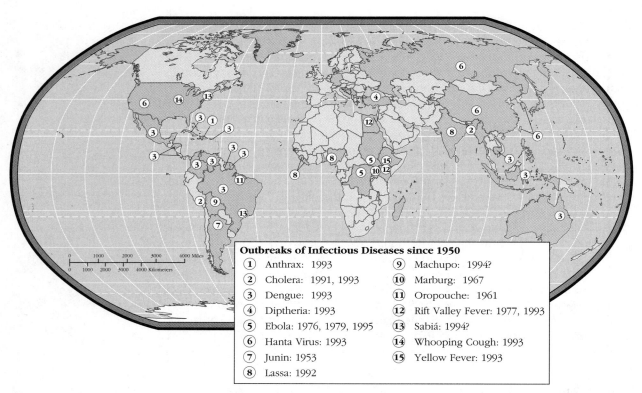

Outbreaks of Infectious Diseases since 1950

①	Anthrax: 1993	⑨	Machupo: 1994?
②	Cholera: 1991, 1993	⑩	Marburg: 1967
③	Dengue: 1993	⑪	Oropouche: 1961
④	Diptheria: 1993	⑫	Rift Valley Fever: 1977, 1993
⑤	Ebola: 1976, 1979, 1995	⑬	Sabiá: 1994?
⑥	Hanta Virus: 1993	⑭	Whooping Cough: 1993
⑦	Junin: 1953	⑮	Yellow Fever: 1993
⑧	Lassa: 1992		

Figure 14.11 **Infectious Disease Outbreaks**
Source: Adapted from Robert S. Boyd, "Threat of Disease Growing Serious," *Houston Chronicle,*
April 10, 1995 (data from Centers for Disease Control and Prevention, 1994); Geoffrey Cowley, "Out-
break of Fear," *Newsweek,* May 22, 1995. Data from Centers for Disease Control and Prevention,
World Health Organization, Pan American Health Organization.

AIDS was relatively difficult to acquire—it was transmitted through bodily fluids
by sexual acts, by transfusion, from mother to child or by accident—it was spreading rapidly, and it was 100 percent lethal. The HIV virus might incubate in a
human body for a decade or more; this made it inordinately difficult to stop the
transmission of HIV, since so many people did not realize they were infected and
took no precautions to prevent infecting others. But once it converted into full-
blown AIDs, only a downward spiral into a deadly series of diseases awaited the
patient.

Furthermore, the HIV virus mutated so rapidly and so efficiently that developing a vaccine to prevent infection appeared to be an impossible task. Consequently, and hesitantly, the international health community began to focus on
ways to prevent transmission of the disease rather than to vaccinate against it,
although the search for a vaccine still goes on. The hesitancy arose largely from
the fact that in the United States at least, AIDS seemed largely a disease of homo-
sexual men or intravenous drug users, and neither group possessed much in the
way of political leverage. The initial AIDS outbreak coincided with the years of
the Ronald Reagan presidency, years in which extreme conservatives and religious leaders argued that to some extent the people who came down with AIDS
deserved it. Reagan administration support for AIDS research and AIDS education
was very slow in coming.

· The source of the disease is still hotly debated today, and so are the projected numbers. The evidence points to Central Africa as the initial source of the outbreak, and to the strong possibility that HIV originally infected monkey populations before becoming one of several recent viruses to cross from one species to another. Because of the political ramifications—what nation or people would want to be blamed for starting such an awful disease?—the question of the source of AIDS has been relatively downplayed. However, there is little question about why it was able to spread so rapidly in Africa and the United States during its incubation period in the late 1970s. In Central Africa, chaos prevailed as the result of multiple wars, major dislocations of populations, ballooning urban populations, and continuing poverty. The highway that stretches across the heart of the continent, from Kinshasa, Zaire, to Mombasa and Dar es Salaam, Tanzania, provided a clear path for the rapid spread of the disease, and transcontinental airline flights permitted its escape from the African continent into the rest of the world. In the United States, the "gay revolution" with its accompanying sexual freedom provided multiple opportunities for the transmission of the disease, as did intravenous drug users' habit of sharing needles.

The Present.   AIDS numbers are daunting (see fig. 14.12). The Global AIDS Policy Coalition, consisting primarily of former members of WHO's Global Project on AIDS, has published grim statistics on the spread and impact of the disease. By 1992, they calculate, nearly 13 million people worldwide had been infected with HIV, and 2.7 million had already developed AIDs. However, they project that by the year 2000, at least 38 million people worldwide would be HIV positive, and that number could range as high as 110 million. Just in the decade from 1990 to 2000, the Coalition projects, AIDS may kill as many as 25 million people (Garrett 1994, 486–87).

WHO's figures are scarcely more comforting. In 1992 WHO estimated the number of AIDS cases at 2 million and calculated that 30 to 40 million people will carry HIV by 2000. So far, according to WHO, the disease is most deadly in the United States and ten African nations, where one-third of AIDS patients are children. In the United States and these African nations, AIDS is the leading cause of death among people aged 20 to 44 (Schoepf 1993, 13–15). And these figures have been compiled largely without factoring in the AIDS epidemic that is beginning to sweep Thailand and other Southeast Asian nations, without much in the way of statistics from India, and with no real statistical evidence, yet, of the spread of AIDS in Russia and China.

The Future.   The consequences of the AIDS epidemic promise to be horrific. Some estimates are that by 2020 the incidence of AIDS in some African nations may reach 80 percent of the population. Direct and indirect costs in Africa, calculated by the United Nations, have already reached $40 billion, and the increasingly steep curve of infection casts serious doubts on Africa's ability to continue economic and thus social and political development. Life expectancies are expected to plummet; without AIDS, life expectancy in Uganda would be 59 by the year 2010; with AIDS, it is predicted to drop to 32 years. The U.S. Census Bureau calculates that in just sixteen nations, primarily in Africa, by 2000 there will be 121 million fewer people than were expected before the onset of AIDs.

Some experts have even predicted net population losses in Central and Eastern Africa, despite the still alarming birth and fertility rates. As many as 35 million AIDS orphans are expected by the year 2000 (Garrett 1994, 486-87). According to

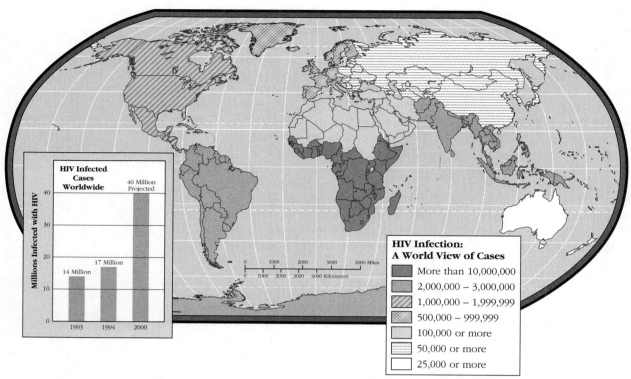

Figure 14.12 **The Demographics of Death**
Since the mid-1970s, HIV has infected more than 17 million people, most of them in Africa. With the epidemic now exploding in Asia, experts say the number of infections worldwide will exceed 40 million by the year 2000.
Source: Adapted, from *Newsweek,* August 22, 1994. Data from World Health Organization.

the United Nations, the populations of Zimbabwe and Zambia will be 6.9 percent smaller than would be expected without AIDS, and the population of Uganda will be 6.1 percent smaller than expected. As a result of the AIDS epidemic, life expectancy in at least four African nations—Zimbabwe, Zambia, Kenya, and Uganda—will be five years lower because of AIDS. In an understatement, the UN notes that "coupled with the demand for resources induced by continued population growth, the strain induced by the AIDS epidemic will present difficult challenges in the next decades" ("AIDS Has a Devastating Toll in Africa but Population Growth Rates Remain High" 1995).

The virus has now spread to Asia, with potentially catastrophic consequences. In early 1996 WHO epidemiologists predict that as many as twelve million people in Asia may carry the HIV virus by the year 2000. The number of people with HIV in Asia exceeded that of Africa in 1995, and epidemiologists fear that by the turn of the century the number of people infected in Asia annually will exceed the number for the rest of the world. Estimates put the percentage of infected individuals at more than 2 percent of the adult population of Thailand, more than 1 percent of the populations of Myanmar and Cambodia, and around 1 percent of the populations of India, Malaysia, and Brunei. By 2000, India alone may have as many as 2 million HIV-infected people (Shenon 1996).

The Mysterious Fevers: Marburg, Lassa, Ebola

Before and while AIDS was cutting its terrible swath through entire populations, much smaller groups were coming down with, and often succumbing to, a series of new and frightening diseases classified together as **hemorrhagic fevers.** These diseases, none of which has yet broken out into a full-scale epidemic, appear to be caused by viruses that, like HIV, have managed to cross the species barrier from monkey to man; the fear is that they, and perhaps their even more lethal cousins, lurk in rainforests simply waiting for the human population to intrude far enough into the rainforest to become massively, epidemically infected.

hemorrhagic fevers Diseases that incapacitate and usually kill their victims through hemorrhaging from the body orifices.

Marburg. The first of these fevers to be identified was Marburg fever, which erupted in Europe in 1967 among workers who were monkey caretakers for pharmaceutical companies, their doctors, and a veterinarian and his wife; although the disease first erupted in the city of Marburg, Germany, it also was reported in Frankfurt, Germany, and in Belgrade, Yugoslavia. It was a vicious disease, causing high fever, several breakage of capillaries that turned the entire body red, neurological symptoms, comas, and bleeding from every opening in the body. Ultimately, seven of the thirty-one who contracted the disease died of it. Extensive research showed that the Marburg virus was something entirely new; not even the largest library of viral agents could find anything that matched it. Warnings were issued to take greater care when dealing with monkeys, but little else seemed possible. Marburg surfaced briefly again in 1975, when a young Australian, his girlfriend, and a nurse all contracted the disease while they were in South Africa. The young man died; the two women lived.

Then Marburg seemed to vanish. But it probably did not. Epidemiologists believe that the virus simply retreated back into its reservoir, an insect or mammal in which it could live without harming its host until some time in the future when it again came into contact with human beings and the virus could "jump its ship for the new, highly susceptible vessel, producing an epidemic" (Garrett 1994, 53–59).

Lassa. The other two frightening hemorrhagic fevers that emerged as "new" diseases in Africa followed similar courses. Lassa fever, caused by a different virus but similar in its effects to Marburg, emerged in Lassa, Nigeria, in 1969; by the mid-1970s, virologists were convinced that the hemorrhagic fever was more or less endemic in areas of Africa, including parts of Nigeria, Sierra Leone, and Liberia, and that the African population often mistakenly dismissed it as malaria or another kind of fever. The virus was spread by contaminated rodent droppings or by direct blood contact—a slip of a surgeon's knife during an autopsy, a nurse accidentally sticking herself with an infected needle. And Lassa was lethal; about 16 percent of its victims died horrifying deaths, hemorrhaging from mouth and anus and nose and eyes and every other body opening. However, caught and diagnosed in its earliest stages, Lassa was treatable. Somewhat like Marburg, Lassa retreated back into its reservoir and dropped off the international epidemiologists' radar in the mid-1970s (Garrett 1994, 71–99).

Ebola. Lassa fever's place in the catalogue of "new" and awful hemorrhagic fevers was quickly taken by Ebola fever, deadliest of the three. The fever first emerged in Zaire in 1976, with its primary locus at a missionary hospital run by Belgian nuns. Because they had so few medical supplies and virtually no medical

A Zairian soldier (center) and a health worker carry a patient infected with the Ebola virus as a doctor (left) follows them during a recent outbreak of the virus in Kikwit.

training, the sisters used and reused hypodermic syringes—sometimes more than four hundred times. And in so doing they transmitted the lethal Ebola virus from person to person at the hospital. In addition to causing high fever and hemorrhage, the virus also attacked connective tissue, so that human faces became slack masks from which "ghost eyes" stared. Of those infected by direct blood-to-blood transmission, either through needles or through direct contamination from the blood of an infected individual, the death rate was above 90 percent. A somewhat less deadly strain of the virus also attacked large numbers of individuals in Sudan (Garrett 1994, 100–152).

A genuinely frightening point in the evolution of these filoviruses (Marburg and Ebola are both caused by long, threadlike viruses) came in 1989, when monkeys imported for research from the Philippine Islands by a firm in Reston, Virginia, less than twenty miles from Washington, D.C., began to manifest signs of a virulent fever. United States Army veterinarians quickly established that the sick monkeys were in fact suffering from Ebola fever, and mounted an expedition to kill all the infected or possibly infected monkeys and completely decontaminate the building in which they were housed. Luckily, this particular form of Ebola, which was an airborne version of the virus, with the possibility of spreading as fast as the common cold or the flu, did not attack human beings. But no one had suspected that monkey populations in the Philippines could harbor Ebola. And no one was prepared to deal with a catastrophic outbreak of Ebola in the United States (Preston, 1994).

When Ebola erupted again in Zaire in early 1995, the epidemic created worldwide headlines, became the subject of television programs and an Internet home page, and had Americans questioning whether they too could fall prey to this disease. In the United States, news of the Ebola outbreak coincided with the opening of *Outbreak,* a film about a contagious tropical disease. Newsmagazines and newspapers ran large headlines: "Killer Outbreak in Zaire" (SoRelle 1995),

"Return to the Hot Zone" (Lemonick 1995), "Outbreak of Fear: Killer Virus Emerges after Eighteen-Year Hiatus" (Cowley, 1995), and "Horror in the Hot Zone" (Ransdell 1995). A shiver of fear raced through populations in and beyond Africa, despite the difficulty of contracting Ebola except through contact with infected bodily fluids. Ebola was reported in the Ivory Coast in December 1995 and in Gabon in February 1996. In the spring of 1996 as well, Ebola was found in monkeys in Texas, but the disease did not spread to humans. (Koffi 1995; "WHO monitors Ebola outbreak in Gabon").

Several articles highlighted the role of the Centers for Disease Control and Prevention (CDC) in keeping infectious diseases out of the United States and its current funding woes. According to CDC officials, the Ebola crisis came at the same time the agency received requests for help on other hemorrhagic fevers in Bolivia, Nigeria, and the United Arab Emirates (Altman 1995). The former director of the National Center for Infectious Diseases at the CDC, Doctor Frederick Murphy, points out that CDC funding for infectious disease research and control has remained constant for the last twelve years; this constitutes a 50 percent reduction in real dollars because of inflation. And funding for the U.S. Army units so vital in dealing with the Reston Ebola outbreak has dwindled substantially as well (Murphy 1995; see futher McCormick and Fisher-Hoch, 1996).

Although the likelihood of Ebola's spreading to the U.S. remains small despite jet travel, scientists warn that the future could bring more problems. In the long run, they explain, new diseases will continue to occur as people, who are generally poor and ill equipped to deal with them, move inexorably into habitats such as the rainforests. As one scientist warns, human beings are moving into the Amazon rainforest at the same time that they are relocating to the rainforests of Africa. "They are going to come into contact with these new viruses," he warns, "and the viruses will infect people" (SoRelle 1995). Recent research has linked human Ebola virus to chimpanzees—most of the people who contracted the disease in Gabon had eaten meat from a dead chimpanzee several children had discovered—but scientists believe that there is still a missing link in the transmission process. Chimpanzees are too susceptible to Ebola to be the ultimate reservoir of the disease—they die as quickly as infected human beings—and research is now centered on the possibility that a small, forest-dwelling animal, perhaps a rodent, harbors the virus (Purvis 1996).

More to Come?

Writers and virologists look at the emergence of these new and often deadly viruses—HIV, Marburg, Lassa, Ebola, and multiple others—as the direct result of population growth and spread. As we have mentioned, they believe that these viruses live in reservoirs, insect or mammal or primate, deep in the world's rainforests. As the ecology of the rainforests is disrupted, the viruses escape from their reservoirs, at least for a while, and burn their way through human populations. And then they retreat to the rainforest, to await their next opportunity to escape and multiply. According to Richard Preston, who wrote a truly hair-raising account of the close brush with Ebola catastrophe in Virginia's rolling hills, "The emergence of AIDS, Ebola, and any number of other rainforest agents appears to be a natural consequence of the ruin of the tropical biosphere. The emerging viruses are surfacing from ecologically damaged parts of the earth. Many of them come from the tattered edges of tropical rain forest, or they come from tropical savanna that is being settled rapidly by people." The tropical rainforests, he writes, are "the deep reservoirs of life on the planet, containing most of the world's plant and animal species"; viruses simply constitute some of those life forms. Preston adds that "the AIDS virus and other emerging viruses are surviving the wreck of the tropical biosphere because they can mutate faster than any changes taking place in their ecosystems." He continues, "AIDS might not be Nature's preeminent display of power. Whether the human race can actually maintain a population of five billion or more without a clash with a hot virus remains an open question. . . . The answer lies hidden in the labyrinth of tropical ecosystems. AIDS is the revenge of the rain forest. It is only the first act of revenge" (Preston 1994, 287–89).

Preston's assessment may be overly dramatic, but it is well worth mulling over. Alison Jacobson, a South African virologist, echoes these predictions. Citing not only Ebola, Lassa, and Marburg but also Rift Valley fever and dengue hemorrhagic fever, Jacobson states that such viruses "cycle throughout their ecological niches and are encountering opportunities in our modern world to spread with a frightening vigour." Jacobson warns that public health crises generally have two stages: "I don't believe you," and "Why didn't you tell me?" Global trade has contributed to the spread of disease as well; for example, the Asian Tiger mosquito, a vector for dengue and dengue hemorrhagic fever, came to Houston, Texas, in a shipment of used tires from Asia and is now established in seventeen states (Jacobson 1995).

According to Jacobson, we are seeing today "spectacular examples of emergence and re-emergence [of viruses] resulting from innocent environmental manipulation or natural environmental change." Seven major trends contribute to the emergence or reemergence of viruses: human intrusion into tropical forests, deforestation, irrigation, uncontrolled urbanization, increased long-distance air travel, long-distance animal transportation, and new routing of long-distance bird migration. "Given the diverse nature of threats from infectious diseases, it is not adequate merely to face each crisis as it emerges, as this may provide a strategy which proves to be too little and too late." To head off catastrophe, we need to "address the issue of infectious disease within the context of shared environmental responsibility." Only a "holistic approach," including improved health care and socioeconomic improvement, can enable us to cope with these viruses (Jacobson 1995).

The Emergence of International Cooperation

Even as the debate over the severity of these intertwined problems—population, the environment, and disease—goes on, governments and nongovernmental organizations are beginning to take steps toward dealing with them, steps that often transcend traditional national boundaries and suggest a growing acceptance of the need for multilateral international action.

Some of these steps are coming from what would seem to be unlikely sources. The United States Department of Defense (DoD), for example, is attempting to carve out a major role for itself in addressing environmental issues, a role far beyond that traditionally claimed by the Army Corps of Engineers. The sources of this new role are multiple. In part, DoD concern with the environment clearly stems from its own miserable record in dealing with sensitive environmental issues such as nuclear waste and hazardous materials; currently, 10 percent of the EPA Superfund sites, the most dangerous places in the United States, are at DoD bases and other DoD locations. Estimated DoD cleanup costs range from a low of twenty-three billion dollars to a staggering high of four hundred billion dollars (Butts 1993, 4–5). Also, there is increasing recognition that environmental issues easily may become national security issues. "For many LDCs [developing nations], environmental issues are survival interests and therefore potential sources of regional conflict" (Butts 1993, vii). And cynics point out that with the Soviet Union no longer *the* enemy, an environmental role gives DoD a whole new dimension for activity, a whole new reason for being, and a whole new justification for larger budgets. Regardless of the causes, the DoD has indeed been increasingly active in environmental projects. In April 1996 United States Secretary of State Warren Christopher announced that, in the future, environmental issues would play a major role in American foreign policy. According to Christopher, global peace and national security depend on the health of the world's natural resources, and diplomats must protect those resources. "We are determined," he said, "to put environmental issues where they belong: in the mainstream of American foreign policy" (Clifford 1996; see further Greenhouse 1995).

Other examples of increasing international environmental awareness abound. Recently, for example, the World Bank has been extending larger and larger loans to enable developing nations to deal with both environmental problems and disease. Long a target of critics who allege that World Bank lending policies have tended to worsen rather than cure environmental problems (see French 1994, as well as this chapter's boxed feature), the Bank has lent more than $750 million since 1986 to help nations battle the AIDS epidemic. These loans stem from both recognition of the dire economic consequences of populations under attack from AIDS and, according to Bank officials, genuine humanitarian concerns. "What strikes the visitor [to areas hardest hit by AIDS] is the human cost," says Jean-Louis Lamboray, a senior public health specialist with the World Bank. Lamboray cites a comment made by a public health official from Zambia to support his statement. "I won't bother you with more figures," the Zambian official told him at a recent AIDS conference. "Let me tell you one thing. Our social life is limited to visits to hospitals, funeral halls, and cemeteries" (Brown 1994).

Finally, there are more and more treaties and international organizations in place to try to ensure global cooperation on economic and population matters. Despite an often rancorous debate, the 1994 United Nations Conference on Population, Women, and Development in Cairo produced a declaration pledging its signatories to pursue policies intended to control population and empower women. International agreements such as the Convention on International Trade in Endangered Species of Wild Fauna and Flora (CITES) are attempting, not always successfully, to preserve animals such as the elephant, tiger, and leopard by using economic leverage, prohibiting the international trade in ivory and spotted cat skins. The success has been mixed (Zaneski 1994). In late 1993 and 1994, four major international agreements on environmental issues came into being: the Law of the Sea Treaty, the Biodiversity Convention, the Climate Convention, and the Ban on Hazardous Waste Exports (Ayres 1994, 6).

However, a short piece in an environmentally activist magazine, *World Watch,* reveals unintentionally but clearly the hazards that still await such international agreements. Proclaiming that "momentum seems to be swinging rapidly toward greater international cooperation in the battle to reverse environmental and human decline," the magazine bills the agreements (on the front cover) as a "grand slam for global governance," and the headline of the article is "Global Governance Gaining" (Ayres, 6). While these may seem triumphal moments for

Villains in Pinstripes?

Environmental activists identify the World Bank as one of the major villains in the ongoing struggle over sustainable development. These critics increasingly see development itself, a major goal of the World Bank, as the primary source of a slowly unfolding global ecological crisis. "Massive internationally financed development schemes [are] increasingly unleashing ecological destruction and social upheaval" over large areas (Rich 1994, 3).

First, critics charge that Bank-funded development projects disrupt traditional social patterns and cause the physical as well as the economic dislocation of massive numbers of people. In Thailand, for example, according to the critics, nearly ten million people have been dislocated by Bank-funded projects, primarily the logging of the teak forests. In India, officially sponsored development projects have turned more than twenty million people, most of them already desperately poor, into virtual nomads and refugees.

Furthermore, critics charge that the World Bank, anxious to find projects to fund and thus justify its own existence, has favored development at the expense of the environment. Although the Bank has guidelines designed to protect the environment, critics allege that in its haste to make loans, and to guide developing nations to profitable export-oriented projects (so that they can repay their loans), Bank officials have simply ignored their own guidelines. The result has been, according to the critics, ecological devastation incurred by Bank-supported projects such as hydroelectric power dams and logging operations, and by its encouragement of monoculture (the dedication of most productive agricultural land

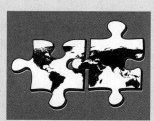

GLOBAL PERSPECTIVES

to a single, exportable commodity). Bank loans have accelerated the destruction of huge swaths of rainforest in Brazil, as well as in Africa and Southeast Asia. Additionally, the critics say, Bank policies have played a key role in the ongoing extermination of more than half the world's species by helping to cause desertification and global warming, as well as rainforest destruction.

Critics also level political charges at the Bank, accusing it of promiscuously lending to authoritarian regimes instead of encouraging democracy. The Bank has substituted "technical rationality and procedural correctness for moral responsibility" (Rich 1994, 154). Thus it has become "a microcosm of a larger global political and economic crisis, a crisis of accountability and sustainability" (Rich 1994, 192).

World Bank officials, not surprisingly, reject such sweeping criticism, pointing to the general rise in global standards of living, income, and mortality rates since 1960 as proof that Bank policies have done a lot of good. (They also point out that Bank loans account for only 3.1 percent of net resources flowing into developing countries.) In the long run, the Bank argues, there will always be hard decisions and tensions between development and the environment, and the Bank has increased dramatically its loans for environmental projects. Finally, the Bank admits that it has made mistakes in the past, but insists that it can learn and change (Lateef 1995).

And an objective observer, writing on the Bank's fiftieth anniversary, concludes that although the Bank is not guilty exactly as charged, change is necessary. The World Bank's "ends and means [must be] radically revised to keep pace with a changing world [and] the time to start changing is now" (Owen 1994).

environmentalists, they are described in terms sure to raise nationalist hackles all over the world among those who cherish the sovereignty of individual nations and are profoundly suspicious of what Clare Boothe Luce once referred to as "globaloney."

There indeed have been important, although halting, steps toward addressing the problems enumerated in this chapter, as well as other major global problems, such as crime, the drug trade, terrorism, and human rights. But virtually all attempts to deal with these problems on a global scale raise serious issues about the nature and continuation of sovereignty. Despite all the talk about "Spaceship

Earth" and the obvious fraility of the global ecosystem as observed from space, powerful forces of nationalism still stand in the way of concerted global effort to deal with these problems, as do North-South suspicions and the fear among developing nations that the developed nations of the world will use environmental issues to keep them in a permanent state of colonialism. However, no matter how skeptical one might be of any individual piece of evidence, the picture of the human future pieced together from all these sources is a grim one, unless unprecedented levels of international cooperation can be achieved and the global resources of technology, communications, and economics brought into play to deal with these issues.

Summary

Several major issues that face both governments and people are far too complex, and far too widespread, to be solved by individual states. Global cooperation will be essential if these problems are to be solved. While crime, terrorism, drugs, and the refugee crisis are all serious problems, we believe that three closely interlinked problems—population, the environment, and disease—present greater longer-range challenges to both human ingenuity and the ability of governments to work together for the solution of truly global problems.

Population: While the direst predictions of Thomas Malthus about population growth outstripping the food supply have yet to come true, the twentieth century has seen enormous increases in global population, and projections indicate that by the middle of the twenty-first century, population may well outstrip the planet's carrying capacity. Urbanization, concentrating more people on smaller patches of land, accentuates the problems of population growth. However, some critics of the "population explosion" theorists view them as alarmists and place their faith in human ingenuity and technological innovation. Attempts to limit population growth have led to opposition within various religious communities and traditional societies, and also raise serious questions about women's role in society in general.

The Global Environment: Warning flags also are flying about what appears to be accelerated degradation of the environment and destruction of key ecological systems. Problems ranging from water and air pollution to shrinking rainforests and global warming raise serious concerns about the future ability of the environment to sustain human life. However, a substantial number of critics of environmental "alarmism" maintain that it is impossible to extrapolate long-term trends from short-term data; again, such critics believe that technological innovation will more than compensate for "incidental" environmental damage.

Disease: The period since 1945 has seen a mixed bag on the question of disease. A handful of major killer diseases, smallpox primary among them, have vanished or all but vanished as a result of medical advances. However, a series of other diseases once thought conquered—malaria and tuberculosis for example—have proven frighteningly resilient; even more frightening is the resistance of many of these diseases to previously effective treatment. Finally, perhaps as a result of population growth and the resultant push of human beings into previously uninhabited forest areas, a whole new range of diseases has appeared in the last quarter-century, including the almost always lethal AIDS and the often lethal hemorrhagic fevers like Ebola and Lassa.

While it is clear that cooperation on a global scale will be necessary to deal with these three interlinked problems, it is not clear that such cooperation is possible. Complicating matters even more, these problems are related not only to one another but also to such issues as poverty, political instability, and North-South relations.

Key Terms

Fertility rate
Replacement fertility rate
Population momentum
Urbanization

Green revolution
Greenhouse effect
Hemorrhagic fevers

Thought Questions

1. What are the implications of unchecked population growth? What steps can be taken to counter this?
2. What are the most important environmental problems facing today's world? How can they be dealt with?
3. What factors have led to the reemergence of diseases once thought conquered? To the emergence of new diseases? What can be done to deal with these diseases?

References

Adams, Douglas, and Mark Carwardine. *Last Chance to See.* New York: Ballantine, 1990.

"AIDS Has a Devastating Toll in Africa but Population Growth Rates Remain High." United Nations Population Division, Population Information Network, Internet. http://opr.princeton.edu/popindex.htm. Downloaded June 10, 1995.

Altman, Lawrence K. "Agency on Front Line of Virus War is Understaffed, Overwhelmed." *Houston Chronicle,* May 29, 1995.

Antrobus, Peggy. "Women and Development." In Joel Krieger, ed. *The Oxford Companion to World Politics.* New York: Oxford, 1993. 978–80.

Ayres, Ed. "Global Governance Gaining." *Worldwatch* (July/August 1994).

Bailey, Ronald, ed. *The True State of the Planet: Ten of the World's Premier Environmental Researchers in a Major Challenge of the Environmental Movement.* New York: Free Press, 1995.

"Battle of the Bulge." *The Economist* (September 3, 1994): 23–25.

Boyd, Robert S. "Threat of Disease Growing Serious." *Houston Chronicle,* April 10, 1995.

Brown, David. "World Bank Lending Policy Links AIDS, Economic Development." *Houston Chronicle,* November 29, 1994.

Brown, Lester R., *State of the World 1993: A World Watch Institute Report on Progress toward a Sustainable Society.* New York: W. W. Norton, 1993.

———. *State of the World 1994: A World Watch Institute Report on Progress Toward a Sustainable Society.* New York: W. W. Norton, 1994.

———, ed. *The World Watch Reader on Global Environmental Issues.* New York: W. W. Norton, 1991.

Budiansky, Stephen. "Ten Billion for Dinner, Please: With Technology and Free Trade, the Earth Can Defy the Doomsayers—and Feed Twice as Many People." *U.S. News & World Report,* September 12, 1994, 57–62.

Butts, Kent Hughes. *Environmental Security: What Is DoD's Role.* Carlisle, Pa.: Strategic Studies Institute, U.S. Army War College, 1993.

Chadwick, Douglas H. *The Fate of the Elephant.* San Francisco: Sierra Club, 1994.

Choukri, Nazli. "Environmentalism." In Joel Krieger, ed. *The Oxford Companion to Politics of the World.* New York: Oxford, 1993. 216–17.

Clifford, Frank. "Christopher links environmental issues to U.S. foreign policy." *Houston Chronicle.* April 10, 1996.

Cowley, Geoffrey. "Outbreak of Fear." *Newsweek,* May 22, 1995.

Cowley, Geoffrey, and Mary Hager. "The Ever-Expanding Plague: AIDS: Experts Point to Asia as the Next Epicenter." *Newsweek,* August 22, 1994, 37.

Crane, Barbara. "Population Policy." In Joel Krieger, ed. *The Oxford Companion to Politics of the World.* New York: Oxford, 1993.

"Crop Patents Raise Concerns: Killer Virus Emerges after Eighteen-Year Hiatus," Associated Press, November 28, 1994. Prodigy Online.

Crosby, Alfred W., Jr. *The Columbian Exchange: Biological and Cultural Consequences of 1492.* Westport, Conn. Greenwood Press, 1972.

Cushman, John H., Jr. "U.N.: Global Warming Poses Threat to Public Health." *New York Times.* July 8, 1996. Downloaded July 8, 1996. http://www.nytimes.com/7/8/96/first/warming.html

Dalrymple, Dana. "Green Parties." In Joel Krieger, ed. *The Oxford Companion to Politics of the World.* New York: Oxford, 1993. 365–67).

Easterbrook, Gregg. *A Moment on the Earth: the Coming Age of Environmental Optimism.* New York: Penguin, 1995.

"Ebola Haemorrhagic Fever." World Health Organization. Internet. http://www.who.ch/programmes/emc/ebola/ebfact.htm. Downloaded March 20, 1996.

"Ebola Virus Hemorrhagic Fever: General Information." Center for Disease Control/Internet, http://www.cdc.gov/ncidod.htm May 29, 1995.

Ehrlich, Paul R. *The Population Bomb.* New York: Ballantine, 1968.

Ehrlich, Paul R., and Anne H. Ehrlich. *The Population Explosion.* New York: Simon and Schuster, 1990.

Elliott, Michael, and Christopher Dickey. "Body Politics: Population Wars." *Newsweek,* September 12, 1994.

"Food Patents in the Wings." Associated Press, November 28, 1994. Prodigy. Downloaded Nov. 28, 1994.

French, Hillary. "The World Bank: Now Fifty But How Fit?" *Word Watch* (July/August 1994).

Garrett, Laurie. *The Coming Plague: Newly Emerging Diseases in a World Out of Balance.* New York: Farrar, Straus and Giroux, 1994.

Gore, Al. *Earth in the Balance: Ecology and the Human Spirit*. New York: Plume/Penguin, 1993.

Greenhouse, Steven. "The greening of foreign policy." *Houston Chronicle*. October 9, 1995.

Hazarike, Sanjoy. "Origins of pneumonic plague in India still puzzle WHO." *Houston Chronicle,* May 2, 1995.

Henson, Carol. "Fast-growing hole in ozone layer doubles in year, agency reports." *Houston Chronicle*. September 13, 1995.

"India Plague: It Was Pneumonic." Associated Press/Prodigy, February 7, 1995.

Jacobson, Alison. "Emerging and Re-Emerging Viruses: An Essay." On Internet "Ebola Page," May 29, 1995. http://www.uct.ac.za/microbiology/ebolaess.html.

Kennedy, Paul. *Preparing for the Twenty-first Century*. New York: Random House, 1993.

Keyfitz, Nathan. "The Scientific Debate: Is Population Growth a Problem?" *Harvard International Review* (Fall 1994), 10–13.

Koffi, Marc. "Health officials confirm Ivory Coast Ebola case." *Houston Chronicle*. December 9, 1995.

Lateef, Sarwar. "Fifty But How Fit? The World Bank Replies." *World Watch* (January/February 1995).

Leakey, Richard, and Roger Lewin. *The Sixth Extinction: Patterns of Life and the Future of Humankind*. New York: Doubleday, 1995.

Lemonick, Michael D. "The Killers All Around." *Time,* September 12, 1994.

———. "Return to the Hot Zone." *Time,* May 22, 1995.

McCormick, Joseph, M.D., and Susan Fisher-Hoch, M.D. *Level 4: Virus Hunters of the CDC*. Atlanta: Turner, 1996.

Miller, Kenton R., Walter V. Reid, and Charles V. Barber. "Deforestation and Species Loss: Responding to the Crisis." In Jessica Tuchman Matthews, ed. *Preserving the Global Environment: The Challenge of Shared Leadership*. New York: W. W. Norton, 1991.

Moffett, George D. *Global Population Growth: Twenty-First Century Challenges*. New York: Foreign Policy Association Headline Series, 1993.

———. *Critical Masses: The Global Population Challenge*. New York: Viking, 1994.

Montalbano, William D. "Ecological Damage: Dark Times for the Black Sea." *Los Angeles Times,* November 27, 1994.

Murphy, Frederick A. "Dr. Frederick A. Murphy Talks about the Ebola Virus." Interview, by Sean Henahan, On Internet, http://outcast.gene.com/ae/WN/NM/interview_murphy.html, Downloaded May 29, 1995.

"New data support fears of a shrinking ozone layer." *Houston Chronicle*. April 25, 1996.

Owen, Henry. "The World Bank: Is 50 Years Enough?" *Foreign Affairs* (September/October 1994).

Petchesky, Rosalind Pollack. "Reproductive Politics." In Joel Krieger, ed. *The Oxford Companion to Politics of the World*. New York: Oxford, 1993. 782–85.

"Plague Kills Twenty-Two in Zimbabwe." Associated Press/Prodigy, December 19, 1994.

Platt, Anne. "Why Don't We Stop Tuberculosis?" *World Watch* (July/August 1994).

Preston, Richard. *The Hot Zone: A Terrifying True Story*. New York: Random House, 1994.

Purvis, Andrew. "Where Does Ebola Hide?" *Time*. March 4, 1996, 43.

Ransdell, Eric. "Horror in the Hot Zone." *U.S. News & World Report,* May 22, 1995.

Raup, David M. *Extinction: Bad Genes or Bad Luck?* New York: W. W. Norton, 1991.

Rich, Bruce. *Mortgaging the Earth: The World Bank, Environmental Impoverishment, and the Crisis of Development*. Boston: Beacon, 1994.

Schoepf, Brooks Grundfest. "AIDS." In Joel Krieger, ed. *The Oxford Companion to Politics of the World*. New York: Oxford, 1993. 13–15.

Sege, Irene. "Missing: Sixty Million Women: Studies, Statistics Point to Grim Mystery." *Houston Chronicle,* February 20, 1992.

Semones, James K. *Sociology: A Core Text*. Fort Worth, Tex.: Holt, Rinehart & Winston, 1990.

Shenon, Philip. "Asia's 'fuse has been lit' for an explosion of AIDS." *Houston Chronicle.* January 28, 1996.

SoRelle, Ruth. "Killer outbreak in Zaire." *Houston Chronicle,* May 12, 1995.

Siebert, Charles. "Smallpox Is Dead—Long Live Smallpox." *New York Times Magazine.* August 31, 1994, 31–37.

Simon, Julian L. *The Ultimate Resource*. Princeton, NJ: Princeton University Press, 1981.

Soto, Alvaro. "A southern Perspective." In Glenn Hastedt, ed. *One World, Many Voices: Global Perspectives on Political Issues*. Englewood Cliffs, N.J.: Prentice Hall, 1995.

Tobias, Michael. *World War III: Population and Biosphere at the End of the Millenium*. Santa Fe, N.M.: Bear and Company, 1994.

Trotta, Dan. "An entire region is going up in smoke." *Houston Chronicle,* June 11, 1995.

Turshen, Meredith. "World Health Organization." In Joel Krieger, ed. *The Oxford Companion to Politics of the World*. New York: Oxford, 1993. 986–87.

"WHO monitors Ebola outbreak in Gabon." *Houston Chronicle.* February 20, 1996.

Zaneski, Cyril T. "Ivory ban, thriving elephants: horns of Africa dilemma." *Houston Chronicle,* November 8, 1994.

Chapter 15

The Dynamics of the Post-Cold War World

Introduction

"The Cold War is over and everybody won!" exclaimed more than just one analyst. The turf over which two archrivals formerly fought suddenly was being perceived as something other than a geopolitical zero-sum game board. Politicians from Washington to Moscow, from Beijing to Johannesburg were proclaiming a **peace dividend,** or a least a reprieve from the chess game of the two superpowers. What had happened? In the words of John Mueller, "over a period of less than three years—from major shifts in Soviet foreign policy by 1988 to the collapse of a conservative coup in Moscow in 1991—the world underwent a cataclysm that was something like the functional equivalent of World War III" (Mueller 1995, 1).

As a result of this nearly bloodless "war," a political anachronism of the twentieth century—the Russian/Soviet empire—was dismembered, and the boundaries of eastern Europe and parts of Asia were reconfigured geographically as well as politically. A defeated ideology had imploded under its own weight. Although stunning, these events were not entirely unprecedented: the world has experienced similar dissolutions in this century, with the demise of the European monarchies at the end of World War I and the defeat of fascism and Nazism at the end of World War II. But stunning the recent changes were—and bearing enormous consequences for the entire human community.

Mueller emphasizes the magnitude of these events and their consequences: "So many people so quickly became so blasé about this phenomenon that it is perhaps worth screaming a little: *over the course of a couple of years, virtually all the major problems that plagued big country (sometimes known as Great Power) international relations for nearly a half century were resolved with scarcely a shot being fired, a person being executed, or a rock being thrown"* (Mueller 1995, 2). Mueller goes on to say that "the issues resolved were the unpopular and often brutal Soviet occupation of Eastern Europe; the artificial and deeply troubling division of Germany; the expensive, virulent, crisis-prone, and apparently dangerous military contest between East and West; and the ideological struggle between authoritarian, expansionist, violence-encountering Communism and reactive, sometimes-panicky, capitalist democracy" (Mueller, 2).

The Cold War, for all of its shortcomings and crisis mentalities, preserved a peace of sorts for almost fifty years. The Cold War can be described in retrospect as an interlude between the defeats of two "evil" ideologies: Nazism/fascism, and communism. The downfalls of these two political philosophies of the twentieth century have left democracy (and implicitly, liberal capitalism) as the only remaining organizing conceptual framework for developing (and newly unleashed) countries to emulate in establishing their polities. And replacing the rather ramshackle but delicately balanced world operating mechanism known as the **Cold War** necessitates some thought, given that the players and issues have changed dramatically as a result of its end.

Thus, this chapter is concerned with anticipating the very crude dimensions of the newly emerging post–Cold War world. Some of the tensions and problems in this new world are not new. They have been subsumed under the rubric (some say, under the rug) of traditional Great Power politics since 1945. Other problems—some even larger and potentially more dangerous in scope—are relatively new, compared to the devils we knew from 1945 to 1989. The array of changes and challenges that we foresee in the post-Cold War world can be overwhelming.

peace-dividend The money supposedly saved in the production of arms by the East and the West due to the end of the Cold War.

Cold War The period between 1945 and 1989 in which the world was basically bipolar, marked by loyalty to either the United States and its allies or the USSR and its allies.

We will attempt to sketch some of these changes as the world whirls itself into the twenty-first century without its familiar anchor, the Cold War.

Listed and discussed in the remaining pages of this chapter are some rather broad questions (not necessarily in order of importance) concerning the direction and scope of the political world as we see it. Put differently, these are some of the reasons we should stay awake politically for the remainder of this century and into the next. The ways these questions are asked, addressed, and answered will impact your lives tremendously. As we warned in chapter 1, what you don't know can hurt you!

New World Order That arrangement of world power that is still to be determined due to the collapse of the former Soviet Union, and hence, the end of the Cold War.

The New World Order?

The end of the Cold War meant a change to a widely hailed yet still evolving **New World Order.** How much order really exists in this new world is indeed questionable. To President George Bush, the New World Order was akin to that envisioned by his predecessor, Woodrow Wilson. Bush declared,

Former United States President George Bush frequently spoke of what he termed the "New World Order," but the disorderly world created by the end of the Cold War has continued to defy attempts to impose any kind of orderly structure on it.

We have a vision of a new partnership of nations that transcends the Cold War. A partnership based on consultation, cooperation, and collective action especially through international and regional organizations. A partnership united by principle and the rule of law and supported by an equitable sharing of both cost and commitment. A partnership whose goals are to increase democracy, increase prosperity, increase the peace, and reduce arms. (Bush 1990, 152 in Kissinger, 1994)

The exact way this noble vision would come about was unclear. The American nation had heard a similar tune twice before: once during the presidency of Woodrow Wilson, who had tried to charm the Europeans at Versailles and the second time during the administrations of Roosevelt and Truman. Each time, states former Secretary of State Henry Kissinger, "America . . . proclaimed its intention to build a new world order by applying its domestic values to the world at large" (Kissinger 1994, 805). One thing *was* clear this latest time: peace was *not* at hand. Iraq, Bosnia, Chechnya, and Rwanda have provided graphic examples of the problems of this new peace.

Why is this so? Given the chance to wipe the international slate clean of the ideological, bipolar politics that has dominated the world since 1945, why has the new international order of cooperation and peace not sprung from the vacuum left by the death of communism? In part, the answer lies in the fact that this new world order is something yet to be crafted. We may not see the contours of the international system's structure until well into the next century. New power centers will have to emerge. Until such time, nations are free to pursue their own individual interests in the absence of restraint by the hegemons. At this time, the United States is the only remaining international power that can flex its military power globally. However, its national capabilities do not necessarily imply its intent. The political resolve on the part of the United States at this time to act as the sole hegemon either geopolitically or geoeconomically is questionable, and probably absent.

International systems or orders are quick to emerge and just as quick to change. Each system though behaves as if it has life eternal. And as we have just stated, it will take some time before the next order is in place. For now, let us examine the current system-in-transition by asking three questions. First, what are the basic units of the international order? Second, what are their means of interacting? And third, what are the goals on behalf of which they interact? (Kissinger 1994, 806)

According to Kissinger, the world now has three typical nation-state systems. The first type includes the "splinter" nations arising from the dissolution of the former Soviet Union and Yugoslavia. Embroiled in battles instigated by long-standing ethnic rivalries and feuds, they are not concerned at this point in more cosmopolitan ventures.

The second type of state is composed of the former colonial states in Africa, Asia, the Middle East, and elsewhere. Wilsonian idealism helped create such artificial geopolitical entities. The end result has been and will continue to be civil war and other attempts to redraw geopolitical boundaries along ethnocentric lines.

A third type of state, the continental state, probably will constitute one of the new actors in the future new world order. Such a state is multiethnic and multireligious in nature. Because of its domestic fault lines, the latitude of its foreign policy is questionable. Several salient continental states (both existing and potential) are India, China, the United States, the European Union (should it fully solidify), and perhaps the Russian Federation (which is now teetering between disintegration and reimperialization—Kissinger 1994, 808).

At this point, how do all these nation-states interact? The international rules of engagement have been altered beyond traditional recognition since 1989. The pre-1989 Cold War world was configured according to the *high politics* of war and peace, while issues of *low politics*—lowering infant mortality rates or raising adult literacy rates—were relegated to a distant second place. However, just because the tension between the two Cold War hegemons now has subsided (for the time being at least), peace has not automatically engulfed the world. The world, moreover, has not automatically oriented itself to unsolved "low political," or quality-of-life, issues. In fact, the world community has done a rather miserable job in maintaining the peace as we knew it in the halcyon days of the Cold War, and attempts to refocus the world community's attention on issues of a human dimension have so far gone unnoticed.

Even with the "successful" multilateral ventures in the Persian Gulf, Namibia, Cambodia, and Haiti (to a certain degree), the United Nations has seen failure multiplied in Bosnia, Somalia, Rwanda, and other places. Clearly, the United Nations and other multilateral or transnational actors have a long way to go before interstate, inter-nation peace is bolstered on a global scale. As we mentioned in chapter 4, there is a qualitative as well as a quantitative difference between *peace-keeping* and *peacemaking*. The intergovernmental organizations usually can keep an established peace; they face an impossible task in attempting to create such a peace.

Another characteristic of international relations in this transition time is *low-intensity conflict,* the conflict signature of the latter part of this century. Instead of shooting across borders, belligerents now are shooting primarily within their own borders, or across new borders at people of different cultures or nationalities, who until recently were their compatriots. Intrastate ethnocentric conflict is now the big problem plaguing both daily human life and the high politics of war and peace.

As we have stressed in previous chapters, the *web of world politics* (see the volume of the same name by Mansbach, Ferguson, and Lampert, 1976) has changed since 1945. Nation-states are no longer the only players in the global game. Other subnational and non-state actors, along with a host of international actors of a transnational character, have emerged. But the interest of the developed world in "going it together" in certain venues and over certain issues has not been echoed in the newly emerging, poorer nations of the world, where basic human needs continue to go unfulfilled because of war, famine, pestilence, and the lack of political will or structure. Nonetheless, nation-states will continue to be the primary actors in world politics, they now will share responsibility with a host of other actors; the NGOs, MNCs, and IGOs that we have identified in chapter 4.

Not only global actors but also the ways they relate are new. The issues that the world will face have changed as well. The focal point of geopolitics is now geoeconomic, rather than geostrategic. The principal engine running world dynamics is economics, at least for most of the developed world. And internecine warfare is rampant in many newly released states in Asia, Africa, central Europe, and Latin America.

It appears that the world is experiencing an implosion of political and economic forces in the newly unleashed nations of the former USSR and Soviet bloc (e.g., the former Yugoslavia and the Baltic states, as well as the southern Islamic nations of Azerbaijan, Turkmenistan, Uzbekistan, etc.). At the same time, the world is experiencing an explosion of supranational cooperation, or at least quasi-regulated conflict, at the level of global economics and politics. For evidence of the latter, witness the growth and power of the European Union, the waiting list for NATO membership, the newly created World Trade Organization, and the North American Free Trade Association.

Ideas Matter . . . The End of History?

Perhaps one of the lessons of the Cold War will be that political ideas matter. People die for them and because of them. In fact, the differences in the world may be largely the result of different ideas as to how the world should work. But while ideas matter, they also can change. As the end of the Cold War has shown, the defeat of certain ideas, such as international communism, can occur naturally, without much bloodshed. And just as political ideologies can die, so too can new (or at least rearranged) ideologies rise up.

Francis Fukuyama's article "The End of History?" (Fukuyama 1989) lays out the provocative thesis that what we have witnessed is not just the end of the Cold War, but the end of history itself. In other words, what we have recently experienced with the demise of communism represents the end point of the world's ideological evolution, and the triumph of Western liberal capitalist democracy as the final form of human government. From now until the end of time, goes this line of reasoning, we are assigned the dismal lot of just tinkering with and fine-tuning the engines of democracy and capitalism—however these are defined.

Others analysts, however, are not so sanguine about the end of tyrannies such as fascism, Nazism, or communism. Those who rebut Fukuyama's thesis argue that history abounds with scores of menaces to plague the political human being. "There were plenty of predatory tyrannies before Lenin arrived at the Finland Station, and there will be plenty more even if a Romanov is restored to a Kremlin throne. Genghis Khan and Caligula did not need a course in dialectical materialism to make their periods of history interesting. . . ." (Talbott 1989, 39).

Even if one political system were acknowledged as superior and preeminent, such a development would probably not mark the end of history, or the end of conflict. As even we in this country are becoming aware, differences in cultures—in their values, their religions, their languages—may combine with ancient animosities to present irreconcilable conflicts. The strange alliance between the Roman Catholic Church and fundamentalist Muslims at the World Population Conference in the spring of 1994 gives some indication of the vehemence with which a given cultural group may hold and fight for one of its values (in this case, vehemence enough to forge such an unlikely coalition, despite the fact that Catholics and most other Christians are miles apart from Muslims on other questions of women's status). This is but one example illustrating the complexity of global concerns about values. Furthermore, the virtual paralysis of the conference shows the power of the commitment to self-identity embodied in the cultural values of particular groups. The end of history? Not likely. People and their groupings are complex. Ideas matter. And these people, groupings, and ideas are far from uniform.

Is Sovereignty Dead?

As we have stated before, the nation-state is a relatively recent phenomenon in human history: as political constructs, states have existed only since the Peace of Westphalia in 1648. And states as we know them will not necessarily continue to exist as they do now. Nation-states are modern; the postmodern structures of governments are barely visible on the horizon.

Good arguments can be advanced for the natural extinction of states, given the multitude of transnational issues that the world faces—for example, problems of the environment, of disease, and of international terrorism—as well as the potential, for good or ill, of instantaneous global communication. All of these issues and developments cannot be addressed simply on a national scale. Therefore, states seem to be undergoing increased pressure for transnational action that may require them to relinquish some of their traditional sovereign duties and responsibilities.

Ironically, although the world may be coming to recognize that the seemingly intractable problems that exist are systemic in nature, not regional or state-specific, states are the only effective managerial units thus far created to cope with such transnational issues. The United Nations, for example, could not exist if it were not for the cooperation of its functional units, the nation-states.

Given the tensions in many nation-states today, one must ponder whether or not such functional units will survive the onslaught of subnational political tensions caused by intense religious fundamentalism and virulent nationalism. In sum, political conflict has been fixed on governmental structure recently, but not always. Even if the world's states were varieties of democracies, we would expect that the purposes and desires of these democracies would be in conflict. The thesis of the end of history asks us to take seriously the end of cultures as well.

Whatever history is and has been, we can not fully know. We cannot doubt, however, that insofar as history documents human life and purposes, destruction and vitality, novelty can not be over. The task of the conscientious political scientist is to imagine the future in light of the past, with recognition of real differences between and among peoples.

The Clash of Cultures

Professor Samuel P. Huntington writes in his seminal article "The Clash of Civilizations?" that

> the fundamental source of conflict in this new world will not be primarily ideological or primarily economic. The great divisions among humankind and the dominating source of conflict will be cultural. Nation states will remain the most powerful actors in world affairs, but the principal conflicts of global politics will occur between nations and groups of different civilizations. The clash of civilizations will dominate global politics. The fault lines between civilizations will be the battle lines of the future. (Huntington 1993, 22; see further Huntington 1996)

Huntington goes on to say that the notational groupings of countries as members of the First, Second, Third, or Fourth World, or the grouping of nations according to their political systems, is no longer relevant. What *is* relevant is grouping nations according to their cultures and civilizations (Huntington 1993, 23). Figure 15.1 shows the world according to Huntington.

The reason the world will experience a **clash of cultures** is sixfold. First, says Huntington, differences between civilizations are real; they are basic. One civilization is differentiated from another by history, language, culture, tradition, and most important, religion. Second, as the world shrinks, the interactions between people of different cultures are increasing. Heightened interaction may increase cultural clashes.

Third, the processes of economic modernization and social change throughout the world are separating people from longstanding local identities. In short, they weaken the nation-state and allow religion (usually of a fundamentalist variety) to fill the gap once occupied by allegiance to the nation-state.

Fourth, "the growth of civilization-consciousness has enhanced the dual role of the West. On the one hand, the West is at a peak of power. At the same time, however, and perhaps as a result, a 'return to the roots' phenomenon is occurring among non-Western civilizations" (Huntington 1993, 26). Thus, one sees the re-Islamization of the Middle East, the debate over the Westernization versus the Russification of Russia, and the questioning of the legacy of Kemal Attaturk in Turkey. But while elites in many non-Western countries are rejecting Western values, the masses are not. They are embracing Western (largely American) culture.

Fifth, cultural characteristics are less mutable than economic and political ones. Communists can become democrats, but Lithuanians cannot become Armenians. People can and do change ideologies; they seldom change religions. They cannot change ethnicities.

clash of cultures What some predict as a result of the end of the Cold War. Culture clashes will replace clashes of ideologies.

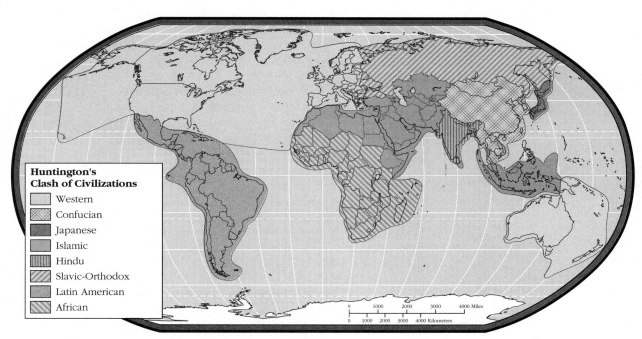

Huntington's Clash of Civilizations

- Western
- Confucian
- Japanese
- Islamic
- Hindu
- Slavic-Orthodox
- Latin American
- African

Figure 15.1
This map shows the globe divided according to Huntington's distinctions among eight major civilizations.

Finally, "economic blocism is now the rage." During the 1980s, intraregional trade rose from 51 percent to 59 percent in Europe, from 33 to 37 percent in East Asia, and from 32 to 36 percent in North America. Increased blocism will only accentuate regional culture. For example, the European Union is essentially Western and Christian. NAFTA is also Western and Christian—but it will succeed only if Mexico is successful in merging with American and Canadian cultures. Common culture is facilitating the rapid expansion of the economic relations between China, Hong Kong, Taiwan, Singapore, and overseas Chinese communities in other Asian countries (Huntington 1993, 28). Culture is also the basis for the Economic Cooperation Organization, which brings together ten non-Arab Muslim countries; for Caricom; for the Central American Common Market; and for other regional bloc efforts in South America and Africa.

Huntington and others who accept his thesis are convinced that the clash of civilizations will be the hallmark of conflict for the foreseeable future. Such conflict will occur at both the micro level—between neighboring groups across the fault line of civilizations—and the macro level, as states compete for economic and military power.

If one agrees with the Huntington thesis, then one accepts the inevitability of conflict within the international system. This viewpoint also calls upon the West to remain vigilant in guarding its power by becoming cognizant of other cultural and religious underpinnings which are antithetical to its own.

Is War Obsolete?

Isn't it ironic that the Cold War was the longest peace between the world's great powers since the seventeenth century? This has given many analysts reason to believe that the concept of global war is now obsolete. The lessons of both world wars, coupled with the technology and refinement of weapons of mass destruction, have led some to proclaim that a new and more civilized paradigm for human behavior has replaced the war paradigm that has characterized the current international system.

The authors, however, are not so optimistic about such a shift in the relations of nations. In fact, the likelihood of war between nations, civilizations, and states has probably never been higher, given the tensions arising from the dissolution of the Soviet empire. With twenty-seven thousand nuclear weapons spread among five former republics of the Soviet Union, the world is poised for a perpetual round of global arms limitations/reduction talks led by the West, which has neither the capability for or an interest in enforcing the Nuclear Nonproliferation Treaty. The security agreement (described in chapter 12) between the United States and the Ukraine could inject the United States into a Russian-Ukrainian crisis over, say, the status of the Crimea, with America risking the safety of New York or Washington to protect Kiev (Bandow 1995, 56).

While the likelihood of global thermonuclear war is difficult to calculate, we think it is far more likely that the world will see an increase in low-intensity conflicts arising from ethnocultural differences. "Ethnic cleansing" may indeed be an increasing threat to the world's minorities, as nations become smaller and more homogeneous. In 1993, the UN High Commissioner on Refugees estimated that one in every 125 humans on this planet had to flee a homeland in search of safety. While war may become a thing of the past for most of the developed world, it probably will remain a fact of life for the dispossessed and their dispossessors, who historically have tended to drag others along with them into the carnage. It is unlikely that the developed world will sit idly by and watch the Third World implode in a sea of conflict. Global stability is in the best interests of the West. Unfortunately, in the eyes of the rest of the world, it is not such a priority.

Geoeconomics versus Geopolitics

Geopolitics as the world has known it since 1945 is dead. As we have mentioned throughout the text, many believe that the newly defined battleground is **geoeconomics** (Rosecrance 1986). The importance of geoeconomics to the stability of the world is open to debate. But it is likely that the world will continue to coagulate into regional trading blocs, which will require nation-state bureaucracies to redefine their missions with respect to economic cooperation or conflict.

As national wealth is translated into political power, national fervor can create increased competition and assertiveness. On the other hand, economic failures could either lead to strife within nations or increase international hostilities fueled by economic dislocations. Whatever the case, the next century's world economic pecking order is likely to be different from today's—largely because of the rise of regional trading blocs. A given nation might find that if it is not a member of a "team," then it will not be able to sit at the table.

geopolitics World affairs viewed primarily from a national security perspective.

geoeconomics World affairs viewed from a macro-economics perspective.

The Third World/NIEO Is Dead

The 1995 Nonaligned Conference held in Bandung, Indonesia, was full of hope for a newer and better postcolonial world. The foremost goal of the nonaligned movement was for the Third World to reorder fundamentally the system of international economic intercourse. But today, the New International Economic Order—a radical restructuring of the liberal economics practiced by the West (and hence dominating the rest of the world)—is dead. Discussion of issues revolving around the reordering of the trilogy of aid, trade, and foreign investment ring hollow when members of the former Third World congregate. For such a congregation includes the newly industrializing nations of the world, many of which boast higher standards of living than some European nations.

The new "imperialists" tend to be lending organizations, like the World Bank and the International Monetary Fund, that have tried to impose stringent fiscal regimes. "The 'neocolonial' tag also has been attached to donor nations asking questions about rights abuses, child labor, religious or sex discrimination, and population policy. At the recent UN population conference in Cairo, some of the hottest buttons and bumper stickers proclaimed angrily, 'No to Contraception Imperialism'" (November 13, 1994).

Poverty and desperation will unquestionably continue to exist, but the end of the Cold War may well make their solution less, not more, likely.

Technological Innovation

Technological innovations offer solutions to some of the world's most pressing problems—but this also has its downside. Technology has created instantaneous communication, which has, in part, facilitated radical economic, political, and social changes. Some of these are wonderful; others, frightening. Technology has solved many of the dilemmas posed by disease; it also has invented new ways to eradicate human life. Agricultural technology has helped feed more people more efficiently; it also has intruded upon cultural norms and mores. As people try to weigh technology's benefits against its drawbacks, a definite tension exists between technological change and human receptivity to it. This is especially true in the developing world.

But regardless of resistance to it, the engine of change in today's world is technology. Changes in telecommunications, medicine, transportation, microelectronics, and many other fields have given rise to a new type of individual, the global technocrat. While such technicians are invaluable at fixing finite problems within their areas of expertise, they may have little comprehension of how the international political system at large works. The danger is that they will fix one problem, only to discover that other, seemingly unrelated, areas are now out of kilter.

The New and Future World Order

John Mueller may be right. Perhaps there was a World War III that started in 1989 and ended in 1991. The axis on which the old world turned, the Cold War, is now obsolete; the world is seeking a new axis on which to revolve. We have attempted to describe this new axis in this chapter using rather broad brush strokes. It includes increased democratization within the world; a newfound appreciation for liberal economics dominated by regional blocs; conflict founded primarily on cultural rather than nation-state loyalties; and a yen for technological innovation, with a simultaneous suspicion of the unknown.

One portrait of the world in the foreseeable future is that of a globe dominated by Western political, economic, and technological culture. It will be a world of "the West versus the rest." However, tides of discontent are not far outside the frame of this picture. The rest of the world may become increasingly resentful of Western culture and all that it stands for, with the already-existing gap between the West and the rest widening as we move into the twenty-first century. The secularized, economically advantaged, pluralistic, democratically governed nations and supranational institutions of the West will be confronted by the religiously fundamental, poor, culturally homogeneous, and undemocratic nations elsewhere in the world. Accentuating the gap between them will be technology at large and telecommunications specifically, for as the world shrinks in perceptual distance, such shrinkage magnifies the real differences between cultures. Cross-cultural tolerance has not been a hallmark of the world in the twentieth century, with its legacy of colonialism, imperialism, nationalism, and religious disputes that have led to wars. To expect a reversal of such deep-seated animosities with the advent of a new century is sophomoric.

Another picture, not quite so gloomy, may yet be a realistic depiction of the world of tomorrow. The twenty-first century may see increased transnationalism and democratization, and as a result, increased cooperation among the functional units. The increased wealth of the West and newly industrializing nations of the East may serve to inspire development in the new states that will be created along ethnocultural lines. Not only will the economic system of the West serve as a model; so too will its system of governance, liberal democracy. Woodrow Wilson's thesis that a world of democratic nations will be more peaceful seems to have stood the test of time. But we do not pretend that even in this scenario, all will be rosy. While democracies may not wage war on one another, conflict in the new world may well assume an uncharacteristic, economic face. Moreover, Wilson's ideal of national self-determination serves peace only in the abstract; in reality, self-determination has proven quite costly in terms of human life.

The fear of war between major powers may have diminished—but the resultant world may be even more deadly in the days to come. Because of the simultaneous integration and disintegration of the world on several fronts simultaneously, the concept of national—as well as personal—security assumes increased dimensions.

Nations of the world today experience tremendous pressures: an abundance of issues on their domestic agendas; increasing economic and cultural spillover influences by trans- or subnational units such as multinational corporations; democracy and liberal economics as the watchwords of the day; increasing economic regionalization; tensions of ethnonationalism abounding; perhaps their accustomed ideologies out of favor; the increased shrinkage of the world due to technology. What lies ahead? Uncertainty, of course. It is uncertainty full of dangers, yet tinged with hope. Einstein was right: around the globe, politics *is* more difficult than physics.

Summary

The end of the Cold War was the functional equivalent of World War III in the enormity and speed of the change it introduced to world affairs. Global relations underwent a sudden and dramatic shift from the half-century of "cold war, hot peace" that had kept the world in relative tranquillity. Now, uncertainty reigned among the nations of the world concerning how they should relate to one another.

When the two superpowers did engage each other politically and militarily during the Cold War, they frequently did so through surrogate nations, which acted as the footsoldiers in the battle of competing ideas that pitted the liberal, Western democracies with their capitalistic systems against the centralized, communistic Soviet bloc with its centrally planned economies. For now at least, the dragon of communism is dead in the lands of the former Soviet empire—but in its place have arisen dozens of small snakes with which the West must contend.

The twentieth century began with rampant fires of nationalism leading to the century's first world war, and quickly witnessed new and virulent ideologies, a whirlpool of conflicting ideas about how the world should work. The waves of National Socialism, fascism, despotism, and communism all battered the liberal, democratic ideals of the Western victors of World War I, who collectively had attempted to "make the world safe for democracy."

Now, as the century draws to a close, we are left with the opportunity to forge what some analysts call the "New World Order." How this new world order will evolve is yet unknown to the policy-makers of the world. Many opportunities and many dangers lie ahead. But one thing is certain: both the issues and the actors have changed substantially since 1900.

The principal figure in the dance of world politics is still the nation-state. Other actors, though—transnational organizations such as the European Community, supranational actors (such as the United Nations), and multinational corporations (such as McDonald's)—have burst upon the world stage to compete with the nation-state for the allegiance of people.

The issues also have shifted, and fall into two contrasting types. Low-intensity conflicts such as those in the Balkans and in eastern Africa beg for attention, as do issues of a more geoeconomic sort. Two phenomena are happening at the same time: the disintegration of former states fueled by a nationalism that was bottled up during the Cold War, and the transnational cooperation brought about by regional economic trading systems worldwide. Which pattern will predominate in the world of the future?

The answer to this question may vary from culture to culture; some predict, accordingly, that the next round of world conflict will be a "conflict of culture," not based upon rigid geographic lines, but cutting across and overlapping national, political, economic, and social boundaries.

In the midst of tremendous global change, many ponder whether the world has outgrown its penchant for global war. We are not so sanguine as to claim that the scourge of the world war will fail to rear its ugly head once more. Human beings seem to have retained a propensity for war: most of the world's present refugees have been displaced by its ravages. Uncertainty about this human tendency, combined with rising nationalism and the nuclear capabilities of volatile groups, causes some observers even to be nostalgic for the ideological tensions of the Cold War era, which enjoyed the longest "peace" since the seventeenth century.

Although the technological revolution of the latter part of this century is extraordinary, it will be neither the world's savior nor, we hope, its downfall. People use technology for their own purposes—people, as we have noted, who have a history and who are driven by ideas. This is the reason the study of global politics is so vitally important to us all. We are those people who, with others, will shape the world of tomorrow. And what we don't know can hurt us.

Key Terms

Peace dividend	Clash of cultures
Cold War	Geopolitics
New World Order	Geoeconomics

Thought Questions

1. The Cold War is over. Describe the contours of the new world order arising from the ashes of the old one.
2. What is the "clash of cultures"?

3. In what ways is technology the engine driving the train of today and tomorrow?

References

Fukuyama, Francis. "The End of History?" *National Interest,* no. 16 (Summer 1989): 3-18.

Huntington, Samuel P. "The Clash of Civilizations?" *Foreign Affairs* (Summer 1993)

———. *The Clash of Civilizations and the Remaking of World Order.* New York: Simon and Schuster, 1996.

Kissinger, Henry. *Diplomacy,* New York: Simon & Shuster, 1994.

Mansbach, Richard, Yale H. Ferguson, and Donald E. Lampert. *The Web of World Politics.* Prentice Hall, 1976.

Mueller, John. *Quiet Catacylsm.* HarperCollins, 1995.

Rosecrance, Richard. *The Rise of the Trading State: Commerce and Conquest in the Modern World.* New York: Basic Books, 1996.

Talbott, Strobe. 1989. "The End of History?" *Newsweek,* December 3, 1989, 39.

Glossary

Aggression An instinct that in natural conditions helps to insure the survival of the individual and the species.

Ambassador A diplomatic representative sent from the home country to a host country to represent the home nation's views and relay data about the host to the home country.

Arms control The overarching concept of weapons control in terms of number, type, and deployment. It includes arms limitation, reduction, and elimination.

Arms limitation The setting of a cap or limit on the number, type, and deployment of weapons systems.

Attitudes Predispositions to react favorably or unfavorably toward a class of objects or people.

Balance of Power Theory Theory of international relations stipulating that peace will ensue when there is a configuration of military power so that no one power dominates the system.

Balance of trade The ratio between what a nation exports compared to what a nation imports.

Belief system Sum of beliefs, attitudes, and opinions an individual holds.

Beliefs Feelings or convictions that given entities either exist or do not exist.

Biological weapons Military weapons that are classified as weapons of mass destruction because of the biological nature of their composition, e.g. anthrax disease.

Bipolarity A world configuration in which there are two centers of power.

Bolshevik Revolution The Marxist-Leninist revolution in Russia in 1917, which established the Union of Soviet Socialist Republics (USSR).

Bolstering Shoring up the attractiveness of a decision once it is made.

Bretton Woods Agreements on rules, institutions, and procedures devised at the end of World War II at Bretton Woods, N.H., to facilitate global economic relations.

Capitalism Economic system based upon the precepts of private ownership of real property, profit maximization, and limited central government.

CFCs Chlorofluorocarbons: chemical compounds believed to contribute to the depletion of the earth's ozone layer.

CFE Conventional Forces Europe (popular name for the Paris Treaty on Conventional Forces Europe): treaty that limited deployment of troops in Europe and opened the way for agreement to widespread destruction of nuclear weapons in the START talks.

Chemical weapons Military weapons that are classified as weapons of mass destruction because of their chemical composition, e.g. mustard gas.

Chokepoint A narrow body of water or land whose possessor can exercise great power through controlling communications.

CIS Commonwealth of Independent States.

Civic nationalism Nationalism predicated upon a shared sense of political ideals; national identity is based on beliefs, not blood.

G–2   ◆   *Glossary*

Clash of cultures   What some predict as a result of the end of the Cold War. Culture clashes will replace clashes of ideologies.

Clausewitz, Karl von   A nineteenth-century German military thinker of the realist school of thought.

Clipper chip   A proposed encoding device that would shield against telephone eavesdropping by everyone except the U.S. federal government.

Cobweb model   The model of international relations that asserts that the world is intricately interconnected. What happens in one part of the world has repercussions in every other quarter of the world no matter how insignificant the event.

Cognitions   Beliefs about the world.

Cohesion   The bonding of individuals in a small group setting generally with the feeling that the group is superior to other groups.

Cold War   The period between 1945 and 1989 in which the world was basically bipolar, marked by loyalty to either the United States and its allies or the USSR and its allies.

Collective security   The original peacekeeping doctrine of the United Nations, which held that an attack against one was an attack against all and should be defeated by the collective action of all.

Communism   An umbrella ideology based upon economic relations between the people and the state, originating with the writings of Karl Marx.

Comparative advantage   An economic principle stating that any two nations will benefit if each specializes in what it can produce best, and acquires through trade what it cannot produce.

Conditionality   The demand by lenders that borrowers meet certain conditions.

Conformity   The propensity of a small decisional group to gel around certain norms of operation. Conformity is used by the group to repel outsiders who disagree with the group's norms and values.

Confucianism   Orthodox Chinese political and ethical belief system that viewed human nature as basically good.

Conventional war   War conducted without the use of nuclear weapons.

Conventional weapons   Nonnuclear arms.

Coser-Simmel thesis   A theory of war that states that if a nation experiences external threat, then internal cohesion will follow.

Counterforce targeting   Nuclear targeting of the enemy's military-industrial components.

Counterintelligence   Intelligence that works against the activities of other nations' intelligence agencies.

Countervalue targeting   Nuclear targeting of the enemy's civilian population centers, in addition to its military-industrial centers.

Covert operations   Undercover or covert intelligence-gathering.

Crisis   An international situation characterized by high threat to system stability, short decision time, and surprise to the foreign policy makers of a nation.

Cultural imperialism   Transference of one culture abroad, displacing the existing culture; usually accomplished via technological means such as television, movies, etc.

Culture   A pattern of beliefs, values, attitudes, customs, and behaviors that is learned by the individual from his or her family and society. It predisposes an individual to act in specific ways that are acceptable to society.

Cyberspace   The theory of communication and control through space.

Deception   The art of subterfuge.

Decision-making   The processes of choosing which policy to adopt; affected by idiosyncratic variables, group composition, setting, and stress factors.

Decisional Extremism   The tendency of small decisional groups to reach more extreme decisions (either riskier or more cautious) than would be predicted from the sum of individual preferences.

Decisional polarization   The predisposition of a group to gravitate to a perceived group norm, i.e., either risk or caution.

Decisional quality   The *processes* used in coming to a final group decision and the successful implementation of the decision.

Decolonization   The withdrawal of former colonial powers after World War II, primarily from Africa, Asia, and Latin America.

Defensive avoidance Avoidance or veering away from making a decision.

Democracy System of government characterized by elections for lawmakers and a nation's leadership. Its philosophical foundation is classical liberalism.

Democratic centralism A decision-making system in which all participants agree publicly with the government's decision, regardless of whether they do so privately or not.

Dependence An economic theory that states that the South is disadvantaged in a neocolonial sense, due to the rules of the international economic system allegedly imposed by the North.

Derivatives Trading instruments not based directly on conditions, but tied to such things as options and futures; i.e., sophisticated bets on what could happen, not what actually is going on.

Deterrence A primarily psychological approach to defense based on the goal of avoiding damage to oneself and on the perception of the retaliatory capability of the enemy.

Development A process that takes a nation from a less developed to a more developed status. Usually measured by a nation's GNP.

Dialecticism A view of history that states that the progression of man is economically determined in stages of action and reaction to the existing order, bringing the political system to a higher state of perfection.

Diplomacy The political craft of discussion and negotiation on a government-to-government level; the management of relations between states and other actors.

Diplomatic immunity Legal status of foreign diplomats in a host nation exempting them from most of the laws of the host state.

Diplomatic recognition The legal acknowledgment granted by one government to another to permit normal international intercourse.

Disarmament A process that would remove the possibility of nuclear war by abolishing nuclear weapons altogether. Today, the term is used primarily in conjunction with nuclear weapons.

Disintegration The explosion or scattering of once sovereign units into much smaller political units, e.g.,

the former republic of Czechoslovakia is now the Czech Republic and the Slovakia—two separate states.

Dumping The sale of surplus products overseas to drive down the cost and potentially dry up competitors' markets.

E-cash Digital or electronic money.

Economic determinism A Marxist belief that all of the superstructure is caused or determined by the substructure; all politics is economically determined.

Economic imperialism Transference of one's economic system or products abroad, displacing the existing system or products produced.

Economic nationalism Belief that the economic interests of the nation are subordinate to the state.

ECOSOC Economic and Social Council of the United Nations.

Endism Theory that humanity has reached the end of history in terms of ideological struggles.

Espionage The gathering of national or commercial intelligence or data through various means of surveillance.

Etatism Government involvement in the building up of industry and the promotion of exports.

Ethnicity The sense of shared historical, linguistic, and socio-religious heritage among a particular group of people.

Ethnic nationalism Fervent loyalty to one's cultural, ethnic, or linguistic community within the nation or nation-state.

Eurocommunism A variant of communism marked by the belief that communism can evolve within the democratically controlled European state without violent revolution.

Eurodollars The common-fund currency of the European Union.

Euromarket The market comprising the members of the European Community.

Facism A virulent form of ethnic nationalism most commonly associated with Mussolini's Italian regime of the same name during World War II.

FDI Foreign direct investment.

Fertility rate The number of births per thousand women of childbearing age, defined as 15 through 44 years.

Fiasco As used regarding the groupthink concept, descriptive term for foreign policy failures when decision-makers have not pursued decisional quality.

FISINT (Foreign Instrumentation Signals Intelligence) The monitoring of telemetry, or machine-to-people communications.

Foreign direct investment Direct investment of capital by foreign nations in a host country.

Functionalism An attempt to foster political integration in a bottom-up approach through transnational organizations and shared sovereignty.

G-7 Group of seven highly industrialized nations—the U.S., Canada, England, France, Italy, Germany, Japan—that meets regularly to discuss international political economy.

Gateway Geographical term for key passages of (usually, but not exclusively) water for shipping of goods.

General Assembly The "legislative" body of the United Nations, composed of all constituent members.

Geneva Protocol, 1925 International agreement that called for the decent treatment of prisoners of war and the sick and wounded. It also banned the use of chemical weapons.

Genocide The intentional destruction of a national, ethnic, racial, or religious group.

Geo-strategic In traditional power politics jargon, the geo(world) configuration of power in a military sense.

Geoeconomic A modern term which denotes the new or transferred orientation to global economics for much of the developed world as opposed to the traditional geostrategic mode of thought.

Geoeconomics World affairs viewed from a macro-economics perspective.

Geopolitics World affairs viewed primarily from a national security perspective.

Gold standard The standard for the world's currency established at the Bretton Woods Conference, based on a rate of 35 U.S. dollars per ounce of gold.

Great War WWII from the Russian perspective. WWI in the eyes of the rest of the world.

Green revolution A dramatic increase in crop production in this century, due to the introduction of new high-yield, drought-resistant grains.

Greenhouse effect The global production of vast amounts of carbon dioxide and other compounds that trap the warmth created by the sun.

Group cohesion The solidarity one feels as a member of a group that exhibits strong cohesion.

Group conformity Agreement with and movement toward a perceived group norm.

Group dynamics The interpersonal working relationships that transpire within a small decisional unit.

Group extremization The propensity of a group to be even more extreme—either to risk or to caution—in their decision compared to the average of individual preferences of the group's members.

Group norms The dominant beliefs and decision rules held by most members of a decision group that help create an unspoken consensus and springboard of behavior.

Group of 77 Group of 77 Third World nations that called for a reordering of global economic relations in North-South trade, aid, and investment, in a New International Economic Order.

Group polarization The group serves as a magnifier of predominant or existing individual values which exist in the group as a unit of decision.

Groupthink The inclination of decisional groups to promote consensus, conformity, and insularity, resulting in a lack of vigilant information-processing, moral judgment, and reality testing.

Guerrilla war Low-intensity, unconventional war, usually fought by an insurgency of irregulars against much stronger forces.

Hegemon A regional or world economic and/or political-military power that seeks to impose the existing world order on others for the sake of its own stability.

Hemorrhagic fevers Human fevers such as Ebola and Marburg, which are often lethal.

H-O-S model The Heckscher-Ohlin-Samuelson theory of international trade, also known as the neoclassical liberal theory of trade (*see* comparative advantage).

Hot money The speed that money is transferred in the electronic casino.

Hypervigilence Panic behavior.

ICBM Intercontinental Ballistic Missile.

Idealism The theory of international relations in the twentieth century that states that human beings are essentially good in nature and that peace depends upon the appropriate concentration of international power.

Ideology A finely honed belief system of how the world works or should work.

Idiosyncratic Personality-level variables.

IGOs Intergovernmental organizations.

IMF International Monetary Fund.

Imperialism Economic theory founded by Hobson and later refined by Lenin to connote the highest stage of capitalism. Belief that surplus capital seeks external markets, raw materials, and cheap labor to the detriment of host nations.

Import substitution strategy Developing alternatives at home for the importation of goods and services.

Industrial espionage Commercial spying for information on product/service development, data, sources, etc.

Information superhighway The National Information Infrastructure, a combined computer-television-telephone net that will allow access to the Internet, viewing of movies, connections to libraries, and other services.

Integration In terms of political science, integration is the melding together of various units, sometimes sovereign nation-states to form a large supra-national unit, e.g., the European Union or NAFTA.

Intelligence The gathering and analysis of information to be used in national policy making.

Intelligence cycle The process of taking information and turning it into useful data for policymakers of a nation. The steps involved are: planning and direction; collection; processing; analysis and production; and dissemination.

Interdependence A situation of mutual dependence.

Interdevelopmental symbiosis A mutually beneficial situation said to be existing between the South with its cheap labor and raw materials, and the North with its markets and technology.

International arms trade The sale of conventional arms by one nation to another for profit and/or geopolitical favor.

International casino Global computerized system in which money, seen as a commodity itself, is traded at superfast speeds (*see* derivatives).

International law Rules governing state-to-state relations. Includes two sectors: public and private international law.

International politics A term often interchanged with international relations, world politics, or global politics that denotes the sum of all political interchange within the world at a given time. In its strictest sense, international politics is the accumulation of all politics that emerge between nations of the world.

Internet Global computer network that constitutes one part of the information superhighway.

IRBM Intermediate Range Ballistic Missile.

Irredentism The desire by one nation to annex territory belonging to another, but that the first nation believes is historically or ethnically linked to itself.

Islamic fundamentalism Muslims who rely upon the ancient works of Islam, the Koran, and Sunn, to guide their lives.

Islamism Post-modern Islamic doctrine that rejects modernity and incorporates some antimodernist western philosophers.

Jihad According to the Islamic faith, a holy war against infidels (nonbelievers).

Just war Doctrine of war concerned with when war is morally justified and how and against whom it should be conducted.

Kellogg-Briand Pact A treaty (1928) that sought to outlaw war as an instrument of national policy.

KGB The former Soviet intelligence agency that paralleled the CIA of the United States.

League of Nations A global intergovernmental organization that was the predecessor of the United Nations.

Leninism The variant of Marxism that led to the ideological establishment of the USSR. Lenin saw the Communist Party as the principal organizing component of the ongoing revolution.

Levels of analysis Perspectives (individual, state, or systemic) from which to view and analyze international politics.

Liberal democracy The set of Jeffersonian political principles that allows for limited government, private property, majority rule, and minority rights.

LIC Low-intensity conflict.

Limited war War in which participants decide not to use their full range of weapons or to attack any and all potential enemy sites.

Linkage Tying your opponent so closely to you that he will not drag you into conflict.

"Loose nukes" Nuclear weapons that have found their way into the hands of renegade nations and militant groups as a result of the dissolution of the former Soviet Union.

Low-intensity conflict Warfare ranging from guerilla war to low-level conventional war between modern armies, but never including the use of nuclear weapons. Under United States doctrine, low-intensity conflict includes: counterinsurgency; pro-insurgency; peacetime contingency operations; and military "shows of force."

Manhattan District Project U.S. project that developed the atomic bomb and launched the atomic (later nuclear) age in weaponry.

Maoism The Chinese variant of Marxism-Leninism that stipulates that the revolution is permanent, not subject to replacement in the dialectic process. Named after the first Chinese Communist leader, Mao Tse-tung.

Marshall Plan The American plan to aid in the reconstruction of its European allies after World War II.

Marxism The ideology named after Karl Marx, the nineteenth-century German philosopher. With Georg Hegel, Marx emphasized the dialectical progression of history—thesis, antithesis, synthesis—which, according to the theory, yielded a higher stage of human being, who is seen as merely an economic animal.

Marxism-Leninism The twentieth-century "refinement" of Marxism by Vladimir Lenin, the Russian Bolshevik. Lenin's contributions to Marxism were twofold: his emphasis on the role of the party within the state, and his assertion that *imperialism* was the highest stage of capitalism.

MFN status Most favored nation status: status granted by the U.S. government to foreign nations, who thereby receive tariff preferences.

Military technological revolution (MTR) The revolution that has occurred since the advent of "smart" weapons which eliminate the direct human element from field operations.

Mirror imaging The inclination of nations and people to view others as operating according to their own motivations or goals.

MNCs Multinational corporations (or TNCs, transnational corporations).

Mole Spy placed by one government or business within another to conduct espionage.

Multilateral diplomacy Two or more nations banding together for some common diplomatic purpose.

Multipolarity A world political configuration with more than one center of power; the existence of multiple hegemons.

NAFTA North American Free Trade Agreement: agreement that incorporates Canada, the U.S., and Mexico economically into a free-trade zone.

Narco terrorism The use of drug trafficking to advance the aims of terrorist organizations.

Nation A body of people who believe that they have racial, ethnic, religious, linguistic, or cultural reasons for a common political identity or purpose.

Nation-state A nation with a political construct, i.e., territorially defined boundaries, legal government, foreign recognition, etc.

Nation-state level The level of analysis that focuses upon the soverign state as the primary player of international relations.

National self-determination One of the principles called for in Wilson's Fourteen Points which advocated the right of people to assert their nationalistic claims to a particular territory and to subsequently establish self-rule or sovereignty over their territory.

National Socialism The doctrine of state fascism exposed by the Nazi party under the rule of Adolf Hitler during World War II.

Nationalism A state of mind in which the individual's loyalty is directed totally toward the nation-state on behalf of a nation.

NATO North Atlantic Treaty Organization: Body established at the end of World War II by the United States and its Western European allies to guard against the encroachment of Soviet communism.

Natural resources Primary materials produced by the earth itself and used in the production of secondary goods and services.

Natural rights Inalienable rights innate to human beings; these are not given by government, and hence cannot be taken away by government.

Nazism National Socialist German Workers' Party: ideology implemented by Adolf Hitler during World War II.

Negotiations Processes in which two or more parties interact in developing potential agreements to provide guidance for and regulation of their future behavior.

Neofunctionalism Political factors directly assessed in a re-constituted functionalist approach to politics.

New trade theory The impact of history and historical accident upon the comparative trade advantages of a nation.

New World Order That arrangement of world power that is still to be determined due to the collapse of the former Soviet Union, and hence, the end of the Cold War.

NGOs Nongovernmental organizations.

Norms The standards or values by which a small decisional group operates.

North-South Debate Controversy between the rich industrialized nations and the lesser developed nations over the rules of international economic engagement.

Nuclear proliferation The spread of nuclear weapons to nations beyond the original circle of nuclear powers (the U.S., the USSR, England, and France) after World War II.

Nuclear winter The freezing and desolate aftermath of hypothetical global nuclear exchange.

Opinions Relatively stable predispositions to react favorably or unfavorably to particular objects or persons.

Partisans Those who fight usually within their nations, sometimes without the tacit support of their government.

Partnership for Peace Association with NATO that may or may not serve to qualify for NATO membership—primarily nations of the former Warsaw Pact and Soviet Union.

Peace dividend The money supposedly saved in the production of arms by the East and the West due to the end of the Cold War.

Peacekeeping An attempt by the United Nations to place itself between international belligerents to maintain an agreed peace.

Peacemaking Imposing or forcing the cessation of hostilities between two or more conflicting parties.

Permanent revolution The primarily Maoist idea that the revolution is never-ending, a permanent stage in the dialectic process.

Political disintegration The explosion of political order and symmetry.

Political integration The composition of forces within a society or system to bind it together.

Political personality The sum of an individual's political beliefs, attitudes, and opinions.

Population momentum The continuing growth of the population long after replacement fertility has been achieved.

Power The core concept of international relations; the totality of a nation's international capabilities, stemming from natural, synthetic, and social-psychological components.

PQLI Physical Quality of Life Index: index used to rank nations according to life expectancy, infant mortality, and literacy rates, in the assessment of progress in terms of basic human needs.

Private international law A somewhat routine form of international law that deals with such issues as diplomatic immunity, passports, extradition, the sharing of data, fishing rights, etc..

Progressivism   Reform movement in early twentieth century United States that sought "fairness" in economic and public life. Both Theodore Roosevelt and Woodrow Wilson were leading Progressives.

Propaganda   The use of information (sometimes false) in an act of psychological warfare directed at an opponent.

Psychological predispositions   Individual perceptions of the world.

Public international law   Government-to-government agreements covering relations on such issues as peace and national security.

Public negotiation; public diplomacy   Intentional use of the world media to jockey for position or outcome in a diplomatic negotiation.

Realism   School of international relations political theory that concentrates on power relationships; power is seen as the essential element for maintaining stability within the international system.

Realpolitik   Belief that politics is based on the pursuit, possession, and application of power; doctrine closely associated with the realist school of thought.

Reformism   Muslims who believe that moral character stems from within, and cannot be imposed by the state.

Religious fundamentalism   A religious return to the basic values of various religions around the world, affecting the political action of the adherents.

Replacement fertility rate   The rate of reproduction at which a constant level of population is maintained.

Republic of insects   What some scientists believe to be the only surviving creatures after a nuclear exchange.

Revolutionary nationalism   Desire for independence, self-determination, and social, political, and economic reform that generally culminates in a revolt against the existing regime.

Scapegoat theory of war   The theory that a nation starts a war to divert attention from its internal turmoils.

Security Council   The fifteen-member main peace-keeping body (with five permanent members) of the United Nations.

Separatism   The desire for nations (usually within multi-national states) to be separate and distinct. The desire to form one's own government.

Shatterbelts   Flashpoints of geostrategic contention.

Signaling   Diplomacy by nuance or indirect communication, rather than face-to-face negotiation.

SLBM   Submarine-launched ballistic missile.

Small groups   Small decisional units that usually range in size from 3–20 members. Such groups are prominent in formulating a nation's foreign policy during crises.

Social contract   Rousseauian construct of the "general will" linking the governed and the government, upon which government rested.

Socialism   Economic theory that denies for the most part the legitimacy of private property; socialism advocates a large role for the central government in policy and planning.

Social-psychological level   Level of analysis that focuses on the intersection of variables between the individual and society.

Sovereignty   The fundamental right of the state to perpetuate and govern itself, subject to no higher political authority.

Stalinism   The form of totalitarianism that occurred in the Soviet Union during the reign of Joseph Stalin (1925–1953).

START   Strategic Arms Reduction Treaty, 1991: agreement between the U.S. and the former USSR to reduce strategic forces.

Star Wars   A proposed anti-ballistic missile system using laser technology.

State   A legal geopolitical entity that has a permanent population, defined territory, and a legitimate government.

Stereotyping   The regarding of all members of a certain group as identical in various attributes.

Strategic location The politically important geographical characteristics and position of a nation.

Strategic trade policy Usually a government's direct, positive involvement in the strategic advantage of a particular industry in that nation.

Stress The anxiety an individual experiences in a situation he or she perceives as posing a severe threat, either to the individual or to one or more values.

Structuralism Dependency school theory that asserts that the structure of the international economy as structured by GATT is designed to work against the development of the Third World.

Substructure In Marxist terms, the economic foundation of a society, which determines the superstructure.

Summitry Negotiations between two or more heads of state.

Superstructure In Marxist terms, the part of society that does not specifically deal with economics, e.g., the arts, sex, religion, etc., but that is determined by the substructure of economics.

Supragovernmental Political dealings at a level that transcends the nation-state(s), e.g., at the level of the United Nations. In other words, politics at a plateau above the nation.

Systems level The level of analysis that focuses on global actors and conditions, e.g., geopolitics and geoeconomics, world technology, etc.

Technology The practical application of knowledge and the application of tools which are used to make work easier.

Tension pull The pressure on smaller nations to acquire arms as a result of the demise of the Cold War; these nations rush to fill the void created by the loss of the superpower rivalry in weapons production.

Terrorism Premeditated political violence perpetuated against a nation's noncombatants.

Technology push The phenomenon that occurs with the advent of technological advances in military weaponry development. One new invention or advancement spurs another in a spiraling effect.

Theory In the political context, the scientific attempt to describe, explain, and predict political phenomena.

TNC Transnational corporations (also called multinational corporations).

Total war Modern form of conventional war in which older distinctions between military and civilian targets no longer exist.

Trade balance The difference between a nation's imports and its exports. If the nation imports more than it exports, it will have an unfavorable balance of trade; conversely, if the opposite occurs, it will have a favorable balance of trade.

Traditionalism Muslims who yearn for a return to traditional or old-fashioned values of village life, economic, social and religious beliefs.

Transfer pricing The trading of commodities between a parent company's subsidiaries in different countries in order to record profits in jurisdictions where taxes are low.

Transgovernmental Term denoting usually agreements, exchanges between governments or sub-units of a government working with their counterparts with other governments.

Transitional societies Societies moving from less developed status to developed status.

Transparency GATT's mechanism to alert all nations to trade barriers imposed by some states.

Treaty of Maastricht Treaty signed by members of the European Union in December 1991 that stipulated greater economic and political unity.

Treaty of Westphalia The 1648 peace treaty that concluded the Thirty Years' War and ultimately led to the establishment of the current nation-state system.

Triffin's dilemma Named after the economist Robert Triffin, who discovered that the United States must run a budget deficit to bolster the world's economy.

Trinitarian war War supported totally by the triad of the people, government, and the military against an enemy.

Ultranationalism Hypernationalism that goes beyond xenophobia to an active attempt both to eliminate those who are not of the same nationality and to extend national power.

Urbanization The concentration of humanity in cities around the world.

CDC/Prevention United States Centers for Disease Control and Prevention.

Versailles Conference The Paris Peace Conference of 1919, which concluded World War I and set the stage of nationalistic expectations around the world.

War The conduct of armed hostilities between states or within states.

Wars of national liberation Wars to gain or restore independence, often fought by small numbers of unconventional forces motivated by revolutionary ideology as well as desire for independence.

World Bank Collective name for the economic institutions of International Bank for Reconstruction and Development, International Development Agency, and International Finance Corporation, which lend money to nations for economic development.

WTO Multilateral world economic trade regulatory agency established as a part of the GATT Moroccan Conference, 1994.

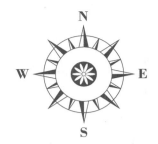

Index